North Carolina DWI Defense:

The Law and Practice

J. Scott Smith
James Nesci

Contributors
Mimi Coffey
James O. Ruane

Lawyers & Judges Publishing Company, Inc.
Tucson, Arizona

Lawyers & Judges Publishing Company, Inc.

P.O. Box 30040 • Tucson, AZ 85751-0040
(800) 209-7109 • FAX (800) 330-8795
e-mail: sales@lawyersandjudges.com
www.lawyersandjudges.com

Library of Congress Cataloging-in-Publication Data

Names: Smith, J. Scott, (Lawyer), author. | Nesci, James, author.
Title: North Carolina DWI defense : the law and practice / J. Scott Smith, James Nesci ; Contributors Mimi Coffey, James O. Ruane.
Description: Tucson, Arizona : Lawyers & Judges Publishing Company, 2016. | Includes bibliographical references and index.
Identifiers: LCCN 2015041420| ISBN 9781936360376 (hardcover : alk. paper) | ISBN 1936360373 (hardcover : alk. paper)
Subjects: LCSH: Drunk driving--North Carolina. | Defense (Criminal procedure)--North Carolina.
Classification: LCC KFN7697.8 .S65 2016 | DDC 345.756/0247--dc23
LC record available at http://lccn.loc.gov/2015041420

ISBN 13: 978-1-936360-37-6
ISBN 10: 1-936360-37-3

Printed in the United States of America
10 9 8 7 6 5 4 3 2 1

How to Use This Book

There are very few practice manuals available in North Carolina that focus on DWI. With the rise of new attorneys opening up their own firms straight out of law school due to the decline in employment opportunities after graduation I see more of a need for a book like this to be written. This book was written for the beginner to the more experienced DWI litigator and offers practice tips as well as relevant scientific data to aid the practitioner in his or her quest to more effectively do battle in the court room. This publication is meant to be a comprehensive guide on DWI practice in North Carolina. While every effort has been made to ensure that the law is up-to-date at the time of printing, please check all citations for accuracy prior to using them.

Contents

Table of Cases

North Carolina Cases

Other State Cases

Federal Cases

Preface

One of the very first things I tell prospective DWI clients that come to my office is that these types of cases are hard to win. Not only is DWI one of the most complicated misdemeanors in the State, it is also one of the most politically charged crimes as well. Let's face it, no one wants drunk drivers to "get off." With organizations like Mothers Against Drunk Driving (MADD) and the fact that political pressure is constantly applied to our State legislature and judiciary only increases the number of convictions in cases involving DWI.

It seems that the Constitution is under an incredible weight when it is used to battle a DWI in the court room. The presumption of innocence and the fundamentally rooted protections in the Bill of Rights seem to shudder when looked at under the microscope of a DWI prosecution. It is for that purpose that we must fight to make sure that these rights are upheld in every case, but especially in a DWI case.

As a DWI lawyer you wear multiple hats: defense attorney; scientist; salesperson; and above all, advocate. I am very blessed to have been able to train younger attorneys and to have mentored a few as well in these areas. One of those attorneys is Andrew M. Newman, one of my associates. Without Mr. Newman's help this book would not have been complete.

Many months of preparation and research have been put into this text to help defense attorneys be better litigators inside the court room. Godspeed and good luck.

— J. Scott Smith

Chapter 1

Lawyer Advertising

Co-Authored by James O. Ruane, Esq.

Synopsis

1.1 Ethical Issues in Advertising

The ethical rules regarding advertising are found in the North Carolina State Bar's Rules of Professional Conduct, which are available online at http://www.ncbar.com/rules/rpcsearch.asp.[1] Common sense applies to advertising. Certainly private attorneys in the DWI defense area are competitors in the marketplace. There is no lack of clients. As laws become more strict and the penalties become more harsh, the defense industry will grow exponentially, but DWI defense attorneys have to realize that although we are competitors in the marketplace we are colleagues in our common desire to defend those accused of DWI. Advertising is our interface with the public, but it is also a prime component of our relationship among defense attorneys. Advertising must be honest and fair. There is nothing in the ethical rules which will prevent you from advertising in a manner that will bring clients to your door. In fact, the ethical rules protect the attorney as much as the consumer.

It was the early 1970s when a couple of Arizona attorneys changed the national landscape of the practice of law by advertising a "legal clinic" to the public in a small and inexpensive printed ad in Phoenix, Arizona. "DO YOU NEED A LAWYER?" is how the ad began. It was nothing like today's personal injury ads seen on national cable and satellite networks which troll for litigants in mass-tort actions. It was a modest ad for divorce, adoption, bankruptcy and changes of name with reasonable flat fees. The State Bar of Arizona took action against the attorneys under the Sherman Act and the Arizona State Bar's own rules. The case was appealed to the United States Supreme Court and became known as: *Bates v. State Bar of Arizona*, 433 U.S. 350, 97 S.Ct. 2961, 53 L.Ed. 2d 810 (1977).

The United States Supreme Court found that although lawyer advertising could be regulated as commercial speech, it could not be barred entirely because of First Amendment protections. The concerns were that members of the public would be misled by unscrupulous attorneys and that advertising would degrade the profession. Mr. Justice Blackmun delivered the opinion of the Court and wrote:

> "It is at least somewhat incongruous for the opponents of advertising to extol the virtues and altruism of the legal profession at one point, and, at another, to assert that its members will seize the opportunity to mislead and distort. We suspect that, with advertising, most lawyers will behave as they always have: They will abide by their solemn oaths to uphold the integrity and honor of their profession and of the legal system. For every attorney who overreaches through advertising, there will be thousands of others who will be candid and honest and straightforward. And, of course, it will be in the latter's interest, as in other cases of misconduct at the bar, to assist in weeding out those few who abuse their trust." *Bates v. State Bar of Arizona*, 433 U.S. 350, 379, 97 S. Ct. 2691, 2707, 53 L. Ed. 2d 810 (1977).

Rule 7.1 Communications concerning a lawyer's services

Nothing should be surprising here. "A lawyer shall not make a false or misleading communication about the lawyer or the lawyer's services." The rule goes on to define a "false or misleading" communication. Lawyers often get a bad rap in the area of honesty. Those of us in the profession hear many jokes about our honesty—or lack of honesty. This hurts us in our presentations to the jury. A simple place to start changing the public view of attorneys is in our advertising. Simply stated, if it isn't true, don't state it.

Rule 7.2 Advertising

Subject to Rule 7.1 and Rule 7.3, lawyers may advertise. Lawyers can't give anything for value to someone for recommending the lawyer's services except for the following: a lawyer may pay for advertising, pay the usual charges of a legal services plan or even pay a referral fee to a not-for-profit qualified lawyer referral service or a prepaid or group legal services plan that has been approved by the appropriate regulatory authority.

Every advertisement must carry the name and office address of at least one lawyer who is responsible for the content of the advertisement unless the communication is that of a lawyer referral service. A lawyer may participate in a lawyer referral service provided that the lawyer is professionally responsible for its operation including the false, deceptive, or misleading name of the referral service. The referral service cannot be operated for profit. The lawyer can pay the referral service only a reasonable amount which would represent a proportionate share of the referral services administrative and advertising costs. The lawyer cannot accept anything of value from the referral service, directly or indirectly, other than the legal fees earned from the representation of clients referred by the referral service. Additionally, employees of the referral service cannot initiate contact with prospective clients and cannot engage in live telephone or in-person solicitation of clients. The referral service cannot collect money from clients or potential clients for the use of the service. All advertisements from the referral service shall state that a list of all of the lawyers participating in the service will be mailed to members of the public upon request and state where that information may be obtained. The referral service advertisement must also explain how the prospective client's needs get matched with the qualifications of the recommended lawyer.

Advertisements on electronic media must adhere to the same rules.

Rule 7.3 Direct contact with potential clients

If you know that someone is in need of your services, and you are not offering your services pro-bono, then you may not contact the prospective client in person, by telephone or real-time electronic form unless the person contacted is a lawyer, or has a familial, close personal or prior professional relationship with you.

Even so, the lawyer may not contact someone if he or she has made known a desire not to be contacted, or if the solicitation involves coercion, duress, harassment, compulsion, intimidation, or threats.

Every written, recorded or electronic communication from a lawyer soliciting employment from a potential client in need shall include the statement in capital letters "THIS IS AN ADVERTISEMENT FOR LEGAL SERVICES" in a font as large as the size of any other printing on the envelope, on the outside of the envelope. The front of the envelope shall contain no other printing other than the name of the lawyer or law firm, the firm's address, the name and address of the recipient and the advertising notice. The advertising notice shall also be printed at the beginning of the body of the letter in a font as large or larger than any other print contained in the letter. For electronic communications, the advertising notice shall appear in the "in reference" box of the address section; no other statement can appear in this section. The same rules apply about font size here as well and the advertising notice must appear at the beginning and the ending of the electronic communication. The advertising notice shall be clearly articulated at the beginning and ending of any recorded electronic communication.

A lawyer may participate with a prepaid or group legal service plan as long as certain rules are followed. These types of plans are defined as any arrangement by which a person, firm, or corporation, not otherwise engaged in the practice of law, in exchange for valuable consideration, offers to provide or to arrange to provide legal services that are paid for in advance of an immediate need for the legal services. These are considered covered services. In addition to covered services a plan can also provide legal services at a lower fee than what a non-member of the plan would pay. The services provided in North Carolina that are offered by the plan must be provided by a licensed lawyer that is not an employee, director, or owner of the plan. A prepaid legal services plan does not include the sale of an identified legal service that is limited, such as drafting a will for a fixed, one-time fee.

To participate in these types of prepaid or group plans, certain conditions must be followed. First, the plan must be operated by an organization that is not owned or directed by the lawyer. Second, the plan must be registered with the

State Bar and comply with all the rules and regulations pertaining to such plans. Third, the lawyer must give notice to the State Bar in writing before participating in the plan and must also give written notice to the State Bar no later than 30 days after the lawyer stops participating in the plan. Fourth, the lawyer must make a reasonable investigation and have a good faith belief that the plan is being operated in compliance with the Revised Rules of Professional Conduct and other pertinent rules. Fifth, the plan's advertisements must represent that the plan is registered with the State Bar and that just because it's registered, doesn't necessarily mean it's approved by the State Bar. The plan may use in-person or telephone contact to solicit membership or subscription as long as the person being solicited is not known to need legal services in a particular matter covered by the plan and the contact doesn't involve coercion, duress, or harassment. The communication must also not be false, deceptive or misleading. A potential client is for the purposes of this rule, defined as a person with whom a lawyer would like to form a client-lawyer relationship.

PRACTICE TIP: Although it may be perfectly legal and ethical to contact specific people whom you believe need your services under certain circumstances, don't do it. The ethical rules provide a minefield of opportunities to misstep and create a giant ethical problem for your firm. Moreover, people who need legal services should have the opportunity to "shop around" rather than retain the first lawyer who contacts them. In fact, make it a practice to suggest that the person take the opportunity to contact other attorneys before he or she makes a decision. If the prospective client likes and trusts you, he will come back to retain you. If you directly solicit a client known to need your services, that client may eventually feel "trapped" and look for excuses to find faults with your work.

The ethical rules regarding advertising contain more detailed and specific information than contained in this chapter. It is wise to take 15 minutes to read the ethical rules regarding advertising at least once a year and any time that your firm chooses to embark on a new ad campaign or use a new media outlet. Fifteen minutes of reading could save you 20 hours of time dealing with a needless bar complaint.

Rule 7.4 Communication of fields of practice and specialization

A lawyer may communicate the fact that the lawyer does or does not practice in a specific field of law. We have all had it happen to us—we advertise that we practice exclusively in the criminal field and we get calls from people seeking bankruptcy counsel or help with child custody issues. Nothing we do will ever stop that from happening. One way we have cut down on calls for services outside our areas of practice is by advertising "specialization" in an area. However, one cannot claim specialization unless one is actually a "specialist" with the State Bar via granted certification. This specialist certification can also be given in North Carolina if the organization giving the certification is accredited by the State Bar or the certification was granted by an organization accredited by the American Bar Association under procedures and criteria endorsed by the State Bar. Additionally, the name of the certifying organization must be clearly identified in the communication.

PRACTICE TIP: The National College for DUI Defense, Inc. is the only organization which grants Board Certification in the specific area of DWI Defense. Board Certification by the NCDD is extremely difficult to obtain as their standards usually exceed any state standards for certification in any area. Board Certification is a nationally-recognized specialty and is recognized by the American Bar Association. Details and application forms can be found at www.NCDD.com and it is well-worth examining. At the time of this printing, no North Carolina attorney has been deemed a specialist in DWI although our State Bar does permit it through certification of the NCDD since they are recognized by the American Bar Association.

Rule 7.5 Firm names and letterheads

A firm name, letterhead or professional designation shall not violate Rule 7.1, and a lawyer in private practice may use a trade name if the trade name does not imply a connection with a government agency or a public or charitable legal services organization. The trade name must also not be misleading in violation of Rule 7.1. Every trade name used must be registered with the State Bar, which then will determine whether the name is misleading. A firm with offices in multiple jurisdictions can use the same name or designation. However, the identification of lawyers in an office of the firm must indicate the jurisdictional limitations on those not licensed to practice in the jurisdiction where the office is located. A law firm that has offices only in North Carolina cannot list a lawyer not licensed to practice law in North Carolina as being affiliated with the law firm unless the listing states that the lawyer is not licensed to practice in North Carolina and states the jurisdiction in which the lawyer is licensed. A lawyer's name can't be used in the name of the law firm or in any communications on behalf of the law firm if the lawyer holds public office during any substantial time that the lawyer is not regularly and actively practicing with the law firm whether or not the lawyer is precluded from practicing law at the time. Lawyers may only say they practice in a partnership or professional organization when it is a fact.

1.2 Advertising Resources

There are plenty of media outlets available for advertising purposes. Clearly, the phone book was the largest source for advertising in the past, but the Internet has now replaced it as the prime source for advertising. You may certainly find, however, that there are specific targeted media in addition to the Internet which are capable of producing a lucrative return on the dollar. These will vary locally and can be found by simply checking out the places that your target audience frequents.

A. Phone Book Advertising

There are a few simple things to keep in mind with any type of phone book advertising. The first consideration is timing the start of your practice with the publication date of the phone book. In other words, do not open the doors of your private practice in October if the phone book is published in September, unless you have finalized phone book advertising first. If you are going to open your practice in October, plan on finalizing your advertisement contract in May. The content of your ad is up to you, but you should listen to your phone book ad representative. Keep in mind that they receive a commission on the ad, so it is in that salesperson's best interest to sell you the largest ad you will purchase; but also keep in mind that the salesperson has an interest in keeping you in business. Graphic artists are generally expensive, but hiring a graphic artist who specializes in advertising is a wise investment. Think of it in these terms: Should someone accused of a crime defend himself? Certainly not. You're probably not a graphic artist, so don't try it yourself.

There are many different types of phone books available to consumers. Phone books are cheap to print and they flood the marketplace nowadays, but have the least impact on client retention. My best advice is to pick the largest phone book available in your area and place a mid-sized ad under both the DWI heading as well as the Criminal Defense heading. Stay away from the large one- or two-page ads at the front of the directory. Those ads pay off well for civil attorneys doing personal injury, medical malpractice and bankruptcy. They simply do not work well for criminal defense and DWI.

B. Internet Advertising

Internet advertising is one of the best ways that a DWI attorney can advertise. Be sure to have your website professionally built and maintained. Many different license agreements are available for attorneys to ensure that their websites are easily found by various search engines. They provide easy access for people to your firm on a 24-hour basis. Be sure, however, to adhere to the following rules: warn potential users not to e-mail confidential information to you and that you have no attorney-client relationship via the website. Also ensure that you have not created such a relationship via the website. There are some attorneys who advertise on the web with fee agreements available to the public along with methods of payment via the web. These are things that could create an attorney-client agreement and cause endless headaches with the state bar.

Links to other sites can help increase your visibility on the web. Do not be afraid to ask other attorneys to link sites with your site. Linking to the National College for DUI Defense, Inc. (NCDD) is a wise thing to do, if you are a member of the NCDD. (You can find them at www.NCDD.com and join the organization, easily.)

Links to the National Highway Traffic Safety Administration (NHTSA) will provide potential and actual clients access to government publications and research regarding driving, impairment, field sobriety testing and statistical information.

Blogs and legal postings drive people to websites. Content is what moves your site further up the chain of results. However, even though blogs and legal postings may drive people to your site, they must be accurate for two reasons. First, inaccurate or outdated material will make you look less professional and less knowledgeable. The second reason to keep it accurate is for ethical purposes. While there may be no direct ethical rule on-point, your advertising could be considered misleading—and that is a basis for discipline.

C. Giveaways

Law firms often give away t-shirts, pens, cup holders, coffee mugs, refrigerator magnets, matchbooks, USB drives, and even poker chips with their firm's information on them. These things can be fun and informative and there is virtually no limit to what you can put your firm's name on these days. People will keep them around for a while as well. Whether you choose to spend your money on something like this or not will depend on your market. Although not required, I always check with the State Bar if I wish to send out these types of items since not all items of this nature require your firm's address to be present on the giveaway.

1.3 Social Media

Whether you are advertising through social media, communicating with clients or other attorneys, or just using it to stay informed, today's practice must address the rising role of social media and how it impacts the criminal defense attorney. Many lawyers do not understand the role that social media plays in your marketing plan as well as the perils and pitfalls that could impact your professional licensing as an attorney. In this section we want to make sure that you understand the social networks that are out there and being used by your staff and your clients. By understanding how they work, we can identify the areas that may pose risks regarding ethical concerns and implement best practices so that you can avoid being the subject of a bar complaint. This will also help you to protect yourself from conduct by employees that could subject you to discipline or a lawsuit.

Social media networks have changed the online dynamic from passive listening and looking to active involvement in the discussion. Clients, jurors, members of the courthouse staff, and others take to social media to express their opinions and give voice to their ideas on how the world should be working.

The easiest way to understand the new realm of social media—such as Facebook®, Twitter®, and other social networks—is to realize that these online programs facilitate a conversation and, just like any kind of social gathering, there are norms and taboos regarding the topics you choose to "discuss" online. It's helpful to think of social media as a perpetually ongoing conversation among friendly people. Just as there are some topics that you would never bring up at a cocktail party, those same topics are not likely good fodder for online discussions and debate. And because of the archival nature of the digital world, any comments you make in the social media world will stick around, forever.

A. Ethical Concerns

Before we begin to talk about social media and how it can help you with your practice, we must first cover some basic ethical rules to make sure we are all on the same page and have the same core understanding of our duties as attorneys. The first issue we must discuss is the concept of attorney-client privilege. For lay people, attorney-client privilege is most likely a term they've heard uttered on their TV screens or read in a crime drama. Attorney-client privilege is, in its simplest terms, an evidentiary rule. It is codified in every formalized rule of evidence along with other traditional privilege exceptions, such as the spousal privilege, in which a person cannot be forced to testify in either a civil or criminal matter about confidential communications with their spouse. The evidentiary rule regarding attorney-client privilege deals with the admissibility of evidence at a formalized proceeding. It requires an attorney to decline to answer questions about certain aspects of the representation of their client. One frequently used example of attorney-client privilege is the notion of a client who confesses to committing a crime when speaking with their attorney. That attorney holds that information as privileged and cannot disclose it without their client's consent. The question then becomes "who holds that privilege?" While it is called the attorney-client privilege, it really should be called the client-attorney privilege. The client holds the privilege and chooses whether it will be enforced or not. This privilege exists in perpetuity, unless revoked by the client, meaning it does not terminate at the end of representation.

B. Confidentiality vs. Privilege

The concept of client confidentiality is one that is often misperceived by the general public, and even some attorneys. They tend to throw all weight behind the idea of privilege because they see it dramatically played out in movies and television. ABA rule 1.6 states, in part:

> **Client lawyer relationship rule 1.6 Confidentiality of Information**
> A lawyer shall not reveal information relating to the representation of a client unless the client gives informed consent (or) the disclosure is impliedly authorized in order to carry out the representation....

This is a very broad rule. The rule doesn't say privileged information is defined only as information regarding illegal activity. It clearly states, "relating to the representation of a client." So we must ask ourselves, what constitutes information related to client representation?

1. Any motions you file, even if they are public record;
2. Transcripts from trials, especially if the trial resulted in an acquittal;
3. The fact that you were their legal representative.

All of those areas and more are covered by your confidentiality requirement. It's important to keep in mind that, in the world of social media, it is much more likely that an attorney will run afoul of their confidentiality requirements than violate their privilege responsibilities.

Now that we have established that the scope of confidentiality extends well beyond privileged information, we need to understand that confidentiality places a greater burden of responsibility upon us, as attorneys, to protect our client's information. When facing a decision of whether to disclose information about your representation of a client you have to step back and look at it from bar counsel's perspective. The number of cases of alleged privilege violation reported to the bar pale in comparison to the reported cases (and lawsuits) that allege violation of confidentiality. The responsibility of confidentiality rests firmly on your shoulders.

You must constantly guard against potential lapses in your judgment regarding confidentiality as well as lapses in the judgment of your employees, associate attorneys, law firm partners, and other staff members. With social media, the information that you or one of your employees discloses online will exist in the world of the internet forever. Not only that, it will be accessible to countless individuals located around the world. You should consider the use of social media akin to the use of a microphone or even a bullhorn. Your social media posts are broadcast far and wide and, therefore, you must be in constant compliance with the duty of confidentiality when using these new digital tools. No lawyer would feel comfortable standing at a microphone and proclaiming that, "John Brown told me he sells heroin daily at the corner of Eighth and Walnut between noon and midnight," because the attorney knows that information is privileged and they could not testify to it in court under oath. That begs the question: Why are so many lawyers comfortable using social media to brag about their triumphs in court and, in the process, possibly violating confidentiality duties? The answer is most likely due to the fact that those lawyers do not understand Rule 1.6 and its depth and breadth.

C. The 3 Tenets of Social Media: Timeliness, Honesty, and Transparency

Unlike traditional media used by law firms and lawyers to broadcast a basic message, like advertisements and press releases, social media moves at a lightning pace and once you engage, you're expected to react immediately and post updates quickly and often. This can create problems with confidentiality when you speak first and think second.

Another social media issue that deserves due consideration is honesty. It is not unusual for attorneys to "gild the lily" when producing marketing materials. This allows them to feel good about all their wonderful accomplishments and, as long as the information is accurate, there is not likely to be much blowback from promoting your accomplishments on traditional media platforms. Social media, however, invites a more intimate exchange and allows for critics to fact check any and all statements you make very quickly. It is an easy medium for people to express dissenting viewpoints, or in cases of maliciousness, attack their competitors. One example that comes readily to mind is when lawyers brag about achieving a not guilty verdict regarding one or more criminal counts in a certain case, yet the attorney neglects to mention his or her client was found guilty on several other counts in the same case.

Transparency is another important issue to consider when dealing with social media. Many lawyers don't realize that if you are about to post something on social media, you should do so with your own name, firm, or brand. Trying to mask yourself, or post as someone else, is unethical and possibly illegal in both the real and social media worlds. Most attorneys don't make this mistake deliberately. Many lawyers will have a generic e-mail address, such as ones that include the terms "Criminal," "DUI," "DWI," or "Drugs" prominently in the address and they may not realize that their email is not obvious or transparent when commenting or putting information out online. Of course, some attorneys do purposely use pseudonyms.

The next thing to consider is the various social media venues that exist, and to weigh their strengths and weaknesses in regards to what they can offer in the way of services for the modern criminal defense attorney.

D. Facebook

Facebook is the king of the social media beasts and it can help you research jurors, clients, and witnesses, and in particular police officer and expert witnesses. Many people find Facebook addictive and because it feels like it's just you and the computer screen, it can be very easy to forget the duties you have as a lawyer as you sit there in court, bored and frustrated, waiting for your case to be called. At the heart of Facebook is the idea that your social network of friends are all interconnected. Many lawyers in local and national organizations are connected as friends on Facebook, and from those friends you gain more friends, and potential business contacts. One of the smartest moves you can make is to choose wisely who you accept as a friend on Facebook. Though it may seem harsh, the act of ignoring and declining some friend requests—much in the way that you may turn away a potential client—may be in your best interest. For those who do use Facebook, there are a few simple things you can do to get the best use of the social network for your legal practice.

1. Add the recommend button to your website. Facebook allows you to add either a "like" or "recommend" button. We suggest "recommend" since as criminal defense lawyers we deal with a certain segment of society that some people on social me-

dia may not want to "like," but they can certainly "recommend" you. Be sure, however, not to trade "recommends" between friends, as this may also breach ethical rules of receiving recommendations for a transfer of value;
2. Add Facebook insights for your own website, which allows you to view the demographics of the people viewing your site;
3. Permit people logged into Facebook to comment on your blog;
4. Create a custom audience and market yourself to people who have already expressed an interest in your services.

Just like there are things that you can do on Facebook, there are several things that you should never do on Facebook.

1. Don't blast friend requests to everyone under the sun;
2. Avoid posting only self-promotional items;
3. Do not refuse to admit that you are human or ignore a problem if you make a mistake. If you make a mistake on Facebook, you should edit your posts or delete the post to avoid offending others and creating bigger problems.

One of the worst potential ethical violations for attorney to commit in the social media world is to create a fake profile or use a real profile to contact a potential victim or the party or parties who are represented by opposing counsel. Some lawyers have landed in hot water for using social media platforms to contact victims or search out and find information that would not have been available otherwise. Remember this: if you wouldn't do something in real life to get the information or contact the person, you shouldn't resort to such tactics online.

E. Twitter

Twitter has gained in popularity as a micro-blogging platform that enables people to blast short messages out to their group of followers on timely issues. It is very popular among the news media as a way to break news and follow up on ongoing investigative articles. The existence of Twitter is perhaps one of the biggest challenges that attorneys who try cases must tackle. There are scores of examples of people who have ruined their careers through the careless use of Twitter. Anthony Weiner is one recent example. Another example is the case of Justine Sacco, the public relations executive who was fired by IAC after issuing a racist and insensitive tweet on a long flight to South Africa.

Attorneys should also be aware of and closely follow the use of Twitter by members of the press who may be sitting in the courtroom, or other areas, and may hear important information meant only for the defense. Reporters can easily tweet out information about your case without your knowledge, so be aware of your surroundings at all times and be careful about the information you discuss in court and in public.

Other social media platforms to consider include:

- Foursquare—Helps you find the hottest restaurants, clubs, and bars, as well as other places of social gathering.
- Vine—A popular site for individuals and businesses to market their services or products through short web videos.
- Instagram—Uses still images to capture moments within your personal and professional life and share them with online followers. Many businesses use it as a marketing platform.
- Pinterest—Also uses pictures, or still images, to feature products, services, ideas, and concepts.

F. Social Media as a Research Tool

Another issue that should be addressed is the use of social media by jurors during court recesses and before and after court. Those jurors can search out your social media profiles, so you should be careful as to what you post and what you say. Privacy controls allow you to limit what others can see about your profile, so make sure to review your privacy settings frequently and update them accordingly.

G. Final Thoughts on Social Media

The use of social media for business practices can be a boom or bust for trial lawyers and other legal counsel. It can help your practice by promoting your brand and reaching even larger numbers of potential clients, or it can sink your practice if you violate basic rules of confidentiality and the trust of those you are tasked to represent and protect. The best approach is one of measured caution. View your practice and your client's information as priceless and do not engage in careless banter or reckless comments online. Be vigilant with the dissemination of all information, whether it's a tweet or a Facebook post or through an official press release. By taking all necessary precautions and employing a thoughtful, deliberate approach, you can use all the modern tools of social media to the benefit, and not the detriment, of your practice and your clients.

Endnotes

1. The adopted ethics opinions of the North Carolina State Bar are public records. This material is the property of the North Carolina State Bar

   The North Carolina State Bar Rules of Professional Conduct are a public record. This material is the property of the North Carolina State Bar.

Chapter 2

Client Relations

2.1 Meeting the Prospective Client

Prospective clients are, in a word, scared. It does not matter if they have never been through the process before or if this is their third or fourth time. They are scared. Knowledge generally alleviates fear, although when a client realizes he is facing ten years in prison, knowledge may have the opposite effect. The most important thing that you can do as an attorney is to give potential clients knowledge about the process and possible defenses. They will calm down, they will appreciate you for it and, if they can afford your fee, they will reward you for it by signing a retainer contract.

Make your office comfortable. Make the client comfortable. Have your support staff offer the person something to drink. Keep a small box of toys or coloring books in your office for clients with children. Keep a box of tissues within reach of the client. Grown men have become tearful when they realize the gravity of the situation that lies ahead. Clearly, you are in the business to make money; but you do a disservice to the legal profession and to the person sitting in your office if you do not answer basic questions in a meaningful way.

There are two schools of thought on client intake forms: short and to the point, or long, detailed multi-page forms. There are advantages and disadvantages to both.

Short intake forms tend to be a relief for the client. If you are having the potential new client fill out a 20-page intake questionnaire solely for the purpose of making the person think that you are more thorough than anybody else they have seen, stop doing it. If that is your reason, chances are you are not using that form efficiently. Moreover, some people dread the idea of filling out long intake forms.

On the other hand, a long and detailed intake form allows you to make a thorough assessment of the case and possible defenses. You still need to call the potential client back into your office for a more thorough interview once that potential new client becomes an actual new client, but your interview will be very detailed.

The other option is to have the client fill out a short portion of the questionnaire regarding biographical matters, and then you can fill out the rest as you discuss the case in your office. This allows you to more fully explore medical issues or Miranda rights and any other relevant aspects of a defense. Be sure to have a checklist in front of you so that you remember to touch upon every relevant subject. Interviews with a short intake form tend to be more free-flowing and informal. It is easy to get caught up in discussing the fact that your client has diabetes and forget to ask about the fact that the police officer did not let the client make a phone call to an attorney.

When interviewing the client, first explain the differences between misdemeanor DWI and habitual or felony DWI. Many people are under the impression that blood alcohol level determines whether the matter is designated as a felony or misdemeanor. Others do not know what the terms misdemeanor and felony mean. Likewise, you should question the client regarding prior offenses, license status and whether there were any passengers under age eighteen (a person with mental development under age eighteen), or a passenger unable to get out of the car unassisted in the car at the time of the offense.

Explain the charges to the client. Most are shocked to find that they have more than one charge pending from one arrest, such as an impairment charge and a lane violation charge. In fact, because many people are released that night without ever being handcuffed, they do not realize that they have been "arrested" as opposed to simply cited for a crime. Go over the elements of each of the charges in order to give the client a framework for relevant comments. You will find that once your client understands the elements, an interview becomes much more productive.

Driver's license consequences need to be discussed. Ensure that your client's address is on file with the Division of Motor Vehicles (DMV) because that is where DMV will correspond with the client. Provide the client with an envelope addressed the DMV Office and ensure that the potential client requests a hearing properly in the event that the person does not retain you. By doing this, you have preserved that person's right to a hearing in cases involving refusals. Discuss general strategies, the investigation, court process, types of witnesses and chemical test issues. It is important to discuss health issues and how they can affect breath, blood and field sobriety testing. Only then should you discuss fees and costs. If you discuss fees and costs before you have this information, you may wind up with a case that has more work than you had imagined, or you may quote a fee that is entirely unreasonable to the client.

Be sure to discuss out-of-pocket expenses such as those for an expert witness, investigators and others. Do not let your client buy the high-performance sports car and not afford to put fuel in the tank.

Above all else—never promise the potential client that you will win. You cannot predict the future.

2.2 Client Intake Questions

While there are many questions that you may want to ask during the client intake interview, or put on your intake questionnaire, the list below contains some essentials. Some are obvious such as asking about balance problems, but why ask about bulimia? Bulimics often force themselves to vomit, which can cause damage to the esophagus and that, over time, can cause GERD. GERD can affect a breath test estimate under specific certain circumstances. Do not use the questions below without knowing what the condition is, or why you want the information.

Medical Conditions

Do you currently have or have you ever been diagnosed with any of the following:

- Attention Deficit Disorder (ADD)
- Attention Deficit Hyperactivity Disorder
- Balance problems of any type
- Cancer
- Diabetes
- Dyslexia
- Dyspepsia
- Gastro Esophogeal Reflux Disease (GERD)
- Inner-ear infections
- Nystagmus
- Tinnitus
- Vertigo
- Have you been treated by a doctor or dentist in the last 6 months?
    - Why?
- Past surgeries?
- Any injuries/soreness to your:
    - Feet
    - Ankles
    - Knees
    - Legs
    - Hips
    - Back
    - Arms
    - Shoulders
    - Neck
    - Head

Medications, Implants and Devices

- Were you taking any medications on the date of the arrest?
- Were there any medications that were prescribed to you that you should have been taking, but did not take on the date of the arrest?
- Do you wear glasses? If not, should you?
- Is there a corrective lens restriction on your driver's license?
- Do you have any trouble hearing?
- Do you have any hearing aids or implants?
- Do you wear dentures, have any false teeth or dental implants?
- Do you have any medical implants?

Psychological Profile

Do you have any of the following:

- Bi-polar disorder
- Bulimia
- Depression
- Schizophrenia
- Chemical dependence
- Alcoholism

Chemical Testing Questions

Did the police administer any of the following:

- Breath test
- Blood test
- Urine test
- DNA swab

Investigatory Questions

- Were Miranda rights read to you?
- Did you ask to contact an attorney?
- Were there any passengers in your vehicle?
- Who were they?
- What were their ages at the time?

Prior Legal History

- Do you have any DUI/DWI/OUI prior offenses?
- Do you have any pending or past traffic offenses?
- Do you have any pending or past criminal offenses?
- Was your license valid at the time of the traffic stop?
- What restrictions or endorsements are on your license?

Professional/Occupational Licenses/Citizenship

- Do you hold any professional licenses?
- Commercial driver's license?
- Pilot's license?
- Nursing license?
- Real estate license?
- Securities license?
- Security clearance?
- Are you in the military?
- Do you hold a teaching certificate?
- Do you have a fingerprint clearance card?
- Is English your primary language?
- Are you a United States citizen?
- If not, what is your status?

2.3 Client Intake Interview

The initial client interview is protected by the attorney-client privilege, irrespective of whether the potential client actually retains you. This means that when you discuss the facts of the case family members and non-investigatory office staff should not be present. Often we find ourselves representing clients whose fees are paid by a third party such as a parent, grandparent or even an employer. We must remember, however, that the attorney-client privilege is held by the client—not the person footing the bill. This can become problematic for attorneys practicing in large college towns where a client's mother or father lives in another state. Often one or both parents will call asking for an update, and the client does not want her parents to know the full details of the arrest. In these types of situations it is imperative that you have a signed letter in your file expressly authorizing you to discuss sensitive matters with the client's parent if that is the client's wish. The letter needs to state specifically whether the parent will be sent copies of certain documents such as police reports or physical evidence such as arrest videos.

After meeting the client and explaining the parameters of the initial interview, you should explain the DWI laws to the client, possible punishments, collateral consequences for a DWI arrest and/or conviction and how the court process might work. A detailed client history should then be taken, including prior criminal history, driving record, medical history, medicines that were being taken by the client (or ones prescribed, but not taken) and events leading up to the DWI arrest. Quite a number of DWI arrestees are diagnosed with some sort of depression. Alcohol is a common way to "self-medicate" for many people. The absence of a medication for depression when it is prescribed and not used may have serious effects on the field sobriety test performance. So too, attention deficit disorders can have an effect on the results.

Immigration consequences can be devastating. Never assume that your client is a United States citizen—always ask. Never assume that your client does not have a professional license or security clearance. There are many people who hold some type of professional license, but are simply not working in that profession at the present time. Military security clearances need to be discussed, as any arrest or conviction for a criminal offense may trigger reporting requirements. Even though one may not be in the military, that person may still hold a clearance as a defense contractor employee.

A thorough client interview is imperative not only to framing the issues for defense, but also to ensuring that you protect the client's interests to the fullest extent possible.

2.4 Retainer Agreements

Clearly define the case. You may refer to it by police report number, docket number or however else you choose to define it, but be sure it is clear. State whether you will represent the client on post-conviction issues, license suspension hearings, reinstatements, and so on. Be sure to differentiate between felonies and misdemeanors. Sometimes the case will be dismissed and re-filed as a felony—are you adequately compensated for a felony under the original fee, or will you require more money? Are out-of-pocket expenses included? Expert fees can be costly—do not forget to make that clear to the client.

The retainer agreement should contain some language about how to resolve misunderstandings between the attorney and client should the retainer agreement itself become a contested issue. Whether you want to include state-initiated appeals, special actions and the like is entirely up to you.

Below is a sample agreement for a DUI case in the Tucson City Court from Nesci & St. Louis PLLC in Tucson, Arizona. If you choose to use it, be sure that it complies with your state's laws and ethical rules. Even if you do not use the entire contract, the "included" and "excluded" boxes below can be conveniently adapted to any contract and serve as a clear notice to the parties. Once it is on your computer, you can then move lines from one side to the other as needed.

Nesci & St. Louis P.L.L.C.
216 North Main Avenue • Tucson, Arizona 85701
Telephone (520) 622-1222

LEGAL SERVICES RETAINER CONTRACT

I. SCOPE OF REPRESENTATION, ATTORNEY FEES AND RETAINER

Nesci & St. Louis, PLLC ("the firm") agrees, and you authorize them, to represent you (hereafter referred to as "Client"), in connection with the following matter(s): **Tucson City Court Docket TR123456789.**

Client hereby agrees to pay a reasonable attorney fee to the firm as set forth below:

A retainer fee of $13,500 which shall be paid upon the date of this Contract. **If the Retainer Fee is paid by credit card, an additional five percent (5%) shall be added to any amount charged to a credit card for credit card processing fees.**

This amount is non-refundable and represents the minimum amount that the firm believes our services are worth in connection with representing the Client.

WHAT THIS CONTRACT INCLUDES	WHAT THIS CONTRACT EXCLUDES
• All necessary investigatory work. • All written pre-trial motions. • All legal and/or evidentiary hearings. • Motor Vehicle Division hearing(s). • Appeal from MVD decision (if appropriate). • State-initiated appeals. • Special actions. • Plea negotiations. • Change-of-plea and sentencing hearing. • Sentencing memorandum (if appropriate). • Jury trial or bench trial.	• Pre-indictment investigatory work. • Post-conviction relief. • Defense-initiated appeals. • Motion for new trial. • Any services not specifically mentioned in this Contract.

At the conclusion of Client's case, the firm shall file a Motion to Withdraw from any further representation of the Client not specified in this Contract.

The firm is undertaking the representation because you have agreed to pay all fees and expenses set forth above. In exchange, the firm agrees to devote its full professional ability to your case and perform all services that may be necessary to represent Client. In the event that Client fails to pay the sums specified above, Client hereby authorizes the firm to withdraw, and agrees to obtain substitute counsel for any remaining proceedings. In the event that legal action is necessary to enforce the terms of this Contract, the prevailing party shall be entitled to receive any costs incurred and is entitled to receive reasonable attorney's fees for the enforcement of this Contract at the rate of Two Hundred Fifty Dollars ($250.00) per hour. Additionally, in the event that Client breaches this Contract, and does not pay an outstanding balance after demand is made in writing for payment in full, Client agrees to pay interest on any outstanding balance at the rate of twelve percent (12%) per annum.

In the event the firm determines that it is not feasible for it to proceed as Client's attorney, because of a disagreement as to how the case should be resolved, or for other good cause, Client understands that the firm may, after due notice to Client and in compliance with the Rules of the Arizona Supreme Court, withdraw.

At the conclusion of the case, the firm shall review the matter to determine that the fee charged was fair to Client, and may refund a portion of the fee if it was not. The attorneys in the firm have been practicing for over forty years collectively, and they give their clients the benefit of the doubt when setting fees, so it is unlikely that the fee being charged is excessive, given Client's charges. It is also anticipated that the firm will turn down other cases in order to handle Client's case. In addition, if Client were to fire the firm before any substantial work was completed in the case, it is possible that Client could have some or all of the attorney's fee returned.

II. DISBURSEMENTS

a. Out of Pocket Expenses

In addition to attorney fees, Client also hereby agrees to pay all reasonable and necessary costs and disbursements incurred by the firm on your behalf, including without limitation and not limited to:

(1) special action filing fees,
(2) transcription charges,
(3) disclosure fees,
(4) out-of-town travel costs,
(5) process service charges,
(6) postage charges,
(7) expert witness/consultant fees and costs,
(8) photography, videography, audio recording,
(9) photocopies,
(10) private investigator,
(11) extraordinary research fees (at the sole discretion of the firm).

b. Trust Account Deposit

In addition to fees as noted above, an expense retainer in the amount of One Thousand Dollars ($1,000.00) was paid to the firm, and placed in a trust account for payment of the out of pocket expenses. Client understands that this Trust Account Deposit may, or may not, cover the entire amount of out-of-pocket expenses and that Client may be asked to replenish such funds from time to time.

c. Expert Witness

It is likely that the use of an Expert Witness will be necessary to adequately defend the Client at trial. The cost of this Expert Witness is to be paid by the Client as mentioned above and such funds must be paid before the Expert Witness is retained. The firm may be willing to take your case to trial without an Expert Witness, but Client must realize that it is often difficult or impossible to adequately defend certain allegations by the State without an Expert Witness.

III. CORRESPONDENCE AND PLEADINGS

As a matter of course, the firm will forward to you photocopies of all correspondence and pleadings generated or received by the firm regarding your case. This is an inexpensive way to keep Client advised of important developments as the case progresses. Client should contact the firm should Client have any questions or comments about documents received, or in the event Client is not receiving such copies.

Client agrees to keep the firm advised of Client's whereabouts at all times and to cooperate in the preparation and trial of the case, to appear on reasonable notice for appointments and court appearances, and to comply with all reasonable requests made of Client in connection with the preparation and presentation of this case.

IV. ATTORNEY/CLIENT PRIVILEGE AND ASSIGNMENT OF ATTORNEY

The attorney/client privilege protects the Client and applies to all work-product and confidential communications between attorney and Client. Disclosure of protected information may not be made without permission of the Client to any third party, including the party funding the representation.

From time-to-time, the attorney assigned to your case may consult with attorneys from other law firms about your case. This will not incur added expense and does not violate the attorney/client privilege.

From time-to-time, the firm may share office space with other attorneys and/or law firms. Nesci & St. Louis PLLC is solely responsible for your representation.

Although a lead-attorney will be assigned to Client's case, other attorneys from the firm may work on the case. Client has retained the firm of Nesci & St. Louis PLLC and not any individual attorney within the firm. Nesci & St. Louis PLLC reserves the right to reassign individual attorneys to use the firm's resources in the manner which the firm chooses in its sole discretion.

V. OUTCOME OF LITIGATION

Litigation is subject to many variables and therefore it is difficult to predict the outcome of any matter. The firm therefore cannot, and does not, guarantee the outcome of any contested matter.

VI. DISPUTES

If there is any disagreement concerning the terms of this Contract or attorneys' fees, Client agrees to binding arbitration with the fee arbitration committee of the State Bar of Arizona.

Any liability arising from representation or services provided by the firm shall be limited solely to Nesci & St. Louis P.L.L.C.

If you have any questions concerning the contents of this Contract, please discuss them with me. If not, please sign the original below and return it to me.

Thank you for allowing us the opportunity to represent you in this matter.

____
James Nesci, Partner
Nesci & St. Louis P.L.L.C.

I have read and understand the provisions of this Contract, have received a copy of it, and accept all of its terms.

DATED: ______________________________
Client: ______________________________
E-mail: ______________________________
Street Address: ______________________________
Tucson, AZ 857__
Home Phone: ______________________________
Cell Phone: ______________________________

2.5 Fees

Fees should be reasonable. When you set your prices, you need to take into account the complexity of the case, your level of expertise (but not necessarily your number of years in practice), your available time and market conditions. There is absolutely nothing wrong with charging more than others around you if you are doing better and more detailed work than those around you.

There are two competing theories in the defense community. The first theory builds a practice around running as many cases through the office as possible, with as little work as possible, and pleading as many cases as possible. Firms that work that way do a disservice to the community, to the law, to the profession and, most importantly, to the client.

The second theory builds a practice around client service and trying to do the right thing. Simply put: a drunk driving defense is expensive and the consequences of losing are too great to "hard sell" someone into a defense, and then sell that client down the river for the price of convenience.

Some good advice is to limit the number of cases that you defend and charge more for the individual case. You might not make more money than those around you, but you will be able to sleep at night, knowing that you were able to do your very best for that client.

In North Carolina, attorneys are permitted to charge flat fees. Since many DWIs are billed as an up-front, non-refundable flat fee, it is important to note that flat fees may not be deemed 'earned upon receipt,' 'non-refundable' or in similar terms unless the client is simultaneously advised in writing that the client may nevertheless discharge the lawyer at any time and in that event may be entitled to a refund of all or part of the flat fee based upon the value of the representation.

Rule 1.5 Fees[1]

(a) A lawyer shall not make an agreement for, charge, or collect an illegal or clearly excessive fee or charge or collect a clearly excessive amount for expenses. The factors to be considered in determining whether a fee is clearly excessive include the following:

(1) the time and labor required, the novelty and difficulty of the questions involved, and the skill requisite to perform the legal service properly;

(2) the likelihood, if apparent to the client, that the acceptance of the particular employment will preclude other employment by the lawyer;

(3) the fee customarily charged in the locality for similar legal services;

(4) the amount involved and the results obtained;

(5) the time limitations imposed by the client or by the circumstances;

(6) the nature and length of the professional relationship with the client;

(7) the experience, reputation, and ability of the lawyer or lawyers performing the services; and

(8) whether the fee is fixed or contingent.

(b) When the lawyer has not regularly represented the client, the scope of the representation and the basis or rate of the fee and expenses for which the client will be responsible shall be communicated to the client, preferably in writing, before or within a reasonable time after commencing the representation.

(c) A fee may be contingent on the outcome of the matter for which the service is rendered, except in a matter in which a contingent fee is prohibited by paragraph (d) or other law. A contingent fee agreement shall be in a writing signed by the client and shall state the method by which the fee is to be determined, including the percentage or percentages that shall accrue to the lawyer in the event of settlement, trial or appeal; litigation and other expenses to be deducted from the recovery; and whether such expenses are to be deducted before or after the contingent fee is calculated. The agreement must clearly notify the client of any expenses for which the client will be liable whether or not the client is the prevailing party. Upon conclusion of a contingent fee matter, the lawyer shall provide the client with a written statement stating the outcome of the matter and, if there is a recovery, showing the remittance to the client and the method of its determination.

(d) A lawyer shall not enter into an arrangement for, charge, or collect:

(1) a contingent fee for representing a defendant in a criminal case; however, a lawyer may charge and collect a contingent fee for representation in a criminal or civil asset forfeiture proceeding if not otherwise prohibited by law; or

(2) a contingent fee in a civil case in which such a fee is prohibited by law.

(e) A division of a fee between lawyers who are not in the same firm may be made only if:

(1) the division is in proportion to the services performed by each lawyer or each lawyer assumes joint responsibility for the representation;

(2) the client agrees to the arrangement, including the share each lawyer will receive, and the agreement is confirmed in writing; and

(3) the total fee is reasonable.

(f) Any lawyer having a dispute with a client regarding a fee for legal services must:

(1) make reasonable efforts to advise his or her client of the existence of the North Carolina State Bar's program of fee dispute resolution at least 30 days prior to initiating legal proceedings to collect the disputed fee; and

(2) participate in good faith in the fee dispute resolution process if the client submits a proper request.

Comment

Appropriate Fees and Expenses

[1] Paragraph (a) requires that lawyers charge fees that are not clearly excessive under the circumstances. The factors specified in (1) through (8) are not exclusive. Nor will each factor be relevant in each instance. Paragraph (a) also requires that expenses for which the client will be charged must not be clearly excessive. A lawyer may seek reimbursement for expenses for in-house services, such as copying, or for other expenses incurred in-house, such as telephone charges, either by charging a reasonable amount to which the client has agreed in advance or by charging an amount that reasonably reflects the cost incurred by the lawyer.

Basis or Rate of Fee

[2] When the lawyer has regularly represented a client, an understanding will have ordinarily evolved concerning the basis or rate of the fee and the expenses for which the client will be responsible. In a new client-lawyer relationship, however, a written understanding as to fees and expenses should be promptly established. Generally, furnishing the client with a simple memorandum or copy of the lawyer's customary fee arrangements will suffice, provided that the writing states the general nature of the legal services to be provided, the basis, rate or total amount of the fee and whether and to what extent the client will be responsible for any costs, expenses or disbursements in the course of the representation. A written statement concerning the terms of the engagement reduces the possibility of misunderstanding.

[3] Contingent fees, like any other fees, are subject to the standard of paragraph (a) of this Rule. In determining whether a particular contingent fee is clearly excessive, or whether it is reasonable to charge any form of contingent fee, a lawyer must consider the factors that are relevant under the circumstances. Applicable law may impose limitations on contingent fees, such as a ceiling on the percentage allowable, or may require a lawyer to offer clients an alternative basis for the fee. Applicable law also may apply to situations other than a contingent fee, for example, government regulations regarding fees in certain tax matters.

Terms of Payment

[4] A lawyer may require advance payment of a fee, but is obliged to return any unearned portion. See Rule 1.16(d). This does not apply when the advance payment is a true retainer to reserve services rather than an advance to secure the payment of fees yet to be earned. A lawyer may accept property in payment for services, such as an ownership interest in an enterprise, provided this does not involve acquisition of a proprietary interest in the cause of action or subject matter of the litigation contrary to Rule 1.8 (i). However, a fee paid in property instead of money may be subject to the requirements of Rule 1.8(a) because such fees often have the essential qualities of a business transaction with the client.

[5] Once a fee agreement has been reached between attorney and client, the attorney has an ethical obligation to fulfill the contract and represent the client's best interests regardless of whether the lawyer has struck an unfavorable bargain. An attorney may seek to renegotiate the fee agreement in light of changed circumstances or for other good cause, but the attorney may not abandon or threaten to abandon the client to cut the attorney's losses or to coerce an additional or higher fee. Any fee contract made or remade during the existence of the attorney-client relationship must be reasonable and freely and fairly made by the client having full knowledge of all material circumstances incident to the agreement. If a dispute later arises concerning the fee,

the burden of proving reasonableness and fairness will be upon the lawyer.

[6] An agreement may not be made whose terms might induce the lawyer improperly to curtail services for the client or perform them in a way contrary to the client's interest. For example, a lawyer should not enter into an agreement whereby services are to be provided only up to a stated amount when it is foreseeable that more extensive services probably will be required, unless the situation is adequately explained to the client. Otherwise, the client might have to bargain for further assistance in the midst of a proceeding or transaction. However, it is proper to define the extent of services in light of the client's ability to pay. A lawyer should not exploit a fee arrangement based primarily on hourly charges by using wasteful procedures.

Prohibited Contingent Fees

[7] Paragraph (d) prohibits a lawyer from charging a contingent fee in a domestic relations matter when payment is contingent upon the securing of a divorce or upon the amount of alimony or support to be obtained. This provision does not preclude a contract for a contingent fee for legal representation in connection with the recovery of post-judgment balances due under support, alimony or other financial orders because such contracts do not implicate the same policy concerns.

Division of Fee

[8] A division of fee is a single billing to a client covering the fee of two or more lawyers who are not in the same firm. A division of fee facilitates association of more than one lawyer in a matter in which neither alone could serve the client as well, and most often is used when the fee is contingent and the division is between a referring lawyer and a trial specialist. Paragraph (e) permits the lawyers to divide a fee either on the basis of the proportion of services they render or if each lawyer assumes responsibility for the representation as a whole. In addition, the client must agree to the arrangement, including the share that each lawyer is to receive, and the agreement must be confirmed in writing. A lawyer may divide a fee with an out-of-state lawyer who refers a matter to the lawyer if the conditions of paragraph (e) are satisfied. Contingent fee agreements must be in a writing signed by the client and must otherwise comply with paragraph (c) of this Rule. Joint responsibility for the representation entails financial and ethical responsibility for the representation as if the lawyers were associated in a partnership. A lawyer should only refer a matter to a lawyer whom the referring lawyer reasonably believes is competent to handle the matter. See Rule 1.1.

[9] Paragraph (e) does not prohibit or regulate division of fees to be received in the future for work done when lawyers were previously associated in a law firm.

Disputes over Fees

[10] Participation in the fee dispute resolution program of the North Carolina State Bar is mandatory when a client requests resolution of a disputed fee. Before filing an action to collect a disputed fee, the client must be advised of the fee dispute resolution program. Notification must occur not only when there is a specific issue in dispute, but also when the client simply fails to pay. However, when the client expressly acknowledges liability for the specific amount of the bill and states that he or she cannot presently pay the bill, the fee is not disputed and notification of the client is not required. In making reasonable efforts to advise the client of the existence of the fee dispute resolution program, it is preferable to address a written communication to the client at the client's last known address. If the address of the client is unknown, the lawyer should use reasonable efforts to acquire the current address of the client. Notification is not required in those instances where the State Bar does not have jurisdiction over the fee dispute as set forth in 27 N.C.A.C. 1D, .0702.

[11] If fee dispute resolution is requested by a client, the lawyer must participate in the resolution process in good faith. The State Bar program of fee dispute resolution uses mediation to resolve fee disputes as an alternative to litigation. The lawyer must cooperate with the person who is charged with investigating the dispute and with the person(s) appointed to mediate the dispute. Further information on the fee dispute resolution program can be found at 27 N.C.A.C. 1D, .0700, et. seq . The lawyer should fully set forth his or her position and support that position by appropriate documentation.

[12] A lawyer may petition a tribunal for a legal fee if allowed by applicable law or, subject to the requirements for fee dispute resolution set forth in Rule 1.5(f), may bring an action against a client to collect a fee. The tribunal's determination of the merit of the petition or the claim is reached by an application of law to fact and not by the application of this Rule. Therefore, a tribunal's reduction or denial of a petition or claim for a fee is not evidence that the fee request violates this Rule and is not admissible in a disciplinary proceeding brought under this Rule.

History Note: Statutory Authority G. 84-23

Adopted July 24, 1997

Amended March 1, 2003

ETHICS OPINION NOTES

CPR 11. An attorney may accept an interest in land as a fee for title examination and representation in an action to clear title.

CPR 37. An attorney may charge interest on delinquent accounts.

CPR 47. A Legal Aid Society may receive fees awarded by the court.

CPR 54. An attorney may submit a fee schedule to a savings and loan association.

CPR 79. An attorney serving as a trustee in bankruptcy or as a fiduciary in state proceedings may receive legal fees for acting as his own attorney.

CPR 129. An attorney may accept payment of legal fees by credit card.

CPR 312. Contingent fees may be charged in equitable distribution cases.

CPR 375. An attorney may agree for his fee to be the interest earned on an amount escrowed at a loan closing to guarantee completion of repairs.

RPC 2. Contingent fees may be charged to collect liquidated amounts of past due child support.

RPC 7. An attorney may employ a collection agency to collect a past due fee so long as the fee agreement out of which the account arose was permitted by law and by the Rules of Professional Conduct; the lawyer, at the time the underlying fee agreement was made, did not believe, and had no reason to believe, that he was undertaking to represent a client who was unable to afford his services; the legal services giving rise to the fee out of which the account arose have been completed so that the lawyer has no further responsibilities as the client's attorney; there is no genuine dispute between the lawyer and the client about the existence, amount, or delinquent status of the indebtedness; and the lawyer does not believe, and has no reason to believe, that the agency which he employs will use any illegal means to collect the account.

RPC 35. An attorney may not charge an elevated contingent fee to collect "med-pay" or any other claim with respect to which liability is clear and there is no real dispute as to the amount due.

RPC 50. A lawyer may charge nonrefundable retainers that are reasonable in amount. (But see 2000 FEO 5)

RPC 52. Opinion describes circumstances under which a lawyer who has been appointed to represent an indigent person may accept payment directly from the client.

RPC 106. Opinion discusses circumstances under which a refund of a prepaid fee is required.

RPC 107. A lawyer and her client may agree to employ alternative dispute resolution procedures to resolve disputes between themselves about legal fees.

RPC 141. An attorney's contingent fee in a case resolved by a structured settlement should, if paid in a lump sum, be calculated in terms of the settlement's present value.

RPC 148. A lawyer may not split a fee with another lawyer who does not practice in her law firm unless the division is based upon the work done by each lawyer or the client consents in writing, the fee is reasonable, and responsibility is joint.

RPC 155. An attorney may charge a contingent fee to collect delinquent child support.

RPC 158. A sum of money paid to a lawyer in advance to secure payment of a fee which is yet to be earned and to which the lawyer is not entitled must be deposited in the lawyer's trust account.

RPC 166. A lawyer may seek to renegotiate a fee agreement with a client provided he does not abandon or threaten to abandon his client to cut his losses or to coerce a higher fee.

RPC 174. A legal fee for the collection of "med-pay" which is based upon the amount collected is unreasonable.

RPC 190. A lawyer who agreed to bill a client on the basis of hours expended may not bill the client on the same basis for reused work product.

RPC 196. A law firm may not charge a clearly excessive fee for legal representation even if the legal fee may be recovered from an opposing party.

RPC 205. A lawyer may receive a fee for referring a case to another lawyer provided that, by written agreement with the client, both lawyers assume responsibility for the representation and the total fee is reasonable.

RPC 222. Prior to the completion of legal services for a client, a lawyer may not obtain a confession of judgment from a client to secure a fee.

RPC 231. A lawyer may not collect a contingent fee on the reimbursement paid to the client's medical insurance provider in addition to a contingent fee on the gross recovery if the total fee received by the lawyer is clearly excessive.

RPC 235. A lawyer may charge a client an hourly rate, or a flat rate, for his or her services plus a contingent fee on the client's recovery provided the ultimate fee paid by the client is not clearly excessive and the client is given an honest assessment of the potential for recovery.

RPC 247. Opinion provides guidelines for receipt of payment of earned and unearned fees by electronic transfers.

97 Formal Ethics Opinion 4. Opinion provides that flat fees may be collected at the beginning of a representation, treated as presently owed to the lawyer, and deposited into the lawyer's general operating account or paid to the lawyer but that if a collected fee is clearly excessive under the circumstances of the representation a refund to the client of some or all of the fee is required.

98 Formal Ethics Opinion 3. Opinion rules that, subject to the requirements of law, a lawyer may add a finance charge to a client's account if the client fails to pay the balance when due as agreed with the client.

98 Formal Ethics Opinion 9. Opinion rules that a lawyer may charge a client the actual cost of retrieving a closed client file from storage, subject to certain conditions, provided the lawyer does not withhold the file to extract payment.

98 Formal Ethics Opinion 14. Opinion rules that a lawyer may participate in the solicitation of funds from third parties to pay the legal fees of a client provided there is disclosure to contributors and the funds are administered honestly.

99 Formal Ethics Opinion 1. Opinion rules that a lawyer may not accept a referral fee or solicitor's fee for referring a client to an investment advisor.

2000 Formal Ethics Opinion 5. Opinion rules that a lawyer may not tell a client that any fee paid prior to the rendition of legal services is "nonrefundable" although, by agreement with the client, a lawyer may collect a flat fee for legal services to be rendered in the future and treat the fee as earned immediately upon receipt subject to certain conditions.

2000 Formal Ethics Opinion 7. Opinion rules that a lawyer may not charge the client a legal fee for the time required to participate in the State Bar's fee dispute resolution program.

2005 Formal Ethics Opinion 11. Opinion examines the requirements for an interim account used to pay the costs for real estate closings and also rules that the actual costs may be marked up by the lawyer provided there is full disclosure and the overcharges are not clearly excessive.

2005 Formal Ethics Opinion 12. Opinion explores a lawyer's obligation to return legal fees when a third party is the payor.

2005 Formal Ethics Opinion 13. Opinion rules that a minimum fee that will be billed against at an hourly rate and is collected at the beginning of representation belongs to the client and must be deposited into the trust account until earned and, upon termination of representation, the unearned portion of the fee must be returned to the client.

2006 Formal Ethics Opinion 14. Opinion rules that when a lawyer charges a fee for a consultation, and the lawyer accepts payment, there is a client-lawyer relationship for the purposes of the Rules of Professional Conduct.

2007 Formal Ethics Opinion 8. Opinion rules that a lawyer may not charge a client for filing and presenting a motion to withdraw unless withdrawal advances the client's objectives for the representation or the charge is approved by the court when ruling on a petition for legal fees from a court-appointed lawyer.

2007 Formal Ethics Opinion 13. Opinion rules that, to insure honest billing predicated on hourly charges, the lawyer must establish a reasonable hourly rate for his services and for the services of his staff; disclose the basis for the amounts to be charged; avoid wasteful, unnecessary, or redundant procedures; and make certain that the total cost to the client is not clearly excessive.

2008 Formal Ethics Opinion 8. A provision in a law firm employment agreement for dividing legal fees received after a lawyer's departure from a firm must be reasonable and may not penalize or deter the withdrawing lawyer from taking clients with her.

2008 Formal Ethics Opinion 10. Opinion surveys prior ethics opinions on legal fees, sets forth the ethical requirements for the different types of fees paid in advance, authorizes minimum fees earned upon payment, and provides model fee provisions.

2010 Formal Ethics Opinion 4. A lawyer may accept barter dollars as payment for legal services but all advance payments of litigation expenses by a barter exchange client must be paid in cash or by check or credit card.

2010 Formal Ethics Opinion 6. If a lawyer associates another law firm in connection with a legal matter, the lawyer may receive a fee in proportion to the services he performs in the matter or he may receive a fee based on his assumption of joint responsibility for the representation.

2010 Formal Ethics Opinion 10. A law firm may charge a client for the expenses associated with a remote consultation, but may not charge a flat fee for the remote consultation irrespective of the actual cost to the firm.

2011 Formal Ethics Opinion 6. A law firm may contract with a vendor of software as a service provided the lawyer uses reasonable care to safeguard confidential client information.

CASE NOTES

Entitlement to Reasonable Value of Services. - An attorney discharged by his client is entitled to recover the reasonable value of the services he has already rendered. The reasonable value of such services is determined by the totality of the circumstances of each case. *O'Brien v. Plumides*, 79 N.C. App. 159, 339 S.E.2d 54, *cert. dismissed* , 318 N.C. 409, 348 S.E.2d 805 (1986).

Plaintiff's attorney brought an action to recover a contingent fee in a personal injury case where the client had discharged the attorney after he had begun working on the client's case. The court held that the attorney was entitled to the reasonable value of the services rendered before his discharge by the client. *Covington v. Rhodes*, 38 N.C. App. 61, 247 S.E.2d 305 (1978) , *disc. rev. denied* , 296 N.C. 410, 251 S.E.2d 468 (1979).

Determination of Reasonable Fees. - Reasonable counsel fees may be determined in part by the amount of the verdict obtained in a condemnation proceeding in light of proposals made to the property owner prior to his employment of an attorney. The results obtained by an attorney are a legitimate consideration in determining the amount of his fee. *Redevelopment Comm'n v. Hyder*, 20 N.C. App. 241, 201 S.E.2d 236 (1973).

The court refused to issue a temporary restraining order where lawyer in fee dispute with client failed to follow the procedures of this section and there was a state court action pending. *Parker v. United States* , 948 F. Supp. 24 (E.D.N.C. 1996).

Contingent Fee Contracts in Domestic Cases. - A contingent fee contract for legal services in a divorce, alimony or child support proceeding is void. *Thompson v. Thompson* , 70 N.C. App. 147, 319 S.E.2d 315 (1984), *rev'd on other grounds* , 313 N.C. 313, 328 S.E.2d 288 (1985).

Contingent Fee Contracts in Obtaining Equitable Distribution. - A contingent fee contract for an attorney's services in obtaining an equitable distribution is valid if the contract does not compensate the attorney for securing a divorce for the same client. *In Re Cooper* , 81 N.C. App. 27, 344 S.E.2d 27 (1986).

Contingent Contract Held Void. - Fee contract which provided that the attorney would receive 20% of the total amount recovered in an action for alimony and child support was void as against public policy. *Townsend v. Harris* , 102 N.C. App. 131, 401 S.E.2d 132, *appeal dismissed* , 328 N.C. 734, 404 S.E.2d 877, *cert. denied* , 502 U.S. 919, 112 S. Ct. 329 116 L. Ed. 2d. 270 (1991).

Quoted in *Robinson, Bradshaw & Hinson, P.A. v. Smith* , 139 N.C. App. 1, 532 S.E.2d 815 (2000).

Cited in *West ex rel . Farris v. Tilley* , 120 N.C. App. 145, 461 S.E.2d 1 (1995).

2.6 IOLTA

Interest on Lawyer Trust Accounts (IOLTA) are for money that does not belong to the firm. Each trust account has the same tax ID number assigned to it and the state bar collects the interest earned on all accounts to use for the benefit of the members of the state bar.

PRACTICE TIP: Although rare for a DWI defense attorney to take in money for such things as settlements in a DWI case, the attorney might share the firm account with other members of the firm who do civil work. It is possible that a deposit could be made by a member of the firm which is the subject of a federal interpleader action. This could cause the entire trust account assets to be frozen pending the outcome of the action. Checks will bounce. The bar will be notified. It will be a huge mess that could have been easily avoided by simply doing the following: If the firm does more than just criminal work, a separate trust account should be maintained for monies deposited by clients for DWI expenses such as expert witnesses, transcripts, retesting of blood vials, and so on. Thus, if the trust account is frozen, it will affect only one trust account.

In addition to electronic records, it is simple, easy and wise to keep a handwritten ledger for clients' funds. Two simple three-ring binders in alphabetical order will work well. One binder is for active cases and the other is for terminated cases. Each record is nothing more than a one- or two-page ledger as follows:

Client: Bell, Brian		**Docket No. TR 123456**	
Date	**Description**	**Check #**	**Amount**
05/23/12	Expenses Retainer	Cash	$2,000
08/02/12	Expert Witness Fee	5004	$1,500
08/06/12	Transcripts	5009	$250
10/26/12	Client Refund	5050	$250
10/26/12	Final Balance Case Closed	N/A	Bal. 0

Three-Way Reconciliation

A three-way reconciliation can be an accurate accounting method of keeping track of client funds when done properly. As with anything, however, it is only as accurate as the information which is used in the accounting. The three-way reconciliation has three components, as the name suggests:

> **Escrow Trial Balance:** This is an accounting of all open client accounts at a specific point in time. It is often helpful to figure this balance on the date of the bank statement. It takes into account all credits and debits, whether checks or funds have cleared or not. It also includes any fees and surcharges.
>
> **Bank Statement**: This is your monthly account statement, listing all debits and credits.
>
> **Check Register**: This is your firm's check register. Keep it up to date.

The first step is to make sure that all Escrow Trial Balance components are accounted for and come up with a balance for each client. Then add all of the balances together for a total sum that should be in the IOLTA account.

Next, compare the Escrow Trial Balance sum to your monthly bank statement. These may differ, based on uncashed checks and other funds which have not yet cleared the account. For example, you may have deposited a client check into the IOLTA on the 14th of the month and your bank statement is printed on the 15th of the month. The client's check may not have cleared at the time that the bank printed the statement and would not appear. That is why the third step exists.

The third step is to compare your check register to the bank statement to reconcile credits and debits which have not yet been accounted for by the bank. If you can find the differences in the check register and they all balance out, then all is fine in the IOLTA account. If not, you have some searching to do to account for the missing or surplus funds.

2.7 Communication

The most frequent bar complaint from clients in every state is for lack of communication. Think about it from the client's perspective: the client has paid you lots of money to take care of a problem that is, most likely, the largest problem that person will ever face—and you don't talk to him.

Taking on fewer cases than other attorneys do and putting more time into the cases is a successful basic strategy, and it allows you to make the personal commitment to your clients. When a letter is written to a client, you may be able to write it yourself.

If your practice is a large operation with attorneys stretched thin, you can accomplish adequate communication by the use of form letters written by office staff. Be sure that if you communicate with clients via e-mail that your e-mail is secure, and that you always print hard-copies of the e-mail for inclusion in the client's file.

Make it a practice to return phone calls within 24 hours. Sometimes you may be in trial and not able to return the call. If so, have someone from your office return the call even if it is only to say that you are in trial, you have received the message and you have not forgotten about the client. Most clients will understand that although you will have enough time to defend her case there might be some periods of time when you will have to focus undivided attention on another client's case. Assure them that when the time comes for hearings and trial, they will have your undivided attention as well.

Copy the client on everything. If you request interviews with witnesses, or correspond with any driver's license agency or the prosecutor, forward a copy of the correspondence. Police reports and transcripts should always be forwarded with instructions for the client to read the material and comment. No matter how much investigation you do, you were not there when your client was arrested. Your client will always have something to add—whether it is helpful or not.

Prepare your client to receive police reports. Often the client will call asking if you have received the police report yet and "does it look bad?" I always tell clients, beforehand, that the police report will probably look bad. This is because the police report says "You did it." I tell clients that the police generally will not write down the good stuff—they only record the things that make you look drunk.

Breath test machine calibration logs, blood test chromatograms and urine test lab documents will likely be gibberish to a client. It is important either to write a detailed explanation of the documents or to call the client in to discuss the documents. Always be sure to give the client an opinion of whether the machine was working properly or whether the test was done properly. If you cannot tell without further investigation, let the client know what needs to be done. Do not be afraid of telling the client that you don't know something—just be sure to find the answer.

Even if you lose the case, your client will appreciate the work that you put into the case, but only if you have treated that client right throughout the representation. One of the most important aspects of that is client communication.

The ABA Model Rules of Professional Conduct (2004) are great rules to live by. Not only will they keep you out of hot water with the bar, they will also be an integral part of a good attorney-client relationship. As passed by the American Bar Association House of Delegates on February 5, 2002, and amended in August 2002, Rule 1.4 states:

> (a) A lawyer shall:
>
> (1) promptly inform the client of any decision or circumstance with respect to which the client's informed consent, as defined in Rule 1.0 (e), is required by these Rules;
>
> (2) reasonably consult with the client about the means by which the client's objectives are to be accomplished;
>
> (3) keep the client reasonably informed about the status of the matter;
>
> (4) promptly comply with reasonable requests for information; and
>
> (5) consult with the client about any relevant limitation on the lawyer's conduct when the lawyer knows that the client expects assistance not permitted by the Rules of Professional Conduct or other law.
>
> (b) A lawyer shall explain a matter to the extent reasonably necessary to permit the client to make informed decisions regarding the representation.

2.8 Client File Retention

The length of time that an attorney must retain a client file, after the case is closed, is governed by bar rules. Closed client files can take up an extraordinary amount of space. However, one may be able to electronically store the client's files for future reference. In addition, consider giving your client a closed file electronically. USB memory stick or "jump drives," are an easy solution to delivering an entire paper file to your client. Many companies will sell USB memory sticks with your company's name and logo on the outside. It is then a simple matter of scanning the documents to the stick. Do not forget to include a message to the client, thanking her for allowing you the opportunity to represent her in the case. You can also include a hot-link to your website, or e-mail. (And, if you want to get rid of the file without the cost of storage, transport or shredding it, offer the physical file to the client when the case is over—problem solved.)

If you do have to delete files from your inventory, be sure to completely destroy it. Shredding is a well-accepted and proper way of disposing of sensitive documents. Many companies have mobile shredders and will come to your office to shred the documents. Be aware that some companies will run special deals where they will destroy the first ten or so boxes for one price. It is best to save up your files for mass-shredding to take advantage of this deal. If the company offers a certificate of destruction, take it (or simply save the receipt with a list of the files that you had destroyed).

Endnotes

1. The North Carolina State Bar Rules of Professional Conduct are a public record. This material is the property of the North Carolina State Bar.

Chapter 3

Driving While Impaired

3.1 Misdemeanor DWI: Many Changes

Since the passage of the Motor Vehicle Driver Protection Act in 2006 (hereafter "The Act"), the DWI laws in North Carolina have only increased in their severity. The Act modified the statutes on checking station and roadblock guidelines as well as many of the pretrial and Court procedures. After the sweeping 2006 changes, the State legislature continued to tinker with DWI legislation by changing penalties and sentencing factors. In the latest revision, our State added more stringent community service and Interlock guidelines for defendants convicted of subsequent DWI offenses in order to conform more closely to the Federal laws.

N.C.G.S. §20-4.01–Definitions

Before one even begins to read the substantive DWI statutes, one must understand the words and phrases which make up the statutes. It is a surprise to most people to find that "alcohol" includes not only the type found in beer and wine (ethanol), but also types of alcohol that were never meant for ingestion such as wood alcohol (methanol) and rubbing alcohol (isopropanol).

§28-101. Definitions

In this title, unless the context otherwise requires:Unless the context requires otherwise, the following definitions apply throughout this Chapter to the defined words and phrases and their cognates:

(1a) Alcohol. - Any substance containing any form of alcohol, including ethanol, methanol, propanol, and isopropanol.

(1b) Alcohol Concentration. - The concentration of alcohol in a person, expressed either as:

a. Grams of alcohol per 100 milliliters of blood; or

b. Grams of alcohol per 210 liters of breath.

The results of a defendant's alcohol concentration determined by a chemical analysis of the defendant's breath or blood shall be reported to the hundredths. Any result between hundredths shall be reported to the next lower hundredth.

(2) Canceled. - As applied to drivers' licenses and permits, a declaration that a license or permit which was issued through error or fraud, or to which G.S. 20-15(a)(3) applies, is void and terminated.

(2a) Class A Motor Vehicle. - A combination of motor vehicles that meets either of the following descriptions:

a. Has a combined GVWR of at least 26,001 pounds and includes as part of the combination a towed unit that has a GVWR of at least 10,001 pounds.

b. Has a combined GVWR of less than 26,001 pounds and includes as part of the combination a towed unit that has a GVWR of at least 10,001 pounds.

(2b) Class B Motor Vehicle. - Any of the following:

a. A single motor vehicle that has a GVWR of at least 26,001 pounds.

b. A combination of motor vehicles that includes as part of the combination a towing unit that has a GVWR of at least 26,001 pounds and a towed unit that has a GVWR of less than 10,001 pounds.

(2c) Class C Motor Vehicle. - Any of the following:

a. A single motor vehicle not included in Class B.

b. A combination of motor vehicles not included in Class A or Class B.

(3a) Chemical Analysis. - A test or tests of the breath, blood, or other bodily fluid or substance of a person to determine the person's alcohol concentration or presence of an impairing substance, performed in accordance with G.S. 20-139.1, including duplicate or sequential analyses.

(3b) Chemical Analyst. - A person granted a permit by the Department of Health and Human Services under G.S. 20-139.1 to perform chemical analyses.

(3c) Commercial Drivers License (CDL). - A license issued by a state to an individual who resides in the state that authorizes the individual to drive a class of commercial motor vehicle. A "nonresident commercial drivers license (NRCDL)" is issued by a state to an individual who resides in a foreign jurisdiction.

(3d) Commercial Motor Vehicle. - Any of the following motor vehicles that are designed or used to transport passengers or property:

a. A Class A motor vehicle that has a combined GVWR of at least 26,001 pounds and includes as part of the combination a towed unit that has a GVWR of at least 10,001 pounds.

b. A Class B motor vehicle.- Any of the following:

a. A single motor vehicle that has a GVWR of at least 26,001 pounds.

b. A combination of motor vehicles that includes as part of the combination a towing unit that has a GVWR of at least 26,001 pounds and a towed unit that has a GVWR of less than 10,001 pounds.

c. A Class C motor vehicle that meets either of the following descriptions:

1. Is designed to transport 16 or more passengers, including the driver.

2. Is transporting hazardous materials and is required to be placarded in accordance with 49 C.F.R. Part 172, Subpart F.

(4) Commissioner. - The Commissioner of Motor Vehicles.

(4a) Conviction. - A conviction for an offense committed in North Carolina or another state:

a. In-State. When referring to an offense committed in North Carolina, the term means any of the following:

1. A final conviction of a criminal offense, including a no contest plea.

2. A determination that a person is responsible for an infraction, including a no contest plea.

3. An unvacated forfeiture of cash in the full amount of a bond required by Article 26 of Chapter 15A of the General Statutes.

4. A third or subsequent prayer for judgment continued within any five-year period.

5. Any prayer for judgment continued if the offender holds a commercial drivers license or if the offense occurs in a commercial motor vehicle.

b. Out-of-State. When referring to an offense committed outside North Carolina, the term means any of the following:

1. An unvacated adjudication of guilt.

2. A determination that a person has violated or failed to comply with the law in a court of original jurisdiction or an authorized administrative tribunal.

3. An unvacated forfeiture of bail or collateral deposited to secure the person's appearance in court.

4. A violation of a condition of release without bail, regardless of whether or not the penalty is rebated, suspended, or probated.

5. A final conviction of a criminal offense, including a no contest plea.

6. Any prayer for judgment continued, including any payment of a fine or court costs, if the offender holds a commercial drivers license or if the offense occurs in a commercial motor vehicle.

(4b) Crash. - Any event that results in injury or property damage attributable directly to the motion of a motor vehicle or its load. The terms collision, accident, and crash and their cognates are synonymous.

(5b) Disqualification. - A withdrawal of the privilege to drive a commercial motor vehicle.

(6) Division. - The Division of Motor Vehicles acting directly or through its duly authorized officers and agents.

(7) Driver. - The operator of a vehicle, as defined in subdivision (25). The terms "driver" and "operator" and their cognates are synonymous.

(7a) Electric Personal Assistive Mobility Device. - A self-balancing nontandem two-wheeled device, designed to transport one person, with a propulsion system that limits the maximum speed of the device to 15 miles per hour or less.

(13) Highway. - The entire width between property or right-of-way lines of every way or place of whatever nature, when any part thereof is open to the use of the public as a matter of right for the purposes of vehicular traffic. The terms "highway" and "street" and their cognates are synonymous.

(14a) Impairing Substance. - Alcohol, controlled substance under Chapter 90 of the General Statutes, any other drug or psychoactive substance capable of impairing a person's physical or mental faculties, or any combination of these substances.

(16) Intersection. - The area embraced within the prolongation of the lateral curblines or, if none, then the lateral edge of roadway lines of two or more highways which join one another at any angle whether or not one such highway crosses the other.
Where a highway includes two roadways 30 feet or more apart, then every crossing of each roadway of such divided highway by an intersecting highway shall be regarded as a separate intersection. In the event that such intersecting highway also includes two roadways 30 feet or more apart, then every crossing of two roadways of such highways shall be regarded as a separate intersection.

(17) License. - Any driver's license or any other license or permit to operate a motor vehicle issued under or granted by the laws of this State including:
a. Any temporary license or learner's permit;
b. The privilege of any person to drive a motor vehicle whether or not such person holds a valid license; and
c. Any nonresident's operating privilege.

(18) Local Authorities. - Every county, municipality, or other territorial district with a local board or body having authority to adopt local police regulations under the Constitution and laws of this State.

(21a) Moped. - A type of passenger vehicle as defined in G.S. 105-164.3

(22) Motorcycle. - A type of passenger vehicle as defined in G.S. 20-4.01(27).

(23) Motor Vehicle. - Every vehicle which is self-propelled and every vehicle designed to run upon the highways which is pulled by a self-propelled vehicle. This shall not include mopeds as defined in G.S. 20-4.01(27)d1.

(24) Nonresident. - Any person whose legal residence is in some state, territory, or jurisdiction other than North Carolina or in a foreign country.

(24a) Offense Involving Impaired Driving. - Any of the following offenses:
a. Impaired driving under G.S. 20-138.1.
b. Any offense set forth under G.S. 20-141.4 when conviction is based upon impaired driving or a substantially similar offense under previous law.
c. First or second degree murder under G.S. 14-17 or involuntary manslaughter under G.S. 14-18 when conviction is based upon impaired driving or a substantially similar offense under previous law.
d. An offense committed in another jurisdiction which prohibits substantially similar conduct prohibited by the offenses in this subsection.
e. A repealed or superseded offense substantially similar to impaired driving, including offenses under former G.S. 20-138 or G.S. 20-139.
f. Impaired driving in a commercial motor vehicle under G.S. 20-138.2, except that convictions of impaired driving under G.S. 20-138.1 and G.S. 20-138.2 arising out of the same transaction shall be considered a single conviction of an offense involving impaired driving for any purpose under this Chapter.
g. Habitual impaired driving under G.S. 20-138.5.

A conviction under former G.S. 20-140(c) is not an offense involving impaired driving.

(25) Operator. - A person in actual physical control of a vehicle which is in motion or which has the engine running. The terms "operator" and "driver" and their cognates are synonymous.

(26) Owner. - A person holding the legal title to a vehicle, or in the event a vehicle is the subject of a chattel mortgage or an agreement for the conditional sale or lease thereof or other like agreement, with the right of purchase upon performance of the conditions stated in the agreement, and with the immediate right of possession vested in the mortgagor, conditional vendee or lessee, said mortgagor, conditional vendee or lessee shall be deemed the owner for the purpose of this Chapter. For the purposes of this Chapter, the lessee of a vehicle owned by the government of the United States shall be considered the owner of said vehicle.

(27) Passenger Vehicles. -
a. Excursion passenger vehicles. - Vehicles transporting persons on sight-seeing or travel tours.
b. For hire passenger vehicles. - Vehicles transporting persons for compensation. This classification shall not include vehicles operated as ambulances; vehicles operated by the owner where the costs of operation are shared by the passengers; vehicles operated pursuant to a ridesharing arrangement as defined in G.S. 136-44.21; vehicles transporting students for the public school system under contract with the State Board of Education or vehicles leased to the United States of America or any of its agencies on a nonprofit basis; or vehicles used for human service or volunteer transportation.
c. Common carriers of passengers. - Vehicles operated under a certificate of authority issued by the Utilities Commission for operation on the highways of this State between fixed termini or over a regular route for the transportation of persons for compensation.

c1. Child care vehicles. - Vehicles under the direction and control of a child care facility, as defined in G.S. 110-86(3), and driven by an owner, employee, or agent of the child care facility for the primary purpose of transporting children to and from the child care facility, or to and from a place for participation in an event or activity in connection with the child care facility.

d. Motorcycles. - Vehicles having a saddle for the use of the rider and designed to travel on not more than three wheels in contact with the ground, including motor scooters and motor-driven bicycles, but excluding tractors and utility vehicles equipped with an additional form of device designed to transport property, three-wheeled vehicles while being used by law-enforcement agencies and mopeds as defined in subdivision d1 of this subsection.

d1. Moped. - Defined in G.S. 105-164.3.

d2. Motor home or house car. - A vehicular unit, designed to provide temporary living quarters, built into as an integral part, or permanently attached to, a self-propelled motor vehicle chassis or van. The vehicle must provide at least four of the following facilities: cooking, refrigeration or icebox, self-contained toilet, heating or air conditioning, a portable water supply system including a faucet and sink, separate 110-125 volt electrical power supply, or an LP gas supply.

d3. School activity bus. - A vehicle, generally painted a different color from a school bus, whose primary purpose is to transport school students and others to or from a place for participation in an event other than regular classroom work. The term includes a public, private, or parochial vehicle that meets this description.

d4. School bus. - A vehicle whose primary purpose is to transport school students over an established route to and from school for the regularly scheduled school day, that is equipped with alternately flashing red lights on the front and rear and a mechanical stop signal, that is painted primarily yellow below the roofline, and that bears the plainly visible words "School Bus" on the front and rear. The term includes a public, private, or parochial vehicle that meets this description.

e. U-drive-it passenger vehicles. - Passenger vehicles included in the definition of U-drive-it vehicles set forth in this section.

f. Ambulances. - Vehicles equipped for transporting wounded, injured, or sick persons.

g. Private passenger vehicles. - All other passenger vehicles not included in the above definitions.

h. Low-speed vehicle. A four-wheeled electric vehicle whose top speed is greater than 20 miles per hour but less than 25 miles per hour.

(28) Person. - Every individual, firm, partnership, association, corporation, governmental agency, or combination thereof of whatsoever form or character.

(30) Private Road or Driveway. - Every road or driveway not open to the use of the public as a matter of right for the purpose of vehicular traffic.

(31a) Provisional Licensee. - A person under the age of 18 years.

(32) Public Vehicular Area. - Any area within the State of North Carolina that meets one or more of the following requirements:

a. The area is used by the public for vehicular traffic at any time, including by way of illustration and not limitation any drive, driveway, road, roadway, street, alley, or parking lot upon the grounds and premises of any of the following:

1. Any public or private hospital, college, university, school, orphanage, church, or any of the institutions, parks or other facilities maintained and supported by the State of North Carolina or any of its subdivisions.

2. Any service station, drive-in theater, supermarket, store, restaurant, or office building, or any other business, residential, or municipal establishment providing parking space whether the business or establishment is open or closed.

3. Any property owned by the United States and subject to the jurisdiction of the State of North Carolina. (The inclusion of property owned by the United States in this definition shall not limit assimilation of North Carolina law when applicable under the provisions of Title 18, United States Code, section 13).

b. The area is a beach area used by the public for vehicular traffic.

c. The area is a road used by vehicular traffic within or leading to a gated or non-gated subdivision or community, whether or not the subdivision or community roads have been offered for dedication to the public.

d. The area is a portion of private property used by vehicular traffic and designated by the private property owner as a public vehicular area in accordance with G.S. 20-219.4.

(32b) Regular Drivers License. - A license to drive a commercial motor vehicle that is exempt from the commercial drivers license requirements or a non-commercial motor vehicle.

(33a) Relevant Time after the Driving. - Any time after the driving in which the driver still has in his body alcohol consumed before or during the driving.

(33b) Reportable Crash. - A crash involving a motor vehicle that results in one or more of the following:

a. Death or injury of a human being.
b. Total property damage of one thousand dollars ($1,000) or more, or property damage of any amount to a vehicle seized pursuant to G. S. 20-28.3.

(34) Resident. - Any person who resides within this State for other than a temporary or transitory purpose for more than six months shall be presumed to be a resident of this State; but absence from the State for more than six months shall raise no presumption that the person is not a resident of this State.

(36) Revocation or Suspension. - Termination of a licensee's or permittee's privilege to drive or termination of the registration of a vehicle for a period of time stated in an order of revocation or suspension. The terms "revocation" or "suspension" or a combination of both terms shall be used synonymously.

(38) Roadway. - That portion of a highway improved, designed, or ordinarily used for vehicular travel, exclusive of the shoulder. In the event a highway includes two or more separate roadways the term "roadway" as used herein shall refer to any such roadway separately but not to all such roadways collectively.

(41a) Serious Traffic Violation. - A conviction of one of the following offenses when operating a commercial or other motor vehicle:

a. Excessive speeding, involving a single charge of any speed 15 miles per hour or more above the posted speed limit.
b. Careless and reckless driving.
c. A violation of any State or local law relating to motor vehicle traffic control, other than a parking violation, arising in connection with a fatal accident.
d. Improper or erratic lane changes.
e. Following the vehicle ahead too closely.
f. Driving a commercial motor vehicle without obtaining a commercial drivers license.
g. Driving a commercial motor vehicle without a commercial drivers license in the driver's possession.
h. Driving a commercial motor vehicle without the proper class of commercial drivers license or endorsements for the specific vehicle group being operated or for the passenger or type of cargo being transported.
i. Unlawful use of a mobile telephone under G.S. 20-137.4A or Part 390 or Part 392 of Title 49 of the Code of Federal Regulations while operating a commercial motor vehicle.

(45) State. - A state, territory, or possession of the United States, District of Columbia, Commonwealth of Puerto Rico, a province of Canada, or the Sovereign Nation of the Eastern Band of the Cherokee Indians with tribal lands, as defined in 18 U.S.C. § 1151, located within the boundaries of the State of North Carolina. For provisions in this Chapter that apply to commercial drivers licenses, "state" means a state of the United States and the District of Columbia.

(46) Street. - A highway, as defined in subdivision (13). The terms "highway" and "street" and their cognates are synonymous.

(47) Suspension. - Termination of a licensee's or permittee's privilege to drive or termination of the registration of a vehicle for a period of time stated in an order of revocation or suspension. The terms "revocation" or "suspension" or a combination of both terms shall be used synonymously.

(48b) Under the Influence of an Impairing Substance. - The state of a person having his physical or mental faculties, or both, appreciably impaired by an impairing substance.

(49) Vehicle. - Every device in, upon, or by which any person or property is or may be transported or drawn upon a highway, excepting devices moved by human power or used exclusively upon fixed rails or tracks; provided, that for the purposes of this Chapter bicycles shall be deemed vehicles and every rider of a bicycle upon a highway shall be subject to the provisions of this Chapter applicable to the driver of a vehicle except those which by their nature can have no application. This term shall not include a device which is designed for and intended to be used as a means of transportation for a person with a mobility impairment, or who uses the device for mobility enhancement, is suitable for use both inside and outside a building, including on

sidewalks, and is limited by design to 15 miles per hour when the device is being operated by a person with a mobility impairment, or who uses the device for mobility enhancement. This term shall not include an electric personal assistive mobility device as defined in G.S. 20-4.01(7a).

Date of offense

Caution: I've written this chapter making an assumption that your client is charged after October 1, 2013. Since North Carolina's DWI laws change so frequently it is important to look at the date of the offense to see what sentencing factors apply. In general, look for offenses committed before December 1, 2011 on or after December 1, 2011, offenses committed on or after December 1, 2012 but before October 1, 2013. If you find a client in that boat, refer to the sentencing statutes in those years. A lot of changes were made which include changing the age of a child in the car and aggravating the level, when CAM began to be allowed instead of active jail time, and when the new Aggravated Level One came to be.

N.C.G.S. §20-138–Misdemeanor DWI

The standard DWI charge in the State is found under this section as well as DWI for CDL holders driving commercial vehicles and for drivers charged that are under the age of twenty one.

The Law:

20-138.1. Impaired Driving.

(a) Offense. - A person commits the offense of impaired driving if he drives any vehicle upon any highway, any street, or any public vehicular area within this State:

(1) While under the influence of an impairing substance; or

(2) After having consumed sufficient alcohol that he has, at any relevant time after the driving, an alcohol concentration of 0.08 or more. The results of a chemical analysis shall be deemed sufficient evidence to prove a person's alcohol concentration; or

(3) With any amount of a Schedule I controlled substance, as listed in G.S. 90-89, or its metabolites in his blood or urine.

(a1) A person who has submitted to a chemical analysis of a blood sample, pursuant to G.S. 20-139.1(d), may use the result in rebuttal as evidence that the person did not have, at a relevant time after driving, an alcohol concentration of 0.08 or more.

(b) Defense Precluded. - The fact that a person charged with violating this section is or has been legally entitled to use alcohol or a drug is not a defense to a charge under this section.

(b1) Defense Allowed. - Nothing in this section shall preclude a person from asserting that a chemical analysis result is inadmissible pursuant to G.S. 20-139.1(b2).

(c) Pleading. - In any prosecution for impaired driving, the pleading is sufficient if it states the time and place of the alleged offense in the usual form and charges that the defendant drove a vehicle on a highway or public vehicular area while subject to an impairing substance.

(d) Sentencing Hearing and Punishment. - Impaired driving as defined in this section is a misdemeanor. Upon conviction of a defendant of impaired driving, the presiding judge shall hold a sentencing hearing and impose punishment in accordance with G.S. 20-179.

(e) Exception. - Notwithstanding the definition of "vehicle" pursuant to G.S. 20-4.01(49), for purposes of this section the word "vehicle" does not include a horse.

The above statute is the gold standard for a prosecutor in North Carolina determined to convict your client of DWI. The first question that comes to mind in reference to this statute is what constitutes operation in the context of the statutory language? The term "drives" can be understood in a wide variety of ways. In North Carolina, to show operation, the State must prove that either the engine of the vehicle was running or that the defendant was in control of the vehicle (see N.C.G.S. §20-4.01(25)) which has been reprinted above in the definitions section). Can the State prove that your client was in a vehicle with the engine running or had actual physical control of the vehicle? The courts have found that operation existed when a person steered the wheel of a vehicle that was being towed by another vehicle.

Okay, so what qualifies as a vehicle? Once again, a vehicle is defined above in our definitions section and can also be found in N.C.G.S. §20-4.01(49). And if we look closely, we can see that the legislature has also included "bicycle" in its definition of vehicle; so yes, you can get a DWI on a bicycle in North Carolina. On the other hand, a horse would not qualify nor would a skate board.

Let's take a look at our next element: street or highway or public vehicular area (PVA). The terms street and highway are pretty much the same and are also defined in the definitions section above as well as in N.C.G.S. §20-4.01(13). The PVA is a different beast; mainly, when we think of PVAs we think of parking lots. N.C.G.S. §20-4.01 (32) goes into more detail on what qualifies as a PVA and is also included in our definitions section above. Keep in mind that PVAs can be private parking areas, private drives, private business parking, and federally owned property in the State.

What does it mean to be under the influence of an impairing substance? That is defined above as well and under N.C.G.S. §20-4.01(48b). It just requires that the person's mental or physical faculties or both be impaired and that impairment needs only to be appreciable (commonly defined as noticeable). An impairing substance is alcohol (defined above and under §20-4.01 (1a) as any form of alcohol including ethanol, methanol, propanol, and isopropanol), any controlled substance in chapter 90 of the North Carolina General Statutes, any other drug or psychoactive substance capable of impairing a person's mental or physical faculties or any combination of these substances (see N.C.G.S. §20-4.01 (14a)).

Our next element deals with the number itself: 0.08 at a relevant time after driving. The mistake a lot of new attorneys make in DWI defense in North Carolina is that they rely far too heavily on this number. Keep in mind that this number is only prima facie evidence that your client is impaired. See *State v. Narron* 193 N.C. App. 76 (2008), holding that if the number is properly admitted, the statutory language "shall be deemed sufficient evidence to prove" does NOT create an unconstitutional mandatory presumption, but does allow for the chemical analysis to be treated as a prima facie evidence of the defendant's alcohol concentration. Also see State v. Simmons 205 N.C. App. 509 (2010), which talks about *Narron*. In jury trials where the number is going to be an issue, I often ask the judge to allow what we North Carolina DWI defense attorneys call a Narron/Simmons instruction.

PRACTICE TIP: The Forsyth County District Attorney's Office often tries DWI cases where the number result is below the ever sought after 0.08. I've tried more than one DWI case where the number in question was a 0.06 or 0.07. The State also likes to bring in their own "expert" witness to testify about retrograde extrapolation in order to artificially raise your client's blood alcohol content by saying that during the time of the actual driving, your client was over the legal limit and should be convicted. I always strongly recommend using an expert witness when confronted with retrograde extrapolation, especially if you are new to the concept or your jurisdiction has begun bringing in experts for the State. We will talk more about retrograde extrapolation in a later chapter.

A relevant time after driving is defined once again in N.C.G.S. §20-4.01 (33a) which basically says that any time after driving when the person has any alcohol remaining in that person's body that was consumed before or during the driving. A common defense strategy is the drinking after driving defense. I have successfully argued this defense in cases where the client tells you that he had an accident, went home, and then proceeded to have a few drinks to calm his nerves. Usually, the police arrive later and then charge your client with DWI even after the client has admitted to the police that they had not had a drink until after the accident.

Keep in mind that ANY amount of a Schedule I drug as defined in N.C.G.S. §90-89 is DWI. The State doesn't have to prove that your client was impaired if they have taken your client's blood and the results come back with any metabolites of a Schedule I drug. A Schedule I drug can be a lot of different things, and for that reason, I've reprinted N.C.G.S. §90-89 here:

§ 90-89. Schedule I controlled substances.

This schedule includes the controlled substances listed or to be listed by whatever official name, common or usual name, chemical name, or trade name designated. In determining that a substance comes within this schedule, the Commission shall find: a high potential for abuse, no currently accepted medical use in the United States, or a lack of accepted safety for use in treatment under medical supervision. The following controlled substances are included in this schedule:

(1) Any of the following opiates, including the isomers, esters, ethers, salts and salts of isomers, esters, and ethers, unless specifically excepted, or listed in another schedule, whenever the existence of such isomers, esters, ethers, and salts is possible within the specific chemical designation:

a. Acetyl-alpha-methylfentanyl (N[1-(1-methyl-2-phenethyl)-4-piperidinyl]-N-phenylacetamide).
b. Acetylmethadol.
c. Repealed by Session Laws 1987, c. 412, s. 2.
d. Alpha-methylthiofentanyl (N-[1-methyl-2-(2-thienyl)ethyl-4-piperidinyl]-N-phenylpropanamide).
e. Allylprodine.
f. Alphacetylmethadol.
g. Alphameprodine.
h. Alphamethadol.
i. Alpha-methylfentanyl (N-(1-(alpha-methyl-beta-phenyl) ethyl-4-piperidyl) propionalilide; 1(1-methyl-2-phenyl-ethyl)-4-(N-propani-

lido) piperidine).
j. Benzethidine.
k. Betacetylmethadol.
l. Beta-hydroxfentanyl (N-[1-(2-hydroxy-2-phenethyl)-4-piperidinyl]-N-phenylpropanamide).
m. Beta-hydroxy-3-methylfentanyl (N-[1-(2-hydroxy-2-phenethyl)-3-methyl-4-piperidinyl]-N-phenylpropanamide).
n. Betameprodine.
o. Betamethadol.
p. Betaprodine.
q. Clonitazene.
r. Dextromoramide.
s. Diampromide.
t. Diethylthiambutene.
u. Difenoxin.
v. Dimenoxadol.
w. Dimepheptanol.
x. Dimethylthiambutene.
y. Dioxaphetyl butyrate.
z. Dipipanone.
aa. Ethylmethylthiambutene.
bb. Etonitazene.
cc. Etoxeridine.
dd. Furethidine.
ee. Hydroxypethidine.
ff. Ketobemidone.
gg. Levomoramide.
hh. Levophenacylmorphan.
ii. 1-methyl-4-phenyl-4-propionoxypiperidine (MPPP).
jj. 3-Methylfentanyl (N-[3-methyl-1-(2-Phenylethyl)-4-Piperidyl]-N-Phenylpropanamide).
kk. 3-Methylthiofentanyl (N-[(3-methyl-1-(2-thienyl)ethyl-4-piperidinyl]-N-phenylpropanamide).
ll. Morpheridine.
mm. Noracymethadol.
nn. Norlevorphanol.
oo. Normethadone.
pp. Norpipanone.
qq. Para-fluorofentanyl(N-(4-fluorophenyl)-N-[1-(2-phen-ethyl)-4-piperidinyl]-propanamide.
rr. Phenadoxone.
ss. Phenampromide.
tt. 1-(2-phenethyl)-4-phenyl-4-acetoxypiperidine (PEPAP).
uu. Phenomorphan.
vv. Phenoperidine.
ww. Piritramide.
xx. Proheptazine.
yy. Properidine.
zz. Propiram.
aaa. Racemoramide.
bbb. Thiofentanyl(N-phenyl-N-[1-(2-thienyl)ethyl-4-piperidinyl]-propanamide.
ccc. Tilidine.
ddd. Trimeperidine.

(2) Any of the following opium derivatives, including their salts, isomers, and salts of isomers, unless specifically excepted, or listed in another schedule, whenever the existence of such salts, isomers, and salts of isomers is possible within the specific chemical designation:
a. Acetorphine.
b. Acetyldihydrocodeine.
c. Benzylmorphine.
d. Codeine methylbromide.
e. Codeine-N-Oxide.
f. Cyprenorphine.
g. Desomorphine.
h. Dihydromorphine.
i. Etorphine (except hydrochloride salt).
j. Heroin.
k. Hydromorphinol.
l. Methyldesorphine.
m. Methyldihydromorphine.
n. Morphine methylbromide.
o. Morphine methylsulfonate.
p. Morphine-N-Oxide.
q. Myrophine.
r. Nicocodeine.
s. Nicomorphine.
t. Normorphine.
u. Pholcodine.
v. Thebacon.
w. Drotebanol.

(3) Any material, compound, mixture, or preparation which contains any quantity of the following hallucinogenic substances, including their salts, isomers, and salts of isomers, unless specifically excepted, or listed in another schedule, whenever the existence of such salts, isomers, and salts of isomers is possible within the specific chemical designation:
a. 3, 4-methylenedioxyamphetamine.
b. 5-methoxy-3, 4-methylenedioxyamphetamine.
c. 3, 4-Methylenedioxymethamphetamine (MDMA).

d. 3,4-methylenedioxy-N-ethylamphetamine (also known as N-ethyl-alpha-methyl-3,4-(me thylenedioxy)phenethylamine, N-ethyl MDA, MDE, and MDEA).
e. N-hydroxy-3,4-methylenedioxyamphetamine (also known as N-hydroxy-alpha-methyl-3,4-(methylenedioxy)phenethylamine, and N-hydroxy MDA).
f. 3, 4, 5-trimethoxyamphetamine.
g. Alpha-ethyltryptamine. Some trade or other names: etryptamine, Monase, alpha-ethyl-1H-indole-3-ethanamine, 3-(2-aminobutyl) indole, alpha-ET, and AET.
h. Bufotenine.
i. Diethyltryptamine.
j. Dimethyltryptamine.
k. 4-methyl-2, 5-dimethoxyamphetamine.
l. Ibogaine.
m. Lysergic acid diethylamide.
n. Mescaline.
o. Peyote, meaning all parts of the plant presently classified botanically as LophophoraWilliam-siiLemaire, whether growing or not; the seeds thereof; any extract from any part of such plant; and every compound, manufacture, salt, derivative, mixture or preparation of such plant, its seed or extracts.
p. N-ethyl-3-piperidyl benzilate.
q. N-methyl-3-piperidyl benzilate.
r. Psilocybin.
s. Psilocin.
t. 2, 5-dimethoxyamphetamine.
u. 2, 5-dimethoxy-4-ethylamphetamine. Some trade or other names: DOET.
v. 4-bromo-2, 5-dimethoxyamphetamine.
w. 4-methoxyamphetamine.
x. Ethylamine analog of phencyclidine. Some trade or other names: N-ethyl-1-phenylcyclohexylamine, (1-phenylcyclohexyl) ethylamine, N-(1-phenylcyclohexyl) ethylamine, cyclohexamine, PCE.
y. Pyrrolidine analog of phencyclidine. Some trade or other names: 1-(1-phenylcyclohexyl)-pyrrolidine, PCPy, PHP.
z. Thiophene analog of phencyclidine. Some trade or other names: 1-[1-(2-thienyl)-cyclohexyl]-piperidine, 2-thienyl analog of phencyclidine, TPCP, TCP.
aa. 1-[1-(2-thienyl)cyclohexyl]pyrrolidine; Some other names: TCPy.
bb. Parahexyl.
cc. 4-Bromo-2, 5-Dimethoxyphenethylamine.
dd. Alpha-Methyltryptamine.
ee. 5-Methoxy-n-diisopropyltryptamine.

(4) Any material compound, mixture, or preparation which contains any quantity of the following substances having a depressant effect on the central nervous system, including its salts, isomers, and salts of isomers whenever the existence of such salts, isomers, and salts of isomers is possible within the specific chemical designation, unless specifically excepted or unless listed in another schedule:
a. Mecloqualone.
b. Methaqualone.
c. Gamma hydroxybutyric acid; Some other names: GHB, gamma-hydroxybutyrate, 4-hydroxybutyrate, 4-hydroxybutanoic acid; sodium oxybate; sodium oxybutyrate.

(5) Stimulants. - Unless specifically excepted or unless listed in another schedule, any material, compound, mixture, or preparation that contains any quantity of the following substances having a stimulant effect on the central nervous system, including its salts, isomers, and salts of isomers:
a. Aminorex. Some trade or other names: aminoxaphen; 2-amino-5-phenyl-2-oxazoline; or 4,5-dihydro-5-phenly-2-oxazolamine.
b. Cathinone. Some trade or other names: 2-amino-1-phenyl-1-propanone, alpha-aminopropiophenone, 2-aminopropiophenone, and norephedrone.
c. Fenethylline.
d. Methcathinone. Some trade or other names: 2-(methylamino)- propiophenone, alpha-(me thylamino)propiophenone, 2-(methylamino)-1-phenylpropan-1-one, alpha-N-methylamino- propiophenone, monomethylproprion, ephedrone, N-methylcathinone, methylcathinone, AL-464, AL-422, AL-463, and UR1432.
e. (+-)cis-4-methylaminorex [(+-)cis-4,5-dihydro-4-methyl-5-phenyl-2-oxazolamine] (also known as 2-amino-4-methyl-5-phenyl-2-oxazoline).
f. N,N-dimethylamphetamine. Some other names: N,N,alpha-tri- methylbenzeneethaneamine; N,N,alpha-trimethylphenethylamine.
g. N-ethylamphetamine.

h. 4-methylmethcathinone (also known as mephedrone).
i. 3,4-Methylenedioxypyrovalerone (also known as MDPV).
j. A compound, other than bupropion, that is structurally derived from 2-amino-1-phenyl-1-propanone by modification in any of the following ways: (i) by substitution in the phenyl ring to any extent with alkyl, alkoxy, alkylenedioxy, haloalkyl, or halide substituents, whether or not further substituted in the phenyl ring by one or more other univalent substituents; (ii) by substitution at the 3-position with an alkyl substituent; or (iii) by substitution at the nitrogen atom with alkyl or diakyl groups or by inclusion of the nitrogen atom in a cyclic structure.
k. N-Benzylpiperazine.
l. 2,5-Dimethoxy-4-(n)-propylthiophenethylamine.

Section (b1) of the impaired driving statute allows a person charged to take an additional test. This additional test can be used to rebut the test given to your client by the State. The State doesn't have to actively seek a third party to come out and give this additional test if it's requested; the State is only required to allow your client access to a telephone (if they are being held and not released) to try and find this third party test administrator.

Section (c) of the statute talks in general terms about the pleadings. It says that it's okay as long as it states the time and place the event occurred as well as alleging that the person drove a motor vehicle while subject to an impairing substance.

PRACTICE TIP: I have had the wonderful occasion to actually have a client's DWI charge dismissed because the arresting officer failed to check the box that said "while subject to an impairing substance" on the citation. The argument was that it was a fatally defective charging document. If you have the opportunity to do this remember not to point it out to the State until the trial has commenced; otherwise, the State can amend the charging document and correct their deficiency.

3.2 DWI Sentencing and Punishment

Under the current law, a DWI by and of itself, (unless it's habitual which we will discuss later) is a misdemeanor. Misdemeanors in North Carolina are subject to structured sentencing EXCEPT for DWI. All sentencing for DWI is under the Fair Sentencing Guidelines. All DWI sentencing is governed by N.C.G.S. §20-179 which I have reprinted for reference below:

§ 20-179. Sentencing hearing after conviction for impaired driving; determination of grossly aggravating and aggravating and mitigating factors; punishments.

(a) Sentencing Hearing Required. - After a conviction under G.S. 20-138.1, G.S. 20-138.2, a second or subsequent conviction under G.S. 20-138.2A, or a second or subsequent conviction under G.S. 20-138.2B, or when any of those offenses are remanded back to district court after an appeal to superior court, the judge shall hold a sentencing hearing to determine whether there are aggravating or mitigating factors that affect the sentence to be imposed.

(1) The court shall consider evidence of aggravating or mitigating factors present in the offense that make an aggravated or mitigated sentence appropriate. The State bears the burden of proving beyond a reasonable doubt that an aggravating factor exists, and the offender bears the burden of proving by a preponderance of the evidence that a mitigating factor exists.

(2) Before the hearing the prosecutor shall make all feasible efforts to secure the defendant's full record of traffic convictions, and shall present to the judge that record for consideration in the hearing. Upon request of the defendant, the prosecutor shall furnish the defendant or his attorney a copy of the defendant's record of traffic convictions at a reasonable time prior to the introduction of the record into evidence. In addition, the prosecutor shall present all other appropriate grossly aggravating and aggravating factors of which he is aware, and the defendant or his attorney may present all appropriate mitigating factors. In every instance in which a valid chemical analysis is made of the defendant, the prosecutor shall present evidence of the resulting alcohol concentration.

(a1) Jury Trial in Superior Court; Jury Procedure if Trial Bifurcated. -

(1) Notice. - If the defendant appeals to superior court, and the State intends to use one or more aggravating factors under subsections (c) or (d) of this section, the State must provide the defendant with notice of its intent. The notice shall be provided no later than 10 days prior to trial and shall contain a plain and concise factual statement indicating the factor or factors it intends to use under the authority of subsections (c) and (d) of this section. The notice must list all the aggravating factors that the State seeks to establish.

(2) Aggravating factors. - The defendant may admit to the existence of an aggravating factor, and the factor so admitted shall be treated as though it were found by a jury pursuant to the procedures in this section. If the defendant does not so admit, only a jury may determine if an aggravating factor is present. The jury impaneled for the trial may, in the same trial, also determine if one or more aggravating factors is present, unless the court determines that the interests of justice require that a separate sentencing proceeding be used to make that determination. If the court determines that a separate proceeding is required, the proceeding shall be conducted by the trial judge before the trial jury as soon as practicable after the guilty verdict is returned. The State bears the burden of proving beyond a reasonable doubt that an aggravating factor exists, and the offender bears the burden of proving by a preponderance of the evidence that a mitigating factor exists.

(3) Convening the jury. - If prior to the time that the trial jury begins its deliberations on the issue of whether one or more aggravating factors exist, any juror dies, becomes incapacitated or disqualified, or is discharged for any reason, an alternate juror shall become a part of the jury and serve in all respects as those selected on the regular trial panel. An alternate juror shall become a part of the jury in the order in which the juror was selected. If the trial jury is unable to reconvene for a hearing on the issue of whether one or more aggravating factors exist after having determined the guilt of the accused, the trial judge shall impanel a new jury to determine the issue.

(4) Jury selection. - A jury selected to determine whether one or more aggravating factors exist shall be selected in the same manner as juries are selected for the trial of criminal cases.

(a2) Jury Trial on Aggravating Factors in Superior Court. -

(1) Defendant admits aggravating factor only. - If the defendant admits that an aggravating factor exists, but pleads not guilty to the underlying charge, a jury shall be impaneled to dispose of the charge only. In that case, evidence that relates solely to the establishment of an aggravating factor shall not be admitted in the trial.

(2) Defendant pleads guilty to the charge only. - If the defendant pleads guilty to the charge, but contests the existence of one or more aggravating factors, a jury shall be impaneled to determine if the aggravating factor or factors exist.

(b) Repealed by Session Laws 1983, c. 435, s. 29.

(c) Determining Existence of Grossly Aggravating Factors. - At the sentencing hearing, based upon the evidence presented at trial and in the hearing, the judge, or the jury in superior court, must first determine whether there are any grossly aggravating factors in the case. Whether a prior conviction exists under subdivision (1) of this subsection, or whether a conviction exists under subdivision (d)(5) of this section, shall be matters to be determined by the judge, and not the jury, in district or superior court. If the sentencing hearing is for a case remanded back to district court from superior court, the judge shall determine whether the defendant has been convicted of any offense that was not considered at the initial sentencing hearing and impose the appropriate sentence under this section. The judge must impose the Aggravated Level One punishment under subsection (f3) of this section if it is determined that three or more grossly aggravating factors apply. The judge must impose the Level One punishment under subsection (g) of this section if it is determined that the grossly aggravating factor in subdivision (4) of this subsection applies or two of the other grossly aggravating factors apply. If the judge does not find that the aggravating factor at subdivision (4) of this subsection applies, then the judge must impose the Level Two punishment under subsection (h) of this section if it is determined that only one of the other grossly aggravating factors applies. The grossly aggravating factors are:

(1) A prior conviction for an offense involving impaired driving if:

a. The conviction occurred within seven years before the date of the offense for which the defendant is being sentenced; or

b. The conviction occurs after the date of the offense for which the defendant is presently being sentenced, but prior to or contemporaneously with the present sentencing; or

c. The conviction occurred in district court; the case was appealed to superior court; the appeal has been withdrawn, or the case has been remanded back to district court; and a new sentencing hearing has not been held pursuant to G.S. 20-38.7.

Each prior conviction is a separate grossly aggravating factor.

(2) Driving by the defendant at the time of the offense while his driver's license was revoked under G.S. 20-28, and the revocation was an impaired driving revocation under G.S. 20-28.2(a).

(3) Serious injury to another person caused by the defendant's impaired driving at the time of the offense.

(4) Driving by the defendant while (i) a child under the age of 18 years, (ii) a person with the mental development of a child under the age of 18 years, or (iii) a person with a physical disability preventing unaided exit from the vehicle was in the vehicle at the time of the offense.

In imposing an Aggravated Level One, a Level One, or a Level Two punishment, the judge may consider the aggravating and mitigating factors in subsections (d) and (e) in determining the appropriate sentence. If there are no grossly aggravating factors in the case, the judge must weigh all aggravating and mitigating factors and impose punishment as required by subsection (f).

(c1) Written Findings. - The court shall make findings of the aggravating and mitigating factors present in the offense. If the jury finds factors in aggravation, the court shall ensure that those findings are entered in the court's determination of sentencing factors form or any comparable document used to record the findings of sentencing factors. Findings shall be in writing.

(d) Aggravating Factors to Be Weighed. - The judge, or the jury in superior court, shall determine before sentencing under subsection (f) whether any of the aggravating factors listed below apply to the defendant. The judge shall weigh the seriousness of each aggravating factor in the light of the particular circumstances of the case. The factors are:

(1) Gross impairment of the defendant's faculties while driving or an alcohol concentration of 0.15 or more within a relevant time after the driving. For purposes of this subdivision, the results of a chemical analysis presented at trial or sentencing shall be sufficient to prove the person's alcohol concentration, shall be conclusive, and shall not be subject to modification by any party, with or without approval by the court.

(2) Especially reckless or dangerous driving.

(3) Negligent driving that led to a reportable accident.

(4) Driving by the defendant while his driver's license was revoked.

(5) Two or more prior convictions of a motor vehicle offense not involving impaired driving for which at least three points are assigned under G.S. 20-16 or for which the convicted person's license is subject to revocation, if the convictions occurred within five years of the date of the offense for which the defendant is being sentenced, or one or more prior convictions of an offense involving impaired driving that occurred more than seven years before the date of the offense for which the defendant is being sentenced.

(6) Conviction under G.S. 20-141.5 of speeding by the defendant while fleeing or attempting to elude apprehension.

(7) Conviction under G.S. 20-141 of speeding by the defendant by at least 30 miles per hour over the legal limit.

(8) Passing a stopped school bus in violation of G.S. 20-217.

(9) Any other factor that aggravates the seriousness of the offense.

Except for the factor in subdivision (5) the conduct constituting the aggravating factor shall occur during the same transaction or occurrence as the impaired driving offense.

(e) Mitigating Factors to Be Weighed. - The judge shall also determine before sentencing under subsection (f) whether any of the mitigating factors listed below apply to the defendant. The judge shall weigh the degree of mitigation of each factor in light of the particular circumstances of the case. The factors are:

(1) Slight impairment of the defendant's faculties resulting solely from alcohol, and an alcohol concentration that did not exceed 0.09 at any relevant time after the driving.

(2) Slight impairment of the defendant's faculties, resulting solely from alcohol, with no chemical analysis having been available to the defendant.

(3) Driving at the time of the offense that was safe and lawful except for the impairment of the defendant's faculties.

(4) A safe driving record, with the defendant's having no conviction for any motor vehicle offense for which at least four points are assigned under G.S. 20-16 or for which the person's license is subject to revocation within five years of the date of the offense for which the defendant is being sentenced.

(5) Impairment of the defendant's faculties caused primarily by a lawfully prescribed drug for an existing medical condition, and the amount of the drug taken was within the prescribed dosage.

(6) The defendant's voluntary submission to a mental health facility for assessment after he was charged with the impaired driving offense for which he is being sentenced, and, if recommended by the facility, his voluntary participation in the recommended treatment.

(6a) Completion of a substance abuse assessment, compliance with its recommendations, and simultaneously maintaining 60 days of continuous abstinence from alcohol consumption, as proven by a continuous alcohol monitoring system. The continuous alcohol monitoring system shall be of a type approved by the Division of Adult Correction of the Department of Public Safety.

(7) Any other factor that mitigates the seriousness of the offense.

Except for the factors in subdivisions (4), (6), (6a), and (7), the conduct constituting the mitigating factor shall occur during the same transaction or occurrence as the impaired driving offense.

(f) Weighing the Aggravating and Mitigating Factors. - If the judge or the jury in the sentencing hearing determines that there are no grossly aggravating factors, the judge shall weigh all aggravating and mitigating factors listed in subsections (d) and (e). If the judge determines that:

(1) The aggravating factors substantially outweigh any mitigating factors, the judge shall note in the judgment the

factors found and his finding that the defendant is subject to the Level Three punishment and impose a punishment within the limits defined in subsection (i).

(2) There are no aggravating and mitigating factors, or that aggravating factors are substantially counterbalanced by mitigating factors, the judge shall note in the judgment any factors found and the finding that the defendant is subject to the Level Four punishment and impose a punishment within the limits defined in subsection (j).

(3) The mitigating factors substantially outweigh any aggravating factors, the judge shall note in the judgment the factors found and his finding that the defendant is subject to the Level Five punishment and impose a punishment within the limits defined in subsection (k).

It is not a mitigating factor that the driver of the vehicle was suffering from alcoholism, drug addiction, diminished capacity, or mental disease or defect. Evidence of these matters may be received in the sentencing hearing, however, for use by the judge in formulating terms and conditions of sentence after determining which punishment level shall be imposed.

(f1) Aider and Abettor Punishment. - Notwithstanding any other provisions of this section, a person convicted of impaired driving under G.S. 20-138.1 under the common law concept of aiding and abetting is subject to Level Five punishment. The judge need not make any findings of grossly aggravating, aggravating, or mitigating factors in such cases.

(f2) Limit on Consolidation of Judgments. - Except as provided in subsection (f1), in each charge of impaired driving for which there is a conviction the judge shall determine if the sentencing factors described in subsections (c), (d) and (e) are applicable unless the impaired driving charge is consolidated with a charge carrying a greater punishment. Two or more impaired driving charges may not be consolidated for judgment.

(f3) Aggravated Level One Punishment. - A defendant subject to Aggravated Level One punishment may be fined up to ten thousand dollars ($10,000) and shall be sentenced to a term of imprisonment that includes a minimum term of not less than 12 months and a maximum term of not more than 36 months. Notwithstanding G.S. 15A-1371, a defendant sentenced to a term of imprisonment pursuant to this subsection shall not be eligible for parole. However, the defendant shall be released from the Statewide Misdemeanant Confinement Program on the date equivalent to the defendant's maximum imposed term of imprisonment less four months and shall be supervised by the Section of Community Supervision of the Division of Adult Correction under and subject to the provisions of Article 84A of Chapter 15A of the General Statutes and shall also be required to abstain from alcohol consumption for the four-month period of supervision as verified by a continuous alcohol monitoring system. For purposes of revocation, violation of the requirement to abstain from alcohol or comply with the use of a continuous alcohol monitoring system shall be deemed a controlling condition under G.S. 15A-1368.4.

The term of imprisonment may be suspended only if a condition of special probation is imposed to require the defendant to serve a term of imprisonment of at least 120 days. If the defendant is placed on probation, the judge shall impose as requirements that the defendant (i) abstain from alcohol consumption for a minimum of 120 days to a maximum of the term of probation, as verified by a continuous alcohol monitoring system pursuant to subsections (h1) and (h3) of this section, and (ii) obtain a substance abuse assessment and the education or treatment required by G.S. 20-17.6 for the restoration of a drivers license and as a condition of probation. The judge may impose any other lawful condition of probation.

(g) Level One Punishment. - A defendant subject to Level One punishment may be fined up to four thousand dollars ($4,000) and shall be sentenced to a term of imprisonment that includes a minimum term of not less than 30 days and a maximum term of not more than 24 months. The term of imprisonment may be suspended only if a condition of special probation is imposed to require the defendant to serve a term of imprisonment of at least 30 days. A judge may reduce the minimum term of imprisonment required to a term of not less than 10 days if a condition of special probation is imposed to require that a defendant abstain from alcohol consumption and be monitored by a continuous alcohol monitoring system, of a type approved by the Division of Adult Correction of the Department of Public Safety, for a period of not less than 120 days. If the defendant is monitored on an approved continuous alcohol monitoring system during the pretrial period, up to 60 days of pretrial monitoring may be credited against the 120-day monitoring requirement for probation. If the defendant is placed on probation, the judge shall impose a requirement that the defendant obtain a substance abuse assessment and the education or treatment required by G.S. 20-17.6 for the restoration of a drivers license and as a condition of probation. The judge may impose any other lawful condition of probation.

(h) Level Two Punishment. - A defendant subject to Level Two punishment may be fined up to two thousand dollars ($2,000) and shall be sentenced to a term of imprisonment that includes a minimum term of not less than seven days and a maximum term of not more than 12 months. The term of imprisonment may be suspended only if a condition of special probation is imposed to require the defendant to serve a term of imprisonment of at least seven days or to abstain from consuming alcohol for at least 90 consecutive days, as verified by a continuous alcohol monitoring system, of a type approved by the Division of Adult Correction of the Department of Public Safety. If the defendant is subject to Level Two punishment based on a finding that the grossly aggravating factor in subdivision (1) or (2) of subsection (c) of this section applies, the conviction for a prior offense involving impaired driving occurred within five years before the date of the offense for which the defendant is being sentenced and the judge suspends all active terms of imprisonment and imposes abstention from alcohol as verified by a continuous alcohol monitory system, then the judge must also impose as an additional condition of special probation that the defendant must complete 240 hours of community service. If the defendant is monitored on an approved continuous alcohol monitoring system during the pretrial period, up to 60 days of pretrial monitoring may be credited against the 90-day monitoring requirement for probation. If the defendant is placed on probation, the judge shall impose a requirement that the defendant obtain a substance abuse assessment and the education or treatment required by G.S. 20-17.6 for the restoration of a drivers license and as a condition of probation. The judge may impose any other lawful condition of probation.

(h1) The judge may impose, as a condition of probation for defendants subject to Level One or Level Two punishments, that the defendant abstain from alcohol consumption for a minimum of 30 days, to a maximum of the term of probation, as verified by a continuous alcohol monitoring system. The defendant's abstinence from alcohol shall be verified by a continuous alcohol monitoring system of a type approved by the Division of Adult Correction of the Department of Public Safety.

(h2) Repealed by Session Laws 2011-191, s. 1, effective December 1, 2011, and applicable to offenses committed on or after that date.

(h3) Repealed by Session Laws 2012-146, s. 9, effective December 1, 2012.

(i) Level Three Punishment. - A defendant subject to Level Three punishment may be fined up to one thousand dollars ($1,000) and shall be sentenced to a term of imprisonment that includes a minimum term of not less than 72 hours and a maximum term of not more than six months. The term of imprisonment may be suspended. However, the suspended sentence shall include the condition that the defendant:

(1) Be imprisoned for a term of at least 72 hours as a condition of special probation; or

(2) Perform community service for a term of at least 72 hours; or

(3) Repealed by Session Laws 2006-253, s. 23, effective December 1, 2006, and applicable to offenses committed on or after that date.

(4) Any combination of these conditions.

If the defendant is placed on probation, the judge shall impose a requirement that the defendant obtain a substance abuse assessment and the education or treatment required by G.S. 20-17.6 for the restoration of a drivers license and as a condition of probation. The judge may impose any other lawful condition of probation.

(j) Level Four Punishment. - A defendant subject to Level Four punishment may be fined up to five hundred dollars ($500.00) and shall be sentenced to a term of imprisonment that includes a minimum term of not less than 48 hours and a maximum term of not more than 120 days. The term of imprisonment may be suspended. However, the suspended sentence shall include the condition that the defendant:

(1) Be imprisoned for a term of 48 hours as a condition of special probation; or

(2) Perform community service for a term of 48 hours; or

(3) Repealed by Session Laws 2006-253, s. 23, effective December 1, 2006, and applicable to offenses committed on or after that date.

(4) Any combination of these conditions.

If the defendant is placed on probation, the judge shall impose a requirement that the defendant obtain a substance abuse assessment and the education or treatment required by G.S. 20-17.6 for the restoration of a drivers license and as a condition of probation. The judge may impose any other lawful condition of probation.

(k) Level Five Punishment. - A defendant subject to Level Five punishment may be fined up to two hundred dollars ($200.00) and shall be sentenced to a term of imprisonment that includes a minimum term of not less than 24 hours and a maximum term of not more than 60 days. The term of imprisonment may be suspended. However, the suspended sentence shall include the condition that the defendant:

(1) Be imprisoned for a term of 24 hours as a condition of special probation; or

(2) Perform community service for a term of 24 hours; or

(3) Repealed by Session Laws 2006-253, s. 23, effective December 1, 2006, and applicable to offenses committed on or after that date.

(4) Any combination of these conditions.

If the defendant is placed on probation, the judge shall impose a requirement that the defendant obtain a substance abuse assessment and the education or treatment required by G.S. 20-17.6 for the restoration of a drivers license and as a condition of probation. The judge may impose any other lawful condition of probation.

(k1) Credit for Inpatient Treatment. - Pursuant to G.S. 15A-1351(a), the judge may order that a term of imprisonment imposed as a condition of special probation under any level of punishment be served as an inpatient in a facility operated or licensed by the State for the treatment of alcoholism or substance abuse where the defendant has been accepted for admission or commitment as an inpatient. The defendant shall bear the expense of any treatment unless the trial judge orders that the costs be absorbed by the State. The judge may impose restrictions on the defendant's ability to leave the premises of the treatment facility and require that the defendant follow the rules of the treatment facility. The judge may credit against the active sentence imposed on a defendant the time the defendant was an inpatient at the treatment facility, provided such treatment occurred after the commission of the offense for which the defendant is being sentenced. This section shall not be construed to limit the authority of the judge in sentencing under any other provisions of law.

(k2) Probationary Requirement for Abstinence and Use of Continuous Alcohol Monitoring. - The judge may order that as a condition of special probation for any level of offense under G.S. 20-179 the defendant abstain from alcohol consumption, as verified by a continuous alcohol monitoring system, of a type approved by the Division of Adult Correction of the Department of Public Safety.

(k3) The court, in the sentencing order, may authorize probation officers to require defendants to submit to continuous alcohol monitoring for assessment purposes if the defendant has been required to abstain from alcohol consumption during the term of probation and the probation officer believes the defendant is consuming alcohol. The defendant shall bear the costs of the continuous alcohol monitoring system if the use of the system has been authorized by a judge in accordance with this subsection.

(k4) Notwithstanding the provisions of subsections (g), (h), (k2), and (k3) of this section, if the court finds, upon good cause shown, that the defendant should not be required to pay the costs of the continuous alcohol monitoring system, the court shall not impose the use of a continuous alcohol monitoring system unless the local governmental entity responsible for the incarceration of the defendant in the local confinement facility agrees to pay the costs of the system.

(l) Repealed by Session Laws 1989, c. 691.

(m) Repealed by Session Laws 1995, c. 496, s. 2.

(n) Time Limits for Performance of Community Service. - If the judgment requires the defendant to perform a specified number of hours of community service, a minimum of 24 hours must be ordered.

(o) Evidentiary Standards; Proof of Prior Convictions. - In the sentencing hearing, the State shall prove any grossly aggravating or aggravating factor beyond a reasonable doubt, and the defendant shall prove any mitigating factor by the greater weight of the evidence. Evidence adduced by either party at trial may be utilized in the sentencing hearing. Except as modified by this section, the procedure in G.S. 15A-1334(b) governs. The judge may accept any evidence as to the presence or absence of previous convictions that he finds reliable but he shall give prima facie effect to convictions recorded by the Division or any other agency of the State of North Carolina. A copy of such conviction records transmitted by the police information network in general accordance with the procedure authorized by G.S. 20-26(b) is admissible in evidence without further authentication. If the judge decides to impose an active sentence of imprisonment that would not have been imposed but for a prior conviction of an offense, the judge shall afford the defendant an opportunity to introduce evidence that the prior conviction had been obtained in a case in which he was indigent, had no counsel, and had not waived his right to counsel. If the defendant proves by the preponderance of the evidence all three above facts concerning the prior case, the conviction may not be used as a grossly aggravating or aggravating factor.

(p) Limit on Amelioration of Punishment. - For active terms of imprisonment imposed under this section:

(1) The judge may not give credit to the defendant for the first 24 hours of time spent in incarceration pending trial.

(2) The defendant shall serve the mandatory minimum period of imprisonment and good or gain time credit may not be used to reduce that mandatory minimum period.

(3) The defendant may not be released on parole unless he is otherwise eligible, has served the mandatory minimum period of imprisonment, and has obtained a substance abuse assessment and completed any recommended treatment or training program or is paroled into a residential treatment program.

With respect to the minimum or specific term of imprisonment imposed as a condition of special probation under this section, the judge may not give credit to the defendant for the first 24 hours of time spent in incarceration pending trial.

(q) Repealed by Session Laws 1991, c. 726, s. 20.

(r) Supervised Probation Terminated. - Unless a judge in his discretion determines that supervised probation is necessary, and includes in the record that he has received evidence and finds as a fact that supervised probation is necessary, and states in his judgment that supervised probation is necessary, a defendant convicted of an offense of impaired driving shall be placed on unsupervised probation if he meets three conditions. These conditions are that he has not been convicted of an offense of impaired driving within the seven years preceding the date of this offense for which he is sentenced, that the defendant is sentenced under subsections (i), (j), and (k) of this section, and has obtained any necessary substance abuse assessment and completed any recommended treatment or training program.

When a judge determines in accordance with the above procedures that a defendant should be placed on supervised probation, the judge shall authorize the probation officer to modify the defendant's probation by placing the defendant on unsupervised probation upon the completion by the defendant of the following conditions of his suspended sentence:

(1) Community service; or

(2) Repealed by Session Laws 1995 c. 496, s. 2.

(3) Payment of any fines, court costs, and fees; or

(4) Any combination of these conditions.

(s) Method of Serving Sentence. - The judge in his discretion may order a term of imprisonment to be served on weekends, even if the sentence cannot be served in consecutive sequence. However, if the defendant is ordered to a term of 48 hours or more, or has 48 hours or more remaining on a term of imprisonment, the defendant shall be required to serve 48 continuous hours of imprisonment to be given credit for time served.

(1) Credit for any jail time shall only be given hour for hour for time actually served. The jail shall maintain a log showing number of hours served.

(2) The defendant shall be refused entrance and shall be reported back to court if the defendant appears at the jail and has remaining in his body any alcohol as shown by an alcohol screening device or controlled substance previously consumed, unless lawfully obtained and taken in therapeutically appropriate amounts.

(3) If a defendant has been reported back to court under subdivision (2) of this subsection, the court shall hold a hearing. The defendant shall be ordered to serve his jail time immediately and shall not be eligible to serve jail time on weekends if the court determines that, at the time of his entrance to the jail,

a. The defendant had previously consumed alcohol in his body as shown by an alcohol screening device, or

b. The defendant had a previously consumed controlled substance in his body.

It shall be a defense to an immediate service of sentence of jail time and ineligibility for weekend service of jail time if the court determines that alcohol or controlled substance was lawfully obtained and was taken in therapeutically appropriate amounts.

To break this down into laymen's terms we will take it a step at a time. The first thing we need to know is if your client has any Grossly Aggravating Factors or GAFs. Listed in the above statute, these include: a prior conviction for impaired driving within the last seven years (this is calculated from the date of conviction of the previous charge to the date of arrest for the current charge); driving while the person's license was revoked due to an impaired driving revocation (see N.C.G.S. §20-28.2(a)); serious injury to another caused by the impaired driving; driving with a child under 18, a person with the mental development of a child under 18, or a disabled person unable to exit the vehicle unaided. Each prior DWI conviction in the last seven years counts as a GAF. So if the client has 2 prior DWI convictions within seven years, they would both be counted as 2 GAFs.

After determining how many GAFs if any your client has you can determine the appropriate level. This isn't always easy. I once had to argue over a leap year for calculation purposes. If your client has ANY GAFs then he or she is at least a Level 2 or higher. If your client has three or more GAFs then he or she is an Aggravated Level One for sentencing purposes. An Aggravated Level One is the most serious punishment level for misdemeanor DWI. At a minimum, the client must serve 120 days of active jail time followed by 120 days of CAM (Continuous Alcohol Monitoring). At the maximum, your client could serve three years in jail, not to mention having to pay up to a $10,000 fine.

If there are no GAFs, go to the Aggravating Factors, or AFs. These factors include the following: gross impairment of faculties or a BAC of 0.15 or higher; especially dangerous or reckless driving; negligent driving that leads to a reportable accident; driving while license revoked; two or more motor vehicle convictions (not involving impaired driving) in which at least three points are assigned or for which that person's license is subject to revocation if the convictions occurred within five years of the date of the offense; any prior impaired driving convictions outside of the seven year look back; speeding to flee or elude (see N.C.G.S. §20-141.5); speeding thirty miles per hour or more over the legal limit (see N.C.G.S. §20-141); passing a stopped school bus (see N.C.G.S. §20-117); any other factor that aggravates.

Figure up the AFs and write them down. Now go to the Mitigating Factors or MFs. These factors include the following: slight faculty impairment resulting from alcohol only and a BAC not exceeding a 0.09; slight faculty impairment resulting solely from alcohol with no chemical analysis having been available; safe and lawful driving at the time of the offense other than the impairment; a safe driving record (see

N.C.G.S. §20-179); impairment was caused by a legally prescribed drug and the drug was taken within the prescribed dosage; a voluntary assessment from a mental health facility and participation in the recommended treatment; completion and compliance with the substance abuse assessment plus 60 days of sobriety monitored by CAM; any other factor that mitigates.

Now take the number of AFs and the number of MFs and compare them. If there are more MFs than AFs, your client will be Level 5 for sentencing purposes. If you have an equal amount of AFs and MFs, your client will be Level 4 for sentencing purposes. If there are more AFs than MFs, your client will be a Level 3 for sentencing purposes.

PRACTICE TIP: At the initial client interview, when you are trying to calculate your client's record level, be sure to advise the client that if they are a Level 1 or Level 2 they CAN NOT get a driving privilege if they are convicted for DWI.

The above statute doesn't leave any room for leniency in many situations. For example, let's say that your client is twenty one years old and is out with some friends. One of the friends is seventeen years old and the other is twenty two. Your client is stopped for speeding and upon subsequent investigation is arrested for DWI. He has no criminal record and no one was injured. What is his punishment? If you guessed Level One, then you would be correct. Since your client has a Grossly Aggravating Factor that falls under sub (4), his sentence would be an active one, with a minimum of 30 days in jail. However, if your client decides to check into an inpatient facility for ten days and agree to wear CAM for 120 days, a judge would not have to give him active jail time. I don't believe that the statute was intended to punish young adults this way; I feel that the legislature was trying to go after people who drive drunk with their children in the car. But, as the above example shows, this can and does happen.

PRACTICE TIP: If you are going to be asking the judge to allow your client credit for inpatient treatment in lieu of active jail time, have the client do this far in advance of your trial date. If you are not successful at trial, the judge is much more likely to allow the credit instead of imposing a jail sentence if the inpatient treatment has already been completed. Likewise, I recommend getting the most out of CAM before trial as well. The Court can allow up to sixty days of credit on CAM to go toward the balance.

In most of your standard first offense cases, a good driving record (see N.C.G.S. §20-179) and an alcohol assessment will put your client at a Level 5 for sentencing. Although a judge can give active jail time for Level 5 punishment, in my experience the judge will substitute 24 hours of community service instead. Remember to keep an eye on the date that your client had his or her assessment since these are only good for six months.

Aider and Abettor Punishment

The concept is simple: if a person knows that someone is impaired and lets them drive the car that the aider and abettor owns, that person can be charged with aiding and abetting a DWI. Aid and Abet DWI is hard for the State to prove. I have seen this charge handled a number of ways. The State used to offer the person charged with aiding and abetting a dismissal in exchange for their testimony against the driver. More recently, those charged with aid and abet in this context have the charge dismissed by the State at the conclusion of the driver's DWI case. The bad news for the person charged with aid and abet is that the punishment is the same as if he or she had been DWI. Although you can technically represent both the driver charged with DWI and (most commonly) the passenger charged with aiding and abetting the DWI (provided both clients have given informed consent) I would recommend sending the other person that was charged to another attorney in your area.

3.3 Impaired Driving in other vehicles

20-138.2. Impaired Driving in a commercial vehicle.

(a) Offense. - A person commits the offense of impaired driving in a commercial motor vehicle if he drives a commercial motor vehicle upon any highway, any street, or any public vehicular area within the State:

(1) While under the influence of an impairing substance; or

(2) After having consumed sufficient alcohol that he has, at any relevant time after the driving, an alcohol concentration of 0.04 or more. The results of a chemical analysis shall be deemed sufficient evidence to prove a person's alcohol concentration; or

(3) With any amount of a Schedule I controlled substance, as listed in G.S. 90-89, or its metabolites in his blood or urine.

(a1) A person who has submitted to a chemical analysis of a blood sample, pursuant to G.S. 20-139.1(d), may use the result in rebuttal as evidence that the person did not have, at a relevant time after driving, an alcohol concentration of 0.04 or more.

(a2) In order to prove the gross vehicle weight rating of a vehicle as defined in G.S. 20-4.01(12e), the opinion of a person who observed the vehicle as to the weight, the testimony of the gross vehicle weight rating affixed to the vehicle, the registered or declared weight shown on the Division's records pursuant to G.S. 20-26(b1), the gross vehicle weight rating as determined from the vehicle identification number, the listed gross weight publications from the manufacturer of the vehicle, or any other description or evidence shall be admissible.

(b) Defense Precluded. - The fact that a person charged with violating this section is or has been legally entitled to use alcohol or a drug is not a defense to a charge under this section.

(b1) Defense Allowed. - Nothing in this section shall preclude a person from asserting that a chemical analysis result is inadmissible pursuant to G.S. 20-139.1(b2).

(c) Pleading. - To charge a violation of this section, the pleading is sufficient if it states the time and place of the alleged offense in the usual form and charges the defendant drove a commercial motor vehicle on a highway, street, or public vehicular area while subject to an impairing substance.

(d) Implied Consent Offense. - An offense under this section is an implied consent offense subject to the provisions of G.S. 20-16.2.

(e) Punishment. - The offense in this section is a misdemeanor and any defendant convicted under this section shall be sentenced under G.S. 20-179. This offense is not a lesser included offense of impaired driving under G.S. 20-138.1, and if a person is convicted under this section and of an offense involving impaired driving under G.S. 20-138.1 arising out of the same transaction, the aggregate punishment imposed by the Court may not exceed the maximum punishment applicable to the offense involving impaired driving under G.S. 20-138.1.

(f) Repealed by Session Laws 1991, c. 726, s. 19.

(g) Chemical Analysis Provisions. - The provisions of G.S. 20-139.1 shall apply to the offense of impaired driving in a commercial motor vehicle.

Driving a commercial vehicle (a tractor trailer or semi) while impaired has the same punishment consequences if convicted, however it is NOT a lesser included offense of DWI. Since CDL DWI is not a lesser included offense, technically your client could be charged with CDL DWI and regular DWI. If that happens to be the case, keep in mind that the Court cannot exceed the maximum punishment under the sentencing outlined in N.C.G.S. §20-179. The sentencing structure is the same. The major difference is the number. Instead of being held to the 0.08, the number needed in this instance is only a 0.04. Note that the State still has to prove that the vehicle was a commercial vehicle (see N.C.G.S. §20-4.01), although this can seemingly be proved by opinion testimony as to the vehicle's weight. The main obstacle here at the beginning of your representation involves the civil revocation of one year which is usually a job killer for your client. I will speak more about that in a later chapter.

20-138.2A. Operating a commercial vehicle after consuming alcohol.

(a) Offense. - A person commits the offense of operating a commercial motor vehicle after consuming alcohol if the person drives a commercial motor vehicle, as defined in G.S. 20-4.01(3d)a. and b., upon any highway, any street, or any public vehicular area within the State while consuming alcohol or while alcohol remains in the person's body.

(b) Implied-Consent Offense. - An offense under this section is an implied-consent offense subject to the provisions of G.S. 20-16.2. The provisions of G.S. 20-139.1 shall apply to an offense committed under this section.

(b1) Odor Insufficient. - The odor of an alcoholic beverage on the breath of the driver is insufficient evidence by itself to prove beyond a reasonable doubt that alcohol was remaining in the driver's body in violation of this section unless the driver was offered an alcohol screening test or chemical analysis and refused to provide all required samples of breath or blood for analysis.

(b2) Alcohol Screening Test. - Notwithstanding any other provision of law, an alcohol screening test may be administered to a driver suspected of violation of subsection (a) of this section, and the results of an alcohol screening test or the driver's refusal to submit may be used by a law enforcement officer, a court, or an administrative agency in determining if alcohol was present in the driver's body.

No alcohol screening tests are valid under this section unless the device used is one approved by the Department of Health and Human Services, and the screening test is conducted in accordance with the applicable regulations of the Department as to its manner and use.

(c) Punishment. - Except as otherwise provided in this subsection, a violation of the offense described in subsection (a) of this section is a Class 3 misdemeanor and, notwithstanding G.S. 15A-1340.23, is punishable by a penalty of one hundred dollars ($100.00). A second or subsequent violation of this section is a misdemeanor punishable under G.S. 20-179. This offense is a lesser included offense of impaired driving of a commercial vehicle under G.S. 20-138.2.

(d) Second or Subsequent Conviction Defined. - A conviction for violating this offense is a second or subsequent conviction if at the time of the current offense the person has a previous conviction under this section, and the previous conviction occurred in the seven years immediately preceding the date of the current offense. This definition of second or subsequent conviction also applies to G.S. 20-17(a)(13) and G.S. 20-17.4(a)(6).

The statute above applies to ANY amount of alcohol. Technically speaking, your client could blow a 0.01 on a Portable Breath Test (PBT) and be charged with this offense. There are many different food variants that can cause a low blow like this to be present. Honey buns and other baked goods as well as some fermented sodas and even some types of peppermint flavored items can show a positive reading on a PBT. When representing a client charged with the above I would recommend reading the instruction manuals on the various Interlock devices on the market; most of these manuals tell their users to be careful about consuming baked goods and other products which may result in a false positive for alcohol.

Notwithstanding the above argument, it's good to point out to a potential client that a first offense conviction under this statute will not revoke their license unless they have had a previous impaired conviction. A subsequent conviction is punished under N.C.G.S. §20-179. This statute only applies to Class A and B motor vehicles, not Class C (see the above statute).

PRACTICE TIP: Remember that odor alone is NOT enough under N.C.G.S. §20-138.2A to convict. I would recommend objecting to any introduction of the PBT on foundation if the State doesn't adequately lay out the foundation required by the North Carolina Administrative Code. See 10A NCAC 41B .0503. Not only should the officer know what type of PBT he or she uses, but should also know whether or not it was calibrated within the last thirty days.

20-138.2B. Operating a school bus, school activity bus, child care vehicle, ambulance, other EMS vehicle, firefighting vehicle, or law enforcement vehicle after consuming alcohol.

(a) Offense. - A person commits the offense of operating a school bus, school activity bus, child care vehicle, ambulance, other emergency medical services vehicle, firefighting vehicle, or law enforcement vehicle after consuming alcohol if the person drives a school bus, school activity bus, child care vehicle, ambulance, other emergency medical services vehicle, firefighting vehicle, or law enforcement vehicle upon any highway, any street, or any public vehicular area within the State while consuming alcohol or while alcohol remains in the person's body. This section does not apply to law enforcement officers acting in the course of, and within the scope of, their official duties.

(b) Implied-Consent Offense. - An offense under this section is an implied-consent offense subject to the provisions of G.S. 20-16.2. The provisions of G.S. 20-139.1 shall apply to an offense committed under this section.

(b1) Odor Insufficient. - The odor of an alcoholic beverage on the breath of the driver is insufficient evidence by itself to prove beyond a reasonable doubt that alcohol was remaining in the driver's body in violation of this section unless the driver was offered an alcohol screening test or chemical analysis and refused to provide all required samples of breath or blood for analysis.

(b2) Alcohol Screening Test. - Notwithstanding any other provision of law, an alcohol screening test may be administered to a driver suspected of violation of subsection (a) of this section, and the results of an alcohol screening test or the driver's refusal to submit may be used by a law enforcement officer, a court, or an administrative agency in determining if alcohol was present in the driver's body. No alcohol screening tests are valid under this section unless the device used is one approved by the

Department of Health and Human Services, and the screening test is conducted in accordance with the applicable regulations of the Department as to its manner and use.

(c) Punishment. - Except as otherwise provided in this subsection, a violation of the offense described in subsection (a) of this section is a Class 3 misdemeanor and, notwithstanding G.S. 15A-1340.23, is punishable by a penalty of one hundred dollars ($100.00). A second or subsequent violation of this section is a misdemeanor punishable under G.S. 20-179. This offense is a lesser included offense of impaired driving of a commercial vehicle under G.S. 20-138.1.

(d) Second or Subsequent Conviction Defined. - A conviction for violating this offense is a second or subsequent conviction if at the time of the current offense the person has a previous conviction under this section, and the previous conviction occurred in the seven years immediately preceding the date of the current offense. This definition of second or subsequent conviction also applies to G.S. 20-19(c2).

This statute is very similar in nature to Operating a commercial vehicle after consuming alcohol. The main difference to look out for is that although it is still punished the same way with the same fine, a first time conviction under this statute will result in a license revocation (see N.C.G.S. §20-17(a)(14)).

20-138.2C. Possession of alcoholic beverages while operating a commercial motor vehicle.

A person commits the offense of operating a commercial motor vehicle while possessing alcoholic beverages if the person drives a commercial motor vehicle, as defined in G.S. 20-4.01(3d), upon any highway, any street, or any public vehicular area within the State while having an open or closed alcoholic beverage in the passenger area of the commercial motor vehicle. This section shall not apply to the driver of a commercial motor vehicle that is also an excursion passenger vehicle, a for-hire passenger vehicle, a common carrier of passengers, or a motor home, if the alcoholic beverage is in possession of a passenger or is in the passenger area of the vehicle.

3.4 Underage Impaired Driving

20-138.3. Driving by person less than 21 years old after consuming alcohol or drugs.

(a) Offense. - It is unlawful for a person less than 21 years old to drive a motor vehicle on a highway or public vehicular area while consuming alcohol or at any time while he has remaining in his body any alcohol or controlled substance previously consumed, but a person less than 21 years old does not violate this section if he drives with a controlled substance in his body which was lawfully obtained and taken in therapeutically appropriate amounts.

(b) Subject to Implied-Consent Law. - An offense under this section is an alcohol-related offense subject to the implied-consent provisions of G.S. 20-16.2.

(b1) Odor Insufficient. - The odor of an alcoholic beverage on the breath of the driver is insufficient evidence by itself to prove beyond a reasonable doubt that alcohol was remaining in the driver's body in violation of this section unless the driver was offered an alcohol screening test or chemical analysis and refused to provide all required samples of breath or blood for analysis.

(b2) Alcohol Screening Test. - Notwithstanding any other provision of law, an alcohol screening test may be administered to a driver suspected of violation of subsection (a) of this section, and the results of an alcohol screening test or the driver's refusal to submit may be used by a law enforcement officer, a court, or an administrative agency in determining if alcohol was present in the driver's body. No alcohol screening tests are valid under this section unless the device used is one approved by the Department of Health and Human Services, and the screening test is conducted in accordance with the applicable regulations of the Department as to its manner and use.

(c) Punishment; Effect When Impaired Driving Offense Also Charged. - The offense in this section is a Class 2 misdemeanor. It is not, in any circumstances, a lesser included offense of impaired driving under G.S. 20-138.1, but if a person is convicted under this section and of an offense involving impaired driving arising out of the same transaction, the aggregate punishment imposed by the court may not exceed the maximum applicable to the offense involving impaired driving, and any minimum punishment applicable shall be imposed.

(d) Limited Driving Privilege. - A person who is convicted of violating subsection (a) of this section and whose drivers license is revoked solely based on that conviction may apply for a limited driving privilege as provided in G.S. 20-179.3. This subsection shall apply only if the person meets both of the following requirements:

(1) Is 18, 19, or 20 years old on the date of the offense.

(2) Has not previously been convicted of a violation of this section.

The judge may issue the limited driving privilege only if the person meets the eligibility requirements of G.S. 20-179.3, other than the requirement in G.S. 20-179.3(b)(1)c. G.S. 20-179.3(e) shall not apply. All other terms, conditions, and restrictions provided for in G.S. 20-179.3 shall apply. G.S. 20-179.3, rather than this subsection, governs the issuance of a limited driving privilege to a person who is convicted of violating subsection (a) of this section and of driving while impaired as a result of the same transaction.

Most North Carolina DWI attorneys call this a "baby DWI" or an "underage DWI." Sometimes this charge is a stand-alone charge, but increasingly we see this charge accompanied by a regular DWI as well. Of special note here is that if your client is charged with both but is subsequently convicted of the "regular" or "adult" DWI, N.C.G.S. §20-138.1 your client will NOT be eligible for a driving privilege. If convicted of just the underage DWI by itself and the client is 18, 19, or 20 years of age at the time of the offense, then you can get a driving privilege for the client.

Once again, odor is NOT sufficient; there must be a reading. Here as with operating a commercial vehicle with alcohol in the body, the number can come into the hearing. It is not just a positive or negative for alcohol, but the actual number that your client blew. See N.C.G.S. §20-138.2A(b2) and N.C.G.S. §20-138.2B(b2) allowing use of the results to N.C.G.S. §20-16.3(d) which speaks in terms of allowing positive or negative results.

PRACTICE TIP: When I have a client that is charged only with an underage DWI, I will generally have the client get a substance abuse assessment and follow through by taking the recommended classes. I also have the client perform 50 hours of community service. Most judges I know will generally allow for a PJC (Prayer for Judgment Continued) on a plea of guilty to this charge if the client has done the assessment and classes plus the community service. Although a PJC is technically an admission of guilt, the DMV will not revoke the license, ergo making it unnecessary to pursue a privilege.

3.5 Habitual DWI (Felony DWI)

§ 20-138.5. Habitual impaired driving.

(a) A person commits the offense of habitual impaired driving if he drives while impaired as defined in G.S. 20-138.1 and has been convicted of three or more offenses involving impaired driving as defined in G.S. 20-4.01(24a) within 10 years of the date of this offense.

(b) A person convicted of violating this section shall be punished as a Class F felon and shall be sentenced to a minimum active term of not less than 12 months of imprisonment, which shall not be suspended. Sentences imposed under this subsection shall run consecutively with and shall commence at the expiration of any sentence being served.

(c) An offense under this section is an implied consent offense subject to the provisions of G.S. 20-16.2. The provisions of G.S. 20-139.1 shall apply to an offense committed under this section.

(d) A person convicted under this section shall have his license permanently revoked.

(e) If a person is convicted under this section, the motor vehicle that was driven by the defendant at the time the defendant committed the offense of impaired driving becomes property subject to forfeiture in accordance with the procedure set out in G.S. 20-28.2. In applying the procedure set out in that statute, an owner or a holder of a security interest is considered an innocent party with respect to a motor vehicle subject to forfeiture under this subsection if any of the following applies:

(1) The owner or holder of the security interest did not know and had no reason to know that the defendant had been convicted within the previous seven years of three or more offenses involving impaired driving.

(2) The defendant drove the motor vehicle without the consent of the owner or the holder of the security interest.

Habitual DWI or Felony DWI can happen at any time on the fourth DWI charge a client receives in a ten year period as long as the previous three charges resulted in convictions for DWI (as of this writing). In order for the State to properly charge a person with Habitual DWI, the State must first take their case to the Grand Jury and receive an indictment. If the State does not indict, the DWI is treated just like any other misdemeanor DWI charge.

PRACTICE TIP: Many times, the State will not act quickly enough in going to the Grand Jury for an indictment. Sometimes, depending on your client's record, it may be best to plead as quickly as possible, before the State indicts so that your client receives less time in District Criminal Court than they would if the felony charge attached.

A key difference to remember about Habitual or Felony DWI is that unlike habitual felon which is a status, habitual DWI is an actual crime by and of itself and not merely a status. In a jury trial for habitual DWI, the defendant has a choice before the trial begins: either admit to the prior DWI convictions or deny them. If your client denies the priors then the State can bring them up at trial because they have to prove them to make their case. In cases like these, I have my client admit the priors outside the presence of the jury so that the jury doesn't know this isn't just a run of the mill DWI being tried. Otherwise, my thoughts are that the jury will tend to punish your client for the continued bad behavior. DWI is not a lesser included offense of habitual DWI.

Since Habitual DWI is a felony and not a misdemeanor, sentencing is proper under structured sentencing. Habitual DWI is a class F felony. The minimum sentence by statute is twelve months active jail time.

3.6 Homicide

DWI can sometimes result in the death of pedestrians, occupants of other vehicles and passengers within the DWI driver's vehicle. Although higher levels of homicide are sometimes charged, the most common forms are Manslaughter and Felony Death by Motor Vehicle. Sometimes a DWI homicide trial will focus on winning the DWI which serves as the only basis for the homicide charge.

The statutes are presented below.

§ 14-18. Punishment for manslaughter. Voluntary manslaughter shall be punishable as a Class D felony, and involuntary manslaughter shall be punishable as a Class F felony.

Involuntary manslaughter is a common law crime defined as "This offense consists in the unintentional killing of one person by another without malice (1) by doing some unlawful act not amounting to a felony or naturally dangerous to human life; or (2) by negligently doing some act which in itself is lawful; or (3) by negligently failing or omitting to perform a duty imposed by law." See *State v. Satterfield*, 198 N.C. 682 (1930).

Ergo, in a prosecution for involuntary manslaughter due to the fact that the defendant was impaired, the State must show that the death was proximately caused by the DWI. Involuntary manslaughter is a class F felony for structured sentencing purposes.

§ 20-141.4. Felony and misdemeanor death by vehicle; felony serious injury by vehicle; aggravated offenses; repeat felony death by vehicle.

(a) Repealed by Session Laws 1983, c. 435, s. 27. (al) Felony Death by Vehicle. – A person commits the offense of felony death by vehicle if: (1) The person unintentionally causes the death of another person, (2) The person was engaged in the offense of impaired driving under G.S. 20-138.1 or G.S. 20-138.2, and (3) The commission of the offense in subdivision (2) of this subsection is the proximate cause of the death.

(a2) Misdemeanor Death by Vehicle. – A person commits the offense of misdemeanor death by vehicle if: (1) The person unintentionally causes the death of another person, (2) The person was engaged in the violation of any State law or local ordinance applying to the operation or use of a vehicle or to the regulation of traffic, other than impaired driving under G.S. 20-138.1, and (3) The commission of the offense in subdivision (2) of this subsection is the proximate cause of the death.

(a3) Felony Serious Injury by Vehicle. – A person commits the offense of felony serious injury by vehicle if: (1) The person unintentionally causes serious injury to another person, (2) The person was engaged in the offense of impaired driving under G.S. 20-138.1 or G.S. 20-138.2, and (3) The commission of the offense in subdivision (2) of this subsection is the proximate cause of the serious injury.

(a4) Aggravated Felony Serious Injury by Vehicle. – A person commits the offense of aggravated felony serious injury by vehicle if: (1) The person unintentionally causes serious injury to another person, (2) The person was engaged in the offense of impaired driving under G.S. 20-138.1 or G.S. 20-138.2, (3) The commission of the offense in subdivision (2) of this subsection is the proximate cause of the serious injury, and (4) The person has a previous conviction involving impaired driving, as defined in G.S. 20-4.01(24a), within seven years of the date of the offense.

(a5) Aggravated Felony Death by Vehicle. – A person commits the offense of aggravated felony death by vehicle if: (1) The person unintentionally causes the death of another person, (2) The person was engaged in the offense of impaired driving under G.S. 20-138.1 or G.S. 20-138.2, (3) The commission of the offense in subdivision (2) of this subsection is the proximate cause of the death, and (4) The person has a previous conviction involving impaired driving, as defined in G.S. 20-4.01(24a), within seven years of the date of the offense.

(a6) Repeat Felony Death by Vehicle Offender. – A person commits the offense of repeat felony death by vehicle if: (1) The person commits an offense under subsection (a1) or subsection (a5) of this section; and (2) The person has a previous conviction under: a. Subsection (a1) of this section; b. Subsection (a5) of this section; or c. G.S. 14-17 or G.S. 14-18, and the basis of the conviction was the unintentional death of another person while engaged in the offense of impaired driving under G.S. 20-138.1 or G.S. 20-138.2. The pleading and proof of previous convictions shall be in accordance with the provisions of G.S. 15A-928.

(b) Punishments. – Unless the conduct is covered under some other provision of law providing greater punishment, the following classifications apply to the offenses set forth in this section: (1) Repeat felony death by vehicle is a Class B2 felony. (1a) Aggravated felony death by vehicle is a Class D felony. Notwithstanding the provisions of G.S. 15A-1340.17, the court shall sentence the defendant in the aggravated range of the appropriate Prior Record Level. (2) Felony death by vehicle is a Class D felony. Notwithstanding the provisions of G.S. 15A-1340.17, intermediate punishment is authorized for a defendant who is a Prior Record Level I offender. (3) Aggravated felony serious injury by vehicle is a Class E felony. (4) Felony serious injury by vehicle is a Class F felony. (5) Misdemeanor death by vehicle is a Class A1 misdemeanor.

(c) No Double Prosecutions. – No person who has been placed in jeopardy upon a charge of death by vehicle may be prosecuted for the offense of manslaughter arising out of the same death; and no person who has been placed in jeopardy upon a charge of manslaughter may be prosecuted for death by vehicle arising out of the same death.

Let's break each of these out and talk about them separately. Felony death by motor vehicle is when a person unintentionally causes the death of another person while driving while impaired or driving while impaired in a commercial vehicle and that the proximate cause of the other person's death is because of the impaired driving. Proximate cause in North Carolina is defined as "as a cause: (1) which, in a natural and continuous sequence and unbroken by any new and independent cause, produces an injury; (2) without which the injury would not have occurred; and (3) from which a person of ordinary prudence could have reasonably foreseen that such a result, or some similar injurious result, was probable under the facts as they existed." See State v. Hall, 60 N.C. App. 450, 454-55 (1983). Felony death by vehicle is a class D felony for structured sentencing purposes.

Misdemeanor death by motor vehicle requires an unintentional death of another person while violating a state law or local ordinance that applies to the use or operation of a vehicle or regulation of traffic (other than DWI) and that's what proximately caused the other person's death. Misdemeanor death by motor vehicle is a class A1 misdemeanor for structured sentencing purposes.

Felony serious injury by vehicle is basically the same as felony death by vehicle, only the person harmed here in only injured and not killed due to the impaired driving. "Serious injury" is not defined by statute or case law and is generally determined by the facts on a case by case basis. Felony serious injury by vehicle is a class F felony for structured sentencing purposes.

Aggravated felony serious injury by vehicle has only one difference when compared to felony serious injury by vehicle and that is a prior conviction for impaired driving within seven years of the date of the offense. Aggravated felony serious injury by vehicle is a class E felony for structured sentencing purposes.

Aggravated felony death by vehicle is also similar to felony death by vehicle except that it also adds the addition of the person having a previous conviction for impaired driving within seven years of the date of offense. Aggravated felony death by vehicle is a class D felony for structured sentencing purposes.

Repeat Felony Death by Vehicle occurs when a person previously convicted of felony death by vehicle, aggravated felony death by vehicle, or murder or manslaughter based on the unintentional death of another person while DWI and now commits felony death by vehicle or aggravated felony death by vehicle. Repeat felony death by vehicle is a class B2 felony for structured sentencing purposes.

3.7 Reckless Driving

Often when a non-DWI plea is offered in a misdemeanor DWI case, it will be to N.C.G.S. §20-140. Clearly, this has some distinct advantages to your client. The primary advantage is that it is not a DWI and does not have the social stigma of a DWI conviction. Jail time is rarely requested in such a plea offer.

PRACTICE TIP: Although a Reckless Driving plea may be welcomed by your client, be sure to think through the disadvantages as well. Reckless driving is a criminal offense; it is a Class 2 misdemeanor. Reckless Driving carries 4 points with it. Be sure that you have checked your client's Motor Vehicle Record for points accumulation.

N.C.G.S. §20-140 Reckless driving.

(a) Any person who drives any vehicle upon a highway or any public vehicular area carelessly and heedlessly in willful or wanton disregard of the rights or safety of others shall be guilty of reckless driving.
(b) Any person who drives any vehicle upon a highway or any public vehicular area without due caution and circumspection and at a speed or in a manner so as to endanger or be likely to endanger any person or property shall be guilty of reckless driving.
(c) Repealed by Session Laws 1983, c. 435, s. 23.
(d) Reckless driving as defined in subsections (a) and (b) is a Class 2 misdemeanor.
(e) Repealed by Session Laws 1983, c. 435, s. 23.
(f) A person is guilty of the Class 2 misdemeanor of reckless driving if the person drives a commercial motor vehicle carrying a load that is subject to the permit requirements of G.S. 20-119 upon a highway or any public vehicular area either:
(1) Carelessly and heedlessly in willful or wanton disregard of the rights or safety of others; or
(2) Without due caution and circumspection and at a speed or in a manner so as to endanger or be likely to endanger any person or property.

3.8 Boating While Impaired

§ 75A-10. Operating vessel or manipulating water skis, etc., in reckless manner; operating, etc., while intoxicated, etc.; depositing or discharging litter, etc.

(a) No person shall operate any motorboat or vessel, or manipulate any water skis, surfboard, or similar device on the waters of this State in a reckless or negligent manner so as to endanger the life, limb, or property of any person.
(b) No person shall manipulate any water skis, surfboard, nonmotorized vessel, or similar device on the waters of this State while under the influence of an impairing substance.
(b1) No person shall operate any vessel while underway on the waters of this State:
(1) While under the influence of an impairing substance, or
(2) After having consumed sufficient alcohol that the person has, at any relevant time after the boating, an alcohol concentration of 0.08 or more.
(b2) The fact that a person charged with violating this subsection is or has been legally entitled to use alcohol or a drug is not a defense to a charge under subsections (b) and (b1) of this section. The relevant definitions contained in G.S. 20-4.01 shall apply to subsections (b), (b1), and (b2) of this section.
(b3) A person who violates a provision of subsection (a) or (b) of this section is guilty of a Class 2 misdemeanor.
(b4) A person who violates subsection (b1) of this section is guilty of a Class 2 misdemeanor, punishable by a fine of not less than two hundred fifty dollars ($250.00).
(c) No person shall place, throw, deposit, or discharge or cause to be placed, thrown, deposited, or discharged on the waters of this State or into the inland lake waters of this State, any litter, raw sewage, bottles, cans, papers, or other liquid or solid materials which render the waters unsightly, noxious, or otherwise unwholesome so as to be detrimental to the public health or welfare or to the enjoyment and safety of the water for recreational purposes.
(d) No person shall place, throw, deposit, or discharge or cause to be placed, thrown, deposited, or discharged on the waters of this State or into the inland lake waters of this State any medical waste as defined by G.S. 130A-290 which renders the waters unsightly, noxious, or otherwise unwholesome so as to be detrimental to the public health or welfare or to the enjoyment and safety of the water for recreational purposes.
(e) A person who willfully violates subsection (d) of this section is guilty of a Class 1 misdemeanor. A person who willfully violates subsection (d) of this section and in so doing releases medical waste that creates a substantial risk of physical injury to any person who is not a participant in the offense is guilty of a Class F felony which may include a fine not to exceed fifty thousand dollars ($50,000) per day of violation.

Many DWI attorneys in North Carolina have not had a ton of experience with what I call BWI or boating while impaired. The best part about dealing with this misdemeanor is that the citation is usually given out by a North Carolina Wildlife Enforcement Officer. While these officers must go through the standard BLET (Basic Law Enforcement Training), they usually have little experience in DWI investigation. This means that they will most likely either not give the standardized tests correctly or will not know what they are. There are more advanced training available through the Coast Guard and other organizations to help Wildlife better understand the investigations of this type of misdemeanor.

The good news is that a conviction for BWI will NOT affect your client's driver's license. The reason is that it is NOT an implied consent offense. Your client can also refuse to blow with no detriment. Usually most counties that handle these types of cases will immediately offer your client a PJC (Prayer for Judgment Continued) with a fine and assessment. This is a good route to take, however be careful if your client is looking to restore a driver's license due to a prior DWI conviction. If that is the case, DMV can count the PJC as a conviction against them and revoke your client's license longer.

The bad news is (at present) a Wildlife officer can board your client's boat for no real reason at all. For example: the officer approaches your boat and wants to board to make sure you have enough life jackets. This is permitted. It seems odd, but the current case law says that there doesn't have to be reasonable articulable suspicion. See State v. Pike 139 N.C. App. 96 (2000).

Most Wildlife officers will use the NHTSA standardized tests. They seem particularly fond of the HGN test followed by the "hand pat" test and the finger dexterity test. All of these tests are usually used prior to having your client return to land for the SFSTs. I always like to argue that if these tests are not given and the client is ordered to come ashore with no tests, he or she has been detained for Constitutional purposes.

3.9 Other related charges

Open container charges (sometimes referred to as 18B violations) fall under N.C.G.S. §20-138.7 which is set forth below. Note that the first subpart is a misdemeanor and the second is an infraction. A moped is also considered a motor vehicle for the purposes of this statute.

§ 20-138.7. Transporting an open container of alcoholic beverage.

(a) Offense. - No person shall drive a motor vehicle on a highway or the right-of-way of a highway:

(1) While there is an alcoholic beverage in the passenger area in other than the unopened manufacturer's original container; and

(2) While the driver is consuming alcohol or while alcohol remains in the driver's body.

(a1) Offense. - No person shall possess an alcoholic beverage other than in the unopened manufacturer's original container, or consume an alcoholic beverage, in the passenger area of a motor vehicle while the motor vehicle is on a highway or the right-of-way of a highway. For purposes of this subsection, only the person who possesses or consumes an alcoholic beverage in violation of this subsection shall be charged with this offense.

(a2) Exception. - It shall not be a violation of subsection (a1) of this section for a passenger to possess an alcoholic beverage other than in the unopened manufacturer's original container, or for a passenger to consume an alcoholic beverage, if the container is:

(1) In the passenger area of a motor vehicle that is designed, maintained, or used primarily for the transportation of persons for compensation;

(2) In the living quarters of a motor home or house car as defined in G.S. 20-4.01(27)d2.; or

(3) In a house trailer as defined in G.S. 20-4.01(14).

(a3) Meaning of Terms. - Under this section, the term "motor vehicle" means any vehicle driven or drawn by mechanical power and manufactured primarily for use on public highways and includes mopeds.

(b) Subject to Implied-Consent Law. - An offense under this section is an alcohol-related offense subject to the implied-consent provisions of G.S. 20-16.2.

(c) Odor Insufficient. - The odor of an alcoholic beverage on the breath of the driver is insufficient evidence to prove beyond a reasonable doubt that alcohol was remaining in the driver's body in violation of this section, unless the driver was offered an alcohol screening test or chemical analysis and refused to provide all required samples of breath or blood for analysis.

(d) Alcohol Screening Test. - Notwithstanding any other provision of law, an alcohol screening test may be administered to a driver suspected of violating subsection (a) of this section, and the results of an alcohol screening test or the driver's refusal to submit may be used by a law enforcement officer, a court, or an administrative agency in determining if alcohol was present in the driver's body. No alcohol screening tests are valid under this section unless the device used is one approved by the Commission for Public Health, and the screening test is conducted in accordance with the applicable regulations of the Commission as to the manner of its use.

(e) Punishment; Effect When Impaired Driving Offense Also Charged. - Violation of subsection (a) of this section shall be a Class 3 misdemeanor for the first offense and shall be a Class 2 misdemeanor for a second or subsequent offense. Violation of subsection (a) of this section is not a lesser included offense of impaired driving under G.S. 20-138.1, but if a person is convicted under subsection (a) of this section and of an offense involving impaired driving arising out of the same transaction, the punishment imposed by the court shall not exceed the maximum applicable to the offense involving impaired driving, and any minimum applicable punishment shall be imposed. Violation of subsection (a1) of this section by the driver of the motor vehicle is a lesser-included offense of subsection (a) of this section. A violation of subsection (a) shall be considered a moving violation for purposes of G.S. 20-16(c).
Violation of subsection (a1) of this section shall be an infraction and shall not be considered a moving violation for purposes of G.S. 20-16(c).

(f) Definitions. - If the seal on a container of alcoholic beverages has been broken, it is opened within the meaning of this section. For purposes of this section, "passenger area of a motor vehicle" means the area designed to seat the driver and passengers and any area within the reach of a seated driver or passenger, including the glove compartment. The area of the trunk or the area behind the last upright back seat of a station wagon, hatchback, or similar vehicle shall not be considered part of the passenger area. The term "alcoholic beverage" is as defined in G.S. 18B-101(4).

(g) Pleading. - In any prosecution for a violation of subsection (a) of this section, the pleading is sufficient if it states the time and place of the alleged offense in the usual form and charges that the defendant drove a motor vehicle on a highway or the right-of-way of a highway with an open container of alcoholic beverage after drinking.
In any prosecution for a violation of subsection (a1) of this section, the pleading is sufficient if it states the time and place of the alleged offense in the usual form and charges that (i) the defendant possessed an open container of alcoholic beverage in the passenger area of a motor vehicle while the motor vehicle was on a highway or the right-of-way of a highway, or (ii) the defendant consumed an alcoholic beverage in the passenger area of a motor vehicle while the motor vehicle was on a highway or the right-of-way of a highway.

(h) Limited Driving Privilege. - A person who is convicted of violating subsection (a) of this section and whose drivers license is revoked solely based on that conviction may apply for a limited driving privilege as provided for in G.S. 20-179.3. The judge may issue the limited driving privilege only if the driver meets the eligibility requirements of G.S. 20-179.3, other than the requirement in G.S. 20-179.3(b)(1)c. G.S. 20-179.3(e) shall not apply. All other terms, conditions, and restrictions provided for in G.S. 20-179.3 shall apply. G.S. 20-179.3, rather than this subsection, governs the issuance of a limited driving privilege to a person who is convicted of violating subsection (a) of this section and of driving while impaired as a result of the same transaction.

In a limited number of cases, you will find yourself defending someone charged with impaired instruction. N.C.G.S. §20-12.1 is reproduced below.

§ 20-12.1. Impaired supervision or instruction.
(a) It is unlawful for a person to serve as a supervising driver under G.S. 20-7(l) or G.S. 20-11 or as an approved instructor under G.S. 20-7(m) in any of the following circumstances: (1) While under the influence of an impairing substance. (2) After having consumed sufficient alcohol to have, at any relevant time after the driving, an alcohol concentration of 0.08 or more. (b) An offense under this section is an implied-consent offense under G.S. 20-16.2.

3.10 Seizure and Forfeiture of a Motor Vehicle

Unfortunately for a lot of clients, losing a car or truck to a pending DWI charge can be a harsh reality. This is especially true when that car or truck is fairly new and still has many outstanding payments. In certain situations, the State can and will take motor vehicles in DWI cases. The governing statute on motor vehicle forfeiture is N.C.G.S. §20-28.3 reproduced here:

§ 20-28.3. Seizure, impoundment, forfeiture of motor vehicles for offenses involving impaired driving while license revoked or without license and insurance, and for felony speeding to elude arrest.

(a) Motor Vehicles Subject to Seizure for Impaired Driving Offenses. -
A motor vehicle that is driven by a person who is charged with an offense involving impaired driving is subject to seizure if:
(1) At the time of the violation, the drivers license of the person driving the motor vehicle was revoked as a result of a prior impaired driving license revocation as defined in G.S. 20-28.2(a); or
(2) At the time of the violation:
a. The person was driving without a valid drivers license, and
b. The driver was not covered by an automobile liability policy.
For the purposes of this subsection, a person who has a complete defense, pursuant to G.S. 20-35, to a charge of driving without a drivers license, shall be considered to have had a valid drivers license at the time of the violation.
(a1) Motor Vehicles Subject to Seizure for Felony Speeding to Elude Arrest. - A motor vehicle is subject to seizure if it is driven by a person who is charged with the offense of felony speeding to elude arrest pursuant to G.S. 20-141.5(b) or (b1).
(b) Duty of Officer. - If the charging officer has probable cause to believe that a motor vehicle driven by the defendant may be subject to forfeiture under this section, the officer shall seize the motor vehicle and have it impounded. If the officer determines prior to seizure that the motor vehicle had been reported stolen, the officer shall not seize the motor vehicle pursuant to this section. If the officer determines prior to seizure that the motor vehicle was a rental vehicle driven by a person not listed as an authorized driver on the rental contract, the officer shall not seize the motor vehicle pursuant to this section, but shall make a reasonable effort to notify the owner of the rental vehicle that the vehicle was stopped and that the driver of the vehicle was not listed as an authorized driver on the rental contract. Probable cause may be based on the officer's personal knowledge, reliable information conveyed by another officer, records of the Division, or other reliable sources. The seizing officer shall notify the Division as soon as practical but no later than 24 hours after seizure of the motor vehicle of the seizure in accordance with procedures established by the Division.
(b1) Written Notification of Impoundment. - Within 48 hours of receipt within regular business hours of the notice of seizure, the Division shall issue written notification of impoundment to any lienholder of record and to any motor vehicle owner who was not operating the motor vehicle at the time of the offense. A notice of seizure received outside regular business hours shall be considered to have been received at the start of the next business day. The notification of impoundment shall be sent by first-class mail to the most recent address contained in the Division's records. If the motor vehicle is registered in another state, notice shall be sent to the address shown on the records of the state where the motor vehicle is registered. This written notification shall provide notice that the motor vehicle has been seized, state the reason for the seizure and the procedure for requesting release of the motor vehicle. Additionally, if the motor vehicle was damaged while the operator was committing an offense resulting in seizure or incident to the seizure, the Division shall issue written notification of the seizure to the owner's insurance company of record and to any other insurance companies that may be insuring other motor vehicles involved in the accident. The Division shall prohibit title to a seized motor vehicle from being transferred by a motor vehicle owner unless authorized by court order.
(b2) Additional Notification to Lienholders. - In addition to providing written notification pursuant to subsection (b1) of this section, within eight hours of receipt within regular business hours of the notice of seizure, the Division shall notify by facsimile any lienholder of record that has provided the Division with a designated facsimile number for notification of impoundment. The facsimile notification of impoundment shall state that the vehicle has been seized, state the reason for the seizure, and notify the lienholder of the additional written notification that will be provided pursuant to subsection (b1) of this section. The Division shall establish procedures to allow a lienholder to provide one designated facsimile number for notification of impoundment for any vehicle for which the lienholder is a lienholder of record and shall maintain a centralized database of the provided facsimile numbers. The lienholder must provide a facsimile number at which the Division may give notification of impoundment at anytime.
(c) Review by Magistrate. - Upon determining that there is probable cause for seizing a motor vehicle, the seizing officer shall present to a magistrate

within the county where the driver was charged an affidavit of impoundment setting forth the basis upon which the motor vehicle has been or will be seized for forfeiture. The magistrate shall review the affidavit of impoundment and if the magistrate determines the requirements of this section have been met, shall order the motor vehicle held. The magistrate may request additional information and may hear from the defendant if the defendant is present. If the magistrate determines the requirements of this section have not been met, the magistrate shall order the motor vehicle released to a motor vehicle owner upon payment of towing and storage fees. If the motor vehicle has not yet been seized, and the magistrate determines that seizure is appropriate, the magistrate shall issue an order of seizure of the motor vehicle. The magistrate shall provide a copy of the order of seizure to the clerk of court. The clerk shall provide copies of the order of seizure to the district attorney and the attorney for the county board of education.

(c1) Effecting an Order of Seizure. - An order of seizure shall be valid anywhere in the State. Any officer with territorial jurisdiction and who has subject matter jurisdiction for violations of this Chapter may use such force as may be reasonable to seize the motor vehicle and to enter upon the property of the defendant to accomplish the seizure. An officer who has probable cause to believe the motor vehicle is concealed or stored on private property of a person other than the defendant may obtain a search warrant to enter upon that property for the purpose of seizing the motor vehicle.

(d) Custody of Motor Vehicle. - Unless the motor vehicle is towed pursuant to a statewide or regional contract, or a contract with the county board of education, the seized motor vehicle shall be towed by a commercial towing company designated by the law enforcement agency that seized the motor vehicle. Seized motor vehicles not towed pursuant to a statewide or regional contract or a contract with a county board of education shall be retrieved from the commercial towing company within a reasonable time, not to exceed 10 days, by the county board of education or their agent who must pay towing and storage fees to the commercial towing company when the motor vehicle is retrieved. If either a statewide or regional contractor, or the county board of education, chooses to contract for local towing services, all towing companies on the towing list for each law enforcement agency with jurisdiction within the county shall be given written notice and an opportunity to submit proposals prior to a contract for local towing services being awarded. The seized motor vehicle is under the constructive possession of the county board of education for the county in which the operator of the vehicle is charged at the time the vehicle is delivered to a location designated by the county board of education or delivered to its agent pending release or sale, or in the event a statewide or regional contract is in place, under the constructive possession of the Department of Public Instruction, on behalf of the State at the time the vehicle is delivered to a location designated by the Department of Public Instruction or delivered to its agent pending release or sale. Absent a statewide or regional contract that provides otherwise, each county board of education may elect to have seized motor vehicles stored on property owned or leased by the county board of education and charge a reasonable fee for storage, not to exceed ten dollars ($10.00) per day. In the alternative, the county board of education may contract with a commercial towing and storage facility or other private entity for the towing, storage, and disposal of seized motor vehicles, and a storage fee of not more than ten dollars ($10.00) per day may be charged. Except for gross negligence or intentional misconduct, the county board of education, or any of its employees, shall not be liable to the owner or lienholder for damage to or loss of the motor vehicle or its contents, or to the owner of personal property in a seized vehicle, during the time the motor vehicle is being towed or stored pursuant to this subsection.

(e) Release of Motor Vehicle Pending Trial. - A motor vehicle owner, other than the driver at the time of the underlying offense resulting in the seizure, may apply to the clerk of superior court in the county where the charges are pending for pretrial release of the motor vehicle.

The clerk shall release the motor vehicle to a nondefendant motor vehicle owner conditioned upon payment of all towing and storage charges incurred as a result of seizure and impoundment of the motor vehicle under the following conditions:

(1) The motor vehicle has been seized for not less than 24 hours;

(2) Repealed by Session Laws 1998-182, s. 3, effective December 1, 1998.

(3) A bond in an amount equal to the fair market value of the motor vehicle as defined by G.S. 20-28.2 has been executed and is secured by a cash deposit in the full amount of the bond, by a recordable deed of trust to real property in the full amount of the bond, by a bail bond under G.S. 58-71-1(2), or by at least one solvent surety, payable to the county school fund and conditioned on return of the motor vehicle, in substantially the same condition as it was at the time of seizure and without any new or additional liens or encumbrances, on the day of any hearing scheduled and noticed by the district attorney under G.S. 20-28.2(c), unless the motor vehicle has been permanently released;

(4) Execution of either:

a. An impaired driving acknowledgment as described in G.S. 20-28.2(a1)(1a) if the seizure was for an offense involving impaired driving; or

b. A speeding to elude arrest acknowledgment as defined in G.S. 20-28.2(a1)(8) if the seizure was for violation of G.S. 20-141.5(b) or (b1).

(5) A check of the records of the Division indicates that the requesting motor vehicle owner has not previously executed an acknowledgment naming the operator of the seized motor vehicle; and

(6) A bond posted to secure the release of this motor vehicle under this subsection has not been previously ordered forfeited under G.S. 20-28.5.

In the event a nondefendant motor vehicle owner who obtains temporary possession of a seized motor vehicle pursuant to this subsection does not return the motor vehicle on the day of the forfeiture hearing as noticed by the district attorney under G.S. 20-28.2(c) or otherwise violates a condition of pretrial release of the seized motor vehicle as set forth in this subsection, the bond posted shall be ordered forfeited and an order of seizure shall be issued by the court. Additionally, a nondefendant motor vehicle owner or lienholder who willfully violates any condition of pretrial release may be held in civil or criminal contempt.

(e1) Pretrial Release of Motor Vehicle to Innocent Owner. - A nondefendant motor vehicle owner may file a petition with the clerk of court seeking a pretrial determination that the petitioner is an innocent owner. The clerk shall consider the petition and make a determination as soon as may be feasible. At any proceeding conducted pursuant to this subsection, the clerk is not required to determine the issue of forfeiture, only the issue of whether the petitioner is an innocent owner. If the clerk determines that the petitioner is an innocent owner, the clerk shall release the motor vehicle to the petitioner subject to the same conditions as if the petitioner were an innocent owner under G.S. 20-28.2(e). The clerk shall send a copy of the order authorizing or denying release of the vehicle to the district attorney and the attorney for the county board of education. An order issued under this subsection finding that the petitioner failed to establish that the petitioner is an innocent owner may be reconsidered by the court as part of the forfeiture hearing conducted pursuant to G.S. 20-28.2(d).

(e2) Pretrial Release of Motor Vehicle to Defendant Owner. -

(1) If the seizure was for an offense involving impaired driving, a defendant motor vehicle owner may file a petition with the clerk of court seeking a pretrial determination that the defendant's license was not revoked pursuant to an impaired driving license revocation as defined in G.S. 20-28.2(a). The clerk shall schedule a hearing before a judge of the division in which the underlying criminal charge is pending for a hearing to be held within 10 business days or as soon thereafter as may be feasible. Notice of the hearing shall be given to the defendant, the district attorney, and the attorney for the county board of education. The clerk shall forward a copy of the petition to the district attorney for the district attorney's review. If, based on available information, the district attorney determines that the defendant's motor vehicle is not subject to forfeiture, the district attorney may note the State's consent to the release of the motor vehicle on the petition and return the petition to the clerk of court who shall enter an order releasing the motor vehicle to the defendant upon payment of all towing and storage charges incurred as a result of the seizure and impoundment of the motor vehicle, subject to the satisfactory proof of the identity of the defendant as a motor vehicle owner and the existence of financial responsibility to the extent required by Article 13 of this Chapter, and no hearing shall be held. The clerk shall send a copy of the order of release to the attorney for the county board of education. At any pretrial hearing conducted pursuant to this subdivision, the court is not required to determine the issue of the underlying offense of impaired driving only the existence of a prior drivers license revocation as an impaired driving license revocation. Accordingly, the State shall not be required to prove the underlying offense of impaired driving. An or-

der issued under this subdivision finding that the defendant failed to establish that the defendant's license was not revoked pursuant to an impaired driving license revocation as defined in G.S. 20-28.2(a) may be reconsidered by the court as part of the forfeiture hearing conducted pursuant to G.S. 20-28.2(d).

(2) If the seizure was for a felony speeding to elude arrest offense, a defendant motor vehicle owner may apply to the clerk of superior court in the county where the charges are pending for pretrial release of the motor vehicle. The clerk shall release the motor vehicle to the defendant motor vehicle owner conditioned upon payment of all towing and storage charges incurred as a result of seizure and impoundment of the motor vehicle under the following conditions:

a. The motor vehicle has been seized for not less than 24 hours;

b. A bond in an amount equal to the fair market value of the motor vehicle as defined by G.S. 20-28.2 has been executed and is secured by a cash deposit in the full amount of the bond, by a recordable deed of trust to real property in the full amount of the bond, by a bail bond under G.S. 58-71-1(2), or by at least one solvent surety, payable to the county school fund and conditioned on return of the motor vehicle, in substantially the same condition as it was at the time of seizure and without any new or additional liens or encumbrances, on the day of any hearing scheduled and noticed by the district attorney under G.S. 20-28.2(c), unless the motor vehicle has been permanently released;

c. A bond posted to secure the release of this motor vehicle under this subdivision has not been previously ordered forfeited under G.S. 20-28.5.

In the event a defendant motor vehicle owner who obtains temporary possession of a seized motor vehicle pursuant to this subdivision does not return the motor vehicle on the day of the forfeiture hearing as noticed by the district attorney under G.S. 20-28.2(c) or otherwise violates a condition of pretrial release of the seized motor vehicle as set forth in this subdivision, the bond posted shall be ordered forfeited, and an order of seizure shall be issued by the court. Additionally, a defendant motor vehicle owner who willfully violates any condition of pretrial release may be held in civil or criminal contempt.

(e3) Pretrial Release of Motor Vehicle to Lienholder. -

(1) A lienholder may file a petition with the clerk of court requesting the court to order pretrial release of a seized motor vehicle. The lienholder shall serve a copy of the petition on all interested parties which shall include the registered owner, the titled owner, the district attorney, and the county board of education attorney. Upon 10 days' prior notice of the date, time, and location of the hearing sent by the lienholder to all interested parties, a judge, after a hearing, shall order a seized motor vehicle released to the lienholder conditioned upon payment of all towing and storage costs incurred as a result of the seizure and impoundment of the motor vehicle if the judge determines, by the greater weight of the evidence, that:

a. Default on the obligation secured by the motor vehicle has occurred;

b. As a consequence of default, the lienholder is entitled to possession of the motor vehicle;

c. The lienholder agrees to sell the motor vehicle in accordance with the terms of its agreement and pursuant to the provisions of Part 6 of Article 9 of Chapter 25 of the General Statutes. Upon sale of the motor vehicle, the lienholder will pay to the clerk of court of the county in which the driver was charged all proceeds from the sale, less the amount of the lien in favor of the lienholder, and any towing and storage costs paid by the lienholder;

d. The lienholder agrees not to sell, give, or otherwise transfer possession of the seized motor vehicle while the motor vehicle is subject to forfeiture, or the forfeited motor vehicle after the forfeiture hearing, to the defendant or the motor vehicle owner; and

e. The seized motor vehicle while the motor vehicle is subject to forfeiture, or the forfeited motor vehicle after the forfeiture hearing, had not previously been released to the lienholder as a result of a prior seizure involving the same defendant or motor vehicle owner.

(2) The clerk of superior court may order a seized vehicle released to the lienholder conditioned upon payment of all towing and storage costs incurred as a result of the seizure and impoundment of the motor vehicle at any time when all interested parties have, in writing, waived any rights that they may have to notice and a hearing, and the lienholder has agreed to the provision of subdivision (1)d. above. A lienholder who refuses to sell, give, or transfer possession of a seized motor vehicle while the mo-

tor vehicle is subject to forfeiture, or a forfeited motor vehicle after the forfeiture hearing, to:

a. The defendant;

b. The motor vehicle owner who owned the motor vehicle immediately prior to seizure pending the forfeiture hearing, or to forfeiture after the forfeiture hearing; or

c. Any person acting on the behalf of the defendant or the motor vehicle owner,

shall not be liable for damages arising out of such refusal. However, any subsequent violation of the conditions of release by the lienholder shall be punishable by civil or criminal contempt.

(f), (g) Repealed by Session Laws 1998-182, s. 3, effective December 1, 1998.

(h) Insurance Proceeds. - In the event a motor vehicle is damaged incident to the conduct of the defendant which gave rise to the defendant's arrest and seizure of the motor vehicle pursuant to this section, the county board of education, or its authorized designee, is authorized to negotiate the county board of education's interest with the insurance company and to compromise and accept settlement of any claim for damages. Property insurance proceeds accruing to the defendant, or other owner of the seized motor vehicle, shall be paid by the responsible insurance company directly to the clerk of superior court in the county where the motor vehicle driver was charged. If the motor vehicle is declared a total loss by the insurance company liable for the damages to the motor vehicle, the clerk of superior court, upon application of the county board of education, shall enter an order that the motor vehicle be released to the insurance company upon payment into the court of all insurance proceeds for damage to the motor vehicle after payment of towing and storage costs and all valid liens. The clerk of superior court shall provide the Division with a certified copy of the order entered pursuant to this subsection, and the Division shall transfer title to the insurance company or to such other person or entity as may be designated by the insurance company. Insurance proceeds paid to the clerk of court pursuant to this subsection shall be subject to forfeiture pursuant to G.S. 20-28.5 and shall be disbursed pursuant to further orders of the court. An affected motor vehicle owner or lienholder who objects to any agreed upon settlement under this subsection may file an independent claim with the insurance company for any additional monies believed owed. Notwithstanding any other provisions in this Chapter, nothing in this section or G.S. 20-28.2 shall require an insurance company to make payments in excess of those required pursuant to its policy of insurance on the seized motor vehicle.

(i) Expedited Sale of Seized Motor Vehicles in Certain Cases. - In order to avoid additional liability for towing and storage costs pending resolution of the criminal proceedings of the defendant, the county board of education may, after expiration of 90 days from the date of seizure, sell any motor vehicle having a fair market value of one thousand five hundred dollars ($1,500) or less. The county board of education may also sell a motor vehicle, regardless of the fair market value, any time the outstanding towing and storage costs exceed eighty-five percent (85%) of the fair market value of the vehicle, or with the consent of all the motor vehicle owners. Any sale conducted pursuant to this subsection shall be conducted in accordance with the provisions of G.S. 20-28.5(a), and the proceeds of the sale, after the payment of outstanding towing and storage costs or reimbursement of towing and storage costs paid by a person other than the defendant, shall be deposited with the clerk of superior court. If an order of forfeiture is entered by the court, the court shall order the proceeds held by the clerk to be disbursed as provided in G.S. 20-28.5(b). If the court determines that the motor vehicle is not subject to forfeiture, the court shall order the proceeds held by the clerk to be disbursed first to pay the sale, towing, and storage costs, second to pay outstanding liens on the motor vehicle, and the balance to be paid to the motor vehicle owners.

(j) Retrieval of Certain Personal Property. - At reasonable times, the entity charged with storing the motor vehicle may permit owners of personal property not affixed to the motor vehicle to retrieve those items from the motor vehicle, provided satisfactory proof of ownership of the motor vehicle or the items of personal property is presented to the storing entity.

(k) County Board of Education Right to Appear and Participate in Proceedings. - The attorney for the county board of education shall be given notice of all proceedings regarding offenses related to a motor vehicle subject to forfeiture under this section. However, the notice requirement under this subsection does not apply to proceedings conducted under G.S. 20-28.3(e1). The attorney for the county board of education shall also have the right to appear and to be heard on all issues relating to the seizure, possession, release, forfeiture, sale, and other matters related to the seized vehicle under this section. With the prior consent of the county board of education, the district attorney may delegate to the attorney for the county board of education any or all of the duties of the district attorney under this section. Clerks of superior court, law enforcement agencies, and all other agencies with information relevant to the seizure, impoundment, release, or forfeiture of motor vehicles are authorized and directed to provide county boards of education with access to that information and to do so by electronic means when existing technology makes this type of transmission possible.

(l) Payment of Fees Upon Conviction. - If the driver of a motor vehicle seized pursuant to this section is convicted of the underlying offense resulting in the seizure of a motor vehicle pursuant to this section, the defendant shall be ordered to pay as restitution to the county board of education, the motor vehicle owner, or the lienholder the cost paid or owing for the towing, storage, and sale of the motor vehicle to the extent the costs were not covered by the proceeds from the forfeiture and sale of the motor vehicle. If the underlying offense resulting in the seizure is felony speeding to elude arrest pursuant to G.S. 20-141.5(b) or (b1) and the defendant's conviction is for misdemeanor speeding to elude arrest pursuant to G.S. 20-141.5(a), whether or not the reduced charge is by plea agreement, the defendant shall be ordered to pay as restitution to the county board of education, the motor vehicle owner, or the lienholder the cost paid or owing for the towing and storage of the motor vehicle. In addition, a civil judgment for the costs under this section in favor of the party to whom the restitution is owed shall be docketed by the clerk of superior court. If the defendant is sentenced to an active term of imprisonment, the civil judgment shall become effective and be docketed when the defendant's conviction becomes final. If the defendant is placed on probation, the civil judgment in the amount found by a judge during the probation revocation or termination hearing to be due shall become effective and be docketed by the clerk when the defendant's probation is revoked or terminated.

(m) Trial Priority. - District court trials of offenses involving forfeitures of motor vehicles pursuant to G.S. 20-28.2 shall be scheduled on the arresting officer's next court date or within 30 days of the offense, whichever comes first.

Once scheduled, the case shall not be continued unless all of the following conditions are met:

(1) A written motion for continuance is filed with notice given to the opposing party prior to the motion being heard.
(2) The judge makes a finding of a "compelling reason" for the continuance.
(3) The motion and finding are attached to the court case record.

Upon a determination of guilt, the issue of vehicle forfeiture shall be heard by the judge immediately, or as soon thereafter as feasible, and the judge shall issue the appropriate orders pursuant to G.S. 20-28.2(d).

Should a defendant appeal the conviction to superior court, any party who has not previously been heard on a petition for pretrial release under subsection (e1) or (e3) of this section or any party whose motor vehicle has not been the subject of a forfeiture hearing held pursuant to G.S. 20-28.2(d) may be heard on a petition for pretrial release pursuant to subsection (e1) or (e3) of this section. The provisions of subsection (e) of this section shall also apply to seized motor vehicles pending trial in superior court. Where a motor vehicle was released pursuant to subsection (e) of this section pending trial in district court, the release of the motor vehicle continues, and the terms and conditions of the original bond remain the same as those required for the initial release of the motor vehicle under subsection (e) of this section, pending the resolution of the underlying offense involving impaired driving in superior court.

(n) Any order issued pursuant to this section authorizing the release of a seized vehicle shall require the payment of all towing and storage charges incurred as a result of the seizure and impoundment of the motor vehicle. This requirement shall not be waived.

As you can see, to actually seize the vehicle the State must show certain things: either, the license of the driver at the time has to have been revoked for a prior impaired driving license revocation at the time of the current offense (see N.C.G.S. §20-28.2 below which also defines fair market value, innocent owner, and the like); or, the driver wasn't validly licensed and didn't have liability insurance at the time. The term motor vehicle is defined in the beginning of this chapter as well as the term of what constitutes an offense involving impaired driving.

§ 20-28.2. Forfeiture of motor vehicle for impaired driving after impaired driving license revocation; forfeiture for felony speeding to elude arrest.

(a) Meaning of "Impaired Driving License Revocation". - The revocation of a person's drivers license is an impaired driving license revocation if the revocation is pursuant to:

(1) G.S. 20-13.2, 20-16(a)(8b), 20-16.2, 20-16.5, 20-17(a)(2), 20-17(a)(12), or 20-138.5; or

(2) G.S. 20-16(a)(7), 20-17(a)(1), 20-17(a)(3), 20-17(a)(9), or 20-17(a)(11), if the offense involves impaired driving; or

(3) The laws of another state and the offense for which the person's license is revoked prohibits substantially similar conduct which if committed in this State would result in a revocation listed in subdivisions (1) or (2).

(a1) Definitions. - As used in this section and in G.S. 20-28.3, 20-28.4, 20-28.5, 20-28.7, 20-28.8, 20-28.9, 20-54.1, and 20-141.5, the following terms mean:

(1) Fair Market Value. - The value of the seized motor vehicle, as determined in accordance with the schedule of values adopted by the Commissioner pursuant to G.S. 105-187.3.

(1a) Impaired Driving Acknowledgment. - A written document acknowledging that:

a. The motor vehicle was operated by a person charged with an offense involving impaired driving, and:

1. That person's drivers license was revoked as a result of a prior impaired drivers license revocation; or

2. That person did not have a valid drivers license, and did not have liability insurance.

b. If the motor vehicle is again operated by this particular person, and the person is charged with an offense involving impaired driving, then the vehicle is subject to impoundment and forfeiture if (i) the offense occurs while that person's drivers license is revoked, or (ii) the offense occurs while the person has no valid drivers license, and has no liability insurance.

c. A lack of knowledge or consent to the operation will not be a defense in the future, unless the motor vehicle owner has taken all reasonable precautions to prevent the use of the motor vehicle by this particular person and immediately reports, upon discovery, any unauthorized use to the appropriate law enforcement agency.

(2) Innocent Owner. - A motor vehicle owner:

a. Who, if the offense resulting in seizure was an impaired driving offense, did not know and had no reason to know that (i) the defendant's drivers license was revoked, or (ii) that the defendant did not have a valid drivers license, and that the defendant had no liability insurance; or

b. Who, if the offense resulting in seizure was an impaired driving offense, knew that (i) the defendant's drivers license was revoked, or (ii) that the defendant had no valid drivers license, and that the defendant had no liability insurance, but the defendant drove the vehicle without the person's expressed or implied permission, and the owner files a police report for unauthorized use of the motor vehicle and agrees to prosecute the unauthorized operator of the motor vehicle, or who, if the offense resulting in seizure was a felony speeding to elude arrest offense, did not give the defendant express or implied permission to drive the vehicle, and the owner files a police report for unauthorized use of the motor vehicle and agrees to prosecute the unauthorized operator of the motor vehicle; or

c. Whose vehicle was reported stolen; or

d. Repealed by Session Laws 1999-406, s. 17.

e. Who is (i) a rental car company as defined in G.S. 66-201(a) and the vehicle was driven by a person who is not listed as an authorized driver on the rental agreement as defined in G.S. 66-201; or (ii) a rental car company as defined in G.S. 66-201(a) and the vehicle was driven by a person who is listed as an authorized driver on the rental agreement as defined in G.S. 66-201 and if the offense resulting in seizure was an impaired driving offense, the rental car company has no actual knowledge of the revocation of the renter's drivers' license at the time the rental agreement is entered, or if the offense resulting in seizure was a felony speeding to elude arrest offense, the rental agreement expressly prohibits use of the vehicle while committing a felony; or

f. Who is in the business of leasing motor vehicles, who holds legal title to the motor vehicle as a lessor at the time of seizure and, if the offense resulting in seizure was an impaired driving offense, who has no actual knowledge of the revocation of the lessee's drivers license at the time the lease is entered.

(2a) Insurance Company. - Any insurance company that has coverage on or is otherwise liable for repairs or damages to the motor vehicle at the time of the seizure.

(2b) Insurance Proceeds. - Proceeds paid under an insurance policy for damage to a seized motor vehicle less any payments actually paid to valid lienholders and for towing and storage costs incurred for the motor vehicle after the time the motor vehicle became subject to seizure.

(3) Lienholder. - A person who holds a perfected security interest in a motor vehicle at the time of seizure.

(3a) Motor Vehicle Owner. - A person in whose name a registration card or certificate of title for a motor vehicle is issued at the time of seizure.

(4) Order of Forfeiture. - An order by the court which terminates the rights and ownership interest of a motor vehicle owner in a motor vehicle and any insurance proceeds or proceeds of sale in accordance with G.S. 20-28.2.

(5) Repealed by Session Laws 1998-182, s. 2.

(6) Registered Owner. - A person in whose name a registration card for a motor vehicle is issued at the time of seizure.

(7) Repealed by Session Laws 1998-182, s. 2.

(8) Speeding to Elude Arrest Acknowledgment. - A written document acknowledging that:

a. The motor vehicle was operated by a person charged with felony speeding to elude arrest pursuant to G.S. 20-141.5(b) or (b1).

b. If the motor vehicle is again operated by this particular person and the person is charged with felony speeding to elude arrest pursuant to G.S. 20-141.5(b) or (b1), then the vehicle is subject to impoundment and forfeiture.

c. A lack of knowledge or consent to the operation will not be a defense in the future unless the motor vehicle owner has taken all reasonable precautions to prevent the use of the motor vehicle by this particular person and immediately reports upon discovery any unauthorized use to the appropriate law enforcement agency.

(b) When Motor Vehicle Becomes Property Subject to Order of Forfeiture; Impaired Driving and Prior Revocation. - A judge may determine whether the vehicle driven by an impaired driver at the time of the offense becomes subject to an order of forfeiture. The determination may be made at any of the following times:

(1) A sentencing hearing for the underlying offense involving impaired driving.

(2) A separate hearing after conviction of the defendant.

(3) A forfeiture hearing held at least 60 days after the defendant failed to appear at the scheduled trial for the underlying offense, and the defendant's order of arrest for failing to appear has not been set aside.

The vehicle shall become subject to an order of forfeiture if the greater weight of the evidence shows that the defendant is guilty of an offense involving impaired driving, and that the defendant's license was revoked pursuant to an impaired driving license revocation as defined in subsection (a) of this section.

(b1) When a Motor Vehicle Becomes Property Subject to Order of Forfeiture; No License and No Insurance. - A judge may determine whether the vehicle driven by an impaired driver at the time of the offense becomes subject to an order of forfeiture. The determination may be made at any of the following times:

(1) A sentencing hearing for the underlying offense involving impaired driving.

(2) A separate hearing after conviction of the defendant.

(3) A forfeiture hearing held at least 60 days after the defendant failed to appear at the scheduled trial for the underlying offense, and the defendant's order of arrest for failing to appear has not been set aside.

The vehicle shall become subject to an order of forfeiture if the greater weight of the evidence shows that the defendant is guilty of an offense involving impaired driving, and: (i) the defendant was driving without a valid drivers license, and (ii) the defendant was not covered by an automobile liability policy.

(b2) When a Motor Vehicle Becomes Property Subject to Order of Forfeiture; Felony Speeding to Elude Arrest. - A judge may determine whether the vehicle driven at the time of the offense becomes subject to an order of forfeiture. The determination may be made at any of the following times:

(1) A sentencing hearing for the underlying felony speeding to elude arrest offense.

(2) A separate hearing after conviction of the defendant.

(3) A forfeiture hearing held at least 60 days after the defendant failed to appear at the scheduled trial for

the underlying offense, and the defendant's order of arrest for failing to appear has not been set aside. The vehicle shall become subject to an order of forfeiture if the greater weight of the evidence shows that the defendant is guilty of felony speeding to elude arrest pursuant to G.S. 20-141.5(b) or (b1).

(c) Duty of Prosecutor to Notify Possible Innocent Parties. - In any case in which a prosecutor determines that a motor vehicle driven by a defendant may be subject to forfeiture under this section and the motor vehicle has not been permanently released to a nondefendant vehicle owner pursuant to G.S. 20-28.3(e1), a defendant owner pursuant to G.S. 20-28.3(e2), or a lienholder, pursuant to G.S. 20-28.3(e3), the prosecutor shall notify the defendant, each motor vehicle owner, and each lienholder that the motor vehicle may be subject to forfeiture and that the defendant, motor vehicle owner, or the lienholder may intervene to protect that person's interest. The notice may be served by any means reasonably likely to provide actual notice, and shall be served at least 10 days before the hearing at which an order of forfeiture may be entered.

(c1) Motor Vehicles Involved in Accidents. - If a motor vehicle subject to forfeiture was damaged while the defendant operator was committing the underlying offense resulting in seizure, or was damaged incident to the seizure of the motor vehicle, the Division shall determine the name of any insurance companies that are the insurers of record with the Division for the motor vehicle at the time of the seizure or that may otherwise be liable for repair to the motor vehicle. In any case where a seized motor vehicle was involved in an accident, the Division shall notify the insurance companies that the claim for insurance proceeds for damage to the seized motor vehicle shall be paid to the clerk of superior court of the county where the motor vehicle driver was charged to be held and disbursed pursuant to further orders of the court. Any insurance company that receives written or other actual notice of seizure pursuant to this section shall not be relieved of any legal obligation under any contract of insurance unless the claim for property damage to the seized motor vehicle minus the policy owner's deductible is paid directly to the clerk of court. The insurance company paying insurance proceeds to the clerk of court pursuant to this section shall be immune from suit by the motor vehicle owner for any damages alleged to have occurred as a result of the motor vehicle seizure. The proceeds shall be held by the clerk. The clerk shall disburse the insurance proceeds pursuant to further orders of the court.

(d) Forfeiture Hearing. - Unless a motor vehicle that has been seized pursuant to G.S. 20-28.3 has been permanently released to an innocent owner pursuant to G.S. 20-28.3(e1), a defendant owner pursuant to G.S. 20-28.3(e2), or to a lienholder pursuant to G.S. 20-28.3(e3), the court shall conduct a hearing on the forfeiture of the motor vehicle. The hearing may be held at the sentencing hearing on the underlying offense resulting in seizure, at a separate hearing after conviction of the defendant, or at a separate forfeiture hearing held not less than 60 days after the defendant failed to appear at the scheduled trial for the underlying offense and the defendant's order of arrest for failing to appear has not been set aside. If at the forfeiture hearing, the judge determines that the motor vehicle is subject to forfeiture pursuant to this section and proper notice of the hearing has been given, the judge shall order the motor vehicle forfeited. If at the sentencing hearing or at a forfeiture hearing, the judge determines that the motor vehicle is subject to forfeiture pursuant to this section and proper notice of the hearing has been given, the judge shall order the motor vehicle forfeited unless another motor vehicle owner establishes, by the greater weight of the evidence, that such motor vehicle owner is an innocent owner as defined in this section, in which case the trial judge shall order the motor vehicle released to the innocent owner pursuant to the provisions of subsection (e) of this section. In any case where the motor vehicle is ordered forfeited, the judge shall:

(1) a. Authorize the sale of the motor vehicle at public sale or allow the county board of education to retain the motor vehicle for its own use pursuant to G.S. 20-28.5; or

b. Order the motor vehicle released to a lienholder pursuant to the provisions of subsection (f) of this section; and

(2) a. Order any proceeds of sale or insurance proceeds held by the clerk of court to be disbursed to the county board of education; and

b. Order any outstanding insurance claims be assigned to the county board of education in the event the motor vehicle has been damaged in an accident incident to the seizure of the motor vehicle.

If the judge determines that the motor vehicle is subject to forfeiture pursuant to this section, but that notice as required by subsection (c) has not been given, the judge shall continue the forfeiture proceeding until adequate notice has been given. In no circumstance shall the sentencing of the defendant be delayed as a result of the failure of the prosecutor to give adequate notice.

(e) Release of Vehicle to Innocent Motor Vehicle Owner. - At a forfeiture hearing, if a nondefendant motor vehicle owner establishes by the greater weight of the evidence that: (i) the motor vehicle was being driven by a person who was not the only motor vehicle owner or had no ownership interest in the motor vehicle at the time of the underlying offense and (ii) the petitioner is an "innocent owner", as defined by this section, a judge shall order the motor vehicle released to that owner, conditioned upon payment of all towing and storage charges incurred as a result of the seizure and impoundment of the motor vehicle.

Release to an innocent owner shall only be ordered upon satisfactory proof of:

(1) The identity of the person as a motor vehicle owner;
(2) The existence of financial responsibility to the extent required by Article 13 of this Chapter or by the laws of the state in which the vehicle is registered; and
(3) Repealed by Session Laws 1998-182, s. 2, effective December 1, 1998.
(4) The execution of:
a. An impaired driving acknowledgment as defined in subdivision (a1)(1a) of this section if the seizure was for an offense involving impaired driving; or
b. A speeding to elude arrest acknowledgment as defined in subdivision (a1)(8) of this section if the seizure was for violation of G.S. 20-141.5(b) or (b1).

If the nondefendant owner is a lessor, the release shall also be conditioned upon the lessor agreeing not to sell, give, or otherwise transfer possession of the forfeited motor vehicle to the defendant or any person acting on the defendant's behalf. A lessor who refuses to sell, give, or transfer possession of a seized motor vehicle to the defendant or any person acting on the behalf of the defendant shall not be liable for damages arising out of the refusal.

No motor vehicle subject to forfeiture under this section shall be released to a nondefendant motor vehicle owner if the records of the Division indicate the motor vehicle owner had previously signed an impaired driving acknowledgment or a speeding to elude arrest acknowledgment, as required by this section, and the same person was operating the motor vehicle at the time of the current seizure unless the innocent owner shows by the greater weight of the evidence that the motor vehicle owner has taken all reasonable precautions to prevent the use of the motor vehicle by this particular person and immediately reports, upon discovery, any unauthorized use to the appropriate law enforcement agency. A determination by the court at the forfeiture hearing held pursuant to subsection (d) of this section that the petitioner is not an innocent owner is a final judgment and is immediately appealable to the Court of Appeals.

(f) Release to Lienholder. - At a forfeiture hearing, the trial judge shall order a forfeited motor vehicle released to the lienholder upon payment of all towing and storage charges incurred as a result of the seizure of the motor vehicle if the judge determines, by the greater weight of the evidence, that:

(1) The lienholder's interest has been perfected and appears on the title to the forfeited vehicle;
(2) The lienholder agrees not to sell, give, or otherwise transfer possession of the forfeited motor vehicle to the defendant or to the motor vehicle owner who owned the motor vehicle immediately prior to forfeiture, or any person acting on the defendant's or motor vehicle owner's behalf;
(3) The forfeited motor vehicle had not previously been released to the lienholder;
(4) The owner is in default under the terms of the security instrument evidencing the interest of the lienholder and as a consequence of the default the lienholder is entitled to possession of the motor vehicle; and
(5) The lienholder agrees to sell the motor vehicle in accordance with the terms of its agreement and pursuant to the provisions of Part 6 of Article 9 of Chapter 25 of the General Statutes. Upon the sale of the motor vehicle, the lienholder will pay to the clerk of court of the county in which the vehicle was forfeited all proceeds from the sale, less the amount of the lien in favor of the lienholder, and any towing and storage costs paid by the lienholder.

A lienholder who refuses to sell, give, or transfer possession of a forfeited motor vehicle to the defendant, the vehicle owner who owned the motor vehicle immediately prior to forfeiture, or any person acting on the behalf of the defendant or motor vehicle owner shall not be liable for damages arising out of such refusal. The defendant, the motor vehicle owner who owned the motor vehicle immediately prior to forfeiture, and any person acting on the defendant's or motor vehicle owner's behalf are prohibited from purchasing the motor vehicle at any sale conducted by the lienholder.

(g) Repealed by Session Laws 1998-182, s. 2, effective December 1, 1998.

(h) Any order issued pursuant to this section authorizing the release of a seized vehicle shall require the payment of all towing and storage charges incurred as a result of the seizure and impoundment of the motor vehicle. This requirement shall not be waived.

Chapter 4

Division of Motor Vehicles

Synopsis

4.1 Overview

When a motorist is cited for DWI, Habitual DWI, or Minor Driving with Alcohol in the Body, the motorist is subject to the requirements of the North Carolina implied consent laws and must submit to a chemical test as chosen by the law enforcement officer. There are three possible scenarios with regard to alcohol:

1. The motorist submits to the test and is not at or over the presumptive limit of .08 (or .04 in a commercial vehicle). In this case, DMV takes no action against the motorist.
2. The motorist submits and is at or over the presumptive limit of .08 (or .04 in a commercial vehicle). In this case, DMV takes action against the motorist.
3. The motorist refuses to submit. In this case, DMV takes action against the motorist as well. (The driver may also be subjected to a forced blood draw if the police obtain a search warrant after refusal to submit to a chemical test).

The motorist may challenge an order of suspension through either a hearing which is governed by the rules set forth in Chapter 20 of the North Carolina General Statutes, which are discussed in detail later in this chapter. DWI with drugs in the system triggers no DMV action unless the person is convicted of the criminal charge. A refusal, however, to submit to a chemical test where the police are looking for drugs only falls into the same category as refusing to submit to a test for alcohol.

4.2 The Role of the Magistrate

When a person is charged with an implied consent offense, the same laws that govern initial appearances in all criminal cases apply as well as other charge specific laws. The role of the magistrate in these types of cases is to determine whether probable cause exists, whether or not to revoke the license of the person charged, whether or not to impound the vehicle of the person charged, whether or not to set a bond, and to inform the person of their rights involving not only the testing procedures but also as to witnesses. The magistrate must also determine if all the conditions are met to civilly revoke a person's driver's license.

4.3 Civil Revocations

N.C.G.S. §20-16.5 sets out the conditions that must be met in order to issue a civil revocation of someone's driver's license. It is reproduced below.

§ 20-16.5. Immediate civil license revocation for certain persons charged with implied-consent offenses.

(a) Definitions. - As used in this section the following words and phrases have the following meanings:

(1) Law Enforcement Officer. - As described in G.S. 20-16.2(a1).

(2) Clerk. - As defined in G.S. 15A-101(2).

(3) Judicial Official. - As defined in G.S. 15A-101(5).

(4) Revocation Report. - A sworn statement by a law enforcement officer and a chemical analyst containing facts indicating that the conditions of subsection (b) have been met, and whether the per-

son has a pending offense for which the person's license had been or is revoked under this section. When one chemical analyst analyzes a person's blood and another chemical analyst informs a person of his rights and responsibilities under G.S. 20-16.2, the report must include the statements of both analysts.

(5) Surrender of a Driver's License. - The act of turning over to a court or a law-enforcement officer the person's most recent, valid driver's license or learner's permit issued by the Division or by a similar agency in another jurisdiction, or a limited driving privilege issued by a North Carolina court. A person who is validly licensed but who is unable to locate his license card may file an affidavit with the clerk setting out facts that indicate that he is unable to locate his license card and that he is validly licensed; the filing of the affidavit constitutes a surrender of the person's license.

(b) Revocations for Persons Who Refuse Chemical Analyses or Who Are Charged With Certain Implied-Consent Offenses. - A person's driver's license is subject to revocation under this section if:

(1) A law enforcement officer has reasonable grounds to believe that the person has committed an offense subject to the implied-consent provisions of G.S. 20-16.2;

(2) The person is charged with that offense as provided in G.S. 20-16.2(a);

(3) The law enforcement officer and the chemical analyst comply with the procedures of G.S. 20-16.2 and G.S. 20-139.1 in requiring the person's submission to or procuring a chemical analysis; and

(4) The person:

a. Willfully refuses to submit to the chemical analysis;

b. Has an alcohol concentration of 0.08 or more within a relevant time after the driving;

c. Has an alcohol concentration of 0.04 or more at any relevant time after the driving of a commercial motor vehicle; or

d. Has any alcohol concentration at any relevant time after the driving and the person is under 21 years of age.

(b1) Precharge Test Results as Basis for Revocation. - Notwithstanding the provisions of subsection (b), a person's driver's license is subject to revocation under this section if:

(1) The person requests a precharge chemical analysis pursuant to G.S. 20-16.2(i); and

(2) The person has:

a. An alcohol concentration of 0.08 or more at any relevant time after driving;

b. An alcohol concentration of 0.04 or more at any relevant time after driving a commercial motor vehicle; or

c. Any alcohol concentration at any relevant time after driving and the person is under 21 years of age; and

(3) The person is charged with an implied-consent offense.

(c) Duty of Law Enforcement Officers and Chemical Analysts to Report to Judicial Officials. - If a person's driver's license is subject to revocation under this section, the law enforcement officer and the chemical analyst must execute a revocation report. If the person has refused to submit to a chemical analysis, a copy of the affidavit to be submitted to the Division under G.S. 20-16.2(c) may be substituted for the revocation report if it contains the information required by this section. It is the specific duty of the law enforcement officer to make sure that the report is expeditiously filed with a judicial official as required by this section.

(d) Which Judicial Official Must Receive Report. - The judicial official with whom the revocation report must be filed is:

(1) The judicial official conducting the initial appearance on the underlying criminal charge if:

a. No revocation report has previously been filed; and

b. At the time of the initial appearance the results of the chemical analysis, if administered, or the reports indicating a refusal, are available.

(2) A judicial official conducting any other proceeding relating to the underlying criminal charge at which the person is present, if no report has previously been filed.

(3) The clerk of superior court in the county in which the underlying criminal charge has been brought if subdivisions (1) and (2) are not applicable at the time the law enforcement officer must file the report.

(e) Procedure if Report Filed with Judicial Official When Person Is Present. - If a properly executed revocation report concerning a person is filed with a judicial official when the person is present before that official, the judicial official shall, after completing any other proceedings involving the person, determine whether there is probable cause to believe that each of the conditions of subsection (b) has been met. If he determines that there is such probable cause, he shall enter an order revoking the person's driver's license for the period required in this subsection. The judicial official shall order the person to surrender his license and if necessary may order a law-enforcement officer to seize the license. The judicial official shall give the person a copy of the revocation order. In addition to setting it out in the order the judicial official shall personally inform the person of his right to a hearing as specified in subsection (g), and that his license remains revoked pending the hearing. The revocation under this subsection begins at the time the revocation order is issued and continues until the person's license has been surrendered for the period specified in this subsection, and the person has paid the applicable costs. The period of revocation is 30 days, if there are no pending offenses for which the person's license had been or is revoked under this section. If at the time of the current offense, the person has one or more pending offenses for which his license had been or is revoked under this section, the revocation shall remain in effect until a final judgment, including all appeals, has been entered for the current offense and for all pending offenses. In no event, may the period of revocation under this subsection be less than 30 days. If within five working days of the effective date of the order, the person does not surrender his license or demonstrate that he is not currently licensed, the clerk shall immediately issue a pick-up order. The pick-up order shall be issued to a member of a local law-enforcement agency if the law enforcement officer was employed by the agency at the time of the charge and the person resides in or is present in the agency's territorial jurisdiction. In all other cases, the pick-up order shall be issued to an officer or inspector of the Division. A pick-up order issued pursuant to this section is to be served in accordance with G.S. 20-29 as if the order had been issued by the Division.

(f) Procedure if Report Filed with Clerk of Court When Person Not Present. - When a clerk receives a properly executed report under subdivision (d)(3) and the person named in the revocation report is not present before the clerk, the clerk shall determine whether there is probable cause to believe that each of the conditions of subsection (b) has been met. For purposes of this subsection, a properly executed report under subdivision (d)(3) may include a sworn statement by the law enforcement officer along with an affidavit received directly by the Clerk from the chemical analyst. If he determines that there is such probable cause, he shall mail to the person a revocation order by first-class mail. The order shall direct that the person on or before the effective date of the order either surrender his license to the clerk or appear before the clerk and demonstrate that he is not currently licensed, and the order shall inform the person of the time and effective date of the revocation and of its duration, of his right to a hearing as specified in subsection (g), and that the revocation remains in effect pending the hearing. Revocation orders mailed under this subsection become effective on the fourth day after the order is deposited in the United States mail. If within five working days of the effective date of the order, the person does not surrender his license to the clerk or appear before the clerk to demonstrate that he is not currently licensed, the clerk shall immediately issue a pick-up order. The pick-up order shall be issued and served in the same manner as specified in subsection (e) for pick-up orders issued pursuant to that subsection. A revocation under this subsection begins at the date specified in the order and continues until the person's license has been revoked for the period specified in this subsection and the person has paid the applicable costs. If the person has no pending offenses for which his license had been or is revoked under this section, the period of revocation under this subsection is:

(1) Thirty days from the time the person surrenders his license to the court, if the surrender occurs within five working days of the effective date of the order; or

(2) Thirty days after the person appears before the clerk and demonstrates that he is not currently licensed to drive, if the appearance occurs within five working days of the effective date of the revocation order; or

(3) Forty-five days from the time:

a. The person's drivers license is picked up by a law-enforcement officer following service of a pick-up order; or

b. The person demonstrates to a law-enforcement officer who has a pick-up order for his license that he is not currently licensed; or

c. The person's drivers license is surrendered to the court if the surrender occurs more than five working days after the effective date of the revocation order; or

d. The person appears before the clerk to demonstrate that he is not currently licensed, if he appears more than five working days after the effective date of the revocation order.

If at the time of the current offense, the person has one or more pending offenses for which his license had been or is revoked under this section, the revocation shall remain in effect until a final judgment, including all appeals, has been entered for the current offense and for all pending offenses. In no event may the period of revocation for the current offense be less than the applicable period of revocation in subdivision (1), (2), or (3) of this subsection. When a pick-up order is issued, it shall inform the person of his right to a hearing as specified in subsection (g), and that the revocation remains in effect pending the hearing. An officer serving a pick-up order under this subsection shall return the order to the court indicating the date it was served or that he was unable to serve the order. If the license was surrendered, the officer serving the order shall deposit it with the clerk within three days of the surrender.

(g) Hearing before Magistrate or Judge if Person Contests Validity of Revocation. - A person whose license is revoked under this section may request in writing a hearing to contest the validity of the revocation. The request may be made at the time of the person's initial appearance, or within 10 days of the effective date of the revocation to the clerk or a magistrate designated by the clerk, and may specifically request that the hearing be conducted by a district court judge. The Administrative Office of the Courts must develop a hearing request form for any person requesting a hearing. Unless a district court judge is requested, the hearing must be conducted within the county by a magistrate assigned by the chief district court judge to conduct such hearings. If the person requests that a district court judge hold the hearing, the hearing must be conducted within the district court district as defined in G.S. 7A-133 by a district court judge assigned to conduct such hearings. The revocation remains in effect pending the hearing, but the hearing must be held within three working days following the request if the hearing is before a magistrate or within five working days if the hearing is before a district court judge. The request for the hearing must specify the grounds upon which the validity of the revocation is challenged and the hearing must be limited to the grounds specified in the request. A witness may submit his evidence by affidavit unless he is subpoenaed to appear. Any person who appears and testifies is subject to questioning by the judicial official conducting the hearing, and the judicial official may adjourn the hearing to seek additional evidence if he is not satisfied with the accuracy or completeness of evidence. The person contesting the validity of the revocation may, but is not required to, testify in his own behalf. Unless contested by the person requesting the hearing, the judicial official may accept as true any matter stated in the revocation report. If any relevant condition under subsection (b) is contested, the judicial official must find by the greater weight of the evidence that the condition was met in order to sustain the revocation. At the conclusion of the hearing the judicial official must enter an order sustaining or rescinding the revocation. The judicial official's findings are without prejudice to the person contesting the revocation and to any other potential party as to any other proceedings, civil or criminal, that may involve facts bearing upon the conditions in subsection (b) considered by the judicial official. The decision of the judicial official is final and may not be appealed in the General Court of Justice. If the hearing is not held and completed within three working days of the written request for a hearing before a magistrate or within five working days of the written request for a hearing before a district court judge, the judicial official must enter an order rescinding the revocation, unless the person contesting the revocation contributed to the delay in completing the hearing. If the person requesting the hearing fails to appear at the hearing or any rescheduling thereof after having been properly notified, he forfeits his right to a hearing.

(h) Return of License. - After the applicable period of revocation under this section, or if the magistrate or judge orders the revocation rescinded, the person whose license was revoked may apply to the clerk for return of his surrendered license. Unless the clerk finds that the person is not eligible to use the surrendered license, he must return it if:

(1) The applicable period of revocation has passed and the person has tendered payment for the costs under subsection (j); or

(2) The magistrate or judge has ordered the revocation rescinded.

If the license has expired, he may return it to the person with a caution that it is no longer valid. Otherwise, if the person is not eligible to use the license and the license was issued by the Division or in another state, the clerk must mail it to the Division. If the person has surrendered his copy of a limited driving privilege and he is no longer eligible to use it, the clerk must make a record that he has withheld the limited driving privilege and forward that record to the clerk in the county in which the limited driving privilege was issued for filing in the case file. If the person's license is revoked under this section and under another section of this Chapter, the clerk must surrender the license to the Division if the revocation under this section can terminate before the other revocation; in such cases, the costs required by subsection (j) must still be paid before the revocation under this section is terminated.

(i) Effect of Revocations. - A revocation under this section revokes a person's privilege to drive in North Carolina whatever the source of his authorization to drive. Revocations under this section are independent of and run concurrently with any other revocations. No court imposing a period of revocation following conviction of an offense involving impaired driving may give credit for any period of revocation imposed under this section. A person whose license is revoked pursuant to this section is not eligible to receive a limited driving privilege except as specifically authorized by G.S. 20-16.5(p).

(j) Costs. - Unless the magistrate or judge orders the revocation rescinded, a person whose license is revoked under this section must pay a fee of one hundred dollars ($100.00) as costs for the action before the person's license may be returned under subsection (h) of this section. Fifty percent (50%) of the costs collected under this section shall be credited to the General Fund. Twenty-five percent (25%) of the costs collected under this section shall be used to fund a statewide chemical alcohol testing program administered by the Injury Control Section of the Department of Health and Human Services. The remaining twenty-five percent (25%) of the costs collected under this section shall be remitted to the county for the sole purpose of reimbursing the county for jail expenses incurred due to enforcement of the impaired driving laws.

(k) Report to Division. - Except as provided below, the clerk shall mail a report to the Division:

(1) If the license is revoked indefinitely, within 10 working days of the revocation of the license; and

(2) In all cases, within 10 working days of the return of a license under this section or of the termination of a revocation of the driving privilege of a person not currently licensed.

The report shall identify the person whose license has been revoked, specify the date on which his license was revoked, and indicate whether the license has been returned. The report must also provide, if applicable, whether the license is revoked indefinitely. No report need be made to the Division, however, if there was a surrender of the driver's license issued by the Division, a 30-day minimum revocation was imposed, and the license was properly returned to the person under subsection (h) within five working days after the 30-day period had elapsed.

(l) Restoration Fee for Unlicensed Persons. - If a person whose license is revoked under this section has no valid license, he must pay the restoration fee required by G.S. 20-7 before he may apply for a license from the Division.

(m) Modification of Revocation Order. - Any judicial official presiding over a proceeding under this section may issue a modified order if he determines that an inappropriate order has been issued.

(n) Exception for Revoked Licenses. - Notwithstanding any other provision of this section, if the judicial official required to issue a revocation order under this section determines that the person whose license is subject to revocation under subsection (b):

(1) Has a currently revoked driver's license;

(2) Has no limited driving privilege; and

(3) Will not become eligible for restoration of his license or for a limited driving privilege during the period of revocation required by this section,

the judicial official need not issue a revocation order under this section. In this event the judicial official must file in the records of the civil proceeding a copy of any documentary evidence and set out in writing all other evidence on which he relies in making his determination.

(o) Designation of Proceedings. - Proceedings under this section are civil actions, and must be identified by the caption "In the Matter of ________" and filed as directed by the Administrative Office of the Courts.

(p) Limited Driving Privilege. - A person whose drivers license has been revoked for a specified period of 30 or 45 days under this section may apply for a limited driving privilege if:

(1) At the time of the alleged offense the person held either a valid drivers license or a license that had been expired for less than one year;

(2) Does not have an unresolved pending charge involving impaired driving except the charge for which the license is currently revoked under this section or additional convictions of an offense involving impaired driving since being charged for the violation for which the license is currently revoked under this section;

(3) The person's license has been revoked for at least 10 days if the revocation is for 30 days or 30 days if the revocation is for 45 days; and

(4) The person has obtained a substance abuse assessment from a mental health facility and registers for and agrees to participate in any recommended training or treatment program.

A person whose license has been indefinitely revoked under this section may, after completion of 30 days under subsection (e) or the applicable period of time under subdivision (1), (2), or (3) of subsection (f), apply for a limited driving privilege. In the case of an indefinite revocation, a judge of the division in which the current offense is pending may issue the limited driving privilege only if the privilege is necessary to overcome undue hardship and the person meets the eligibility requirements of G.S. 20-179.3, except that the requirements in G.S. 20-179.3(b)(1)c. and G.S. 20-179.3(e) shall not apply. Except as modified in this subsection, the provisions of G.S. 20-179.3 relating to the procedure for application and conduct of the hearing and the restrictions required or authorized to be included in the limited driving privilege apply to applications under this subsection. Any district court judge authorized to hold court in the judicial district is authorized to issue such a limited driving privilege. A limited driving privilege issued under this section authorizes a person to drive if the person's license is revoked solely under this section. If the person's license is revoked for any other reason, the limited driving privilege is invalid.

4.4 The Pre-arrest Test

If law enforcement is investigating a person for suspicion of DWI, but has not yet made the probable cause decision to arrest, the suspicious person may request that the officer give them a pre-arrest test. This test is also mentioned in the above statue N.C.G.S. §20-16.5. When this test is requested, the officer must take the person directly to the testing facility and read the person their chemical analysis rights with regard to the pre-test.

4.5 Implied Consent to Chemical Analysis

After arrest and prior to taking a chemical test, in most cases the police must read the North Carolina Implied Consent Rights to the arrestee. Obviously, if the motorist is dead or unconscious, or otherwise incapable of consenting, the admonitions need not be read. Blood may also be taken as part of a medical draw without the form being read (see N.C.G.S. §20-16.2 reproduced below).

§ 20-16.2. Implied consent to chemical analysis; mandatory revocation of license in event of refusal; right of driver to request analysis.

(a) Basis for Officer to Require Chemical Analysis; Notification of Rights. - Any person who drives a vehicle on a highway or public vehicular area thereby gives consent to a chemical analysis if charged with an implied-consent offense. Any law enforcement officer who has reasonable grounds to believe that the person charged has committed the implied-consent offense may obtain a chemical analysis of the person.

Before any type of chemical analysis is administered the person charged shall be taken before a chemical analyst authorized to administer a test of a person's breath or a law enforcement officer who is authorized to administer chemical analysis of the breath, who shall inform the person orally and also give the person a notice in writing that:

(1) You have been charged with an implied-consent offense. Under the implied-consent law, you can refuse any test, but your drivers license will be revoked for one year and could be revoked for a longer period of time under certain circumstances, and an officer can compel you to be tested under other laws.

(2) Repealed by Session Laws 2006-253, s. 15, effective December 1, 2006, and applicable to offenses committed on or after that date.

(3) The test results, or the fact of your refusal, will be admissible in evidence at trial.

(4) Your driving privilege will be revoked immediately for at least 30 days if you refuse any test or the test result is 0.08 or more, 0.04 or more if you

were driving a commercial vehicle, or 0.01 or more if you are under the age of 21.

(5) After you are released, you may seek your own test in addition to this test.

(6) You may call an attorney for advice and select a witness to view the testing procedures remaining after the witness arrives, but the testing may not be delayed for these purposes longer than 30 minutes from the time you are notified of these rights. You must take the test at the end of 30 minutes even if you have not contacted an attorney or your witness has not arrived.

(a1) Meaning of Terms. - Under this section, an "implied-consent offense" is an offense involving impaired driving, a violation of G.S. 20-141.4(a2), or an alcohol-related offense made subject to the procedures of this section. A person is "charged" with an offense if the person is arrested for it or if criminal process for the offense has been issued.

(b) Unconscious Person May Be Tested. - If a law enforcement officer has reasonable grounds to believe that a person has committed an implied-consent offense, and the person is unconscious or otherwise in a condition that makes the person incapable of refusal, the law enforcement officer may direct the taking of a blood sample or may direct the administration of any other chemical analysis that may be effectively performed. In this instance the notification of rights set out in subsection (a) and the request required by subsection (c) are not necessary.

(c) Request to Submit to Chemical Analysis. - A law enforcement officer or chemical analyst shall designate the type of test or tests to be given and may request the person charged to submit to the type of chemical analysis designated. If the person charged willfully refuses to submit to that chemical analysis, none may be given under the provisions of this section, but the refusal does not preclude testing under other applicable procedures of law.

(c1) Procedure for Reporting Results and Refusal to Division. - Whenever a person refuses to submit to a chemical analysis, a person has an alcohol concentration of 0.15 or more, or a person's drivers license has an alcohol concentration restriction and the results of the chemical analysis establish a violation of the restriction, the law enforcement officer and the chemical analyst shall without unnecessary delay go before an official authorized to administer oaths and execute an affidavit(s) stating that:

(1) The person was charged with an implied-consent offense or had an alcohol concentration restriction on the drivers license;

(2) A law enforcement officer had reasonable grounds to believe that the person had committed an implied-consent offense or violated the alcohol concentration restriction on the drivers license;

(3) Whether the implied-consent offense charged involved death or critical injury to another person, if the person willfully refused to submit to chemical analysis;

(4) The person was notified of the rights in subsection (a); and

(5) The results of any tests given or that the person willfully refused to submit to a chemical analysis.

If the person's drivers license has an alcohol concentration restriction, pursuant to G.S. 20-19(c3), and an officer has reasonable grounds to believe the person has violated a provision of that restriction other than violation of the alcohol concentration level, the officer and chemical analyst shall complete the applicable sections of the affidavit and indicate the restriction which was violated. The officer shall immediately mail the affidavit(s) to the Division. If the officer is also the chemical analyst who has notified the person of the rights under subsection (a), the officer may perform alone the duties of this subsection.

(d) Consequences of Refusal; Right to Hearing before Division; Issues. - Upon receipt of a properly executed affidavit required by subsection (c1), the Division shall expeditiously notify the person charged that the person's license to drive is revoked for 12 months, effective on the tenth calendar day after the mailing of the revocation order unless, before the effective date of the order, the person requests in writing a hearing before the Division. Except for the time referred to in G.S. 20-16.5, if the person shows to the satisfaction of the Division that his or her license was surrendered to the court, and remained in the court's possession, then the Division shall credit the amount of time for which the license was in the possession of the court against the 12-month revocation period required by this subsection. If the person properly requests a hearing, the person retains his or her license, unless it is revoked under some other provision of law, until the hearing is held, the person withdraws the request, or the person fails to appear at a scheduled hearing. The hearing officer may subpoena any witnesses or documents that the hearing officer deems necessary. The person may request the hearing officer to subpoena the charging officer, the chemical analyst, or both to appear at the hearing if the person makes the request in writing at least three days before the hearing. The person may subpoena any other witness whom the person deems necessary, and the provisions of G.S. 1A-1, Rule 45, apply to the issuance and service of all subpoenas issued under the authority of this section. The hearing officer is authorized to administer oaths to witnesses appearing at the hearing. The hearing shall be conducted in the county where the charge was brought, and shall be limited to consideration of whether:

(1) The person was charged with an implied-consent offense or the driver had an alcohol concentration restriction on the drivers license pursuant to G.S. 20-19;

(2) A law enforcement officer had reasonable grounds to believe that the person had committed an implied-consent offense or violated the alcohol concentration restriction on the drivers license;

(3) The implied-consent offense charged involved death or critical injury to another person, if this allegation is in the affidavit;

(4) The person was notified of the person's rights as required by subsection (a); and

(5) The person willfully refused to submit to a chemical analysis.

If the Division finds that the conditions specified in this subsection are met, it shall order the revocation sustained. If the Division finds that any of the conditions (1), (2), (4), or (5) is not met, it shall rescind the revocation. If it finds that condition (3) is alleged in the affidavit but is not met, it shall order the revocation sustained if that is the only condition that is not met; in this instance subsection (d1) does not apply to that revocation. If the revocation is sustained, the person shall surrender his or her license immediately upon notification by the Division.

(d1) Consequences of Refusal in Case Involving Death or Critical Injury. - If the refusal occurred in a case involving death or critical injury to another person, no limited driving privilege may be issued. The 12-month revocation begins only after all other periods of revocation have terminated unless the person's license is revoked under G.S. 20-28, 20-28.1, 20-19(d), or 20-19(e). If the revocation is based on those sections, the revocation under this subsection begins at the time and in the manner specified in subsection (d) for revocations under this section. However, the person's eligibility for a hearing to determine if the revocation under those sections should be rescinded is postponed for one year from the date on which the person would otherwise have been eligible for the hearing. If the person's driver's license is again revoked while the 12-month revocation under this subsection is in effect, that revocation, whether imposed by a court or by the Division, may only take effect after the period of revocation under this subsection has terminated.

(e) Right to Hearing in Superior Court. - If the revocation for a willful refusal is sustained after the hearing, the person whose license has been revoked has the right to file a petition in the superior court district or set of districts defined in G.S. 7A-41.1, where the charges were made, within 30 days thereafter for a hearing on the record. The superior court review shall be limited to whether there is sufficient evidence in the record to support the Commissioner's findings of fact and whether the conclusions of law are supported by the findings of fact and whether the Commissioner committed an error of law in revoking the license.

(e1) Limited Driving Privilege after Six Months in Certain Instances. - A person whose driver's license has been revoked under this section may apply for and a judge authorized to do so by this subsection may issue a limited driving privilege if:

(1) At the time of the refusal the person held either a valid drivers license or a license that had been expired for less than one year;

(2) At the time of the refusal, the person had not within the preceding seven years been convicted of an offense involving impaired driving;

(3) At the time of the refusal, the person had not in the preceding seven years willfully refused to submit to a chemical analysis under this section;

(4) The implied consent offense charged did not involve death or critical injury to another person;

(5) The underlying charge for which the defendant was requested to submit to a chemical analysis has been finally disposed of:

a. Other than by conviction; or

b. By a conviction of impaired driving under G.S. 20-138.1, at a punishment level authorizing issuance of a limited driving privilege under G.S. 20-179.3(b), and the defendant has complied with at least one of the mandatory conditions of probation listed for the punishment level under which the defendant was sentenced;

(6) Subsequent to the refusal the person has had no unresolved pending charges for or additional convictions of an offense involving impaired driving;

(7) The person's license has been revoked for at least six months for the refusal; and

(8) The person has obtained a substance abuse assessment from a mental health facility and successfully completed any recommended training or treatment program.

Except as modified in this subsection, the provisions of G.S. 20-179.3 relating to the procedure for application and conduct of the hearing and the restrictions required or authorized to be included in the limited driving privilege apply to applications under this subsection. If the case was finally disposed of in the district court, the hearing shall be conducted in the district court district as defined in G.S. 7A-133 in which the refusal occurred by a district court judge. If the case was finally disposed of in the superior court, the hearing shall be conducted in the superior court district or set of districts as defined in G.S. 7A-41.1 in which the refusal occurred by a superior court judge. A limited driving privilege issued under this section authorizes a person to drive if the person's license is revoked solely under this section or solely under this section and G.S. 20-17(2). If the person's license is revoked for any other reason, the limited driving privilege is invalid.

(f) Notice to Other States as to Nonresidents. - When it has been finally determined under the procedures of this section that a nonresident's privilege to drive a motor vehicle in this State has been revoked, the Division shall give information in writing of the action taken to the motor vehicle administrator of the state of the person's residence and of any state in which the person has a license.

(g) Repealed by Session Laws 1973, c. 914.

(h) Repealed by Session Laws 1979, c. 423, s. 2.

(i) Right to Chemical Analysis before Arrest or Charge. - A person stopped or questioned by a law enforcement officer who is investigating whether the person may have committed an implied consent offense may request the administration of a chemical analysis before any arrest or other charge is made for the offense. Upon this request, the officer shall afford the person the opportunity to have a chemical analysis of his or her breath, if available, in accordance with the procedures required by G.S. 20-139.1(b). The request constitutes the person's consent to be transported by the law enforcement officer to the place where the chemical analysis is to be administered. Before the chemical analysis is made, the person shall confirm the request in writing and shall be notified:

(1) That the test results will be admissible in evidence and may be used against you in any implied consent offense that may arise;

(2) Your driving privilege will be revoked immediately for at least 30 days if the test result is 0.08 or more, 0.04 or more if you were driving a commercial vehicle, or 0.01 or more if you are under the age of 21.

(3) That if you fail to comply fully with the test procedures, the officer may charge you with any offense for which the officer has probable cause, and if you are charged with an implied consent offense, your refusal to submit to the testing required as a result of that charge would result in revocation of your driving privilege. The results of the chemical analysis are admissible in evidence in any proceeding in which they are relevant.

If the motorist submits and the results indicate a BAC less than .08 (.04 in a commercial vehicle), no action is taken by DMV, although the motorist may still be subject to criminal charges.

If the motorist submits to a breath or blood test that shows a BAC of .08 or more (or .04 in a commercial vehicle), the Magistrate will suspend the motorist's license by serving an Affidavit of Revocation on the motorist.

If the motorist refuses to take the test, DMV will attempt to suspend the motorist's license for one year under N.C.G.S. §20-16.2 by serving an Order of Suspension on the motorist (irrespective of whether police forcibly drew blood after they had obtained a search warrant and irrespective of the BAC results).

A license suspended pursuant to N.C.G.S. §20-16.2 remains suspended for 30 days. If the motorist has no other serious violations on his or her record, the motorist can obtain a restricted driving privilege for the last 20 days of the 30-day suspension.

A license suspended pursuant to N.C.G.S. §20-16.2 remains suspended for one year, unless there is a prior implied consent refusal on the motorist's record within the previous seven years.

There is no administrative sanction for the presence of illegal drugs in a motorist's body, although one may certainly be criminally prosecuted in that instance.

In addition to being arrested for DWI, a vehicle operator also gives consent to be tested in the event of an accident with death or serious physical injury as defined by statute.

4.6 Chemical Analysis Procedures

The law enforcement officer doing the chemical analysis decides which test he or she wants the accused to submit; it is solely in the officer's discretion. Unless drugs are suspected as the impairing substance, most officers will opt for a breath analysis. The procedures for the chemical analysis are laid out in N.C.G.S. §20-139.1 which is reproduced below.

§ 20-139.1. Procedures governing chemical analyses; admissibility; evidentiary provisions; controlled-drinking programs.

(a) Chemical Analysis Admissible. - In any implied-consent offense under G.S. 20-16.2, a person's alcohol concentration or the presence of any other impairing substance in the person's body as shown by a chemical analysis is admissible in evidence. This section does not limit the introduction of other competent evidence as to a person's alcohol concentration or results of other tests showing the presence of an impairing substance, including other chemical tests.

(b) Approval of Valid Test Methods; Licensing Chemical Analysts. - The results of a chemical analysis shall be deemed sufficient evidence to prove a person's alcohol concentration. A chemical analysis of the breath administered pursuant to the implied-consent law is admissible in any court or administrative hearing or proceeding if it meets both of the following requirements:

(1) It is performed in accordance with the rules of the Department of Health and Human Services.

(2) The person performing the analysis had, at the time of the analysis, a current permit issued by the Department of Health and Human Services authorizing the person to perform a test of the breath using the type of instrument employed.

For purposes of establishing compliance with subdivision (b)(1) of this section, the court or administrative agency shall take notice of the rules of the Department of Health and Human Services. For purposes of establishing compliance with subdivision (b)(2) of this section, the court or administrative agency shall take judicial notice of the list of permits issued to the person performing the analysis, the type of instrument on which the person is authorized to perform tests of the breath, and the date the permit was issued. The Department of Health and Human Services may ascertain the qualifications and competence of individuals to conduct particular chemical analyses and the methods for conducting chemical analyses. The Department may issue permits to conduct chemical analyses to individuals it finds qualified subject to periodic renewal, termination, and revocation of the permit in the Department's discretion.

(b1) When Officer May Perform Chemical Analysis. - Any person possessing a current permit authorizing the person to perform chemical analysis may perform a chemical analysis.

(b2) Breath Analysis Results Preventive Maintenance. - The Department of Health and Human Services shall perform preventive maintenance on breath-testing instruments used for chemical analysis. A court or administrative agency shall take judicial notice of the preventive maintenance records of the Department. Notwithstanding the provisions of subsection (b), the results of a chemical analysis of a person's breath performed in accordance with this section are not admissible in evidence if:

(1) The defendant objects to the introduction into evidence of the results of the chemical analysis of the defendant's breath; and

(2) The defendant demonstrates that, with respect to the instrument used to analyze the defendant's breath, preventive maintenance procedures required by the regulations of the Department of Health and Human Services had not been performed within the time limits prescribed by those regulations.

(b3) Sequential Breath Tests Required. - The methods governing the administration of chemical analyses of the breath shall require the testing of at least duplicate sequential breath samples. The results of the chemical analysis of all breath samples are admissible if the test results from any two consecutively collected breath samples do not differ from each other by an alcohol concentration greater than 0.02. Only the lower of the two test results of the consecutively administered tests can be used to prove a particular alcohol concentration. A person's refusal to give the sequential breath samples necessary to constitute a valid chemical analysis is a refusal under G.S. 20-16.2(c).

A person's refusal to give the second or subsequent breath sample shall make the result of the first breath sample, or the result of the sample providing the lowest alcohol concentration if more than one breath sample is provided, admissible in any judicial or administrative hearing for any relevant purpose, including the establishment that a person had a particular alcohol concentration for conviction of an offense involving impaired driving.

(b4) Repealed by Session Laws 2006-253, s. 16, effective December 1, 2006, and applicable to offenses committed on or after that date.

(b5) Subsequent Tests Allowed. - A person may be requested, pursuant to G.S. 20-16.2, to submit to a chemical analysis of the person's blood or other bodily fluid or substance in addition to or in lieu of a chemical analysis of the breath, in the discretion of a law enforcement officer; except that a person charged with a violation of G.S. 20-141.4 shall be requested to provide a blood sample in addition to or in lieu of a chemical analysis of the breath. However, if a breath sample shows an alcohol concentration of .08 or more, then requesting a blood sample shall be in the discretion of a law enforcement officer. If a subsequent chemical analysis is requested pursuant to this subsection, the person shall again be advised of the implied consent rights in accordance with G.S. 20-16.2(a). A person's willful refusal to submit to a chemical analysis of the blood or other bodily fluid or substance is a willful refusal under G.S. 20-16.2. If a person willfully refuses to provide a blood sample under this subsection, and the person is charged with a violation of G.S. 20-141.4, then a law enforcement officer with probable cause to believe that the offense involved impaired driving or was an alcohol-related offense made subject to the procedures of G.S. 20-16.2 shall seek a warrant to obtain a blood sample. The failure to obtain a blood sample pursuant to this subsection shall not be grounds for the dismissal of a charge and is not an appealable issue.

(b6) The Department of Health and Human Services shall post on a Web page a list of all persons who have a permit authorizing them to perform chemical analyses, the types of analyses that they can perform, the instruments that each person is authorized to operate, the effective dates of the permits, and the records of preventive maintenance. A court or administrative agency shall take judicial notice of whether, at the time of the chemical analysis, the chemical analyst possessed a permit authorizing the chemical analyst to perform the chemical analysis administered and whether preventive maintenance had been performed on the breath-testing instrument in accordance with the Department's rules.

(c) Blood and Urine for Chemical Analysis. - Notwithstanding any other provision of law, when a blood or urine test is specified as the type of chemical analysis by a law enforcement officer, a physician, registered nurse, emergency medical technician, or other qualified person shall withdraw the blood sample and obtain the urine sample, and no further authorization or approval is required. If the person withdrawing the blood or collecting the urine requests written confirmation of the law enforcement officer's request for the withdrawal of blood or collecting the urine, the officer shall furnish it before blood is withdrawn or urine collected. When blood is withdrawn or urine collected pursuant to a law enforcement officer's request, neither the person withdrawing the blood nor any hospital, laboratory, or other institution, person, firm, or corporation employing that person, or contracting for the service of withdrawing blood or collecting urine, may be held criminally or civilly liable by reason of withdrawing the blood or collecting the urine, except that there is no immunity from liability for negligent acts or omissions. A person requested to withdraw blood or collect urine pursuant to this subsection may refuse to do so only if it reasonably appears that the procedure cannot be performed without endangering the safety of the person collecting the sample or the safety of the person from whom the sample is being collected. If the officer requesting the blood or urine requests a written justification for the refusal, the medical provider who determined the sample could not be collected safely shall provide written justification at the time of the refusal.

(c1) Admissibility. - The results of a chemical analysis of blood or urine reported by the North Carolina State Crime Laboratory, the Charlotte, North Carolina, Police Department Laboratory, or any other laboratory approved for chemical analysis by the Department of Health and Human Services (DHHS), are admissible as evidence in all administrative hearings, and in any court, without further authentication and without the testimony of the analyst. For the purposes of this section, a "laboratory approved for chemical analysis" by the DHHS includes, but is not limited to, any hospital laboratory approved by DHHS pursuant to the program resulting from the federal Clinical Laboratory Improvement Amendments of 1988 (CLIA).

The results shall be certified by the person who performed the analysis. The provisions of this subsection may be utilized in any administrative hearing, but can only be utilized in cases tried in the district and superior court divisions, or in an adjudicatory hearing in juvenile court, if:

(1) The State notifies the defendant at least 15 business days before the proceeding at which the evidence would be used of its intention to introduce the report into evidence under this subsection and provides a copy of the report to the defendant, and

(2) The defendant fails to file a written objection with the court, with a copy to the State, at least five business days before the proceeding at which the report would be used that the defendant objects to the introduction of the report into evidence.

If the defendant's attorney of record, or the defendant if that person has no attorney, fails to file a written objection as provided in this subsection, then the report shall be admitted into evidence without the testimony of the analyst. Upon filing a timely objection, the admissibility of the report shall be determined and governed by the appropriate rules of evidence.

The report containing the results of any blood or urine test may be transmitted electronically or via facsimile. A copy of the affidavit sent electronically or via facsimile shall be admissible in any court or administrative hearing without further authentication. A copy of the report shall be sent to the charging officer, the clerk of superior court in the county in which the criminal charges are pending, the Division of Motor Vehicles, and the Department of Health and Human Services.

Nothing in this subsection precludes the right of any party to call any witness or to introduce any evidence supporting or contradicting the evidence contained in the report.

(c2) Repealed by Session Laws 2013-194, s. 1, effective June 26, 2013.

(c3) Procedure for Establishing Chain of Custody Without Calling Unnecessary Witnesses. -

(1) For the purpose of establishing the chain of physical custody or control of blood or urine tested or analyzed to determine whether it contains alcohol, a controlled substance or its metabolite, or any impairing substance, a statement signed by each successive person in the chain of custody that the person delivered it to the other person indicated on or about the date stated is prima facie evidence that the person had custody and made the delivery as stated, without the necessity of a personal appearance in court by the person signing the statement.

(2) The statement shall contain a sufficient description of the material or its container so as to distinguish it as the particular item in question and shall state that the material was delivered in essentially the same condition as received. The statement may be placed on the same document as the report provided for in subsection (c1) of this section.

(3) The provisions of this subsection may be utilized in any administrative hearing, but can only be utilized in cases tried in the district and superior court divisions, or in an adjudicatory hearing in juvenile court, if:

a. The State notifies the defendant at least 15 business days before the proceeding at which the statement would be used of its intention to introduce the statement into evidence under this subsection and provides a copy of the statement to the defendant, and

b. The defendant fails to file a written notification with the court, with a copy to the State, at least five business days before the proceeding at which the statement would be used that the defendant objects to the introduction of the statement into evidence.

If the defendant's attorney of record, or the defendant if that person has no attorney, fails to file a written objection as provided in this subsection, then the statement shall be admitted into evidence without the necessity of a personal appearance by the person signing the statement. Upon filing a timely objection, the admissibility of the report shall be determined and governed by the appropriate rules of evidence.

(4) Nothing in this subsection precludes the right of any party to call any witness or to introduce any evidence supporting or contradicting the evidence contained in the statement.

(c4) Repealed by Session Laws 2013-194, s. 1, effective June 26, 2013.

(c5) The testimony of an analyst regarding the results of a chemical analysis of blood or urine admissible pursuant to subsection (c1) of this section, and reported by that analyst, shall be permitted by remote testimony, as defined in G.S. 15A-1225.3, in all administrative hearings, and in any court, if all of the following occur:

(1) The State has provided a copy of the report to the attorney of record for the defendant, or to the de-

fendant if that person has no attorney, as required by subsections (c1) and (c3) of this section.

(2) The State notifies the attorney of record for the defendant, or the defendant if that person has no attorney, at least 15 business days before the proceeding at which the evidence would be used of its intention to introduce the testimony regarding the chemical analysis into evidence using remote testimony.

(3) The defendant's attorney of record, or the defendant if that person has no attorney, fails to file a written objection with the court, with a copy to the State, at least five business days before the proceeding at which the testimony will be presented that the defendant objects to the introduction of the remote testimony.

If the defendant's attorney of record, or the defendant if that person has no attorney, fails to file a written objection as provided in this subsection, then the analyst shall be allowed to testify by remote testimony.

The method used for remote testimony authorized by this subsection shall allow the trier of fact and all parties to observe the demeanor of the analyst as the analyst testifies in a similar manner as if the analyst were testifying in the location where the hearing or trial is being conducted. The court shall ensure that the defendant's attorney, or the defendant if that person has no attorney, has a full and fair opportunity for examination and cross-examination of the analyst.

Nothing in this section shall preclude the right of any party to call any witness. Nothing in this subsection shall obligate the Administrative Office of the Courts or the State Crime Laboratory to incur expenses related to remote testimony absent an appropriation of funds for that purpose.

(d) Right to Additional Test. - Nothing in this section shall be construed to prohibit a person from obtaining or attempting to obtain an additional chemical analysis. If the person is not released from custody after the initial appearance, the agency having custody of the person shall make reasonable efforts in a timely manner to assist the person in obtaining access to a telephone to arrange for any additional test and allow access to the person in accordance with the agreed procedure in G.S. 20-38.5. The failure or inability of the person who submitted to a chemical analysis to obtain any additional test or to withdraw blood does not preclude the admission of evidence relating to the chemical analysis.

(d1) Right to Require Additional Tests. - If a person refuses to submit to any test or tests pursuant to this section, any law enforcement officer with probable cause may, without a court order, compel the person to provide blood or urine samples for analysis if the officer reasonably believes that the delay necessary to obtain a court order, under the circumstances, would result in the dissipation of the percentage of alcohol in the person's blood or urine.

(d2) Notwithstanding any other provision of law, when a blood or urine sample is requested under subsection (d1) of this section by a law enforcement officer, a physician, registered nurse, emergency medical technician, or other qualified person shall withdraw the blood and obtain the urine sample, and no further authorization or approval is required. If the person withdrawing the blood or collecting the urine requests written confirmation of the charging officer's request for the withdrawal of blood or obtaining urine, the officer shall furnish it before blood is withdrawn or urine obtained. A person requested to withdraw blood or collect urine pursuant to this subsection may refuse to do so only if it reasonably appears that the procedure cannot be performed without endangering the safety of the person collecting the sample or the safety of the person from whom the sample is being collected. If the officer requesting the blood or urine requests a written justification for the refusal, the medical provider who determined the sample could not be collected safely shall provide written justification at the time of the refusal.

(d3) When blood is withdrawn or urine collected pursuant to a law enforcement officer's request, neither the person withdrawing the blood nor any hospital, laboratory, or other institution, person, firm, or corporation employing that person, or contracting for the service of withdrawing blood, may be held criminally or civilly liable by reason of withdrawing that blood, except that there is no immunity from liability for negligent acts or omissions. The results of the analysis of blood or urine under this subsection shall be admissible if performed by the State Crime Laboratory or any other hospital or qualified laboratory.

(e) Recording Results of Chemical Analysis of Breath. - A person charged with an implied-consent offense who has not received, prior to a trial, a copy of the chemical analysis results the State intends to offer into evidence may request in writing a copy of the results. The failure to provide a copy prior to any trial shall be grounds for a continuance of the case but shall not be grounds to suppress the results of the chemical analysis or to dismiss the criminal charges.

(e1) Use of Chemical Analyst's Affidavit in District Court. - An affidavit by a chemical analyst sworn to and properly executed before an official authorized to administer oaths shall be admissible in evidence without further authentication and without the testimony of the analyst in any hearing or trial in the District Court Division of the General Court of Justice with respect to the following matters:

(1) The alcohol concentration or concentrations or the presence or absence of an impairing substance of a person given a chemical analysis and who is involved in the hearing or trial.

(2) The time of the collection of the blood, breath, or other bodily fluid or substance sample or samples for the chemical analysis.

(3) The type of chemical analysis administered and the procedures followed.

(4) The type and status of any permit issued by the Department of Health and Human Services that the analyst held on the date the analyst performed the chemical analysis in question.

(5) If the chemical analysis is performed on a breath-testing instrument for which regulations adopted pursuant to subsection (b) require preventive maintenance, the date the most recent preventive maintenance procedures were performed on the breath-testing instrument used, as shown on the maintenance records for that instrument.

The Department of Health and Human Services shall develop a form for use by chemical analysts in making this affidavit.

(e2) Except as governed by subsection (c1), (c2), or (c3) of this section, the State can only use the provisions of subsection (e1) of this section if:

(1) The State notifies the defendant at least 15 business days before the proceeding at which the affidavit would be used of its intention to introduce the affidavit into evidence under this subsection and provides a copy of the affidavit to the defendant, and

(2) The defendant fails to file a written notification with the court, with a copy to the State, at least five business days before the proceeding at which the affidavit would be used that the defendant objects to the introduction of the affidavit into evidence.

The failure to file a timely objection as provided in this subsection shall be deemed a waiver of the right to object to the admissibility of the affidavit. Upon filing a timely objection, the admissibility of the report shall be determined and governed by the appropriate rules of evidence. The case shall be continued until the analyst can be present. The criminal case shall not be dismissed due to the failure of the analyst to appear, unless the analyst willfully fails to appear after being ordered to appear by the court. Nothing in subsection (e1) or subsection (e2) of this section precludes the right of any party to call any witness or to introduce any evidence supporting or contradicting the evidence contained in the affidavit.

(f) Evidence of Refusal Admissible. - If any person charged with an implied-consent offense refuses to submit to a chemical analysis or to perform field sobriety tests at the request of an officer, evidence of that refusal is admissible in any criminal, civil, or administrative action against the person.

(g) Controlled-Drinking Programs. - The Department of Health and Human Services may adopt rules concerning the ingestion of controlled amounts of alcohol by individuals submitting to chemical testing as a part of scientific, experimental, educational, or demonstration programs. These regulations shall prescribe procedures consistent with controlling federal law governing the acquisition, transportation, possession, storage, administration, and disposition of alcohol intended for use in the programs. Any person in charge of a controlled-drinking program who acquires alcohol under these regulations must keep records accounting for the disposition of all alcohol acquired, and the records must at all reasonable times be available for inspection upon the request of any federal, State, or local law-enforcement officer with jurisdiction over the laws relating to control of alcohol. A controlled-drinking program exclusively using lawfully purchased alcoholic beverages in places in which they may be lawfully possessed, however, need not comply with the record-keeping requirements of the regulations authorized by this subsection. All acts pursuant to the regulations reasonably done in furtherance of bona fide objectives of a controlled-drinking program authorized by the regulations are lawful notwithstanding the provisions of any other general or local statute, regulation, or ordinance controlling alcohol.

(h) Disposition of Blood Evidence. - Notwithstanding any other provision of law, any blood or urine sample subject to chemical analysis for the presence of alcohol, a controlled substance or its metabolite, or any impairing substance pursuant to this section may be destroyed by the analyzing agency 12 months after the case is filed or after the case is concluded in the trial court and not under appeal, whichever is later, without further notice to the parties. However, if a Motion to Preserve the evidence has been filed by either party, the evidence shall remain in the custody of the analyzing agency or the agency that collected the sample until dispositive order of a court of competent jurisdiction is entered.

4.7 Affidavits, Revocation Reports, and Procedures

When law enforcement determines that a person meets the criteria for civil revocation he or she must file the Administrative Office of the Courts form AOC-CVR-1A. This form is available for free online by visiting www.nccourts.org and clicking on the Forms tab at the top of the page. From that point just enter in the form number and a downloadable pdf file will appear. This form serves as a sworn statement by the officer and chemical analyst. The arresting officer in some cases is both and as such must check both the "law enforcement officer" and "chemical analyst" boxes at the top of the form. If they are two different people (one administering the test and the other the arresting officer) then both must fill out the form in their appropriate capacities. If the person is present, the magistrate must then complete the order revoking the person's license. The magistrate is not required to issue the order if the person is currently revoked, or doesn't have a privilege, or isn't eligible for restoration during the civil revocation. If this applies the magistrate must file and set out in writing what he or she relied on to make that determination (see N.C.G.S. §20-16.5).

The magistrate must fill out a different AOC form than the officers. The magistrate will use AOC-CVR-2 if the person is present. This form is also available on the www.nccourts.org. This form is titled "Revocation Order When Person Present." It informs the driver that they must pay a revocation fee of $100.00 to get their license back following the revocation. This revocation can be no shorter than thirty days. At this point, the magistrate will order the person to surrender his or her license. If the person has lost their license, the magistrate should have them complete another AOC form, AOC-CVR-8 entitled "Affidavit No License." If the person doesn't have his or her license with them, they can surrender them within five working days. If the license is not surrendered at that time, the DMV may issue a pick up order.

If the person is NOT present (this happens a lot in accident cases where the driver is taken to the hospital) the same AOC forms are used by the officers and analyst but the clerk must mail a revocation order to the person using AOC form AOC-CVR-3 (also available online). N.C.G.S. §20-16.5 also lays out the revocation periods of 30 or 45 days. The only difference between these revocation periods is if the person doesn't timely submit his or her license to the Court. After the revocation period is passed (assuming the person didn't contest the revocation) a trip to the clerk's office and the payment of the civil revocation fee will get the license returned and reinstated pending the outcome of the case.

4.8 Fighting the Civil Revocation

This is an option that can be useful if used sparingly in my opinion. I only use the provisions allowed under N.C.G.S. §20-16.5 for my clients that are CDL carriers. One reason I do this is because the revocation time for a CDL DWI is one year versus the revocation period of thirty days for a regular license. You don't see these often because of the various time constraints involved in the statute. First, you only have ten days to request the hearing using AOC form AOC-CVR-5 (available online). Next, you need to select whether you want the hearing to be in front of a District Court Judge or a magistrate. I always opt for the District Court Judge. The hearing must be set within three days of your request (if you want a magistrate) or within five days if you want a District Court Judge to hear it. If the hearing is not held within three working days (if a magistrate is requested) or within five working days (if a Judge is requested) then the revocation must be rescinded. Keep in mind that the burden of proof in this hearing is the greater weight of the evidence.

PRACTICE TIP: Many of the clerks are not familiar with this AOC form and thus are not aware that the clerk's office must set a hearing within the time limits stated in the statute. Most of the cases I've had rescinded were due to the clerk not scheduling these hearings within the time constraints. I don't tell the clerks how to do their job, I just file the form and hand it to the clerk. The more knowledgeable clerks will know what to do and set your hearing. Be sure to follow the statute and set out all of your arguments in writing. I usually attach a separate sheet of paper. Also, be sure to subpoena the magistrate that ordered the revocation if you want to contest any of the findings.

4.9 Refusal Revocations

North Carolina's implied consent is just what it says it is, you've consented to a search of your person if an officer finds probable cause to arrest you for an implied consent crime. In order to coerce most people to take a chemical test, the State has decided to revoke their license for one year if they do not consent to the chemical analysis. All of this is laid out above in N.C.G.S. §20-16.2. The refusal then usually goes one of two ways: 1. a search warrant to draw blood is obtained; or 2. the person is just marked as a refusal and no further testing occurs. If your client is marked a refusal (and hires you quickly enough to ask the DMV for a hearing) it's in your client's best interests to have a DMV hearing. Your client only has ten days to ask for this hearing so it's very important to look at the timing of the revocation letter. Once a hearing is set, your client's revocation is lifted until the hearing takes place. The hearing is limited to the things set out in N.C.G.S. §20-16.2 but many hearing officers will give you leeway to discover more facts about your case.

PRACTICE TIP: I always ask the officer about the stop and the clues on the SFSTs as well as the revocation questions. Since we get only limited discovery in these cases I like to find out all I can about what the officer will later testify to in Court. I also always ask the hearing officer if I can record the hearing. Later, you can have the recording transcribed by a local Court reporting service. I always do this because the police officer is under oath at the hearing just like he will be in Court. If the story changes, you then have some ammo in Court.

If your client is not successful at the DMV hearing the refusal can still be appealed to the Superior Court. However, this appeal is not de novo. It is limited to the record.

4.10 Driving Privileges

The Division of Motor Vehicles was given the authority as an executive agency to revoke a person's license. The Courts have the authority through the judicial branch to allow for limited privileges to drive during a suspension or revocation from the DMV. We will go through the many different types of privileges that the Court generally allows. These privileges are controlled by the General Statutes. N.C.G.S. §20-179.3 and N.C.G.S. §20-16.2 and N.C.G.S. §20-16.5 (the last two statutes have already been reproduced above) are controlling. Here is N.C.G.S. §20-179.3.

§ 20-179.3. Limited driving privilege.

(a) Definition of Limited Driving Privilege. - A limited driving privilege is a judgment issued in the discretion of a court for good cause shown authorizing a person with a revoked driver's license to drive for essential purposes related to any of the following:

(1) His employment.

(2) The maintenance of his household.

(3) His education.

(4) His court-ordered treatment or assessment.

(5) Community service ordered as a condition of the person's probation.

(6) Emergency medical care.

(b) Eligibility. -

(1) A person convicted of the offense of impaired driving under G.S. 20-138.1 is eligible for a limited driving privilege if:

a. At the time of the offense he held either a valid driver's license or a license that had been expired for less than one year;

b. At the time of the offense he had not within the preceding seven years been convicted of an offense involving impaired driving;

c. Punishment Level Three, Four, or Five was imposed for the offense of impaired driving;

d. Subsequent to the offense he has not been convicted of, or had an unresolved charge lodged against him for, an offense involving impaired driving; and

e. The person has obtained and filed with the court a substance abuse assessment of the type required by G.S. 20-17.6 for the restoration of a drivers license.

A person whose North Carolina driver's license is revoked because of a conviction in another jurisdiction substantially similar to impaired driving under G.S. 20-138.1 is eligible for a limited driving privilege if he would be eligible for it had the conviction occurred in North Carolina. Eligibility for a limited driving privilege following a revocation under G.S. 20-16.2(d) is governed by G.S. 20-16.2(e1).

(2) Any person whose licensing privileges are forfeited pursuant to G.S. 15A-1331.1 is eligible for a limited driving privilege if the court finds that at the time of the forfeiture, the person held either a valid drivers license or a drivers license that had been expired for less than one year and

a. The person is supporting existing dependents or must have a drivers license to be gainfully employed; or

b. The person has an existing dependent who requires serious medical treatment and the defendant is the only person able to provide transportation to the dependent to the health care facility where the dependent can receive the needed medical treatment. The limited driving privilege granted under this subdivision must restrict the person to essential driving related to the purposes listed above, and any driving that is not related to those purposes is unlawful even though done at times and upon routes that may be authorized by the privilege.

(c) Privilege Not Effective until after Compliance with Court-Ordered Revocation. - A person convicted of an impaired driving offense may apply for a limited driving privilege at the time the judgment is entered. A person whose license is revoked because of a conviction in another jurisdiction substantially similar to impaired driving under G.S. 20-138.1 may apply for a limited driving privilege only after having completed at least 60 days of a court-imposed term of nonoperation of a motor vehicle, if the court in the other jurisdiction imposed such a term of nonoperation.

(c1) Privilege Restrictions for High-Risk Drivers. - Notwithstanding any other provision of this section, any limited driving privilege issued to a person convicted of an impaired driving offense with an alcohol concentration of 0.15 or more at the time of the offense shall:

(1) Not become effective until at least 45 days after the final conviction under G.S. 20-138.1;

(2) Require the applicant to comply with the ignition interlock requirements of subsection (g5) of this section; and

(3) Restrict the applicant to driving only to and from the applicant's place of employment, the place the applicant is enrolled in school, any court ordered treatment or substance abuse education, and any ignition interlock service facility.

For purposes of this subsection, the results of a chemical analysis presented at trial or sentencing shall be sufficient to prove a person's alcohol concentration, shall be conclusive, and shall not be subject to modification by any party, with or without approval by the court.

(d) Application for and Scheduling of Subsequent Hearing. - The application for a limited driving privilege made at any time after the day of sentencing must be filed with the clerk in duplicate, and no hearing scheduled may be held until a reasonable time after the clerk files a copy of the application with the district attorney's office. The hearing must be scheduled before:

(1) The presiding judge at the applicant's trial if that judge is assigned to a court in the district court district as defined in G.S. 7A-133 or superior court district or set of districts as defined in G.S. 7A-41.1, as the case may be, in which the conviction for impaired driving was imposed.

(2) The senior regular resident superior court judge of the superior court district or set of districts as defined in G.S. 7A-41.1 in which the conviction for impaired driving was imposed, if the presiding judge is not available within the district and the conviction was imposed in superior court.

(3) The chief district court judge of the district court district as defined in G.S. 7A-133 in which the conviction for impaired driving was imposed, if the presiding judge is not available within the district and the conviction was imposed in district court.

If the applicant was convicted of an offense in another jurisdiction, the hearing must be scheduled before the chief district court judge of the district court district as defined in G.S. 7A-133 in which he resides. G.S. 20-16.2(e1) governs the judge before whom a hearing is scheduled if the revocation was under G.S. 20-16.2(d). The hearing may be scheduled in any county within the district court district as defined in G.S. 7A-133 or superior court district or set of districts as defined in G.S. 7A-41.1, as the case may be.

(e) Limited Basis for and Effect of Privilege. - A limited driving privilege issued under this section authorizes a person to drive if his license is revoked solely under G.S. 20-17(a)(2) or as a result of a conviction in another jurisdiction substantially similar to impaired driving under G.S. 20-138.1; if the person's license is revoked under any other statute, the limited driving privilege is invalid.

(f) Overall Provisions on Use of Privilege. - Every limited driving privilege must restrict the applicant to essential driving related to the purposes listed in subsection (a), and any driving that is not related to those purposes is unlawful even though done at times and upon routes that may be authorized by the privilege. If the privilege is granted, driving related to emergency medical care is authorized at any time and without restriction as to routes, but all other driving must be for a purpose and done within the restrictions specified in the privilege.

(f1) Definition of "Standard Working Hours". - Under this section, "standard working hours" are 6:00 A.M. to 8:00 P.M. on Monday through Friday.

(g) Driving for Work-Related Purposes in Standard Working Hours. - In a limited driving privilege, the court may authorize driving for work-related purposes during standard working hours without specifying the times and routes in which the driving must occur. If the applicant is not required to drive for essential work-related purposes except during standard working hours, the limited driving privilege must prohibit driving during nonstandard working hours unless the driving is for emergency medical care or is authorized by subsection (g2). The limited driving privilege must state the name and address of the applicant's place of work or employer, and may include other information and restrictions applicable to work-related driving in the discretion of the court.

(g1) Driving for Work-Related Purposes in Nonstandard Hours. - If the applicant is required to drive during nonstandard working hours for an essential work-related purpose, he must present documentation of that fact before the judge may authorize him to drive for this purpose during those hours. If the applicant is self-employed, the documentation must be attached to or made a part of the limited driving privilege. If the judge determines that it is necessary for the applicant to drive during nonstandard hours for a work-related purpose, he may authorize the applicant to drive subject to these limitations:

(1) If the applicant is required to drive to and from a specific place of work at regular times, the limited driving privilege must specify the general times and routes in which the applicant will be driving to and from work, and restrict driving to those times and routes.

(2) If the applicant is required to drive to and from work at a specific place, but is unable to specify the times at which that driving will occur, the limited driving privilege must specify the general routes in which the applicant will be driving to and from work, and restrict the driving to those general routes.

(3) If the applicant is required to drive to and from work at regular times but is unable to specify the places at which work is to be performed, the limited driving privilege must specify the general times and geographic boundaries in which the applicant will be driving, and restrict driving to those times and within those boundaries.

(4) If the applicant can specify neither the times nor places in which he will be driving to and from work, or if he is required to drive during these nonstandard working hours as a condition of employment, the limited driving privilege must specify the geographic boundaries in which he will drive and restrict driving to that within those boundaries.

The limited driving privilege must state the name and address of the applicant's place of work or employer, and may include other information and restrictions applicable to work-related driving, in the discretion of the court.

(g2) Driving for Other than Work-Related Purposes. - A limited driving privilege may not allow driving for maintenance of the household except during standard working hours, and the limited driving privilege may contain any additional restrictions on that driving, in the discretion of the court. The limited driving privilege must authorize driving essential to the completion of any community work assignments, course of instruction at an Alcohol and Drug Education Traffic School, or substance abuse assessment or treatment, to which the applicant is ordered by the court as a condition of probation for the impaired driving conviction. If this driving will occur during nonstandard working hours, the limited driving privilege must specify the same limitations required by subsection (g1) for work-related driving during those hours, and it must include or have attached to it the name and address of the Alcohol and Drug Education Traffic School, the community service coordinator, or mental health treatment facility to which the applicant is assigned. Driving for educational purposes other than the course of instruction at an Alcohol and Drug Education Traffic School is subject to the same limitations applicable to work related driving under subsections (g) and (g1).

(g3) Ignition Interlock Allowed. - A judge may include all of the following in a limited driving privilege order:

(1) A restriction that the applicant may operate only a designated motor vehicle.

(2) A requirement that the designated motor vehicle be equipped with a functioning ignition interlock system of a type approved by the Commissioner. The Commissioner shall not unreasonably withhold approval of an ignition interlock system and shall consult with the Division of Purchase and Contract in the Department of Administration to ensure that potential vendors are not discriminated against.

(3) A requirement that the applicant personally activate the ignition interlock system before driving the motor vehicle.

(g4) The restrictions set forth in subsection (g3) and (g5) of this section do not apply to a motor vehicle that meets all of the following requirements:

(1) Is owned by the applicant's employer.

(2) Is operated by the applicant solely for work-related purposes.

(3) Its owner has filed with the court a written document authorizing the applicant to drive the vehicle, for work-related purposes, under the authority of a limited driving privilege.

(g5) Ignition Interlock Required. - If a person's drivers license is revoked for a conviction of G.S. 20-138.1, and the person had an alcohol concentration of 0.15 or more, a judge shall include all of the following in a limited driving privilege order:

(1) A restriction that the applicant may operate only a designated motor vehicle.

(2) A requirement that the designated motor vehicle be equipped with a functioning ignition interlock system of a type approved by the Commissioner, which is set to prohibit driving with an alcohol concentration of greater than 0.00. The Commissioner shall not unreasonably withhold approval of an ignition interlock system and shall consult with the Division of Purchase and Contract in the Department of Administration to ensure that potential vendors are not discriminated against.

(3) A requirement that the applicant personally activate the ignition interlock system before driving the motor vehicle.

For purposes of this subsection, the results of a chemical analysis presented at trial or sentencing shall be sufficient to prove a person's alcohol concentration, shall be conclusive, and shall not be subject to modification by any party, with or without approval by the court.

(h) Other Mandatory and Permissive Conditions or Restrictions. - In all limited driving privileges the judge shall also include a restriction that the applicant not consume alcohol while driving or drive at any time while he has remaining in his body any alcohol or controlled substance previously consumed, unless the controlled substance was lawfully obtained and taken in therapeutically appropriate amounts. The judge may impose any other reasonable restrictions or conditions necessary to achieve the purposes of this section.

(i) Modification or Revocation of Privilege. - A judge who issues a limited driving privilege is authorized to modify or revoke the limited driving privilege upon a showing that the circumstances have changed sufficiently to justify modification or revocation. If the judge who issued the privilege is not presiding in the court in which the privilege was issued, a presiding judge in that court may modify or revoke a privilege in accordance with this subsection. The judge must indicate in the order of modification or revocation the reasons for the order, or he must make specific findings indicating the reason for the order and those findings must be entered in the record of the case.

(j) Effect of Violation of Restriction. - A holder of a limited driving privilege who violates any of its restrictions commits the offense of driving while his license is revoked under G.S. 20-28(a) and is subject to punishment and license revocation as provided in that section. If a law-enforcement officer has reasonable grounds to believe that the holder of a limited driving privilege has consumed alcohol while driving or has driven while he has remaining in his body any alcohol previously consumed, the suspected offense of driving while license is revoked is an alcohol-related offense subject to the implied-consent provisions of G.S. 20-16.2. If a holder of a limited driving privilege is charged with driving while license revoked by violating a restriction contained in his limited driving privilege, and a judicial official determines that there is probable cause for the charge, the limited driving privilege is suspended pending the resolution of the case, and the judicial official must require the holder to surrender the limited driving privilege. The judicial official must also notify the holder that he is not entitled to drive until his case is resolved. Notwithstanding any other provision of law, an alcohol screening test may be administered to a driver suspected of violating this section, and the results of an alcohol screening test or the driver's refusal to submit may be used by a law enforcement officer, a court, or an administrative agency in determining if alcohol was present in the driver's body. No alcohol screening tests are valid under this section unless the device used is one approved by the Department of Health and Human Services, and the screening test is conducted in accordance with the applicable regulations of the Department as to the manner of its use.

(j1) Effect of Violation of Community Service Requirement. - Section of Community Corrections of the Division of Adult Correction staff shall report significant violations of the terms of a probation judgment related to community service to the court that ordered the community service. The court shall then conduct a hearing to determine if there was a willful failure to comply. The hearing may be held in the district where the requirement was imposed, where the alleged violation occurred, or where the probationer resides. If the court determines that there was a willful failure to pay the prescribed fee or to complete the work as ordered within the applicable time limits, the court shall revoke any limited driving privilege issued in the impaired driving case until community service requirements have been met. In addition, the court may take any further action authorized by Article 82 of Chapter 15A of the General Statutes for violation of a condition of probation.

(k) Copy of Limited Driving Privilege to Division; Action Taken if Privilege Invalid. - The clerk of court or the child support enforcement agency must send a copy of any limited driving privilege issued in the county to the Division. A limited driving privilege that is not authorized by this section, G.S. 20-16.2(e1), 20-16.1, 50-13.12, or 110-142.2, or that does not contain the limitations required by law, is invalid. If the limited driving privilege is invalid on its face, the Division must immediately notify the court and the holder of the privilege that it considers the privilege void and that the Division records will not indicate that the holder has a limited driving privilege.

(l) Any judge granting limited driving privileges under this section shall, prior to granting such privileges, be furnished proof and be satisfied that the person being granted such privileges is financially responsible. Proof of financial responsibility shall be in one of the following forms:

(1) A written certificate or electronically-transmitted facsimile thereof from any insurance carrier duly authorized to do business in this State certifying that there is in effect a nonfleet private passenger motor vehicle liability policy for the benefit of the person required to furnish proof of financial responsibility. The certificate or facsimile shall state the effective date and expiration date of the nonfleet private passenger motor vehicle liability policy and shall state the date that the certificate or facsimile is issued. The certificate or facsimile shall remain effective proof of financial responsibility for a period of 30 consecutive days following the date the certificate or facsimile is issued but shall not in and of itself constitute a binder or policy of insurance or

(2) A binder for or policy of nonfleet private passenger motor vehicle liability insurance under which the applicant is insured, provided that the binder or policy states the effective date and expiration date of the nonfleet private passenger motor vehicle liability policy.

The preceding provisions of this subsection do not apply to applicants who do not own currently registered motor vehicles and who do not operate nonfleet private passenger motor vehicles that are owned by other persons and that are not insured under commercial motor vehicle liability insurance policies. In such cases, the applicant shall sign a written certificate to that effect. Such certificate shall be furnished by the Division. Any material misrepresentation made by such person on such certificate shall be grounds for suspension of that person's license for a period of 90 days.

For the purpose of this subsection "nonfleet private passenger motor vehicle" has the definition ascribed to it in Article 40 of General Statute Chapter 58.

The Commissioner may require that certificates required by this subsection be on a form approved by the Commissioner. Such granting of limited driving privileges shall be conditioned upon the maintenance of such financial responsibility during the period of the limited driving privilege. Nothing in this subsection precludes any person from showing proof of financial responsibility in any other manner authorized by Articles 9A and 13 of this Chapter.

All of the privileges issued in North Carolina are based on AOC forms. Each privilege has its own unique AOC form. I will talk about each of the forms and give their respective numbers when going over the differences. These AOC forms are also available online for free at the nccourts website.

The first limited driving privilege I am going to talk about is the one that most clients are most eager to hear about. The civil revocation limited driving privilege is the most popular because it allows the client to drive again fairly quickly after the arrest. This privilege is available to a client that has already been revoked for ten days and meets the eligibility requirements of the statute. Usually this allows the client to drive the remaining twenty days of the thirty day civil revocation under certain limitations. The requirements for obtaining this type of privilege are: 1. At the time of the alleged offense your client had a valid driver's license or one that had been expired less than a year; 2. The client doesn't have another pending charge for impaired driving other than the charge for which his or her license is currently revoked and your client doesn't have any additional convictions for impaired driving since being charged with the current charge; 3. Your client's license has been revoked for at least ten days if the revocation was for thirty days or at least thirty days if the revocation was for forty five days; 4. Your client has obtained a substance abuse assessment from an approved facility and has agreed to participate in training or treatment (see N.C.G.S. §20-16.5).

To obtain this type of privilege, you must first file the petition with the clerk's office. The petition is AOC-CVR-9. This is also the same AOC form used for indefinite suspensions. The driving privilege itself is AOC-CVR-10 for civil license revocations. By looking at the privilege form you can see that the second page of the privilege sets out certain restrictions by statute. Driving for medical emergencies is permitted at any time. Driving is only permitted by the privilege for the following purposes: work or school during standard working hours (standard working hours is defined as Monday through Friday from 6 a.m. to 8 p.m.); maintenance of household during standard working hours; community service assignments and Adult Drug and Education Traffic School (ADETS) and substance abuse treatment. As you can see from the form, the privilege also allows your client to drive during non-standard hours for work and school. To show these outside hours I attach a letter from the employer explaining the non-standard hours or a school class schedule showing my client's enrollment.

A client that is revoked indefinitely under N.C.G.S. §20-16.5 can also apply for a limited privilege using the same petition form. The requirements for indefinite relief are similar to the requirements for the civil revocation and are laid out in the statute. The AOC form for this type of privilege is AOC-CR-11.

Privileges following in State convictions are different as well. To obtain a driving privilege after a DWI conviction your client must be sentenced at Level three, four, or five. A client sentenced at levels one, two, or aggravated level one is not eligible to receive a limited driving privilege. If your client is convicted, the length of the revocation can be one year, four years, or permanent depending on their situation. Your client's ability to receive a driving privilege after conviction is controlled by N.C.G.S. §20-179.3 which is reproduced above. A client that is convicted of DWI in another state or in Federal Court may also be eligible for driving privileges (see AOC-CV-350) subject to N.C.G.S. §20-179.3 as long as the Chief District Court Judge of your client's home district is available.

If your client is under the age of 21 at the time of the DWI arrest, he or she is NOT eligible for a driving privilege following conviction. DMV considers your client revoked under two different statutes (N.C.G.S. §20-13.2(b) and N.C.G.S. §20-17(a)(2) which N.C.G.S. §20-179.3 does not allow) and DMV will send the privilege back and, in my experience, also write the Judge that issued the privilege a letter telling them that he or she is not authorized to give your client a privilege. What makes this even stranger is the fact that a person who is revoked solely under N.C.G.S. §20-138.3 (the underage DWI only) is eligible for a privilege if they meet the requirements. The AOC has provided a form for this privilege also: AOC-CR-312.

4.11 Driver's License Restoration and Alcohol Restrictions

Your client's license restoration and the implications regarding the alcohol restrictions placed on that restoration are found in part in N.C.G.S. §20-19, which is reproduced below.

§ 20-19. Period of suspension or revocation; conditions of restoration.

(a) When a license is suspended under subdivision (8) or (9) of G.S. 20-16(a), the period of suspension shall be in the discretion of the Division and for such time as it deems best for public safety but shall not exceed six months.

(b) When a license is suspended under subdivision (10) of G.S. 20-16(a), the period of suspension shall be in the discretion of the Division and for such time as it deems best for public safety but shall not exceed a period of 12 months.

(c) When a license is suspended under any other provision of this Article which does not specifically provide a period of suspension, the period of suspension shall be not more than one year.

(c1) When a license is revoked under subdivision (2) of G.S. 20-17, and the period of revocation is not determined by subsection (d) or (e) of this section, the period of revocation is one year.

(c2) When a license is suspended under G.S. 20-17(a)(14), the period of revocation for a first conviction shall be for 10 days. For a second or subsequent conviction as defined in G.S. 20-138.2B(d), the period of revocation shall be one year.

(c3) (Effective until December 1, 2016) Restriction; Revocations. - When the Division restores a person's drivers license which was revoked pursuant to G.S. 20-13.2(a), G.S. 20-23 when the offense involved impaired driving, G.S. 20-23.2, subdivision (2) of G.S. 20-17(a), subdivision (1) or (9) of G.S. 20-17(a) when the offense involved impaired driving, G.S. 20-138.5(d), or this subsection, in addition to any other restriction or condition, it shall place the applicable restriction on the person's drivers license as follows:

(1) For the first restoration of a drivers license for a person convicted of driving while impaired, G.S. 20-138.1, or a drivers license revoked pursuant to G.S. 20-23 or G.S. 20-23.2 when the offense for which the person's license was revoked prohibits substantially similar conduct which if committed in this State would result in a conviction of driving while impaired under G.S. 20-138.1, that the person not operate a vehicle with an alcohol concentration of 0.04 or more at any relevant time after the driving;

(2) For the second or subsequent restoration of a drivers license for a person convicted of driving while impaired, G.S. 20-138.1, or a drivers license revoked pursuant to G.S. 20-23 or G.S. 20-23.2 when the offense for which the person's license was revoked prohibits substantially similar conduct which if committed in this State would result in a conviction of driving while impaired under G.S. 20-138.1, that the person not operate a vehicle with an alcohol concentration greater than 0.00 at any relevant time after the driving;

(3) For any restoration of a drivers license for a person convicted of driving while impaired in a commercial motor vehicle, G.S. 20-138.2, habitual impaired driving, G.S. 20-138.5, driving while less than 21 years old after consuming alcohol or drugs, G.S. 20-138.3, felony death by vehicle, G.S. 20-141.4(a1), manslaughter or negligent homicide resulting from the operation of a motor vehicle when the offense involved impaired driving, or a revocation under this subsection, that the person not operate a vehicle with an alcohol concentration of greater than 0.00 at any relevant time after the driving;

(4) For any restoration of a drivers license revoked pursuant to G.S. 20-23 or G.S. 20-23.2 when the offense for which the person's license was revoked prohibits substantially similar conduct which if committed in this State would result in a conviction of driving while impaired in a commercial motor vehicle, G.S. 20-138.2, driving while less than 21 years old after consuming alcohol or drugs, G.S. 20-138.3, a violation of G.S. 20-141.4, or manslaughter or negligent homicide resulting from the operation of a motor vehicle when the offense involved impaired driving, that the person not operate vehicle with an alcohol concentration of greater than 0.00 at any relevant time after the driving.

In addition, the person seeking restoration of a license must agree to submit to a chemical analysis in accordance with G.S. 20-16.2 at the request of a law enforcement officer who has reasonable grounds to believe the person is operating a motor vehicle on a highway or public vehicular area in violation of the restriction specified in this subsection. The person must also agree that, when requested by a law enforcement officer, the person will agree to be transported by the law enforcement officer to the place where chemical analysis is to be administered.

The restrictions placed on a license under this subsection shall be in effect (i) seven years from the date of restoration if the person's license was permanently revoked, (ii) until the person's twenty-first birthday if the revocation was for a conviction under G.S. 20-138.3, and (iii) three years in all other cases.

A law enforcement officer who has reasonable grounds to believe that a person has violated a restriction placed on the person's drivers license shall complete an affidavit pursuant to G.S. 20-16.2(c1). On the basis of information reported pursuant to G.S. 20-16.2, the Division shall revoke the drivers license of any person who violates a condition of reinstatement imposed under this subsection. An alcohol concentration report from an ignition interlock system shall not be used as the basis for revocation under this subsection. A violation of a restriction imposed under this subsection or the willful refusal to submit to a chemical analysis shall result in a one-year revocation. If the period of revocation was imposed pursuant to subsection (d) or (e), or G.S. 20-138.5(d), any remaining period of the original revocation, prior to its reduction, shall be reinstated and the one-year revocation begins after all other periods of revocation have terminated.

(c3) (Effective December 1, 2016) Restriction; Revocations. - When the Division restores a person's drivers license which was revoked pursuant to G.S. 20-13.2(a), G.S. 20-23 when the offense involved impaired driving, G.S. 20-23.2, subdivision (2) of G.S. 20-17(a), subdivision (1) or (9) of G.S. 20-17(a) when the offense involved impaired driving, or this subsection, in addition to any other restriction or condition, it shall place the applicable restriction on the person's drivers license as follows:

(1) For the first restoration of a drivers license for a person convicted of driving while impaired, G.S. 20-138.1, or a drivers license revoked pursuant to G.S. 20-23 or G.S. 20-23.2 when the offense for which the person's license was revoked prohibits substantially similar conduct which if committed in this State would result in a conviction of driving while impaired under G.S. 20-138.1, that the person not operate a vehicle with an alcohol concentration of 0.04 or more at any relevant time after the driving;

(2) For the second or subsequent restoration of a drivers license for a person convicted of driving while impaired, G.S. 20-138.1, or a drivers license revoked pursuant to G.S. 20-23 or G.S. 20-23.2 when the offense for which the person's license was revoked prohibits substantially similar conduct which if committed in this State would result in a conviction of driving while impaired under G.S. 20-138.1, that the person not operate a vehicle with an alcohol concentration greater than 0.00 at any relevant time after the driving;

(3) For any restoration of a drivers license for a person convicted of driving while impaired in a commercial motor vehicle, G.S. 20-138.2, driving while less than 21 years old after consuming alcohol or drugs, G.S. 20-138.3, felony death by vehicle, G.S. 20-141.4(a1), manslaughter or negligent homicide resulting from the operation of a motor vehicle when the offense involved impaired driving, or a revocation under this subsection, that the person not operate a vehicle with an alcohol concentration of greater than 0.00 at any relevant time after the driving;

(4) For any restoration of a drivers license revoked pursuant to G.S. 20-23 or G.S. 20-23.2 when the offense for which the person's license was revoked prohibits substantially similar conduct which if committed in this State would result in a conviction of driving while impaired in a commercial motor vehicle, G.S. 20-138.2, driving while less than 21 years old after consuming alcohol or drugs, G.S. 20-138.3, a violation of G.S. 20-141.4, or manslaughter or negligent homicide resulting from the operation of a motor vehicle when the offense involved impaired driving, that the person not operate vehicle with an alcohol concentration of greater than 0.00 at any relevant time after the driving.

In addition, the person seeking restoration of a license must agree to submit to a chemical analysis in accordance with G.S. 20-16.2 at the request of a law enforcement officer who has reasonable grounds to believe the person is operating a motor vehicle on a highway or public vehicular area in violation of the restriction specified in this subsection. The person must also agree that, when requested by a law enforcement officer, the person will agree to be transported by the law enforcement officer to the place where chemical analysis is to be administered.

The restrictions placed on a license under this subsection shall be in effect (i) seven years from the date of restoration if the person's license was permanently revoked, (ii) until the person's twenty-first birthday if the revocation was for a conviction under G.S. 20-138.3, and (iii) three years in all other cases.

A law enforcement officer who has reasonable grounds to believe that a person has violated a restriction placed on the person's drivers license shall complete an affidavit pursuant to G.S. 20-16.2(c1). On the basis of information reported pursuant to G.S. 20-16.2, the Division shall revoke the drivers license of any person who violates a condition of reinstatement imposed under this subsection. An alcohol concentration report from an ignition interlock system shall not be used as the basis for revocation under this subsection. A violation of a restriction imposed under this subsection or the willful refusal to submit to a chemical analysis shall result in a one-year revocation. If the period of revocation was imposed pursuant to subsection (d) or (e), any remaining period of the original revocation, prior to its reduction, shall be reinstated and the one-year revocation begins after all other periods of revocation have terminated.

(c4) Applicable Procedures. - When a person has violated a condition of restoration by refusing a chemical analysis, the notice and hearing procedures of G.S. 20-16.2 apply. When a person has submitted to a chemical analysis and the results show a violation of the alcohol concentration restriction, the notification and hearing procedures of this section apply.

(c5) Right to Hearing Before Division; Issues. - Upon receipt of a properly executed affidavit required by G.S. 20-16.2(c1), the Division must expeditiously notify the person charged that the person's license to drive is revoked for the period of time specified in this section, effective on the tenth calendar day after the mailing of the revocation order unless, before the effective date of the order, the person requests in writing a hearing before the Division. Except for the time referred to in G.S. 20-16.5, if the person shows to the satisfaction of the Division that the person's license was surrendered to the court and remained in the court's possession, then the Division shall credit the amount of time for which the license was in the possession of the court against the revocation period required by this section. If the person properly requests a hearing, the person retains the person's license, unless it is revoked under some other provision of law, until the hearing is held, the person withdraws the request, or the person fails to appear at a scheduled hearing. The hearing officer may subpoena any witnesses or documents that the hearing officer deems necessary. The person may request the hearing officer to subpoena the charging officer, the chemical analyst, or both to appear at the hearing if the person makes the request in writing at least three days before the hearing. The person may subpoena any other witness whom the person deems necessary, and the provisions of G.S. 1A-1, Rule 45, apply to the issuance and service of all subpoenas issued under the authority of this section. The hearing officer is authorized to administer oaths to witnesses appearing at the hearing. The hearing must be conducted in the county where the charge was brought, and must be limited to consideration of whether:

(1) The charging officer had reasonable grounds to believe that the person had violated the alcohol concentration restriction;

(2) The person was notified of the person's rights as required by G.S. 20-16.2(a);

(3) The drivers license of the person had an alcohol concentration restriction; and

(4) The person submitted to a chemical analysis upon the request of the charging officer, and the analysis revealed an alcohol concentration in excess of the restriction on the person's drivers license.

If the Division finds that the conditions specified in this subsection are met, it must order the revocation sustained. If the Division finds that any of the conditions (1), (2), (3), or (4) is not met, it must rescind the revocation. If the revocation is sustained, the person must surrender the person's license immediately upon notification by the Division.

(c6) Appeal to Court. - There is no right to appeal the decision of the Division. However, if the person properly requested a hearing before the Division under subsection (c5) and the Division held such a hearing, the person may within 30 days of the date the Division's decision is mailed to the person, petition the superior court of the county in which the hearing took place for discretionary review on the record of the revocation. The superior court may stay the imposition of the revocation only if the court finds that the person is likely to succeed on the merits of the case and will suffer irreparable harm if such a stay is not granted. The stay shall not exceed 30 days. The reviewing court shall review the record only and shall be limited to determining if the Division hearing officer followed proper procedures and if the hearing officer made sufficient findings of fact to support the revocation. There shall be no further appeal.

(d) When a person's license is revoked under (i) G.S. 20-17(a)(2) and the person has another offense involving impaired driving for which he has been convicted, which offense occurred within three years immediately preceding the date of the offense for which his license is being revoked, or (ii) G.S. 20-17(a)(9) due to a violation of G.S. 20-141.4(a3), the period of revocation is four years, and this period may be reduced only as provided in this section. The Division may conditionally restore the person's license after it has been revoked for at least two years under this subsection if he provides the Division with satisfactory proof that:

(1) He has not in the period of revocation been convicted in North Carolina or any other state or federal jurisdiction of a motor vehicle offense, an alcoholic beverage control law offense, a drug law offense, or any other criminal offense involving the possession or consumption of alcohol or drugs; and

(2) He is not currently an excessive user of alcohol, drugs, or prescription drugs, or unlawfully using any controlled substance. The person may voluntarily submit themselves to continuous alcohol monitoring for the purpose of proving abstinence

from alcohol consumption during a period of revocation immediately prior to the restoration consideration.

a. Monitoring periods of 120 days or longer shall be accepted by the Division as evidence of abstinence if the Division receives sufficient documentation that reflects that the person abstained from alcohol use during the monitoring period.

b. The continuous alcohol monitoring system shall be a system approved under G.S. 15A-1343.3.

c. The Division may establish guidelines for the acceptance of evidence of abstinence under this subdivision.

If the Division restores the person's license, it may place reasonable conditions or restrictions on the person for the duration of the original revocation period.

(e) When a person's license is revoked under (i) G.S. 20-17(a)(2) and the person has two or more previous offenses involving impaired driving for which the person has been convicted, and the most recent offense occurred within the five years immediately preceding the date of the offense for which the person's license is being revoked, (ii) G.S. 20-17(a)(2) and the person was sentenced pursuant to G.S. 20-179(f3) for the offense resulting in the revocation, or (iii) G.S. 20-17(a)(9) due to a violation of G.S. 20-141.4(a4), the revocation is permanent.

(e1) Notwithstanding subsection (e) of this section, the Division may conditionally restore the license of a person to whom subsection (e) applies after it has been revoked for at least three years under subsection (e) if the person provides the Division with satisfactory proof of all of the following:

(1) In the three years immediately preceding the person's application for a restored license, the person has not been convicted in North Carolina or in any other state or federal court of a motor vehicle offense, an alcohol beverage control law offense, a drug law offense, or any criminal offense involving the consumption of alcohol or drugs.

(2) The person is not currently an excessive user of alcohol, drugs, or prescription drugs, or unlawfully using any controlled substance. The person may voluntarily submit themselves to continuous alcohol monitoring for the purpose of proving abstinence from alcohol consumption during a period of revocation immediately prior to the restoration consideration.

a. Monitoring periods of 120 days or longer shall be accepted by the Division as evidence of abstinence if the Division receives sufficient documentation that reflects that the person abstained from alcohol use during the monitoring period.

b. The continuous alcohol monitoring system shall be a system approved under G.S. 15A-1343.3.

c. The Division may establish guidelines for the acceptance of evidence of abstinence under this subdivision.

(e2) Notwithstanding subsection (e) of this section, the Division may conditionally restore the license of a person to whom subsection (e) applies after it has been revoked for at least 24 months under G.S. 20-17(a)(2) if the person provides the Division with satisfactory proof of all of the following:

(1) The person has not consumed any alcohol for the 12 months preceding the restoration while being monitored by a continuous alcohol monitoring device of a type approved by the Division of Adult Correction of the Department of Public Safety.

(2) The person has not in the period of revocation been convicted in North Carolina or any other state or federal jurisdiction of a motor vehicle offense, an alcoholic beverage control law offense, a drug law offense, or any other criminal offense involving the possession or consumption of alcohol or drugs.

(3) The person is not currently an excessive user of drugs or prescription drugs.

(4) The person is not unlawfully using any controlled substance.

(e3) (Effective until December 1, 2016) If the Division restores a person's license under subsection (e1), (e2), or (e4) of this section, it may place reasonable conditions or restrictions on the person for any period up to five years from the date of restoration.

(e3) (Effective December 1, 2016) If the Division restores a person's license under subsection (e1) or (e2) of this section, it may place reasonable conditions or restrictions on the person for any period up to five years from the date of restoration.

(e4) (Expires December 1, 2016) When a person's license is revoked under G.S. 20-138.5(d), the Division may conditionally restore the license of that person after it has been revoked for at least 10 years after the completion of any sentence imposed by the court, if the person provides the Division with satisfactory proof of all of the following:

(1) In the 10 years immediately preceding the person's application for a restored license, the person has not been convicted in North Carolina or in any other state or federal court of a motor vehicle offense, an alcohol beverage control law offense, a

drug law offense, or any other criminal offense.

(2) The person is not currently a user of alcohol, unlawfully using any controlled substance, or an excessive user of prescription drugs.

(f) When a license is revoked under any other provision of this Article which does not specifically provide a period of revocation, the period of revocation shall be one year.

(g) When a license is suspended under subdivision (11) of G.S. 20-16(a), the period of suspension shall be for a period of time not in excess of the period of nonoperation imposed by the court as a condition of the suspended sentence; further, in such case, it shall not be necessary to comply with the Motor Vehicle Safety and Financial Responsibility Act in order to have such license returned at the expiration of the suspension period.

(g1) When a license is revoked under subdivision (12) of G.S. 20-17, the period of revocation is six months for conviction of a second offense and one year for conviction of a third or subsequent offense.

(g2) When a license is revoked under G.S. 20-17(a)(16), the period of revocation is 90 days for a second conviction and six months for a third or subsequent conviction. The term "second or subsequent conviction" shall have the same meaning as found in G.S. 20-17(a)(16).

(h) Repealed by Session Laws 1983, c. 435, s. 17.

(i) (For applicability, see Editor's note) When a person's license is revoked under G.S. 20-17(a)(1) or G.S. 20-17(a)(9), and the offense is one involving impaired driving and a fatality, the revocation is permanent. The Division may, however, conditionally restore the person's license after it has been revoked for at least five years under this subsection if he provides the Division with satisfactory proof that:

(1) In the five years immediately preceding the person's application for a restored license, he has not been convicted in North Carolina or in any other state or federal court of a motor vehicle offense, an alcohol beverage control law offense, a drug law offense, or any criminal offense involving the consumption of alcohol or drugs; and

(2) He is not currently an excessive user of alcohol or drugs.

If the Division restores the person's license, it may place reasonable conditions or restrictions on the person for any period up to seven years from the date of restoration.

(j) The Division is authorized to issue amended revocation orders issued under subsections (d) and (e), if necessary because convictions do not respectively occur in the same order as offenses for which the license may be revoked under those subsections.

(k) (Effective until December 1, 2016) Before the Division restores a driver's license that has been suspended or revoked under G.S. 20-138.5(d), or under any provision of this Article, other than G.S. 20-24.1, the person seeking to have his driver's license restored shall submit to the Division proof that he has notified his insurance agent or company of his seeking the restoration and that he is financially responsible. Proof of financial responsibility shall be in one of the following forms:

(1) A written certificate or electronically-transmitted facsimile thereof from any insurance carrier duly authorized to do business in this State certifying that there is in effect a nonfleet private passenger motor vehicle liability policy for the benefit of the person required to furnish proof of financial responsibility. The certificate or facsimile shall state the effective date and expiration date of the nonfleet private passenger motor vehicle liability policy and shall state the date that the certificate or facsimile is issued. The certificate or facsimile shall remain effective proof of financial responsibility for a period of 30 consecutive days following the date the certificate or facsimile is issued but shall not in and of itself constitute a binder or policy of insurance or

(2) A binder for or policy of nonfleet private passenger motor vehicle liability insurance under which the applicant is insured, provided that the binder or policy states the effective date and expiration date of the nonfleet private passenger motor vehicle liability policy.

The preceding provisions of this subsection do not apply to applicants who do not own currently registered motor vehicles and who do not operate nonfleet private passenger motor vehicles that are owned by other persons and that are not insured under commercial motor vehicle liability insurance policies. In such cases, the applicant shall sign a written certificate to that effect. Such certificate shall be furnished by the Division and may be incorporated into the restoration application form. Any material misrepresentation made by such person on such certificate shall be grounds for suspension of that person's license for a period of 90 days.

For the purposes of this subsection, the term "nonfleet private passenger motor vehicle" has the definition ascribed to it in Article 40 of General Statute Chapter 58.

The Commissioner may require that certificates required by this subsection be on a form approved by the Commissioner. The financial responsibility required by this subsection shall be kept in effect for not less than three years after the date that the license is restored. Failure to maintain financial responsibility as required by this subsection shall be grounds for suspending the restored driver's license for a period of thirty (30) days. Nothing in this subsection precludes any person from showing proof of financial responsibility in any other manner authorized by Articles 9A and 13 of this Chapter.

(k) (Effective December 1, 2016) Before the Division restores a driver's license that has been suspended or revoked under any provision of this Article, other than G.S. 20-24.1, the person seeking to have his driver's license restored shall submit to the Division proof that he has notified his insurance agent or company of his seeking the restoration and that he is financially responsible. Proof of financial responsibility shall be in one of the following forms:

(1) A written certificate or electronically-transmitted facsimile thereof from any insurance carrier duly authorized to do business in this State certifying that there is in effect a nonfleet private passenger motor vehicle liability policy for the benefit of the person required to furnish proof of financial responsibility. The certificate or facsimile shall state the effective date and expiration date of the nonfleet private passenger motor vehicle liability policy and shall state the date that the certificate or facsimile is issued. The certificate or facsimile shall remain effective proof of financial responsibility for a period of 30 consecutive days following the date the certificate or facsimile is issued but shall not in and of itself constitute a binder or policy of insurance or

(2) A binder for or policy of nonfleet private passenger motor vehicle liability insurance under which the applicant is insured, provided that the binder or policy states the effective date and expiration date of the nonfleet private passenger motor vehicle liability policy.

The preceding provisions of this subsection do not apply to applicants who do not own currently registered motor vehicles and who do not operate nonfleet private passenger motor vehicles that are owned by other persons and that are not insured under commercial motor vehicle liability insurance policies. In such cases, the applicant shall sign a written certificate to that effect. Such certificate shall be furnished by the Division and may be incorporated into the restoration application form. Any material misrepresentation made by such person on such certificate shall be grounds for suspension of that person's license for a period of 90 days.

For the purposes of this subsection, the term "nonfleet private passenger motor vehicle" has the definition ascribed to it in Article 40 of General Statute Chapter 58.

The Commissioner may require that certificates required by this subsection be on a form approved by the Commissioner. The financial responsibility required by this subsection shall be kept in effect for not less than three years after the date that the license is restored. Failure to maintain financial responsibility as required by this subsection shall be grounds for suspending the restored driver's license for a period of thirty (30) days. Nothing in this subsection precludes any person from showing proof of financial responsibility in any other manner authorized by Articles 9A and 13 of this Chapter.

After your client's privilege expires and he or she is eligible to get his or her license back, the client must first pay a restoration fee to the DMV. The fee for this restoration for clients revoked under 20-17(a)(2) is one hundred dollars. Following your client's restoration, the DMV will impose either a 0.04 restriction on his or her license or a 0.00 restriction. The 0.04 restriction means that your client cannot operate a motor vehicle with a result of 0.04 or more; if the client does operate at this restriction, they will be subject to being charged with a license restriction violation and having their license revoked again until a final determination is made. This restriction applies generally to first offenders either in-state, in another state, or Federal convictions.

The 0.00 restriction is applied the same way as it is above in those cases where there is a subsequent conviction. However, the zero tolerance restriction also applies to first timers convicted of CDL DWI, habitual DWI, underage DWI, felony death by vehicle, or manslaughter or homicide (see N.C.G.S. §20-19). This also applies to violation of alcohol restriction, and substantially similar conduct if committed in North Carolina that would result in a conviction of DWI CDL, underage DWI, death or serious injury be vehicle, and death or homicide resulting from impaired driving (see N.C.G.S. §20-19). The length of time that the alcohol restriction remains in place will vary by the revocation. If your client is like most, the revocation will be removed in three years. If your client was convicted of underage DWI, the restriction will end when he or she turns twenty one. If your client has a permanent revocation the restriction will last for seven years following restoration (see N.C.G.S. §20-19, above). If your client is suspected of violating the alcohol restriction imposed by DMV, another revocation is issued, and your client is notified of his or her rights to a DMV hearing under N.C.G.S. §20-19.

4.12 Ignition Interlock Requirements and Restrictions

Just as DMV put an interlock restriction on your client if he or she was convicted for DWI and the result was a 0.15 or higher for his or her limited privilege (after the 45 day lock down) the same applies once the license is restored. Since there still remains in most cases, a 45 day interlock requirement after restoration, or longer, DMV will use interlock as a further restriction. Ignition interlock can be tricky. I advise all of my clients at the initial consultation that if they blew over a 0.15 or if in the case of a blood draw, the number comes back at a 0.15 or higher then they will be subject to having to install interlock in ALL of the vehicles registered to them. Another key provision I like to point out is that the interlock privilege is different from a regular impaired driving privilege. Interlock does NOT allow for driving outside of work or school. There is no time allowed for standard household maintenance as with the other privilege. I also advise my clients that there will be a forty five day period post conviction that no privilege will be available to them. When a client gets a ticket for driving a car without interlock installed and the client is restricted, a conviction will result in another revocation. I have found that so far, the DMV will not count a PJC as a conviction for purposes of revocation in this situation.

Interlock is primarily just a fuel cell machine similar in nature to the PBTs that the officers carry with them to test drivers on the roadside. The interesting note is that while the roadside devices that the officers carry must be calibrated every thirty days for accuracy, the interlock unit only must be serviced and calibrated every sixty days. The interlock unit is also exposed to all the outside elements of extreme heat during the summer months and extreme cold in the winter.

It's generally a good idea to read through the specific manual for the model of interlock device your client has had installed. Most of the manuals will admit that there are numerous contaminants that will supply a false positive reading for alcohol (examples include certain baked goods like cakes or pies or marinated meats or even inhalants). I tell my clients to keep a bottle of water with them and to rinse out their mouths before attempting to give a sample to the machine.

Each time the interlock device reports a positive result that the interlock company flags as a possible violation, the DMV can choose to hold a revocation hearing based upon a positive result for alcohol reported by the interlock company. These hearings are held at the DMV office and a DMV Hearing Officer records them. If the DMV decides to revoke your client after a hearing is held for this type of violation, there is a thirty day window of time to appeal the case to the Superior Court. The appeal is actually in the form of a civil action suing the Commissioner of the DMV in the Superior Court. The Attorney General's office handles these appeals. Be sure to get a judge to sign a TRO or Temporary Restraining Order to bar the DMV from revoking your client's license until after the matter can be heard in the Superior Court; a District Court Judge can even sign these TROs. Those restrictions are contained in N.C.G.S. §20-17.8 which is reproduced below.

§ 20-17.8. Restoration of a license after certain driving while impaired convictions; ignition interlock.

(a) Scope. - This section applies to a person whose license was revoked as a result of a conviction of driving while impaired, G.S. 20-138.1, and:

(1) The person had an alcohol concentration of 0.15 or more;

(2) The person has been convicted of another offense involving impaired driving, which offense occurred within seven years immediately preceding the date of the offense for which the person's license has been revoked; or

(3) The person was sentenced pursuant to G.S. 20-179(f3).

For purposes of subdivision (1) of this subsection, the results of a chemical analysis, as shown by an affidavit or affidavits executed pursuant to G.S. 20-16.2(c1), shall be used by the Division to determine that person's alcohol concentration.

(a1) (Expires December 1, 2016) Additional Scope. - This section applies to a person whose license was revoked as a result of a conviction of habitual impaired driving, G.S. 20-138.5.

(b) (Effective until December 1, 2016) Ignition Interlock Required. - Except as provided in subsection (l) of this section, when the Division restores the license of a person who is subject to this section, in addition to any other restriction or condition, it shall require the person to agree to and shall indicate on the person's drivers license the following restrictions for the period designated in subsection (c):

(1) A restriction that the person may operate only a vehicle that is equipped with a functioning ignition interlock system of a type approved by the Commissioner. The Commissioner shall not unreasonably withhold approval of an ignition interlock system and shall consult with the Division of Purchase and Contract in the Department of Administration to ensure that potential vendors are not discriminated against.

(2) A requirement that the person personally activate the ignition interlock system before driving the motor vehicle.

(3) An alcohol concentration restriction as follows:

a. If the ignition interlock system is required pursuant only to subdivision (a)(1) of this section, a requirement that the person not drive with an alcohol concentration of 0.04 or greater;

b. If the ignition interlock system is required pursuant to subdivision (a)(2) or (a)(3) of this section, or subsection (a1) of this section, a requirement that the person not drive with an alcohol concentration of greater than 0.00; or

c. If the ignition interlock system is required pursuant to subdivision (a)(1) of this section, and the person has also been convicted, based on the same set of circumstances, of: (i) driving while impaired in a commercial vehicle, G.S. 20-138.2, (ii) driving while less than 21 years old after consuming alcohol or drugs, G.S. 20-138.3, (iii) a violation of G.S. 20-141.4, or (iv) manslaughter or negligent homicide resulting from the operation of a motor vehicle when the offense involved impaired driving, a requirement that the person not drive with an alcohol concentration of greater than 0.00.

(b) (Effective December 1, 2016) Ignition Interlock Required. - Except as provided in subsection (l) of this section, when the Division restores the license of a person who is subject to this section, in addition to any other restriction or condition, it shall require the person to agree to and shall indicate on the person's drivers license the following restrictions for the period designated in subsection (c):

(1) A restriction that the person may operate only a vehicle that is equipped with a functioning ignition interlock system of a type approved by the Commissioner. The Commissioner shall not unreasonably withhold approval of an ignition interlock system and shall consult with the Division of Purchase and Contract in the Department of Administration to ensure that potential vendors are not discriminated against.

(2) A requirement that the person personally activate the ignition interlock system before driving the motor vehicle.

(3) An alcohol concentration restriction as follows:

a. If the ignition interlock system is required pursuant only to subdivision (a)(1) of this section, a requirement that the person not drive with an alcohol concentration of 0.04 or greater;

b. If the ignition interlock system is required pursuant to subdivision (a)(2) or (a)(3) of this section, a requirement that the person not drive with an alcohol concentration of greater than 0.00; or

c. If the ignition interlock system is required pursuant to subdivision (a)(1) of this section, and the person has also been convicted, based on the same set of circumstances, of: (i) driving while impaired in a commercial vehicle, G.S. 20-138.2, (ii) driving while less than 21 years old after consuming alcohol or drugs, G.S. 20-138.3, (iii) a violation of G.S. 20-141.4, or (iv) manslaughter or negligent homicide resulting from the operation of a motor vehicle when the offense involved impaired driving, a requirement that the person not drive with an alcohol concentration of greater than 0.00.

(c) Length of Requirement. - The requirements of subsection (b) shall remain in effect for:

(1) One year from the date of restoration if the original revocation period was one year;

(2) Three years from the date of restoration if the original revocation period was four years; or

(3) Seven years from the date of restoration if the original revocation was a permanent revocation.

(c1) Vehicles Subject to Requirement. - A person subject to this section shall have all registered vehicles owned by that person equipped with a functioning ignition interlock system of a type approved by the Commissioner. The Commissioner shall not issue a license to a person subject to this section until presented with proof of the installation of an ignition interlock system in all registered vehicles owned by the person. In order to avoid an undue financial hardship, a person subject to this section may seek a waiver from the Division for any vehicle registered to that person that is relied upon by another member of that person's family for transportation and that the vehicle is not in the possession of the person subject to this section. The Division shall determine such waiver on a case-by-case basis following an assessment of financial hardship to the person subject to this restriction. The Commissioner shall cancel the drivers license of any person subject to this section for registration of a motor vehicle owned by the person without an installed ignition interlock system or removal of the ignition interlock system from a motor vehicle owned by the person, other than when changing ignition interlock providers or upon sale of the vehicle.

(d) Effect of Limited Driving Privileges. - If the person was eligible for and received a limited driving privilege under G.S. 20-179.3, with the ignition interlock requirement contained in G.S. 20-179.3(g5), the period of time for which that limited driving privilege was held shall be applied towards the requirements of subsection (c).

(e) Notice of Requirement. - When a court reports to the Division a conviction of a person who is subject to this section, the Division must send the person written notice of the requirements of this section and of the consequences of failing to comply with these requirements. The notification must include a statement that the person may contact the Division for information on obtaining and having installed an ignition interlock system of a type approved by the Commissioner.

(f) Effect of Violation of Restriction. - A person subject to this section who violates any of the restrictions of this section commits the offense of driving while license revoked under G.S. 20-28(a) and is subject to punishment and license revocation as provided in that section. If a law enforcement officer has reasonable grounds to believe that a person subject to this section has consumed alcohol while driving or has driven while he has remaining in his body any alcohol previously consumed, the suspected offense of driving while license is revoked is an alcohol-related offense subject to the implied-consent provisions of G.S. 20-16.2. If a person subject to this section is charged with driving while license revoked by violating a condition of subsection (b) of this section, and a judicial official determines that there is probable cause for the charge, the person's license is suspended pending the resolution of the case, and the judicial official must require the person to surrender the license. The judicial official must also notify the person that he is not entitled to drive until his case is resolved. An alcohol concentration report from the ignition interlock system shall not be admissible as evidence of driving while license revoked, nor shall it be admissible in an administrative revocation proceeding as provided in subsection (g) of this section, unless the person operated a vehicle when the ignition interlock system indicated an alcohol concentration in violation of the restriction placed upon the person by subdivision (b)(3) of this section.

(g) Effect of Violation of Restriction When Driving While License Revoked Not Charged. - A person subject to this section who violates any of the restrictions of this section, but is not charged or convicted of driving while license revoked pursuant to G.S. 20-28(a), shall have the person's license revoked by the Division for a period of one year.

(h) Beginning of Revocation Period. - If the original period of revocation was imposed pursuant to G.S. 20-19(d) or (e), any remaining period of the original revocation, prior to its reduction, shall be reinstated and the revocation required by subsection (f) or (g) of this section begins after all other periods of revocation have terminated.

(i) Notification of Revocation. - If the person's license has not already been surrendered to the court, the Division must expeditiously notify the person that the person's license to drive is revoked pursuant to subsection (f) or (g) of this section effective on the tenth calendar day after the mailing of the revocation order.

(j) Right to Hearing Before Division; Issues. - If the person's license is revoked pursuant to subsection (g) of this section, before the effective date of the order issued under subsection (i) of this section, the person may request in writing a hearing before the Division. Except for the time referred to in G.S. 20-16.5, if the person shows to the satisfaction of the Division that the person's license was surrendered to the court and remained in the court's possession, then the Division shall credit the amount of time for which the license was in the possession of the court against the revocation period required by subsection (g) of this section. If the person properly requests a hearing, the person retains the person's license, unless it is revoked under some other provision of law, until the hearing is held, the person withdraws the request, or the person fails to appear at a scheduled hearing. The hearing officer may subpoena any witnesses or documents that the hearing officer deems necessary. The person may request the hearing officer to subpoena the charging officer, the chemical analyst, or both to appear at the hearing if the person makes the request in writing at least three days before the hearing. The person may subpoena any other witness whom the person deems necessary, and the provisions of G.S. 1A-1, Rule 45, apply to the issuance and service of all subpoenas issued under the authority of this section. The hearing officer is authorized to administer oaths to witnesses appearing at the hearing. The hearing must be conducted in the county where the charge was brought, except when the evidence of the violation is an alcohol concentration report from an ignition interlock system, the hearing may be conducted in the county where the person resides. The hearing must be limited to consideration of whether:

(1) The drivers license of the person had an ignition interlock requirement; and

(2) The person:

a. Was driving a vehicle that was not equipped with a functioning ignition interlock system; or

b. Did not personally activate the ignition interlock system before driving the vehicle; or

c. Drove the vehicle in violation of an applicable alcohol concentration restriction prescribed by subdivision (b)(3) of this section.

If the Division finds that the conditions specified in this subsection are met, it must order the revocation sustained. If the Division finds that the condition of subdivision (1) is not met, or that none of the conditions of subdivision (2) are met, it must rescind the revocation. If the revocation is sustained, the person must surrender the person's license immediately upon notification by the Division. If the revocation is sustained, the person may appeal the decision of the Division pursuant to G.S. 20-25.

(k) Restoration After Violation. - When the Division restores the license of a person whose license was revoked pursuant to subsection (f) or (g) of this section and the revocation occurred prior to completion of time period required by subsection (c) of this section, in addition to any other restriction or condition, it shall require the person to comply with the conditions of subsection (b) of this section until the person has complied with those conditions for the cumulative period of time as set forth in subsection (c) of this section. The period of time for which the person successfully complied with subsection (b) of this section prior to revocation pursuant to subsection (f) or (g) of this section shall be applied towards the requirements of subsection (c) of this section.

(l) Medical Exception to Requirement. - A person subject to this section solely for the reason set forth in subdivision (a)(1) of this section and who has a medically diagnosed physical condition that makes the person incapable of personally activating an ignition interlock system may request an exception to the requirements of this section from the Division. The Division shall not issue an exception to this section unless the person has submitted to a physical examination by two or more physicians or surgeons duly licensed to practice medicine in this State or in any other state of the United States and unless such examining physicians or surgeons have completed and signed a certificate in the form prescribed by the Division. Such certificate shall be devised by the Commissioner with the advice of those qualified experts in the field of diagnosing and treating physical disorders that the Commissioner may select and shall be designed to elicit the maximum medical information necessary to aid in determining whether or not the person is capable of personally activating an ignition interlock system. The certificate shall contain a waiver of privilege and the recommendation of the examining physician to the Commissioner as to whether the person is capable of personally activating an ignition interlock system.

The Commissioner is not bound by the recommendations of the examining physicians but shall give fair consideration to such recommendations in acting upon the request for medical exception, the criterion being whether or not, upon all the evidence, it appears that the person is in fact incapable of personally activating an ignition interlock system. The burden of proof of such fact is upon the person seeking the exception.

Whenever an exception is denied by the Commissioner, such denial may be reviewed by a reviewing board upon written request of the person seeking the exception filed with the Division within 10 days after receipt of such denial. The composition, procedures, and review of the reviewing board shall be as provided in G.S. 20-9(g)(4). This subsection shall not apply to persons subject to an ignition interlock requirement under this section for the reasons set forth in subdivision (a)(2) or (a)(3) of this section.

4.13 Suspension for Out-Of-State Convictions

Pursuant to N.C.G.S. §20-23, if DMV receives notice of a conviction of the person for an offense that would be grounds for suspension had the conviction occurred in North Carolina, DMV may revoke.

4.14 Validity of Out-of-State Licenses

If one's license or privilege to drive is suspended by the State of North Carolina, an out-of-state license is equally invalid within North Carolina. See N.C.G.S. §20-21.

4.15 Out-of-State Licensees

In the case of an out-of-state driver, the law enforcement officer has no legal authority to confiscate the out-of-state license. This is because the license remains the property of the home state of the driver, and while North Carolina may have the authority to suspend nonresident driving privileges, North Carolina has no authority to confiscate a license issued by another sovereign entity. North Carolina will confiscate the out of state license for the period of the civil revocation (see State v. Streckfuss 171 NC App 81). However, North Carolina has adopted an interstate driver license compact (referred to by DMV as the "Non-Resident Violator Compact") which requires the reporting of certain offenses as described below. The effect of this compact is that the licensee's home state will be aware of any restriction imposed by North Carolina, which will allow the home state both to suspend the driver's license pending resolution of the North Carolina infractions and implement their own punishment if they choose to do so.

Alaska, California, Michigan, Montana, Oregon and Wisconsin ***are not*** part of the compact.

N.C.G.S. §20-4.21 to 20-4.30–Adoption of Compact

The driver's license compact is entered into and enacted into law as follows:

Driver License Compact
Article I
Findings and Declaration of Policy

(a) The party states find that:

(1) The safety of their streets and highways is materially affected by the degree of compliance with state and local ordinances relating to the operation of motor vehicles.

(2) Violation of such a law or ordinance is evidence that the violator engages in conduct which is likely to endanger the safety of persons and property.

(3) The continuance in force of a license to drive is predicated upon compliance with laws and ordinances relating to the operation of motor vehicles, in whichever jurisdiction the vehicle is operated.

(b) It is the policy of each of the party states to:

(1) Promote compliance with the laws, ordinances and administrative rules and regulations relating to the operation of motor vehicles by their operators in each of the jurisdictions where such operators drive motor vehicles.

(2) Make the reciprocal recognition of licenses to drive and eligibility therefor more just and equitable by considering the overall compliance with motor vehicle laws, ordinances and administrative rules and regulations as a condition precedent to the continuance or issuance of any license by reason of which the licensee is authorized or permitted to operate a motor vehicle in any of the party states.

Article II
Definitions

As used in this compact:

(a) "State" means a state, territory or possession of the United States, the District of Columbia, or the Commonwealth of Puerto Rico.

(b) "Home state" means the state which has issued and has the power to suspend or revoke the use of the license or permit to operate a motor vehicle.

(c) "Conviction" means a conviction of any offense related to the use or operation of a motor vehicle which is prohibited by state law, municipal ordinance or administrative rule or regulation, or a forfeiture of bail, bond or other security deposited to secure appearance by a person charged with having committed any such offense, and which conviction or forfeiture is required to be reported to the licensing authority.

Article III
Reports of Conviction

The licensing authority of a party state shall report each conviction of a person from another party state occurring within its jurisdiction to the licensing authority of the home state of the licensee. Such report shall clearly identify the person convicted, describe the violation, specifying the section of the statute, code or ordinance violated, identify the court in which action was taken, indicate whether a plea of guilty or not guilty was entered, or the conviction was a result of the forfeiture of bail, bond or other security, and shall include any special findings made in connection therewith.

Article IV

Effect of Conviction

(a) The licensing authority in the home state, for the purposes of suspension, revocation or limitation of the license to operate a motor vehicle, shall give the same effect to the conduct reported, pursuant to article III of this compact, as it would if such conduct had occurred in the home state, in the case of convictions for:

(1) Manslaughter or negligent homicide resulting from the operation of a motor vehicle.

(2) Driving a motor vehicle while under the influence of intoxicating liquor or a narcotic drug or under the influence of any other drug to a degree which renders the driver incapable of safely driving a motor vehicle.

(3) Any felony in the commission of which a motor vehicle is used.

(4) Failure to stop and render aid in the event of a motor vehicle accident resulting in the death or personal injury of another.

(b) As to other convictions, reported pursuant to article III, the licensing authority in the home state shall give such effect to the conduct as is provided by the laws of the home state.

(c) If the laws of a party state do not provide for offenses or violations denominated or described in precisely the words employed in subdivision (a) of this article, such party state shall construe the denominations and descriptions appearing in subdivision (a) hereof as being applicable to and identifying those offenses or violations of a substantially similar nature and the laws of such party state shall contain such provisions as may be necessary to ensure that full force and effect is given to this article.

Article V

Applications for New Licenses

Upon application for a license to drive, the licensing authority in a party state shall ascertain whether the applicant has ever held, or is the holder of a license to drive issued by any other party state. The licensing authority in the state where application is made shall not issue a license to drive to the applicant if:

(1) The applicant has held such a license, but the same has been suspended by reason, in whole or in part, of a violation and if such suspension period has not terminated.

(2) The applicant has held such a license, but the same has been revoked by reason, in whole or in part, of a violation and if such revocation has not terminated, except that after the expiration of one year from the date the license was revoked, such person may make application for a new license if permitted by law. The licensing authority may refuse to issue a license to any such applicant if, after investigation, the licensing authority determines that it will not be safe to grant to such person the privilege of driving a motor vehicle on the public highways.

(3) The applicant is the holder of a license to drive issued by another party state and currently in force unless the applicant surrenders such license.

Article VI

Applicability of Other Laws

Except as expressly required by provisions of this compact, nothing contained herein shall be construed to affect the right of any party state to apply any of its other laws relating to licenses to drive to any person or circumstance nor to invalidate or prevent any driver license agreement or other cooperative arrangement between a party state and a non-party state.

Article VII

Compact Administrator

and Interchange of Information

(a) The head of the licensing authority of each party state shall be the administrator of this compact for his state. The administrators, acting jointly, shall have the power to formulate all necessary and proper procedures for the exchange of information under this compact.

(b) The administrator of each party state shall furnish to the administrator of each other party state any information or documents reasonably necessary to facilitate the administration of this compact.

Article VIII

Entry Into Force and Withdrawal

(a) This compact shall enter into force and become effective as to any state when it has enacted the same into law.

(b) Any party state may withdraw from this compact by enacting a statute repealing the same, but no such withdrawal shall take effect until six months after the executive head of the withdrawing state has given notice of the withdrawal to the executive heads of all other party states. No withdrawal shall affect the validity or applicability by the licensing authorities of states remaining party to the compact of any report of conviction occurring prior to the withdrawal.

Article IX
Construction and Severability

This compact shall be liberally construed so as to effectuate the purposes thereof. The provisions of this compact shall be severable and if any phrase, clause, sentence or provision of this compact is declared to be contrary to the constitution of any party state or of the United States or the applicability thereof to any government, agency, person or circumstance is held invalid, the validity of the remainder of this compact and the applicability thereof to any government, agency, person or circumstance shall not be affected thereby. If this compact shall be held contrary to the constitution of any state party thereto, the compact shall remain in full force and effect as to the remaining states and in full force and effect as to the state affected as to all severable matters.

4.16 DMV Driver Points System

DMV operates on a "points" system as defined under N.C.G.S. §20-16. Traffic violations carry points which are assessed against a motorist's license. There are several different levels that attorneys need to be aware of when representing clients in traffic cases. The Driver Point System is defined as follows:

§ 20-16. Authority of Division to suspend license.

(a) The Division shall have authority to suspend the license of any operator with or without a preliminary hearing upon a showing by its records or other satisfactory evidence that the licensee:

(1) through (4) Repealed by Session Laws 1979, c. 36;

(5) Has, under the provisions of subsection (c) of this section, within a three-year period, accumulated 12 or more points, or eight or more points in the three-year period immediately following the reinstatement of a license which has been suspended or revoked because of a conviction for one or more traffic offenses;

(6) Has made or permitted an unlawful or fraudulent use of such license or a learner's permit, or has displayed or represented as his own, a license or learner's permit not issued to him;

(7) Has committed an offense in another state, which if committed in this State would be grounds for suspension or revocation;

(8) Has been convicted of illegal transportation of alcoholic beverages;

(8a) Has been convicted of impaired instruction under G.S. 20-12.1;

(8b) Has violated on a military installation a regulation of that installation prohibiting conduct substantially similar to conduct that constitutes impaired driving under G.S. 20-138.1 and, as a result of that violation, has had his privilege to drive on that installation revoked or suspended after an administrative hearing authorized by the commanding officer of the installation and that commanding officer has general court martial jurisdiction;

(9) Has, within a period of 12 months, been convicted of (i) two or more charges of speeding in excess of 55 and not more than 80 miles per hour, (ii) one or more charges of reckless driving and one or more charges of speeding in excess of 55 and not more than 80 miles per hour, or (iii) one or more charges of aggressive driving and one or more charges of speeding in excess of 55 and not more than 80 miles per hour;

(10) Has been convicted of operating a motor vehicle at a speed in excess of 75 miles per hour on a public road or highway where the maximum speed is less than 70 miles per hour;

(10a) Has been convicted of operating a motor vehicle at a speed in excess of 80 miles per hour on a public highway where the maximum speed is 70 miles per hour; or

(11) Has been sentenced by a court of record and all or a part of the sentence has been suspended and a condition of suspension of the sentence is that the operator not operate a motor vehicle for a period of time.

However, if the Division revokes without a preliminary hearing and the person whose license is being revoked requests a hearing before the effective date of the revocation, the licensee retains his license unless it is revoked under some other provision of the law, until the hearing is held, the person withdraws his request, or he fails to appear at a scheduled hearing.

(b) Pending an appeal from a conviction of any violation of the motor vehicle laws of this State, no driver's license shall be suspended by the Division of Motor Vehicles because of such conviction or because of evidence of the commission of the offense for which the conviction has been had.

(c) The Division shall maintain a record of convictions of every person licensed or required to be licensed under the provisions of this Article as an operator and shall enter therein records of all convictions of such persons for any violation of the motor vehicle laws of this State and shall assign to the record of such person, as of the date of commission of the offense, a number of points for every such conviction in accordance with the following schedule of convictions and points, except that points shall not be assessed for convictions resulting in suspensions or revocations under other provisions of laws: Further, any points heretofore charged for violation of the motor vehicle inspection laws shall not be considered by the Division of Motor Vehicles as a basis for suspension or revocation of driver's license:

Schedule of Point Values	
Passing stopped school bus	5
Aggressive driving	5
Reckless driving	4
Hit and run, property damage only	4
Following too close	4
Driving on wrong side of road	4
Illegal passing	4
Failure to yield right-of-way to pedestrian pursuant to G.S. 20-158(b)(2)b.	4
Failure to yield right-of-way to bicycle, motor scooter, or motorcycle	4
Running through stop sign	3
Speeding in excess of 55 miles per hour	3
Failing to yield right-of-way	3
Running through red light	3
No driver's license or license expired more than one year	3
Failure to stop for siren	3
Driving through safety zone	3
No liability insurance	3
Failure to report accident where such report is required	3
Speeding in a school zone in excess of the posted schoolzone speed limit	3
Failure to properly restrain a child in a restraint or seat belt	2
All other moving violations	2
Littering pursuant to G.S. 14-399 when the littering involves the use of a motor vehicle	1

Schedule of Point Values for Violations While Operating a Commercial Motor Vehicle	
Passing stopped school bus	8
Rail-highway crossing violation	6
Careless and reckless driving in violation of G.S. 20-140(f	6
Speeding in violation of G.S. 20-141(j3	6
Aggressive driving	6
Reckless driving	5
Hit and run, property damage only	5
Following too close	5
Driving on wrong side of road	5
Illegal passing	5
Failure to yield right-of-way to pedestrian pursuant to G.S. 20-158(b)(2)b	5
Failure to yield right-of-way to bicycle, motor scooter, or motorcycle	5
Running through stop sign	4
Speeding in excess of 55 miles per hour	5
Failing to yield right-of-way	4
Running through red light	4
No driver's license or license expired more than one year	4
Failure to stop for siren	4
Driving through safety zone	4
No liability insurance	4
Failure to report accident where such report is required	4
Speeding in a school zone in excess of the posted school zone speed limit	4
Possessing alcoholic beverages in the passenger area of a commercial motor vehicle	4
All other moving violations	3
Littering pursuant to G.S. 14-399 when the littering involves the use of a motor vehicle	1

The above provisions of this subsection shall only apply to violations and convictions which take place within the State of North Carolina. The Schedule of Point Values for Violations While Operating a Commercial Motor Vehicle shall not apply to any commercial motor vehicle known as an "aerial lift truck" having a hydraulic arm and bucket station, and to any commercial motor vehicle known as a "line truck" having a hydraulic lift for cable, if the vehicle is owned, operated by or under contract to a public utility, electric or telephone membership corporation or municipality and used in connection with installation, restoration or maintenance of utility services.

No points shall be assessed for conviction of the following offenses:

- Overloads
- Over length
- Over width
- Over height
- Illegal parking
- Carrying concealed weapon
- Improper plates
- Improper registration
- Improper muffler
- Improper display of license plates or dealers' tags
- Unlawful display of emblems and insignia
- Failure to display current inspection certificate.

In case of the conviction of a licensee of two or more traffic offenses committed on a single occasion, such licensee shall be assessed points for one offense only and if the offenses involved have a different point value, such licensee shall be assessed for the offense having the greater point value.

Upon the restoration of the license or driving privilege of such person whose license or driving privilege has been suspended or revoked because of conviction for a traffic offense, any points that might previously have been accumulated in the driver's record shall be cancelled.

Whenever any licensee accumulates as many as seven points or accumulates as many as four points during a three-year period immediately following reinstatement of his license after a period of suspension or revocation, the Division may request the licensee to attend a conference regarding such licensee's driving record. The Division may also afford any licensee who has accumulated as many as seven points or any licensee who has accumulated as many as four points within a three-year period immediately following reinstatement of his license after a period of suspension or revocation an opportunity to attend a driver improvement clinic operated by the Division and, upon the successful completion of the course taken at the clinic, three points shall be deducted from the licensee's conviction record; provided, that only one deduction of points shall be made on behalf of any licensee within any five-year period.

When a license is suspended under the point system provided for herein, the first such suspension shall be for not more than 60 days; the second such suspension shall not exceed six months and any subsequent suspension shall not exceed one year.

Whenever the driver's license of any person is subject to suspension under this subsection and at the same time also subject to suspension or revocation under other provisions of laws, such suspensions or revocations shall run concurrently.

In the discretion of the Division, a period of probation not to exceed one year may be substituted for suspension or for any unexpired period of suspension under subsections (a)(1) through (a)(10a) of this section. Any violation of probation during the probation period shall result in a suspension for the unexpired remainder of the suspension period. Any accumulation of three or more points under this subsection during a period of probation shall constitute a violation of the condition of probation.

(d) Upon suspending the license of any person as authorized in this section, the Division shall immediately notify the licensee in writing and upon his request shall afford him an opportunity for a hearing, not to exceed 60 days after receipt of the request, unless a preliminary hearing was held before his license was suspended. Upon such hearing the duly authorized agents of the Division may administer oaths and may issue subpoenas for the attendance of witnesses and the production of relevant books and papers and may require a reexamination of the licensee. Upon such hearing the Division shall either rescind its order of suspension, or good cause appearing therefor, may extend the suspension of such license. Provided further upon such hearing, preliminary or otherwise, involving subsections (a)(1) through (a)(10a) of this section, the Division may for good cause appearing in its discretion substitute a period of probation not to exceed one year for the suspension or for any unexpired period of suspension. Probation shall mean any written agreement between the suspended driver and a duly authorized representative of the Division and such period of probation shall not exceed one year, and any violation of the probation agreement during the probation period shall result in a suspension for the unexpired remainder of the suspension period. The authorized agents of the Division shall have the same powers in connection with a preliminary hearing prior to suspension as this subsection provided in connection with hearings held after suspension. These agents shall also have the authority to take possession of a surrendered license on behalf of the Division if the suspension is upheld and the licensee requests that the suspension begin immediately.

(e) The Division may conduct driver improvement clinics for the benefit of those who have been convicted of one or more violations of this Chapter. Each driver attending a driver improvement clinic shall pay a fee of fifty dollars ($50.00).

(e1) Notwithstanding any other provision of this Chapter, if the Division suspends the license of an operator pursuant to subdivisions (a)(9), (a)(10), or (a)(10a) of this section, upon the first suspension only, a district court judge may allow the licensee a limited driving privilege or license for a period not to exceed 12 months, provided he has not been convicted of any other motor vehicle moving violation within the previous 12 months. The limited driving privilege shall be issued in the same manner and under the terms and conditions prescribed in G.S. 20-16.1(b)(1), (2), (3), (4), and (5).

(e2) If the Division revokes a person's drivers license pursuant to G.S. 20-17(a)(16), a judge may allow the licensee a limited driving privilege for a period not to exceed the period of revocation. The limited driving privilege shall be issued in the same manner and under the terms and conditions prescribed in G.S. 20-16.1(b)(1), (2), (3), (4), (5), and (g).

4.17 Commercial Driver's License Disqualifications

There are severe consequences for those who drive commercial vehicles if convicted of DWI. First, pursuant to N.C.G.S. §20-17.4, the Motor Vehicle Division will disqualify a person from driving a commercial vehicle for at least one year from the date a person is convicted of driving a commercial vehicle while under the influence of .04 or more or for a violation of any DWI or admin per se violation while operating a non-commercial vehicle.

§ 20-17.4. Disqualification to drive a commercial motor vehicle.

(a) One Year. - Any of the following disqualifies a person from driving a commercial motor vehicle for one year if committed by a person holding a commercial drivers license, or, when applicable, committed while operating a commercial motor vehicle by a person who does not hold a commercial drivers license:

(1) A first conviction of G.S. 20-138.1, driving while impaired, for a holder of a commercial drivers license that occurred while the person was driving a motor vehicle that is not a commercial motor vehicle.

(2) A first conviction of G.S. 20-138.2, driving a commercial motor vehicle while impaired.

(3) A first conviction of G.S. 20-166, hit and run.

(4) A first conviction of a felony in the commission of which a commercial motor vehicle was used or the first conviction of a felony in which any motor vehicle is used by a holder of a commercial drivers license.

(5) Refusal to submit to a chemical test when charged with an implied-consent offense, as defined in G.S. 20-16.2.

(6) A second or subsequent conviction, as defined in G.S. 20-138.2A(d), of driving a commercial motor vehicle after consuming alcohol under G.S. 20-138.2A.

(7) A civil license revocation under G.S. 20-16.5, or a substantially similar revocation obtained in another jurisdiction, arising out of a charge that occurred while the person was either operating a commercial motor vehicle or while the person was holding a commercial drivers license.

(8) A first conviction of vehicular homicide under G.S. 20-141.4 or vehicular manslaughter under G.S. 14-18 occurring while the person was operating a commercial motor vehicle.

(9) Driving a commercial motor vehicle during a period when the person's commercial drivers license is revoked, suspended, cancelled, or the driver is otherwise disqualified from operating a commercial motor vehicle.

(a1) Ten-Day Disqualification. - A person who is convicted for a first offense of driving a commercial motor vehicle after consuming alcohol under G.S. 20-138.2A is disqualified from driving a commercial motor vehicle for 10 days.

(b) Modified Life. - A person who has been disqualified from driving a commercial motor vehicle for a conviction or refusal described in subsection (a) who, as the result of a separate incident, is subsequently convicted of an offense or commits an act requiring disqualification under subsection (a) is disqualified for life. The Division may adopt guidelines, including conditions, under which a disqualification for life under this subsection may be reduced to 10 years.

(b1) Life Without Reduction. - A person is disqualified from driving a commercial motor vehicle for life, without the possibility of reinstatement after 10 years, if that person is convicted of a third or subsequent violation of G.S. 20-138.2, a fourth or subsequent violation of G.S. 20-138.2A, or if the person refuses to submit to a chemical test a third time when charged with an implied-consent offense, as defined in G.S. 20-16.2, that occurred while the person was driving a commercial motor vehicle.

(c) Life. - A person is disqualified from driving a commercial motor vehicle for life if that person either uses a commercial motor vehicle in the commission of any felony involving the manufacture, distribution, or dispensing of a controlled substance, or possession with intent to manufacture, distribute, or dispense a controlled substance or is the holder of a commercial drivers license at the time of the commission of any such felony.

(c1) Life. - A person shall be disqualified from driving a commercial motor vehicle for life, without the possibility of reinstatement, if that person has had a commercial drivers license reinstated in the past and is convicted of another major disqualifying offense as defined in 49 C.F.R. § 383.51(b).

(d) Less Than a Year. - A person is disqualified from driving a commercial motor vehicle for 60 days if that person is convicted of two serious traffic violations, or 120 days if convicted of three or more serious traffic violations, arising from separate incidents occurring within a three-year period, committed in a commercial motor vehicle or while holding a commercial drivers license. This disqualification shall be in addition to, and shall be served at the end of, any other prior disqualification. For purposes of this subsection, a "serious violation" includes violations of G.S. 20-140(f) and G.S. 20-141(j3).

(e) Three Years. - A person is disqualified from driving a commercial motor vehicle for three years if that person is convicted of an offense or commits an act requiring disqualification under subsection (a) and the offense or act occurred while the person was transporting a hazardous material that required the motor vehicle driven to be placarded.

(f) Revocation Period. - A person is disqualified from driving a commercial motor vehicle for the period during which the person's regular or commercial drivers license is revoked, suspended, or cancelled.

(g) Violation of Out-of-Service Order. - Any person convicted for violating an out-of-service order, except as described in subsection (h) of this section, shall be disqualified as follows:

(1) A person is disqualified from driving a commercial vehicle for a period of 90 days if convicted of a first violation of an out-of-service order.

(2) A person is disqualified for a period of one year if convicted of a second violation of an out-of-service order during any 10-year period, arising from separate incidents.

(3) A person is disqualified for a period of three years if convicted of a third or subsequent violation of an out-of-service order during any 10-year period, arising from separate incidents.

(h) Violation of Out-of-Service Order; Special Rule for Hazardous Materials and Passenger Offenses. - Any person convicted for violating an out-of-service order while transporting hazardous materials or while operating a commercial vehicle designed or used to transport more than 15 passengers, including the driver, shall be disqualified as follows:

(1) A person is disqualified for a period of 180 days if convicted of a first violation of an out-of-service order.

(2) A person is disqualified for a period of three years if convicted of a second or subsequent violation of an out-of-service order during any 10-year period, arising from separate incidents.

(i) Disqualification for Out-of-State Violations. - The Division shall withdraw the privilege to operate a commercial vehicle of any resident of this State or person transferring to this State upon receiving notice of the person's conviction or Administrative Per Se Notice in another state for an offense that, if committed in this State, would be grounds for disqualification, even if the offense occurred in another jurisdiction prior to being licensed in this State where no action had been taken at that time in the other jurisdiction. The period of disqualification shall be the same as if the offense occurred in this State.

(j) Disqualification of Persons Without Commercial Drivers Licenses. - Any person convicted of an offense that requires disqualification under this section, but who does not hold a commercial drivers license, shall be disqualified from operating a commercial vehicle in the same manner as if the person held a valid commercial drivers license.

(k) Disqualification for Railroad Grade Crossing Offenses. - Any person convicted of a violation of G.S. 20-142.1 through G.S. 20-142.5, when the driver is operating a commercial motor vehicle, shall be disqualified from driving a commercial motor vehicle as follows:

(1) A person is disqualified for a period of 60 days if convicted of a first violation of a railroad grade crossing offense listed in this subsection.

(2) A person is disqualified for a period of 120 days if convicted during any three-year period of a second violation of any combination of railroad grade crossing offenses listed in this subsection.

(3) A person is disqualified for a period of one year if convicted during any three-year period of a third or subsequent violation of any combination of railroad grade crossing offenses listed in this subsection.

(l) Disqualification for Testing Positive in a Drug or Alcohol Test. - Upon receipt of notice of a positive drug or alcohol test, or of refusal to participate in a drug or alcohol test, pursuant to G.S. 20-37.19(c), the Division must disqualify a CDL holder from operating a commercial motor vehicle for a minimum of 30 days and until receipt of proof of successful completion of assessment and treatment by a substance abuse professional in accordance with 49 C.F.R. § 382.503.

(m) Disqualifications of Drivers Who Are Determined to Constitute an Imminent Hazard. - The Division shall withdraw the privilege to operate a commercial motor vehicle for any resident of this State for a period of 30 days in accordance with 49 C.F.R. § 383.52.

(n) Disqualification for Conviction of Criminal Offense That Requires Registration Under the Sex Offender and Public Protection Registration Programs. - Effective December 1, 2009, except as otherwise provided by this subsection, a person convicted of a violation that requires registration under Article 27A of Chapter 14 of the General Statutes is disqualified from driving a commercial motor vehicle that requires a commercial drivers license with a P or S endorsement for the period of time during which the person is required to maintain registration under Article 27A of Chapter 14 of the General Statutes. If a person who is registered pursuant to Article 27A of Chapter 14 of the General Statutes on December 1, 2009, also has a valid commercial drivers license with a P or S endorsement that was issued on or before December 1, 2009, then the person is not disqualified under this subsection until that license expires, provided the person does not commit a subsequent offense that requires registration under Article 27A of Chapter 14 of the General Statutes.

(o) Disqualification for Passing Stopped School Bus. - Any person whose drivers license is revoked under G.S. 20-217 is disqualified from driving a commercial motor vehicle for the period of time in which the person's drivers license remains revoked under G.S. 20-217.

4.18 Commercial Driver's License Notification Requirements

Commercial license holders and applicants have certain notification requirements not just for DWI, but for other moving violations as well.

§ 20-37.18. Notification required by driver.

(a) Any driver holding a commercial driver license issued by this State who is convicted of violating any State law or local ordinance relating to motor vehicle traffic control in any other state, other than parking violations, shall notify the Division in the manner specified by the Division within 30 days of the date of the conviction.

(b) Any driver holding a commercial driver license issued by this State who is convicted of violating any State law or local ordinance relating to motor vehicle traffic control in this or any other state, other than parking violations, shall notify his employer in writing of the conviction within 30 days of the date of conviction.

(c) Any driver whose commercial driver license is suspended, revoked, or cancelled by any state, or who loses the privilege to drive a commercial motor vehicle in any state for any period, including being disqualified from driving a commercial motor vehicle, or who is subject to an out-of-service order, shall notify his employer of that fact before the end of the business day following the day the driver received notice of that fact.

(d) Any person who applies to be a commercial motor vehicle driver shall provide the employer, at the time of the application, with the following information for the 10 years preceding the date of application:

(1) A list of the names and addresses of the applicant's previous employers for which the applicant was a driver of a commercial motor vehicle;

(2) The dates between which the applicant drove for each employer; and

(3) The reason for leaving that employer.

The applicant shall certify that all information furnished is true and complete. Any employer may require an applicant to provide additional information.

4.19 Expungement of Motor Vehicle Record (MVR)

If a driver's license is suspended due to a violation of N.C.G.S. §20-138.1 (suspension for .08 or more), and the driver is later acquitted of the DWI charges, DMV is required to expunge the driver's motor vehicle record pursuant to N.C.G.S. §15A-146. The licensee must submit a copy of the court record indicating a dismissal or acquittal for the violation on which the suspension is based.

§ 15A-146. Expunction of records when charges are dismissed or there are findings of not guilty.

(a) If any person is charged with a crime, either a misdemeanor or a felony, or was charged with an infraction under G.S. 18B-302(i) prior to December 1, 1999, and the charge is dismissed, or a finding of not guilty or not responsible is entered, that person may apply to the court of the county where the charge was brought for an order to expunge from all official records any entries relating to his apprehension or trial. The court shall hold a hearing on the application and, upon finding that the person had not previously received an expungement under this section, G.S. 15A-145, 15A-145.1, 15A-145.2, 15A-145.3, 15A-145.4, or 15A-145.5, and that the person had not previously been convicted of any felony under the laws of the United States, this State, or any other state, the court shall order the expunction. No person as to whom such an order has been entered shall be held thereafter under any provision of any law to be guilty of perjury, or to be guilty of otherwise giving a false statement or response to any inquiry made for any purpose, by reason of his failure to recite or acknowledge any expunged entries concerning apprehension or trial.

(a1) Notwithstanding subsection (a) of this section, if a person is charged with multiple offenses and all the charges are dismissed, or findings of not guilty or not responsible are made, then a person may apply to have each of those charges expunged if the offenses occurred within the same 12-month period of time or if the charges are dismissed or findings are made at the same term of court. Unless circumstances otherwise clearly provide, the phrase "term of court" shall mean one week for superior court and one day for district court. There is no requirement that the multiple offenses arise out of the same transaction or occurrence or that the multiple offenses were consolidated for judgment. The court shall hold a hearing on the application. If the court finds (i) that the person had not previously received an expungement under this subsection, or that any previous expungement received under this subsection occurred prior to October 1, 2005 and was for an offense that occurred within the same 12-month period of time, or was dismissed or findings made at the same term of court, as the offenses that are the subject of the current application, (ii) that the person had not previously received an expungement under G.S. 15A-145, 15A-145.1, 15A-145.2, 15A-145.3, 15A-145.4, or 15A-145.5, and (iii) that the person had not previously been convicted of any felony under the laws of the United States, this State, or any other state, the court shall order the expunction. No person as to whom such an order has been entered shall be held thereafter under any provision of any law to be guilty of perjury, or to be guilty of otherwise giving a false statement or response to any inquiry made for any purpose, by reason of his failure to recite or acknowledge any expunged entries concerning apprehension or trial.

(b) The court may also order that the said entries, including civil revocations of drivers licenses as a result of the underlying charge, shall be expunged from the records of the court, and direct all law-enforcement agencies, the Division of Adult Correction of the Department of Public Safety, the Division of Motor Vehicles, and any other State or local government agencies identified by the petitioner as bearing record of the same to expunge their records of the entries, including civil revocations of drivers licenses as a result of the underlying charge being expunged. This subsection does not apply to civil or criminal charges based upon the civil revocation, or to civil revocations under G.S. 20-16.2. The clerk shall notify State and local agencies of the court's order as provided in G.S. 15A-150. The clerk shall forward a certified copy of the order to the Division of Motor Vehicles for the expunction of a civil revocation provided the underlying criminal charge is also expunged. The civil revocation of a drivers license shall not be expunged prior to a final disposition of any pending civil or criminal charge based upon the civil revocation. The costs of expunging the records, as required under G.S. 15A-150, shall not be taxed against the petitioner.

(b1) Any person entitled to expungement under this section may also apply to the court for an order expunging DNA records when the person's case has been dismissed by the trial court and the person's DNA record or profile has been included in the State DNA Database and the person's DNA sample is stored in the State DNA Databank. A copy of the application for expungement of the DNA record or DNA sample shall be served on the district attorney for the judicial district in which the felony charges were brought not less than 20 days prior to the date of the hearing on the application. If the application for expungement is granted, a certified copy of the trial court's order dismissing the charges shall be attached to an order of expungement. The order of expungement shall include the name and address of the defendant and the defendant's attorney and shall direct the North Carolina State Crime Laboratory to send a letter documenting expungement as required by subsection (b2) of this section.

(b2) Upon receiving an order of expungement entered pursuant to subsection (b1) of this section, the North Carolina State Crime Laboratory shall purge the DNA record and all other identifying information from the State DNA Database and the DNA sample stored in the State DNA Databank covered by the order, except that the order shall not apply to other offenses committed by the individual that qualify for inclusion in the State DNA Database and the State DNA Databank. A letter documenting expungement of the DNA record and destruction of the DNA sample shall be sent by the North Carolina State Crime Laboratory to the defendant and the defendant's attorney at the address specified by the court in the order of expungement.

(c) The clerk shall notify State and local agencies of the court's order as provided in G.S. 15A-150.

(d) A person charged with a crime that is dismissed pursuant to compliance with a deferred prosecution agreement or the terms of a conditional discharge and who files a petition for expunction of a criminal record under this section must pay the clerk of superior court a fee of one hundred seventy-five dollars ($175.00) at the time the petition is filed. Fees collected under this subsection are payable to the Administrative Office of the Courts. The clerk of superior court shall remit one hundred twenty-two dollars and fifty cents ($122.50) of each fee to the North Carolina Department of Public Safety for the costs of criminal record checks performed in connection with processing petitions for expunctions under this section. The remaining fifty-two dollars and fifty cents ($52.50) of each fee shall be retained by the Administrative Office of the Courts and used to pay the costs of processing petitions for expunctions under this section. This subsection does not apply to petitions filed by an indigent.

Chapter 5

Pre-Trial Investigations

Synopsis

5.1 Overview

No matter how many times you ask your client to describe the events of the investigation and arrest, no matter what you obtain in discovery, no matter how many photos you take of the scene, you were not there when the arrest and investigation took place. There will always be parties to the event and witnesses who will know details and subtle nuances that will escape your grasp. This is a fact of life for attorneys everywhere and in every line of criminal work. However, this does not mean that you cannot have an intimate knowledge of the facts and circumstances surrounding the investigation. This also does not mean that you cannot adequately prepare for trial. It simply means that you have to do the work to know your case before you try your case. You must take advantage of every opportunity to learn and catalog your investigatory findings.

5.2 Proper Filing Techniques

You cannot catalog your investigatory findings properly, unless your client file is organized. We have all seen attorneys walk into the courtroom with a "thin" file and no reference books on the day of trial. Clients, spectators and jurors have no idea what that means, but judges, attorneys and court staff all know that the attorney is unprepared. The "thin-file" attorneys have done little, if any, work on the case. They do, however, have one advantage over those of us who show up with a file and materials—they can find things easily. This section is meant to alleviate that disadvantage.

Organization is one of the keys to a successful defense. Information is useless if you cannot find it after you have collected it, so start organizing it the moment that you open the file because that is the easiest time to do it. There are as many different filing systems as there are attorneys. In fact, there are probably more systems than attorneys because most attorneys have started with one system and abandoned it in favor of another. If you are a newly-minted attorney and doubt that, just wait—you'll change one day, just like the rest of us.

Below is a good, basic system with a few simple tips. It will work for the basic case, right up to the most complex. However, the most complex may need to use banker boxes instead of individual file folders. Feel free to add, subtract or combine folders. Just remember that when you combine folders, you may lose some ability to quickly find what you need. Some attorneys prefer to use three-ring binders, but have the same strategy described below.

CLIENT INFORMATION FOLDER

Contents: Client biographical information, client intake form, retainer agreement.

PRE-TRIAL INTERVIEW FOLDER

Contents: All transcripts from all pre-trial interviews. Sometimes transcripts become too wieldy for a folder because of their size and need to be organized into more than one folder. Some attorneys prefer to have transcript folders for each person or event (i.e., "Deputy Ziffel Transcript" or "August 2nd Evidentiary Hearing").

DIVISION OF MOTOR VEHICLES

Contents: All DMV correspondence, briefs, decisions, orders, suspensions, revocations, etc. It is handy to have a list, on the left, of all actions regarding the client's license.

STATE'S MOTIONS FOLDER

Contents: All motions filed by the prosecution (chronological order with the oldest on bottom). Keep a list on the left side of the dates and descriptions of all filings.

DEFENSE MOTIONS FOLDER
Contents: All motions filed by the defense (chronological order with the oldest on bottom). Keep a list on the left side of the dates and descriptions of all filings.

PRIOR OFFENSES FOLDER
Contents: This may be divided into two segments if necessary: priors that the prosecutor alleges and priors unknown to the prosecutor.

POLICE REPORTS FOLDER
Contents: Complete police reports. Despite the fact that some parts of the police reports may also appear in other folders as duplicates, keep the entire report as disclosed.

COURT ORDERS
Contents: Court Orders.

GRAND JURY FOLDER
Contents: Grand Jury transcript, proposed indictment, actual indictment and summons.

ROADBLOCK FOLDER
Contents: All reports, notes, briefings and diagrams related to any roadblock or DWI checkpoint.

ACCIDENT REPORT FOLDER
Contents: Accident reports, Event Data Recorder (Black Box) disclosure.

BLOOD TEST FOLDER
Contents: Blood test results, chain of custody, chromatograms, maintenance logs, repair logs, bench notes and documentation for all calibrators, standards, controls and blanks.

BREATH TEST FOLDER
Contents: Breath test results, quality assurance documents, repair orders, and so on.

URINE TEST FOLDER
Contents: Urine test results, chain of custody, chromatograms, maintenance logs, repair logs, bench notes and documentation for all calibrators, standards, controls and blanks.

VICTIM FOLDER
Contents: Statements, restitution claims, investigatory materials regarding victim's history.

CORRESPONDENCE FOLDER
Contents: All correspondence. It may be helpful to have sub-categories with physical dividers to separate client correspondence from correspondence with prosecutors or expert witnesses, and so on.

EVIDENCE FOLDER
Contents: Photos, DVDs (put them in a protective sleeve), tapes, documents for trial, and so on. At times, there will be pieces of evidence too large to fit inside of a folder, such as your client's high-heeled shoes which were worn during FSTs, or even a vehicle's punctured tire. If something is too large to fit, simply keep a list of evidence in the folder and store the bulky items elsewhere.

EXPERT FOLDER
(Note that this folder can be for either defense or prosecution witnesses.) Contents: expert witness's curriculum vitae, statements, transcripts from prior testimony. Use as many folders as are necessary to accommodate all of the experts.

RESEARCH FOLDER
Contents: Case law, other research.

NOTES/WORK PRODUCT FOLDER
Contents: Trial notes, thoughts, ideas, and so on.

5.3 Visiting the Scene

Simply put: Go visit the scene! Do it quickly, before things change. Construction is a huge issue in some areas. Sometimes it seems as if new highways and loops spring up overnight. The conditions under which your client took field sobriety tests *will* change not only with construction, but also with weather. One only has to look at the differences in the area around the Gulf Coast before and after Hurricane Katrina to see major changes from a catastrophic weather event, but the simple growth and trimming of foliage may make a difference over time as well.

The more time that passes, the more difficult it will be to describe the scene to a jury. Ideally, you should visit the scene before you interview the police witnesses, so that you have first-hand knowledge of the scene. If you are not doing the investigation yourself, ensure that your investigator visits the scene. Drive the route that your client took leading to the arrest. Even if you have an investigator preparing the case, you should drive the route and visit the scene. If the arrest and investigation took place at night, it can beneficial to visit at nighttime and daytime.

Figure 5.1 *This photo is less desirable than that shown in Figure 5.2 because it fails to capture the traffic that may have been present during the stop.*

Figure 5.2 *Highway photo with traffic.*

Figure 5.3 *This roadway appears to be level in this photo, but see Figure 5.4.*

Figure 5.4 *The level and soda can show just how sloped this roadway really is.*

5.4 Photography and Videos

With digital photography and color printers so readily available, there is no excuse for not taking photographs at the scene when you visit. Even if you choose not to use the photographs, they will help you understand how the investigation took place. Consider bringing a digital recorder to record the sound of passing traffic. You might not be able to lay the proper foundation for admissibility, but then again, your investigator with a sound meter in hand might. One thing is for sure: if you do not create the photos, videos and sound recordings, you will not be able to introduce them at trial.

If your client drove a long and winding roadway with no traffic violations other than, perhaps, an inoperative taillight, video the route over which your client traveled. Then point out to the jury that no one who was impaired could have traversed the roadway with no moving violations.

If your client was stopped by the side of the interstate highway or on a well-traveled state highway, be sure that the photographs have a semi-tractor trailer in them. In other words, do not wait for a period of time when there is no traffic passing in order to take your photo (see Figures 5.1 and 5.2).

You need to show the real conditions under which your client took the FSTs. The prosecutor will always argue that you cannot prove that a semi-truck passed during field sobriety tests. He may be right, but the prosecutor cannot prove that one did not pass by and affect the tests. Moreover, many police will testify that trucks passed the location on the interstate. Your client or a passenger in the car may be able to testify that trucks were passing.

Have your investigator take photographs of any slope where your client performed the FSTs. Use a six-foot or eight-foot level in the photograph to show the jury how a level plane would appear (see Figures 5.3 and 5.4).

Another interesting technique is to record your investigator while he places a basketball on the ground and releases it. If a slope is present, the ball will roll away (see Figures 5.5, 5.6, and 5.7).

Figure 5.5 *Ball at rest.*

Figure 5.6 *Ball beginning to roll.*

Figure 5.7 *Ball far away.*

5.5 Diagrams and Aerial Photography

Scale diagrams are usually preferable to non-scale diagrams drawn in the courtroom. Aerial photography is quite cheap so long as you are not hiring someone to do the actual photography. Virtually every county has aerial photographs of every section of the county. They are available for minimal cost and are sometimes free for the asking. Check with your local county or city planning and zoning office for photographs. Aerial photography is also available online through various sources. However, the advantages to purchasing aerial photographs from a governmental agency over an Internet source are that the governmental agency can often supply a high-quality photograph, the photographs can generally be purchased already enlarged, and they may carry an official declaration of authenticity which would provide an alternative method of admission as an exhibit.

Often, locally available aerial photographs will have street names superimposed on the photograph. It then becomes very easy to mount the photograph on foam-core and present it to the jury. The exhibit will look very professional and can be drawn upon by the witness. If they do not have street names superimposed, do it yourself. Print mailing labels from your computer with street names in bold, easy-to-read print and label the photo yourself (be sure your witness can lay the proper foundation). Consider labeling buildings and familiar landmarks prior to trial to make it easier to identify. A path of travel of an automobile can be diagramed in red. In fact, sometimes it is easier to prepare the diagram completely beforehand and simply have the witness testify to the events using the exhibit, rather than having the witness draw on the exhibit before the jury. This also removes the potential for the witness to misidentify the particulars of the diagram or photograph. Be sure to work with the witness and the exhibit in detail before she takes the stand.

Google Earth© is a tremendously helpful resource. Many times, highly detailed photos and maps are available. Since they are digital images, they can be cut and pasted right into a slide presentation for the jury. Street-level views are also available in many parts of the country. Remember, however, that such images are still subject to the traditional rules of admissibility. Unless you can stipulate to admission, you will have to have a witness lay the foundation for admissibility. If you are planning on using an image in a slide presentation in closing, be sure to have a hard-copy for admission as an exhibit. Also, be sure that if you do use an image in a slide presentation that has been admitted, you have not altered it from the admitted image when you use it on the big screen. Whether you can use a "zoom" image to enlarge small details is a question for the court to decide. A prosecutor may certainly object to the image, but you can quell that argument before it even starts by simply announcing that you are going to zoom in on a particular detail of the image.

PRACTICE TIP: When you get the aerial photograph, look carefully for cars in the photograph. Sometimes one can identify a vehicle making the same traffic mistake (like a wide turn or driving the wrong way on a one-way street) as the one made by your client.

5.6 Accident Reconstruction

You cannot do it yourself unless you are an accident reconstructionist. Even then, you shouldn't do it yourself because you will end up being a witness. Hire a knowledgeable and competent accident reconstructionist. Check out the reconstructionist's background. Ask other attorneys about their experiences with the reconstructionist. Interview that person. Get transcripts from prior testimony. Good accident reconstructionists aren't cheap, and cheap accident reconstructionists aren't good. Be sure to discuss fees and costs with your client.

In court, consider using model cars to have your accident reconstructionist witness describe how the accident occurred. One-eighteenth scale, die-cast metal model cars are inexpensive and just the right size to be handled by a witness and to be seen by jurors several feet away. The cars can be used to show point of impact, how the vehicle moved and many other things as well. One-eighteenth scale models are available for most years, makes and models of real cars. Even where the exact type of car is unavailable as a scale model, a similar one may be used to show vehicle movement as an illustration to a jury. The drawback, of course, is that such testimony does not translate well into a written record for appellate purposes.

Driver Identification

Whether the accused can be proven to be the driver may be an issue. Accident reconstruction will include not just physical evidence, but also observations of eyewitnesses, if any. Witnesses may include other drivers and pedestrians. Emergency personnel can be witnesses to post-accident evidence of driving and may have heard statements about driving.

Physical evidence may include DNA, blood, hair, and fingerprint analysis. Airbags can be examined for traces of blood and DNA to prove who was sitting in the driver or passenger seat. In many vehicles the passenger-side airbag will not deploy if no one is sitting in the passenger seat. A head-strike on a windshield will often leave hair, skin, and blood stuck in the windshield. A corresponding, or inconsistent, injury to the occupant may be noted. Likewise, other occupant injuries should be noted to be either consistent or inconsistent with placement in the vehicle. Impressions of the driver's footwear may be left on the brake, gas, or clutch pedals. Likewise, impressions of the pedals may be left on the driver's footwear. Even clothing may be fused onto a seat.

"Pattern injury" from striking the steering wheel may be left on the driver's chest. Although fingerprints from the driver may be left on the steering wheel or other control surfaces, if the driver was a passenger in his own car at the time of the accident, his prints would likely be present anyway. Fingerprints of another occupant on control surfaces may provide evidence that another person was driving. Brake pedals, although they seem very strong to the average driver, can actually break off during an accident due to the force of the driver's leg on it. Likewise, the driver's leg and foot may sustain injuries consistent with such an event.

Seatbelt marks or trauma can be powerful evidence as to the location of the occupants. A mark from the left shoulder across the chest and down to the right hip would indicate the person was in the driver seat, while the opposite mark would indicate that the person was in the passenger seat. Injuries to the knees may be present from striking the underside of the dashboard. Some vehicles are equipped with knee-airbags as well.

Just about any interior surface of the car can cause injury to an occupant and leave marks on the occupant's body. Because of the set-up of the interior, door handles may leave marks on either the right or left side of the body, depending on the position of the occupant. Interior mirrors may be broken, leaving valuable trace evidence. Impressions of teeth could be left on softer surfaces. Multiple small lacerations (called "dicing") may be the result of window glass imploding.

Simple logic also plays a role in determining the position of the occupants. Is the car equipped with a standard or automatic transmission? If the car involved is equipped with a standard transmission and the accused driver does not know how to drive a car with a standard transmission, that fact may be the key to reasonable doubt. Seat position is also another common-sense piece of evidence that may be overlooked. Is the accused driver 5'0" tall? Was the driver seat positioned for someone 6'6" tall?

Evidence obtained outside of the car may be available, such as gas receipts for a fill-up moments before the accident. Traffic-camera videos or security cameras from nearby businesses or residences may be available. Don't overlook the fact that witnesses may have whipped out a cell-phone and started filming the aftermath of the accident. Such evidence may be valuable both to show who was driving and how the accident occurred.

Speed

Speed is often the main focus of an accident-reconstruction analysis. A moving vehicle has "kinetic energy" which is dependent upon the vehicle's mass and speed. When brakes are applied, the kinetic energy of the car is converted to heat energy produced by friction. When the car is brought to a complete stop, most of the kinetic energy has been transferred to the brakes and dissipated in the form of heat. In fact, on some race cars, the brake discs can be seen glowing cherry-red as they enter a corner and brake. This is an extreme example of kinetic energy being converted to heat as the car slows.

In addition to the brakes, some of the kinetic energy of a car being brought to a stop is transferred via tire friction with the roadway which is why skid-mark analysis is important. The smallest transfer is through wind-drag and is negligible.

Another way to transfer kinetic energy is when a car collides with another object. The object, be it another vehicle, a wall, a pole, farm animal, or a pedestrian absorbs some or all of that kinetic energy and helps to slow or stop the vehicle.

"Crush damage analysis" is the term used when the deformation of vehicles is measured in an attempt to determine speed. NHTSA does extensive crash-testing of vehicles at different speeds and sometimes comparison of real-life crush damage can be used to help determine speed, but a myriad of other factors have to be taken into account. For example, the crush damage from the NHTSA tests were retrieved from vehicles at specific speeds, striking objects at specific angles. Rotation of the vehicle must be known for a more accurate analysis. Approach angles, especially of turning vehicles, must be accounted for in the analysis.

"Yaw" is the vehicle slipping or skidding sideways out of a turn. The vehicle's attachment to the ground is through the "tire patch." A "tire patch" is the area of contact between the tire and the ground. Many things affect the size of tire patch such as inflation of the tire, size of the tire, camber, and movement of the vehicle. In a car, there are four tire patches. No matter what else occurs, there is a definite limit on the available friction from the tire patch. In a drag race car, the rear tires are specially suited to deliver as much grip as possible to forward motion produced by the engine. Drag race tires are notoriously bad at cornering and braking. On the other hand, circle-track race cars have a component built in to them to allow good grip while cornering. Normal, everyday passenger car tires have been engineered to factor in grip devoted to acceleration, braking, and cornering along with overall tread-wear economics. Although the equation may be complex, the principle is simple: if a tire is both accelerating and cornering, it has to divide the available grip (or friction) between the two forces.

Skid marks (or lack of skid marks) have to be taken into consideration in a reconstruction analysis. Police accident reconstructionists are fond of measuring road surface friction with a drag sled and determining speed based on the distance of skid marks without taking into account vehicle weight. Simple physics will tell you that a 3,000 lb. vehicle and a 6,000 lb. vehicle traveling at the same speeds with the same tires will leave differing length skid marks when their brakes are locked up. Did the vehicle become airborne at any point? No skid marks will be left by a vehicle vaulting into the air.

Things to take into consideration when a drag sled is used are that, during measurement, the bouncing of thee drag sled may produce considerable uncertainty in the measurement. Multiple measurements must be made to ensure reproducibility of measurements. Like any measuring device, anything used to measure friction must be properly calibrated.

Vehicle lighting may be an important issue as well. What position was the light switch in at the time of the in-

Figure 5.8 *Light bulb with deformed filament. Photo by Ken Dagostino*

Figure 5.9 *Light bulb with normal filament.*

vestigation? Certainly a light switch could be moved during or after the accident, but it is an important piece of the puzzle that could produce reasonable doubt. The filaments in light bulbs will deform if they are struck while they are on because the filament will deform when it is struck while hot. Thus, examination of the headlights, taillights or brake lights may be important. For example, in figure 5.8 below, we can see that the filament in the bulb is deformed. This is because it was still on while it was being struck. If the filament was not hot when it was struck, there would be no deformation as in figure 5.9. Note that a filament may still deform if it is off, but still very hot as it is being struck—usually within less than four seconds of it being on.

5.7 Event Data Recorders (Black Boxes)

Event Data Recorders (EDR) or "black boxes" are computer data-recording devices which record the last few seconds of vehicle movement data prior to a crash. Unlike aircraft black boxes which are typically orange in color, automobile black boxes are, actually, black (or unpainted metal). Also, unlike aircraft black boxes, those contained inside of an automobile do not record voices.

Most black boxes are located inside of the passenger compartment underneath the driver's seat. They are connected to sensors and other computer modules located throughout the vehicle. Black boxes will "fix" or "lock in" data under certain circumstances and cannot be rewritten. Once the data is locked, the black box can be downloaded and has a feature which will allow a person to determine how many times the data has been accessed since the data was locked.

Removing or disconnecting a black box will typically render the vehicle inoperable. Sensors placed throughout the vehicle sense when forward velocity changes rapidly as when in a crash. If the velocity change is great enough, it activates the recording feature. If the change in forward velocity is not great enough to activate the data recording feature, it will record nothing. Thus, your client could have been driving at speeds well in excess of 100 miles per hour, taking turns like a Formula One race car driver and if she never crashes, the black box will not have recorded anything. The data recording feature is governed by a "sensing algorithm," which is a calculation based upon data received from all of the sensors. If the parameters of the calculation are met, the black box records and stores data from the sensors. If the parameters of the calculation are not met, it will not record data. See Figure 5.10. Black boxes only record two types of crash events: Non-Deployment Events and Deployment Events. There are only two types of recorded data: Pre-Crash Data and Crash Data.

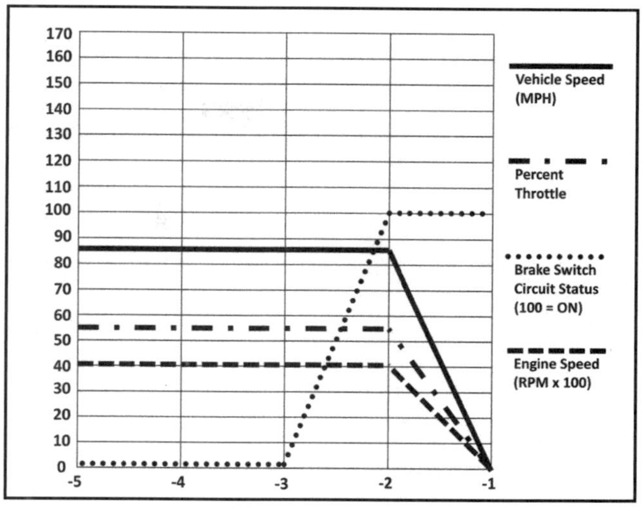

Figure 5.10 *Pre-crash data showing four parameters (vehicle speed, percent throttle, brake switch status and engine speed) over the last 5 seconds prior to a Deployment or Non-Deployment Event. This graph must be read in conjunction with other charts indicating system status.*

1. Non-Deployment Event. A Non-Deployment Event is an event severe enough to activate the sensing algorithm but not severe enough to deploy the air bag(s). It contains both Pre-Crash and Crash Data. The data module can store only one Non-Deployment Event. The stored event will be overwritten by an event that has a greater vehicle forward velocity change (i.e., a worse crash). With most black boxes, the recorded event will be cleared (not "overwritten") by the black box after the ignition has been turned on and off ("cycled") 250 times.
2. Deployment Event. The Deployment Event data will contain both Pre-Crash and Crash Data. The black box can store up to two different Deployment Events, if they occur within 5 seconds of one another. Deployment Events cannot be overwritten or cleared from the black box. Once the black box has deployed the air bag, the black box itself must be replaced. The Pre-Crash Data in the non-deployment file will be "fixed" or "locked" after a deployment, if the Non-Deployment Event occurs within 5 seconds prior to the deployment.

The black box does not sense a "crash" in terms of contact with another vehicle or fixed object. Starting with the triggering event, it senses a crash by recording the change in forward velocity over time, but not the speed that the vehicle was traveling before the event. It also does not sense the "Barrier Equivalent Velocity" (BEV) which is the energy required to produce the damage associated with an impact. The black box is not the infallible cornucopia of irrefutable data that some police investigators would like to claim that it is. The black box data is one piece of evidence that should be examined in conjunction with other available physical evidence from the vehicle and scene when assessing occupant or vehicle forward velocity change.

Certain limitations of the black box have to be kept in mind. For example, the crash may be so severe as to damage the black box itself. It is possible that the entire event may not have been recorded in this instance, but the black box should indicate whether the data from the recorded event has been fully written to the black box memory or if it has been interrupted and not fully written. If power to the black box is lost during a crash event, all or part of the crash record may not be recorded. A "Data Invalid" message may appear where the black box does not receive a valid message.

Black boxes have several status indicators which can record the status of the brake switch circuit (i.e., when did the driver step on the brake pedal) and a driver's seatbelt switch circuit which indicates whether the driver's seatbelt was latched. Be aware that a crash could sever either of these connections.

System Status At Non-Deployment

SIR Warning Lamp Status	OFF
Driver's Belt Switch Circuit Status	BUCKLED
Ignition Cycles At Non-Deployment	77
Ignition Cycles At Investigation	79
Maximum SDM Recorded Velocity Change (MPH)	-2.72
Algorithm Enable to Maximum SDM Recorded Velocity Change (msec)	52.5
Event Recording Complete	YES
Multiple Events Associated With This Record	NO
One Or More Associated Events Not Recorded	NO

This chart shows the system status prior to the Deployment Event. "SDM" is the Sensing Diagnostic Module or "black box." "SIR" is the acronym for "Supplemental Inflatable Restraint" or "airbags." Note that when the airbag lamp is off, the system is ready.

The recorded vehicle speed accuracy can be affected if the vehicle has had the tire size or the final drive axle ratio changed from the factory build specifications. If the vehicle is not on the ground, vehicle speed may be inaccurate.

The black box measures data both internally and externally. All data is measured, calculated, and stored internally, except for: vehicle speed, engine speed (RPM), and percent throttle data which are transmitted once per second by the Powertrain Control Module (PCM). The PCM governs engine and transmission functions.

The brake switch circuit status data is transmitted once per second by either the Anti-Lock Braking System (ABS) module or the PCM. In many vehicles, the driver's seatbelt switch circuit is wired directly to the black box. However, in some vehicles, the driver's seatbelt switch circuit status data is transmitted from the Body Control Module (BCM). The BCM controls various non-powertrain functions such as power windows, anti-theft devices and environmental controls.

Not all black boxes are created equal. For example. The Ford module may store 25 seconds of 16-parameter data continually as long as the vehicle's ignition switch is in the "on" position. If a deployment or near-deployment event occurs, the Airbag Control Module (ACM) will send a Restraint Deployment Signal (RDS) to the PCM. The PCM will then lock in the 20 seconds of pre-crash data already stored in its flash memory. It will then record another 5 seconds of post-crash data. The captured data will be locked in the flash memory for a significant number of ignition cycles before it is overwritten.

With all of the information recorded, the black box data is clearly something that the police would want to examine in the course of an accident investigation. The defense should be concerned in regards to privacy and ownership issues. For example: the vehicle owner certainly owns the black box, but who owns the data? If the owner of the vehicle was not the driver involved in the crash, what privacy interest does the driver have? Can the rights of the owner of the vehicle trump the rights of the driver?

Search Warrants & Data Retrieval

While legal retrieval of the data may be complicated, the physical retrieval of the data is a simple affair. If the vehicle's electrical system is intact after the collision, download is achieved through the vehicle's Data Link Connector (DLC). The DLC is the same port used by emissions testing facilities to gather emissions data and also by mechanics to check error and diagnostic codes. If the electrical system is not intact, then the module, itself, can be accessed by removing the data cable which connects it to the vehicle and plugging in a cable to retrieve the data.

Most software systems will record whether data has been accessed previously. The Bosch software requires the input of the investigator's name, a case number, investigation date, and crash date, which will become part of the final downloaded data. The Ford/Bosch software even has a "privacy question" built into its version of the data retrieval software that must be answered before data is downloaded: "Do you have written permission from the owner of this vehicle to collect data or other legal authority such as a subpoena or search warrant?"

Certainly, data can be retrieved via a search warrant, but like any other warrant, it can only be issued based upon probable cause. It is highly unlikely that there would be any exigent circumstances that would ever allow police to access the data because it is facing imminent destruction. Typically, where data is sought in an investigation, the vehicle has already been impounded by police and is being stored at a secure facility.

Manufacturer's Obligations

Where the police seek to retrieve data, the vehicle manufacturer does not necessarily have to supply their own proprietary software necessary to decode it. However, that is becoming an increasingly irrelevant issue.

A company called Vertronix began making software used to download and interpret data. They began their relationship with General Motors (GM) in 1984 and developed the first event data retrieval system in 1990 (GM only). The system became available to the public in 2000. Ford then contracted with Vertronix and in 2003 the system became available for Ford products. Bosch purchased Vertronix and now supplies software and hardware necessary to download and interpret various makes of vehicles including: Oldsmobile, Saturn, Hummer, Saab, Mercury, Lincoln, Chrysler, Dodge, Jeep, Mitsubishi, Isuzu, Sterling Corporation, Suzuki, and others.

Admissibility of Data & Expert Testimony

Like any data produced from a computerized device, the admissibility of data from a black box is subject to the Rules of Evidence, statutes, and case law. Assumptions which are made from the data will also be subject to certain rules of admissibility, especially if they are scientific in nature.

One of the chief areas of attack of the black box is its ability to accurately measure and record data. If we think of this in terms of another scientific instrument commonly used in DWI cases, the point becomes clear. If we have a case with a breath testing device, we can look at calibration and maintenance history of a specific device used in a specific case. We can look at a specific history of calibration checks both before and after a breath test to determine whether it was working within proper parameters. If the breath testing device has a computer memory, we can look at other subject tests for errors as well. However, this is impossible to do with a black box.

Once the black box has commanded the airbags to deploy, the data is fixed in the memory. No other data exists to compare with the fixed crash data. We have no way of knowing whether it was calibrated properly because there are no calibration checks. Moreover, the sensing devices which sent signals to the black box, causing it to command the airbag deployment, may have been damaged in the collision. Realistically, the closest we can get to checking the accuracy of the data is to rely on the manufacturer's and government information on crash tests done on identical vehicles equipped with identical black boxes (note that in 2011, General Motors, alone, had at least 20 different black box modules in use).

If we go back to the breath testing analogy, it would be as if a breath test was given on a device with no maintenance or calibration history, that had never been used before, and that was destroyed right after it printed the breath test result. Instead of having such information, you only have information from the manufacturer and government which says that identical models of the breath testing device worked properly and accurately when tested. If courts would not admit the results of a breath test under these conditions, then it should not admit the data from a black box under the same circumstances. Consider other devices such as RADAR and LIDAR. Without any indication that these devices were calibrated and functioning properly, speed readings would be inadmissible as well. Yet, courts seem to have few problems admitting the results of a device which cannot be tested and has no history.

For example, in the Massachusetts appellate case *Commonwealth v. Zimmermann Michelle M.*, 70 Mass. App. Ct. 357, 873 N.E.2d 1215 (2007 Mass. App.) the court took testimony of an expert who had conducted 200 tests on black boxes, had taught and published on the subject, and had testified as an expert on black boxes in other states. The expert testified that the technology behind the black box had been known for many years; that he and others had tested the speed of motor vehicles by other methods to compare information provided by black boxes and had found them to be reliable. Without any foundation, however, the expert also testified that black boxes need no maintenance and calibration for ten years.

The expert's calculations based on the physical and other evidence in this case were consistent with the black box data from the vehicle. Despite the fact that this was a vehicular homicide case, the accused presented no opposing expert testimony at the motion hearing and the judge ruled that evidence from the black box met the standard of admissibility set forth in Massachusetts law.

Black box data has been admissible throughout most of the country under the *Frye* and *Daubert* standards. See;

Matos v. State of Florida, 899 So.2d 403 (Fla. Dist. Ct. App. 2005); *State of New Jersey v. Shabazz*, 400 N.J. Super. 203, 946 A.2d 626 (N.J. Super. Ct. Law Div. 2005); *People v. Slade*, 2005 N.Y. Misc. Lexis 3217; 233 N.Y.L.J. 11). One New York court even refused to hold an admissibility hearing, finding that the admissibility of the data was so obvious as to not require a hearing (*People v. Christmann*, 776 N.Y.S. 2d 437, (N.Y.J. Ct. 2004)).

5.8 Roadblock (a.k.a. "DWI Checkpoint") Investigations

There is no excuse for a police agency not to have full and complete documentation regarding any roadblock that they created. Anyone, including the police, who want to block off a public roadway have to get permission from local governmental agencies. At the very least, fire department and ambulance providers will have to be notified so that they can make arrangements for travel through or around the affected area. Safety of the officers, observers and the public must be taken into account. Plans must be drawn up and approved prior to the implementation of the roadblock. Signage must be documented and approved. The police will have to plan for an area where suspects can be administered field sobriety tests and, possibly, on-site chemical tests. Prisoner holding areas must be designated and transportation must be arranged for both arrestees and passengers who cannot drive the vehicle. Parking and vehicle storage areas must be designated, or tow truck arrangements must be made. But, what does all of this mean to the defense attorney? The simple, one-word answer is: *discovery*.

There should be a detailed and comprehensive list of every person involved in the roadblock. The chain of command will start with the person in charge of the entire roadblock. Sub-commanders may be assigned to various details such as approaching vehicles and greeters (officers who make first-contact with the public). The officers who make first contact will also often have designated personnel to move suspect vehicles off the roadway if the driver is detained for further investigation. Watch for the situation where a driver is identified as a suspected drunk driver and is then asked to drive her car to a designated location and park it pending further investigation. The obvious issue for attack is: if the officer really believed that the person was such a danger that she should be removed from the roadway for an investigation, she shouldn't have been directed to drive anywhere by the officer.

There may be a DWI investigation sub-commander who is in charge of the officers who are conducting the DWI investigations on those suspects who are detained by the greeters. The sub-commander may also be responsible for chemical testing and prisoner detention.

Police will often have "chase vehicles" as well to deal with people who do not stop for the roadblock or who avoid it. When a driver avoids a roadblock, police will often follow that driver for some period of time to make a traffic stop for any actual or "suspected" traffic violation. In many instances, the "suspected" traffic violation is nothing more than the officer's desire to stop anyone who avoids a roadblock.

Moreover, because a roadblock is an intrusion upon the liberty of the public, strict guidelines have to be met by the law enforcement agency running the roadblock. Often, there will be a sub-commander who is in charge of the traffic flow, signage and permits from local governmental agencies. Diagrams are an integral part of the set-up procedures. Aerial photos of the area may also be available and part of the plan. See Figure 5.11.

To justify a roadblock, the police must have statistics which show that a roadblock is necessary (see Figure 5.12). Such statistics are often presented to the participating personnel in the form of a pre-checkpoint briefing and are kept to justify the roadblock in later court proceedings when challenged by the defense. It is often a simple matter of asking for such discovery to get the entire briefing material.

Because everything should be well-documented and planned, the police agency may have virtually everything that you need in terms of investigating the driving, area for field sobriety tests, witness lists and chemical testing. Moreover, by virtue of the fact that it is a roadblock and not a random traffic stop, more than one arrest may have taken place at the same location. If you can find out the names of the other arrestees and talk to them, you may be able to see trends in arrest procedures and defects in police investigations. Be sure to find out, however, if the other arrestees are represented before you speak to them about the roadblock.

Finally, be aware that many law enforcement agencies also conduct a post-checkpoint debriefing to discuss the success of the checkpoint, problems and suggestions for future checkpoints.

In North Carolina, our general statutes operate to show how a roadblock or checking station should be set up. The statute is reprinted below.

§ 20-16.3A. Checking stations and roadblocks.

(a) A law-enforcement agency may conduct checking stations to determine compliance with the provisions of this Chapter. If the agency is conducting a checking station for the purposes of determining compliance with this Chapter, it must:

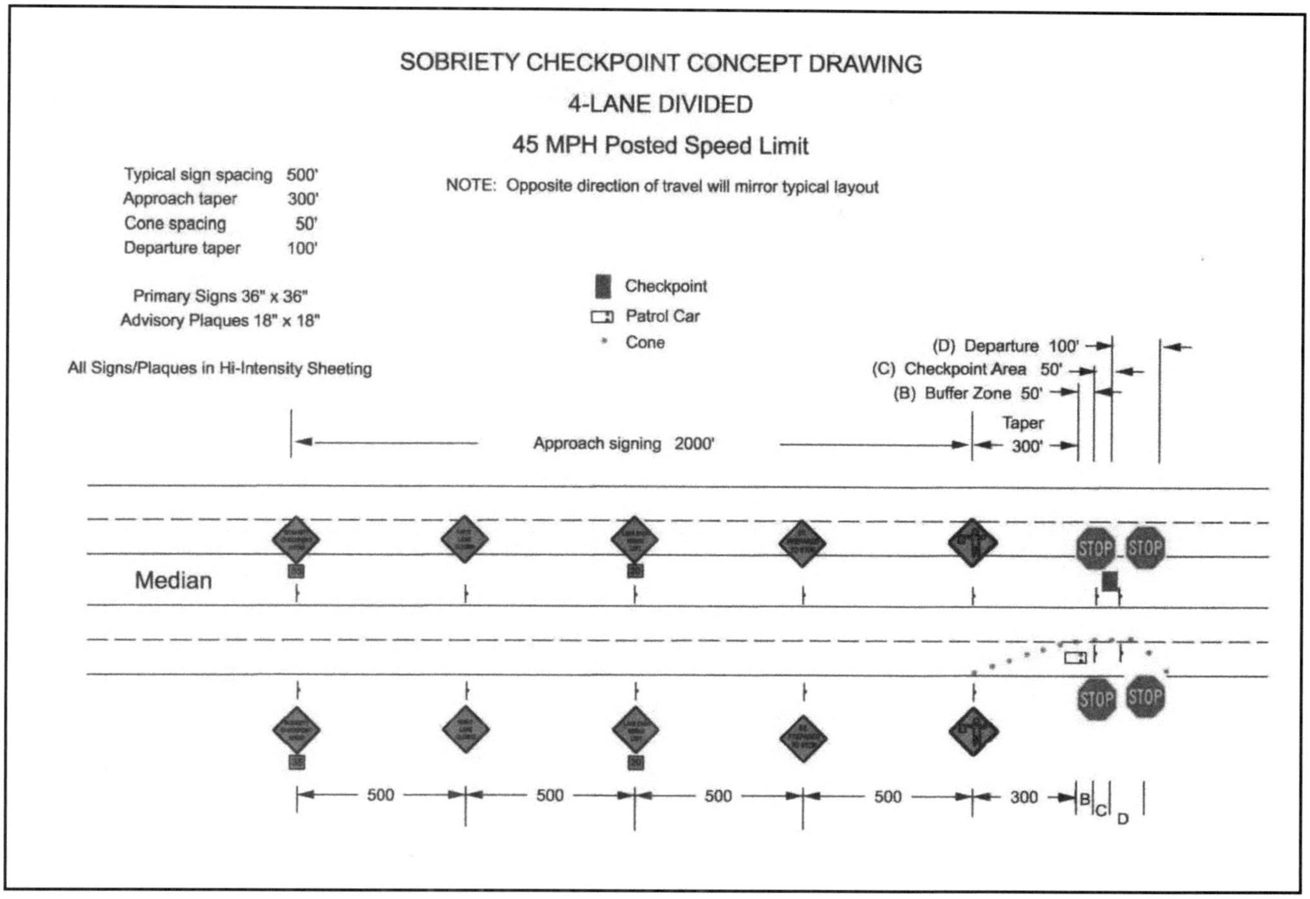

Figure 5.11 Typical roadblock signage plan

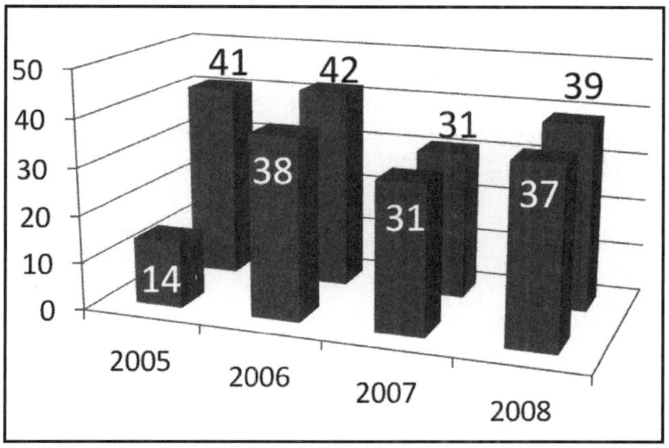

Figure 5.12 Plots number of roadblocks (front) vs. number of fatal accidents (rear) as justification for more roadblocks from 2005 to 2008 as shown to police at a pre-checkpoint briefing.

(1) Repealed by Session Laws 2006-253, s. 4, effective December 1, 2006, and applicable to offenses committed on or after that date.

(2) Designate in advance the pattern both for stopping vehicles and for requesting drivers that are stopped to produce drivers license, registration, or insurance information.

(2a) Operate under a written policy that provides guidelines for the pattern, which need not be in writing. The policy may be either the agency's own policy, or if the agency does not have a written policy, it may be the policy of another law enforcement agency, and may include contingency provisions for altering either pattern if actual traffic conditions are different from those anticipated, but no individual officer may be given discretion as to which vehicle is stopped or, of the vehicles stopped, which driver is requested to produce drivers license, registration, or insurance information. If officers of a law enforcement agency are operating under another agency's policy, it must be stated in writing.

(3) Advise the public that an authorized checking station is being operated by having, at a minimum, one law enforcement vehicle with its blue light in operation during the conducting of the checking station.

(a1) A pattern designated by a law enforcement agency pursuant to subsection (a) of this section shall not be based on a particular vehicle type, except that the pattern may designate any type of commercial motor vehicle as defined in G.S. 20-4.01(3d). The provisions of this subsection shall apply to this Chapter only and are not to be construed to restrict any other type of checkpoint or roadblock which is lawful and meets the requirements of subsection (c) of this section.

(b) An officer who determines there is a reasonable suspicion that an occupant has violated a provision of this Chapter, or any other provision of law, may detain the driver to further investigate in accordance with law. The operator of any vehicle stopped at a checking station established under this subsection may be requested to submit to an alcohol screening test under G.S. 20-16.3 if during the course of the stop the officer determines the driver had previously consumed alcohol or has an open container of alcoholic beverage in the vehicle. The officer so requesting shall consider the results of any alcohol screening test or the driver's refusal in determining if there is reasonable suspicion to investigate further.

(c) Law enforcement agencies may conduct any type of checking station or roadblock as long as it is established and operated in accordance with the provisions of the United States Constitution and the Constitution of North Carolina.

(d) The placement of checkpoints should be random or statistically indicated, and agencies shall avoid placing checkpoints repeatedly in the same location or proximity. This subsection shall not be grounds for a motion to suppress or a defense to any offense arising out of the operation of a checking station.

The statute above is what the Court relies on when the defense challenges the admissibility of the roadblock. The Court must also consider the constitutionality of the roadblock. The Court must use a fact based two part inquiry and balance the State's interest in conducting the roadblock versus the individual's Fourth Amendment interests and the effectiveness of the checkpoint. See *State v. Rose* 170 N.C. App. 284 (2005) and *Indianapolis v. Edmond* 531 US 32(2000). The burden of proof is on the State.

The Court must first determine the "primary programmatic purpose" of the checkpoint (see *Edmond* at 46). If there's nothing in the record that contradicts the State's offered purpose, the Court can rely solely on the officer's testimony as to a legitimate purpose as long as the Court determines the officer's testimony is reliable (see *State v. Burroughs* 185 N.C. App. 496). However, if there is evidence in the record that would support either a lawful or unlawful purpose, the trial Court cannot just accept the State's proffered purpose, but must instead review the scheme at issue closely; see *State v. Veazey* 191 N.C. App. 181 (2008). The Court must then make findings of fact regarding the primary programmatic purpose (see *Rose* at 289-290). This is done so that an illegal multipurpose checkpoint isn't made legal by simply assigning the primary purpose to one objective over another (see *Veazey* at 688). When the Court must make findings of fact in regard to the primary programmatic purpose of the checkpoint, the Court cannot rely on just the testimony of the officer, but the State must present evidence from the policy making level of the agency conducting the checkpoint (see *Rose* at 289). If the Court finds that there was no permissible primary programmatic purpose, the Court should grant the defendant's motion to dismiss. If the Court finds that there is a permissible purpose, the Court must then make findings regarding the reasonableness of the checkpoint (see *Rose* at 293).

The Court is guided in making these findings of reasonableness by using a three pronged test, commonly referred to as the Brown factors. See *Brown v. Texas* 443 US 47 (1979). The first Brown factor is the gravity of the public concerns served by the seizure. This is achieved by identifying the primary programmatic purpose and assessing the importance of that particular stop to the public (see *Rose* at 294). The State must present sufficient evidence to the Court so that the Court can adequately assess the State's interests and make findings of fact on that issue.

The second Brown factor is the degree to which the seizure advances the public interest. In other words, did the State appropriately tailor this particular checkpoint to advance its stated programmatic purpose (see *Rose* at 294). For the Court's consideration in evaluating this prong, our Courts have laid out certain factors for the trial Court to consider including: 1. whether police spontaneously decided to set up the checkpoint on a whim; 2. whether police offered any reason for the particular road or stretch of road was chosen for the checkpoint; 3. whether the checkpoint had a predetermined starting or ending time; 4. whether police offered any reason why that particular time span was selected (see *Rose* at 295). If the Court does not make findings of fact on this second Brown factor, the Court cannot conclude the checkpoint was reasonable as a matter of law (see *Veazey* at 690).

The third Brown factor reaches the severity of interference with individual liberty. The Court must look at the level of intrusion into the domain of the individual's Fourth Amendment interests occasioned by the officers acting at the scene (see *Veazey* at 690). Courts consistently require restrictions on officer discretion when conducting checkpoints so that the intrusion on individual liberty is no greater than necessary to achieve the checkpoint's objectives (see *Veazey* at 691). As with the second prong, for this third prong, Courts have also provided some guidance for the trial court in determining these factors. These nonexclusive factors include: 1. The checkpoint's potential interference with legitimate traffic; 2. Whether police took steps to put drivers on notice; 3. Whether the location of the checkpoint was selected by a supervising official, rather than by officers in the field; 4. Whether police stopped every vehicle that passed through the checkpoint, or stopped vehicles pursuant to a set pattern; 5. Whether drivers could see visible signs of the officers' authority; 6. Whether police operated the checkpoint pursuant to any oral or written guidelines; 7. Whether the officers were subject to any form of supervision; and 8. Whether the officers received permission from their supervising officer to conduct the checkpoint (see *Veazey* at 691).

If the State can present sufficient evidence to support findings of fact for the three Brown factors, the Court must then determine whether or not the checkpoint was reasonably conducted as a matter of law after weighing the State's interest in conducting the checkpoint against the individual's Fourth Amendment interests (see *Veazey* at 692). If the checkpoint was not reasonable, the motion to suppress should be allowed. If the Court finds that the checkpoint was reasonable, the motion should be denied. Special thanks to my good friend and excellent DWI attorney, James R. McMinn, for his motion on which the above roadblock discussion is based.

5.9 Pre-Trial Interviews, Law Enforcement

Make no mistake about it, the trial starts at the pre-trial interview. This is not a time for cross-examination. This is not the time to go for the jugular. This is the time to let the state's witness answer open-ended questions. That's not to say that you cannot pin the witness down to a specific statement, but do not get so caught up in one particular statement that you ignore other possibilities. The officer may give you answers that hurt your client's case. In a way, that's a good thing—at least you will know how the officer will testify in court on that particular subject, and you can prepare for it. Remember that preparation includes knowing what subjects to stay away from during trial as much as it means highlighting the good subjects.

As you know, there is NO discovery in a District Court DWI case; with that being said, most jurisdictions will give you access to police reports and most police officers are willing to speak with you about your case. You can usually find the officer either in the back hallway of the court house or many times they will even agree to speak with you while on duty if you call them during their shift. Remember, however, that the police officer is NOT required to speak with you about your case or provide you with any reports or videos that accompany your case. I find that this is the exception and not the rule. As long as you are courteous and friendly, the officer is usually willing to share what he or she has and speak to you about it.

Be pleasant and courteous during the interview. You may be on the other side of the case from the state's witness, but that is no excuse to be rude. You are doing a job and so is the state's witness—act professionally. Moreover, being courteous will generally get you what you want and more.

Police interviews

Audio record the interview. Always start off with the time, date and location of the interview. State for the record who is present. Make a clear statement for the officer about how the interview will proceed. For example:

> Officer, I first want to go through your background and training as it relates to law enforcement and DWIs. Next I want to talk about what you did during the investigation. I will want to know why you did what you did. If you answer a question in a way that is favorable to my client, I am going to ask you that question again in court and hold you to your answer. If you answer a question in a way that is not favorable to my client, I probably won't ask you that question again in court. Fair enough?
>
> If you ever have any questions about my questions, or don't understand my question, please let me know and I will do my best to clarify it. I'm not here to cross-examine you. I'm here to find out what you are going to say in court.
>
> When I'm done with all of my interviews, I will typically have them transcribed, and I will send you a copy. Where would you like it sent? When you get it, please read it over for content and, if you say, "Hey, I didn't say that," call me up. I will review the recording, and review the transcript and make corrections as necessary. Is that alright with you?
>
> If I have not heard from you within two weeks after sending the transcript, I will assume that it is accurate.

Next, go into the officer's background and training. Sample questions include:

- How long have you been with the department?
- Do you have any prior law enforcement training or experience (when, where)?
- If the officer left a previous police job, ask why.
- Have you ever held a rank higher than the one you hold now?
- Have you ever been disciplined by any law enforcement agency?
- Do you have any military training? What branch? Were you in law enforcement in the military?
- Do you have any medical training? What, when, where?
- Have you ever worked where alcohol has been sold in a retail capacity, such as a bartender, doorman, server? Did you have any training on recognizing when someone has had too much to drink from that job?
- Have you, a friend or a family members ever been injured by a drunk driver?
- Have you ever attended a MADD vigil, protest or event as part of your duties or on your own time?
- Have you ever been nominated for or received any awards for making DWI arrests?
- What type of DWI training have you had? What manuals did you use? Do you still have them?

At the end of the interview always allow the officer to clear up any matters or add anything to the transcript. Example:

> Officer, is there anything that you would like to add, change, or delete from this interview? If not, thank you for the interview (state the ending time of the interview).

Police Radio Codes

If you have obtained police radio-traffic recordings, it is important to understand what the police are saying before you do the interview. Police use radio codes to describe incidents for several reasons. Chief among those reasons is to alleviate confusion as to what the officer needs. Radio codes also allow quicker transmission of information, and they also allow police to relay information right in front of a suspect, with little chance that the suspect will understand what was being said. For example, a SHP officer might call in a license plate of a vehicle that he is about to stop along Interstate 40. Having stopped the driver, he gets the driver's license and walks back toward his patrol car and says "10-27" to the dispatcher, giving the dispatcher the driver's license number or name. The dispatcher begins a license check (10-27). He then returns to the driver to keep an eye on him while the license is being checked by dispatch. The dispatcher then says "10-30" and "Signal 1" over the radio which can be heard by the driver, but the driver has no idea that those two codes mean Danger/Caution and Suspect Armed and Dangerous. The Trooper can then simply say "10-33" (Help Me Quick) while acting nonchalantly.

In the DWI context, understanding 10-Codes can be very helpful. The 10-Codes can reveal that a DWI suspect was "in-custody" long before an officer's police report indicates. They can show that an officer called for a tow-truck moments after the stop, thus converting the stop to an arrest. They can also be used to show that an officer thought that certain conduct was against regulations.

Unfortunately, there is little consistency between radio codes used by different police agencies. Below is a list of available codes. Be aware that computer dispatch codes are not the same as radio codes.

10-Codes

North Carolina State Highway Patrol 10-Codes:

10-1 Signal weak
10-2 Signal good
10-3 Stop transmitting
10-4 Affirmative (OK)
10-5 Relay (to)
10-6 Busy
10-7 Out-of-Service
10-8 In-Service
10-9 Say Again (Repeat)
10-10 Negative
10-12 Stand by (Stop)
10-13 Existing Conditions
10-14 Message/Information
10-15 Message Delivered
10-16 Reply to Message
10-17 En Route
10-18 Urgent
10-19 (In) contact
10-20 Location
10-21 Call ____ by phone
10-22 Disregard
10-23 Arrived at Scene
10-24 Assignment Completed
10-25 Report to (Meet)
10-26 Estimated Arrival Time
10-27 License/Permit Information
10-28 Ownership Info (Vehicle)
10-29 Records Check
10-30 Danger/Caution
10-31 Pick Up

10-32 ____ Units Needed (Specify)
10-33 Help Me Quick
10-34 Time
10-35 Valid Concealed Handgun Permit
10-36 Restraint Violation
10-40 Fight in Progress
10-41 Beginning Tour of Duty
10-42 Ending Tour of Duty
10-43 Chase
10-44 Riot
10-45 Bomb Threat
10-46 Bank Alarm
10-47 Complete Assignment Quickly
10-48 Detaining Suspect, Expedite
10-49 Drag Racing
10-50 Collision PD, PI, F
10-51 Wrecker Needed
10-52 Ambulance Needed
10-53 Road Blocked
10-54 Hit and Run PD, PI, F
10-55 Intoxicated Driver
10-56 Intoxicated Pedestrian
10-57 Request Chemical Analyst on Duty to Meet ___
10-58 Direct Traffic
10-59 Convoy or Escort
10-60 Investigate Suspicious Vehicle
10-61 Stopping Suspicious Vehicle
10-62 Burglary/Breaking and Entering
10-63 Investigate ___ at ___
10-64 Crime in Progress
10-65 Report of Armed Robbery
10-66 Notify Medical Examiner
10-67 Investigate Report of Death
10-68 Livestock on Highway
10-69 Advise Present Telephone Number
10-70 Improperly Parked Vehicle
10-71 Improper Use of Radio
10-72 Have Prisoner in Custody
10-73 Mental Subject
10-74 Prison or Jail Break
10-75 Records Indicate Wanted or Stolen
10-76 Report of Prowler
10-77 Assist Fire Department with Traffic
10-78 Report of Abandoned Vehicle
10-79 Report of Vehicle Fire
10-80 Report of Careless and Reckless Driving
10-81 Report of High Speed
10-82 Report of Disabled Motorist
10-83 Report of Improper Registration
10-84 Report of Operator's License Violation
10-85 Report of Mini Bike/Go Cart Violation
10-86 Beginning Authorized Travel
10-87 Ending Authorized Travel
10-88 Unlawful Use of Mobile Device While Operating Motor Vehicle
10-90 Rest Area/Welcome Center Check
10-91 CMV Inspection
Signal 1 Suspect Armed and Dangerous
Signal 2 Report of Suspected Drug Trafficking (vehicle/suspect description, direction of travel and "Signal 1" if applicable)
Signal 3 Confidential Traffic
Signal 4 Report of Vehicle Stored/Recovered
Signal 5 Situation under control, no further assistance necessary
Signal 6 Violator on active probation/parole
Signal 7 Report to District Office/Troop HQ without delay (disturbance)
Signal 8 Your equipment is ready for service.
Signal 9 Meet at ____ Troop or District meeting.
Signal 10 Possible Suicidal Person
Signal 11 All members affected by this signal should immediately prepare for emergency duty and maintain radio contact.
Signal 12 Report to ___ at ____ for emergency duty.
Signal 13 Conviction/Revocation
Signal 14 Current Suspension/Revocation Information other than DWI
Signal 15 Protection Order
Signal 16 Registered Sex Offender
Signal 17 Gang Member
Signal 18 Accident/Incident Involving Hazardous Material
Signal 19 Report of Aircraft Crash at ___
Signal 20 Report of Aircraft in Difficulty at ___
Signal 21 Request for radio or car repair
Signal 22 Fatal Collision Report
Signal 23 Message requiring special handling (answer requested)
Signal 24 Daily Fatality Summary
Signal 25 ___ needs immediate assistance to make arrest of resisting person. Report at once to ____.
Signal 26 Computer terminal is temporarily out-of-service
Signal 27 Pick-Up License Revocation Confirmed
Signal 28 Pick-Up Registration Plate Revocation Confirmed
Signal 30 Individual of the opposite sex must be placed within the Patrol vehicle for the purpose of public service or enforcement contacts

Winston-Salem Police Department 10-Codes:

10-0 Use Caution
10-1 Weak Signal
10-2 Good Signal
10-3 Stop Transmitting
10-4 Affirmative
10-5 Relay to/from
10-6 Busy
10-7 Out of Service
10-8 In Service
10-9 Say Again
10-10 Negative
10-11 Employee Number
10-12 Stand By
10-13 Weather Conditions
10-14 Message / Information
10-15 Message Delivered
10-16 Reply to Message
10-17 Enroute
10-18 Urgent
10-19 In Contact
10-20 Location
10-21 Call by phone
10-22 Disregard
10-23 Arrived at Scene
10-24 Assignment Completed
10-25 Report to ______
10-26 ETA
10-27 Drivers License Inquiry
10-28 Vehicle Inquiry
10-29 Records Check
10-30 Danger
10-31 Pick-up
10-32 ____ Units Needed
10-33 Need Immediate Assistance
10-34 Current Time
10-40 Fight in Progress
10-41 Beginning Tour of Duty
10-42 Ending Tour of Duty
10-43 In Pursuit
10-44 Riot 10-45 Bomb Threat
10-46 Bank Alarm
10-47 Complete Assignment Quickly
10-48 Detaining Suspect, Expedite
10-49 Drag Racing
10-50 Vehicle Accident, PD, PI, F
10-51 Dispatch Wrecker
10-52 Dispatch Ambulance
10-53 Road Blocked
10-54 Hit and Run Accident, PD, PI, F
10-55 Intoxicated Driver
10-56 Intoxicated Pedestrian
10-57 Request BT Operator
10-58 Direct Traffic
10-59 Escort
10-60 Suspicious Vehicle
10-61 Stopping Suspicious Vehicle
10-62 B&E in Progress
10-63 Prepare to Receive an Assignment
10-64 Crime in Progress
10-65 Armed Robbery
10-66 Notify Medical Examiner
10-67 Report of Death
10-68 Livestock in Roadway
10-69 Advise Telephone Number
10-70 Improper Parked Vehicle
10-71 Improper Use of Radio
10-72 Prisoner in Custody
10-73 Mental Subject
10-74 Prison/Jail Break
10-75 Wanted or Stolen
10-76 Prowler
10-77 Direct Traffic at Fire Scene
10-80 Fire Alarm
10-81 Nature of Fire
10-82 Fire in Progress
10-83 Smoke Visible
10-84 No Smoke Visible
10-85 Respond without Blue Lights/Siren

Town of Kernersville Police Department 10-Codes:

Not available to the public.

Forsyth County Sheriff's Department 10-Codes:

Not available to the public.

Greensboro Police Department 10-Codes:

Not available to the public.

Guilford County Sheriff's Department 10-Codes:

10-0 Use caution
10-1 Unable to copy
10-2 Signal is good
10-3 Stop transmitting
10-4 Acknowledgment
10-5 Relay
10-6 Busy- standby unless urgent
10-7 Out of service
10-8 In service
10-9 Repeat

10-10 Fight in progress
10-11 Animal case/ dog bite
10-12 Standby
10-13 Weather information
10-14 Prowler
10-15 Patient
10-16 Domestic/ civil disturbance
10-17 See the complainant
10-18 Complete assignment quickly
10-19 Return to....
10-20 Location
10-21 Call by telephone
10-22 Disregard
10-23 Arrived at scene
10-24 Assignment complete
10-25 Report in person to....
10-26 Detaining subject
10-27 Driver's license check
10-28 Registration check
10-29 Wanted/ stolen check
10-30 Unauthorized use of radio
10-31 In progress
10-32 Subject armed with.....
10-33 Emergency
10-34 Large disturbance/ riot
10-35 Noise disturbance/ loud party
10-36 Correct time
10-37 Suspicious vehicle or person
10-38 Stopping a vehicle
10-39 Emergency run - lights and siren
10-40 Routine run- no lights or siren
10-41 Beginning tour of duty
10-42 Ending tour of duty
10-43 Information
10-44 Leaving beat for.....
10-45 Animal carcass in road
10-46 Assist motorist/ disabled vehicle
10-47 Emergency road repair needed
10-48 Utility pole/ sign repair needed
10-49 Traffic control out
10-50 Vehicle accident
PD- Property damage
PI- Personal Injury
F- Fatality
10-51 Wrecker needed
10-52 EMS needed
10-53 Fire equipment needed
10-54 Livestock in road
10-55 Impaired driver
10-56 Impaired pedestrian
10-57 Hit and run vehicle accident
PD- Property damage
PI- Personal Injury
F- Fatality
10-58 Direct traffic
10-59 Escort
10-60 Burglar alarm
10-61 Reported burglary
10-62 Check for traffic violations
10-63 Prepare to make written copy
10-64 Debris in road
10-65 Power/ phone lines down
10-66 Message cancellation
10-67 Ice/ snow removal needed
10-68 Check road conditions/ flooding
10-69 Assault
10-70 Fire
10-71 Advise nature of fire
10-72 Report progress on fire
10-73 Smoke report
10-74 Negative
10-75 Advise status
10-76 Enroute
10-77 Estimated time of arrival
10-78 Need assistance
10-79 Subject deceased
10-80 Vehicle pursuit
10-81 Breathalyzer requested
10-82 Foot pursuit
10-83 Hostage situation
10-84 Rape/ sexual assault
10-85 Alcohol/ narcotic violation
10-86 Employee/ partner on-duty
10-87 Pick up papers
10-88 Advise a phone number
10-89 Bomb threat
10-90 Robbery alarm
10-91 Reported robbery
10-92 Illegally parked vehicle
10-93 Roadblock
10-94 Racing
10-95 Subject in custody
10-96 Mental subject
10-97 Pick up prisoner
10-98 Prisoner escape
10-99 Wanted/ stolen
10-100 No assist car available

10-7 Codes

Code 1 Follow up
Code 2 Training

Code 3 Court
Code 4 Legal paper
Code 5 Special assignment
Code 6 Equipment/ vehicle
Code 7 Premises check
Code 8 Administrative
Code 9 Interagency assignment
Code 10 Meal
Code 11 Break
Code 12 Personal

10-22 Codes
Code 1 No one injured
Code 2 Patient(s) refused
Code 3 Transported POV
Code 4 Handled by law/ fire
Code 5 False call
Code 9 Other

10-24 Codes
Code 1 Report (All) Arrest (GPD)
Code 2 Information Given
Code 3 Arrest (SO)
Code 4 Assistance Provided
Code 5 Unfounded/Not Located

Hospital Transport destinations
61- Moses Cone Hospital
62- Wesley Long Hospital
63- Women's Hospital
64- Vencor Hospital
65- High Point Regional Hospital

Patient condition codes
Code 44- Patient DOA / dead at scene
Code 47- CPR in progress

Aircraft alerts
Alert 1- aircraft in flight with minor problems
Alert 2- aircraft in flight with major problems
Alert 3- aircraft crash
Amber Alert 3- aircraft crash off PTIA property

County Fire Clearance
Condition 10- all apparatus are clear the scene & available

Signals
0 - In trouble, need immediate assistance
1 - Self-initiated activity/ event
2 - Computer system/ file is down
3 - Handicapped address
4 - Hazardous materials
5 - Radioactive materials
6 - Willie M. subject
7- reserved for future use
8 - Meet another unit
9 - reserved for future use
10- Radio reception problems in a structure
11- At base
12- Radio emergency button activation
18- Reported pin-in
19- Confirmed pin-in
20- Meal break
25- Field personnel held hostage
33- Sensitive radio information to follow, advise when radio is secure
40- Fueling unit
50- Situation under control, no further assistance needed
75- Fire scene under control/ Fans needed

State's criminalist

Before the interview begins, be sure that you have all relevant documentation regarding the chemical test. If you are going to ask the state's criminalist to do calculations regarding blood alcohol concentration, be sure to have all your facts summarized, such as body weight, type of drink (if known) and time that drinking started and ended. The time of the traffic stop and time of the chemical tests are also important to have. Do the calculations ahead of time, yourself, and ask about discrepancies between your answers and the criminalist's answers.

It is important to ask if the criminalist has ever been wrong about a test. Either way, the answer will not hurt your case. On the one hand, a criminalist who admits to having been incorrect in the past allows you to argue that no one is perfect and maybe there was an error in your client's case. On the other hand, a criminalist who claims perfection will be viewed with suspicion by the jury if you are able to frame the questions properly. No one is perfect.

Always ask the criminalist for scientific research and names of articles that back up her claims. Often, such articles and research will be kept by the crime lab in its own library. Many times criminalists have been kind enough to photocopy the articles for me when asked.

Do not be afraid to send scientific articles to a criminalist ahead of the interview. There are many articles and publications which help the defense. Criminalists who read the article may agree or disagree with the findings. If they agree, and if the article is helpful to your client, this may mean that you will not have to retain your own expert for the trial. If they disagree, find out why they disagree. Sometimes, however, the criminalist will refuse to even read articles and publications sent by defense attorneys. Some crime labs and police departments have standing policies that inform defense attorneys not to send such items as they have prohibited their criminalists from reading articles supplied by defense attorneys. This provides wonderful opportunities for cross-examination on the subject of bias.

5.10 Pre-Trial Interviews, Emergency Personnel

Every emergency response agency has a protocol governing their conduct. It does not matter whether it is an official city ambulance crew responding to an accident, a volunteer fire crew, or a private, for-profit rural fire department. They all have written protocols governing conduct.

With the exception of patient-privacy laws, there is probably no scenario under which they can deny access to reports made for an accident response or rescue operation. Even where access is denied, you can still get a copy of their blank report forms which will indicate what type of information may have been recorded by the response personnel.

Where your client was treated or evaluated, your client has the absolute right to a copy of the report. Get a copy of the report to determine the extent of injuries to your client. Perhaps your client suffered a head-injury which would invalidate some or all of the field sobriety tests. Yet, it is likely that the emergency responder also documented alcohol or drug use. In this scenario, you may be able to use the patient-privacy laws to shield your client from the introduction of such evidence.

Prior to interviewing the emergency personnel, it is important to have reviewed both the protocol and the responder's report. Make distinctions between alcohol intoxication and simple consumption of alcohol. Many times the responder will only be able to state that alcohol was consumed, but not be able to state an opinion on level of intoxication or amount of alcohol. Other times, the responder may have the ability to render an opinion that your client was drunk. Either way, you need to know about it.

5.11 Pre-Trial Interviews, Civilians

Often, civilian witnesses are passengers in your client's car, witnesses to an accident or 911 callers. It is rare to have a civilian witness who does not fall into one of these broad categories.

Passengers

Passengers are generally friendly witnesses to your case. Most often, however, they have been drinking as well. The initial interview should attempt to discern if that passenger will help or hurt. Clearly, testimony along the lines of "We were all pretty tanked, but Joe was the most sober of all of us so he drove" is not good testimony. Try to nail down exactly what the passenger saw the driver drink. Also, do not forget to ask the passenger how much he had to drink. An entirely sober passenger is a double-edged sword. On the one hand, the passenger certainly had clearness of intellect to remember the events of the evening and could make a reasoned decision to let your client drive. On the other hand, juries often have a problem with a situation where the driver had four beers while the passenger is alcohol free. The obvious question that runs through their minds is—why didn't the passenger drive?

Accident witnesses

Accident witnesses may be either favorable or not, depending upon what they saw. Often, however, a favorable accident witness will become unfavorable once she learns that your client has been charged with DWI. There is a widespread prejudice against people charged with DWI, and a witness's recollection of events or willingness to help you may suddenly become problematic. When requesting an interview, it is best to simply tell the witness that you represent one of the parties to the accident and would like a statement regarding the event. Obviously, you should not lie to the witness by saying that your client was not charged with a crime, but you do not need to specify anything unless asked.

Check for statements made by the witness to police. Usually a statement is taken in the form of an oral assertion by the witness and recorded in the police report in the officer's own words. However, some police agencies have witness report forms on which the witness records his recollections. Some forms even have areas for a diagram that can be drawn by the witness.

911 callers

The most problematic of all third-party witnesses are 911 callers. By virtue of the fact that the witness saw something that she believed warranted the attention of the police, that witness will often be a bad witness for the defense. Sometimes the prosecutor will not be able to find this witness. In that case, you might not want to look for the witness, either. The statements of a 911 caller who is not present at trial may be excluded as hearsay, depending on what is in the statement and under what conditions it was given. If it was a present sense impression, that is, a statement made which describes the event at or near the time of the event, it may be admissible.

The United States Supreme Court took up this issue in *Davis v. Washington*, 547 U.S. 813, 126 S. Ct. 2266, 165 L. Ed. 2d 224 (2006): "The question before us in *Davis,* then, is whether, objectively considered, the interrogation that took place in the course of the 911 call produced testimonial statements." The Court weighed the reasons for the 911 call in the context of whether it was interrogation and whether it was likely to produce an unreliable statement. The Court wrote: "A 911 call, on the other hand, and at least the initial interrogation conducted in connection with a 911 call, is ordinarily not designed primarily to "establis[h] or prov[e]" some past fact, but to describe current circumstances requiring police assistance." They found that a 911 call may be admissible as a present sense impression, but cautioned that the statement could turn into inadmissible hearsay if they go beyond describing the event. Yet, this does not mean that they are admissible absent other requirements. The 911 call, for instance, must still be authenticated. It also must not be the result of threats or coercion as is the rule for any other statement to be used against the accused.

Calls to 911 are always recorded. A request for the 911 recording may be made either through the prosecuting agency or through the 911 call center. Recordings of 911 calls are not kept forever by every agency. A standard disclosure request should at least ask that the 911 recording be preserved. If you ask for it to be preserved and it is destroyed, you will certainly at least have preserved an argument for suppression, preclusion or even dismissal.

5.12 Prior Offenses

If your client has prior offenses, investigation of those priors is important. Priors are going to be divided into two main categories—those that are known and those that are unknown. Clearly, if your client has priors that the prosecutor and courts do not know about, you will want to tread lightly around any investigation of those priors lest you tip them off. Your ethical duty to your client requires the utmost in secrecy. Sometimes, it is best not to check the court records anywhere but online to find unknown priors. As a practical matter, however, you don't really need to investigate a prior that has not been alleged.

Documents supplied to you by the prosecutor which allege a prior offense must be analyzed carefully for accuracy and defects. If there is a transcript of the previous sentencing hearing, you need to get it—especially where a prior conviction is the result of a plea bargain. Un-counseled prior convictions present a host of opportunities to invalidate a prior offense. While there are many online services which can provide documents, the courthouse where the prior conviction was made will have copies that you can obtain.

If it is an out-of-state prior offense, it is best to contact a local attorney familiar with that state for help. Driver's license facilities will also have a neat summary of traffic-related offenses and that is a good place to start gathering information.

Chapter 6

Pre-Trial Motions Practice

6.1 Overview

Pre-trial motions can be broken down into three main categories: Procedural, Substantive and Motions in Limine. Procedural motions must be filed in every case and are usually discovery related. Substantive motions are filed in an effort to suppress evidence and dismiss charges. Motions in limine are filed immediately prior to trial and are usually aimed at limiting evidence at trial or allowing exploration of certain issues during questioning.

6.2 Procedural Motions

Procedural motions must be filed in every case in the Superior Court. In District Court however, where most of these cases begin and usually end, these types of motions are made orally in front of the Judge. The most important procedural motions in the District Court are those that give notice to the State that you will be contesting the stop, arrest, search, or a Knoll motion, which will be discussed later in this chapter. For Superior Court, these motions are still important and need to be more thoroughly drafted and accompanied by a sworn affidavit. For District Court purposes, I use a very vanilla style of motion that just consists of a form with boxes next to what I may argue that I can check off. This way, I've met my notice requirement but I haven't given the State a detailed narrative of what I will be arguing. Keep in mind, as all of the prosecutors in this State are more than happy to point out, "there is no discovery in District Court."

The absence of our ability to gain discovery in the District Court can at times be annoying, however sometimes it benefits us as well. For example, when I want to use an expert witness in one of my DWI cases I don't have to tell the State; I just show up with the expert and his CV. The no discovery rule also makes trial by ambush the new norm. Most jurisdictions in the State have an open file type of discovery when dealing with these kinds of cases, but there are still a few jurisdictions that will offer you nothing at all, including even a copy of the police report. Remember that the Superior Court rules take over if your client is charged with Habitual DWI, since that is a felony and its proper place is in the Superior Court. In these types of cases, you would have to follow the local rules and of course, notice the State of any expert witnesses and their opinions if you intend to call them.

Notice of Appearance

A Notice of Appearance is not complex in a DWI case in North Carolina. It is made in the District Court, orally, in front of the Judge.

Notice of Defenses

Generally speaking, the only time you need to give notice of defenses in North Carolina is in the Superior Court. These notices are limited to the following: alibi, duress, entrapment, insanity, mental infirmity, diminished capacity, self defense, accident, automatism, and voluntary and involuntary intoxication. Also, any tests or, obviously in Superior Court, any expert witnesses and a summary of the expert's testimony needs to be incorporated in your notice.

Notice of Pre trial Motions

A Notice of Pre trial Motions is required in every case that will proceed to trial in cases which you intend to suppress any evidence obtained as the result of an improper stop or an arrest lacking in probable cause. I submit these notices of pre trial motions as follows:

1. Stop
2. Arrest
3. Search/Seizure
4. Statements made
5. Implied Consent
6. Knoll (355 NC 535)

7. Ferguson (90 N.C. App. 513)
8. Hernandez (188 NC App 193) and NCGS 20-166.1
9. Suppress results of EC/IR ii machine
10. Statute of Limitations
11. Improper service of summons (if case is too old)

§ 20-38.6. Motions and district court procedure.

(a) The defendant may move to suppress evidence or dismiss charges only prior to trial, except the defendant may move to dismiss the charges for insufficient evidence at the close of the State's evidence and at the close of all of the evidence without prior notice. If, during the course of the trial, the defendant discovers facts not previously known, a motion to suppress or dismiss may be made during the trial.

(b) Upon a motion to suppress or dismiss the charges, other than at the close of the State's evidence or at the close of all the evidence, the State shall be granted reasonable time to procure witnesses or evidence and to conduct research required to defend against the motion.

(c) The judge shall summarily grant the motion to suppress evidence if the State stipulates that the evidence sought to be suppressed will not be offered in evidence in any criminal action or proceeding against the defendant.

(d) The judge may summarily deny the motion to suppress evidence if the defendant failed to make the motion pretrial when all material facts were known to the defendant.

(e) If the motion is not determined summarily, the judge shall make the determination after a hearing and finding of facts. Testimony at the hearing shall be under oath.

(f) The judge shall set forth in writing the findings of fact and conclusions of law and preliminarily indicate whether the motion should be granted or denied. If the judge preliminarily indicates the motion should be granted, the judge shall not enter a final judgment on the motion until after the State has appealed to superior court or has indicated it does not intend to appeal.

Request for Discovery

Below is an all-purpose Request for Discovery in a DWI case with a breath or blood test. If it is a breath test case, eliminate the blood testing case questions, and vice versa if it is a blood test case. If there is no chemical test, eliminate all questions regarding chemical testing.

COMES NOW the defendant, John Doe, by and through counsel undersigned, pursuant to Rules 15A-901 through 15A-910 North Carolina Rules of Criminal Procedure, and the decision of the United States Supreme Court in Brady v. Maryland, 373 U.S. 83, 83 S.Ct. 1194, 10 L.Ed.2d 215 (1963), and hereby requests that the Court order the State to furnish the defendant with the following information forthwith:

1. The names, agencies and addresses of all police officers or government employees who investigated this case.
2. The names, addresses and phone numbers of all civilian witnesses.
3. The name, address, and phone number of any Expert Witness that the State may call at trial, including:
    a) a list and description of any and all chemical and/or scientific tests or experiments about which the State's expert will testify;
    b) a list of any and all publications relied upon by the State's Expert Witness;
    c) whether the State's Expert Witness will render an opinion concerning the supposed Blood Alcohol Level of the defendant.
4. All police or agency reports created in connection with this case including accident reports, if any.
5. All books, papers, documents, photographs, sound or video recordings, tangible objects, and other exhibits which are intended for use by the State as evidence at the trial or were obtained from or belong to the Defendant John Doe.
6. A copy of the Implied Consent Affidavit.
7. Any and all photographs, diagrams, videos, audio tapes created with respect to this case.
8. Whether there was any type of special operation in effect on the date of the arrest, including, but not limited to: roadblocks, sobriety checkpoints, saturation patrols, zero-tolerance patrols, North Carolina DWI Task Force Operations, Operation Safe Streets, etc. And, if there was such an operation in effect:
    a) any official or unofficial reports stemming from the operation;
    b) any descriptions, instructions or rules involved, whether made public or not;

c) statistics on the number of stops, investigations and arrests made;

d) the names of all participants in the operation;

e) payroll records for the officers who participated in the operation.

9. The names of any Field Sobriety Tests that were given as well as the
results of such tests if they are not listed in the disclosed police reports.

10. If one or more HGN tests were administered:

a) the HGN logs of the person(s) who administered the test;

b) the date such person(s) was first qualified for HGN;

c) the date and location such person(s) attended HGN training;

d) the score of the person(s) on his or her HGN test;

e) the results of the HGN administered to John Doe.

11. All reports or records of prior convictions of Defendant John Doe, and reports or records of prior convictions of persons whom the attorney for the State expects to call as witnesses (including police officers). Defendant John Doe further requests all reports or records of prior convictions the State intends to use for impeachment purposes for all defense witnesses within 15 days of defense disclosure of the names of such witnesses.

12. All material now known to the State, or which may become known, or which through due diligence may be learned by the State, which is exculpatory in nature or favorable to the Defendant John Doe or which may lead to exculpatory material.

13. Any other evidence obtained by observation of police witnesses intended to be used against Defendant John Doe at trial that is not part of a written police report furnished to defense counsel.

14. All DMV records regarding the Defendant John Doe.

15. Proof of any alleged prior DWI conviction that the State plans to introduce at trial.

16. A list of any prior felony convictions of the Defendant John Doe that the State plans to introduce at trial.

17. Any and all documents signed by, read to or offered to John Doe as part of the police contact including, but not limited to, waivers of preserved chemical samples, breath/blood advisory forms and independent test option forms.

18. The times of all breath tests administered and the respective results.

19. All breath testing checklists, forms and memoranda used in preparation of the breath test.

20. The name of the operator and the date that the operator was certified by the Department of Health and Human Services to operate the type of breath instrument used to test John Doe along with a properly certified copy of his or her operator's permit.

21. A description or syllabus of any training course or seminar taken along with a description of the curriculum used and a copy of any written materials used to train the operator.

22. The following information about the breath instrument used:

a) type of instrument;

b) serial number;

c) date of acquisition;

d) date first entered into service (first certification);

e) whether the instrument was acquired new or used;

f) complete repair records of the instrument used;

g) the location of the instrument on the date of the arrest, if it was not being used as a mobile unit.

23. The name, address and phone number of the person(s) who maintains the instrument.

24. The monthly Quality Assurance Calibration Check sheets for the instrument in question for the period immediately prior to the date of arrest and immediately following the date of arrest.

25. The Function and Accuracy Calibration Sheets for the instrument in question for the period immediately prior to the date of arrest and immediately following the date of the arrest which are kept in accord with Department of Health and Human Services.

26. If the breath testing machine has a computer data memory, the Defendant requests all data that exist that are now and ever stored in the memory from the beginning of time to the date of this request.

27. The Gas Chromatograph or Titration Results for the Stock Solution and the Simulator Solution

This demand is made pursuant to Rules 15A-901 through 15A-910 Rules of Criminal Procedure. The requested materials have a direct bearing on the guilt or innocence of the Defendant.

28. If blood or urine testing was done, identify:
    a) the testing method used,
    b) the qualifications of the person who administered the test,
    c) the date, time and place of the test,
    d) whether the test was performed using enzymatic analysis, calorimetric distillation, alcohol separation or any other procedure,
    e) whether the Defendant John Doe signed any waiver form or other document allowing the results of the test to be released to the State,
    f) whether a sample of the blood or urine has been retained for independent testing,
    g) whether any preservatives, anticoagulants or other reagents were added to the blood or urine and, if so, the name of that preservative, anticoagulant or reagent, the amount added by whom it was added and the time it was added, and
    h) a complete list of all persons in the chain of custody and in possession of the blood or urine sample.
29. Defendant by and through counsel undersigned, hereby demands that the State, pursuant to Rules 15A-901 through 15A-910 Rules of Criminal Procedure, disclose in writing the existence of and permit the Defendant to inspect, copy, photograph and/or gain access to any and all of the following:
    a) Copies of the Forensic Crime Lab's written procedures for the testing of a blood sample, including, but not limited to a description of the correct and/or standard method for the testing and handling blood samples.
    b) Copies of Defendant's blood alcohol test result printouts created by (or in connection with) the blood testing devices used to analyze Defendant's blood, including printouts of all chromatograms for the Defendant's blood, all calibrators, controls, standard mix, blanks and verifiers.
    c) Copies of any other notes, charts, graphs or memorandum created in connection with the testing of the Defendant's blood including all Calibration Curve Reports.
    d) If the calibration standard, control, blank or verifier run at the time of the testing of Defendant's blood was produced in the Forensic Crime Lab:
        I. All notes, charts, graphs or memorandum created regarding the batch used;
        II. The identification of the person who created the batch, and when it was created.
    e) If the calibration standard, control, blank or verifier run at the time of the testing of Defendant's blood was purchased:
        I. The name of the manufacturer;
        II. The date of purchase;
        III. Copies of all certificates, literature or other information provided to the Lab by the manufacturer;
        IV. Copies of the results of any tests performed upon the standard.
    f) All repair and maintenance records maintained on the blood testing device used to analyze Defendant's blood as well as any pipettes and autosamplers.
    g) The identification of the type of swab used on Defendant's arm at the time of the blood draw; including the name of the manufacturer, expiration date and any other identifying information, and copies of the results of any test run on this type of swab.
    h) All documentation and information on the blood tubes use to collect and store Defendant's blood, including:
        I. The name of the manufacturer;
        II. The date of purchase;
        III. Copies of all certificates, literature of other information provided to the Lab by the manufacturer;
        IV. Copies of the results of any tests performed upon the test tubes.
    i) The identification of all preservatives and anti- coagulants that were added to Defendant's blood sample, including:
        I. The name of the manufacturer;
        II. The date of purchase;
        III. Copies of all certificates, literature or other information provided to the Lab by the manufacturer;
        IV. Copies of the results of any tests performed upon the preservatives or anticoagulants.

Defendant is charged with at least one count of DWI. The state intends to use the results of a blood alcohol test performed by the state's criminalist at the Forensic Crime Laboratory. All of the items requested to be produced herein relate to that test.

As to the reasons the specific items requested are necessary to the defense:

> **Item (a)** will allow Defendant to verify that the procedure used to analyze his blood was performed correctly and in conformance with the requirements of the laboratory performing the tests.
> **Items (b), (c) and (f)** will allow Defendant to evaluate the analysis performed by the blood testing device, and the criminalist's interpretation of those results.
> **Items (d)-(g), (h) and (i)** will allow the Defendant to determine whether any ingredient was added to his blood which could have produced a false positive reading for alcohol or increased the blood alcohol reading.

All of the requested information pertains directly to the validity of the test results obtained on Defendant's blood and pertains to whether the tests were performed within the requirements set forth by the North Carolina Department of Health Services regulations. As such, the information is necessary to the defense of Defendant's case. All of the information requested is within the control of the state, is easily obtainable by the state's agents, can be easily reproduced, and the disclosure of this information will present no burden on the state. On the other hand, Defendant has no independent access to this information.

This demand is made pursuant to Rules 15A-901 through 15A-910 of the North Carolina Rules of Criminal Procedure. The requested materials have a direct bearing on the guilt or innocence of the Defendant.

The Defendant John Doe has substantial need for these materials to prepare a defense and would otherwise be unable to obtain them without undue hardship. In the alternative, if the state is not able to produce the requested material, counsel will move the Court to suppress any and all evidence of the Defendant's chemical analysis, equipment, procedures and results.

6.3 Substantive Motions

Reasonable suspicion

All traffic stops must be performed with reasonable suspicion that the driver has either violated the motor vehicle code (Chapter 20) or with reasonable suspicion that the driver is engaged in some type of criminal activity. Usually, if there is no violation of Chapter 20, the officer making the stop will claim that there was some sort of traffic movement which is legal but gave him or her cause to believe that the driver was impaired. Generally, the police officer will refer to the National Highway and Traffic Safety Administration (NHTSA) cues for detecting impaired drivers to justify the stop.

The defense, however, does not have to show that there were no such movements. The burden on the defense is simply to show that there was no warrant issued for the defendant's seizure on the date that he was detained. The resulting statement of facts for a reasonable suspicion motion should only include those two facts and should never make any admissions to any element of any crime. Thus, the motion would state the following:

> All information contained herein has been gathered through review of the police reports, state's disclosure, and witness statements. John Doe makes no admissions as to any of the elements of the charges. John Doe was seized on January 1, 2012. There was no arrest warrant ever issued.

Case law directly on point shows that the defendant must do no more than establish that there was a warrantless search. A search and seizure " 'conducted outside the judicial process, without prior approval by judge or magistrate, [is] per se unreasonable under the Fourth Amendment—subject only to a few specifically established and well delineated exceptions.' " *State v. Summey*, 150 N.C. App. 662, 666, 564 S.E.2d 624, 627 (2002). Where a defendant shows that the search was warrantless, it is the state's burden to show a valid exception to the Fourth Amendment search warrant requirement. The state carries the burden of proof as well as the burden of going forward with the evidence. The Court of Appeals held: "Hence, when the State seeks to admit evidence discovered by way of a warrantless search in a criminal prosecution, it must first show how the former intrusion was **55 exempted from the general constitutional demand for a warrant." *State v. Cooke* 306 N.C. 132, 135 (1982).

These cases require the state to prove that the stop was reasonable.

In many instances, it is advantageous for the defense to require that the court take judicial notice of the warrantless stop. This avoids exposing the accused to cross-examination by having to call the accused to the stand to establish the warrantless stop. Rule 201 of the North Carolina Rules of Evidence provides the basis for mandatory judicial notice.

> **Rule 201. Judicial Notice of Adjudicative Facts**
> (a) Scope of rule. This rule governs only judicial notice of adjudicative facts.
> (b) Kinds of facts. A judicially noticed fact must be one not subject to reasonable dispute in that it is either (1) generally known within the territorial jurisdiction of the trial court or (2) capable of accurate and ready determination by resort to sources whose accuracy cannot reasonably be questioned.
> * * *
> (d) When mandatory. A court shall take judicial notice if requested by a party and supplied with the necessary information.
> * * *
> (f) Time of taking notice. Judicial notice may be taken at any stage of the proceeding.

The proper procedure is to request that the court take judicial notice of the North Carolina Traffic Ticket and Complaint in the court's own file under Rule 201(d). This establishes that the defendant was arrested on the date in question. Then request that the court take judicial notice of the absence of a warrant in the court's file. This satisfies the burden on the defense to show a warrantless seizure without resorting to putting a witness on the stand. If the state has no witnesses to rebut this evidence, the motion should be granted.

An investigative stop will be deemed reasonable where the officer can demonstrate some basis from which the court can determine that the police were not arbitrary or harassing. *United States v. Walling*, 486 F.2d 229 (9th Cir. 1973), cert. denied, 415 U.S. 923, 94 S.Ct. 1427, 39 L.Ed.2d 479 (1974). *United States v. Walling*; *Wilson v. Porter*, 361 F.2d 412, 415 (9th Cir. 1966); *United States v. Contreras-Diaz*, 575 F.2d 740 (9th Cir.), *cert. denied*, 439 U.S. 855, 99 S.Ct. 167, 58 L.Ed.2d 161 (1978).

Constitutional parameters are spelled out in *Terry v. Ohio*, 392 U.S. 1, 88 S.Ct. 1868, 20 L.Ed.2d 889 (1968). There, the Supreme Court of the United States held that a police officer may effect a limited detention of an individual, not amounting to an arrest, if the officer's actions were reasonable under the circumstances.

> Terry requires a dual inquiry into the reasonableness of an investigatory stop. The reviewing court must determine: (1) whether the facts warranted the intrusion on the individual's Fourth Amendment rights, and (2) whether the scope of the intrusion was reasonably related "to the circumstances which justified the interference in the first place." *Carpenter v. Sigler*, 419 F.2d 169, 171 (8th Cir. 1969). *United States v. Stevie*, 578 F.2d 204, 207 (8th Cir. 1977).

An investigative detention is lawful if the officer is "able to point to specific and articulable facts which, taken together with rational inferences from those facts, reasonably warrant … [the officer's] intrusion" upon the person's Fourth Amendment rights. *Terry v. Ohio*, 392 U.S. 1, 21, 88 S.Ct. 1868, 1880, 20 L.Ed.2d 889, 906 (1968). If the totality of the circumstances provides a "particularized and objective basis" for the officers to suspect that the person is engaged in criminal activity, the stop is permissible. *United States v. Cortez*, 449 U.S. 411, 417, 101 S.Ct. 690, 695, 66 L.Ed.2d 621, 629 (1981). *See also, State v. Barnard* 362 N.C. 244, 256 (2008). If the state puts a witness on the stand who merely testifies that the accused demonstrated "signs and symptoms" of impairment, but that witness does not elaborate on the specifics of those signs and symptoms, it is best not to cross-examine the witness for the details. The often used term "signs and symptoms" will generally not be enough to overcome the "particularized and objective basis" for the officers to suspect that the accused was violating the law. To pass muster in court, the fact finder must be able to listen to what the officer says he or she saw and make an independent decision as to whether the officer acted reasonably. Because "signs and symptoms" are vague and open to many interpretations, they cannot be particularized and objective, by definition.

Whether an officer's conduct was "reasonable" or "appropriate" depends on the facts and circumstances of the particular case, so that the decision in one case seldom furnishes a pat answer in another case. A principle to be applied generally, however, is that in judging the reasonableness of the actions of the officer the circumstances before him are not to be dissected and viewed singly; rather they must be considered as a whole. So considered, they are to be viewed through the eyes of a reasonable and cautious officer on the scene, guided by his or her experience and training. See *United States v. Davis*, 147 U.S.App.D.C. 400, 458 F.2d 819 (1972), and *United States v. Hall*, 174 U.S.App.D.C. 13, 15, 525 F.2d 857, 859 (1976).

The Supreme Court in *Pennsylvania v. Mimms*, 434 U.S. 106, 108-09, 98 S.Ct. 330, 332, 54 L.Ed.2d 331, 335-36 (1977), set forth the test for Fourth Amendment violations in this fashion:

> The touchstone of our analysis under the Fourth Amendment is always "the reasonableness in all

> the circumstances of the particular governmental invasion of a citizen's personal security." *Terry v. Ohio*, 392 U.S. 1, 19, 88 S.Ct. 1868, 20 L.Ed.2d 889 (1968). Reasonableness, of course, depends "on a balance between the public interest, and the individual's right to personal security free from arbitrary interference by law officers." *United States v. Brignoni-Ponce*, 422 U.S. 873, 878, 95 S.Ct. 2574, 45 L.Ed.2d 607 (1975).

In the opinion of *Brown v. Texas*, 443 U.S. 97, 99 S.Ct. 2637, 2640, 61 L.Ed.2d 357 (1979), the Supreme Court said that a central concern in balancing these competing considerations "has been to assure that an individual's reasonable expectation of privacy is not subject to arbitrary invasions solely at the unfettered discretion of officers."

Where a person has been seized unlawfully, an incidental search is also unlawful, and fruits of the search are inadmissible and cannot be used against the person. *Wong Sun v. United States*, 371 U.S. 471, 83 S.Ct. 407, 2640, 9 L.Ed.2d (1963). Thus, any evidence obtained after the seizure must be suppressed.

Probable cause

Once again, it is the state's burden to show that there is a valid exception to the search warrant requirement of the Fourth Amendment just as they had to do for reasonable suspicion. Once again, the defense can satisfy their burden of going forward without putting any witnesses on the stand by having the court take mandatory judicial notice of the North Carolina Traffic Ticket and Complaint in the court's file as well as the absence of a warrant for the seizure.

Where a defendant shows that the search was warrantless, it is the state's burden to show a valid exception to the warrantless search requirement. The state carries the burden of proof as well as the burden of going forward with the evidence.

A warrantless search is presumptively unreasonable under the Fourth Amendment "subject only to a few specifically established, jealously and carefully drawn exceptions." *Jones v. United States*, 357 U.S. 493, 78 S.Ct. 1253. In the probable cause motion, the defendant challenges the arrest, which must be based on probable cause. *Beck v. Ohio*, 379 U.S. 89, 84 S.Ct. 223 (1964);

In North Carolina, "Probable cause for an arrest has been defined to be a reasonable ground of suspicion supported by circumstances sufficiently strong in themselves to warrant a cautious man in believing the accused to be guilty.... To establish probable cause the evidence need not amount to proof of guilt, or even to prima facie evidence of guilt, but it must be such as would actuate a reasonable man acting in good faith." 5 Am.Jur.2d, Arrest § 44 (1962); *State v. Harris*, 279 N.C. 307, 182 S.E.2d 364 (1971). When the constitutional validity of an arrest is challenged, it is the function of a court to determine whether the facts available to the officers at the moment of the arrest would "warrant a man of reasonable caution in the belief" that an offense has been committed. *Carroll v. United States*, 267 U.S. 132, 162, 45 S.Ct. 280, 288, 69 L.Ed. 543.

If there are circumstances that would tend to show sobriety, they may be listed in the probable cause motion if there is a good faith belief that such evidence would come out at the evidentiary hearing. Some examples are:

1. Only a faint odor of alcohol.
2. No speech problems.
3. No bad driving.
4. No properly administered FSTs.
5. No HGN.
6. No balance problems during the HGN.
7. No balance problems while exiting the car.
8. No balance problems walking.
9. No balance problems while standing in a stationary position.
10. No "flushed" or "pale" face.
11. No PBT or any other indicator of a blood alcohol content.

Be mindful of the fact that even where the police have established reasonable suspicion, the driving behavior is still relevant to a determination of probable cause. Take, for example, the situation where a person is stopped for a Chapter 20 equipment violation of having no license plate light but was driving fine. Clearly, there is reasonable suspicion to stop, but having an inoperable license plate light has nothing to do with impairment. Driving well militates against impairment, and such facts should be used by the defense.

If the police have clearly insufficient evidence to believe that an offense had been committed, then the seizure was without probable cause.

An arrest without a warrant bypasses the safeguards provided by an objective predetermination of probable cause and substitutes instead the far less reliable procedure on an after-the-event justification for the arrest or search, too likely to be subtly influenced by the familiar shortcomings of hindsight judgment. *Beck v. Ohio*, 379 U.S. 89, 84 S.Ct. 223 (1964).

As *Beck* clearly demonstrates, the court must weigh the reasons for the arrest with great care. This court must be able to separate the information that the officer had at the time of the arrest with what he learned after the arrest. To allow the state to blur the lines between the two will render the term *probable cause* meaningless.

It is always important to point out to the court that if the court would not have issued a warrant for arrest had the police requested one, then probable cause did not exist. Whether or not the requirements of reliability and particularity of the information on which an officer may act are more stringent where an arrest warrant is absent, they surely cannot be less stringent then where an arrest warrant is obtained. Otherwise, a principal incentive now existing for the procurement of arrest warrants would be destroyed. *Wong Sun v. United States*, 371 U.S. 471, 83 S.Ct. 407, 9 L.Ed.2d 441.

This standard exists for the safety and security from government intrusions for all citizens. The court in *Wong Sun* noted that there is a history of use and abuse of the power to arrest, and they caution that the relaxation of the probable cause standards would "leave law-abiding citizens at the mercy of the officer's whim or caprice." *Wong Sun*, *supra*, quoting *Brinegar v. United States*, 338 U.S. 160, 176, 69 S.Ct. 1302, 1311, 93 L.Ed. 1879.

A warrantless investigative detention is only lawful if the officer is "able to point to specific and articulable facts which, taken together with rational inferences from those facts, reasonably warrant … [the officer's] intrusion" upon the person's Fourth Amendment rights. *Terry v. Ohio*, 392 U.S. 1, 21, 88 S.Ct. 1868, 1880, 20 L.Ed.2d 889, 906 (1968). Like many reasonable suspicion motions, many probable cause motions have been won by the defense when the state's witnesses simply testify to "signs and symptoms" of impairment and do not describe the actual signs and symptoms individually. Merely stating that there were "signs and symptoms" of impairment does not provide "specific and articulable facts" from which a court can determine whether the officer acted reasonably.

Whether an officer's conduct was "reasonable" or "appropriate" depends on the facts and circumstances of the particular case, so that the decision in one case seldom furnishes a definitive answer in another case. A principle to be applied generally, however, is that in judging the reasonableness of the actions of the officer the circumstances are not to be dissected and viewed singly; rather they must be considered as a whole. So considered, they are to be viewed through the eyes of a reasonable and cautious officer on the scene, guided by experience and training. See *United States v. Davis*, 147 U.S.App.D.C. 400, 458 F.2d 819 (1972); *United States v. Hall*, 174 U.S.App.D.C. 13, 15, 525 F.2d 857, 859 (1976).

The Supreme Court of the United States in *Pennsylvania v. Mimms*, 434 U.S. 106, 108-09, 98 S.Ct. 330, 332, 54 L.Ed.2d 331, 335-36 (1977), set forth the test for Fourth Amendment violations in this fashion:

> The touchstone of our analysis under the Fourth Amendment is always 'the reasonableness in all the circumstances of the particular governmental invasion of a citizen's personal security.' *Terry v. Ohio*, 392 U.S. 1, 19, 88 S.Ct. 1868, 20 L.Ed.2d 889 (1968). Reasonableness, of course, depends 'on a balance between the public interest, and the individual's right to personal security free from arbitrary interference by law officers.' *United States v. Brignoni-Ponce*, 422 U.S. 873, 878, 95 S.Ct. 2574, 45 L.Ed.2d 607 (1975).

There are many North Carolina cases and one statute which support the position that identification is an integral part of any determination of probable cause.

North Carolina General Statute §15A-401 reads, in relevant part:

> An officer may arrest without a warrant any person who the officer has probable cause to believe has committed a criminal offense or has violated a pretrial release order entered under G.S. 15A-534 or G.S. 15A-534.1(a)(2), in the officer's presence.
>
> Without a doubt, for a misdemeanor, probable cause consists of two distinct elements:
>
> One: That a crime was committed in the officer's presence.
>
> and,
>
> Two: That the person to be arrested has committed the offense.

The statute is very clear on its face: the officer must have probable cause to believe that the person arrested committed the offense.

Relevant case law

A warrantless arrest is based upon probable cause if the facts and circumstances known to the arresting officer warrant a prudent man in believing that a felony has been committed and the person to be arrested is the felon. *McCray v. Illinois*, 386 U.S. 300, 18 L.Ed.2d 62, 87 S.Ct. 1056 (1967). "Probable cause for an arrest has been defined to be a reasonable ground of suspicion supported by circumstances sufficiently strong in themselves to warrant a cautious man in believing the accused to be guilty.... To establish probable cause the evidence need not amount to proof of guilt, or even to prima facie evidence of guilt, but it must be such as would actuate a reasonable man acting in good faith." 5 Am.Jur.2d, Arrest § 44 (1962); *State v. Harris*, 279 N.C. 307, 182 S.E.2d 364 (1971).

Probable cause for an arrest is a reasonable ground of suspicion, supported by circumstances sufficiently strong in themselves to warrant a cautious man in believing the accused to be guilty.

State v. Harris, 279 N.C. 307, 311, 182 S.E.2d 364, 367 (1971)

An arrest does not always first occur when the police utter the words "You're under arrest." In fact, many times it occurs long before those words are said. Thus, it is possible to persuade the court that although the police had probable cause at the time that they officially informed the suspect that he or she was under arrest, the arrest had actually occurred much earlier in the investigation before probable cause existed.

One test is to determine whether a reasonable person would have felt free to leave. When deciding if an arrest occurred, a significant consideration is the extent to which freedom of movement is curtailed and the degree and manner of force used. *United States v. Beck*, 598 F.2d 497 (9th Circuit 1979). Another significant factor is the display of official authority such that "a reasonable person would have believed he was not free to leave."*Florida v. Royer*, 460 U.S. 491, 501, 103 S.Ct. 1319, 1326, 75 L.Ed.2d 229 (1983). In determining whether a defendant is "in custody" for *Miranda* purposes, however, the reviewing court may rely upon neither the subjective intent of the police to restrain him nor the subjective belief of the defendant as to what the police would do if he attempted to leave. Instead, the reviewing court must determine whether the suspect was in custody based upon an objective test of whether a reasonable person in the suspect's position would believe that he had been taken into custody or otherwise deprived of his freedom of action in any significant way or, to the contrary, would believe that he was free to go at will. *State v. Davis* 305 N.C. 400 (1982) *quoting United States v. Mendenhall*, 446 U.S. 544, 554, 100 S.Ct. 1870, 1877, 64 L.Ed.2d 497, 509 (1980).

While an arrest definitely occurs with the use of physical restraint, an arrest certainly may occur without physical restraint by the police or even the magic words "You're under arrest" being uttered. The varied forms of arrest without physical restraint or an express statement are documented as follows:

- *United States v. Harris*, 313 F.3d 1228 (10th Circuit, 2002) (Officers ordered suspect to stop, take hands out of pockets, and escorted accused to a police car constituted seizure).
- *United States v. Wood*, 981 F.2d 536 (D.C. Cir. 1992) (Officers ordered suspect to halt right there, stop, constituted seizure).
- *People v. Boodle*, 47 N.Y. 2d 398, 391 N.E. 2d 1329 (1979) (Order by police officer to keep hands where I can see them amounted to seizure).
- *Brown v. Texas*, 443 U.S. 47 (1979) (Officers asking suspect for identification and to explain what he was doing in an alleyway constituted seizure).
- *State v. Jones*, 283 S.E. 2d 483, (1983) (Seizure occurred when officer ordered man to step back from the vehicle with his hands in plain view).
- *United States v. Bowles*, 625 F.2d 526 (5th Cir. 1980) (Agent sees suspect and others engaged in suspicious activity. Suspect starts walking down hallway in airport. Agent's action of walking past the accused, showing his identification, and asking him if he could talk to him for a moment, while identifying himself as a narcotics agent amounted to a seizure).
- *United States v. Turpin*, 920 F.2d 1377 (8th Cir. 1990) (Seizure occurred when officer with drug-sniffing dog displayed credentials and requested that suspect sit down).
- *Commonwealth v. Houle*, 35 Mass. App. 474, 622 N.E. 2d 638 (1993) (Seizure occurred when officer asked accused if his name was "Bill," and upon seeing something in the accused's mouth ordered that he spit it out).

An arrest can certainly occur where there is a show of force. A seizure justified under the *Terry* standards can soon become a full-blown arrest requiring probable cause when the seizure is other than momentary. For instance, when the accused is ordered to halt and lie face down on the street, this conduct amounts to an arrest and not a temporary detention. *United States v. Delgadill-Velasquez*, 856 F.2d 1292 (9th Cir. 1988); *United States v. Del Vizo*, 918 F.2d 821 (9th Cir. 1990) (officers stopping a vehicle and forcing defendants at gunpoint to lie in the street while handcuffed was an arrest).

The passage of time may also convert an investigative detention into an arrest, although there is no black-letter law on what that amount of time is in minutes or hours. The simple fact that the accused believes that she would be detained for a lengthy period of time without freedom to leave can be considered an arrest without actual force being used. See *Florida v. Royer* 460 U.S. 491, 103 S.Ct. 139, 75 L.Ed 2d 229 (1983); *State of Arizona v. Winegar*, 147 U.S. 440, 711 P.2d 579 (1985); *Washington v. Lambert*, 98 F.3d 1181 (9th Cir. 1996) (police action in shining searchlight into suspect's car, handcuffing occupants and placing them in the back of a patrol car for 5 to 25 minutes amounted to an arrest).

The fruits of the illegal search must be suppressed. Thus, the correct remedy for a court is to suppress all evidence once it has determined that an illegal search has been made. Where a person has been seized unlawfully, an incidental search is also unlawful and fruits of the search are inadmissible and cannot be used against the person. *Wong Sun v. United States, supra*.

Motion to Suppress Statements Taken in Violation of Miranda Rights

It is the state's burden to show that Miranda rights were properly given, that they were understood and that they were knowingly, voluntarily and intelligently waived before statements may be admitted as evidence. Thus, upon a simple request by the defendant, the state must make such a showing before it can use any statements. One important strategy that should be employed by the defense is to use the probable cause argument to shift the time of arrest to an earlier point in the investigation, prior to the reading of the Miranda rights. The idea is simple: the police can conduct a non-custodial interrogation of a suspect without first advising the suspect of Miranda warnings. If the police read Miranda warnings, then that must mean that the suspect was in custody. Clearly, the prosecutor will argue that it was an investigatory detention and not a full-blown arrest. It is your job to convince the judge otherwise.

To satisfy *Miranda v. Arizona*, 384 U.S. 436, 86 S.Ct. 1602, 16 L.Ed.2d 694 (1966), the state must show that a suspect understood her rights and intelligently and knowingly relinquished those rights before custodial interrogation began.

The triggering event for *Miranda* is custodial interrogation. Simply put, if the suspect is not in custody, the police may ask any question that they choose and the answers will likely be admissible. This is one reason that police have such great success in admitting statements made over the telephone. It is common practice for the police to call a suspect at home and ask incriminating questions. It is a difficult prospect to argue that one is in custody when the police call a suspect at home and ask questions about a crime.

The North Carolina Supreme Court has ruled that suspects are entitled to notice of right to counsel pursuant to Miranda when they are in custody and are being asked questions about the crime. *State v. Steptoe*, 296 N.C. 711, 716, 252 S.E.2d 707, 710 (1979).

Miranda held that a person "deprived of his freedom in any significant way" could not be questioned unless a valid waiver of those rights was obtained after being adequately advised of them. In general, *Miranda* requires that, before custodial interrogation begins, criminal suspects must be advised that they have the right to remain silent, to consult with counsel, to have counsel appointed if the suspect cannot afford counsel and that anything that they say may be used against them in a court of law. *Miranda v. Arizona*, 384 U.S. 436, at 444, 86 S.Ct. 1602, at 1612, 16 L.Ed.2d 694 (1966).

Miranda warnings are a prophylactic measure, required at the outset of custodial interrogation, to prevent the state from extracting involuntary confessions from a criminal suspect. *Miranda*, 384 U.S. at 444, 86 S.Ct. at 1612. *Miranda* applies to "questioning initiated by law enforcement officers after a person has been taken into custody or otherwise deprived of his freedom of action in any significant way." *Id.*; . The triggering event for Miranda warnings is custodial interrogation by state law enforcement agents. *Miranda*, 384 U.S. at 444-56, 86 S.Ct. at 1612-13.

If the interrogation is commenced without benefit of being advised of Miranda warnings, all statements taken in violation of Miranda rights should be suppressed. However, suppression because of a violation of Miranda rights will not allow the accused to testify differently from the suppressed statements; it is not a license to lie on the stand. If the accused chooses to testify, there are a myriad of ways she can open the door to the suppressed statements. For example, assume the suppressed statement is an admission by the accused that she drank a twelve-pack of beer before driving. If she takes the stand at trial, the prosecutor can certainly ask her how much she had to drink before driving. If her answer is "two beers," then all your hard work to suppress the statements for violation of Miranda goes down the drain because the prosecutor can impeach her with her previously inadmissible statement.

Motion to Suppress Involuntarily Made Statements

The factual basis for this motion is that the defendant objects to the use of any statements at trial by the state without a ruling on the voluntariness of the statements. Notice that this motion does not state that statements were made by use of force or in an involuntary manner. This motion simply objects to the use of any statements without an express ruling on voluntariness. This is because statements made by a defendant are *prima facie* involuntary. *Jackson v. Denno*, 378 U.S. 368, 84 S.Ct. 1774, 12 L.Ed.2d 908 (1964). The burden is always on the state to show that statements by a defendant were voluntary, and therefore admissible, when the defendant moves for their suppression or objects to their admission.

It is reversible error for a court not to make a ruling on voluntariness when statements are objected to by the defense. More than 40 years ago the United States Supreme Court held that before a confession can be admitted into evidence, the trial judge must hold a hearing outside the presence of the jury and make a clear finding of voluntariness. *Jackson v. Denno*, 378 U.S. 368, 84 S.Ct. 1774, 12 L.Ed.2d 908 (1964). Since then the court has consistently held that failure to make a definite ruling on voluntariness before admission requires either a remand for the trial court to make such a finding or reversal unless the admission of the evidence itself was harmless error. For the purposes of compliance with *Jackson v. Denno*, *supra*, there is no difference between confessions and admissions.

It is always best to make the motion for voluntariness prior to trial. This has two advantages. The first is that it allows the defense to prepare adequately for trial, knowing what is and is not admissible. The second advantage is that it does not waste the jury's time. It is never helpful to object to the admission of statements, excuse the jury for argument on the issue and then have the jury return and hear the statements be admitted. That simply draws too much attention to the statements.

Motion to Dismiss Charges for Violation of the Right to Counsel and its relationship to Knoll

Unlike Reasonable Suspicion, Probable Cause, Miranda, and Voluntariness motions, a Motion to Dismiss for Violation of the Right to Counsel must affirmatively state the facts of the violation, and the defendant has the burden of showing such a violation. This can be done with video or audio tape of the investigation, through the state's own witnesses or by putting on defense witnesses at a hearing. As with Knoll, a witness has a right to see counsel for the purposes of examination, advisement, and witnessing the chemical test.

Violation of the Right to an Independent Test

The denial of the Right to an Independent Test takes several forms. The first is where the arrestee is taken into custody, the second is where the arrestee is field released and the third is where the police do not administer their own chemical test and they do not inform the arrestee of the right to an independent test. The violation of the Right to an Independent Test is something that must be affirmatively pled by the defendant. Thus, it is not a condition precedent to the admission of the chemical test result for the state to prove that they did not violate the Right to an Independent Test.

State v. Bumgarner 97 N.C. App. 567 (1990) sets the stage for the independent test. Although your client must be informed that he or she has a right to have an independent test, our Courts have held firm that all law enforcement is required to do at that point is make a telephone available and allow for medical personnel access. As *Bumgarner* states "Defendant in the case before us contends that the failure of law enforcement officers to take him to the hospital also violated his due process rights as guaranteed **429 by the United States Constitution. While this challenge apparently was not raised in *State v. Bunton*, we now reject such an assertion. Again, the majority rule is that beyond allowing a telephone call, there are few constitutional demands on officers in this situation. *See* Annotation, 45 A.L.R. 4th 11. Law enforcement officers may not hinder a driver from obtaining an independent sobriety test, but their constitutional duties in North Carolina go no further than allowing a defendant access to a telephone and allowing medical personnel access to a driver held in custody." *State v. Bumgarner*, 97 N.C. App. 567, 573, 389 S.E.2d 425, 428-29 (1990).

The Knoll Motion

In North Carolina, the Knoll motion is one of the defense attorney's best tools against the State. That being said, Knoll comes up very rarely since the prosecutors also know its inherent value. Knoll refers to a series of cases that were all combined and heard at the same time by our State Supreme Court. In 1988, three cases were consolidated under the title *State v. Knoll* 322 N.C. 535 (1988) and concerned pretrial motions based on statutory and constitutional rights violations. The basis of the Knoll cases is a denial of access. This was first brought to the Court's attention in *State v. Hill* 277 N.C. 547 (1971). In *Hill*, the Court established that the defendant's rights were violated (Sixth Amendment) because he was denied access to family and friends (witnesses) to be used in his defense. Even though a family member posted bond, he was not allowed to see anyone until his release the next morning. Since the only witnesses to Hill's alleged intoxication were the jailers that held him, the Court felt this was a problem. Later, the State Legislature passed it into law which became N.C.G.S. 15A-954 which says the following:

§ 15A-954. Motion to dismiss - Grounds applicable to all criminal pleadings; dismissal of proceedings upon death of defendant.

(a) The court on motion of the defendant must dismiss the charges stated in a criminal pleading if it determines that:

(1) The statute alleged to have been violated is unconstitutional on its face or as applied to the defendant.

(2) The statute of limitations has run.

(3) The defendant has been denied a speedy trial as required by the Constitution of the United States and the Constitution of North Carolina.

(4) The defendant's constitutional rights have been flagrantly violated and there is such irreparable prejudice to the defendant's preparation of his case that there is no remedy but to dismiss the prosecution.
(5) The defendant has previously been placed in jeopardy of the same offense.
(6) The defendant has previously been charged with the same offense in another North Carolina court of competent jurisdiction, and the criminal pleading charging the offense is still pending and valid.
(7) An issue of fact or law essential to a successful prosecution has been previously adjudicated in favor of the defendant in a prior action between the parties.
(8) The court has no jurisdiction of the offense charged.
(9) The defendant has been granted immunity by law from prosecution.
(10) The pleading fails to charge an offense as provided in G.S. 15A-924(e).
(b) Upon suggestion to the court that the defendant has died, the court upon determining that the defendant is dead must dismiss the charges.
(c) A motion to dismiss for the reasons set out in subsection (a) may be made at any time.

The Legislature using subpart (a)(4) in response to the Hill decision. Hill did lay out that this was "drastic relief" and that it should be granted "most sparingly."

Knoll combined three cases, as I mentioned earlier. Needless to say, there were three defendants: Knoll, Warren, and Hicks. Knoll was stopped in the afternoon and had a breath test result of 0.30; the Magistrate set his bond at $300.00 and allowed him to use the phone to call his father. His father wanted to come and get him but was told he would have to wait until 11:00 p.m. Based on the conversations with his son, his father didn't seem to think he was impaired.

The next defendant, Warren, was stopped shortly after 10 p.m. His breath test result was a 0.25. His bond was set by the Magistrate at $500.00. Two friends stopped by to try and get him. The first witness came during his breath test and was allowed to see him; he had only $300.00 in cash but told the Magistrate he would take responsibility for Warren. The Magistrate told him that his friend could not be released until 6:00 a.m. the following morning. A second person came in after 1:00 a.m. with $200.00 requesting Warren's release. He was also told that Warren would not be released until 6 a.m. Warren was finally released at 8:00 a.m. after posting bond.

The third defendant in the Knoll trilogy is Hicks. Hicks was arrested close to 1:00 a.m. His breath test result was a 0.18. The Magistrate set his bond at $200.00. Hicks had over two thousand dollars in cash with him but was not allowed to post his own bond. He was allowed to call his wife who had no way to get there at the time. He was released the next morning at 6 a.m.

The Court in *Knoll* concluded that the first two defendants, Knoll and Warren should have been released to their respective witnesses. They determined that the third defendant, Hicks, should have been released since he had the money to post his bond and could have hired a taxi to get home to his wife. The crux of this case is the defendant's ability to have access to friends and family that would be able to see the defendant and his condition. The Court found that the defendant's inability to have witnesses observe them at the time limited the defendant's ability to have him observed prejudiced his case. The Court also held, that in cases like these, dismissal was the only remedy.

The Ferguson Motion

State v. Ferguson 90 N.C. App. 513 (1988) was decided by the Court of Appeals shortly before the State Supreme Court decided Knoll. After Ferguson was arrested and informed of his right to a witness, he called his wife. Ferguson told his wife to be at the jail within twenty minutes to witness his test. When his wife arrived, within the twenty minutes, she was told by an officer that she was late. Ferguson refused the test since his wife was not present. The Court ruled that because his witness arrived in time, but was denied access, it constituted a "flagrant violation" of his Constitutional rights and that the results would require a dismissal of charges.

The Myers Motion

A few years later, in 1995, the Court of Appeals came to a similar but different conclusion in *State v. Myers* 118 N.C. App. 452 (1995). Myers was arrested for DWI and taken down to the police station to blow into the breath machine. Since Myers had a statutory right to have someone witness his breath test, he asked if his wife could witness it. The officer told Myers "that might not be a good idea." The Court of Appeals held that since his right to have a witness present had been refused the results of the test should not be admitted.

6.4 Motions in Limine

The following set of Motions in Limine should cover just about every circumstance possible at a DWI trial. Simply choose the ones from the below list that are relevant to the particular DWI case to be tried and disregard the rest.

To pre-instruct the jury panel on the issue of reasonable doubt by reading the following jury instruction to them:

"The state has the burden of proving the defendant guilty beyond a reasonable doubt. In civil cases, it is only necessary to prove that a fact is more likely true than not or that its truth is highly probable. In a criminal case such as this, the state's proof must be more powerful than that. It must be proof beyond a reasonable doubt.

Proof beyond a reasonable doubt is proof that leaves you firmly convinced of the defendant's guilt. There are very few things in this world that we know with absolute certainty, and in criminal cases the law does not require proof that overcomes every doubt. If, based on your consideration of the evidence, you are firmly convinced that the defendant is guilty of the crime charged, you must find him/her guilty. If, on the other hand, you think that there is a real possibility that he/she is not guilty, then you must give him/her the benefit of the doubt and find him/her not guilty."

To preclude any mention of any recorded questions that were asked or answers that were given to the police that have not been disclosed to the defense. Counsel understands that a witness may suddenly "regain" his memory while on the stand. Such conduct is not highly unusual and can be dealt with appropriately on cross-examination. This motion is directed toward information contained in documents or materials not disclosed to the defense, but which should have been disclosed. [*Brady v. Maryland*, 373 U.S. 83, 83 S.Ct 1194, 10 L.Ed.2d 215 (1963)].

To preclude the officer's opinion as to the existence or degree of impairment of the defendant. To preclude the officer's opinion as to the ultimate issue of intoxication or impairment. The North Carolina Supreme Court has previously ruled that the ultimate issue of fact is squarely within the sole province of the jury, and testimony by the police to the ultimate issue of fact violates that province. [*State v. Carr* 196 N.C. 129, Rule 403, North Carolina Rules of Evidence].

To preclude the state from asking their police witnesses to compare the number of DUI arrests to the number of DUI investigations. While it may be proper to ask an officer about the number of DUI investigations performed to gauge experience level, it would be improper to compare the number to the number of investigations to arrests without complete disclosure of the police reports and number of convictions obtained from those arrests. Such a comparison puts the defendant at the disadvantage of not being able to verify the officer's truthfulness and memory. Such testimony would be more highly prejudicial than probative of any fact. In other words, the state would be presenting the information to show that the defendant was investigated and arrested—and is therefore guilty—because the officer lets innocent people go free. Such an analogy is improper, especially in light of the standard pre-trial instruction given to juries that the fact that a defendant has been arrested is not proof of guilt—in fact it is not proof of anything. [*Brady v. Maryland*, 373 U.S. 83, 83 S.Ct 1194, 10 L.Ed.2d 215 (1963); N.C.G.S.15A-901-910].

To preclude any demonstration (or "mimicking") by any officer as to how the defendant performed on the Field Sobriety Test(s) since such tests are not reproducible in court and such demonstration would be more prejudicial that probative. Note: this does not include a demonstration as to how they are supposed to be performed or as to how the officer demonstrated the tests at the time of the investigation. [Rule 403, North Carolina Rules of Evidence].

To preclude any comment by the prosecutor or state's witnesses on the defendant's post-arrest silence, including invocation of Miranda rights. [*State v. Ward* 354 N.C. 231 (2001)]. A defendant's right to due process is violated when a witness introduces a statement at trial that the defendant asserted his or her right to remain silent. [*State v. Mendoza* 206 N.C. App. 391 (2010)].

To preclude the state from mentioning that the defendant had and waived the opportunity to have an independent chemical test completed or that the defendant was advised of the right to obtain an independent chemical test. Such information is neither an element of any offense charged, nor is it a prerequisite to the introduction of the state's chemical test. Such information could only be used improperly to influence the jury by shifting the burden to the defense to prove innocence. Such information is more highly prejudicial than probative of any fact. [Fifth and Sixth Amendments, U.S. Constitution; *In re Winship*, 397 U.S. 358, 361, 90 S.Ct. 1068, 1071 (1970)].

To preclude the state from mentioning that there were two tubes of blood drawn and that one remains intact for testing by the defense. Such information is neither an element of any offense charged, nor is it a prerequisite to the introduction of the state's chemical test. Such information could only be used improperly to influence the jury by shifting the burden to the defense to prove innocence. Such information is more highly prejudicial than probative of any fact. [Fifth and Sixth Amendments, U.S. Constitution].

To preclude any comment by the prosecutor or state's witnesses that the defendant had asked to speak with an attorney or that the defendant was following an attorney's advice by not submitting to any test. Such comment would amount to a due process violation, requiring a mistrial.

To preclude the prosecutor from asking the defendant if the police officer is lying in the event the police officer's version of events differs from the defendant's version of events. United States v. Henke, 222 F.3d 633 (9th Circuit). In United States v. Sanchez, 176 F.3d 1214 (1999), in the Ninth Circuit, the prosecutor's cross-examination of the defendant that forced the defendant to call a U.S. Marshall a liar constituted prosecutorial misconduct because it called for an opinion on the credibility of a witness. While the court found that it was prosecutorial misconduct, the case was reversed on other grounds so the court never reached the issue as to whether this was reversible error or not.

To preclude any mention of a prior DWI during the state's case-in-chief for the reasons that the probative value of such evidence is substantially outweighed by its prejudicial effect and that such evidence is irrelevant. Any questions offered by the prosecution designed to elicit evidence of a prior DWI conviction or arrest. Except in Habitual DWI cases where the defendant has not stipulated to the prior convictions. [Rules 401 and 403, North Carolina Rules of Evidence].

To preclude the state from rendering any opinion as to whether the passenger was intoxicated if the passenger does not testify. Such evidence is entirely irrelevant as the state cannot show "guilt by association," and any such evidence is much more highly prejudicial than probative on any issue that is of consequence to a jury. [Rules 401 and 403, North Carolina Rules of Evidence].

To preclude the prosecutor from asking any witness who was not a passenger in the defendant's vehicle if he or she "would feel comfortable" as a passenger in a vehicle driven by the defendant or if he or she would be a passenger in a vehicle driven by the defendant. Such testimony amounts to nothing more than mere speculation on the part of the witness, takes into account myriad variables which cannot be thoroughly explored at trial, is more highly prejudicial than probative of any point and is irrelevant to any issue. [Rules 401 and 403, North Carolina Rules of Evidence].

The state is put on notice that in the event of a violation of any of the above motions granted by this court, defense counsel will move for a mistrial and dismissal of charges pending for prosecutorial misconduct. The state has the duty to inform its witnesses of all Motions in Limine granted to ensure their cooperation with the court.

6.5 Evidentiary Hearings

The primary purpose of the evidentiary hearing is to win the motions to suppress and/or dismiss. However, the great collateral benefit is that the defense has the opportunity to cross-examine the state's witnesses under oath and on the record. Think of the evidentiary hearing as being able to play poker where you get to see your opponent's hand without showing your own cards, unless there is some compelling reason (such as in a motion to dismiss for violation of right to counsel). The evidentiary hearing on the motions above should be heard sufficiently before trial in order to create a transcript of the state's testimony.

Remember that hearsay is usually admissible at an evidentiary hearing because the court is interested in finding out what the police knew and when they knew it. An evidentiary hearing will, generally, be less formal than a trial. Often foundational requirements are not enforced because both sides will stipulate to them for purposes of the hearing only.

If you know that the police officer is HGN-certified, and his certification is not at issue, you may want to stipulate to the foundational prerequisite for purposes of the evidentiary hearing, only. This will speed the hearing up and all parties will be appreciative. Clearly, though, if the officer's certification is at issue, attack it in the manner necessary to win the issue and the motion.

PRACTICE TIP: Sometimes it is unwise to challenge certain aspects of the state's evidence in a pre-trial hearing. For example, if you find something wrong with the police officer's HGN certification, and it is a defect that could be cured prior to trial, you might want to wait until they need to make the foundational showing of certification at trial before you tip your hand and attack. This has the dual effect of striking when the prosecutor is least prepared to defend the attack as well as making the state look unprepared and incompetent before the jury.

Should your client testify at an evidentiary hearing? In a reasonable suspicion or probable cause motion, the answer is generally in the negative. Reasonable suspicion for the stop and probable cause for the arrest are based on what the officer knew at the time of arrest. Thus, your client could have been having a diabetic seizure at the time of the arrest and if the officer arrested because of impaired balance, slurred speech and the smell of acetone which he mistook for alcohol, nothing your client says will change the reasonableness of the arrest. The only possible way it could have helped would be if your client had communicated this to the officer before the arrest.

Sometimes clients do have to testify at an evidentiary hearing, as in a Miranda motion or one based on voluntariness of statements where there is a real issue that amounts to more than simply making the state prove the lawfulness of the acquisition of the statements.

Chapter 7

Plea Offers

7.1 Overview

DWI plea offers are different in many respects from other plea offers. In the DWI area, prosecutors' hands are tied by mandatory sentencing laws, legislation which requires prosecution, and their own office policies.

DWI is not a political crime, but it is a highly politicized crime. Chief prosecutors are elected and appointed using the same "Get Tough on Crime" message, not a "Let's Do Justice" message. Since DWI is so highly politicized and blown out of proportion, it is easy for a would-be County or City Attorney to campaign on the promise of no plea bargaining in DWI cases. Yet, anyone who practices in this area knows that they have to offer plea bargains in order to function. If every defense attorney set every DWI case for trial, the system would collapse.

As a result, we find that many plea offers are made that ask the defendant to plead "guilty" or "no contest," and receive the bare minimum sentence, and all other traffic charges will be dismissed.

When deciding whether or not to take a plea offer, an attorney should not push the client into a decision. That's not to say, however, that you should withhold your advice. Remember that the client has employed you not only for your legal skills, but also because you have some experience in these types of situations. There are times when a client should reject the plea because there is a strong defense case. There are other times when your client will be slaughtered at trial, and you are only playing for the fumble. Remember, in either situation and in all of the situations in between, it is your client who will have to live with the conviction should you plead or take the matter to trial and lose. There is nothing more difficult than advising your client to go to trial, then having to stand there after the guilty verdict is read and the court security staff handcuffs your client and leads her off through a different exit than you will use to leave the courtroom.

Make it a practice to inform the client fully of all the ramifications of the decision. Putting it in writing is a good method. Writing not only protects the attorney if a client claims ineffective assistance of counsel, but it will also allow the client to read the material over at her leisure.

PRACTICE TIP: Guilty versus no contest: How should my client plead?

In simple terms, a plea of "guilty" means that your client admits to all of the facts alleged in the plea offer. A plea of "no contest" means that your client, although not admitting to the facts, agrees that if there were a trial, he would lose. Either way, the judge finds the accused guilty.

The advantage to a "no contest" plea is that if there is a civil suit arising out of the incident (such as where there is an accident), your client will not have admitted to the facts which will then have to be proved at a civil trial. There is no advantage to a "no contest" plea over a "guilty" plea where there is no possibility of a civil action arising out of the incident.

7.2 Waiver of Rights

Clients must always be informed of their waiver of rights prior to taking a plea. Most judges do it properly, but some do not. In either event, a competent attorney always advises the client of the rights waived prior to entering the courtroom to accept a plea offer. This should be done in writing as well as in a discussion with the client. A good practice is to write a letter to the client that explains the rights, then sit with the client and go over each right, line-by-line. Those rights are:

- The right to a trial by jury.
- The right to confront and cross-examine witnesses for the state.
- The right to compel favorable witnesses by subpoena to testify.
- The right to remain silent and have the state prove each element of every charge.
- The right to a direct appeal.
- The right to counsel, should the client not be able to afford an attorney.

In Superior Court, judges will ask if the accused has had any alcohol or drugs during the 24 hours preceding the change-of-plea proceeding that would affect the decision. The judge will also ask if the accused is a United States citizen, his or her age, and how much school the accused completed. If the person is not a United States citizen, a DWI conviction may have immigration consequences.

7.3 Collateral Consequences

As we know, a DWI conviction can have onerous collateral consequences. Be sure to discuss with your client the adverse effects on immigration, professional licenses, security clearances, military discipline, auto insurance, health insurance, license loss, commercial driver status, ignition interlock requirements, FAA reporting requirements and the like. A DWI conviction restricts travel to certain countries.

There may be questions that you cannot answer—that will occur frequently. But the proper thing to do is to raise the possible issues with your client and seek out the answer. Sometimes it is best left to the client to seek the answer; after all, you cannot say whether a particular workers' union will support your client in the event of termination based upon a DWI conviction. Have your client seek the advice of the union's workers' representative.

7.4 Immigration Consequences

A DWI conviction, whether as a result of trial or plea, may affect immigration status of a noncitizen. It could result in the deportation or removal of a person from this country. It could prevent the person from ever gaining legal status in the United States or becoming a citizen. Each case is as different as each person's status. Always ask your client about immigration status if he is not a United States citizen (see *Padilla v. Kentucky*, 559 U.S. 356, 130 S.Ct. 1473, 176 L.Ed.2d 284 (2010))). Always consult with an attorney who is knowledgeable in the immigration area if you do not know the answer to an immigration question.

Entry into Canada

Non-Canadian citizens may be barred from entry into Canada upon conviction of a misdemeanor DWI. The entry question turns on whether the crime, if it had been committed in Canada, would be a felony or indictable offense in Canada. DWI is both a felony and an indictable offense in Canada. A senior immigration officer or adjudicator may grant entry to a person who is barred from entering because of a DWI conviction subject to such terms and conditions as the officer deems to be appropriate for admission. However, the person cannot remain in Canada for more than 30 days.

Once a minimum of five years has passed from the time that the sentence was completed—not imposed—permission to enter Canada is more easily obtained provided that there were no more than two convictions which would bar entry. Application for entry can be made at a port of entry, but is not recommended as the applicant might still be turned down. Application for entry may be less risky to make at one of the five Canadian Consulate offices in the United States (Buffalo, New York; New York, New York; Detroit, Michigan; Los Angeles, California and Seattle, Washington). It may take up to six months to approve entry. A person may also apply for temporary residency in Canada.

In a nutshell, entry into Canada less than five years after a conviction is an administrative nightmare with little chance of success. When the conviction is more than five, but less than ten years old, entry is more easily obtained upon payment of a fee and a criminal background check. If the conviction is more than ten years old, entry will be permitted with just a background check. Multiple convictions and the seriousness of the crimes will play a pivotal role in the decision to bar entry. In any event, if the client wishes to enter Canada, competent Canadian counsel should be retained.

7.5 Exposure of Prior Offenses

Read the plea offer carefully before your client accepts it, especially if your client has a prior offense. A plea offer may carry language that forces the defendant to acknowledge that she has no prior DWI convictions or pending cases and is not on probation for any other offenses at the time of signing the plea offer. Some offers will even go as far as requiring the defense attorney to acknowledge that the client has no priors and nothing pending. Sometimes the prosecution does not know about a prior offense, but you do.

If the attorney knows of a prior offense, he cannot sign a plea agreement that requires him to acknowledge that nothing exists. That would be a clear ethical violation of being honest with the tribunal and fairness to opposing counsel. Asking the prosecutor to strike such language will certainly tip her off to the fact that your client has a prior offense or something pending. The attorney has limited choices in this situation.

The first choice is not to enter into the plea and take the matter to trial.

The second choice is not to enter into the plea and plead to the court.

The third choice is to withdraw and let the client do as he chooses, but this might raise some red flags. Remember that an attorney has a duty to inform the client that the client should not commit a fraud upon the court and opposing counsel by signing the agreement, should the client decide to proceed in a *pro se* fashion.

7.6 Subsequent Offenses

Clients must be informed about the effect of a conviction on any subsequent conviction. Most clients will tell you that they do not "plan on" getting another DWI, but remind them that they didn't plan on getting the first one. A second conviction within seven years of the first can include mandatory jail time as well as the fine and period of license suspension. In determining the seven year period, the date of conviction of the first charge runs to the date of arrest on the next charge.

Moreover, a fourth DWI within a ten year period (at the time of this writing this is true but check the statute since the legislature is currently trying to amend this to three within ten years) will result in a charge of Felony Habitual DWI as well. The determination of the ten year period in this case looks back to find three convictions in the ten year period with the current charge also within that ten year look back.

7.7 Out of State Offenses

North Carolina allows out-of-state prior offenses to be used as if the offense were committed in North Carolina, under certain circumstances. In these cases, the State has to prove that the DWI statute in the other state is substantially similar to North Carolina's statute beyond a reasonable doubt.

7.8 Misdemeanor Plea Offers

In most instances, misdemeanor prosecutors have their hands tied because of statutory and political consequences of pleading a DWI case.

The most common non-DWI plea offer is to Reckless Driving. While still a criminal offense, Reckless Driving offers several advantages. Although it is a Class Two Misdemeanor, punishable by up to sixty days in jail, it is the rare Reckless plea that results in any jail time. Most often, Reckless pleas will carry a fine in the hundreds of dollars as well as some sort of alcohol-abuse screening and treatment. Along with the primary advantage of no jail time, it will also not result in the loss of a driver's license, by itself. If your client has other offenses on his or her record, it may result in a loss of license.

Generally, the plea offered in a misdemeanor DWI case will dismiss all traffic violations and all but one count of DWI. Most prosecuting agencies will offer the minimum, or near-minimum, stipulated penalty. Even in bad cases, where the trial prospects look grim, it might not be wise to accept the state's plea offer. Remember: no matter how bad the facts of the case look, no matter how high the blood alcohol results are, your client still has a fighting chance at trial. One hundred percent of people who plead guilty are found guilty. As long as the plea does not offer your client anything better than he or she would get if he or she went to trial and lost, the client should seriously consider rejecting the plea offer and taking the matter to trial.

7.9 Felony Plea Offers

Oddly enough, the more serious felony cases offer more room for a plea bargain than do the less serious misdemeanor cases. Typically, a plain vanilla felony DWI can be pled to the minimum active time of twelve months. If your client has no previous felonies on his or her record, going to trial can increase the minimum active time to sixteen months if you lose at trial. Keep in mind that once your client is charged with Felony Habitual DWI the crime now falls under our Structured Sentencing Guidelines instead of the Fair Sentencing Guidelines if it were a misdemeanor.

Chapter 8

Trial

8.1 Overview

If you have done your job properly during the pre-trial stages, either you will not need to try the case or you will be exceedingly prepared for the trial. At all stages throughout the proceedings, you should have been gathering transcripts of evidentiary hearings, witness interviews, DMV hearings and cross-referencing them against the police reports and each other. Organization leads to strategy. Most times, the best way to proceed with your case is in a chronological order with respect to the DWI investigation itself. While the charges will determine the range of defenses needed, never let the prosecutor dictate the method or order of your defense. In other words, don't be reactionary. You do not have to rebut every point made by the prosecutor—just the ones that are important. Every part of a trial is important, but cross-examination is the cornerstone of every defense practice. In fact, you may try case after case without doing a direct examination. Your skill on cross is a likely predictor of your success at trial.

8.2 Voir Dire and Jury Selection

Voir Dire in North Carolina is as varied as the number of courtrooms, perhaps even more so. Some judges will conduct Voir Dire themselves, while others will allow the attorneys free rein to question the jurors. Most styles combine the two. The most important thing is to know what your particular judge's style of Voir Dire will be.

While it has been said that the trial begins with the first police witness interview, it is won or lost with the jury selected. Jury selection is not a "black art," but no one can read a juror's mind. The only way we have to understand a potential juror's thoughts is to ask for them and trust in the juror's understanding of the question and the truthfulness of the answer provided.

Keeping track of juror answers to Voir Dire questions is highly important. Logically organized and clear notes are the keys to good jury selection. This will vary from courtroom to courtroom and also with the number of jurors, but it is the best way I have figured out to do jury selection.

I have a simple piece of thin (1/4-inch thick) hardboard that I bought at a lumber store. It is cut to about 20 inches wide and about 15 inches tall. The corners have been slightly rounded so as not to dig into anything in my trial suitcase.

I then take mailing labels, which I have pre-printed from my computer's printer and place them on the hardboard in the pattern of jury seats. I then write my Voir Dire notes on the pre-printed labels. They appear as below:

The first thing that is written is the information that I deem important from the jurors' questionnaires provided by the court. At the top left of the mailing label I write the juror's name. On the top right I write the assigned juror number. At the bottom, in the middle, I write the juror's rating number. The rating number is 0 to 10 and may certainly be crossed out and change throughout the Voir Dire (that is the idea of the number). The number represents desirability as a juror for the defense. A "0" is considered the worst possible juror. (I must confess, at times I have ignored my own rating system and have assigned negative numbers after having been absolutely appalled at the attitudes of some jurors.) A

"10" is considered the best juror for the defense. A "5" on the scale is considered an absolutely neutral juror who is capable of understanding reasonable doubt and does not begin the trial with a bias. In the right case, a panel of 5s will theoretically acquit every time. You want a panel of 10s.

The reason to use mailing labels is that when a juror is stricken for cause, you can remove the mailing label from the board and replace it with a clean mailing label. I often prepare a few more mailing labels than will be necessary for the first 10 (or 20) because I know that some will be struck and replaced.

The individual labels will appear as follows:

Juror#____

Name______________________ Age______ Kids______

M F M S D W Sep Area______________ W B H A I ME NA

Job/Co.______________________________________

Education________________Language ______________

Car____________ BS__________________________

Spouse______________________ ______________

Religion________________CSI__________________

Dress__________________ND__________________

LEE ____

Military_____ Media____________Prior DUI/Crim________

Disabled - Overweight - MADD - Alcoholism - Religious - L C R

____

____

____

____

0 1 2 3 4 5 6 7 8 9 10

While most designations are obvious, the shorthand notes are:

M F: Male/Female

M S D Sep W: Married, Single, Divorced, Separated, Widow/Widower

W B H A I ME NA: White, Black, Hispanic, Asian, Indian (India), Middle-Eastern, Native American

BS: Bumper Stickers

CSI: Is the person a fan of the TV show CSI?

Dress: Messy, Casual, Neat, Inappropriate for Court, T-Shirt slogans?

ND: Non-Drinker (and reason).

LEE: Law Enforcement Experience

L C R: Political leanings—Left, Center, Right (circle one)

You can write whatever you want on the label, just be sure that it is accurate, uniform, and decipherable. The idea of designations is not to copy the ones above (although feel free to do so), it is to create your own designations that are easily recognizable and useful to your own particular style of Voir Dire and jury selection. The notes have to be quickly taken and easily understood. The most valuable part is the 0 to 10 scale. At the end of the Voir Dire, when it comes time for the peremptory strikes, I already know whom should be struck, and in what order. The only last-minute strike decisions that need to be made are where there is more than one person with the same 0 to 10 scale rating.

Generally, a few hands will rise for "guilty." One or none will rise for "not guilty." And the majority of the hands will remain down because the jurors believe that they cannot vote either way because they have heard no evidence.

This is where you strike: ask the jury, by a show of hands, if they think that our Constitution of the United States is a good thing. Every hand should rise (watch out for the ones that don't). Remind them that our Constitution says that every person is innocent unless proved guilty by proof beyond a reasonable doubt and that they have heard no proof at this point in time. Then ask them as follows:

> Knowing that our Constitution says that a person is innocent unless proved guilty by proof beyond a reasonable doubt, and knowing that you have not heard any evidence yet, how would you have to vote, if you were to vote right now? Please show me hands for "guilty," and show me hands for "not guilty."

This set of questions opens the door for further education as to the burden of proof. It also links your client's rights to the Constitution and shows the jury that they can raise their hands in support of a "not guilty" verdict and be correct. The problem that plagues the defense in every criminal case is that most jurors think that it is their duty to vote "guilty" unless you can convince them otherwise. The courthouse is replete with messages that tell jurors that the police, prosecutors and court system are all linked as partners against crime. Next time you are in a courthouse, stop and look at the state's witnesses—they are all wearing police uniforms. Next look at the courthouse security—they are all wearing uniforms. The bailiff, who takes orders directly from the judge and serves him or her exclusively, may likely be wearing the uniform of the same agency as the police who made the arrest. These subtle messages align the court with the police.

In a breath test case there is the constant danger that the jurors will simply believe the test results because they are produced by a machine. The defense must be prepared to question the jury about their knowledge and experience with mechanical and electronic measuring devices. Some people have extensive experience with calibration standards. The defense attorney should ask the jury: "Would you require the state to prove the results of the breath machine by proof beyond a reasonable doubt just like any other evidence?" Asking the jury why, or why not, as a follow-up question tends to get some good dialogue going.

When you find an undesirable juror, it is always best to attempt to have the judge strike that juror for cause rather than having to use one of your limited peremptory strikes. Asking the juror if he or she can "be fair and honest" usually does not work. Everybody wants to be fair and honest. Not many people want to think of themselves as unfair and dishonest. And those that do will lie to you anyway.

The better way to approach the subject is to explain to the jurors that there are no right or wrong answers—just honest ones. A great approach is to explain that there are many types of jury trials that take place in the court system. Explain that people are tried by juries for drug possession, assault, theft and many other crimes. Some people may not want to sit on a child molestation jury because they have children of a similar age to the victim and just couldn't bear to hear the evidence, but they might be fine to sit on a DWI case. Then suggest to the potential juror in the form of a question: "Maybe this just isn't the right case for you?"

"I think I can be fair." "I'll try to be fair." I'll do my best." These are all phrases that cannot be left without further questioning. As a defense attorney, you need clear, unequivocal answers. People who say that they "will try to be fair" are going to convict your client. Those answers are weasel words—they will allow the juror to weasel out of a tough decision.

Never forget that while your first duty is to win the trial your second duty is to prepare for appeal. If the judge will not let you make a record on the subject of the denial of a motion to strike for cause, then make a record of the fact that the judge would not let you make a record.

When you run into a situation where the potential juror will not give you more of a definite answer than "I'll try," use the following analogy:

> Suppose a husband was going off to Las Vegas for a week-long business trip and he is saying goodbye to his wife at the airport. She knows that there are some romantic temptations in Las Vegas so she asks him to be faithful to her while he's gone. His response to her is "I'll try my best." Is that good enough? Most jurors see the response as problematic and then come to realize that they need to give a clear answer.

8.3 Jury Instructions

It makes sense to consider jury instructions before you step into the courtroom for trial because they should be made part of your theme of the case. While many cases have unexpected twists and turns, the general defense theme of your case usually will remain the same throughout the trial. Reviewing and preparing defense jury instructions will allow you to weave the language of the jury instructions throughout the defense case. Consider framing your questions in terms of the jury instructions. For example, when you have almost finished your examination of your own expert, you might ask him or her if there is a "real possibility" that your client might never have been over the prohibited alcohol limit, thus echoing the words of the *Portillo* reasonable doubt jury instruction.

You might also consider using phrases right out of the instructions during opening and closing statements without announcing that the words come from the instructions. It does not take much time or effort to memorize the reasonable doubt instruction. At some point later, the judge will instruct the jury and use the very same language that you uttered to the jury. On a subconscious level, at least, the jury will see the judge allied with you, and it will raise your stature before the jury. There is no legal or ethical requirement that you submit adverse jury instructions for trial. Make it a practice to submit only those instructions that you feel are advantageous to your case and leave the others out. The prosecutor may fail to ask for jury instructions that would hurt your case. If you feel that you are entitled to an instruction, ask for it. If the instruction does not already exist in the PJIs or case law, write it yourself. As noted earlier in text, I feel that some cases need a *Narron* instruction.

8.4 Opening Statements

If what the lawyers say is not evidence, then why say it? The simple answer is "to win." The rules clearly state that openings are not argument, but a statement of what each party believes the evidence will show. It is the defense attorney's obligation to tell the jury that the evidence will show his client is not guilty.

There is nothing wrong with explaining the standard of reasonable doubt in the opening statement, then showing why the state's evidence will not measure up to the standard. That is not argument.

Do not make promises that you cannot keep in opening. Unless you know that your client must testify, don't go near that subject. Unless you know that you will be able to show that the chemical test was faulty, don't promise the jury that it is faulty.

Many times the prosecutor will thank the jury for their service and claim that he or she is a representative of the people of the State of North Carolina. Remember that you too are a representative of the people of the State of North Carolina—you just represent them one at a time.

Always start out with a bold statement and a story. Prosecutors lose jurors with their platitudes and insincere expressions of thanks to the jury for taking time out of their lives to sit on this case. You must engage the jurors immediately. If you are a poor storyteller, switch to insurance defense work and leave the criminal cases to your storytelling colleagues. Humanize your client. It is easy for a jury to convict "the defendant," but it is entirely different to convict a person with a name, family, friends, co-workers, a home and a cat named "Fluffy."

Touch your client during opening statement. Stand near your client and put your hand on his shoulder at least once while delivering your opening. This subtly allows the jurors to understand that your client is not a criminal, but a human being. Some attorneys lean away from their clients and keep a distance between them. Such body-language portrays a cold feeling. After all, if the person's own attorney cannot stand to be close to him, he must be an evil person. Yet, if the attorney can portray a feeling of warmth toward the client (whether it is heartfelt or simply an act) the jury may feel some of that warmth and friendliness.

If your strategy relies on the error factors of the breath or blood test result, name the error factors and explain how they add up to a margin of error which spans across your client's test results. If your strategy, however, relies on a surprise for the prosecutor, do not reveal it until you are at the appropriate point in testimony.

PRACTICE TIP: Do not reveal the chemical test results during opening argument. Years ago I chose to reveal the breath test result during opening because my client's result was exactly at the legal limit, and the calibration logs before and after my client's test showed that the machine was reading at least 5 percent high. It was a good, strong opening.

Through nothing more than dumb luck on my part and sheer incompetence on the part of the prosecutor, I was able to have the test results suppressed at trial—after I had disclosed them to the jury. There were no grounds for a mistrial because I was the one who disclosed them to the jury!

Fortunately, there was a "not guilty" verdict and a valuable lesson learned. No matter what—don't reveal the results to the jury during opening statement.

— James Nesci

Do not tell the jury to keep an "open mind" and make their decision at the close of all evidence. Their minds should be closed. Keeping an open mind until they have heard all of the evidence is an incorrect application of the constitutional principle of innocent unless proved guilty. At any point in time before the close of evidence, they should vote "not guilty"—especially before they have heard any evidence at all.

Lastly, move into reasonable doubt and the reasons to vote "not guilty." Never sit down without telling the jury to vote "not guilty" at the end of the evidence. Just like your client cannot take the stand without denying the allegations, you cannot present an opening without asking for a "not guilty" verdict.

Should you reserve opening for the start of the defense case? That is a call for the defense attorney to make, but it is not wise to wait. We have all heard anecdotal evidence that shows that jurors make up their minds by the end of opening statements. It is probably true. Think about it—if the jurors are allowed to hear a one-sided argument from the state (prosecutors and police), you have given them nothing to sway them in your favor.

If you let the prosecutor give an opening, then put on all of his or her witnesses, introduce all of his or her evidence, then give your opening, your first real chance to sway the jurors will be after they have already made up their minds against you. It is easier to sway one who has no opinion, or a lightly held opinion, than it is to change the mind of someone who has a firmly held belief.

8.5 Cross-Examination

The method of cross-examination should be tailored to your own style as well as the personality, education and experience of the officer. Every DWI defense lawyer knows that you cannot "beat up" an honest and affable officer. Likewise, if the officer is a pushy, overreaching, jack-booted thug, you can take the initiative to be mean and condescending to the officer, and the jury will appreciate your style. Choose your method carefully, but don't be so hampered by caution that you fail to take calculated risks.

Much of cross-examination in a DWI case is asking the right set of questions and stopping before you blow it. The idea is to ask just enough questions to get your point across and allow you to argue reasonable inferences from the answers during closing argument, when you do not have a hostile witness on the stand to contradict your points. Questions asked by lawyers are not evidence, but they can be used to give meaning to the answers.

Before you can cross-examine, however, you need to have a framework of events that took place in this particular investigation. The framework is best done simply and chronologically with an elapsed time column as described in the example below:

Chronology and Data

Date	September 4, 2006 (Labor Day))
Day of Week	Monday
Stop	Midnight (Elapsed time from stop)
HGN	12:03 A.M. (3)
Start Deprivation	12:04 A.M. (4)
Tow Truck Called	12:04 A.M. (4)
FSTs	12:04-12:09 A.M.
PBT	12:10 A.M. (10)
Miranda	12:12 A.M. (12)
Arrest	12:16 A.M. (16)
First Breath Test	12:25 A.M. (25) Result .094
Second Breath Test	12:32 A.M. (32) Result .098
Release Time	12:45 A.M. (45)
Time Report Written	4:00 A.M. (4:00)
Videotape?	None
Photographs?	None
Audiotape?	Yes—Stop officer recorded first encounter
Dispatch/911 Tape?	None
Arresting Officer	Ofc. Arnold Ziffle
Backup	Ofc. C. McBride
Breath Test Operator	Ofc. S. Barnard
QAS	M. Bloom, TPD Crime lab
Passengers	None

The framework can also include other relevant times and names as seen fit. In blood cases, the phlebotomist's name and others in the chain of custody can be listed. Civilian witnesses and other events such as the arrival and departure times of paramedics, the issuance of a search warrant and the time that a tow truck is called should be documented. Think of it as a quick-reference guide or a cheat-sheet for the defense. It might even be helpful to have the officer record the times as they occurred on an easel and introduce it as a defense exhibit for the jury.

The framework can be very helpful in determining the officer's subjective intent during the investigation. Note that in the example above, the deprivation period preceding the breath tests was started only four minutes after the stop. One could argue that the officer had already made up his mind at that point to arrest. The officer could certainly say that he chose to start the deprivation period only in the event that he arrested—and if he did not arrest, there was no harm in starting the deprivation period. The damning evidence that he made up his mind, however, is that he called for a tow truck only four minutes after the stop. This is something often overlooked by defense counsel. A police officer will not call for a tow truck unless he knows that the car is going to be towed. Imagine what would happen to the officer if he called for a tow truck three times in a row, then sent the tow truck driver away because he decided not to arrest the person. That officer would be in for a serious discussion with a sergeant regarding the efficient use of departmental resources.

Below, cross-examination is broken into several categories defined by the role that the officer will play. It is quite possible, even likely, that some or all of the different law enforcement roles will be played by one officer.

The stop officer

Clearly, the stop officer's cross-examination has to be linked to the driving. Good driving has to be highlighted, while bad driving needs to be minimized. Sometimes bad driving behavior exists, but it is not defined as one of the NHTSA cues from *The Visual Detection of DWI Motorists* pamphlet provided to law enforcement officers, and the distinction has to be made obvious to the jury. For example, your client may have struck an object or another car (or even a person). The NHTSA cue is "almost striking an object" not actually making contact. Therefore, your client may not have displayed one of the cues recognized by NHTSA.

The best case scenario is where your client is stopped for an equipment violation and nothing more. A non-operative taillight or license plate light has nothing to do with impairment. Thus, you get to argue to the jury that this is a drunk driving case with no drunk driving. Break the stop officer's testimony into four categories and attack each one in chronological order: Driving, Stop, First Contact and Exit. If the officer's training and experience offer an area of attack, use it. If it does not, then leave that area alone.

The following questions and areas of inquiry should be used or avoided—depending upon the facts of the case.

Officer's background and training

Some officers have poor DWI training, some have average DWI training and some have extraordinarily good training. Officers' intelligence runs from I.Q. levels hovering at around room temperature, while others are very bright. Education levels run from G.E.D. to postgraduate work. There are even some officers who take the time to do independent research on DWI issues.

One trick that prosecutors often like to use is to ask the officer how many DWI cases he or she has investigated. This is a fair question if properly asked. Where it becomes improper is where the prosecutor then asks the officer how many of those DWI investigations resulted in an arrest. While it may be proper to ask an officer about the number of DWI investigations performed to gauge experience level, it would be improper to compare the number of investigations to arrests without complete disclosure of the police reports and number of convictions obtained from those arrests. Such a comparison puts the defendant at the disadvantage of not being able to verify the officer's truthfulness and memory. Such testimony would be more highly prejudicial than probative of any fact. In other words, the state would be presenting the information to show that the defendant was investigated and arrested—and is therefore guilty—because the officer lets innocent people go free. Such an analogy is improper, especially in light of the standard pretrial instruction given to juries that the fact that a defendant has been arrested is not proof of guilt—in fact it is not proof of anything. See *Brady v. Maryland*, 373 U.S. 83, 83 S.Ct 1194, 10 L.Ed.2d 215 (1963).

If the officer is well trained and has years of experience, do not go into his background and training. Time after time I see defense attorneys asking officers open-ended questions about their training and education simply because the defense attorney does not know where to go with the cross-examination. This will hurt your client.

On the other hand, if the officer is new, poorly trained or has little experience with DWI investigation, this is the time to attack the officer's background and training. For instance, if you know that the officer has not done any of these things, you could ask if he has ever been part of a DWI Squad. Or ask if he has ever been part of the DWI Task Force, or worked a DWI roadblock, etc. Even ask the officer if he has met other officers with more DWI training than himself.

Driving

Compare time that the officer saw the violations to the time that there were no violations. Someone who makes a wide turn and is stopped four blocks later will likely have spent 2 to 3 seconds making the turn and a few minutes driving without incident.

If your client made one of the 24 NHTSA recognized driving cues, such as driving on a lane divider, ask the officer to name the other 23 cues that your client did not display. (See Chapter 9 for a complete list of all 24 cues.)

Do not forget other causes for the driving behavior. Perhaps your client was observed talking on a cell phone by the police or offered that as an excuse. While this certainly opens your client up to an attack for not being able to divide his or her attention, that can be easily thwarted with the relatively well known evidence that people who drive while talking on cell phones are inattentive without any alcohol.

Lastly, when the driving is inexcusably bad, use the prosecution's own tactics for cases with good driving. In cases where there is no bad driving, the prosecution will emphasize the fact that they do not have to prove bad driving in order to convict—they simply have to prove that the person was impaired to at least the slightest degree. If that is the case, then the opposite should be true—bad driving is not the focus of the investigation. This can be partially accomplished with the officer on cross by asking if he or she has ever stopped anyone for a license plate or equipment violation and then made a DWI arrest and if he or she has ever stopped someone for multiple moving violations where the driver turns out to be stone cold sober.

The logical implication now set up for closing argument is that while bad driving may be due to impairment the state cannot prove that it was impairment by proof beyond a reasonable doubt. If the state cannot prove that the bad driving was due to impairment by proof beyond a reasonable doubt, then the jury must acquit.

Speed, time and distance calculations

Speed calculations are important for a defense attorney to understand and to be able to use on the fly. Many times we see police officers testify that they pursued our clients over a certain distance and it took our clients an extraordinarily long time to react to the patrol vehicle's lights. Other times they claim to have observed our clients make many traffic violations over a specific distance and within a certain time period, but when you calculate the time and distance, you find that the speed does not make sense.

For example, I once saw an officer testify at trial that my client was speeding at about 60-65 miles per hour in a 40 mile per hour zone. The officer was traveling in the opposite direction, made a U-turn and was able to reach a point where he could see my client pull into a parking lot, jump out of the car and hop a fence in an attempt to get away. With the help of an accident reconstructionist, we calculated that if what the officer said was accurate, and if we allowed no time whatsoever for him to make the U-turn, he would have had to travel at over 250 mph to put him in a position to see what he claimed to have seen. If we counted in a reasonable amount of time for the U-turn, he would have had to break 325 mph.

Obviously, this led to an effective cross-examination: "Tell me, Officer. Just how many top-fuel dragsters does your police department own?"

Below is a chart that can be used "on the fly" for speed calculations:

MPH	1 Mile (seconds)	½ Mile (seconds)	¼ Mile (seconds)	1/8 Mile (seconds)	Feet/ Second (fps)
90	40	20	10	5	132 fps
85	42.35	21.18	10.59	5.29	124.67 fps
80	45	22.5	11.25	5.63	117.33 fps
75	48	24	12	6	110 fps
70	51.43	25.72	12.86	6.43	102.67 fps
65	55.39	27.70	13.85	6.92	95.33 fps
60	60	30	15	7.5	88 fps
55	65.45	32.73	16.36	8.18	80.67 fps
50	72	36	18	9	73.33 fps
45	80	40	20	10	66 fps
40	89.99	45	22.5	11.25	58.67 fps
35	102.86	51.43	25.72	12.86	51.33 fps
30	120	60	30	15	44 fps

Distance Chart

1 mile = 5,280 feet
$^1/_2$ mile = 2,640 feet
$^1/_4$ mile = 1,320 feet
$^1/_8$ mile = 660 feet

If a car travels at 60 miles per hour, in one hour it has traveled 316,800 feet:

5,280 feet × 60 miles = 316,800 feet

If it has traveled 316,800 feet in an hour, then divide by 60 minutes to solve for feet per minute (fpm):

316,800 feet ÷ 60 minutes = 5,280 fpm

If it has traveled 5,280 feet in one minute, divide by 60 seconds to solve for feet per second (fps):

5,280 feet ÷ 60 seconds = 88 fps

To solve for time (in seconds) to drive one mile, divide 5,280 feet by the feet/second value:

For example, where x is the time in seconds:
x = 5,280 feet ÷ 88 fps
x = 60 seconds to travel one mile.

The stop

Your client either made a flawless stop, or did not. Did your client respond to the police emergency lights in an appropriate amount of time? If he did, then that shows an acute awareness of the surroundings and a sober response.

Did he stop in appropriate place? Was it safe? Out of the flow of traffic? Was it on the right side of the roadway? In other words—*could he divide his attention?*

Try to turn every good point into three good points. For example, most people will stop on the right side of the roadway for the police as required by law. In this instance, ask these questions:

Stop Facts

- He reacted to your lights in a timely manner?
- He reacted in an appropriate manner?
- You did not have to use your **siren**?

- He stopped on the **right side** of road?
- That's where one should stop?
- That's required by law?

- It was out of the flow of traffic?
- It was about where you figured he would stop?
- It was an appropriate place to stop?

- It wasn't a quick, jerky stop?
- It wasn't a long, rolling stop?
- There was ***nothing inappropriate*** about the stop?

Divided Attention Trap

- You're familiar with the term "divided attention" as it applies to driving?
- In order to drive well, a driver has to be able to do more than one thing at the same time?
- A driver has to be able to pay attention to surroundings and the roadway conditions while reacting to other vehicles?
- So, he found an appropriate place to stop, and stopped in an appropriate manner,
- That demonstrates that he could divide his attention between the mental activity and the physical activity of pulling over?
- … And he was able to properly divide his attention between these two things while your bright, flashing emergency strobe lights, wig-wag headlights

and take-down lights (and siren) were creating a major distraction behind him?

By breaking this simple traffic movement down into three questions, your client now has more "points" in his favor for the jury to consider.

First contact

Alcohol has no odor. Most officers realize this and will state that alcohol has no odor, but what one is really smelling are the additives or "congeners" added to alcoholic beverages for their flavor. Many officers will then go on to refer to the odor as an "odor of intoxicants" instead of an odor of alcohol. Yet this will lead the officer to the exact point he or she sought to avoid. The intoxicant in an alcoholic beverage is alcohol. If he is smelling the intoxicant, then he is smelling alcohol, but he just said that alcohol has no odor. If this is true, then the officer must just be using the term "intoxicants" to sway the jury as opposed to actually describing what he had smelled.

Putting that argument aside, there is also a very direct way of discounting the testimony, especially where your client acknowledged (not "admitted") drinking. It goes like this:

- You can't tell *what* she was drinking by the odor alone, can you?
- You can't tell *when* she was drinking by the odor alone, can you?
- You can't tell *how much* she was drinking by the odor alone, can you?
- And she *told you* she had been drinking?
- So the fact that you smelled an odor adds *nothing* to your investigation?

In addition to being a symptom of allergies or of being in a smoky environment, red or bloodshot eyes can be a result of alcohol consumption. That is because alcohol is a vasodilator. In other words, it makes capillaries expand, which is why people feel warm when they drink. (Expanding the capillaries actually makes the body lose heat to the outside air, but a rush of warm blood near the skin makes the skin feel warmer). In addition to the obvious allergies, smoke and other eye-irritants, time of day can certainly play a role in red or bloodshot eyes. Since most of our clients are arrested at or after midnight, this point should be exploited. Witness the following line of questioning:

- Officer, you testified that you saw red eyes?
- You first made contact in the early morning hours after midnight?
- If you were going to take a trip and your flight was scheduled to leave after midnight, that flight would commonly be called the "red eye" wouldn't it?
- And that's because many people have red eyes in the early morning hours after midnight?

Look for contradictions in the symptoms as well. Red or bloodshot eyes should also be seen with a flushed face because alcohol dilates not only the capillaries in the eyes, but also in the skin. If the eyes are red or bloodshot, they should also be watery because the increase in heat at the eyeballs will make the eyes watery. If any one of these elements is missing, then you can more easily question whether the symptoms seen are due to alcohol or some other cause.

Another effective method of impeachment regarding the initial observations is to play one officer's observations off against another officer's observations. Many DWI reports have boxes with typical attributes listed for an officer to check or circle if he or she observes them. Make a chart that enumerates the attributes from different officer's reports and question the discrepancies. Generally, this will lead to an admission by the officers that their observations are subjective in nature and may vary from person to person. Sometimes officers' accounts will vary widely and you can ask the officer if he is sure that he and the other officer were observing the same person. Below is an example of the chart for two officers. If there is a third officer, add his or her observations to the chart in another column.

DWI Reports

Attribute	Arresting Officer	Backup Officer
Eyes	watery/bloodshot	bloodshot only
Pupils	poor reaction	(nothing noted in report)
Face	flushed	normal
Alcoholic Breath	strong	moderate
Speech	slurred	confused
Clothing	orderly	orderly
Balance	swaying	swaying
Unusual Actions	none	none
Attitude	cooperative	cooperative
Lighting	streetlights	streetlights

Attribute	Arresting Officer	Backup Officer
Weather	calm, dry, cool	(nothing noted in report)
Traffic Conditions	medium	light

Cooperative attitudes are always appreciated by juries. Many a DWI case has been lost not on the facts, but because the jury did not like the fact that your client used profanity toward the police. If your client was cooperative and had a stable mood, make the officer testify to that fact. Try this general line of questioning:

- Mr. Doe was cooperative with you?
- He said "please" and "thank you"?
- He addressed you as "sir," didn't he?
- In fact, he was more than cooperative. He was downright polite?
- You've seen people display mood swings when they're under the influence, haven't you?
- In fact, mood swings are so common among intoxicated people that there even a box on your police report called "mood swings" that you can check if they are present?
- He didn't have any mood swings?
- Mr. Doe's demeanor was calm, quiet and stable?

If the officer noted that your client's pupils reacted to light properly, you can ask about the effects of alcohol as a depressant. Bring out the fact that depressants can slow down respiration, heart rate and other automatic bodily functions. Yet your client's pupils were not slow to react to light. Once this is established, leave it alone and move onto the next set of questions. You can argue the point in closing when the officer is not on the stand to fight back.

When the officer asks for a driver's license, insurance and registration, the officer is looking for several things. Where your client had no difficulty retrieving the documents, remember to build this up in the questioning. Most officers will testify that at the police academy they were trained that officer safety is a high priority and that a traffic stop is a dangerous situation because of the unknown factors involved. The officer may be stopping someone for a civil traffic violation who has just robbed a liquor store and is heavily armed. Or, the person may be mentally unstable and dangerous. The person may have a warrant out for his arrest and be a fugitive.

The officer was very likely taught that, for officer safety, he should keep his eyes on the driver's hands because the driver may reach for a weapon. This is especially possible where the driver accesses the glove box for some of the vehicle's documents. In the DWI situation, this is quite helpful because you can question the officer about how he kept his eyes on the driver's hands not only to look for signs of impairment but also for his own safety. Indeed, because of this close scrutiny, we can trust the officer's observations when he testifies that your client had no difficulty retrieving the documents.

Moreover, by asking the driver to produce a license, insurance and registration, the officer is also giving the driver a divided attention task similar to a Field Sobriety Test. Question the officer about this:

Good Dexterity/Divided Attention Trap

- A traffic stop is a dangerous situation for any officer?
- You never know whom you have stopped?
- It could be a simple civil traffic violation and nothing more?
- It could be someone who has just committed a violent crime and is trying to get away?
- Since you don't know whom you're dealing with, you want to keep a close eye on the driver's hands—for your own safety?
- And, since you smelled some alcohol, you also wanted to keep an eye on the driver's actions because you might use that for investigatory purposes?
- So, it's fair to say that you kept your eyes on his hands both for the ***investigation*** and for your own personal ***safety***?
- If you saw some problem with him handling his documents, you would have noted it?
- And you would testify to it here, in court?
- You asked for his ***license***?
    - He had no troubles retrieving it?
    - He had no troubles handling it?
    - He didn't fumble for it?
    - He didn't drop it?
    - He didn't hand you something else?
    - He didn't forget what you asked?
- You asked for his ***registration***?
    - He had no troubles retrieving it?
    - He had no troubles handling it?
    - He didn't fumble for it?
    - He didn't drop it?
    - He didn't hand you something else?
    - He didn't forget what you asked?

- You asked for his ***insurance card***?
  - He had no troubles retrieving it?
  - He had no troubles handling it?
  - He didn't fumble for it?
  - He didn't drop it?
  - He didn't hand you something else?
  - He didn't forget what you asked?
- So, he demonstrated that he could ***divide his attention*** between the mental task of remembering what you wanted, recalling where the documents were located and the physical task of handling those documents?
- So, not only could he properly divide his attention between finding a place to stop and actually stopping, but we have a ***second instance*** where he demonstrated that he could divide his attention between the mental activity of finding his documents and presenting them to you?

Even if your client had some trouble finding or handing over these documents, if they were valid, these are "points" in your client's favor. Think about it—no one likes the idea of someone else driving without insurance. Jurors surely think to themselves that if they have to pay for insurance, everyone else ought to be paying for insurance. Moreover, they surely feel that if they are struck by someone driving without insurance, they will be stuck with the repair bill. This is a basic issue of fairness and responsibility that we all share. Where the documents are all valid, ask the following questions:

- His license was valid?
- His registration was current?
- He had valid proof of insurance?

Where your client's license, insurance, or registration was invalid, move in limine to suppress that fact. This may mean, however, that your client will have to plead to the civil infraction prior to trial. In a felony trial based on a suspended license, you will not be able to suppress the fact that your client's license was suspended. However, you may be able to suppress the reason for the suspension if it was for a previous DWI.

Exit from vehicle

Getting out of a car may not seem like a big deal until your client forgets to remove his seatbelt before he tries to get out. DWI officers have seen it all—from people who exit flawlessly to those who fall out to those who refuse to exit and have to be forcibly removed.

Although it seems like a simple movement, it takes a considerable amount of coordination to shift your weight and rise from a car. Keep in mind that the type of car can make it even more difficult to exit. A very high truck or a low sports car can add to the difficulty. Factors such as having been driving for many hours, resulting in stiff legs, need to be explored. Be especially aware of this possibility when your client is stopped on an interstate highway. Sometimes your client might have driven for three or four hours without stopping. Clearly, being stiff from sitting that long can lead to a less than graceful exit. Start the cross on exiting the car with this line of questions about lighting:

- When you made the traffic stop, you used special lights on your patrol car?
- You have, not only flashing lights, but lights that you use to illuminate the car that you have stopped?
- You have overhead take-down lights?
- You have a very, very bright spotlight?
- You're trained to shine that spotlight through the back window of the car on the rearview mirror or on the driver's side mirror?
- That illuminates the inside of the car for your own safety?
- Very bright lights are also used to hide your approach to the car?
- At the academy, they may have called that a "curtain of light"?
- It works by temporarily blinding the driver with light to make you less of a target?

Then use the appropriate set of questions, below, depending on whether she had trouble getting out, or exited without difficulty:

Troubles Exiting/Walking

- You said Ms. Doe was slow to get out?
- That it seemed like she didn't know where the ground was?
- That her walk to the rear of the car was slow and deliberate?
- And you observed this after you blinded her with several million candlepower of spotlights and take-down lights?

No Troubles Exiting/Walking

- She had no trouble unbuckling the seatbelt?
- I'll bet you've even seen people try to get out without taking off the seatbelt?
- The car was not left out of gear?

- It did not roll anywhere?
- She did not stumble out?
- She did not stagger out?
- She certainly did not fall out?

Never use the term "motor vehicle" in front of the jury, unless you are trying to make a point. That term is for prosecutors with cheap suits and flat-top haircuts. "Motor vehicle" is cop-speak. Drop it from your vocabulary and talk like a real person. If it was a car, use the word "car." If it was a pickup, use the word "pickup."

The investigating officer

The investigating officer will usually be the same as the stop officer. If it is a different officer, then determine if you want to go into his or her background and training before you start with the facts of the case. Generally, however, you will need to touch on the subject as you go through the cross-examination because even if the officer is well-trained the officer might not have followed the NHTSA protocol perfectly as is required. In that case, you can point out that he or she did not follow significant, expensive, and complex training protocols.

HGN (Horizontal Gaze Nystagmus or "Here Goes Nothing")

HGN is the most widespread fraud perpetrated on jurors. It lacks scientific basis, and the studies are so skewed in favor of validity, that it often becomes a basis for an improper conviction. There are two basic methods of HGN cross-examination. One is a good method and the other is even better—but you cannot use both in the same trial.

A good method of conquering the HGN during cross-examination is to show how much the officer does not know about HGN. Take the following thematic questions, for example:

- Ask the officer: Are you a Doctor? Neurologist? Registered Nurse? Physician's Assistant? Ophthalmologist? Optometrist? Optician? EMT? Paramedic?
- You've had a first aid course?
- Name the muscles that control eye movement?
- Tell us how many muscles there are?

You can use the chart below to ask if the officer knows what the different types of nystagmus are. Ask if he or she can differentiate between HGN and the other types below.

Use this rhetorical question ***in closing argument:*** If the officer cannot differentiate between them, then how can he or she know that the alcohol is the cause?

Types of Nystagmus

anticipatory
arthrokinetic
somatosensory
Stransky's
audio kinetic
Bartel's
Brun's
cervical
vestibular-basilar artery insufficiency
circumduction
dissociated disjunctive
downbeat
ictal
deviational
gaze-paretic neurasthenic
Baer's
latent/manifest latent
lateral medullary
Miner's
muscle-paretic myasthenic
sigma
talantropic,
physiologic end-point
pursuit after-induced
pursuit defect
pseudo-spontaneous
rebound
ageotropic
geotropic
Bechterew's
electrical/faradic/galvanic
labyrinthine

Ask him or her *how far* the eye has to jerk back and forth when checking for nystagmus at maximum deviation and *how many times* it has to jerk back and forth. There is no set number or distance mandated by NHTSA. It is left up to the discretion of each officer. In other words, it is subjective. One officer might call what he sees "nystagmus," and another officer might not. NHTSA guidelines simply tell the officer to look for a "distinct" jerking movement of the eyes, but the term "distinct" is not defined in the NHTSA materials.

SFSTs (or RAMs—Roadside Agility Maneuvers)

Stay away from calling them *Field Sobriety Tests*—unless your client passed them. Think about it—what does the name say? It says that these are tests, but not just any old tests, they are ones that test sobriety. And where do these Sobriety Tests take place? In the field, just like where your client took them. And why is your client in court? Is it because he or she passed those Field Sobriety Tests? No, your client is in court because he or she failed them. FSTs should be called Roadside Exercises, Balance Maneuvers, Coordination Exercises, or my personal favorite—RAMs—Roadside Agility Maneuvers.

General theme for the deconstruction of "standardization"

While you might formulate some fantastic and specific questions for cross-examination regarding the roadside exercises, you are better off simply having a theme to attack the FSTs before you get into specific performance by your client.

In general, different people might have differing physical abilities. Some people are in wheelchairs, while others compete in the Olympics. Some people cannot even dribble a basketball, while others can play in the NBA. We have all met people who are just clumsy. Think for a moment, where did the term "two left feet" come from?

Some people are forgetful. Have you ever had a waiter or waitress who just could not remember your order? Most people have had the experience of walking into a room and forgetting what they were looking for. That certainly does not mean that these people are drunk—it is a natural phenomenon. Add to that natural forgetfulness, the stress of a police officer standing over you while demanding that you do these roadside exercises, rattling off instructions in a rapid form, and possibly having your friends in the car and passersby watching. Is it any wonder that people who are sober might have troubles performing these maneuvers?

Often, the police will try to portray the word "standardized" as meaning scientific. Standardization needs to be deconstructed in front of the jury. Standardization is nothing special. It just means that you do the same thing, the same way, every time. And, everybody else does it the same way every time.

Plenty of things are standardized. Put standardization in terms that the cop will understand. For example: If a cop goes into a Dunkin' Donuts® on Tuesday and has a jelly donut, it's going to taste the same as the one he had last Friday. A glazed donut from a Krispy Kreme® in Phoenix will taste the same as a glazed donut from a Krispy Kreme® in Tucson. That's because they do the same thing, the same way, every time. Doors are standardized. Exit signs are standardized. Street signs are standardized. Standardization is nothing magical, and it does not make anything scientific.

Look to the things that your client did right. If your client removed her shoes to do the FSTs and had no trouble removing them, point that out to the jury. If she walked without difficulty to the area where they were administered, point that out to the jury. Break the FSTs into their component parts and highlight the things the client did properly.

Lighting, location, debris, distractions, weather, illness, injury, disease, mental abilities, and intimidation factors all are proper grounds for attacking FSTs. Never forget that FSTs are done under inherently coercive conditions. The mere fact that the officer is armed and in uniform creates the basis for coercion.

FSTs not given

Occasionally, police DWI reports will contain Field Sobriety Tests that were not administered. Sometimes they are part of the three-test battery of SFSTs, but more often they are tests that are not validated. The Tucson Police Department has a great example of this type of test. It is a written evaluation where the subject is asked to write the English alphabet in capital letters, the even numbers 0 to 30, sign it and write the date and time that he or she thinks it is without looking at a watch. Most officers do not administer this test because it is not a validated test. They are usually attacked heavily under cross-examination for administering the test. But under the "damned-if-you-do, damned-if-you-don't" principle, you should attack the officer for not giving such a test as well. Assuming your client did not refuse to do any FSTs offered, the cross goes like this:

- Officer, I see that there's a test on your report that you did not administer. What is that one called?
- You did not administer it?
- There was nothing preventing you from administering it?
- Mr. Doe did all of the other roadside exercises that you asked him to do, so there's not reason to expect that he would refuse this one?
- You wouldn't be reprimanded for giving it?
- Will the other officers laugh at you and not be your friends anymore for giving it? (No)
- Would the department dock your paycheck for giving it? (No)
- Would they fire you for giving it? (No)
- If you had had Mr. Doe complete this Written Evaluation, that would be a piece of physical evidence?
- In fact, the jury might even have the chance to hold it, examine it and even take it with them back into the jury room if it were admitted as a piece of evidence?
- Who deprived this jury of that important piece of physical evidence?

Another good tactic is to give the officer a divided attention test right in front of the jury. Do not use their tests, however. Make up tests of your own. For instance, you can show the officer four or five colored markers in your hand and ask him to draw the scene where the stop was made and tests were performed. Ask him to use different colors, that you have specified, to label street names, mark the location and direction of patrol cars, draw the line for the Walk-and-Turn test, location of street signs and streetlights, etc. Ask the officer to do all of these things in rapid fire procession, then hand him the markers and tell him to begin. When he cannot do it, ask him if he had been drinking before he came to court.

General theme for deconstruction of skills tested relative to driving

The skills needed to drive are not tested by the FSTs. The police say that the skills needed to drive were tested by other means. Most jurors have drivers' licenses and had to take a test to get them. They didn't have to stand on one leg to get their licenses. They were required to take a driving test when they first applied for a license and probably walked out to their respective cars with the road test examiner, but they were allowed to walk normally—not heel-to-toe. DMV gives no divided attention tests in order to get a license.

They were required to take an eye test. Maybe they had to read a chart on a wall or look into a machine. The examiner did not give an HGN test, however. In fact, DMV does not even ask if an applicant has naturally occurring HGN.

License applicants take a written exam. The DMV manual is available to applicants before they take the exam. What constitutes a passing score is known before taking the exam. Yet the person taking the FSTs is not told what a passing score would be and is not provided the opportunity to practice the maneuvers before the exam.

The police should have tested these skills, but did not

It is important to consider the human factors required for safe driving and whether they were tested by the FSTs. Point out to the jury that FSTs have nothing to do with driving. Reaction time is important to driving, but they did not test reaction time. Vision is important, but they did not test it. Depth perception is important, but they did not test it. Hand/eye coordination is important, but they did not test it. Balance is not important to driving, but they did test it.

***Miranda* and interrogation**

My clients have never been "questioned" by the police. They have only been "interrogated" by the police. Just like we should never use the words "crash" or "defendant" in front of a jury, we should also never let the jury think that the interrogation was anything but an intrusion upon a person's right to privacy.

If Miranda rights were read and your client invoked his rights, then the jury should never be informed that the rights were even read—let alone invoked. A prosecutor cannot hold the invocation of one's rights against that person and use it as evidence of guilt.

One way is to ask the officer on cross-examination if he or she took into account everything said by your client, both good and bad, when he or she made the decision to arrest. Then you can ask about the statements made by your client because they are not being offered for the truth of the matter asserted in the statements. They are being offered for the effect on the officer and his decision to arrest. The jury is clearly entitled to evaluate whether they thought that the officer was acting reasonably when he made the arrest.

The third and final method, assuming that the prosecutor has objected to the use of the answers and the judge has improperly ruled against the defense on the first two methods, is to ask the officer about the questions that he asked. For example:

- Officer, you asked Ms. Doe the question; "Do you feel the effects of the alcohol you drank?"
- She answered that question?
- You recorded that answer on your police report?

- You asked Ms. Doe the question; "Do you feel that the alcohol you drank affected your driving to the slightest degree?"
- She answered that question?
- You recorded that answer on your police report?

- You asked Ms. Doe how much she had drank?
- She answered that question?
- You recorded that answer on your police report?

In this manner, not only do you clearly make the jury understand that these answers were favorable to your client, but you also punish the prosecutor for making an improper objection. The prosecutor looks bad in front of the jury for hiding evidence. While you cannot comment on objections that were sustained and ask the jury to speculate as to what the answers were, you can certainly comment on the prosecutor's failure to present evidence that we know exists, and the prosecutor cannot comment on your client's failure to take the stand. Generally, a prosecutor who has been down this path will not do it again with you as the defense attorney.

If your client agreed to the interrogation after Miranda rights were read, use this to show that he or she had nothing to hide—only a dishonest person who is hiding information would refuse to answer questions.

Sometimes the police will use a "1 to 10 scale" question as follows:

1 = Someone Drinking, Not Feeling the Effects									10 = Falling Down Drunk
1	2	3	4	5	6	7	8	9	10

The person is asked to rate him- or herself on the scale, with "1" being someone who was drinking but not feeling the effects and "10" being falling down drunk. The person then circles the number and places his or her initials by it. Realize that this is a trick question. Only two numbers are defined, nine answers are bad for someone accused of DWI, and it may have nothing to do with impairment. Some people circle the number of drinks that they had. Other people don't want to rate themselves at the extreme on either end of any scale. "Effects" are not necessarily "impairment." These criticisms need to be pointed out to a jury—unless your client actually circled a "1."

Sometimes the person is asked directly if he or she feels the effects of the alcohol. Note that effects may be different from impairment. Someone could be influenced by alcohol to feel happy, sad, talkative, quiet, angry or sleepy. These are all effects, but are not impairment.

The coherence trap

The state's case is always premised on a logical progression of intoxication. The police are taught that when one becomes intoxicated by alcohol, the first thing that is affected is a person's ability to think and reason. Judgement is affected. Mental abilities such as memory are compromised as well.

The next thing that is affected by alcohol intoxication is fine motor coordination. Things like finger dexterity are problematic. Signing documents may become difficult.

Finally, gross motor incoordination becomes apparent. People sway, stagger and stumble. They have trouble standing unsupported. They may have difficulty with simple tasks such as speech.

The prosecution, however, is stymied by the fact that in order to use post-Miranda statements, the defendant must have understood Miranda warnings. Likewise, the Implied Consent/Admin *per se* consent is premised upon understanding. The officers certainly would not have let the defendant go after the arrest if the defendant did not acknowledge that by signing the citation he or she was not admitting guilt, but simply promising to appear in court at a later date. These things are a goldmine of opportunity for cross-examination and should be used at the end of cross for maximum effect. I have dubbed this "the coherence trap," and it is described in cross-examination form that follows. Each question is broken into a trilogy for maximum effect. Note that none of the questions asks if the defendant understood the direction or request—they ask if the defendant seemed to understand, and if the defendant gave any indication that he did not, and if the officer was satisfied that he or she understood. This avoids a sustainable speculation objection. Use or delete the appropriate lines as your needs dictate.

- He seemed to understand your request for documents?
- He gave you no indication that he did not understand?
- You were satisfied he understood?

- He seemed to understand your request to get out of the car?
- He gave you no indication that he did not understand?
- You were satisfied he understood?

- He seemed to understand the Roadside Exercise instructions?
- He gave you no indication that he did not understand?
- You were satisfied he understood?

- He seemed to understand his Miranda warnings?
- He gave you no indication that he did not understand?
- You were satisfied he understood?

- He seemed to understand the post-Miranda interrogation questions?
- He gave you no indication that he did not understand?
- You were satisfied he understood?

- He seemed to understand that he was under arrest?
- Did he give you any indication that he did not understand that?
- You were satisfied he understood?

- He seemed to understand the Implied Consent requirements?

- He gave you no indication that he did not understand?
- You were satisfied he understood?

- He seemed to understand the Blood/Breath Advisory?
- He gave you no indication that he did not understand it?
- You were satisfied he understood?

- He seemed to understand the breath testing instructions?
- He gave you no indication that he did not understand them?
- You were satisfied he understood?

- He seemed to understand that by signing the ticket, he was promising to appear in court?
- He gave you no indication that he did not understand that?
- You were satisfied he understood?

- He was coherent?

After the officer has agreed to this litany of coherence exemplars, how can he or she then say that your client was not coherent? Presumably, you have already shown that your client handled and signed documents without difficulty, thus establishing good fine motor coordination. Now you can take away from the prosecution the first two elements of a logical progression of alcohol intoxication, and they are left with gross motor incoordination, which may be due to something, but it is not alcohol.

Sample cross-examination of the stop/investigating officer

The following is a sample cross-examination of a stop/investigating officer from a real trial. It has been edited for non-fluencies such as "ums" and "uhs," but remains true to the content. Names have been changed.

BY MR. NESCI:
Q. Mr. Smith, you're a member of the night motor squad, correct?
A. Yes, sir.
Q. How long have you been a member of the night motor squad?
A. Since it started, I believe, I think we're going on seven or eight years.
Q. This arrest occurred in year 2003, correct?
A. I believe so, yes.
Q. And in year 2003 the night motor squad had a goal of making 55 percent more DWI arrests than they did in 2002, correct?
MR. CLARK. Objection. Relevance.
JUDGE. Mr. Nesci, what's the relevance?
MR. NESCI. I think it goes to credibility as to where he's sitting, what he's looking for, how he's pulling people over.
JUDGE. Okay. Objection's overruled.
BY MR. NESCI:
Q. Is that correct?
A. We did have a goal, yes, put together by our supervisor.
Q. And that goal was 55 percent more DWI arrests in 2003 than in 2002, correct?
A. I believe so. There was an actual number. I don't remember hearing a percentage.
Q. Do you remember what the actual number was?
A. I don't.
Q. Was it 1,575 DWI arrests in 2002, plus another 55 percent for 2003?
A. I don't, I don't recall. I'd have to see the supervisor's form that he asked us to do or the percentage that he put down somewhere or whatever numbers you're referring to. I'm sure it's written somewhere. I just don't recall what they were.
Q. Now, we had a lot of talk about Mr. Jones driving off of the sidewalk, but there was no real sidewalk there, correct?
A. That's correct.
Q. So it's illegal to drive along the sidewalk, correct?
A. It is illegal to drive on a sidewalk, yes. Not across the sidewalk area, but on a sidewalk or sidewalk area.
Q. Are you saying it's a sidewalk or a sidewalk area?
A. Simply because there's no actual concrete sidewalk there is why I referred to that as an area. The city refers to that when looking at parking ordinances that you can't park in a sidewalk area. Even if there's no sidewalk there, they have designated sidewalk areas. The city owns that, and it's normally, from what I've been told from traffic engineers, it's about 8 or 10 feet inside the curb area, which is their easement area where they put their water meters or sidewalks, all that kind of stuff owned by the city.

Q. But pulling out in a vehicle across this area in the manner in which Mr. Jones is not illegal?
A. I don't believe so, no.
Q. In fact sometimes if you go up a sidewalk straight, even if it's a curved one, you might have kind of a big drop as opposed to going off on an angle, correct?
A. If you go straight, yeah, that's correct, especially on low profile vehicles.
Q. So it might be a little bit more comfortable for a driver to exit a parking lot in that manner, correct?
A. Yes, sir.
Q. You were 162 feet away when you used your laser gun; is that correct?
A. That's when I got the stop sign violation. He was 162 feet away. It would have been right about where the stop line was where I got him from where my vehicle was positioned.
Q. And did he disturb any other traffic when he made that right turn from Williams Center onto Williams Circle?
A. No, sir.
Q. Was there any other traffic coming in any direction?
A. Not that I recall, no, sir.
Q. He did stop appropriately at the light at Broadway?
A. Yes, sir.
Q. And he made his right turn onto Broadway, correct?
A. That's correct.
Q. Did he disturb any other traffic when he made his right turn onto Broadway?
A. No, sir.
Q. Now, you don't know if Mr. Jones was making a left turn anyway when he got onto Broadway, correct?
A. You mean at the Toys-R-Us?
Q. Yeah.
A. I don't know that.
Q. What's the speed limit there on Broadway?
A. Through that section there is 40.
Q. Did Mr. Jones ever exceed the speed limit?
A. I don't believe so, no.
Q. Did he get up to about the speed limit?
A. He may have been close. I wasn't paying attention to speed at that point. I was trying to get turned behind him and get him pulled over.
Q. At what point did you turn on your lights on your motorcycle?
A. As soon as he made that right turn and was across into that lane, I immediately got behind him and put on my lights, so, just as fast as my bike would make that turn. Probably 20 or 30 feet east of the intersection there.
Q. So that would maybe be about roughly 280, 270 feet until he gets to the left-turn bay?
A. That's correct.
Q. So you had your lights on for 270, 280 feet roughly?
A. I had my lights on the whole time. I had my siren on for a small portion of that time.
Q. About how many seconds does it take for somebody to go oh, 270 feet or so accelerating up to the speed limit?
A. Well, if you take a fixed speed, say he's going 35 miles an hour. We'll kind of put him a little below the speed limit there. He's going 47½ feet per second. So round it off to 50 feet, feet per second. six seconds to go the 300 feet. So you're probably down to five with that turn and acceleration into the lane.
Q. So basically, you had your lights on for about three to four seconds. He didn't respond, and you thought that was too long, so then you turned on your siren; is that correct?
A. Yes, sir.
Q. Three to four seconds, is that an unusually long amount of time for somebody?
MR. CLARK. Object. Calls for speculation.
JUDGE. Sustained.
Q. How long you been a cop?
A. Twenty-four years.
Q. How long you been doing traffic out of that twenty-four years?
A. Well, the entire time, but I've been in the traffic division for all but about a year and a half of it.
Q. How many traffic stops do you think you made using lights and/or siren?
A. Over 100,000 probably.
Q. And based on your vast training and experience, do you think three to four seconds is an unusually long amount of time?
A. Not when you put it that way, no.
Q. The fact that it took three to four seconds may have nothing to do with alcohol, correct?
A. He may have never seen me, that's correct.
Q. When he turned left into the parking lot, did he have any troubles making the turn. In other words, a wide turn, too narrow, cut anybody off, anything like that?

A. No, sir.
Q. When he pulled in, was it a safe place to stop?
A. Yes.
Q. You said that when you first met him, you smelled an odor of an intoxicant; is that correct?
A. Yes.
Q. But you can't tell what he was drinking, correct?
A. No, sir.
Q. You can't tell when he was drinking, correct?
A. No.
Q. Can't tell how much he was drinking, correct?
A. No.
Q. And you asked him if he had something to drink and he said that he did?
A. Yes.
Q. You asked him for his license, insurance, and registration?
A. Yes, sir.
Q. One of the things you're trained to look for at the academy is if somebody's having trouble with his license, insurance, registration, or other documents, correct?
A. Looking for dexterity and things, yes.
Q. And you're also checking to see if he can divide his attention equally between listening to what you said and remembering to get these three things, correct?
A. Yes, sir.
Q. That's a divided attention task in and of itself?
A. That and dexterity combined, yes, sir.
Q. He had no problems with either of those, correct?
A. He did not.
Q. Did you ask him to get out?
A. I did.
Q. He had no troubles exiting his truck, did he?
A. He did not.
Q. Didn't hang on the door or the roof for support or stumble or stagger or any of that, correct?
A. No, sir.
Q. Have you ever seen somebody forget to take off their seat belt and try and get out?
A. I did.
Q. Ever see somebody fall out?
A. I have.
Q. He didn't, he didn't do any of that stuff, right?
A. No, sir.
Q. Once you got him out, you had him stand for the HGN exam?
A. Yes, sir.
Q. Did you have him put his arms down by his side?
A. I did.
Q. Did you have him put his feet together?
A. I did.
Q. Did he have any balance problems during the HGN?
A. He did not.
Q. Now, you'd agree with me that having somebody stand with their arms down by their sides, feet together, is a position where they're more likely to sway than if they were standing as people typically stand with their feet slightly apart?
MR. CLARK. Objection. Calls for speculation.
JUDGE. Given the testimony of Officer Smith on direct examination pertaining to his expertise as a law enforcement officer assigned to traffic, as well as his expertise with regard to HGN and Field Sobriety Tests, the court is satisfied that with regard to these types of questions by the defense, the officer is qualified to testify or to answer those questions. So the objection is overruled.
A. Could you ask the question again, please?
Q. Now, you'd agree with me that having somebody stand with their arms down by their sides, feet together, is a position where they're more likely to sway than if they were standing as people typically stand with their feet slightly apart?
A. They may, yes.
Q. You said he had 6 out of 6 cues on HGN?
A. That's correct.
Q. When we're talking about, for example, distinct nystagmus at maximum deviation, let's just look at that one cue right there. We have an eye socket. You're looking for a jerking in this direction, correct, back and forth?
A. Jerking, yes, sir.
Q. Both directions, right?
A. Yes, sir.
Q. When you're doing distinct nystagmus at maximum deviation, how many times does the eyeball have to jerk back and forth before NHTSA says you can call it nystagmus?
A. There's no specific number.
Q. How fast does it have to move back and forth before NHTSA says you can call it nystagmus?
A. There's nothing indicated about that.
Q. But it has to be distinct, correct?
A. Distinct nystagmus, yes.

Q. NHTSA has guidelines for doing HGN, correct?
A. Yes, sir.
Q. They have guidelines as to how the person's supposed to stand, correct?
A. Yes.
Q. They have guidelines as to what questions you're supposed to ask the person before you do the HGN test, correct?
A. Yes, sir.
Q. They have guidelines as to how far you're supposed to hold the stimulus away from the person's face, correct?
A. Yes, sir.
Q. They have guidelines as to how fast you're supposed to move that stimulus back and forth when you're doing the various cues, correct?
A. That's correct.
Q. They have guidelines for how long you're supposed to hold it out there for maximum deviation, correct?
A. Yes, sir.
Q. They have guidelines for determining what a 45 degree angle is, correct?
A. Yes, sir.
Q. And I'm sure that they, have defined the term "distinct" somewhere in their regulations, haven't they?
A. I don't know if they have or not.
Q. You agree with me that "distinct" is a very important term when we're talking about distinct nystagmus at maximum deviation, correct?
A. It is.
Q. And you're also looking for distinct nystagmus when you're doing the lack of smooth pursuit, correct?
A. Yes.
Q. And you're also looking for distinct nystagmus when you're doing angle of onset prior to 45 degrees, correct?
A. Yes, sir.
Q. Yet you can't tell me where it's defined or even if it is defined; is that correct?
A. I'm not sure if it's in there. I mean, we're instructed in the instructions of, of looking for distinct, which is very visible or obvious or there's a lot of different terms you can use for that in watching the eye jerk.
Q. But it's up to the individual officer as to what to call distinct and, I guess indistinct, correct?
A. I guess if that's a word.
Q. Yes, indistinct is a word. All right. So it can be a subjective determination, correct?
A. I suppose, yes.
Q. When you gave these roadside agility maneuvers did you use a real line for him to walk on?
A. We did. We used a parking line there. We're right in the parking lot with the striped lines.
Q. And he's wearing flip-flops; am I correct?
A. He was.
Q. He didn't take them off for the Walk-and-Turn test, did he?
A. He did not want to take them off. I asked him if he felt comfortable in those, and if he wanted to remove those, he was welcome to do so, and, being that they were flip-flops, I had a discussion with him about those, and he did not want to take them off.
Q. So he had his choice of either doing the tests in flip-flops or bare feet on a parking lot, correct?
A. I suppose, unless he had some other shoes in his truck.
Q. Neither one of those are ideal conditions for taking Field Sobriety Tests, correct?
A. I'd disagree with that. I've done a lot of workshops where people wear flip-flops and did Field Sobriety Tests. In fact the last workshop probably half the class had flip-flops on.
Q. And these tests are standardized for people wearing flip-flops?
A. I don't know. I don't know what the standard type of shoe was that they were worn. I know there's, there's some shoes that you're to tell them that they're recommended not to do by looking at, at big heels and things like that, but I'm not sure if anything about flip-flops is indicated.
Q. On the One-Leg-Stand, when did he use his arms for balance?
A. I didn't indicate the exact numbers.
Q. Did you tell him to lock his knee when he was doing the One-Leg-Stand?
A. I did.
Q. That is not in the new instructions for the One-Leg-Stand test, correct?
A. It is not. There's a couple things that I continue to do as the old instructions when I give my instructions. They basically tell you to extend your knee, which is the same as locking your knee. They also tell you to—I just—I give what I learned in my head, paraphrase the old instructions, and it covers

everything that's in the new ones and little bit more, which gives them actually more of an instruction of something to listen to that they're not told in the new instructions that we're, we're still looking for because it's not, like you just said, you tell them to lock their knee, no, but they're told to extend their knee straight out. That's the same as locking their knee. It's just an additional word that they've taken out of there, and I still leave it in.
Q. These are, these are standardized Field Sobriety Tests, correct?
A. They are.
Q. That means that one officer is supposed to do the same things as the next officer, correct?
A. That's correct.
Q. One officer is supposed to give the same instructions as the next officer, correct?
A. That's correct.
Q. One officer is supposed to evaluate the results the same as the next officer, correct?
A. That's correct.
Q. But now we may have a situation where you at least are doing these things differently than other officers, correct?
A. I disagree with that. I don't see any difference.
Q. Yet you're not giving the exact same instructions as other officers?
A. I'm not.
Q. And part of the standardization is to give the exact same instructions as other officers?
A. There's nothing that says that you have to read those verbatim. They're put on the sheet if you want to read them. Some officers paraphrase them. I suppose if you paraphrase but you didn't put a couple words that I put in there, you'd still be different than what's on the form, but you're still giving the same instructions. You're still looking for the same thing and still grading them the same way. I don't feel that that's a difference.
Q. Did he seem to follow all your commands?
A. He did.
Q. Produce documents you wanted him to produce?
A. He did.
Q. You read him Miranda rights?
A. Yes, sir.
Q. Did he seem to understand those?
A. He did.
Q. Did he give you any indication he did not understand those?
A. He did not.
Q. Were you satisfied he understood them?
A. Yes, sir.
Q. You did a post-Miranda interrogation. You have questions and answers reflected on your police report?
A. Yes.
Q. Did he seem to understand those questions?
A. He did.
Q. Did he give you any indication he did not understand them?
A. No.
Q. Were you satisfied he understood them?
A. Yes.
Q. Did he seem to know roughly where he was, what time it was, what was happening to him?
A. I believe so, yes.
Q. Was Mr. Jones polite?
A. He was.
Q. Was he cooperative?
A. He was.
Q. Was he coherent?
A. He was.
I don't have any further questions.

The back-up officer

Often there is a second or third officer on scene to provide security backup, to do an accident investigation or administer a breath test, or maybe it will be the officer who actually made the stop and then called for a DWI officer to do the DWI investigation.

In any event, these officers are generally not focused on your client which means that they may not notice the subtle nuances of a DWI investigation that the investigating officer will notice. These officers can be very helpful to your cross-examination of the main investigating officer.

For example, take the real life case of an elderly man who had been in an accident. Once the DWI investigation was over and he had been cited, the officer who completed the accident investigation walked him across the street to a car driven by his wife so that she could take him home.

The officer walked him across a parking lot, over a curb, across a bike lane, three lanes of eastbound traffic, across the median, across three lanes of westbound traffic, another bike lane, up and over another curb, across a lawn, up three concrete stairs and watched as he got into his wife's car. The officer stated that he had no trouble negotiating the obstacles and that he walked like he would expect an eighty-year-old man to walk after being in an accident.

During a pretrial interview the officer stated that he walked my client across the street because he was nearly eighty years old, the roadway was dark and busy, and there was no crosswalk. Due to his department's safety policy, he did not think it was wise to let him cross the roadway on his own.

The first thing to do with this officer is to build his credibility. Go through the officer's training and experience in a positive light with the jury. You will want to talk about his ample training rather than the lack of training. Focus on what's there—not on what's missing.

The next set of questions should deal with the walk across the street. Just like the prosecutors use words such as "crash" and "collision" to describe an accident, we need to use more descriptive words to describe everyday objects. The curb can be described as a "tall curb." Intermittently call the median an "obstacle." The lawn can become "tufts of grass" which will evoke the picture of an uneven surface which could reach out and trip someone—especially in the darkness. Go into detail about the walk across the busy, darkened highway. Did Mr. Smith trip? Did he stumble? Did he use you for support? Was he able to step over the tall curb without help?

The final set of questions should deal with the conditions in the area not only for driving but also for FSTs. If the roadway is dark and busy, chances are the area where FSTs were conducted was also dark and had cars whizzing by. Maybe the cars were moving fast enough to feel the wind from them as they passed?

This officer is your witness. Align yourself with this officer and show the jury that you like him and he likes you. If the investigating officer comes off as a jack-booted thug before the jury, compare the two during closing argument.

Victims

Victims are not always as difficult to handle as one might expect. For the most part, victims who have been injured will not have seen or interacted with your client to any extent which would allow them to assess sobriety. Under many circumstances it may be wise to consider not cross-examining a victim at trial. If your client clearly ran into the back of a car waiting at a stoplight, and the driver of the other car was taken to the hospital with neck injuries, and your pretrial investigation concluded that the car's brake and taillights were operative, what would be the subject of the cross examination? Get the victim off of the stand and out of the jury's minds as soon as possible.

Victims who testify will want to tell the jury about all the pain and suffering, injuries, and loss of income they experienced. Prosecutors will ask questions about these topics in detail. They will ask about the ambulance ride to the hospital, surgery, rehabilitation, loss of work, pain, etc. This is all irrelevant unless an aggravated assault is charged based on the extent of the injuries. Victim's injuries are irrelevant to whether your client was driving while under the influence. Rules 401 and 402 of the North Carolina Rules of Evidence should be cited in an objection to such testimony.

> **Rule 401. Definition of "relevant evidence."**
> "Relevant evidence" means evidence having any tendency to make the existence of any fact that is of consequence to the determination of the action more probable or less probable than it would be without the evidence.
>
> **Rule 402. Relevant evidence generally admissible; irrelevant evidence inadmissible.**
> All relevant evidence is admissible, except as otherwise provided by the Constitution of the United States, by the Constitution of North Carolina, by Act of Congress, by Act of the General Assembly or by these rules. Evidence which is not relevant is not admissible.
>
> Irrelevant evidence is not admissible.

Ground rules for dealing with victims are simple: get them off of the stand quickly and never attack a victim unless you are positive that you can show that the victim is lying about something important. Some examples come to mind.

Take the situation where your client has struck the rear of the victim's car. The victim claims that the rear of his car was pristine prior to the accident and all damage was due to your client. But you find that the victim had backed into a tree the week before and is simply lying to place the blame and financial liability on your client. Or perhaps the victim had been injured previously and is blaming your client for the injury because he or she has no insurance or does not want to make a claim.

The victim's scam may be as simple as padding the number of miles (for restitution) in a roundtrip between the victim's home and doctor's office for treatment. I can think of one case where the doctor had an east side office and a west side office. The victim claimed 80 miles roundtrip to the doctor's west side office, three times a week, for several months. Some simple investigation matched the dates of her treatments to the days of the week that the doctor was at the east side office. This showed that she was making those trips to the east side office three times a week—just 10 miles roundtrip!

Many times victims will be legitimately injured and will ask for just compensation. But rest assured that the number of scams that can be run by victims is as wide and diverse as the victims themselves. This is why it is important to have a private investigator check out every aspect of the victim's claim.

8.6 Direct Examination

The accused

There is no antacid made anywhere that is strong enough to counteract the effects of watching my client be cross-examined for an hour by a prosecutor in a DWI case. Nonetheless, I sometimes have to suffer through it.

Whether to put your client on the stand has to account for many variables. First and foremost is your client's right to testify or remain silent. This is always the client's right and choice, but it should be made in consultation with you. If your client trusts you, he or she will take your advice.

Sometimes you know that your client cannot take the stand no matter what. For example, your client told the officer he had two beers, but he really had eight beers. If he testifies, he cannot commit perjury, and you do not want the jury to hear him say that not only did he lie to the police, but that he really had all those beers.

Sometimes you know that your client has to testify. For example, your client was simply using the car as a stationary shelter in an actual physical control case and was not driving.

Most of the time, however, the decision is less clear. In those cases, you must prepare your client to testify and make the decision after the end of the state's case. Preparation is key. Not only should you go over, in detail, the direct examination, but you should also take the time to play prosecutor and cross-examine your client. If you have another attorney available, have that attorney cross your client prior to trial. Do not be soft on the client during the pretend cross-examination. I have had more than one client become angry with me for a brutal pretend cross-examination prior to trial. Simply explain to the client that you are trying to be tougher than any prosecutor would be in the courtroom in order to prepare the client for the worse possible circumstance. Weaknesses in your client's testimony need to be ferreted out before he or she takes the stand and risks loss of liberty.

The following simple three-part outline for direct examination of your client should be used. Write questions within the framework that are tailored to your client's individual needs and background.

Introduction

If your client testifies, the jurors must like your client. If they don't, they will convict. The introduction allows the jury to learn about your client and gives them the opportunity to get to like him. Some humor is acceptable, but joking around is not. Ask if your client is nervous. An affirmative answer will help the jury to understand certain mannerisms are natural. Allowing your client to answer introductory questions also allows your client to get used to speaking in front of the jury. He will not have to think about his answers, and he can concentrate on relieving the inherent nervousness that comes with testifying before a jury.

If he is married and has children, have him describe them. Let the jury know his occupation. Hobbies, pets and education are all fair game. Just don't bore the jury. They do not need a day-by-day accounting of his routine. They need just enough to humanize and like him.

Just the facts

Ask for the facts, and just the facts. Chronological is the best order. Generally, you should start off earlier in the day, before your client went out and had something to drink. Maybe he played softball earlier and was tired from that activity. Maybe he was at the doctor being treated for rheumatoid arthritis, gout, an inner-ear infection or general balance problems and slurred speech of unknown cause (we can always hope).

Your client now has the opportunity to tell the jury of the fear and nervousness he experienced when he was stopped. He can explain the embarrassment and distractions he felt doing the tests by the side of the road while people drove by and honked their horns.

He can explain about the knee injury that prevented him from balancing on one leg. Or, that his breathing was irregular while doing the breath test.

Most importantly, however, he must be sure about what he had to drink and not deviate from it. Inconsistency within a defendant's own testimony is death to the case. If he does not remember exactly what he had to drink, he needs to state that he does not remember exactly and give an estimate. He needs to be able truthfully to stick to that estimate under cross-examination.

Denial

Your client cannot take the stand without denying the crime. These five questions should be asked in rapid-fire succession with no hesitation in the answers. If your client cannot answer these simple questions with a firm "no" answer, he cannot testify in the typical DWI case. Work with your client and practice so that he knows that when this last part of the direct exam comes up, his answers are all "no", and he does not have to think about the questions.

- Were you drunk?
- Were you buzzed?
- Were you impaired?
- Were you impaired even to the slightest degree?
- Did you have too much to drink to drive safely?

Passengers

Passengers are a double-edged sword. If they have been drinking, then their testimony will be viewed with suspicion regarding their ability to remember. If they were stone cold sober, then at deliberation time, the jurors will be asking each other why the passenger did not drive.

Passengers will generally have a favorable bias toward the driver. Most passengers will be friends, relatives or co-workers of the driver. It is rare to have a passenger who is a stranger or who has very little connection to the driver.

Be sure that the passenger's story matches the account given by any other defense witnesses. If your client's account differs from the passenger's account, one of them should not testify. Be sure to tell the passenger/witness what you would tell any witness: if you do not remember a specific fact, say that you do not remember that specific fact. Do not guess. Do not speculate. Do not lie.

The passenger's direct testimony should be very similar to the client's direct testimony in regard to the sections. Section One should detail the passenger's biographical information, though not in as much detail as the client's history. Section Two should cover the facts, and Section Three should be the denial:

- Have you ever seen Bob drunk? Yes.
- Have you seen him sober? Yes.
- Can you tell the difference between the two? Yes.
- On the night that Bob was arrested, was he drunk or sober? Sober.

If the passenger cannot answer the questions above as indicated, the passenger should not be called by the defense.

8.7 Closing Argument

Closing arguments are nothing more than drawing inferences for the jury. There are certain things that we can infer in everyday life:

- The first person to open an oyster and think that the contents were edible was either really hungry, or blind.
- The person who named blueberries "blueberries" lacked imagination.

These are humorous inferences that we can draw from common experiences. Juries will draw inferences from common experience as well as from specific facts that are given to them at trial. They will equate personality types of the lawyers and witnesses with people they know. They will compare and contrast witnesses with others they have encountered throughout their lives. Bias, prejudice, reasonable and unreasonable beliefs will hold sway with their opinions.

Jurors will project themselves into the story that is being told and make assumptions based upon what they would do if they were in the same position as the police or your client. This is not a bad thing if you are aware of it and have the ability to shape it. We can shape the manner in which the jury perceives our arguments by the use of persuasive words.

Words and names have meaning, and although words are only a representation of everyday objects, some words can evoke emotions so strong that it could be argued that they have taken on an intrinsic value. The word "gold" does not have the same value as the metal itself. But have you noticed that people don't name their kids "Adolf" anymore? Why not? It is nothing more than a name—yet it has taken on an ominous and evil meaning. Introducing your friend named "Adolf" will always cause a pause in the conversation—at least for the next few hundred years.

"Used cars" are now "pre-owned vehicles" because it sounds better. Faux pearls may be fashionable, but fake pearls are simply cheap. Check out the following examples:

What They Say	What We Should Say
FSTs (Field Sobriety Tests)	RAMs (Roadside Agility Maneuvers)
admitted drinking	acknowledged drinking
questioned	interrogated
crash	accident or fender bender
defendant	client's name
prosecutor	government's lawyer
restrained	hog-tied
pressure-hold	choke-hold
blood alcohol content	blood alcohol estimate

Words and thought are an attorney's stock-in-trade and must be used wisely. Use the words with the most value for your point. Saying that your client "admitted" drinking makes it sound as if he or she did something wrong when drinking is perfectly legal. Think about your words and your style as an attorney.

Reasonable doubt is not mentioned by many prosecutors during the state's closing argument. This is because reasonable doubt is such a powerful standard. DWI is a crime of opinion. One cannot have hard evidence such as that involved in a theft case where the defendant is found with the stolen article. In a DWI case a jury has to collect the evidence given to them and form an opinion as to not only whether the defendant was under the influence, but an opinion as to what "under the influence" actually means.

Even a chemical test value is an opinion if it is properly presented by the defense. Any scientist will tell you that no chemical test result value is conclusive. It is impossible to know the exact value of any scientific measurement. Keeping this in mind, there are only two routes that can be taken with any chemical test by an expert: (1) In the expert's opinion the results are incorrect or (2) In the expert's opinion the results are correct within the test's margin of error. This means that where the state's expert opines that the chemical test is accurate and reliable and the defense expert disagrees there is reasonable doubt.

Never fall into the trap of thinking that you must prove that your client was under the legal limit. You do not have to prove that fact, and it is likely that you will not be able to prove it. It is the state that must prove that your client is over the legal limit by proof beyond, and to the exclusion of, every reasonable doubt. Remember that the breath testing machine or the headspace gas chromatograph is an unsworn witness, incapable of cross-examination. Remind the jury of this fact.

Reasonable doubt can be described for a jury in terms of other standards of proof such as reasonable suspicion, probable cause, preponderance of the evidence and clear and convincing evidence. It could be described as a ladder or steps ascending toward the ultimate level of proof.

A jury must be made to realize that they do as much justice when they find someone "guilty" who has been proven guilty by proof beyond a reasonable doubt as they do when they find someone "not guilty" when the proof does not add up. It is not a bad thing to tell the jury that you cannot prove your client innocent—no one can do that. But by the same token, the state cannot prove him guilty because there is reasonable doubt.

"Not guilty" does not mean innocent.

"Not guilty" means "not proven."

The jury must be given a charge. They must be told what they must do—find your client "not guilty." They just watched highly choreographed theater. They do not know any of the witnesses, the judge, the lawyers, your client or each other. Yet these strangers are going to make a decision that will affect your client's life—possibly forever. Tell them that if they have a doubt tomorrow morning at the breakfast table, it is too late. They must express their doubts in the jury room. If they are convinced, they should stick by their decision.

It is not their duty to argue points in the jury room. It is not their duty to sway or persuade other jurors. It is each juror's duty to listen to the evidence and decide the case for himself or herself after consultation with the other jurors, if they can do so. During closing argument the defense attorney should let the jurors know that it is perfectly acceptable to remain undecided. A hung jury is not a conviction. Living to fight another day is far better than a conviction.

In closing, the state goes first if you don't put on any evidence and you get to argue last. However, if you do put on any evidence, the State gets final argument. It is your duty to object to improper argument on the part of the prosecutor. Always ask for surrebuttal as a remedy. You may get it only once during your career, but all you have to do is to ask for it.

Juries should be given alternate verbiage for reasonable doubt. Slide presentations are a great way of drilling the concept of reasonable doubt into a juror's head and all it takes are a few simple slides. The first is a variant of the National College for DUI Defense's "steps" trial graphic used for closing argument. The word "Guilty" has been removed from the graphic and some more subtle changes make it more powerful. The idea of the steps (which is sometimes represented as a glass of water being filled to increasing levels) is to compare reasonable doubt to other legal standards to show just how high of a burden it really is.

Another way of describing reasonable doubt is to discuss how positive a juror must be, without going into percentages for surety. While you cannot ethically tell a juror

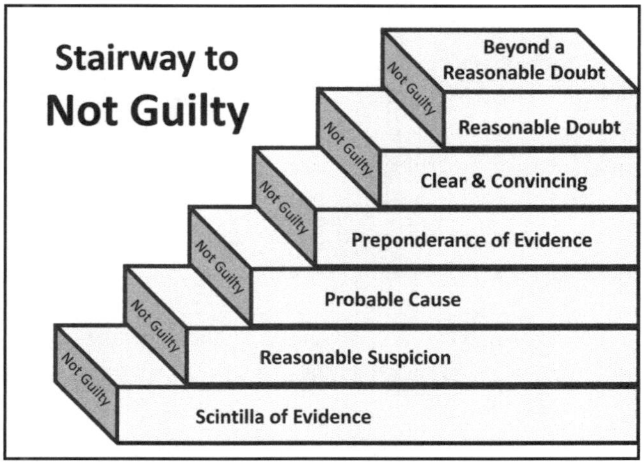

Figure 8.1

that he must be 100 percent sure of his decision, you can say that he must be 100 percent free of reasonable doubt.

8.8 Sentencing

The Four Reasons for Sentencing

There are only four reasons for imposing a sentence on anyone: General Deterrence, Specific Deterrence, Rehabilitation, and Retribution.

General Deterrence is the notion that if you make an example out of someone, other members of the public will take heed and not commit the same offense. This is the mainstay of MADD advertising campaigns. But whether it works or not is open to debate. There is such a great proliferation of general deterrence messages which range from punishment to education, that no one can isolate punishment as a driving force behind any decline in DWI cases. To gauge the efficacy of harsh punishment as a deterrent, one would have to cancel out all other messages to see the effect of this one variable.

Specific Deterrence is the idea that you can deter a specific person from committing the crime again by putting him in prison or limiting driving privileges, thus protecting the community. In misdemeanor cases, this is fruitless as the court never has any significant power in this area. In felony cases, however, specific deterrence is a real possibility—especially where there are multiple criminal convictions and the court has the option of consecutive rather than concurrent sentencing.

Retribution is a very personal idea. In foreign countries, punishment may be accomplished by torture and physical pain. In our country, we accomplish the objective by deprivation, isolation, and—in some cases—death. Each judge, as well as each person on the street has his or her own idea about what punishment should "fit the crime." Some are more harsh, while others are particularly lenient. Some find their roots in religions, while others seem to have no roots at all. Societal ideas of appropriate punishment change over time as well. Sometimes a heavy-handed approach is in vogue, while other times it is a slap on the wrist. Retribution generally only comes into play when it is more than a simple DWI, such as an accident or death case.

Rehabilitation is a hit-or-miss proposition in DWI cases. Clearly, some of our clients are substance-abusers and need rehabilitation. However, the bulk of our clients are simply normal, average, everyday people who had a little too much to drink (or maybe not) and were convicted of DWI. As the presumptive level decreased from 0.15 to 0.10, then to 0.08, more social drinkers were caught in the government's net. There are even rumors afoot which point to a movement to lower the level to 0.05. The problem with the DWI sentencing laws is that while we are punitive at different levels based on BAC, we do not assign rehabilitative measures on the same basis. Surely, most counseling agencies make an attempt to assess and treat the client, however some unscrupulous agencies have realized that they have a captive audience and can oversell the number of hours of counseling required—and the courts will enforce the sale.

On the other end of the spectrum are the clients who are in need of real treatment which is far beyond the capabilities of the government-approved agency. In-patient treatment is a necessity for some people, but limitations on the court's power and the client's finances can make this an impossibility. Rehabilitative efforts in the DWI arena are handed out on a one-size-fits-all basis, which often amounts to little more than a requirement which looks good on paper to the legislature that created the sentencing laws.

PRACTICE TIP: A list of approved North Carolina assessment and treatment agencies can be found at the North Carolina Division of Mental Health, Developmental Disabilities and Substance Abuse Services website by visiting www.ncdmh.net/providerlist/CountyList.idc. These are the State approved agencies that can be used for ADETS and other counseling and treatment. If the agency is not approved by the State the Court will NOT count it.

Mitigation

One can simultaneously prepare for war and peace. Remember that while you are planning to win, you must also prepare for loss. The first thing to do is to get your client into counseling. Generally, in a misdemeanor, this is not going to have any real effect. Many, if not most, defendants receive the minimum sentence, or very nearly the minimum. In a felony, however, or where you expect that the judge might impose more than the minimum, get your client into counseling right away. Make sure that the counselor is a licensed Substance Abuse Counselor by the State of North Carolina, otherwise the counseling may not be given credit by the court.

Have a real evaluation completed, offer the results to the court ahead of any sentencing hearing where that is possible, and have the counseling documented by any form you deem acceptable to the court.

If your client attends AA (Alcoholics Anonymous), have him or her keep track of the AA meetings in a notebook. The notebook should contain the date and time of the meeting, the group name for the particular meeting, and have a signature from the group leader acknowledging that your client was present.

Substance abuse counseling

As noted above, be sure that the counselor is a state licensed Substance Abuse Counselor. In general, one of two types of assessments will be given to someone who is convicted of DWI and is referred for counseling. The assessments are used to determine what level of counseling is appropriate. However, as virtually every DWI defense practitioner has seen, once the substance abuse counselor is told that the person was convicted of an extreme DWI, the results of the assessment are ignored and the person is assigned to the highest level of counseling available.

One of the assessments given is known as the MAST (Michigan Alcoholism Screening Test). It is a 25-question yes/no assessment administered by another person (i.e., not self-assessment). Answers are weighted according to importance. If one scores 5 or higher, alcoholism is highly suspected. The MAST test virtually assures that everyone who takes it as a result of a court order or on the advice of an attorney is labeled as an alcoholic. For example, having attended one AA meeting nets 5 points. Having been arrested for DWI nets 2 points.

Thus, anyone who has been arrested for DWI and has attended an AA meeting at the request of an attorney or by order of the court scores 7 points and is labeled an alcoholic.

Another test given is the SASSI© (Substance Abuse Subtle Screening Inventory). The SASSI-3© is for adults eighteen and over, with a reading grade level slightly above third grade, and takes about 15 minutes to administer. It uses 65 true/false questions. It too contains questions that will hurt anyone assigned to counseling as the result of a DWI conviction. For example, one true/false question is "I have sometimes drunk too much." Clearly, if you have been convicted of a DWI, you might feel that even one drink was too much. Another question is: "When I drink and use drugs I tend to get into trouble." How does one answer that question if one does not use drugs at all? If you answer "false," does that mean that you drink and use drugs but get away with it?

Home monitoring

Home monitoring is a valuable alternative to jail time where allowed. Home monitoring will require approval of the court, usually gained by a court staff member or probation monitor visit to the home. Alcohol generally will not be allowed in the home during the period of home monitoring. It will require a telephone land line and the deactivation of call waiting and other features. If your client is still living in the 90s and has dial-up internet access, he or she must have a second line installed.

Home monitoring requires an ankle bracelet and a device hooked up to the phone line. Like an invisible fence for dogs, your client cannot wander off. If your client strays too far from the monitoring device hooked up to the telephone, the telephone device will call the monitoring company, which will, in turn, notify the probation department that your client has escaped.

At regularly scheduled intervals, your client may be free to leave home for work or school. Generally, upon arrival back, he or she must call the monitoring company. The monitoring company will call your client at regular and random intervals and have the client activate a small button on the ankle monitor. The telephone device may be equipped with a breath tester for random or regular use. The device will have photo-capture capability which will allow the monitor to confirm that the person blowing into the machine is actually the defendant.

Home monitoring charges will generally be charged to your client. They can be significantly less expensive than the costs of incarceration.

Letters to the judge

Any letters to the judge on behalf of your client need to be screened by you before they are sent to the judge. Typically, the best way to do this is to gather letters from all those people who are willing to help and send them in at the same time. Screen them for content, spelling grammar, and to be sure that they have the judge's name right. If they are not perfect, send them back with instructions as to how to correct them.

Each letter writer should be given an outline. The outline should contain the following points:

- Name of the letter writer.
- Relationship to the defendant.
- Short statement of the defendant's good points.
- Acknowledgment of the seriousness of the crime.
- A statement of willingness to help the defendant get back on track.

The letter to the judge is not a forum for the writers to dispute the charges or badmouth the prosecutor, police, witnesses or court system. If the letter-writer feels poorly toward any of them, he should keep it to himself. The writer also should not try to explain, or even mention, other bad acts committed by the defendant. If the defendant has many out-of-wedlock children that he must care for, now is not the time to mention it. The judge may get the feeling of a general lack of responsibility on the part of the defendant.

The letters should only emphasize the good points, not explain the bad points. Do not submit any letter you feel is detrimental to your client's fate, unless your client demands that it be submitted.

Chapter 9

DWI Investigations: Driving and Field Sobriety Testing

Synopsis

9.1 Overview: National Highway Traffic Safety Administration (NHTSA)

NHTSA is a federal agency responsible for reducing deaths, injuries and economic loss from motor vehicle crashes. This broad and vague mission statement has empowered it to leave its mark on virtually every aspect of motorized ground transportation with the exception of railroad and boat travel. Although many of us in the DWI arena think of NHTSA only as the backers of standardized field sobriety test studies, impaired driving studies, purveyors of DWI police officer training materials, and authors of the Conforming Products List, its mission goes much further than that.

NHTSA investigates safety defects in motor vehicles and odometer fraud. It promotes the use of child safety seats, seat belts and air bags. It provides consumer information on crash tests for new cars, and sets and enforces fuel economy standards. NHTSA also sets and enforces safety standards for motor vehicles. Not many federal agencies have a greater impact on everyday life in the United States than NHTSA.

A relatively small part of NHTSA is its anti-drunk driving effort. Yet that effort seems to garner more media attention than all other parts of NHTSA combined. The reason for this is obvious when one compares drunk driving to odometer fraud. Odometer fraud is a large scale problem, but no one dies from it. One will never find a group calling themselves MAOF (Mothers Against Odometer Fraud). It is simply neither an emotionally compelling topic nor a catchy acronym.

The subjects examined in this chapter cover the broad topics of driving behavior, standardized field sobriety testing and non-standardized field sobriety testing, along with their underlying studies.

An important thing to keep in mind is that NHTSA does none of its own studies. The studies are contracted out to individuals and groups that manage to write a grant proposal that is approved by NHTSA. Because of the political climate, there is an incentive for NHTSA to grant money for a proposed study that shows that all drivers are impaired at .08 BAC (or less), while there is little incentive to award a grant to a group that proposes that people are not affected until they reach .15 BAC.

Moreover, none of the studies that back the driving and SFST manuals are peer reviewed. Peer review is one of the most basic and important premises for any scientific study. Peer review allows other scientists and researchers in the field to investigate, evaluate and replicate the study itself. Without peer review, anybody could publish any study and call it the "scientific foundation" for any proposition.

9.2 Driving Behavior

Validation studies

The seminal study in this arena is titled *Visual Detection of Driving While Intoxicated*, by Douglas H. Harris, Anacapa Sciences, Inc., Santa Barbara, CA. ©1980 The Human Factors Society, Inc. It is an eight-page study which first reviewed literature from other researchers on the issue of identifying DWI drivers, then involved ten law enforcement agencies throughout the United States which attempted to demonstrate the effectiveness of the identified visual cues.

The stated purpose of the study was to study the effectiveness of DWI detection because it is "a function of the frequency with which patrol officers see and recognize cues indicative of DWI and the extent to which observed cues discriminate between DWI and driving while sober (DWS)." (*Visual Detection of Driving While Intoxicated, supra.*)

The first issue noted in the study is that the author uses the terms DWI (Driving While Impaired) and DWS (Driving While Sober), yet the study itself is not correlated to sobriety or drunkenness; it is correlated to a specific blood alcohol level (BAC) and arrest rates. The study does not correlate to actual impairment or conviction rates. Moreover, the study concerns only those people driving at night—not during the daylight hours.

The study developed its own list of visual driving cues and reviewed lists of potential driving cues from a 1974 Michigan State University Study, *DWI Law Enforcement Training Project, Student Manual*, DOT Contract No. HS-334-3-645 by Carnahan, Holmes, Keyes, Stempler and Dreveskracht. They analyzed 1,288 DWI arrest reports from nine agencies and found 3,658 visual detection cues. They prepared the data for analysis by dividing the cues into several categories and came up with a preliminary listing of 129 visual cues that they believe were useful for DWI detection. Think about it—129 visual cues are a staggering number and could cover almost every conceivable driving violation. In fact, some of the cues were not violations of the law at all. Take, for example, weaving within the lane. There are no statutes that make it illegal to use the entire lane.

The detection study found that 39 percent of the drivers had a BAC less than .05, while 23 percent had a BAC greater than .05 but less than .10, and 38 percent had a .10 or higher BAC. In other words, more drivers who were stopped based on the cues were under .05 BAC than were over .10 BAC. The researchers condensed the visual driving cues into 23 cues that accounted for 92 percent of the 1,681 cue occurrences in the detection study.

The most common reason for a stop was weaving, with an occurrence of 145 per 1,000 detections of DWI. The least common occurrence was slow response to traffic signals, which had an occurrence of 20 times per 1,000 detections of DWI. The average number of "cue events" was 2.6 per stop. However, there was no statistical correlation between the types of cues that normally occurred together. In other words, one does not see a correlation of weaving going hand-in-hand with headlights being off at night, or there is no correlation between being slow to react to a signal light with the frequency of almost striking a vehicle or object.

There was, however, a cumulative effect noted. Where two cues were seen together, 5 percent could be added to the percentage chance of DWI for the larger cue. If three or more were present, 10 percent could be added. The cumulative effect works as follows:

- Drifting at night had a 45 percent correlation to .10 BAC or more.
- Braking erratically at night had a 35 percent correlation to .10 BAC or more.
- Where both drifting and erratic braking were seen in the same driver, the correlation was 50 percent to a BAC of .10 or more.

If we add a third cue of turning with a wide radius at 60 percent for the same driver, the correlation would be 70 percent.

PRACTICE TIP: "Almost Striking an Object or Vehicle" is a cue recognized by NHTSA, but actually striking an object or vehicle is not. Often, prosecutors will argue that an accident is proof of impaired driving, but actually having an accident did not occur with enough frequency to become even a poor cue.

Ten law enforcement agencies involved in the field study reported an overall increase in arrests of 12 percent during the testing period as compared to the baseline period. Five agencies increased their arrest rate by 94 percent, four did not change significantly and one agency had a significant decrease. The study had some major flaws. One was that when comparing the "Guide" to the actual test values, "... the probabilities contained in the guide were derived from data collected using procedures that were substantially different from those employed for collecting data in the field test." This is problematic, to say the least, when the study claims that the field test portion was to investigate and confirm the data previously collected. It is simply comparing apples to oranges.

The guide probabilities were based on breath testing of subjects, and the officers were accompanied by observers. The field test probabilities were obtained by the use of special forms filled out by the officers themselves—with no observers present. The police obviously knew that they were being monitored on the number and type of DWI arrests made. Without a neutral observer present, one cannot discount the possibility that the police officers were dishonest in the reporting of their results.

The final conclusion of the study was that: "The basis exists for the development and evaluation of a DWI detection guide to facilitate the application of research findings to on-the-road detection of DWI by police patrol officers."

The result of the study was the publication, by NHTSA, of several guides to detecting drunk drivers at night. The first was called *The Guide to Detecting Drunk Drivers at Night*.

Figure 9.1 *NHTSA Guide*

NHTSA Guide to Visual Detection of Impaired Motorists
The Guide to Detecting Drunk Drivers at Night contained 20 cues that the police should look for while on patrol at night. The cues were published in a small-format pamphlet along with a quick reference card that officers could keep in a shirt pocket. NHTSA also produced and distributed at least two instructional videos for police training purposes. The first is part of a two-tape series titled *DWI Detection and SFST Training*. Each tape is one-hour long and contains sections regarding driving behaviors, SFSTs, in-court testimony, report writing, and so on. It is published by the U.S. Department of Transportation, Transportation Safety Institute (TSI). It is no longer available from the DOT.

The second video deals exclusively with driving behaviors and is titled *The Visual Detection of DWI Motorists*. It is just over 16 minutes and was published by the U.S. Department of Transportation, National Highway Traffic Safety Institute (NHTSA) in July 1997. It is still available from NHTSA. NHTSA also released a pamphlet for law enforcement with the same title as the video, *The Visual Detection of DWI Motorists.*

The current list of driving cues as published by NHTSA in *The Visual Detection of DWI Motorists* can be divided into four categories: maintaining lane position, speed and braking, vigilance, and judgment. It is important to realize that somewhere along the way of development, evolution and revision of the NHTSA *Guide to Detecting Drunk Drivers at Night*, to the current pamphlet *The Visual Detection of DWI Motorists*, the nighttime aspect of the guide went missing, yet there are no studies to explain why it went missing.

The Visual Detection of DWI Motorists assigns the following probabilities to a chance that a driver exhibiting the following cues is "DWI." Of course, now "DWI" means .08 or more BAC, yet there is little actual scientific evidence to show that the research done previously on the .10 standard will apply to a .08 standard.

The *Guide* also states that the probability of detecting DWI by random traffic enforcement stops at night has been found to be about 3 percent.

The *Guide* assigns the following probabilities to driving observations in four categories:

Problems Maintaining Proper Lane Position
(50% to 75%)
Weaving, Weaving across lane lines, Straddling a lane line, Swerving, Turning with a wide radius, Drifting, Almost striking a vehicle or other object.

NHTSA describes the "Problems Maintaining Proper Lane Position" category on its website as follows:

> Maintaining proper lane position can be a difficult task for an impaired driver. For example, we have all seen vehicles weaving before. Weaving means that the vehicle alternately moves toward one side

of the lane and then the other. The pattern of lateral movement can be fairly regular, as one steering correction is closely followed by another. In extreme cases, the vehicle's wheels even cross the lane lines before a correction is made. You might even observe a vehicle straddling a center or lane line. That is, the vehicle is moving straight ahead with either the right or left tires on the wrong side of the lane line or markers.

Drifting means that a vehicle is moving in a generally straight line, but at a slight angle to the lane. The driver might correct his or her course as the vehicle approaches a lane line or other boundary, or fail to correct until after a boundary has been crossed. In extreme cases, the driver fails to correct in time to avoid a collision.

Course corrections can be gradual or abrupt. For example, you might observe a vehicle to swerve, making an abrupt turn away from a generally straight course, when a driver realizes that he or she has drifted out of proper lane position, or to avoid a previously-unnoticed hazard.

A related DWI cue is almost striking a vehicle or other object. You might observe a vehicle, either at slow speeds or moving with traffic, to pass unusually close to a sign, barrier, building, or other object. This cue also includes almost striking another vehicle, either moving or parked, and causing another vehicle to maneuver to avoid a collision.

Turning with a wide radius, or drifting during a curve, is the final cue in this category of driver behaviors. A vehicle appears to drift to the outside of the lane, or into another lane, through the curve or while turning a corner. Watch for this cue and stop the driver when you see it. Many alcohol-involved crashes are caused by an expanding turn radius, or drifting out of lane position during a curve.

Figure 9.2 *Weaving*

Figure 9.3 *Drifting*

Figure 9.4 *Swerving*

Speed and Braking Problems

(45% to 70%)

Stopping problems (too far, too short or too jerky), Accelerating or decelerating for no apparent reason, Varying speed, Slow speed (10+ mph under the limit).

NHTSA describes the "Speed and Braking Problems" category on its website as follows:

> The research showed that braking properly can be a difficult task for an impaired driver. For example, there is a good chance the driver is DWI if you observe any type of stopping problem. Stopping

Figure 9.5 *Turning with a wide radius*

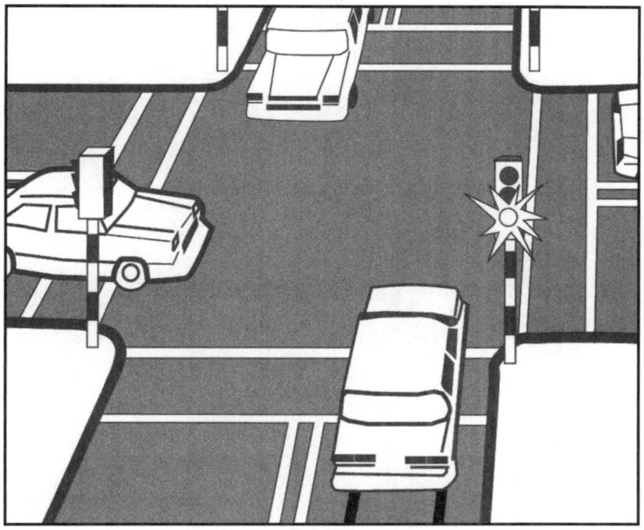

Figure 9.6 *Stopping beyond a limit line*

Figure 9.7 *Signaling inconsistent with driving actions*

problems include; stopping too far from a curb or at an inappropriate angle, stopping too short or beyond a limit line, and jerky or abrupt stops.

Impaired drivers also can experience difficulty maintaining an appropriate speed. There is a good chance the driver is DWI if you observe a vehicle to accelerate or decelerate rapidly for no apparent reason, vary its speed, alternating between speeding up and slowing down, or be driven at a speed that is ten miles per hour or more under the limit.

Vigilance Problems

(55% to 65%)

Driving in opposing lanes or wrong way on one-way, Slow response to traffic signals, Slow or failure to respond to officer's signals, Stopping in lane for no apparent reason, Driving without headlights at night*, Failure to signal or signal inconsistent with action* (*50 percent when combined with any other cue).

NHTSA describes the "Vigilance Problems" category on its website as follows:

> Vigilance concerns a person's ability to pay attention to a task or notice changes in surroundings. A driver whose vigilance has been impaired by alcohol might forget to turn his or her headlights on when required.
>
> Similarly, impaired drivers often forget to signal a turn or lane change, or their signal is inconsistent with their maneuver, for example, signaling left, but turning right.
>
> Alcohol-impaired vigilance also results in motorists driving into opposing or crossing traffic, and turning in front of oncoming vehicles with an insufficient headway.
>
> Driving is a complex task that requires accurate information about surrounding traffic conditions. Failing to yield the right of way and driving the wrong way on a one-way street are dangerous examples of vigilance problems.
>
> A driver whose vigilance has been impaired by alcohol also might respond more slowly than normal to a change in a traffic signal. For example, the vehicle might remain stopped for an unusually long period of time after the signal has turned green. Similarly, an impaired driver might be unusually slow to respond to an officer's lights, siren, or hand signals.
>
> The most extreme DWI cue in the category of vigilance problems is to find a vehicle stopped in a lane for no apparent reason. Sometimes when you

Figure 9.8 *Driving into opposite or crossing traffic*

Figure 9.9 *Turning illegally*

Figure 9.10 *Driving on other than designated roadway*

Figure 9.11 *Appearing to be impaired*

observe this behavior the driver will be just lost or confused, but more than half of the time the driver will be DWI—maybe even asleep at the wheel.

Judgment Problems

(35% to 90%)

Following too closely, Improper or unsafe lane change, Illegal or improper turn (too fast, jerky, sharp, etc.), Driving on other than the designated roadway, Stopping inappropriately in response to officer, Inappropriate or unusual behavior (throwing, arguing, etc.), Appearing to be impaired.

NHTSA describes the "Judgment Problems" category on its website as follows:

> Operating a motor vehicle requires continuous decision-making by the driver. Unfortunately, judgment abilities can be affected by even small amounts of alcohol. For example, alcohol-impaired judgment can cause a driver to follow another vehicle too closely, providing an unsafe stopping distance.
>
> Alcohol-impaired judgment also can result in a driver taking risks or endangering others. If you observe a vehicle to make improper or unsafe lane changes, either frequently or abruptly, or with apparent disregard for other vehicles, there is a good chance the driver's judgment has been impaired by alcohol.
>
> Similarly, impaired judgment can cause a driver to turn improperly. For example, misjudgments about speed and the roadway can cause a driver to take a turn too fast, or to make sudden corrections during the maneuver. These corrections can appear to the observer as jerky or sharp vehicle movements during the turn.
>
> Alcohol-impaired judgment can affect the full range of driver behaviors. For example, the research found that impaired drivers are less inhibited about making illegal turns than unimpaired drivers.
>
> Driving on other than the designated roadway is another cue exhibited by alcohol-impaired driv-

ers. Examples include driving at the edge of the roadway, on the shoulder, off the roadway entirely, and straight through turn-only lanes.

In some cases, impaired drivers stop inappropriately in response to an officer, either abruptly as if they had been startled, or in an illegal or dangerous manner.

In fact, the research has shown that there is a good chance a driver is DWI if you observe the person to exhibit any inappropriate or unusual behavior. Unusual behavior includes throwing something from the vehicle, drinking in the vehicle, urinating at the roadside, arguing with another motorist, or otherwise being disorderly. If you observe inappropriate or unusual behavior, there is a good probability that the driver is DWI.

Appearing to be Impaired: The final cue is actually one or more of a set of indicators related to the personal behavior or appearance of a driver. These indicators include, gripping the steering wheel tightly, driving with one's face close to the windshield, slouching in the seat, and staring straight ahead with eyes fixed. Some officers routinely scrutinize the faces of drivers in oncoming traffic, looking for the indicators of impairment. If you observe a driver who appears to be impaired, the research showed that there is an excellent probability that you are correct in your judgment.

One can visit the NHTSA website and find explanations for the 24 driving cues. The NHTSA website general address is www.nhtsa.gov and the web address which will take you directly to the driving cues is: www.nhtsa.dot.gov/people/injury/alcohol/dwi/dwihtml/index.htm.

PRACTICE TIP: When your client did not exhibit any of the NHTSA cues, such as speeding, cross-examine the stop officer on the *DWI Detection Guide* to show that your client did not display any of the common cues, with the inference that he was not impaired.

When your client did display one of the cues, ask the stop officer to name the other 23 cues that he did not display.

Literature review

Effects of Low Doses of Alcohol on Driving-Related Skills: A Review of the Evidence SRA Technologies, Inc. Alexandria, VA July, 1988 DOT HS 807 280, Moskowitz and Robinson.

1. **Reaction Time**: for simple, complex, visual, auditory, and choice reaction times there are twenty-two studies that show no impairment from .11 to .20.
2. **Tracking**: for compensatory, pursuit, and critical task tracking there are twelve studies that show no impairment from .11 to .20.
3. **Concentrated Attention**: for visual signal detection and visual vigilance there are three studies that show no impairment from .12 to .17.
4. **Divided Attention**: for compensatory tracking, response to central stimuli, peripheral stimuli, meter monitoring, signal detection, and visual search/recognition there are five studies that show no impairment from .11 to .12.
5. **Information Processing**: for Meter Monitoring, Visual Backward Masking, Response Latency, Information Processing Rate, Character recognition, Verbal recognition and recall, Information registration, recall and organization, and Eye Dwell there are eleven studies that show no impairment from .11 to .18.
6. **Psychomotor Performance**: for coordination, Purdue pegboard, key press response, motor coordination, handwriting, and finger tapping there are twenty-five studies that show no impairment at .11 to .21.
7. **Driver Performance**: for following speed maintenance, accelerating and braking, speed changes, reaction time (peripheral), time/distance estimation, steering, vehicle position, signal errors, distance judgment and speed maintenance there are fourteen studies that show no impairment from .11 to .16.

   Total: Ninety-two studies covering seven areas from .11 to .21 that show no impairment at levels above .10.

Detecting impaired motorcyclists

In addition to the videos regarding the detection of impaired motorists, NHTSA also produced two training videos regarding motorcyclists: *The Detection of DWI Motorcyclists* and *Detecting Impaired Motorcyclists* (April 2000).

The first thing that should be apparent is that it is a special guide for motorcyclists, separate and apart from the *DWI Detection Guide*, which applies only to automobiles. In fact, although the study does not explicitly state it, logically it should not apply to large trucks either. For example, a semi tractor trailer may have to make a wide radius turn in certain instances because of its length. It may also have to drive ten or more miles an hour below the speed limit because of the weight of its load. So too, motorcycles do not drive like automobiles by virtue of the fact that they have two wheels instead of four.

The impetus claimed by NHTSA for the motorcycle guide, *The Detection of DWI Motorists* (U.S. Department of Transportation, National Highway Traffic Safety Administration DOT HS 807 856, Revised; March, 2005), was the NHTSA estimate that in 2003, 36 percent of motorcycle operators who were involved in fatal crashes had a BAC of .01 or higher. Remember that .01 BAC in a 150-pound male is less than one drink, and there is very limited data to suggest that a BAC of .01 will produce any effects of impairment in a human being. Moreover, the phrase "motorcycle operators who were involved in fatal crashes" does not necessarily mean that the operator of the motorcycle was impaired. The phrase easily encompasses sober motorcyclists who were hit by drunk automobile drivers. Based on this, however, NHTSA concluded:

> Clearly, enforcing impaired driving laws is a key to reducing the number of alcohol-related motorcyclist fatalities. *But which cues should be used to detect impaired motorcyclists?*
>
> (Emphasis in original)

NHTSA sponsored a study published in 1993 which interviewed police officers and examined 1,000 arrest reports. (*The Detection of DWI Motorcyclists*, DOT HS 807 839, March 1993; Jack W. Stuster, Anacapa Sciences, Inc.). They did field evaluations in two separate studies and eventually narrowed a list of over 100 cues to 14 cues, seven of which they claim are "excellent" predictors of impairment with the remaining seven as "good" predictors of impairment.

What does NHTSA mean by "excellent" predictors? They mean 50 percent or greater—somewhere from a coin toss and up.

What does NHTSA mean by "good" predictor? They mean 30 to 50 percent—less than the probability of a coin toss.

Clearly, from the lack of evidence showing that anyone is impaired at a .01 BAC and their labeling of "good" predictors and "excellent" predictors which amount to the probability of a coin toss, there is fertile ground for attacking the NHTSA motorcycle cues in court. The guide published by NHTSA gives ample ammunition for cross-examination. Page 3 of the guide states: "... some officers, even those with many years of experience, reported they believe there are no cues that can be used to distinguish DWI from unimpaired motorcycle operation." The cues are:

Figure 9.12 *NHTSA Motorcycle Guide*

Excellent Cues (50% or greater probability)

- Drifting during a turn or curve
- Trouble with a dismount
- Trouble with balance at a stop
- Turning problems (unsteady, sudden corrections, late braking, improper lean angle)
- Inattentive to surroundings

- Inappropriate or unusual behavior (carrying or dropping an object, urinating at roadside, disorderly conduct)
- Weaving

Good Cues (30% to 49% probability)

- Erratic movement while going straight
- Operating without lights at night
- Recklessness
- Following too closely
- Running stop light or sign
- Evasion
- Wrong way

If we deconstruct the cues listed above, it becomes more than clear that they run the gamut from highly objective to highly subjective. Obviously, driving the wrong way on a one-way street, running a stop sign/light or riding without lights on at night would be highly objective. Weaving, following too closely or erratic movements are toward the middle of the spectrum. Finally, trouble with balance/dismount, recklessness and inattentiveness to surroundings are most subjective. View, however, the cue labeled "carrying an object." NHTSA claims that this is a cue. But motorcycles certainly have limited storage space so sometimes it is a necessity for a driver to carry an object. Does lack of storage space create a cue?

Moreover, the "evasion" cue either is speculative or should be renamed "attempted evasion" because anyone who evaded the officers would not have his BAC measured to contribute to the study.

There were some cues that had a high correlation in the study but did not make it into the final guide. Among the cues was pushing a motorcycle either on or off road. This cue had the same probability as did striking an object while riding. Perhaps it was not included because the motorcyclist was not actually riding.

Likewise, riding a stolen motorcycle had predictors as high as or higher than some cues that actually made it into the guide. Failure to pay a toll, coasting downhill, "wearing silly headgear" and a category called "facial expression" all had high correlations yet did not make the final guide.

Finally, note that the published guide for automobile drivers at least correlates to a percentage probability that the driver is at or above a particular BAC. The published motorcycle guide makes no such claims—they simply predict that the driver is "DWI" without defining "DWI" in terms of a BAC. The study, however, does correlate to a particular BAC. This means that an officer who has read only the motorcycle guide and not the underlying study may be unaware of the percentages, whereas an officer who reads only the automobile guide and not the underlying study should be aware of the percentages.

Older drivers

Like the pamphlets published to help police identify impaired drivers and motorcyclists, NHTSA has also published a pamphlet to help police identify older drivers who may be a hazard to themselves and others on the roadway. The pamphlet "Older Drivers: Cues for Law Enforcement" (DOT HS 808 778, September 1998) list cues and explanations for driving behavior attributed to drivers aged 65 and older. In the DWI situation, some of these cues can be used in at least two ways.

The NHTSA pamphlet can certainly be used to identify alternative explanations to drunk driving when you have a client who is accused of DWI and is an older driver (defined by the pamphlet as 65-years-of-age and older—the same age as the upper limit for validation of field sobriety testing). But don't overlook the fact that some of the explanations mentioned can be used for drivers of any age. For example, NHTSA includes explanations such as seats that cannot be adjusted to accommodate a driver's shape or size. This could be used to provide an alternative explanation for poor driving with a person who is extremely overweight or obese. Couple that explanation along with the fact that field sobriety tests are not validated for someone 50 lbs or more overweight, and you may have the beginning of a good defense.

While most of us think of the dash of a car being well-thought-out and logical, NHTSA explains that "illogical dash design and displays" may be a barrier to safe driving. Think of this when you have a client who has been diagnosed with Attention Deficit Disorder (ADD) or Attention Deficit Hyperactivity Disorder (ADHD). People with ADD or ADHD function much better in an organized and logically-designed environment. Moreover, if your client was driving a rental car, he might be confused by a particular and unfamiliar auto-manufacturer's dash and control layout. At least one automaker has a car model in which the headlights can be turned on separately from the taillights. Logically speaking, there should be a reason for this feature, but the author of this book hasn't figured that one out, yet.

Some of the cues listed are similar, if not the same as cues that police are taught to look for in a DWI investigation. The pamphlet asks if the driver knows the current time of day, or day of the week. Whether the driver has difficulty communicating or stumbles over words are listed as cues. In terms of balance, stumbling, falling, and lacking coordination are all identified as well.

In the pamphlet, NHTSA recognizes many "engineering barriers to safe operational mobility" which include: small width on all inner, outer, and center highway divider

Figure 9.13 NHTSA Older Drivers Pamphlet

lines; worn, damaged/ or missing roadway markings and signs; illegible and unreasonably sized fonts on traffic control devices; work zone areas that are not distinctly marked with official traffic control devices to warn of substandard width lanes, slower posted speed, pedestrian traffic; lack of a vigorous maintenance schedule for traffic control devices, and; traffic control devices that, due to placement off the roadway, are not effective. These issues serve as reminders as to why we need to visit the area where our clients were driving and stopped to properly assess how the investigation was conducted.

The pamphlet states "The cues listed were field analyzed by Florida State Troopers in Pinellas County, Florida during the month of April, 1998. The responses obtained from using the cues assisted these law enforcement officers in the assessment of the older citizen drivers they encountered during traffic crash investigations and traffic stops." However, NHTSA fails to explain how the cues were first developed, what the frequency of observation of the cues was, what percentage of drivers under 65 years of age displayed the cues, the sample size, or how the cues were "field analyzed" by the police.

The pamphlet's bibliography cites to many sources, including the American Medical Association, American Traffic Safety Services Association, United States National Institute on Aging, United States Department of Commerce Bureau of the Census, United States National Institutes of Health, United States Department of Health and Human Services Center for Disease Control and Prevention, National Center of Health Statistics, United States National Academy of Sciences, United States Department of Transportation National Highway Traffic Safety Administration and others.

Excerpts from the "Older Drivers: Cues for Law Enforcement" appear, below:

> **Cues for Law Enforcement**
> **Introduction**
> **Older Drivers**
> America is aging. By 2020, America will have 50 million citizens 65-years-of-age and older. By 2020, eight states will double their 65-years-of-age and older population and nineteen states will have one million or more older citizens.
> California and Florida will rank first and second in the older citizen population by 2025. These citizens are mobility minded; they are electing to drive longer. They are self-assessment oriented in questions pertaining to safely operating their motor vehicles. However, some older drivers are not able to correctly access their capabilities; they will require assistance to continue operating motor vehicles safely. Every person, not just older citizens, faces a progressive, natural history of functional decline. Self-evaluation and self-assessment of driving ability are essential elements in the decision to restrict or eliminate certain styles of driving. Older drivers

may avoid limited access roadways, scale back or eliminate nighttime driving, and rarely operate a motor vehicle in inclement weather. They want to drive safely. They are not opposed to fair and unbiased evaluations. However, the evaluations should be based on performance, not age. Older drivers are seeking to keep autonomy and mobility. Many older drivers, who have virtually been abandoned by their immediate family and cannot be reached by sparse or at times non-existent governmental social services, view their driving privileges and their motor vehicle as the last vestige of independence. This independence is difficult to relinquish.

Purpose

The purpose of this pamphlet is to provide law enforcement officers cues for determining the safe operational needs of older drivers.

Barriers To Safe Mobility

Older drivers face a multitude of medical and non-medical barriers that may affect their safe operation of a motor vehicle. Some of the medical barriers that confront older drivers and impede their ability to operate a motor vehicle include:

- Alzheimer's Disease
- Other dementia such as multi-infarction
- Field of vision loss, low vision, cataracts and the onset of glaucoma
- Arthritis, Parkinson's Disease, and stroke
- Slowed reaction time due to advanced age and/or poor physical condition

Non-medical barriers to safe driving operation also hinder older drivers. These include:

Interior design of a motor vehicle:

- seats that cannot be adjusted to accommodate a driver's shape, size, or medical condition
- interior seating that does not provide for the comfort of the operator
- illogical dash design and displays
- seat belt/shoulder harness placement that is difficult to reach

Exterior design of motor vehicles:

- motor vehicle exterior doors that are heavy and cumbersome
- visibility problems due to pillar post placement
- motor vehicles that are large in overall size

Engineering barriers to safe operational mobility:

- small width on all inner, outer, and center highway divider lines
- worn/damaged/missing roadway markings and signs
- illegible and unreasonably sized fonts on traffic control devices
- work zone areas that are not distinctly marked with official traffic control devices to warn of substandard width lanes, slower posted speed, pedestrian traffic, etc.
- lack of a vigorous maintenance schedule for traffic control devices
- traffic control devices that, due to placement off the roadway, are not effective

CUES

Does the driver know the current:

- time of day?
- day of the week?
- month of the year?
- year?

Does the driver recall where they are coming from?

Does the driver know their destination?

Is the driver far from their residence?

Does the driver:

- have difficulty communicating?
- stumble over words?
- ramble in short, unattached, meaningless sentences or explanations of their driving ability?

Is the driver's clothing:

- disheveled?
- non-matching?
- incomplete or too much for existing weather conditions?
- Does the driver exhibit poor personal hygiene? (EXAMPLE: Urine/feces stains on clothing, on the person, in the motor vehicle.)

- Does the driver launch into accusations of perceived victimization by criminals?
- Does the driver appear to be suffering from dementia such as Alzheimer's Disease?
- Is the driver wearing an identification bracelet or necklace indicating dementia that would affect safe driving mobility?

• Does the driver have large amounts of prescription medicines, prescribed by different doctors, visible in the motor vehicle?
• If the driver is out of the motor vehicle or exits the motor vehicle, do they have difficulty finding and removing driver's license, motor vehicle registration, insurance card from wallet/purse or producing other requested documents?
• Do they take a long period of time to walk a short distance, stumble/fall, shake excessively, or lack coordination when accomplishing simple tasks?

9.3 Standardized Field Sobriety Testing (SFST) Validation Studies

Many tests have been suggested and tested for police to use to determine whether to arrest or let a suspected DWI driver go free. The National Highway Traffic Safety Administration (NHTSA) has spent millions of tax dollars on grants to determine which tests are the most effective for law enforcement purposes. NHTSA settled on a three-test battery which it recommends for use by law enforcement. The tests are Horizontal Gaze Nystagmus (HGN), Walk-and-Turn (WAT) and One-Leg-Stand (OLS). NHTSA claims that these tests are both "standardized" and "validated."

"Validated" versus "standardized"

Many times these terms are confused and incorrectly interchanged. The term "standardized" refers to a method of administering and interpreting the SFSTs. Standardized tests are supposed to be administered and interpreted in the same manner and under the same conditions no matter where they take place. The theory is that a police officer in New York should be able to administer the tests and interpret them in the same manner as an officer in California. Standardization is not a complex issue. We live with standardization in many respects. For example, copy paper is standardized at 8-$^1/_2$ × 11 inches, EXIT signs are standardized as to color and size, even fast-food is standardized. In fact, one could standardize the way one puts on shoes and socks in the morning by simply doing it the same way, every day, without change. Cronbach (1970) defines a standardized test as being "one in which the procedures, apparatus, and scoring have been fixed so that precisely the same testing procedures can be followed at different times and places." Cronbach, L., *Essentials of Psychological Testing*, New York: Harper & Row, 1970.

The term "validated" refers to the correlation between performance on an SFST and a particular blood alcohol content (BAC). Contrary to what the prosecution says in virtually every state across the nation, the SFSTs have no correlation to impairment. They merely (and crudely) predict BAC. Moreover, there is no "pass" or "fail" with regard to FSTs. However, some police and prosecutors will consistently use those terms to describe a suspect's performance on FSTs. Also, do not confuse the term "validated" with the term "valid." As previously mentioned, "validated" is the term used by the authors of the studies to describe a correlation to a particular BAC. "Valid" has the connotation of truth. Prosecutors and police often attempt to portray SFSTs as valid indicators of impairment, when they are not.

The six major studies regarding FSTs are listed in chronological order as follows:

1. June, 1977 SFST Study
Title: *Psychophysical Tests for DWI Arrests*
Authors: Marcelline Burns and Herbert Moskowitz, 132 pages
Performing Organization: Southern California Research Institute
Department of Transportation Number DOT HS 802 424

2. March, 1981 SFST Study
Title: *Development & Field Test of Psychophysical Tests for DWI Arrests*
Authors: V. Tharp, Marcelline Burns, and Herbert Moskowitz, 98 pages
Performing Organization: Southern California Research Institute
Department of Transportation Number DOT HS 805 864

3. September, 1983 SFST Study
Title: *Field Evaluation of a Behavioral Test Battery for DWI*
Authors: Theodore E. Anderson, Robert M. Schweitz, and Monroe B. Snyder
Performing Organization: Office of Driver & Pedestrian Research, Problem-Behavior Research Division
Department of Transportation Number DOT HS 806 475

4. Florida, 1998
Title: *A Florida Validation Study of the Standardized Field Sobriety Test (S.F.S.T.) Battery*
Authors: Marcelline Burns
Performing Organization: Institute of Police Technology & Management, University of North Florida, Pinellas County Sheriff's Office, Southern California Research Institute
Department of Transportation Number: None

5. San Diego, August 1998
Title: *Validation of the Standardized Field Sobriety Test Battery at BACs Below .10 Percent*
Authors: Jack Stuster and Marcelline Burns
Performing Organization: ANACAPA Sciences, Inc.
Department of Transportation Number: DOT HS 808 839

6. Colorado, November 1995
Title: *A Colorado Validation Study of the Standardized Field Sobriety Test (SFST) Battery*, November 1995, Second Printing: September, 1996
Authors: Ellen Anderson and Marcelline Burns
Performing Organization: Southern California Research Institute
Department of Transportation Number: None

9.4 Legal Analysis and Summary of the SFST Validation Studies

In this section, each study is analyzed and summarized from the defense view with an eye toward understanding and deconstructing the study for use in court.

Analysis: The 1977 SCRI Study

Psychophysical Tests for DWI Arrests, June, 1977; Authors: Marcelline Burns and Herbert Moskowitz, 132 Pages; Performing Organization: Southern California Research Institute; Department of Transportation Number DOT HS 802 424.

More commonly known as "The 1977 Study," this is the seminal study on SFSTs. It was prepared for the U.S. Department of Transportation, National Highway Traffic Administration, under contract number DOT-HS-5-01242. The study was conducted from June 30, 1975 to February 28, 1977, which is a twenty-month period.

The primary focus of the study was to evaluate police sobriety tests and to develop more sensitive and reliable measures. Standardization was also a stated purpose.

Ten police officers administered six tests to 238 participants who were light, moderate and heavy drinkers. BACs ranged from zero to .150. Some participants received placebo drinks. Officers scored the participants on a 1 to 10 scale, basing an arrest/release decision on the entire six-test battery. The correlation was to a BAC of .10. There were 168 men and 70 women. Their ages ranged from 20 to 71 years old, with an average age of 26 years, 6 months. Of the participants, 62 were classified as light drinkers, 86 as moderate and 90 as heavy drinkers.

The six-test battery comprised the Walk-and-Turn (WAT), One-Leg-Stand (OLS), Alcohol Gaze Nystagmus (AGN—not administered exactly as the more recently known test: "HGN"), Tracing and alternate tests such as Romberg Body Sway, Subtraction, Counting Backward, and Letter Cancellation.

All tests were found to be alcohol sensitive to one degree or another. The officers made a correct arrest/release decision 76 percent of the time. The "best" battery of tests was found to be the three-test battery of AGN, Walk-and-Turn and One-Leg-Stand commonly used by officers today. The study found that the three-test battery can be administered in less than five minutes at roadside with an almost 84 percent accuracy rate. The tests can be adapted for a more accurate evaluation if done at the station in a more controlled environment. The officers made the correct decision to release the subject 73 percent of the time. The study notes that officers indicated that they would have arrested 101 people, 47 of whom had BACs below .10. Of special note is the fact that there were six subjects who had no alcohol at all, but officers indicated that they would have arrested them anyway. Research observers indicated that they would have arrested one of the same six. The study faults itself for the fact that the police may have been more likely to make an "arrest" in the laboratory situation than in the field because of the negative consequences of a false arrest. The researchers stated: "In actual practice, the most common error at roadside is a false negative; unless an officer has a high degree of certainty that an individual's BAC is over .10, he is most likely to release rather than arrest." Yet the researchers give no basis for this statement, which DWI defense attorneys all over the country know, anecdotally, to be false.

The authors state that the study shows that "substantial impairment typically occurs at a BAC lower than .10, the current arbitrarily defined level for DWI arrest." The authors suggest a "more appropriate" legal limit of .08.

The original list of tests and explanation that were examined for use in the study is as follows:

> **Alcohol Gaze Nystagmus (AGN)**. The jerking movement of the eye, which is known as Alcohol Gaze Nystagmus, occurs upon lateral gaze when the BAC exceeds approximately .06. The eye jerks in the direction of the gaze, independent of head position.
>
> The person is asked to cover one eye and follow the movement of a small light or object with the other eye without changing head position. The light is moved slowly to points requiring 30 degree and 40 degree lateral deviation of the gaze. The test is then repeated with the other eye. Each eye is observed for jerking movement.

Walk-and-Turn. The person is instructed to walk a straight line, touching heel to toe on each step for nine steps, then turn and return along the same line and in the same manner. A demonstration is given.

Romberg (Balance). The person is instructed to stand with feet together, head tipped back, eyes closed, and arms down at the sides. An anterior-posterior sway is noted. The test lasts for 45 seconds.

Finger-to-Nose. The subject stands erect with eyes closed and arms extended horizontally. The subject is then instructed to touch the nose with the index finger, alternating right and left hands as instructed. A demonstration is given.

One-Leg-Stand. The subject is instructed to stand with one leg straight, slightly elevated off the floor (forward), for 30 seconds. Eyes remain open.

Finger Count. The subject is instructed to touch and count each finger in succession, counting aloud. The test is demonstrated as "Watch what I do. 1-2-3-4-5-5-4-3-2-1."

Tongue Twisters. The person is asked to repeat such words and phrases as "Methodist, episcopal, sophisticated statistics."

Subtraction, Addition, Count Backwards. The subject is instructed to subtract by threes, beginning for example at 102, and to continue to some specified number. The subject may also be asked to add continuously. The same general instructions are given for counting backwards.

Tapping Rate. The subject is instructed to tap a telegraph key as rapidly as possible. The number of taps is recorded by an electronic counter during a ten-second period.

Letter Cancellation. The subject is asked to cancel all occurrences of a given letter in a paragraph of text during a thirty-second time period.

Tracing. The subject is asked to trace a paper pathway or maze in twenty seconds. The test is repeated a total of three times.

Grip Strength. The subject is instructed to squeeze a dynamometer as hard as possible. The dynamometer is shaped like a pistol grip with grooves for each finger. The instrument measures force exerted in isometric contraction.

Coin Pick-Up. Three coins, chips or matches are placed on the floor. The subject is then asked to stand in one location, pick up the objects one at a time and hand them to an examiner. A demonstration is given.

Two-Point Tactile Discrimination. The person is given a two-point tactile stimulation on the forearm or on the back of the hand. Beginning with no separation of the two points, the person is asked "How many places am I touching your arm?" Trials are repeated with increasing separation. Response measure is the first separation to which the person responds "two."

Color Naming (Attention Diagnostic Method, modified). A card presents numbers 10 to 59, in random order and in four colors by row. The person is instructed to find a sequence of ten numbers, beginning with some designated number, and to report the color of each. A verbal response, for example, might be; "Ten-blue, eleven-white, twelve-yellow, thirteen-red ...." The response measure is the time to report the colors of ten numbers.

Serial Performances. The device consists of a small box. Five toggle switches and a small bulb are mounted on the face of the box. The box is presented to the subject with all switches in the center position. The subject is told to move the switches and that when they are in the correct sequence of up-down positions the red light will turn on.

Note that the AGN test used a device to position the light for the officer performing the test. One eye was always covered while the opposite eye was being tested. Floor markings were used for the Walk-and-Turn and One-Leg-Stand. Vertical wall stripes provided contrast for body movements on videotape. Examiners were provided with stopwatches to time the various portions of the tests.

Test subjects were instructed not to eat or use any stimulants for four hours prior to testing, and they were to arrive alcohol free. These conditions were violated by a number of subjects, and some even arrived with positive BACs. The violations were ignored by the researchers.

The final test battery of AGN, Walk-and-Turn and One-Leg-Stand was chosen not only because of the individual reliability of the results, but also because they could be used in the field with little or no specialized equipment and because they did not take an inordinate amount of time to complete. Of special note, however, is that tracing was the second most accurate test next to nystagmus when single-test data were examined. See the chart below:

Test	% Overall Correct	% <.10% Correct	% >.10% Correct
Walk-and-Turn	75.1	80.0	59.7
Finger-to-Nose	70.4	75.6	56.5
Finger Count	67.1	70.8	57.1
Tracing	76.5	84.4	55.6
One-Leg-Stand	75.5	79.6	64.5
Nystagmus—Left	80.1	89.9	54.0
—Right	82.7	87.5	69.8
—Total	81.8	86.0	68.3

The study's authors claim that all three of the objectives set forth in the work statement were achieved:

1. Evaluate currently used tests to determine their relationship to intoxication and driving impairment.
2. Develop more sensitive tests to provide better evidence of impairment and to have a closer relationship to driving impairment.
3. Standardize the tests and observation procedures.

It is important for the defense attorney to note that comparison for a relationship to driving impairment was never made with actual driving. The researcher used only visual tracking and other non-driving-based tests for comparison. The researchers did not develop any new tests at all and only correlated the results to a BAC above or below .10. And, finally, they did standardize the tests and observation procedures.

Analysis: The 1981 SCRI Study

Development & Field Test of Psychophysical Tests for DWI Arrests, March, 1981; Authors: V. Tharp, Marcelline Burns and Herbert Moskowitz, 98 pages; Performing Organization: Southern California Research Institute; Department of Transportation Number DOT HS 805 864.

This is probably the most important SFST study. It serves as the basis for the three-test battery of HGN, Walk-and-Turn and One-Leg-Stand, and its results have been quoted in every NHTSA SFST manual to date. Studies prior to this served as the basis for this study, and those since have only reinterpreted the findings. Intimate knowledge of this study is essential to any DWI defense attorney who contemplates becoming competent in the field.

The administration and scoring procedures for the three-test battery of the HGN, Walk-and-Turn and One-Leg-Stand were standardized for this study. The battery was examined in the laboratory and, to a limited extent, in the field. The study was started in August 1978, and ended in March 1981.

Ten officers from Los Angeles area police agencies examined 297 drinking volunteers in the lab from zero BAC to .18 BAC. There were 202 male subjects and 95 females. One of the female subjects became ill during the research and was unable to return for the second round of testing. None of the laboratory subjects was under 21 years of age, and only two were 65 or older.

Officers in the lab were able to classify correctly 81 percent of the volunteers as above or below .10 BAC.

In the field, officers filled out 3,128 data forms, each representing a driver stopped within a three-month period. The forms included an estimate of the driver's BAC. Drivers who were released were breath tested anonymously.

As in the 1977 study, participants were asked not to eat, drink or use drugs prior to their arrival at the testing facility. Not all complied with those instructions. In fact, three subjects arrived with BACs of .05 or more. Illicit drug use was a major concern of the researchers as they did not want any cumulative effect of drugs and alcohol to skew their results. No drug testing was performed to rule out the possible effects of any drugs on the results. The researchers administered an HGN test to the subjects to check for drug use. Those people who displayed moderate to strong nystagmus at maximum deviation were given placebo doses of alcohol. These people were classified as being high risk for a false positive result—in other words, the police might see the nystagmus and improperly classify the subject as being over .10. One of these individuals, even though at a zero BAC, was classified as being over .10 by the police, and four other subjects at a zero BAC were classified as being over .10 by research staff.

The researchers also relied on the truthfulness of the subjects to report any illegal drug use in a study that used police officers to test the subjects.

Walk-and-Turn

Results for the Walk-and-Turn test showed that asking the subject to balance heel-to-toe while listening to instructions increased the sensitivity to alcohol. Asking people to watch their feet while performing the test also increased sensitivity to alcohol, but made the test difficult for people with monocular vision and poor depth perception. Performing the test with one's eyes open with enough light to see a frame of reference was essential if sober participants were to perform the test without difficulty. The study also found that people over 65 years of age, people with back, leg or middle-ear problems and people wearing high-heeled shoes (over 2 inches) had difficulty performing the tests even when sober. The researchers recommended that only the HGN test be used with people over 65 or those with back, leg or middle-ear problems and that those wearing high-heeled shoes be asked to remove them.

One-Leg-Stand

Few variables were found to alter the sensitivity of the One-Leg-Stand test. It was found that a subject at a BAC of .10 might keep balance for 20 to 25 seconds but would likely falter after that point. The officer must ask the subject to count from 1,001 to 1,030 in order to estimate the passage of 30 seconds. Yet the standardization states that the officer is to ask the subject to count "rapidly" from 1,001 to 1,030, and nowhere in the instructions does the officer tell the subject to estimate the passage of 30 seconds.

More important, however, is that the study found that the subject must be able to see in order to orient herself and that the police officer must stand back from the subject in order not to provide an artificial frame of reference which could distract the subject. The study clearly states: "Generally, if the stopee cannot see or orient with respect to a perpendicular frame of reference, then this test will be difficult to perform even if sober."

Experience tells us that if we ask an officer whether he gave the defendant a perpendicular or vertical frame of reference as a guide while doing the test, the officer will generally say "no," fearing that he administered the test in the wrong manner. This gives the defense attorney ample opportunity to impeach the officer with the study.

The study also found that certain individuals will have difficulty performing this test under sober conditions. Those people over 65 years of age, people with back, leg or middle-ear problems, people 50 pounds or more overweight and people wearing high-heeled shoes (over 2 inches) had difficulty performing the tests even when sober. The researchers recommended that only the HGN test be used with such people and that those wearing high-heeled shoes be asked to remove them. The researchers state: "These individuals should only be given the nystagmus test."

The One-Leg-Stand test should be performed only on a hard, dry, level, non-slippery surface under relatively safe conditions. Note that the research requires a level surface—not "relatively level" or "level-enough" as some officers testify is the requirement. Often, all it takes is an investigator with a level and a camera to show just how bad the test conditions were for this test.

"Relatively safe conditions" can certainly be argued to exclude tests conducted by the side of a busy interstate highway or where there is any chance of being struck by passing traffic.

Horizontal Gaze Nystagmus

There is a strong correlation between the angle of onset and BAC. As the angle of onset decreases, the BAC increases.

In the pilot study there were a number of variables found not to affect the test: stimulus brightness, room brightness, fixation distance, velocity of the stimulus movement, monocular versus binocular fixation, instructions to inhibit nystagmus and the vertical positioning of the eyes. Some of the variables, however, were found to be important in aiding the observer to record the nystagmus. For example, if done in poorly lit conditions, a flashlight must be used to illuminate the subject's eyes. The stimulus must be held slightly above eye level in order to reduce squinting and allow the observer to see the eye movements clearly.

The researchers found that the gaze nystagmus test may not be applicable to certain individuals. People wearing hard contact lenses may not be able to complete the test because it requires lateral eye movement that may be inhibited by the lenses. Also, about 3 percent of the population will show early-onset nystagmus, and impaired balance, with no alcohol in their systems. This could be due to drugs other than alcohol, brain damage, illness, or unknown cause.

The study found that, "Since police officers often arrest intoxicated individuals after midnight, possible effects of fatigue or circadian rhythms on gaze nystagmus could be significant." It was found that the angle of onset after midnight was decreased in a segment of the participants.

They also found that while speed of the stimulus is not critical, if the speed drops below 10 degrees per second while looking for the angle of onset, natural oscillations of the eye may be mistaken for nystagmus.

Analysis: 1983 SFST Field Evaluation

Field Evaluation of a Behavioral Test Battery for DWI, September, 1983; Authors: Theodore E. Anderson, Robert M. Schweitz, and Monroe B. Snyder; Performing Organization: Office of Driver and Pedestrian Research, Problem-Behavior Research Division; Department of Transportation Number DOT HS 806 475.

The first thing to realize about this study is that it was small, both in scope and length. The study itself took only three months to perform. Its objective was to evaluate the use of the three-test battery crafted during the 1981 SCRI Study.

Police agencies from four jurisdictions were used (Arlington County, Virginia; Maryland State Police; North Carolina State Police; and Washington, D.C. Police). The study lasted from November 15, 1982, through February 15, 1983. The Arlington County Police data were for only two months instead of three. They had issues with the legality of the breath tests used in their jurisdiction.

There were major problems with the accuracy of the study. Although the officers were given a one-day training class as well as a manual, it was difficult for the researchers to monitor the police data collection in the field. The study notes this issue:

> It was not possible for researchers to routinely accompany the patrols and supervise the actual data collection. Therefore, no statements can be made as to how closely the requested data collection procedures were followed.

In fact, the data relating to the frequency of the monitors riding with the police are not mentioned in the study which leads one to believe that it was very, very low. Moreover, with the exception of the North Carolina State Police, all agencies equipped their officers with PBTs. Since the focus of the study was to determine the efficacy of the three-test battery, the presence and use of PBTs would certainly interfere with the officers' decisions as to arrest or not arrest. Do not forget—this was a study with real drivers, on real roadways, who could be charged with real crimes. If an officer stopped and tested someone with FSTs and determined that the driver was not impaired, yet used a PBT that showed a .150 BAC, that officer would have to arrest the driver. One could only imagine the liability incurred if the officer let the driver go and she killed someone. The converse is also true—imagine the scenario where the officer administers the "new" and unproven test battery, the driver fails all three tests, yet blows a .003 BAC on the PBT. Instead of releasing that individual, the officer arrests for the sake of the research results. The study acknowledges this flaw:

> There are a number of problems in using these data. We do not know how those given a PBT differ from or are representative of the rest. Perhaps most significant of all, except for North Carolina, all agencies had PBTs available, and in the great majority of the cases, PBT data were available to the officer for a driver before he was arrested. Thus most arrest decisions were based on PBT data, rather than just the test battery data.

The table below shows the percentage of drivers stopped for suspicion of DWI that plots the usage of the Horizontal Gaze Nystagmus (HGN), Walk-and-Turn (WAT), One-Leg-Stand (OLS), all three tests (All 3), and a Preliminary Breath Test (PBT).

Police Agency	**HGN**	**WAT**	**OLS**	**All 3**	**PBT**
Arlington County	84%	76%	72%	70%	92%
Maryland State	92%	91%	90%	88%	63%
North Carolina State	91%	85%	85%	82%	0%
Washington, DC	82%	78%	76%	74%	97%
All Police Agencies	89%	84%	82%	80%	N/A
Washington, DC Control	0	0	0	0	94%

As one can plainly see, a whopping 97 percent of Washington, D.C. police used PBTs during the investigation. Moreover, all drivers were stopped for suspicion of DWI which adds another factor not contemplated by the study. Clearly, driving behavior had something to do with the ultimate arrest/not arrest decision made by the police. Unlike the laboratory evaluation, the police decision to arrest was already affected, if not skewed *toward* arrest, by the fact that all subjects were already suspected of DWI before the officers even met the subjects.

The use of the control groups is laudable. Arlington police stopped 345 people, Maryland stopped 451, North Carolina stopped 434 and Washington, D.C. stopped 276. The control groups operated in Washington, D.C. and North Carolina, collecting PBT data only on 195 and 813 drivers, respectively.

The combined accuracy rate of all police agencies (83 percent) was not far from the laboratory study (80 percent). Of the misclassifications, however, 16 percent of the drivers were incorrectly classified as having a BAC of .10 or more. That means that 197 drivers were falsely arrested.

Analysis: The Colorado Study

A Colorado Validation Study of the Standardized Field Sobriety Test (SFST) Battery, November 1995, Colorado; Authors: Ellen Anderson and Marcelline Burns; Performing Organization: Southern California Research Institute; Department of Transportation Number: None.

The Colorado study is among the most detailed of the six major studies and had two major differences from the other five. First, Colorado's weather was of particular concern to the researchers. Although in the end the study concluded that weather did not affect any of the results in a meaningful fashion, the study does say that, "In particular, note that controlled laboratory conditions are less variable and, therefore, may be less challenging than the highly varied conditions which officers routinely encounter in the field."

Secondly, the Colorado study is based on a differing legal standard. Note that correct/incorrect decision to arrest or release may be skewed as compared to the other studies by Colorado's two-tiered laws which allow arrests at .10 (DUI) and at .05 (DWAI). Thus, the correct/incorrect arrest/release matrix is based on a .05 standard, not on a .10 or a .08 standard.

	Subjects		Arrests		Releases	
	No.	%	No.	%	No.	%
Correct Decisions	201	86%	163	93%	38	64%
Incorrect Decisions	33	14%	12	7%	21	36%
Total	234	100%	175		59	

The study looked at data from 234 investigations. Officers used only the three-test battery and were not equipped with PBTs. Trained observers were only with the officers 41 percent of the time (125 investigations). The observers, however, were all associated with law enforcement in some capacity. In fact, some were sworn police officers and some of those were in a dual-role of observer and participant. This is hardly the detached, neutral observer that one would hope for in a scientific study. It is not surprising that, "The errors by officers that they reported were relatively minor in nature."

Women made up 18 percent of the total sample group of 305 drivers, yet they were 38 percent of the incorrect releases and 25 percent of the incorrect arrests. These numbers are hardly statistically insignificant.

No allowances were made for instrument error in BAC analysis. In fact, no allowances were made for instrument error in any of the six major studies, but the Colorado study is the only one of the six studies to admit it.

With respect to HGN, the study noted: "It is possible that lack of smooth pursuit and distinct nystagmus at maximum deviation occur at low BACs with some subjects, but not with others, or on some occasions, but not others."

The Colorado study recorded but did not correct for many variables that the other five studies did not record. In particular, the Colorado study recorded:

- Weather conditions
- Temperature
- Type of roadway
- Roadway conditions
- Conditions of the surface used for the SFSTs
- Reason for the stop
- Related circumstances (major recreational events, holidays, taverns, bars and restaurants nearby)
- Open containers in the vehicle
- Driver's clothing (whether it was adequate for weather conditions)
- Driver's footwear
- Observer (present/absent)
- BAC by PBT (Yes/No)
- If yes, measured BAC

The Colorado study, to its credit, published the most complete and varied list of factors which were noted throughout each investigation. Compare this with the San Diego study that has not released its raw data for analysis.

The data gathering took place between February 22, 1995, and July 30, 1995, yielding 305 records from six Colorado law enforcement agencies. (Seven agencies initially participated, but one agency provided no data.)

The study notes in its conclusion: "The records collected and analyzed during this study provide evidence that the SFSTs, as used at roadside by trained and experienced law enforcement officers, are valid indices of the presence of alcohol." Since this study used an arrest/release decision matrix of .05, it really tells us nothing about the effectiveness of the three-test battery at BACs of .08 or .10 because a segment of the "correctly identified" arrestees was lower than .08.

Overall, for 234 cases confirmed by chemical tests, the officers' decisions to arrest and release were 86 percent correct, and 93 percent of their arrest decisions were correct—keeping in mind that the correct/incorrect decision was based on a statutory limit of .05.

Analysis: The San Diego Study

Validation of the Standardized Field Sobriety Test Battery at BACs Below .10 Percent, August 1998, San Diego; Authors: Jack Stuster and Marcelline Burns; Performing Organization: ANACAPA Sciences, Inc.; Department of Transportation Number: DOT HS 808 839.

Only seven officers from one agency in San Diego took part in this study. The results of the HGN were adjusted to assume that four of six cues indicated a BAC of .08 or more, as opposed to .10 or more, and that two cues or more indicated a BAC of .04 or more. The study does not mention which of the six cues were noted for the correlation. Two or more cues on the Walk-and-Turn and the One-Leg-Stand were said to represent .08 or more. The study group was similarly small in scale at only 297 motorists who were ultimately examined and given breath tests. Just 12.1 percent of the motorists were females.

HGN was found to be the most effective of the three-test SFST battery used, and the addition of the Walk-and-Turn and the One-Leg-Stand to the HGN did not raise the probability of determining the BAC significantly. The study asked officers to determine whether a person's BAC was above .08 and if below .08, to estimate whether the person's BAC was above .04. The study claims not only good correlation between SFSTs and the .08 limit but also claims good correlation between SFSTs and a .04 level.

The officers were asked not only to estimate whether the motorist was over or under the aforementioned levels but also to estimate an actual BAC. The mean estimation for the entire group was .117. The actual mean of the recorded BACs was .122. Being averages, this tells us nothing about the efficacy of the individual estimations made and provides only "fluff" for the police and prosecution witnesses to cast the study in a more favorable light.

The study claims a very suspect 91 percent accuracy rate at the .08 level and 94 percent for .04. The officers were advised not to use any other tests besides the SFST battery for their initial determination of estimated BAC. Note that *all* officers were equipped with NHTSA-approved portable breath testing devices. They were asked to confirm the BACs of all people who were examined and ultimately arrested or released so that the study could report the results of those people who had both failed the SFST battery, as well as those who passed it. The study claims to have avoided the problems of officers administering a breath test before recording their estimation of the BAC by requiring them to estimate the BAC before using the breath tester. There was little supervision. Project staff monitors "periodically" rode with participating officers.

There were 24 false positive cases. That means that 24 people were arrested who should have been let go. The researchers note that nine of the 24 were within the margin of error of the breath testing machine, clearly implying that those drivers might have actually been over the limit. Yet the study does not find it important enough to mention the number of motorists who were over the limit but also fell within the margin of error. Moreover, the study notes that one of the false positives was a minor. Thus, it was a correct arrest decision because California has a zero-tolerance law for those under 21. They also discount a false positive because, although she had a measured BAC of .05, she was a "psychiatric patient." It seems, even to the casual observer, that this study is slanted in favor of the police.

Officers were required to be trained formally and to have significant DWI experience in order to be part of the study. The study says that, "Only trained and experienced test administrators could be permitted to participate in the *current* study to avoid confounding study results with the effects of substantially different officer skill and experience levels in SFST administration and scoring." This statement clearly helps the defense community in the situation where an inexperienced officer made the arrest. In other words, the San Diego findings apply only to experienced officers, with an intimate knowledge of the SFSTs. If we look back to the earlier studies with untrained and inexperienced officers, those studies claim a much lower correlation percentage at a much higher BAC.

The study contains two important quotes for the defense, both found at page 28:

> Horizontal gaze nystagmus lacks face validity because it does not appear to be linked to the requirements of driving a motor vehicle. The reasoning is correct, but it is based on the incorrect assumption that field sobriety tests are designed to measure driving impairment.

and

> It is unlikely that complex human performance, such as that required to safely drive an automobile, can be measured at roadside .... The link between BAC and driving impairment is a separate issue, involving entirely different research methods.

Analysis: The Florida Study

A Florida Validation Study of the Standardized Field Sobriety Test (S.F.S.T.) Battery 1998, Florida; Authors: Marcelline Burns; Performing Organization: Institute of Police Technology and Management, University of North Florida, Pinellas County Sheriff's Office, Southern California Research Institute; Department of Transportation Number: None.

Chronologically, this is the last of the six major studies. Although it was a small sample group of drivers, the study seems to have been done with many (but not all) clinical controls in place. For example, there were 379 drivers stopped, but only 256 were evaluated for the final report. This is because in 13 cases SFSTs were not administered, in 53 cases other tests were used in addition to the three-test battery (most often the Finger-to-Nose and the Romberg), and 57 drivers refused the breath test, leaving a paltry 256 drivers who were used in the study.

Supposedly the officers were not equipped with PBTs, but observers were present only 63 percent of the time. In other words, 140 of the original 379 investigations were not observed. There is no breakdown as to the percentage of the final 256 investigations that went without observation. The study used only eight police officers and lasted from June 1, 1997, to September 4, 1997.

Measured BAC	Arrested	Released	Total
> .08	197 Correct Arrest	9 Incorrect Release	206 Greater than 0.08%
< .08	9 Incorrect Arrest	41 Correct Release	50 Less than 0.08%
	206 Arrested	50 Released	256 Investigations

As you can see from the chart above, nine people were incorrectly arrested and nine were incorrectly released. Those drivers who were released had no legal obligation to take a breath test but took one anyway at the request of the observers. They were told that if they were over the limit, they would not be arrested unless they chose to drive away from the scene. Alternative transportation was provided. Four of the nine incorrectly arrested had BACs below .05.

The study shows that failures to arrest alcohol-impaired drivers included subjects who were able to perform the Walk-and-Turn and the One-Leg-Stand with little difficulty, but who displayed four or more cues on the HGN. The study opines that the incorrect release decisions may have been due to the officers being "misled" by the lack of psychomotor impairment.

The author of *this* book opines that the reason the officers were "misled" is because not all people are impaired at levels of .08 BAC and above.

9.5 Standardized Field Sobriety Test Battery

The Standardized Field Sobriety Test Battery (better known as SFSTs) is a series of three tests modified, standardized and validated for law enforcement use since the mid-1980s. It is important to realize that many of the SFSTs, as well as the non-standardized FSTs, have a real basis in the medical setting. HGN has been used for years to diagnose gross neurological dysfunction. The Walk-and-Turn test has been used by physicians and neurologists. The Romberg Sway test was used to assess patients in the tertiary stages of syphilis.

Because the tests have been used in the medical setting, it was thought that they may have application in the DWI setting. This is not entirely implausible. Alcohol intoxication is a neurological dysfunction and has certain symptoms which may be measured by physical tests. A brain tumor may also cause a neurological dysfunction with certain symptoms which may be measured by physical tests. This does not mean, however, that minimally trained police officers can accurately diagnose alcohol intoxication by the side of the road, in poor lighting, with a nervous subject, with no medical history and with only crude tests. Yet this is exactly what they do on a daily basis.

The SFSTs are all, with two exceptions, divided attention tasks. That is, they require subjects to divide their attention between a mental task (remembering and following instructions) and a physical task (generally balancing). The two exceptions are Horizontal Gaze Nystagmus and Vertical Gaze Nystagmus which are not divided attention tasks, but merely show an involuntary muscle movement.

The SFSTs are not a measure of one's ability to drive. They merely correlate to a percentage chance that a person is at or above a specific BAC.

The New 2013 NHTSA SFST Manual

NHTSA has published several SFST manuals over the years. The first SFST manual was published in 1984 and was called *Improved Sobriety Testing*, (DOT HS 806 512, January, 29 1984). It was just eleven pages long and was probably the best SFST training manual published by NHTSA. With just eleven pages, it provided little fodder for cross examination by defense attorneys. It mentioned some of the underlying principles of the SFST studies but it neither named them nor gave specifics. The 1984 manual was more of a "how-to" guide than anything else. It was simple and to the point. While all subsequent manuals contain sections on case-law, statistics regarding impaired driver deaths, injury, and property damage, the 1984 manual concentrated on what the three-test battery was and how to administer it. It had one major mistake, however. It listed the maximum age for administration of the Walk-and-Turn and One-Leg-Stand as 60 years. The original studies listed it as 65 years.

Later years would see the publication in 1987 (HS 178 R5/87), 1992 (HS 178 R 6/92), 1995 (HS 178 R10/95), 2000 (HS 178 R2/00), 2002 (HS 178 R1/02), 2004 (HS 178

R9/04), 2006 (HS 178 R2/06). All were titled, *DWI Detection & Standardized Field Sobriety Testing*. All were approximately 400 pages.

Also in 2004: *SFST Refresher Course* was published, which is exactly what the name states—it was a refresher and not much more. From 1987 to 2006, all manuals carried the cautionary language, below, in some form or another warning the officers not to alter the standardized elements or the manner in which they are evaluated. The 1984 language was:

> "The three tests you will study are the Gaze Nystagmus Test, the Walk-and-Turn Test and the One-Leg- Stand Test. If the standardized testing and scoring procedures presented in this Manual are not followed, the decision making guidelines will not be accurate."

From 1995 to 2006 the cautionary language was:

> "It is necessary to emphasize this validation applies only when:
> The tests are administered in the prescribed, standardized manner.
> The standardized clues are used to assess the suspect's performance.
> The standardized criteria are employed to interpret that performance.
> If any one of the standardized field sobriety test elements are changed, the validity is compromised."

In 2013 *DWI Detection & Standardized Field Sobriety Testing* (HS 178 R5/13) was reworked and published. This time, it was published in conjunction with the International Association of Chiefs of Police (IACP). All cautionary language was stricken from the 2013 manual. And, while all manuals from 1992–2006 contained a courtroom component, in 2013, we now see "Testimonial Tips" for police and prosecutors. The manual is light on specifics and refers students to the power point slide show that accompanies each lesson. Compare 2006 and 2013 manuals in Figure 9.15 at the end of the chapter. Less information means less opportunities for discovery by the defense. Moreover, it is more important now than ever to attempt to subpoena the officer's individual manual that was used during training as it contains spaces for the officer's handwritten classroom notes.

The 2013 manual is also heavy on statistical information regarding drunk driving deaths, injury and property damage. It contains a heavy primer on the Drug Evaluation and Classification Protocol (DECP) (see Chapter 10 of this book for an in-depth discussion of the DECP). Poly-drug use as well as the combination of drugs and alcohol are discussed. It is not a substitution for the DECP certification as a Drug-Recognition Expert, but it gives the most in-depth explanation to date, outside of the certification program. Page 29 of the preface states: "Although this course is not designed to qualify you as a DRE, it is intended to make you more knowledgeable when encountering drivers impaired by substances other than alcohol."

9.6 Horizontal Gaze Nystagmus (HGN)

Like all FSTs, HGN does not predict impairment but actually correlates performance on the test with a percentage probability that the subject is at or above a particular BAC. HGN is not intended to be a divided attention task.

Of all the field sobriety tests, the HGN is clearly purported to be based on science. As such, our State Supreme Court ruled in 1998 that HGN test results testimony from an officer was not admissible unless the State could show that HGN was scientifically reliable. *See State v. Helms*, 348 NC 578 (1998). The State legislature then amended Rule 702 in 2006 to allow officers trained in HGN to testify as to the results. *State v. Smart* 195 NC App 752 (2009) seemed to agree and said that the State did not have to prove that the HGN testing method is sufficiently reliable.

The best strategy for HGN is the simplest strategy. We, as defense attorneys, tend to get caught up in the minutia of HGN. There are subtle nuances involved with deciphering HGN that we take for granted. The moment that we assume that a jury understands HGN, we have lost the HGN battle. In a nutshell, your cross-examination should convey the following message:

- HGN is a very scientific, complex examination.
- Under the proper circumstances, and with much education, competent medical personnel can use HGN as a diagnostic tool for measuring gross neurological dysfunction.
- The officer has neither the training nor the intelligence properly to administer or evaluate the HGN exam, and therefore the results are worthless.
- The circumstances under which the HGN was administered make the test results a virtual nullity.
- It is important to realize that HGN is not a police-developed test. HGN is a medical test used by doctors to diagnose head injuries and other pathological brain dysfunction. HGN only made its way into police use through NHTSA.

Use the chart, "Eighty-Six Types of Nystagmus," to form six or seven questions as follows:

Eighty-Six Types of Nystagmus

1. Acquired
2. Ageotropic
3. Alternating Windmill
4. Anticipatory
5. Arthrokinetic
6. Associated
7. Audio Kinetic
8. Baer's
9. Bartel's
10. Bechterew's
11. Bow Tie
12. Brun's
13. Caloric
14. Centripetal
15. Cervical
16. Circular/Oblique
17. Circumduction
18. Compensatory
19. Congenital
20. Convergence
21. Convergence-evoked
22. Diagonal
23. Dissociated
24. Disjunctive
25. Downbeat
26. Drug-induced
27. Elliptic
28. Epileptic
29. Faradic
30. Flash-induced
31. Galvanic
32. Gaze-evoked Deviational
33. Gaze-paretic
34. Geotropic
35. Gyratory
36. Hereditary
37. Horizontal
38. Ictal
39. Induced
40. Intermittent Vertical
41. Jerk
42. Labyrinthine
43. Latent/Manifest Latent
44. Lateral Medullary
45. Lid
46. Miner's
47. Monocular Fixation
48. Muscle-Paretic
49. Myasthenic
50. Neurasthenic
51. Oblique
52. Occupational
53. Optokinetic
54. Optomotor
55. Optokinetic After-Induced
56. Panoramic
57. Pendular
58. Periodic/Aperiodic Alternating
59. Physiologic Endpoint
60. Physiologic Fatigue
61. Positional Alcohol Nystagmus I (PAN I)
62. Positional Alcohol Nystagmus II (PAN II)
63. Post-Optokinetic
64. Pseudo Caloric
65. Pursuit After-induced
66. Pursuit Defect
67. Pseudo Spontaneous
68. Radiary
69. Railway
70. Rebound
71. Reflex
72. Reverse Post-Optokinetic
73. See-Saw
74. Sigma
75. Somatosensory
76. Spontaneous
77. Stepping Around
78. Stransky's
79. Talantropia
80. Torsional
81. Unimacular
82. Uniocular
83. Upbeat
84. Vertical
85. Vestibular
86. Vestibular-Basilar Artery Insufficiency

- Officer, do you know what *Muscle-Paretic Nystagmus* is?
- Can you differentiate between that and Horizontal Gaze Nystagmus?
- Do you know what *Physiologic End-Point Nystagmus* is?
- Can you differentiate between that and Horizontal Gaze Nystagmus?
- Do you know what *Arthrokinetic Nystagmus* is?
- Can you differentiate between that and Horizontal Gaze Nystagmus?

You may notice that officers almost always testify that they have turned off their overhead emergency lights before administering an HGN exam so that the lights will not interfere with the administration or evaluation of the test. This is a goldmine of opportunities for cross-examination. Even if the officer has said that the overhead lights were off, get him to admit that outside forces can affect both the administration and evaluation of the test. Then, through another witness, show that there were cars whizzing by with bright headlights intermittently piercing the darkness, or that neon signs close by were distracting, and so on. Go to the scene yourself and observe the distractions first hand.

According to the NHTSA training on HGN administration, officers are to look for "distinct" nystagmus at maximum deviation. Yet, nowhere in their training is the term "distinct" defined for them. This gives rise to a series of cross-examination questions as follows.

Start by drawing a simple schematic diagram of an eye within an eye-socket on an easel in the courtroom. It needs to be nothing more than an oval-shaped figure with a circle in the middle for the iris and a dot in the middle of the iris to represent the pupil. Ask the officer if HGN is a jerking movement in the horizontal plane while you draw a double-ended arrow as in Figure 9.13.

Then ask the officer how far NHTSA says that the eye has to jerk before one can call it "nystagmus." When he says that NHTSA does not give a distance, ask how many times it must jerk back and forth in that horizontal plane before NHTSA says it can be called "nystagmus." Hopefully, this will lead the officer into saying that there is not a distance and there is not a set number of times, but it must be "distinct" nystagmus. Then ask the officer to show the jury where his training manual defines the term "distinct" in relation to nystagmus. The officer will be unable to do so, because none of the manuals, up to and including the latest one published, define the term "distinct."

It is at this point that the officer's so-called "objective evidence" becomes as subjective as red, watery, bloodshot eyes, or slurred speech or strong odor of intoxicants evidence.

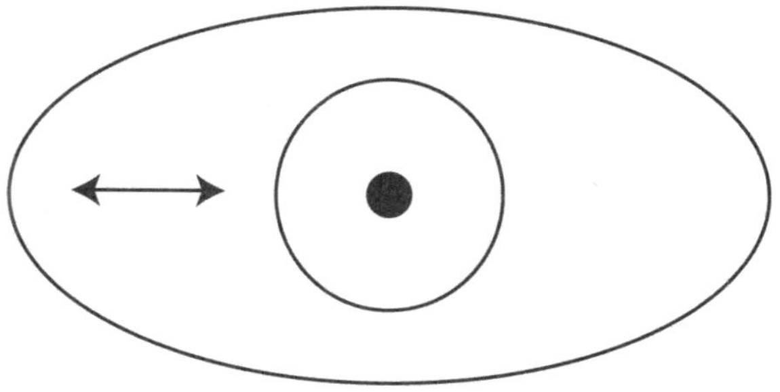

- How many *times* does it have to move back and forth before NHTSA says you can call it "nystagmus"?
- How *far* does it have to move back and forth before NHTSA says you can call it nystagmus?

Figure 9.14

PRACTICE TIP: Do not call the stimulus a "stimulus." Call it what it really is: a pen, a finger, a penlight, etc. Calling it a "stimulus" as the police and prosecutors do gives it an imprimatur of scientific validity for the jury that you don't want it to have. Do not make your job any more difficult than it already is by adopting their language.

HGN instructions (2004 & 2006 Manuals)

The instructions as given in *DWI Detection and Standardized Field Sobriety Testing*, Participant Manual, 2004 and 2006 Editions (HS 178 R2/06 and HS 178 R9/04, Session VIII, "Concepts and Principles for the Standardized Field Sobriety Tests") are as follows:

> If the suspect is wearing eyeglasses, have them removed.
>
> Give the suspect the following instructions from a safe position. (FOR OFFICER SAFETY KEEP YOUR WEAPON AWAY FROM THE SUSPECT):
>
> "I am going to check your eyes."
> "Keep your head still and follow the stimulus with your eyes only."
> "Keep following the stimulus with your eyes until I tell you to stop."
>
> Position the stimulus approximately 12–15 inches from the suspect's nose and slightly above eye level. Check to see that both pupils are equal in size. If they are not, this may indicate a head in-

jury. You may observe Resting Nystagmus at this time, then check the suspect's eyes for the ability to track together. Move the stimulus smoothly across the suspect's entire field of vision. Check to see if the eyes track the stimulus together or one lags behind the other. If the eyes don't track together, it could indicate a possible medical disorder, injury or blindness.

Check the suspect's left eye by moving the stimulus to your right. Move the stimulus smoothly, at a speed that requires approximately two seconds to bring the suspect's eye as far to the side as it can go. While moving the stimulus, look at the suspect's eye and determine whether it is *able to pursue smoothly*. Now, move the stimulus all the way to the left, back across the suspect's face checking if the right eye pursues smoothly. Movement of the stimulus should take approximately two seconds out and two seconds back for each eye. Repeat the procedure.

After you have checked both eyes for lack of smooth pursuit, check the eyes for *distinct and sustained nystagmus at maximum deviation* beginning with the suspect's left eye. Simply move the object to the suspect's left side until the eye has gone as far to the side as possible. Usually, no white will be showing in the corner of the eye at maximum deviation. Hold the eye at that position for a minimum of four seconds, and observe the eye for distinct and sustained nystagmus. Move the stimulus all the way across the suspect's face to check the right eye holding that position for a minimum of four seconds.

PRACTICE TIP: Watch for officers intentionally or negligently inducing "fatigue nystagmus" which can occur when a subject's eyes are kept at maximum deviation for more than 30 seconds. Interview your client and the officer thoroughly about how long the stimulus was kept at maximum deviation.

Next, check for *onset of nystagmus prior to 45 degrees*. Start moving the stimulus towards the right (suspect's left eye) at a speed that would take approximately four seconds for the stimulus to reach the edge of the suspect's shoulder. Watch the eye carefully for any sign of jerking. When you see it, stop and verify that the jerking continues. Now, move the stimulus to the left (suspect's right eye) at a speed that would take approximately four seconds to reach the edge of the suspect's shoulder. Watch the eye carefully for any sign of jerking. When you see it, stop and verify that the jerking continues. Repeat the procedure. NOTE: It is important to use the full four seconds when checking for onset of nystagmus. If you move the stimulus too fast, you may go past the point of onset or miss it altogether.

PRACTICE TIP: Unlike the cue of distinct and sustained nystagmus at maximum deviation, the instructions tell the officer only to check for "any sign of jerking" when checking for onset prior to 45 degrees. This can easily lead to a subjective determination of onset and makes for good cross-examination.

If the suspect's eyes start jerking before they reach 45 degrees, check to see that some white of the eye is still showing on the side closest to the ear. If no white of the eye is showing, you either have taken the eye too far to the side, (that is more than 45 degrees) or the person has unusual eyes that will not deviate very far to the side.

NOTE: Nystagmus may be due to causes other than alcohol. These other causes include seizure medications and some other drugs. A large disparity between the performance of the right eye and the left eye may indicate a medical condition.

Test Interpretation

You should look for three clues of nystagmus in each eye.

1. The eye cannot follow a moving object smoothly.
2. Nystagmus is distinct and sustained when the eye is held at maximum deviation for a minimum of four seconds.
3. The angle of onset of nystagmus is prior to 45 degrees.

HGN instructions (2013 Manual)

The instructions as given in *DWI Detection and Standardized Field Sobriety Testing*, DWI Detection and Standardized Field Sobriety Testing, 2013 Participant Manual,

Session 8 HS178 R 5/13 are below. Note that Vertical Gaze Nystagmus (VGN) is casually thrown in as part of the HGN procedures.

> *Procedures of Horizontal Gaze Nystagmus Testing: The Three Clues*
> The test you will use at roadside is "Horizontal Gaze Nystagmus" -- an involuntary jerking of the eyes occurring as the eyes gaze to the side. When a person is impaired by alcohol or certain drugs, some jerking will be seen if the eyes are moved far enough to the side.
>
> • The Lack of Smooth Pursuit (Clue Number One) - The eyes can be observed to jerk or "bounce" as they follow a smoothly moving stimulus, such as a pencil or penlight. The eyes of an impaired person will not follow smoothly, i.e., a marble rolling across sand paper, or windshield wipers moving across a dry windshield.
>
> • Distinct and Sustained Nystagmus At Maximum Deviation (Clue Number Two) - Distinct and sustained nystagmus is evident when the eye is held at maximum deviation for a minimum of four seconds and continues to jerk toward the side.
>
> • Onset of Nystagmus Prior To 45 Degrees (Clue Number Three) - The point at which the eye is first seen jerking. If the jerking begins prior to 45 degrees it is evident that the person has a BAC above 0.08, as shown by recent research.
>
> The higher the degree of impairment, the sooner the nystagmus will be observable. Horizontal and Vertical Gaze Nystagmus can be observed directly and does not require special equipment. You will need a contrasting stimulus for the subject to follow with their eyes. This can be a penlight or pen. The stimulus used should be held slightly above eye level, so that the eyes are wide open when they look directly at it. It should be held approximately 12 - 15 inches in front of the nose. Remain aware of your position in relation to the subject at all times.
>
> • Check for eyeglasses
> • Verbal instructions
> • Position stimulus (12-15 inches and slightly above eye level)
> • Check for equal pupil size and resting nystagmus
> • Check for equal tracking
> • Lack of smooth pursuit
> • Distinct and sustained nystagmus at maximum deviation
> • Onset of nystagmus prior to 45 degrees
> • Total the clues
> • Check for vertical nystagmus
>
> *Administrative Procedures for Horizontal Gaze Nystagmus*
> It is important to administer the Horizontal Gaze Nystagmus test systematically using the following steps, to ensure that nothing is overlooked. There are 10 steps in the systematic administration of the Horizontal Gaze Nystagmus test.
>
> Step 1: Check for Eyeglasses.
> Begin by instructing the subject to remove eyeglasses, if worn. It does not matter whether the subject can see the stimulus with perfect clarity, as long as subject can see it at all.
>
> Step 2: Verbal Instructions.
> Give the subject the appropriate verbal instructions:
> Point out that officers' should note whether subject sways, wobbles, etc. while trying to balance.
>
> • Put feet together, hands at the side
> • Keep head still
> • Look at the stimulus
> • Follow movement of the stimulus with the eyes only
> • Keep looking at the stimulus until told the test is over
>
> Step 3: Position the Stimulus.
> Position the stimulus approximately 12 - 15 inches (30 - 38 cm) in front of subject's nose, and slightly above eye level to commence the test. Resting Nystagmus may be observed at this time. Officers should note whether the subject displays Resting Nystagmus.
>
> Step 4: Equal Pupil Size and Resting Nystagmus. Check for equal pupil size and resting nystagmus.
>
> Step 5: Equal Tracking. Check for equal tracking. Move the stimulus rapidly from center to far right, to far left and back to center.

Step 6: Lack of Smooth Pursuit. Check the left eye for lack of the "Smooth Pursuit" clue. If the eye is observed to jerk while moving, that is one clue. Check the right eye for lack of the "Smooth Pursuit" clue and compare.

Step 7: Check the right and left eye for the "distinct and sustained nystagmus at maximum deviation" clue. If the jerkiness is distinct and sustained, that is one clue.

Step 8: Onset of Nystagmus Prior to 45 Degrees. Check the left eye for the "onset of nystagmus prior to 45 degrees" clue. If the jerking begins prior to 45 degrees, that is one clue. Check the right eye for "onset of nystagmus prior to 45 degrees" clue, and compare.

Step 9: Total the clues
Maximum number of clues possible for each eye: 3
Total maximum number of clues possible for both eyes: 6.

Step 10: Check for Vertical Nystagmus
It is possible that all three clues definitely will be found in one eye, while only two (or sometimes only one) will show up in the other eye. It is always necessary to check both eyes, and to check them independently. Notwithstanding, it is unlikely that the eyes of someone under the influence of alcohol will behave totally different. Thus, if one eye shows all three clues distinctly while the other eye gives no evidence of nystagmus, the person may be suffering from one of the pathological disorders covered previously.

PRACTICE TIP: Watch for officers "taking a shortcut" in the administration of HGN. Although it may be difficult to prove in court, some officers will only check for onset of nystagmus prior to 45 degrees and assume that the other four cues are present. While someone who displays onset prior to 45 degrees due to alcohol should display the other four cues, it is not a certainty.

Although there have been newer studies that correlate HGN to a percentage chance that the subject is .08 or more, the 2004 NHTSA SFST manual still refers the student to the original studies conducted in the 1970's and 1980's which correlate six out of six cues with a 77 percent chance that the subject is .10 or higher.

PRACTICE TIP: To demonstrate or not to demonstrate? That is the question.

A constant debate between DWI defense attorneys concerns the issue of in-court demonstrations of the FSTs. Should one ask the officer to demonstrate the FSTs before the jury? My advice is "no" for the HGN and an emphatic "yes" for the other FSTs.

Asking the officer to demonstrate the HGN does you no good unless you know that the officer will make a mistake in the administration of the test. Having the officer do the test before the jury makes him appear quite professional and imparts an image of one with scientific or medical knowledge.

Performing the Walk-and-Turn or One-Leg-Stand, however, is quite different. If the officer does well, you can point out that the conditions are perfect—a well-lit, smooth, dry, level surface, no threat of arrest, and the officer has probably done them before.

If the officer makes mistakes, ask the officer if he had something to drink before he entered the courtroom. Asking the officer to demonstrate the FSTs is a win-win proposition for the defense.

9.7 Walk and Turn

The Walk-and-Turn (WAT) test is a divided attention task that requires a subject to listen to and follow instructions as given and demonstrated by the officer. Generally, it requires the subject to stand in a heel-to-toe fashion for a period of time, then to walk heel-to-toe nine steps down a straight line, turn at the ninth step in the manner demonstrated and walk back nine steps in the same fashion.

PRACTICE TIP: By definition, divided attention tasks such as the Walk-and-Turn and the One-Leg-Stand require a subject to concentrate on more than one thing in order to perform the task properly. People with forms of Attention Deficit Disorder (ADD) may have trouble dividing their attention with no alcohol in their systems. The initial intake interview with your client should include questions about ADD.

Walk-and-Turn Instructions (2004 & 2006 Manuals)

The instructions as given in *DWI Detection and Standardized Field Sobriety Testing*, Participant Manual, 2004 and

2006 Editions (HS 178 R2/06 and HS 178 R9/04) Session VIII, "Concepts and Principles for the Standardized Field Sobriety Tests") are as follows:

1. Instructions Stage: Initial Positioning and Verbal Instructions

For standardization in the performance of this test, have the suspect assume the heel-to-toe stance by giving the following verbal instructions, accompanied by demonstrations:

- "Place your left foot on the line" (real or imaginary). Demonstrate.
- "Place your right foot on the line ahead of the left foot, with the heel of right foot against toe of left foot." Demonstrate.
- "Place your arms down by your sides." Demonstrate.
- "Maintain this position until I have completed the in instructions. Do not start to walk until told to do so."
- "Do you understand the instructions so far?" (Make sure the suspect indicates understanding.

2. Demonstrations and Instructions for the Walking Stage

Explain the test requirements, using the following verbal instruction, accompanied by demonstrations:

- "When I tell you to start, take nine heel-to-toe steps, turn, and take nine heel-to-toe steps back." (Demonstrate 3 heel-to-toe steps).
- "When you turn, keep the front foot on the line, and turn by taking a series of small steps with the other foot, like this." (Demonstrate).
- "While you are walking, keep your arms at your sides, watch your feet at all times, and count your steps out loud."
- "Once you start walking, don't stop until you have completed the test."
- "Do you understand the instructions?" (Make sure the suspect understands.)
- "Begin, and count your first step from the heel-to-toe position as 'One'."

3. Test Interpretation

You may observe a number of different behaviors when a suspect performs this test. Original research demonstrated the behaviors listed below are likely to be observed in someone with a BAC above 0.10. Look for the following clues each time this test is given:

A. **Cannot keep balance while listening to instructions**. Two tasks are required at the beginning of this test. The suspect must balance heel-to-toe on the line, and at the same time, listen carefully to the instructions. Typically, the person who is impaired can do only one of these things. The suspect may listen to the instructions, but not keep balance. Record this clue if the *suspect does not maintain the heel-to-toe position throughout the instructions*. (Feet must actually break apart.) *Do not* record this clue if the suspect sways or uses arms to balance but maintains the heel-to-toe position.

B. **Starts before the instructions are finished**. The impaired person may also keep balance, but not listen to the instructions. Since you specifically instructed the suspect not to start walking "until I tell you to begin," record the clue if the suspect does not wait.

C. **Stops while walking**. The suspect pauses for several seconds. *Do not* record this clue if the suspect is merely walking slowly.

D. **Does not touch heel-to-toe**. The suspect leaves a space of more than one-half inch between the heel and toe on any step.

E. **Steps off the line**. The suspect steps so that one foot is entirely off the line.

F. **Uses arms to balance**. The suspect raises one or both arms more than 6 inches from the sides in order to maintain balance.

G. **Improper turn**. The suspect removes the front foot from the line while turning. Also record this clue if the suspect has not followed directions as demonstrated, i.e., spins or pivots around.

H. **Incorrect number of steps**. Record this clue if the suspect takes more or fewer than nine steps in either direction.

Note: If suspect can't do the test, record observed clues and document the reason for not completing the test, e.g., suspect's safety.

If the suspect has difficulty with the test (for example, steps off the line), continue from that point, not from the beginning. This test may also lose its sensitivity if it is repeated several times.

Observe the suspect from a safe distance and limit your movement which may distract the suspect during the test. **Always consider officer safety**.

Based on the original research, if the suspect exhibits two or more clues on this test or fails to complete it, classify the suspect's BAC as above 0.10. Using this criterion, you will be able to accurately classify 68% of your suspects.

PRACTICE TIPS: If the officer demonstrates an even number of steps as opposed to three steps, she will turn in the wrong direction. This could easily confuse a subject taking the test.

Missing heel-to-toe by more than a half inch is a clue, but always be aware of the officer's perspective when viewing the Walk-and-Turn test. It is difficult to see whether someone missed by one half inch versus three quarters of an inch from a distance of 10 feet and at an angle that is not exactly perpendicular to the line.

Sometimes a suspect will step off the line (note that the foot must be entirely off the line) which will also mean that he did not touch heel-to-toe. Since two or more clues is the threshold level for determination of .10 or more, the police may claim that the subject "failed" the test. Nowhere in the manual is this problem addressed.

Test Conditions

Walk-and-Turn test requires a designated straight line, and should be conducted on a reasonably dry, hard, level, non-slippery surface. There should be sufficient room for suspects to complete nine heel-to-toe steps. Note: Recent field validation studies have indicated that varying environmental conditions have not affected a suspect's ability to perform this test.

The original research indicated that individuals over 65 years of age, back, leg or middle ear problems had difficulty performing this test. Individuals wearing heels more than 2 inches high should be given the opportunity to remove their shoes.

PRACTICE TIP: Note that the test requires a designated straight line—not an imaginary line. If you want to be sarcastic, but make your point during cross-examination where the officer used an imaginary line, try this line of questioning:

- Officer, how long was this imaginary line?
- How wide was it?
- What color was it?
- What material was it made of?
- Did my client imagine the same line that you imagined?
- Maybe you just imagined that he stepped off the imaginary line?

Walk and Turn Instructions (2013 Manual)

Walk and Turn

Walk and Turn is a test that has been validated through extensive research sponsored by the National Highway Traffic Safety Administration. The original research was conducted by the SCRI and used to develop the initial curriculum showing this test was 68% accurate at detecting subjects at or above a 0.10 BAC.

Walk and Turn is a divided attention test consisting of two stages:

- Instructions stage
- Walking stage

The Instructions Stage divides the subject's attention between a balancing task (standing while maintaining the heel to toe position) and an information processing task (listening to and remembering instructions).

In the Instructions Stage, the subject must stand with their feet in a heel to toe position, keep their arms at their sides, and listen to the instructions.

In the Walking Stage the subject takes nine heel to toe steps, turns in a prescribed manner, takes nine heel to toe steps back, counts the steps out loud, and watches their feet. During the turn, the subject keeps their front foot on the line, turns in a prescribed manner, and uses the other foot to take several small steps to complete the turn. The Walking Stage divides the subject's attention among a balancing task (walking heel to toe and turning); a small muscle control task (counting out loud); and a short term memory task (recalling the number of steps and the turning instructions).

The walking stage divides the subject's attention between a task of listening, comprehending and carrying out the instruction.

> The Walk and Turn test is administered and interpreted in a standardized manner, i.e., the same way every time. Officers administering the Walk and Turn test observe the subject's performance for eight clues:
>
> • Cannot keep balance while listening to the instructions
> • Starts too soon
> • Stops while walking
> • Does not touch heel to toe
> • Steps off the line
> • Uses arms to balance
> • Improper turn
> • Incorrect number of steps
>
> Inability to complete the Walk and Turn test may occur when the subject is in danger of falling or otherwise cannot complete the test.

Test conditions have always been important to the administration and interpretation of the SFSTs. The manual clearly lays out the conditions:

> Whenever possible, the Walk and Turn test should be conducted on a reasonably dry, hard, level, non-slippery surface. There should be sufficient room for subjects to complete nine heel to toe steps. Recent field validation studies have indicated that varying environmental conditions have not affected a subject's ability to perform this test.

Watch for police using the words "whenever possible" from the quote above as an excuse for administering the tests under improper test conditions. While it is certainly true that the police may not always have conditions suitable for testing, that does not mean that the results of such testing should be admissible. The second sentence of the test conditions paragraph, which reads: "Recent field validation studies have indicated that varying environmental conditions have not affected a subject's ability to perform this test" did not alter the first sentence. And, in fact, it was not "recent field validation studies," it was one, non-peer-reviewed study. It was *A Colorado Validation Study of the Standardized Field Sobriety Test (SFST) Battery*, November 1995, Colorado, mentioned earlier in this chapter. The basic conclusion was that cold temperatures did not affect the results of the tests.

The 2013 manual goes on the give the familiar warning:

> The original SCRI studies suggested that individuals over 65 years of age or people with back, leg or inner ear problems had difficulty performing this test. Less than 1.5% of the test subjects in the original studies were over 65 years of age. Also, the SCRI studies suggest that individuals wearing heels more than 2 inches high should be given the opportunity to remove their shoes. Officers should consider all factors when conducting SFSTs.

The instructions as given in *DWI Detection and Standardized Field Sobriety Testing*, DWI Detection and Standardized Field Sobriety Testing, 2013 Participant Manual, Session 8 HS178 R 5/13 are below.

> *Procedures for Walk and Turn Testing*
> *Instructions Stage: Initial Positioning and Verbal Instructions*
> For standardization in the performance of this test, have the subject assume the heel to toe stance by giving the following verbal instructions, accompanied by demonstrations:
>
> Place your left foot on the line (real or imaginary).
>
> Place your right foot on the line ahead of the left foot, with the heel of your right foot against the toe of the left foot.
>
> Place your arms down at your sides.
>
> Maintain this position until I have completed the instructions. Do not start to walk until told to do so.
>
> Do you understand the instructions so far? (Make sure subject indicates understanding.)
>
> *Demonstrations and Instructions for the Walking Stage*
> Explain the test requirements by giving instructions, accompanied by demonstrations:
>
> When I tell you to start, take nine heel to toe steps on the line, turn, and take nine heel to toe steps down the line.
>
> When you turn, keep the front (lead) foot on the line, and turn by taking a series of small steps with the other foot, like this.
>
> While you are walking, keep your arms at your sides, watch your feet at all times, and count your steps out loud.

Once you start walking, don't stop until you have completed the test.

Do you understand the instructions? (Make sure subject understands.)

Instruct the person to begin the test.

While walking:
- Keep watching feet
- Arms down at sides
- Count steps out loud
- Don't stop during walk

The 2013 manual also gives rules for interpretation, such as:

Cannot keep balance while listening to the instructions.
"Record this clue if the subject does not maintain the heel to toe position throughout the instructions. (Feet must actually break apart or step off the line.) Do not record this clue if the subject sways or uses the arms to balance but maintains the heel to toe position."

Starts too soon.
"The impaired person may also keep balance, but not listen to the instructions. Since you specifically instructed the subject not to start walking "until I tell you to begin," record this clue if the subject does not wait."

Stops while walking.
"The subject stops while walking. Do not record this clue if the subject is merely walking slowly."

Does not touch heel to toe.
"The subject leaves a space of more than one half inch between the heel and toe on any step."

Steps off the line.
"The subject steps so that one foot is entirely off the line."

Uses arms to balance.
"The subject raises one or both arms more than 6 inches from the sides in order to maintain balance."

Improper turn.
"The subject removes the front foot from the line while turning. Also record this clue if the subject has not followed directions as demonstrated, i.e., spins or pivots around or loses balance while turning."

Incorrect number of steps.
"Record this clue if the subject takes more or fewer than nine steps in either direction."

Remember that the SFSTs are a tool to assist you in seeing visible signs of impairment and are not a pass/fail test. If the subject has difficulty with the test (for example, steps off the line), Continue from that point, not from the beginning. This test may lose its sensitivity if it is repeated several times."

(DWI Detection and Standardized Field Sobriety Testing, 2013 Participant Manual, Session 7 HS178 R 5/13)

9.8 One-Leg-Stand

The One-Leg-Stand (OLS) test is a divided attention task that requires a subject to listen to and follow instructions as given and demonstrated by the officer. Generally, it requires the subject to stand on one leg, arms at the subject's side, while the subject watches his raised foot and counts out loud for 30 seconds.

One-Leg-Stand (2004 & 2006 Manuals)

The instructions as given in *DWI Detection and Standardized Field Sobriety Testing*, Participant Manual, 2004 and 2006 Editions (HS 178 R2/06 and HS 178 R9/04) Session VIII, "Concepts and Principles for the Standardized Field Sobriety Tests") are as follows:

1. Instructions Stage: Initial Positioning and Verbal Instructions
Initiate the test by giving the following verbal instructions, accompanied by demonstrations.

- "Please stand with your feet together and your arms down at the sides, like this." (Demonstrate).
- "Do not start to perform the test until I tell you to do so."
- "Do you understand the instructions so far"? (Make sure suspect indicates understanding).

2. Demonstrations and Instructions for the Balance and Counting Stage
Explain the test requirements, using the following verbal instructions, accompanied by demonstrations.

- "When I tell you to start, raise one leg, either leg, with the foot approximately 6 inches off the ground, keeping your raised foot parallel to the ground." (Demonstrate one leg stance.)
- "You must keep both legs straight, arms at your side."
- "While holding this position, count out loud in the following manner: "one thousand and one, one thousand and two, one thousand and three, until told to stop." (Demonstrate and count, as follows: "one thousand and one, one thousand and two, one thousand and three, etc." Officer should not look at his foot when conducting the demonstration—OFFICER SAFETY.)
- "Keep your arms at your sides at all times and keep watching the raised foot."
- "Do you understand?" (Make sure the suspect indicates understanding.)
- "Go ahead and perform the test." (Officer should always time the 30 seconds. Test should be discontinued after 30 seconds.)

Observe the suspect from a safe distance. If the suspect puts the foot down, give instructions to pick the foot up again and continue counting from the point at which the foot touched the ground. If the suspect counts very slowly, terminate the test after 30 seconds.

3. Test Interpretation

You may observe a number of different behaviors when a suspect performs this test. The original research found the behaviors listed below are the most likely to be observed in someone with a BAC above 0.10. Look for the following clues each time the One-Leg-Stand test is administered.

A. **The suspect sways while balancing**. This refers to side-to-side or back-and-forth motion while the suspect maintains the one-leg stand position.

B. **Uses arms for balance**. Suspect moves arms 6 or more inches from the side of the body in order to keep balance.

C. **Hopping**. Suspect is able to keep one foot off the ground, but resorts to hopping to maintain balance.

D. **Puts foot down**. The suspect is not able to maintain the one-leg stand position, putting foot down one or more times during the 30-second count.

Note: If suspect can't do the test, record observed clues and document the reason for not completing the test, e.g., suspect's safety.

Remember that time is critical in this test. The original research has shown that a person with a BAC above 0.10 can maintain balance for up to 25 seconds, but seldom as long as 30.

Based on original research, if an individual displays two or more clues or fails to complete the One-Leg Stand, there is a good chance the BAC is above 0.10. Using that criterion, you will accurately classify 65% of the people you test as to whether their BAC's are above 0.10.

Observe the suspect from a safe distance and remain as motionless as possible during the test so as not to interfere. If the suspect puts the foot down, give instructions to pick the foot up again and continue counting from the point at which the foot touched the ground. If the suspect counts very slowly, terminate the test after 30 seconds.

4. Test Conditions

One-Leg Stand requires a reasonable dry, hard, level, and non-slippery surface. Suspect's safety should be considered at all times. The original research indicated that certain individuals over 65 years of age, back, leg or middle ear problems, or people who are overweight by 50 or more pounds had difficulty performing this test. Individuals wearing heels more than 2 inches high should be given the opportunity to remove their shoes.

One Leg Stand Instructions (2013 Manual)

One Leg Stand

The One Leg Stand has also been validated through NHTSA sponsored research. The original research was conducted by the SCRI and used to develop the initial curriculum showing this test was 65% accurate at detecting subjects at or above a 0.10 BAC.

It is a divided attention test consisting of two stages:

- Instructions stage
- Balance and counting stage

In the Instruction Stage, the subject must stand with their feet together, keep their arms at their sides, and listen to instructions.

In the Balance and Counting Stage, the subject must raise one foot, either foot, with the raised foot approximately six inches off the ground, with both legs straight and the raised foot parallel to the ground. While looking at the elevated foot, count out loud in the following manner: "one thousand one", "one thousand two", "one thousand three" until told to stop. This divides the subject's attention between balancing (standing on one foot) and small muscle control (counting out loud).

The timing for a thirty second period by the officer is an important part of the One Leg Stand test. The original research conducted by SCRI in 1977 showed that many impaired subjects are able to stand on one leg for up to 25 seconds, but that few can do so for 30 seconds. One Leg Stand is also administered and interpreted in a standardized manner. Officers carefully observe the subject's performance and look for four specific clues:

- Sways while balancing
- Uses arms to balance
- Hopping
- Puts foot down

Inability to complete the One Leg Stand test occurs when the subject is in danger of falling or otherwise cannot complete the test.

Test conditions have always been important to the administration and interpretation of the SFSTs. The manual clearly lays out the conditions for the One Leg Stand, but they differ slightly than the conditions necessary for the Walk and Turn in that it adds a warning that if the test cannot be performed under the proper conditions, it should be performed elsewhere or not at all. See below:

> One Leg Stand requires a reasonably dry, hard, level, and non-slippery surface. Subject's safety should be considered at all times. Standardizing this test for every type of road condition is unrealistic. The original research study recommended that this test be performed on a dry, hard, level, non-slippery surface and relatively safe conditions. If not, the research recommends:
>
> • subject be asked to perform the test elsewhere, or
>
> • only HGN be administered

Contrast the One Leg Stand requirements for conditions with those for the Walk and Turn test which starts out: "*Whenever possible*, the Walk and Turn test *should be* conducted on a reasonably dry, hard, level, non-slippery surface." (Emphasis added).

Why does the One Leg Stand have an absolute requirement and the Walk and Turn does not? And, if the conditions for the One Leg Stand are not met then "only HGN be administered," does that mean that it is improper to administer the Walk and Turn as well under the same conditions? The conflict is evident, but good for the defense in that if an officer testifies that the conditions were good for the Walk and Turn, but not good for the One Leg Stand, the defense can argue that only HGN should have been given pursuant to the One Leg Stand warning.

The One Leg Stand test conditions warning goes on to state: "However, recent field validation studies have indicated that varying environmental conditions have not affected a subject's ability to perform this test." But this broad statement is misleading. In fact, it was not "recent field validation studies," it was one, non-peer-reviewed study. It was *A Colorado Validation Study of the Standardized Field Sobriety Test (SFST) Battery*, November 1995, Colorado, mentioned earlier in this chapter. The basic conclusion was that cold temperatures did not affect the results of the tests.

Additionally, like the Walk and Turn test, the 2013 manual goes on the give the familiar warning for the One Leg Stand test. Be aware that the One Leg Stand Test has the added restriction of weight in that a person who is 50 lbs or more overweight should not be given the test. The warning is as follows:

> The original SCRI studies suggested that individuals over 65 years of age; people with back, leg or inner ear problems; or people who are overweight by 50 or more pounds may have difficulty performing this test. Less than 1.5% of the test subjects in the original studies were over 65 years of age. There was no data containing the weight of the test subjects included in the final report. Also, the SCRI studies suggest that individuals wearing heels more than 2 inches high should be given the opportunity to remove their shoes.

The instructions as given in *DWI Detection and Standardized Field Sobriety Testing*, DWI Detection and Standardized Field Sobriety Testing, 2013 Participant Manual, Session 8 HS178 R 5/13 are below.

> *Instructions Stage: Initial Positioning and Verbal Instructions*
>
> Initiate the test by giving the following instructions, accompanied by demonstrations.
>
> Please stand with your feet together and your arms down at the sides, like this.

Do not start to perform the test until I tell you to do so.
Do you understand the instructions so far?

Demonstrations and Instructions for the Balance and Counting Stage
Explain the test requirements, using the following verbal instructions, accompanied by demonstrations:

When I tell you to start, raise either leg with the foot approximately six inches off the ground.

Keep both legs straight and your arms at your side.

While holding that position, count out loud in the following manner: "one thousand one, one thousand two, one thousand three," and so on until told to stop.

Keep your arms at your sides at all times and keep watching the raised foot.
Do you understand?

Go ahead and perform the test. (Officer should always time the 30 seconds. Test should be discontinued after 30 seconds.)
Observe the subject from a safe distance. If the subject puts the foot down, give instructions to pick the foot up again and continue counting from the point at which the foot touched the ground. If the subject counts very slowly, terminate the test after 30 seconds.

Test Interpretation
You may observe a number of different behaviors when a subject performs this test. The original research found the behaviors listed below are the most likely to be observed in someone with a BAC at or above 0.08. When administering the One Leg Stand test, we look for certain specific behaviors. Each behavior or action is considered one clue.
There is a maximum number of 4 clues on this test.
Look for the following clues each time the One leg Stand test is administered.
The subject sways while balancing. This refers to side to side or back and forth motion while the subject maintains the one leg stand position.
Slight tremors of the foot or body should not be interpreted as swaying.
Uses arms to balance. Subject moves arms 6 or more inches from the side of the body in order to keep balance.
Hopping. Subject is able to keep one foot off the ground, but resorts to hopping in order to maintain balance.
Puts foot down. The subject is not able to maintain the one leg stand position, putting the foot down one or more times during the 30 second count.
If the subject puts the foot down, give instructions to pick the foot up again and continue counting from the point at which the foot touched.

If subject can't do the test, record observed clues and document the reason for not completing the test, e.g. subject's safety.
Remember that time is critical in this test. The original SCRI research has shown a person with a BAC above 0.10 can maintain balance for up to 25 seconds, but seldom as long as 30.

PRACTICE TIPS: Although the police are supposed to explain the requirements for the test, they never explain what two or more clues means. This is a basic lack or fairness issue that should be pointed out to the jury either in cross-examination, or closing argument, or both.

If the subject puts her foot down, the officer is supposed to tell her to raise it again and continue counting, but this is another issue of basic fairness. Shouldn't the officer tell the subject before the test that if she puts the raised foot down, that will count as a clue and two clues mean a "failure" in the eyes of the officer?

The OLS instructions state that the officer should not look at his foot when conducting the demonstration for officer safety reasons. While this may be a good safety practice for the officer, it also makes the test much easier to do. Watch for this and point it out to the jury if the officer demonstrates the test in court.

The officer is to "observe the suspect from a safe distance and remain as motionless as possible during the test so as not to interfere," but the instructions do not mention anything about giving the subject a perpendicular frame of reference to act as a guide. This is very important because the original research states:

> Generally, if the stopee cannot see or orient with respect to a perpendicular frame of reference, then this test will be difficult to perform even if sober.

Development and Field Test of Psychophysical Tests for DWI Arrests, March, 1981, Southern California Research Institute, DOT HS 805 864.

Be aware that some police agencies are using NHTSA manuals in their training, but they are not issuing the manuals to the cadets. This means that when the cadet leaves the police academy, he will not have the manual to study from or to be available to the defense under local discovery rules. You cannot disclose what you do not have.

9.9 Correlation Between BAC and HGN or FSTs

Correlation between performance on FSTs and a particular BAC is impermissible. Even after North Carolina's recent changes to Rule 702 of the North Carolina Rules of Evidence, which allows in the results of an HGN test when the test is given by someone who has successfully completed training in HGN, a correlation between BAC and the HGN results is not permitted. As we can see in *State v. Turbyfill* 775 S.E.2d 249 (2015): "Officer Lovelace asked defendant to submit to a series of field sobriety tests. At trial, Officer Lovelace was accepted as an expert on the horizontal gaze nystagmus (HGN) test, a test requiring a subject to follow a stimulus with his or her eyes from side to side on a horizontal plane. Officer Lovelace testified that during the course of the HGN test defendant exhibited six "clues" of impairment: "a lack of smooth pursuit in both eyes"; an involuntary jerking, or sustained nystagmus, in both eyes when defendant moved his eyes to the maximum deviation point of the test; and "the onset of nystagmus prior to forty-five degrees." "Officer Lovelace testified that the onset of any nystagmus prior to forty-five degrees is a point one or greater BAC." Officer Lovelace further testified that "[m]ost of the time four clues would show a BAC of point one." Defendant exhibited six clues: three for each eye. Officer Lovelace's testimony appears to have violated Rule 702(a1) on the issue of specific alcohol concentration level as it is related to the results of the Horizontal Gaze Nystagmus (HGN) Test defendant performed."

9.10 Refusal of SFSTs and General Admissibility

In North Carolina, there is no statutory requirement to perform field sobriety tests, but evidence of refusal to perform such tests may be admissible.

9.11 Commonly Used Non-Standardized/ Non-Validated Field Sobriety Tests

Non-standardized and non-validated FSTs provide wonderful fodder for cross-examination. These tests fall under the "damned-if-you-do, damned-if-you-don't" principle. If the officers use the tests and your client passes them, build them up as the best predictors of intoxication known to humankind. Clearly there is no statistical evidence that shows that the non-standardized/non-validated FSTs have any value, but the common-sense argument would be to ask how someone who is so unsafe to drive could touch the tip of his finger to the tip of his nose, while his eyes are closed, by the side of the road. If the officer starts to discount the efficacy of the test, you can easily hammer him with the fact that his police agency certainly would not administer bogus tests to the public. In fact, had the subject "failed" the test, it would be used against him without mercy.

If, on the other hand your client failed the test, you can attack the officer on grounds of lack of research to support the tests. Clearly, you will want to stay away from the subject of correlation to BAC, but you can use the prosecutor's trick of asking if the tests are standardized and validated.

Practice Tip: Not that long ago, I had a client charged with DWI that was confined to a wheel chair. Obviously, the officer could not get my client to perform the walk and turn test or the one leg stand test. Instead, the officer asked my client to do the HGN test followed by a series of non-validated tests which included the finger dexterity test, the alphabet test, and the counting test. At trial, I hammered the officer on the HGN not being standardized since my client was in a seated position as well as the officer's lack of being on the same level as my client (he was standing over him while giving the test). My argument then consisted of punching holes in these remaining tests by comparing them to some of the others (tracing, coin pick up, etc.) that were considered by NHTSA but never adopted for validation.

You can ask if they are used by the police all over the country. You can ask if they are used and evaluated the same way, every time by different officers. Finally, you can ask if they are "approved" for use on human beings by the National Highway Traffic Safety Administration.

Vertical Gaze Nystagmus (VGN)

Vertical Gaze Nystagmus is taught to police officers in some states as part of their HGN training. VGN is a jerking movement of the eyes in the vertical (up/down) plane as the subject follows a stimulus that is moved from about eye-level to well above the subject's head. The subject's head remains still as the subject follows the stimulus using only her eyes.

The police are taught that VGN, unlike HGN, does not correlate to any particular BAC. Rather they are told that VGN indicates a particularly high BAC for that subject. Obviously, this leads to some serious questions of validity. First and foremost, one would have to determine what "a particularly high BAC" would be for the subject in question.

Moreover, there is a relevance problem involved. Even if the basic premise of VGN were correct, of what relevance would such evidence be to a jury? Suppose a .03 is a particularly high BAC for the individual. VGN would neither suggest that the person is over the limit of .08 nor suggest intoxication. It would simply show that the subject does not normally have a BAC of .03.

Suppose .315 is a particularly high BAC for the individual. VGN would neither suggest that the person is over the limit of .08 (no correlation) nor suggest that the person is intoxicated. It adds nothing to the elements that must be proved by the prosecution.

Be aware that the 2013 NHTSA Manual now includes VGN as part of the official curriculum. Officers in many courts are now claiming that VGN is part of HGN, which allows prosecutors to falsely claim that it is admissible. The manual describes VGN as follows:

> "Vertical Gaze Nystagmus is an involuntary jerking of the eyes occurring as the eyes are held at maximum elevation. For VGN to be recorded, it must be distinct and sustained for a minimum of four seconds at maximum elevation." (DWI Detection and Standardized Field Sobriety Testing, 2013 Participant Manual, Session 7 HS178 R 5/13).

PRACTICE TIP: When your client does well on FSTs, prosecutors typically use the "tolerance argument" to claim that the reason for your client's good performance is that she is tolerant to the effects of alcohol. While it is pure speculation, many judges will still allow prosecutors to make such a baseless argument. If the VGN test was performed and VGN was present, bring this fact out for the jury, then use it to thwart the tolerance argument. If VGN indicates a particularly high dose of alcohol for that individual, then she wouldn't be tolerant and should have done poorly on the FSTs. This is a three-for-one bonus issue at trial. You can highlight the fact that she did well on the FSTs, thwart the tolerance argument, and talk about how the prosecution's case has internal conflicts.

Romberg modified

Part of the original studies, the Romberg test was also researched in the later NHTSA-funded studies. The Romberg (commonly misspelled as "Rhomberg") test is a real, medical test used by neurologists throughout the world. It was first developed by Dr. Moritz Romberg in the mid-1800's and the sway was called "Romberg Sign" which is short for a sign of static ataxia in the tabes dorsalis (in laymen's terms, it is a measure of postural control in darkness). Ironically, he taught a well-attended "propaedeutic clinic" which used practical demonstrations to emphasize the importance of careful medical examinations that would ensure a correct diagnosis. Dr. Romberg would likely be shocked to find that his test is used at the roadside by minimally trained officers to diagnose alcohol impairment.

To perform the test, the person is instructed to stand with feet together, head tipped back, eyes closed and arms down at the sides. An anterior-posterior sway is noted. The test lasts for 45 seconds.

There is nothing noted in Dr. Romberg's description of the test to suggest that the head be tipped back as required by the police. Moreover, there is no time limit to his test. The results of the Romberg test could as easily diagnose alcohol impairment as it could diagnose a person in the tertiary stages of syphilis.

Finger-to-Nose

The instructions are that the subject stand erect with eyes closed and arms extended horizontally. The subject is then instructed to touch the nose with the index finger, alternating right and left hands as instructed. A demonstration is given by the officer.

The instructions above are from the original research into the efficacy of the FSTs. There have been no rewrites of the instructions or official modifications to the instructions. Watch for officers asking that the person touch the "tip" of their finger to the "tip" of their noses and then counting the subject off for using the pad of the finger. Notice that the instructions say nothing about the "tip" of either the finger or the nose. The instructions simply ask the person to "touch the nose with the index finger." This could presumably mean that one could touch the bridge of the nose with any part of the index finger.

Also, watch for officers who demonstrate this test in court, before the jury. If one scratches the end of one's nose before performing the test, it makes it much easier to strike that spot with your eyes closed. Also, point out to the jury that the officer does not close her eyes while demonstrating the test.

Finger Count

Also one of the original FSTs considered for use in the three-test battery, the Finger Count was rejected for use. The instructions are that the subject must touch and count each finger in succession, using the thumb, while counting aloud. The test is demonstrated as "Watch what I do. 1-2-3-4-4-3-2-1."

The Finger Count is probably one of the most difficult tests to perform, although it sounds like it would be the easiest to perform. Some people simply do not have good manual dexterity.

9.12 Videotaping the Driving and Investigation

Now that video recording methods have become more compact and reliable, some jurisdictions are seeing an increase in videos available from the police. Whether they help the defense or the prosecution depends on who is rendering the opinion. As defense attorneys, we have seen tapes that help and hurt, but mostly we see individual video recordings with a mixture of the good, the bad and the ugly. It is often a struggle to show the video portion that helps our clients, while arguing to suppress the portion that hurts. Sometimes the decision is clear, such as when there is mention of an inadmissible prior DWI offense on the audio portion of the tape. Other times, the decision is not so clear, such as when your client makes an unfavorable admission, but says it clearly and enunciates every syllable. This might be used to impeach the officer's ubiquitous testimony as to slurred speech.

Whether it is traditional video or digital recording, with or without audio, whether to use the tape or move to suppress it can only be decided based upon the circumstances of the individual case. In any event, however, there is likely to be a police/prosecuting agency policy on the use of such equipment. In fact, NHTSA published a brochure titled *In-Vehicle Videotaping of DWI Suspects (Driving While Intoxicated)* in July 1996 (DOT HS 808 427). The brochure examined information provided to NHTSA from 68 police departments in 13 states that use in-vehicle videotaping. It also examined first-hand discussions with 93 officers from 10 of those departments (Suffolk County, New York Police Department; City of Binghamton, New York Police Department; North Dakota Highway Patrol; City of Bismarck, North Dakota Police Department; Texas Highway Patrol; City of Houston, Texas Police Department; Utah State Highway Patrol; City of West Valley, Utah Police Department; Kanawha County Sheriff's Department, West Virginia Sheriff's Department; and the City of Clarksburg, West Virginia Police Department).

The research found both advantages and disadvantages noted by the police:

Advantages

- 100% Protects the officers from false allegations and liability suits.
- 97% Provides evidence as to what happened at the time of the arrest.
- 95% Training for other officers and self-critique.
- 93% Enhances evidence-gathering process.
- 90% Ensures officers follow correct procedures.
- 89% Convinces defendant to plead guilty.
- 86% Protects the rights of suspects.
- 83% Helps officers testify in court.
- 68% Limits officers' time in court.

Disadvantages

- 72% Some suspects do not appear impaired on video.
- 61% Forget to activate the camera.
- 47% Equipment operation problems or failures.
- 30% Procedural error may be taped and damage case.
- 28% Operating equipment may interfere with officer safety.

Policies

- Types of incidents to record.
- When to activate and terminate recording.
- Whether to articulate probable cause on tape.
- Responsibility for equipment.
- Evidentiary issues.
- No erasure or re-recording.
- Labeling, storage and retention period.
- Responsibility for handling tapes.
- Release of tape or copies to third parties.
- Supervisory review of tapes.
- Training use.

References

Anderson, Ellen and Marcelline Burns. *A Colorado Validation Study of the Standardized Field Sobriety Test (SFST) Battery.* Southern California Research Institute. November 1995 (Second Printing: September, 1996).

Anderson, Theodore E., R. M. Schweitz, and M. B. Snyder (1983). *Field Evaluation of a Behavioral Test Battery for DWI,* Office of Driver & Pedestrian Research, Problem-Behavior Research Division. U.S. Department of Transportation, National Highway Traffic Safety Administration (NHTSA). DOT HS 806 475, September 1983.

Burns, Marcelline. *A Florida Validation Study of the Standardized Field Sobriety Test (S.F.S.T.) Battery*, Institute of Police Technology & Management, University of North Florida, Pinellas County Sheriff's Office, Southern California Research Institute, Florida, 1988.

Burns, Marcelline and Herbert Moskowitz. *Psychophysical Tests for DWI Arrests,* 132 pages. Southern California Research Institute. DOT HS 802 424, June 1977.

Carnahan, Holmes, Keyes, Stempler and Dreveskracht. 1974. *DWI Law Enforcement Training Project, Student Manual*, Michigan State University Study, DOT Contract No. HS-334-3-645.

Cronbach, L., *Essentials of Psychological Testing, Third Edition*, New York: Harper & Row, 1970.

DWI Detection and Standardized Field Sobriety Testing, Participant Manual, 2004 Edition (HS 178 R2/06 Session VIII, "Concepts and Principles for the Standardized Field Sobriety Tests").

Harris, Douglas H. 1980. "Visual Detection of Driving While Intoxicated." *Human Factors Society* 22(6): 725–32.

Moskowitz, H. and C. D. Robinson. "Effects of Low Doses of Alcohol on Driving-Related Skills: A Review of the Evidence," SRA Technologies, Inc., sponsored by the National Highway Traffic Safety Administration (NHTSA), Washington, DC. July 1988. DOT HS 807-280.

Stuster, Jack W. (Anacapa Sciences, Inc.) *The Detection of DWI Motorcyclists*, Prepared for the U.S. Department of Transportation, National Highway Traffic Safety Administration (NHTSA). DOT HS 807 839. March 1993.

Stuster, Jack and Marcelline Burns (ANACAPA Sciences, Inc.). *Validation of the Standardized Field Sobriety Test Battery at BACs Below .10 Percent,* U.S. Department of Transportation, National Highway Traffic Safety Administration (NHTSA). DOT HS 808 839, August 1988.

Tharp, V., M. Burns, and H. Moskowitz (1981). *Development and Field Test of Psychophysical Tests for DWI Arrest.* U.S. Department of Transportation, National Highway Traffic Safety Administration (NHTSA), DOT HS 805 864, Washington, D.C.

U.S. Department of Transportation, National Highway Traffic Safety Administration (NHTSA). *The Guide to Detecting Drunk Drivers at Night*. DOT HS 805 711.

U.S. Department of Transportation, National Highway Traffic Safety Administration (NHTSA). *The Visual Detection of DWI Motorists.* July 1997. DOT HS 808 677.

U.S. Department of Transportation, National Highway Traffic Safety Administration (NHTSA). *In-Vehicle Videotaping of DWI Suspects (Driving While Intoxicated)* in July 1996 (DOT HS 808 427).

U.S. Department of Transportation, National Highway Traffic Safety Administration (NHTSA). *The Detection of DWI Motorcyclists* and *Detecting Impaired Motorcyclists*. April 2000.

U.S. Department of Transportation, National Highway Traffic Safety Administration (NHTSA). *The Detection of DWI Motorists*. Revised, March 2005. DOT HS 807 856.

Check the suspect's left eye by moving the stimulus to your right. Move the stimulus smoothly, at a speed that requires approximately two seconds to bring the suspect's eye as far to the side as it can go. While moving the stimulus, look at the suspect's eye and determine whether it is able to pursue smoothly. Now, move the stimulus all the way to the left, back across suspect's face checking if the right eye pursues smoothly. Movement of the stimulus should take approximately two seconds out and two seconds back for each eye. Repeat the procedure.

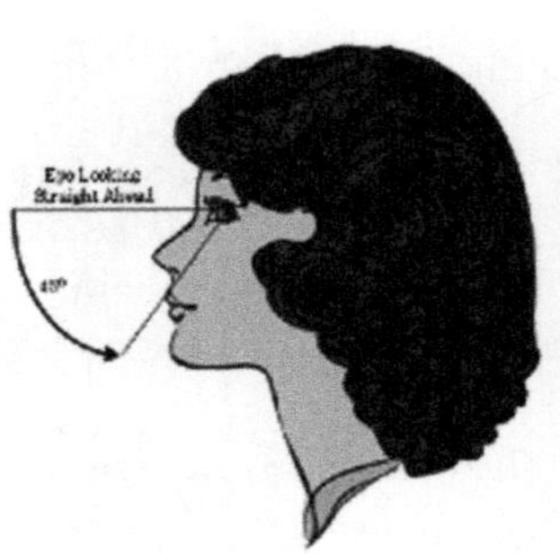

After you have checked both eyes for lack of smooth pursuit, check the eyes for distinct and sustained nystagmus at maximum deviation beginning with the suspect's left eye. Simply move the object to the suspect's left side until the eye has gone as far to the side as possible. Usually, no white will be showing in the corner of the eye at maximum deviation. Hold the eye at that position for a minimum of four seconds, and observe the eye for distinct and sustained nystagmus. Move the stimulus all the way across the suspect's face to check the right eye holding that position for a minimum of four seconds. Repeat the procedure.

Note: Fatigue Nystagmus. This type of nystagmus may begin if a subject's eyes are held at maximum deviation for more than 30 seconds.

Next, check for onset of nystagmus prior to 45 degrees. Start moving the stimulus towards the right (suspect's left eye) at a speed that would take approximately four seconds for the stimulus to reach the edge of the suspect's shoulder. Watch the eye carefully for any sign of jerking. When you see it, stop and verify that the jerking continues. Now, move the stimulus to the left (suspect's right eye) at a speed that would take approximately four seconds for the stimulus to reach the edge of the suspect's shoulder. Watch the eye carefully for any sign of jerking. When you see it, stop and verify that the jerking continues. Repeat the procedure. NOTE: It is important to use the full four seconds when checking for onset of nystagmus. If you move the stimulus too fast, you may go past the point of onset or miss it altogether.

If the suspect's eyes start jerking before they reach 45 degrees, check to see that some white of the eye is still showing on the side closest to the ear. If no white of the eye is showing, you either have taken the eye too far to the side (that is more than 45 degrees) or the person has unusual eyes that will not deviate very far to the side.

ADMINISTRATIVE PROCEDURES

1. CHECK FOR EYEGLASSES
2. VERBAL INSTRUCTIONS
3. POSITION STIMULUS (12-15 INCHES)
4. EQUAL PUPIL SIZE AND RESTING NYSTAGMUS
5. TRACKING
6. LACK OF SMOOTH PURSUIT
7. DIST. & SUSTAINED NYSTAGMUS @ MAX. DEV.
8. ONSET OF NYSTAGMUS PRIOR TO 45°
9. TOTAL THE CLUES
10. CHECK FOR VERTICAL GAZE NYSTAGMUS

HS 178 R2/06 VIII-7

Figure 9.15 *2006 Manual (left) and 2013 Manual (right).*

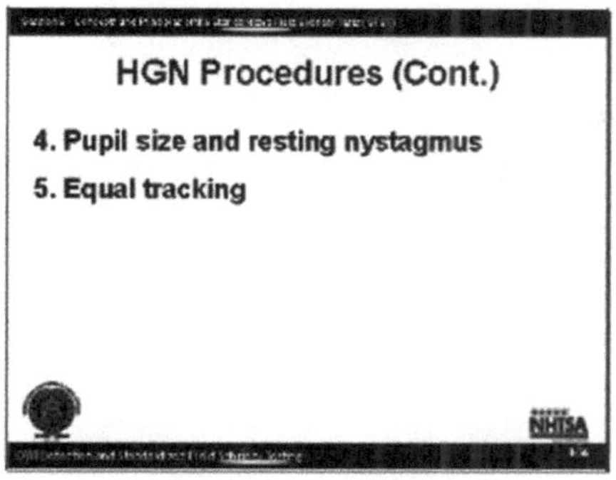

Notes:

Step 4: Equal Pupil Size and Resting Nystagmus. Check for equal pupil size and resting nystagmus.

Step 5: Equal Tracking.

Check for equal tracking. Move the stimulus rapidly from center to far right, to far left and back to center.

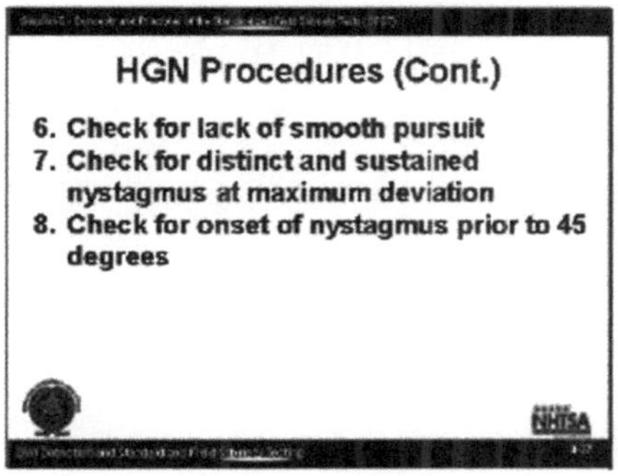

Notes:

Step 6: Lack of Smooth Pursuit. Check the left eye for lack of the "Smooth Pursuit" clue. If the eye is observed to jerk while moving, that is one clue.

Check the right eye for lack of the "Smooth Pursuit" clue and compare.

Step 7: Check the right and left eye for the "distinct and sustained nystagmus at maximum deviation" clue. If the jerkiness is distinct and sustained, that is one clue.

Step 8: Onset of Nystagmus Prior to 45 Degrees. Check the left eye for the "onset of nystagmus prior to 45 degrees" clue. If the jerking begins prior to 45 degrees, that is one clue.

Check the right eye for "onset of nystagmus prior to 45 degrees" clue, and compare.

HS 178 R5/13 23 of 62

Figure 9.15(cont.)

Chapter 10

Drug Recognition Evaluation

Synopsis

10.1 Overview

Aspirin is a drug. Penicillin is a drug. Heroin is a drug. Only one of the three preceding examples can impair your ability to drive a car. While society has a very broad definition of the term "drug," the law enforcement community has a much more narrow definition which has never changed in any DRE Manual from the very first to the most recent:

> A drug is any substance, which, when taken into the human body, can impair the ability of the person to operate a vehicle safely.

HS 172 R5/13.

This is the definition that law enforcement works from and, for their purposes, it is a good working definition. Clearly, the focus is on the effect, not on the chemical composition of the substance. Alcohol is certainly included in the definition, but so are other substances not included in general society's definition. For example, one typically does not think of spray paint as a drug, but some people will spray it into a pail or a bag, then breathe the concentrated vapors to get high. This act is called "huffing."

Despite the prevalence of drug use in our society, drugged driving has very little comparative literature and studies as does alcohol-related driving behavior. Drugged driving also has far less statutory and case law throughout the nation. In many instances, it appears that drugged driving statutes were an afterthought by the legislatures throughout the nation. So too, it seems that detection and prevention measures were afterthoughts. One only has to look at the 12-Step Drug Recognition Evaluation to see that the first step is to determine the suspect's BAC via a breath testing device. If the person's BAC is consistent with the level of impairment noted by the officer, then a Drug Recognition Evaluation will not ensue.

Additionally, because of the wide array of drugs available, it takes special and costly training to diagnose and identify impairment. On a practical level, not many departments have the resources to train many officers as "DREs" (Drug Recognition Experts). Moreover, because many people who use drugs other than alcohol often combine their use with alcohol, officers might not recognize the impairment resulting from drugs other than the alcohol, thus attributing all impairment to alcohol. An officer might easily declare a person with a low BAC, but high level of impairment, as a "lightweight" and not think to check further for drug-induced impairment.

PRACTICE TIP: The police refer to themselves as "Drug Recognition Experts" in court. In the past, they have been known as "Drug Recognition Evaluators" and "Drug Recognition Technicians" (DiRT Officers). One can surmise that they preferred not to be called "DiRT Officers," and thus the names were changed. One should move the court to prevent the prosecutors from referring to the officers as "experts" as this usurps the court's power and would be misleading to the jury. See Section 6.4, *Motions in Limine,* in Chapter 6 for a complete motion on this subject.

The "Three-Step DRE Process" as explained by NHTSA in every DRE manual published to date, is a simple one which encompasses the 12-Step DRE Protocol explained in full detail later in this chapter.

The Three-Step DRE Process:

1. Verify that the suspect is impaired and verify that the suspect's BAC is inconsistent with the degree of impairment evident.
2. Determine whether the impairment is drug or medical related.
3. Use proven diagnostic procedures to determine the category of drugs that is the likely source of impairment.

Note that the first obligation is to determine BAC and make a very subjective determination as to whether the level of impairment matches the suspect's BAC. The proper interpretation of the SFSTs correlates performance to a percentage chance that the subject is at or above a particular BAC. So if an officer administers the SFSTs properly and sees, for example, four out of six cues on the HGN, two on the Walk-and-Turn and two on the One-Leg-Stand, that officer should conclude that the person's BAC is at or above .080, based on his training. If the person's BAC is only .020, that should be an indication to the officer that there is another cause for the impairment. Yet because of problems with the validity of the SFST studies, the individual predilections of the officers and training issues, the objectivity of the DRE process becomes subverted in many instances.

The second obligation is for the officer to "play doctor" and make medical determinations. Even some of the most brilliant doctors in the world may have problems separating medically related impairment issues from drug-induced impairment when given only the tools used by law enforcement, by the side of the road and under less than ideal examination conditions. Frankly, it is unreasonable to put such a burden on law enforcement personnel with minimal training and, in many instances, little formal education.

The third step is for the officer to "use proven diagnostic procedures to determine the category of drugs that is the likely source of impairment." NHTSA refers to "proven diagnostic procedures" as if they have actually been proven. They have not. Like the SFST studies, the DRE studies generally have not been peer reviewed as a whole. Certainly individual parts of the 12-Step DRE Protocol have proven scientific validity, but there is very little evidence, if any, to suggest that the entire protocol has validity. Even the DRE workshop called for by the *NHTSA Training Manual* is highly flawed. One glaring problem is that the training calls for an alcohol workshop, not a drug workshop. In other words, volunteers are dosed with varying amounts of alcohol and not other drugs before they are examined. This means that the police only get to see what a central nervous system depressant (alcohol) does to a person. From a practical standpoint, one can understand the reasons behind not dosing volunteers with PCP for a law enforcement workshop, yet that still does not alleviate the problem resulting from the workshop—that the police leave the workshop with no real examples of impairment via drugs other than alcohol.

It is also important to note that the DRE manuals teach DRE officers to skew their police reports in favor of convictions. The DRE officer is no mere observer—he is actively encouraged to twist the facts to help the prosecution obtain a guilty verdict. This is clear when one reads what the DRE candidates are taught in their DRE manuals as in these examples from DRE Student manuals from 1989 through 2007 (HS172 R6/89 Page XXVI-1, HS172 R3/91 Page XXVI-1, HS172 R4/93 Page XXVI-1, and; HS172 R8/99 Page XXVI-1, HS172, R5/02 Page XXVI-1, sections titled; *The Importance of a Good DRE Report*, and; HS172 R1/07 Page XXVI-1 *The Importance of Documentation*):

> The chemical test simply cannot prove that the suspect was impaired, or under the influence at the time the violation occurred. It is up to you to prove that, and to prove that the nature of the impairment was consistent with some category or categories of drugs. Your observations, examinations and your expertise are the prosecution's strongest weapons. In some cases, they will be the *only* weapons. You have to get your evidence across, and you have to make it as believable as possible. You start doing this in your DRE report.

(Note that HS172 R3/91 Page XXVI-1states: "You start doing this in your DRT report." The short-lived term "DRT" stood for "Drug Recognition Technician").

This is hardly a neutral mandate to the DRE officers. It describes their reports as weapons. By demanding that the DRE "prove that the nature of the impairment was consistent with some category or categories of drugs" the IACP places an undue burden upon the officers to falsify their observations. The IACP attempts to make the DRE responsible for the prosecutor's win or loss in court. Moreover, telling the officer that they have to make their evidence "as believable as possible" is a clear acknowledgment to the investigatory frailty of the DRE protocol. If it was truly a valid and reliable classification program, no officer would have to make it "as believable as possible."

In 2013 NHTSA and the IACP published a new set of manuals, consistent with the 2013 SFST manuals. The instructor manual is titled *Drug Recognition Expert Course (DRE) 7-Day Course, Instructor Guide*, (HS 172 R5/13) and is 1077 pages long. The participant manual is titled *Drug Recognition Expert Course (DRE) 7-Day Course,*

Participant Manual, (HS 172 R5/13) and is 706 pages long. Powerpoint presentations are an integral part of instruction. The 2013 curriculum is broken down into the following sessions:

Session 1: Introduction and Overview. The primary emphasis is on the glossary of terms which will be used throughout the course.
Session 2: Drugs in Society and in Vehicle Operation
Session 3: Development and Effectiveness of the DEC Program. The primary emphasis is on DRE law including Frye and Daubert decisions regarding admissibility of DRE Testimony. There is also a special HGN case law summary written by the American Prosecutors Research Institute along with scientific publications and research Reports Addressing Nystagmus.
Session 4: Overview of the Drug Recognition Expert Procedures. In this session, the student is first introduced to the DRE Face Sheet.
Session 5: Eye Examinations. Students learn how to use a pupil size chart and they are introduced to the SFST Proficiency Examination Form.
Session 6: Physiology and Drugs: An Overview. Students learn how to use a logical progression of inquiry to determine what physiological factors are present with certain drug categories
Session 7: Examinations of Vital Signs. Students learn to examine and record a subject's vital signs such as blood pressure, pulse and muscle tone.
Session 8: Demonstrations of the Evaluation Sequence. The 12-Step DECP is demonstrated.
Session 9: Central Nervous System Depressants. "Drug Exemplar Reports" are studied to show examples of CNS Depressants.
Session 10: Central Nervous System Stimulants. "Drug Exemplar Reports" are studied to show examples of CNS Stimulants.
Session 11: Practice Eye Examinations. Students participate in eye examinations.
Session 12: Alcohol Workshop. This is a wet-workshop where volunteers are dosed and examined by the students who then make an arrest/no-arrest decision.
Session 13: Physician's Desk Reference and Other Reference Resources. Students learn about various medical reference literature and resources available to them during the course of an investigation.
Session 14: Hallucinogens. "Drug Exemplar Reports" are studied to show examples of hallucinogens.
Session 15: Practice: Test Administration. Five "Drug Exemplar Reports" are studied to show the effects of various types of drug categories.
Session 16: Dissociative Anesthetics. "Drug Exemplar Reports" are studied to show examples of dissociative anesthetics.
Session 17: Narcotic Analgesics. "Drug Exemplar Reports" are studied to show examples of narcotic analgesics.
Session 18: Practice: Test Administration
Session 19: Inhalants. "Drug Exemplar Reports" are studied to show examples of inhalants.
Session 20: Practice: Vital Signs Examinations
Session 21: Cannabis. Marijuana use is discussed and "Drug Exemplar Reports" are studied.
Session 22: Overview of Signs and Symptoms. Students study a comparison of DRE symptomatology sources.
Session 23: Curriculum Vitae Preparation and Maintenance. Students learn how to prepare a curriculum vitae for litigation purposes. They are shown two sample curriculum vitae as examples.
Session 24: Drug Combinations. Students are introduced to poly-drug use and shown how to use the Drug Categories Chart in poly-drug use investigations.
Session 25: Practice: Test Interpretation. Students are given five drug exemplar reports to interpret.
Session 26: Preparing the Narrative Report. Unlike the language of previous manuals, the DRE report is not referred to as a "weapon" and students are not told to make their DRE reports "as believable as possible." Instead, they are told:

"Successful prosecution depends on how clearly, completely and convincingly the DRE presents their observations, measurements, and conclusions. A well written, clear, and convincing drug evaluation report increases the likelihood that the suspect will be convicted.

• A prosecutor is more likely to file the charge if the evidence is organized, clearly documented and compelling.

• The defense is less likely to contest the charge when the report is descriptive, detailed, and complete."

"Many prosecutors, judges, and jurors won't know how to interpret the face sheet.

• It is up to you to take all of the information you work so hard to obtain, and put it into a clear, plain English, written report so that the prosecutor, the judge, and the jury will understand what you observed and what it means.

As a DRE, you have a special ability to secure powerful, scientific evidence that can make the difference between success and failure in court. It would be a shame to waste that special ability by submitting an inadequate written report."

Session 27: Practice: Test Administration

Session 28: Case Preparation and Testimony. Not only are students shown what to expect from a prosecutor, but they are also given practice DRE Defense Cross Examination Questions. There is a review of the DRE School, and a Self Quiz.

Session 29: Classifying a Suspect (Role Play). This session is devoted to practical examinations of subjects who are pretending to be under the influence of specific drugs.

Session 30: Transition to Certification Phase of Training. Instructors give the guidelines for the Final Examination. DRE Log of Drug Influence Evaluations (Rolling Log) are prepared and examined.

10.2 DRE Statutory Law

Drugged-driving laws vary from state to state. Nationwide, enforcement ranges from almost non-existent to the most draconian measures imaginable. Because of the lack of uniformity across the nation, coupled with the perceived increasing danger of driving while under the influence of drugs, NHTSA sponsored a study titled, *A State-by-State Analysis of Laws Dealing With Driving Under the Influence of Drugs*, U.S. Department of Transportation, National Highway traffic Administration, DOT HS 811 236, December, 2009. The study classified three types of DWI-Drugs laws:

1. Statutes that require drugs to render the driver "incapable" of driving safely;
2. Statutes requiring that the drug impair the driver's ability to operate safely or require a driver to be "under the influence or affected by an intoxicating drug," and;
3. "Per se" laws that make it a criminal offense to have a drug or metabolite in one's body (or bodily fluids) while driving (also known as "zero tolerance laws").

10.3 Per Se Statutes Comparison

There are seventeen states with "per se" DWI Drugs laws on the books. The seven most restrictive states make it illegal for a driver to have any amount of a prohibited drug ***or its metabolite*** in the body while operating a vehicle. Those states are: Arizona, Delaware, Georgia, Indiana, Minnesota, Pennsylvania and Utah. Note that Minnesota specifically exempts marijuana from the list of prohibited drugs.

In five states, it is illegal to have any amount of a prohibited drug, but not the metabolite of the drug in the body while driving. In other words, it has to be any amount of the active drug. Those states are: Illinois, Iowa, Michigan, Rhode Island and Wisconsin.

In only three states (Nevada, Ohio and Virginia) it is illegal to drive with a specified amount of a prohibited drug in the body.

In laws that make no rational sense, whatsoever, the states of North Carolina and South Dakota make it illegal for any driver under age 21 to drive with any amount of a prohibited drug in the body. Once the driver is 21 or older it is not illegal, per se, to drive with the prohibited drug in the body.

Both Colorado and Washington have legalized recreational marijuana. Both states are currently grappling with defining a per se limit for THC. While Washington has chosen 5 ng/mL as a per se limit, Colorado has chosen no per se limit, but there is a permissive inference of impairment at 5 ng/mL.

In Arizona, the case of *State ex re. Montgomery v. Harris*, 234 Ariz. 343, 322 P.3d 160 (Ariz. 2014) held that the inactive metabolite of marijuana, Carboxy-THC, is not one of the drugs prohibited by A.R.S. 13-3401. Thus, it is legal to drive with any amount of Carboxy-THC in the blood in Arizona.

10.4 Impairment Statutes Comparison

Many states have laws which make it illegal to drive while impaired by either a prohibited or non-prohibited drug in addition to, or in place of, per se statutes. Only Hawaii and New York have DWI Drug statutes separate from DWI-alcohol statutes.

In all 48 other states, the District of Columbia and Puerto Rico, it is illegal to drive under the influence of drug or alcohol or with a combination of the two. In these states, the penalties for DWI Drugs and DIO-Alcohol are the same with the exception of Arizona (where there is a one-year license suspension instead of 90-days for an alcohol-related DWI) and in Washington.

10.5 Defenses

It is no defense to the impairment charge that the driver had a valid prescription for the drug in Alabama, Arizona, Arkansas, Delaware, Georgia, Idaho, Illinois, Kansas, Kentucky, Montana, North Carolina, Oklahoma, Pennsylvania, Rhode Island, South Dakota, Tennessee, Texas, Vermont, Washington, West Virginia and Puerto Rico. Maryland will allow such a defense, however, if either of the following circumstances apply: (1) where the accused was unaware that the drug would render him or her incapable of driving safely, or (2) where the accused was legally entitled to use the controlled substance.

10.6 Implied Consent Laws Comparison

In five states, a driver can refuse to provide a sample for drug analysis. Alabama, Alaska, Massachusetts, New Jersey and West Virginia do not extend their implied consent laws to include providing a sample for analysis to determine drug content.

Thirty four states allow blood or urine to be used, but Maryland, Montana, New Mexico, Rhode Island, Vermont, Virginia, Texas and Washington only allow blood to be used for analysis.

Alabama, Arizona, Georgia, Indiana, Kansas, Louisiana, North Carolina, South Dakota and Puerto Rico allow "other bodily substances" to be used for analysis. This means that not only can ocular fluids be used from a cadaver, but organs can be removed, dissected and analyzed for drug content as well.

Colorado, Missouri, New York, North Dakota, Oklahoma and Utah permit saliva to be used.

Massachusetts, New Jersey and West Virginia laws do not specify what substances are to be used because their implied consent laws do not extend to DWI-Drugs.

10.7 DRE Case Law

One cannot simply assume that the 12-Step DRE Protocol is admissible in every jurisdiction. Even in jurisdictions where it has been admitted, there is still room to challenge further admissibility and conclusions drawn from the DRE testimony. The following is a compilation of precedent setting law from around the nation regarding admissibility of DRE testimony, in chronological order. Many states have never addressed the issue on any precedent setting level.

People v. Quinn, 158 Misc.2d 1015 (1993) New York, 1993. The defense submitted the matter to a judge on stipulated facts rather than face a jury in order to challenge the DRE Protocol on appeal. The case was reversed, however, because there was no waiver of a jury before submission on stipulated facts. Thus, the court did not consider the questions regarding the scientific reliability of a Drug Influence Evaluation. Yet the court felt obliged to write: "However, we would note that in light of the overwhelming evidence of guilt, any error in admitting such testimony would clearly be harmless."

State v. Klawitter, 518 N.W.2d 577 (1994) Minnesota, 1994. Visual exam to determine nystagmus and convergence is scientific in nature but satisfies the *Frye* requirement. The remainder of the 12-Step DRE Protocol is not scientifically new and, therefore, is not subject to *Frye*. The court specifically found that the 12-Step Protocol is "essentially the same components that are used by police officers in evaluations for alcohol impairment or are routine examinations that can be competently performed by the police officer."

One thing to keep in mind—the officer involved in this case was qualified to take medical vital signs and do an examination because he was a certified EMT.

The dissent is great. It finds that while the individual 12 steps are not new or novel, basing an opinion upon them is new and novel. The dissent reminds the rest of the court that the prosecution relies on the totality of the circumstances—not on 12 individual steps, isolated from each other.

U.S. v. Everett, 972 F.Supp. 1313 (1997) Nevada, 1997. DRE testimony is not scientific in nature, is based upon observations, training and experience and, therefore, is governed by Rule 702, not *Daubert*. The federal court wrote: "the otherwise qualified DRE cannot testify as to scientific knowledge, but can testify as to "specialized knowledge which will assist the trier or fact to understand the evidence."

Williams v. State, 710 So.2d 24 (1998) Florida, 1998. The court concluded that the 12-Step DRE Protocol is not subject to *Frye* because tests are within the common experience and understanding of the average person and are not scientific within the meaning of *Frye*. The court wrote: "Contrary to the defendant's assertion, The DRE's opinion is not derived from the symptomology matrix and does not constitute a medical diagnosis."

Horizontal Gaze Nystagmus (HGN), Vertical Gaze Nystagmus (VGN) and Lack Of Convergence (LOC) are scientific within the meaning of

Frye, but *Frye* does not apply because the tests are not new or novel. However, they do not immunize particular areas or principles based on longevity, but go on to say that longevity is helpful to exclude certain evidence from *Frye* analysis which would be wasteful of judicial resources. The court cites to the Minnesota case, *Klawitter*.

State v. Baity, 140 Wash.2d 1, 991 P.2d 1151 (2000) Washington, 2000. DRE Protocol meets *Frye*'s requirements, although many of the DRE steps are not scientific. HGN is scientific but is generally accepted and satisfies *Frye* requirements. With regard to DRE testimony, the court wrote: "This Court finds that the DRE can testify to the probabilities, based upon his or her observations and clinical findings, but cannot testify by way of scientific opinion, that the conclusion is an established fact by any reasonable scientific standard."

The court cautioned that their opinion is confined to situations where all 12 steps of the DRE protocol have been used.

State v. Sampson, 167 Or.App. 489, 6 P.3d 543 (2000) Oregon, 2000. DRE protocol and testimony are scientific evidence and admissible because they have achieved a significant degree of acceptance within the relevant scientific community to be sufficiently established. Scientific parts of the DRE include the following: BAC, VGN, LOC, vital signs, toxicological analysis. Other parts of the DRE are not scientific, yet admissible.

Evidence of the DRE examination is not more highly prejudicial than probative of any fact.

State v. Aman, 194 Or.App. 463, 95 P.3d 244 (2004) Oregon, 2004. Incomplete 12-Step DREs are not admissible as scientific evidence. In this case the urine sample was not taken because the defendant could not produce one. Reversed and remanded. Note that the state admitted that toxicology results do not directly relate to a suspect's impairment but furnish only circumstantial evidence to corroborate a DRE officer's opinion.

10.8 The 12-Step DRE Protocol

The following 12-Step DRE Protocol is taken from *Drug Evaluation and Classification Training, The Drug Recognition Expert School*, 2013 Student Edition.

Drug Influence Report Checklist

_____ 1. Breath Alcohol test
_____ 2. Interview of Arresting Officer
(Note: Gloves must be worn from this point on.)
_____ 3. Preliminary Examination and First Pulse
_____ 4. Eye examinations.
_____ 5. Divided Attention Tests:
    _______ Romberg Balance
    _______ Walk-and-Turn
    _______ One-Leg-Stand
    _______ Finger-to-Nose
_____ 6. Vital Signs and Second Pulse
_____ 7. Dark Room Examinations and Ingestion Examination
_____ 8. Check for Muscle Tone
_____ 9. Check for Injection Sites and Third Pulse
_____ 10. Interrogation, Statements, and Other Observations
_____ 11. Opinion of Evaluator
_____ 12. Toxicological Evaluation

See: Drug Influence Evaluation report at end of this chapter.

1. **Breath Alcohol test**—to determine the suspect's blood alcohol concentration (BAC).

By obtaining an accurate and immediate measurement of BAC, the drug recognition expert can determine whether alcohol may be contributing to the suspect's observable impairment, and whether the concentration of alcohol is sufficient to be the sole cause of that impairment.

It is always possible that a person suspected of being under the influence of drugs other than alcohol may actually have consumed only alcohol. However, it is also very common to find that a suspect has consumed alcohol and other drugs.

2. **Interview of arresting officer**—to take advantage of the things that he or she may have seen or heard during earlier contact with the suspect.

Most arresting officers are not as knowledgeable about drugs as are drug recognition experts. The arresting officers may have uncovered some drug paraphernalia, or overheard the suspect using drug-related "street" terms, without recognizing their significance. A few minutes spent in a careful discussion with the arresting officer can alert the drug recognition expert to the most promising areas of investigation to be explored with the suspect.

3. The **preliminary examination**, which is a structured series of questions, specific observations and simple tests that provide the first opportunity to examine the suspect closely and directly. **Note: to avoid infection, the drug recognition expert must wear gloves from this portion of the examination on.**

One major purpose of the preliminary examination is to determine if the suspect may be suffering from an injury or some other condition not necessarily related to drugs. Another major purpose is to begin systematically assessing the suspect's appearance, behavior, etc. for signs of possible drug influence.

4. The **examination of the eyes**, which include Horizontal Gaze Nystagmus, Vertical Gaze Nystagmus, and a check for Lack of Convergence.

Nystagmus will be caused with certain categories of drugs. Nystagmus, an involuntary jerking that may occur as the eyes gaze to the side or as they are elevated. The presence of nystagmus, and the points at which it becomes observable, can shed light on the possible presence of those categories and the extent to which they may be affecting the suspect.

The inability of the eyes to converge toward the bridge of the nose also gives evidence of the possible presence of certain categories of drugs.

5. **Divided attention psychophysical tests**, which include the Romberg Balance; the Walk-and-Turn; One-Leg-Stand; and, the Finger-to-Nose.

The suspect's performance of these tests produces articulable evidence of their psychophysical impairment. The specific errors of omission or commission may point towards the categories of drugs that are behind that impairment.

6. **Vital signs examinations**, which include systematic checks of the suspect's blood pressure; pulse rate; and, temperature.

Certain categories of drugs may elevate blood pressure, pulse rate and raise the body temperature. Other drugs would have precisely the opposite effects. Vital signs as well as physical observations thus provide valuable evidence of the presence and influence of a variety of drug categories.

7. **Dark room examinations**, which include systematic checks of the size of the pupils of the suspect's eyes; the reaction of the pupils to light; and, evidence of ingestion of drugs by nose or mouth.

Certain categories of drugs affect the eyes, and especially the pupils, in predictable ways. By examining the eyes under carefully controlled lighting conditions, important evidence of those drug categories may be obtained.

8. **Examination for muscle tone**. Certain categories of drugs will cause the muscles to become rigid. Some other categories may cause the muscles to become flaccid.

Begin with the left arm, firmly grasp the upper arm and slowly moving down to determine whether the muscle tone is flaccid, normal or rigid.

9. **Examination for injection sites**, e.g., via hypodermic needles.

Users of certain categories of drugs routinely or occasionally ingest their drugs via injection. Evidence of Needles use (scars, "tracks", etc.) may be found on veins along the neck, arms, legs, etc.

10. **Suspect's statements and other observations**.

Based on the nine previous components of the drug examination, the drug recognition expert should have formed at least an articulable suspicion as to the category or categories of drugs that may be present. The expert then can proceed, *in full conformance with the suspect's Constitutional rights*, to attempt to interview the suspect concerning the drug or drugs involved.

11. **Opinions of the evaluator**.

Based on all of the evidence and observations obtained during the previous ten steps, the drug recognition expert should be able to reach an informed opinion concerning:

Whether the suspect is under the influence of a drug or drugs; and if so, the category or combination of categories of drugs that is the probable cause of the suspect's impairment.

These conclusions should be documented, along with a narrative capsule summary of the observed facts that led to the conclusions.

12. The **toxicological examination**, which is a chemical test or tests that can provide scientific, admissible evidence to substantiate the drug recognition expert's conclusions.

10.9 Deconstruction and Analysis of the 12-Step DRE Protocol

Step 1: Breath Alcohol test

Note that there is neither a standard as to what type of breath alcohol test must be used for Step 1 nor any type of guideline as to what an acceptable BAC would be to determine whether the DRE will continue with the DRE investigation or treat the case as an alcohol-related DWI.

Under the protocol, it is quite possible that the officer might use an unapproved, uncalibrated device for determination of BAC. Moreover, since there is no guide as to what particular BAC would trigger the full 12-Step DRE Protocol, it is left to the individual predilection of the DRE. Suppose the DRE obtains a BAC of .090; this would surely be enough to prosecute a driver for DWI. Yet, the DRE might feel that he needs some overtime hours on his next paycheck, so he launches into a full-blown DRE investigation. Yet another officer with the same facts might not do the DRE. This leads to unequal enforcement of the laws and a possible due process violation.

Step 2: Interview of the arresting officer

Many times the DRE is not the one who makes the initial stop or arrest of the driver. The stop officer is supposed to be interviewed by the DRE. Clearly, the most helpful information would be if the stop officer observed the smell of burning marijuana at the stop or had some other plain indicia of ingestion, especially statements by the driver. Be wary of the fact that the stop officer's statements to the DRE might guide the DRE to a particular conclusion. It is very helpful to note the actual signs of impairment gathered by the DRE and compare them with the end result. Many times you will find that the DRE's opinion matches the type of drug that the driver admitted to ingesting but does not match the conclusion demanded by the results of the protocol.

Another area to watch is probable cause for the arrest. If the driver is already under arrest at the time of the arrival of the DRE, examine the probable cause for that arrest. Sometimes you will find that the person has been placed under arrest for DWI-Drugs before the 12-Step Protocol has begun. This is problematic for the prosecution, to say the least. Examination of the arresting officer should be complete and demanding. If the arresting officer is not a DRE and determined that the driver had a .000 BAC but should be placed under arrest for DWI nonetheless, what was the probable cause?

Step 3: Preliminary examination

The protocol states that the preliminary examination uses "a structured series of questions, specific observations and simple tests" without further definition. This leaves the contents of the section up to the discretion of each officer, agency and jurisdiction. Since this protocol is supposed to be standardized and obtains its alleged validity from that standardization, section 3 leaves the defense attorney ample opportunity to attack admissibility.

Step 4: Examination of the eyes

The results of these tests should be no more admissible under the DRE Protocol than they would be under a traditional alcohol-related DWI investigation. Even if HGN is admissible under certain circumstances in an alcohol-related DWI, the physiological mechanism for causation by drugs is entirely different. Horizontal Gaze Nystagmus, Vertical Gaze Nystagmus, and Lack of Convergence need appropriate expert medical testimony to pass the admissibility test.

The *DRE Manual* charts the effects of various drug categories on the eyes in a very easy to follow chart. Note that there are some exceptions to the rules. Without citation, the manual states that normal pupil size is 3.0 to 6.5 mm.

CNSD = Central Nervous System Depressants
CNSS = Central Nervous System Stimulants
H = Hallucinogens
PCP = Phencyclidine
N/A = Narcotic Analgesics
I = Inhalants
CAN = Cannabis

	CNSD	CNSS	H	PCP	N/A	I	CAN
HGN	Present	None	None	Present	None	Present	None
VGN	Present*	None	None	Present	None	Present*	None
LOC	Present	None	None	Present	None	Present	Present
Pupil Size	Normal +	Dilated	Dilated	Normal	Constricted	Normal ★	Dilated ★★
Reaction to Light	Slow	Slow	Normal	Normal ++	Little or None	Slow	Normal

* High dose for the individual
\+ SOMA, Quaaludes usually dilate pupils
★ Normal, but may be dilated
★★ Pupil size may be normal
++ Certain psychedelic amphetamines
Note that there is no standard to measure whether the suspect's reaction to light is slow, normal or rapid.

Some key technical terms used by the manual in regard to the eyes:

- *Accommodation Reflex* means automatic constriction of the pupils as an object moves closer to them.
- *Hippus* means a rhythmic pulsating of the pupils as they dilate and constrict within fixed limits.
- *Miosis* means an abnormally constricted pupil (less than 3mm in diameter).
- *Mydriasis* means an abnormally enlarged or dilated pupil (more than 6.5mm in diameter).
- *Ptosis* is the term for "droopy eyelids."
- *Pupillary Light Reflex* means the pupils of the eyes will constrict and dilate depending on changes in lighting.
- *Rebound Dilation* is a period of constriction followed by dilation with a change equal to or greater than 2mm.

Step 5: Divided attention psychophysical tests

Note that the Romberg Balance and the Finger-to-Nose tests are not NHTSA validated tests. The Walk-and-Turn and One-Leg-Stand have only been validated by NHTSA for alcohol-related purposes (specifically related to a particular BAC). Yet the DRE uses them to diagnose impairment—not any specific level of drug. And in all cases, none of the tests has been published in peer-reviewed articles as having the validity claimed by NHTSA.

Step 6: Vital signs examinations

While checks of the suspect's blood pressure, pulse rate and temperature are not new or novel, having someone evaluate these vital signs and interpret them as part of a DRE is new and novel. Alcohol and other drugs can certainly cause a neurological impairment as can other organic causes such as a brain tumor or chemical imbalance within the body. Police officers are no more qualified to diagnose alcohol and drug impairment than they are to diagnose a brain tumor.

Step 7: Dark room examinations

DREs are supposed to use a pupillometer to compare the suspect's pupil size with a standard. A pupillometer is nothing more than a card with differing sizes of dots arranged in an ascending order from smallest to largest. Generally, a pupillometer will start at 1mm and move in half-millimeter increments to about 9mm, although there is no standard for a pupillometer. Note that if a pupillometer is a photocopy of another pupillometer, the size of the dots may have varied through the photocopy process. A reliable pupillometer will be an engraved card that has had each of the dots verified by measurement.

A dark room examination can be quite dangerous for an officer. He will be in an enclosed, dark space, and in very close proximity to a suspect who may be high on drugs with unpredictable effects. Violence might certainly occur. This is why the NHTSA manual always requires a back-up officer in the room while the DRE performs the evaluation.

The effect on the suspect might also be affected by the close quarters and intensive examination. Someone who is anxious or hypertensive might be even more so because of this portion of the examination. It is realistic to expect an already nervous person's heart rate to increase as well as producing more perspiration. These are signs easily mistaken for the effects of drugs.

Step 8: Examination for muscle tone

There is no standard for determination as to whether the muscle tone is flaccid, normal or rigid.

Step 9: Examination for injection sites

Certainly evidence of injection sites can provide valuable information for the DRE, but the DRE must be able to distinguish between recent and old sites, along with normal abrasions to the skin.

Step 10: Suspect's statements and other observations

Compare carefully the results of this step (as well as Step 2) with the end result. Many times the 12-Step Protocol will lead to the conclusion that the suspect is under the influence of a category of drugs that are entirely inconsistent with the opinion of the evaluator, yet consistent with what the suspect admitted to ingesting.

Step 11: Opinions of the evaluator

Watch for broad conclusions that ignore the signs and symptoms recorded by the officer. Also note that sometimes an individual step is ignored in the process.

Step 12: Toxicological examination

The toxicological examination is the culmination of the 12-Step process and is used to confirm the DRE's opinions. It is helpful to gather the results of toxicological exams from other DRE examinations done by the same officer and calculate a percentage of competence for the officer.

10.10 Effects of Various Drugs

The following chart is helpful for evaluating whether the DRE officer actually arrived at the proper conclusions dictated by the 12-Step Protocol. Note that it is in a different order of drug categories than the previous NHTSA DRE chart.

CNSD = Central Nervous System Depressants
I = Inhalants
PCP = Phencyclidine
(The three above are commonly known as "DIP Drugs.")

CNSS = Central Nervous System Stimulants
H = Hallucinogens
N/A = Narcotic Analgesics
CAN = Cannabis (marijuana)

From the chart below, we can state some simple, general rules:

Rule 1: DIP drugs cause HGN.

Rule 2: DIP drugs cause HGN and VGN. (Note that VGN absent HGN is indicative of a non-drug-induced neuropathy.)

Rule 3: DIP drugs and cannabis cause Lack of Convergence (LOC).

Rule 4: Depressants and Narcotic Analgesics depress vital signs. The other five categories elevate vital signs. (A near-normal pulse is 60–90 beats per minute, and near-normal blood pressure is 120–140 over 70–90.)

Rule 5: Depressants and cannabis have no effect on temperature; stimulants and hallucinogens elevate temperature; narcotic analgesics lower it; and inhalants may do either or nothing to temperature. (Near-normal temperature is 97.6°F to 99.6°F.)

Rule 6: DIP drugs do not affect pupil dilation. (Normal pupil size is 3mm to 6mm.)

Rule 7: Only Narcotic Analgesics constrict pupils. (Narcotic Analgesics usually cause *very* constricted pupils, sometimes known as "pinpoint" pupils.)

Just like the term "DiRT Officers" suddenly became "Drug Recognition Experts," the term "DIP Drugs" has changed without scientific explanation as well. "DIP Drugs" (Depressants, Inhalants and PCP) are now known as "DID Drugs" (Depressants, Inhalants and Disassociative Anesthetics). On the one hand, it is good to see that the police have become more appreciative of the subtle nuances of the English language. On the other hand, the use of such language only serves to persuade a jury to convict the accused on a standard less than proof beyond every reasonable doubt.

10.11 Drug Evaluation Classification Protocol (DECP)

The International Association of Chiefs of Police (IACP) has established a national standard for training and certification for DREs. Although there are no statutory requirements for DRE certification, police will generally have to be qualified in order to testify to the results of a drug recognition evaluation.

To obtain an IACP certification, a DRE's performance is evaluated under certain guidelines that make it nearly impossible for the DRE not to obtain a certification. In order to become certified, the DRE must pass a practical exam. There are seven categories of drugs as defined by the DRE protocol. In order to successfully complete the exam, the DRE must link impairment with a drug in one of the seven categories.

Toxicological results must confirm the drug, *or its metabolite*, as being present in the subject. This is problematic for two reasons. First, the metabolite generally has no impairing effect on the subject. But if it has no impairing effect, then what was the basis for the officer's observations and subsequent conclusion of impairment? Logically speaking, there would be no effect except to artificially inflate the DRE candidate's chances of passing the DECP.

Secondly, the DRE manual states: "The chemical test simply cannot prove that the suspect was impaired, or under the influence at the time the violation occurred." (HS172 R8/99 Page XXVI-1, section titled; *The Importance of a Good DRE Report*). If the chemical test simply cannot prove impairment, then how do they justify using it as a confirmation for the officer's conclusions? Simply put, the DECP is a mess of twisted government logic outright contradictions.

When being tested under the DECP, DREs are not expected to identify all drugs in the subject—just the ones that account for impairment. Under IACP Standard 18, the following rules apply:

1. The DRE "calls" one drug class: one drug from that class of drugs must be confirmed.
   (The DRE receives a 100% grade).

2. The DRE "calls" two drug classes: one drug from either class must be confirmed.
   (The DRE receives a 100% grade).

3. The DRE "calls" three drug classes: two of the classes must be confirmed.
   (The DRE receives a 100% grade).

4. The DRE "calls" four drug classes: two of the classes must be confirmed.
(The DRE receives a 100% grade).

5. The DRE "calls" five drug classes: two of the classes must be confirmed.
(The DRE receives a 100% grade).

6. The DRE "calls" six drug classes: two of the classes must be confirmed.
(The DRE receives a 100% grade).

7. The DRE "calls" all seven drug classes: only two of the classes must be confirmed.
(The DRE receives a 100% grade).

Clearly, a smart DRE candidate will always call all seven categories of drugs whenever more than one drug is suspected, thus assuring himself of a 100% passing grade for the DECP. Moreover, the DECP is highly flawed in that it requires either the active drug or its metabolite to be present in the confirming toxicological evaluation. This makes no sense as the metabolites of certain drugs, such as marijuana, have no effect on the subject. The savvy DRE candidate may simply ask the subject if he has smoked marijuana in the last 30 days, then tailor the evaluation to indicate presence of marijuana without ever seeing the actual symptoms. The DECP process is a fraud perpetrated upon the legal system and unsuspecting juries who equate the title "Drug Recognition Expert" with science and reliable evidence. In reality, the DECP is neither scientific nor reliable.

The DECP was evaluated in the *Journal of Analytical Toxicology* (Vol. 22, October 1988). The *Journal* reported that of the 280 valid DECP evaluations, the DREs found impairment in 112 subjects. Of the 112 subjects, only 85 subjects actually had an active drug in their systems.

Using the IACP standards, the DRE classification predictions were correct in only 36 cases (32.1% correct). Ranges were found to be from 10.5% to 45.2% for any particular category of drug.

10.12 Drug Evaluation Classification Training Program

The DRE program has three phases that must be completed for an officer to receive DRE certification. The DRE program guidelines are set by the International Association of Chiefs of Police (IACP) and DRE certification is a nationally recognized certification.

As of the end of December 2012, there were 6,940 DREs in the nationwide IACP database, 1,242 of whom are also classified as DRE instructors. Connecticut was the 49th approved DECP State at the end of 2011 and held their first DRE class in the spring of 2012. West Virginia is the only state not part of the DRE program. (Source: *The 2012 Annual Report of the Drug Recognition Section, IACP*)

The three phases of the DECP are summarized below:

Phase I: DRE Preschool. The preschool is a 16-hour-long program taught over two days. Phase I familiarizes officers with the techniques of the DECP. The term "drug" is defined as it is used in terms of the DECP.

Phase II: Classroom Training. Phase II is a 56-hour-long program taught over seven days. Officers receive instruction in the techniques of the

	CNSD	I	PCP	CAN	CNSS	H	N/A
HGN	Present	Present	Present	None	None	None	None
VGN	Present	Present	Present	None	None	None	None
LOC	Present	Present	Present	Present	None	None	None
Pulse	Lowered	Elevated	Elevated	Elevated	Elevated	Elevated	Lowered
Blood Pressure	Lowered	Elevated	Elevated	Elevated	Elevated	Elevated	Lowered
Core Body Temp.	No Change	Elevated, Lowered or No Change	Elevated	No Change	Elevated	Elevated	No Change
Pupil Dilation	None	None	None	Present	Present	Present	None: Very Constricted
Pupil Constriction	None	None	None	None	None	None	Present

drug evaluation examination, limited physiology, and effects of drugs on the human body. Officers are also instructed on the law regarding the DECP and driving under the influence of drugs. There is a written examination that officers must pass before they can move on to Phase III.

Phase III: Field Certification. Over 60-90 days, while being observed by a certified instructor, officers must evaluate subjects who are suspected of being under the influence of drugs other than alcohol. After conducting and documenting the results of at least twelve drug evaluations, and after completing an examination, the student may be certified as a DRE.

DRE certification is valid for only two years and DRE officers must recertify every two years. In many states, to be considered for training, applicants must meet the following criteria:

- Minimum of two years of service as a police officer.
- Must be off probation with the police agency.
- Must be SFST and Intoxilyzer certified.
- Must have "reasonable" background and experience in level in making DWI arrests and/or dealing with subjects under the influence of alcohol or drugs.
- Must be willing to appear before an oral interview board that will assess the officer's background and qualifications.
- Must attend and successfully complete Advanced Roadside Impaired Driver Enforcement (ARIDE) training.
- Must have the approval of agency coordinator and immediate supervisor.

In Arizona, as of the end of 2012, there were 416 DREs, 133 DRE Instructors, and 58 police agencies that have DREs. In 2012, there were 2,234 DRE Enforcement Evaluations, 396 Training Evaluations for a total of 2,633 DRE Evaluations. The Arizona Governor's Office of Highway Safety provided overtime funding to support DRE certification nights, hosted by the Maricopa County Sheriff's Office. In 2012, the Maricopa County Sheriff's Office hosted 94 "DRE Cert Nights" at the Maricopa County 4th Avenue Jail for law enforcement from Arizona and 15 other states, completing more than 2,800 training evaluations. (Source: *The 2012 Annual Report of the Drug Recognition Section, IACP*, Arizona report submitted by Bridget Reutter, Arizona DRE Coordinator)

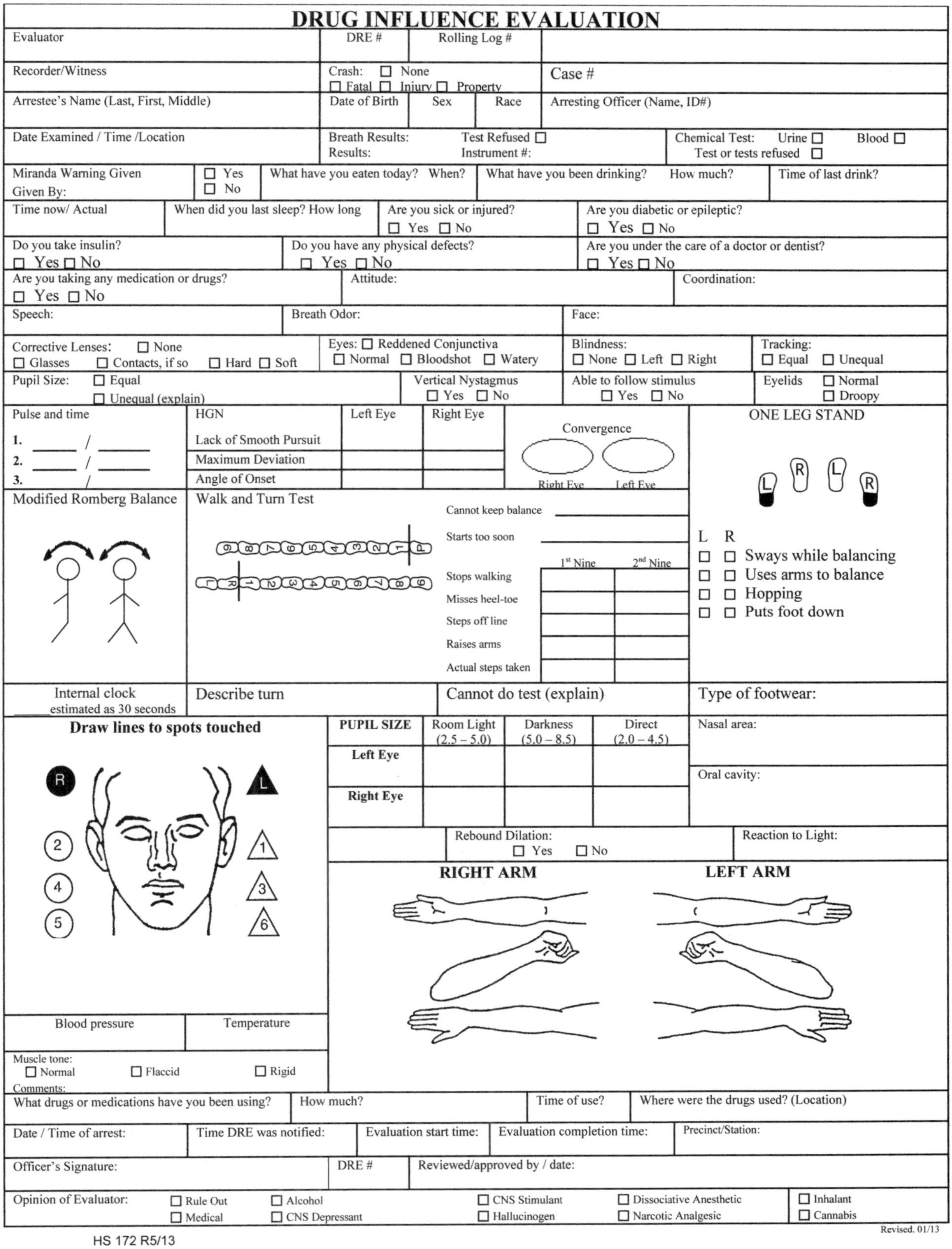

DRUG INFLUENCE EVALUATION

Evaluator | DRE # | Rolling Log #

Recorder/Witness | Crash: ☐ None ☐ Fatal ☐ Injury ☐ Property | Case #

Arrestee's Name (Last, First, Middle) | Date of Birth | Sex | Race | Arresting Officer (Name, ID#)

Date Examined / Time /Location | Breath Results: Test Refused ☐ Results: Instrument #: | Chemical Test: Urine ☐ Blood ☐ Test or tests refused ☐

Miranda Warning Given ☐ Yes ☐ No Given By: | What have you eaten today? When? | What have you been drinking? How much? | Time of last drink?

Time now/ Actual | When did you last sleep? How long | Are you sick or injured? ☐ Yes ☐ No | Are you diabetic or epileptic? ☐ Yes ☐ No

Do you take insulin? ☐ Yes ☐ No | Do you have any physical defects? ☐ Yes ☐ No | Are you under the care of a doctor or dentist? ☐ Yes ☐ No

Are you taking any medication or drugs? ☐ Yes ☐ No | Attitude: | Coordination:

Speech: | Breath Odor: | Face:

Corrective Lenses: ☐ None ☐ Glasses ☐ Contacts, if so ☐ Hard ☐ Soft | Eyes: ☐ Reddened Conjunctiva ☐ Normal ☐ Bloodshot ☐ Watery | Blindness: ☐ None ☐ Left ☐ Right | Tracking: ☐ Equal ☐ Unequal

Pupil Size: ☐ Equal ☐ Unequal (explain) | Vertical Nystagmus ☐ Yes ☐ No | Able to follow stimulus ☐ Yes ☐ No | Eyelids ☐ Normal ☐ Droopy

Pulse and time	HGN	Left Eye	Right Eye
1. ____ / ____	Lack of Smooth Pursuit		
2. ____ / ____	Maximum Deviation		
3. ____ / ____	Angle of Onset		

Convergence — Right Eye, Left Eye

ONE LEG STAND — L R L R

Modified Romberg Balance

Walk and Turn Test — 9 8 7 6 5 4 3 2 1 P; L R 1 2 3 4 5 6 7 8 9

Cannot keep balance ____
Starts too soon ____

	1st Nine	2nd Nine
Stops walking		
Misses heel-toe		
Steps off line		
Raises arms		
Actual steps taken		

L R
☐ ☐ Sways while balancing
☐ ☐ Uses arms to balance
☐ ☐ Hopping
☐ ☐ Puts foot down

Internal clock ____ estimated as 30 seconds | Describe turn | Cannot do test (explain) | Type of footwear:

Draw lines to spots touched — R, L, 2, 4, 5, 1, 3, 6

PUPIL SIZE	Room Light (2.5 – 5.0)	Darkness (5.0 – 8.5)	Direct (2.0 – 4.5)
Left Eye			
Right Eye			

Nasal area:

Oral cavity:

Rebound Dilation: ☐ Yes ☐ No | Reaction to Light:

RIGHT ARM **LEFT ARM**

Blood pressure | Temperature

Muscle tone: ☐ Normal ☐ Flaccid ☐ Rigid
Comments:

What drugs or medications have you been using? | How much? | Time of use? | Where were the drugs used? (Location)

Date / Time of arrest: | Time DRE was notified: | Evaluation start time: | Evaluation completion time: | Precinct/Station:

Officer's Signature: | DRE # | Reviewed/approved by / date:

Opinion of Evaluator: ☐ Rule Out ☐ Medical ☐ Alcohol ☐ CNS Depressant ☐ CNS Stimulant ☐ Hallucinogen ☐ Dissociative Anesthetic ☐ Narcotic Analgesic ☐ Inhalant ☐ Cannabis

Revised. 01/13

HS 172 R5/13

Figure 10.1 *Drug Influence Evaluation Report*

Chapter 11

Chemical Testing

Synopsis

11.1 Preliminary Breath Testing

Preliminary Breath Tests (PBT) are often used for probable cause purposes. Because they carry neither the safeguards nor the documentation of evidential breath testers, from a scientific viewpoint they should not be admitted as evidence. Sometimes the prosecutor will attempt to admit the results to show "presence of alcohol" but with no quantification. If your client has acknowledged drinking, there is no real danger in admitting the result to show presence of alcohol only. The real danger, however, is when the courts are lulled into a sense of routine admission where the next step is to allow the prosecutor to admit the quantitative results. This violates several rules of admissibility and the cornerstone principles of reliability of a breath test result. Keep in mind, however, that in cases involving someone underage or in commercial DWI cases the number is actually admissible.

11.2 Law

SECTION .0500 - ALCOHOL SCREENING TEST DEVICES

10A NCAC 41B .0501 SCREENING TESTS FOR ALCOHOL CONCENTRATION

(a) This Section governs the requirement of G.S. 20-16.3 that the Department examine devices suitable for use by law enforcement officers in making on-the-scene tests of drivers for alcohol concentration and that the Department approve these devices and their manner of use. In examining devices for making chemical analyses, the Department finds that at present only screening devices for testing the breath of drivers are suitable for on-the-scene use by law enforcement officers. (b) This Section does not address or in any way restrict the use of screening tests for impairment other than those based on chemical analyses, including various psychophysical tests for impairment. History Note: Authority G.S. 20-16.3; 20-16.3A; Eff. February 1, 1976; Readopted Eff. December 5, 1977; Amended Eff. April 1, 2007; October 1, 1993; October 1, 1983; January 1, 1982.

10A NCAC 41B .0502 APPROVAL: ALCOHOL SCREENING TEST DEVICES: USE

(a) Alcohol screening test devices that measure alcohol concentration through testing the breath of individuals are approved on the basis of results of evaluations by the Forensic Tests for Alcohol Branch. Devices shall meet the minimum requirements as set forth in the Department specifications for Alcohol Screening Test Devices. Evaluations are not limited in scope and may include any factors deemed appropriate to insure the accuracy, reliability, stability, cost, and ease of operation and durability of the device being evaluated. On the basis of evaluations to date, approved devices are listed in 10A NCAC 41B .0503 of this Section. (b) When the validity of an alcohol screening test of the breath of a driver administered by a law enforcement officer depends upon approval by the Department of the test device and its manner of use, the test shall be administered as follows: (1) The officer shall determine that the driver has removed all food, drink, tobacco products, chewing gum and other substances and objects from his mouth. Dental devices or oral jewelry need not be removed. (2) Unless the driver volunteers the information that he has consumed an alcoholic beverage within the previous 15 minutes, the officer shall administer a screening test as soon as feasible. If a test made without observing a waiting period results in an alcohol concentration reading of 0.08 or more, the officer shall wait five minutes and administer an additional test. If the results of the additional test show an alcohol concentration reading more than 0.02 under the first reading, the officer shall disregard the first reading. (3) The officer may request that the driver submit to one or more additional screening tests. (4) In administering any screening test, the officer shall use an alcohol screening test device approved under 10A NCAC 41B .0503 of this Section in accordance with the operational instructions supplied by the Forensic Tests for Alcohol Branch and listed on the device. History Note: Authority G.S. 20-16.3; Eff. February 1, 1976; Readopted Eff. December 5, 1977; Amended Eff. April 1, 2007; April 1, 2001; September 1, 1990; January 1, 1990; October 1, 1983.

10A NCAC 41B .0503 APPROVED ALCOHOL SCREENING TEST DEVICES: CALIBRATION

(a) The following breath alcohol screening test devices are approved as to type and make: (1) ALCO-SENSOR (with two-digit display), made by Intoximeters, Inc. (2) ALCO-SENSOR III (with three-digit display), made by Intoximeters, Inc. (3) ALCO-SENSOR IV, manufactured by Intoximeters, Inc. (4) ALCO-SENSOR FST, manufactured by Intoximeters, Inc. (5) S-D2, manufactured by CMI, Inc. (6) S-D5, manufactured by CMI, Inc. (b) The agency or operator shall verify instrument calibration of each alcohol screening test device at least once during each 30 day period of use. The verification shall be performed by employment of an alcoholic breath simulator using simulator solution in accordance with the rules in this Section or an ethanol gas canister. (c) Alcoholic breath simulators used exclusively to verify instrument calibration of alcohol screening test devices shall have the solution changed every 30 days or after 25 calibration tests, whichever occurs first. (d) Ethanol gas canisters used exclusively to verify instrument calibration of alcohol screening test devices shall not be utilized beyond the expiration date on the canister. (e) Requirements of Paragraphs (b), (c), and (d) of this Rule shall be recorded on an alcoholic breath simulator log or an ethanol gas canister log designed by the Forensic Tests for Alcohol Branch and maintained by the user agency. History Note: Authority G.S. 20-16.3; Eff. February 1, 1976; Readopted Eff. December 5, 1977; Amended Eff. July 1, 2007; November 1, 2005; April 1, 2001; January 1, 1995; January 4, 1994; April 1, 1993; January 4, 1993.

PRACTICE TIP: Always object to foundation when the State wants to introduce whether or not the result of the PBT was positive or negative for alcohol. Many times you'll find that the prosecutor doesn't know how to lay the proper foundation for admission. On the other hand, if your client has already made an admission to drinking there's no real reason to object since the Judge or jury has already been made aware of the admission.

11.3 Safeguards

Unless an evidential breath testing device is used for the PBT, there may be no safeguards against mouth alcohol. Even where an evidential machine is used, the other safeguards of replicate testing and a deprivation period will not be used. Thus, mouth alcohol can certainly be a factor. In North Carolina, the officer is instructed by law to wait a period of five minutes between each PBT test in order to avoid any possible mouth alcohol contaminants as noted in the administrative code above.

A PBT device should be checked at least once a month for accuracy. Logs should be kept by the department that issues the devices; often, an officer will NOT have these logs when they testify.

Unless an evidential breath testing machine is used as a PBT, radio frequency interference (RFI) may be present and interfere with the test, unknown to the officer.

All of the PBTs described below use fuel-cell technology to determine alcohol concentration. Infrared technology, described later in this chapter, is far too bulky and delicate and uses too much energy to be practical as used in a PBT. In its simplest form, the alcohol fuel cell consists of a porous, chemically inert disk coated on both sides with finely divided platinum (called platinum black). The porous disk is impregnated with an acidic electrolyte solution. Platinum wire electrical connections are applied to the platinum black surfaces. The entire assembly is mounted in a plastic case, which has a gas inlet that allows a fixed volume of breath to be introduced to the upper portion of the fuel cell.

In general terms, the reaction on the cell surface is simple: alcohol is converted to acetic acid. In the conversion process, two free electrons per molecule of alcohol are produced. The reaction takes place on the upper surface of the fuel cell. During the process, H+ ions are freed and migrate to the lower surface of the cell where they combine with atmospheric oxygen to form water, consuming one electron per H+ ion in the reaction. The process causes the upper surface of the disk to have an excess of electrons while the lower surface has a corresponding deficiency of electrons. When the two surfaces are connected electrically, a current flows through the external circuit to neutralize the charge. The current is called a "signal." The signal is electronically amplified and software interprets the amplified signal as a specific amount of alcohol consumed by the fuel cell (see Figure 11.1).

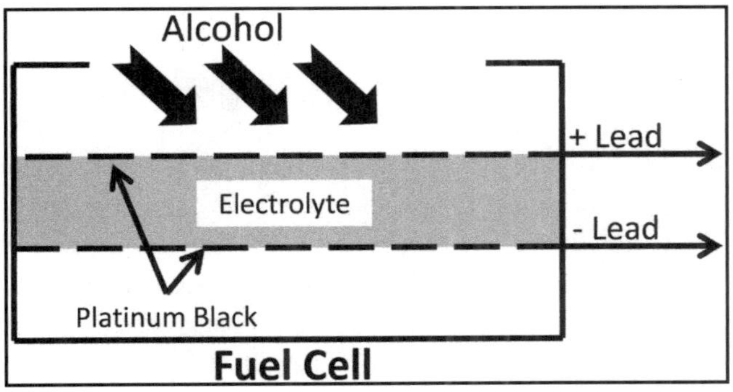

Figure 11.1

11.4 Commonly Used PBT Devices

The Intoxilyzer® 300

The Intoxilyzer® 300 is a small, handheld, lightweight and portable device. It is so lightweight, in fact, that it comes with a wrist strap attached to the base. It weighs approximately one pound and is 3-1/4 inches wide by 1-3/4 inches thick by 6-3/4 inches tall. The Intoxilyzer 300 is powered by five AA batteries with no provision for outside power sources, although a rechargeable power supply is optional. The batteries should last for about 1,000 tests.

It has a four-digit LCD backlit digital display, but no printing capabilities. The memory has a last-test recall feature but is not capable of downloading any stored information.

The machine is designed to be used in ambient temperature conditions between 23°F and 104°F which could create various problems in hot climates.

The Intoxilyzer 300 is a fuel-cell device as opposed to an infrared device such as the Intoxilyzer 5000 and 8000 models. That means that it uses two platinum electrodes that react chemically with alcohol, consuming the alcohol and converting it to an electrical signal that is then interpreted by software to be a particular breath alcohol concentration. All of the traditional breath testing errors applicable to infrared evidential machines apply, such as expired breath temperature, partition ratio, hematocrit levels and breathing patterns. The machine is claimed to be specific to alcohol, so it will not mistake other compounds, such as acetone, for alcohol. There is much dispute about specificity, however.

There is no slope-detector for purposes of determining the presence of mouth alcohol. The machine's manual states that a 20-minute observation period must be maintained to ensure that there is no mouth alcohol affecting the result. Moreover, PBTs are generally only used as a screening device, so replicate testing is rarely performed with a PBT.

The manufacturer claims that the machine is "immune to high levels of radio frequency interference." This claim seems suspect because most electronic devices are affected in some manner by high levels of radio frequency interference.

The machine must be used carefully. Rapidly testing one subject after another could create false readings. At least two minutes must pass after a test of an alcohol-positive subject to allow the fuel cell to clear, otherwise the alcohol from the previous subject may have an additive effect to the next subject's reading. There is no ambient air check or air blank mode. Testing of a subject may be done sooner than two minutes after testing of an alcohol-free subject. The most commonly seen rapid-test problem occurs at parties where the police suspect underage drinking. The police may be hasty in their attempts to test all the underage subjects and not wait the proper amount of time between subjects. An alcohol-free subject may thus be deemed to have had alcohol because of the residual amount left in the machine and the lack of replicate testing and air blank safeguards.

The Intoxilyzer 300 will sample a specimen of breath automatically, but a manual sample can be taken by the operator in the event that the operator believes that the subject is not blowing hard enough to trip the automatic sensor.

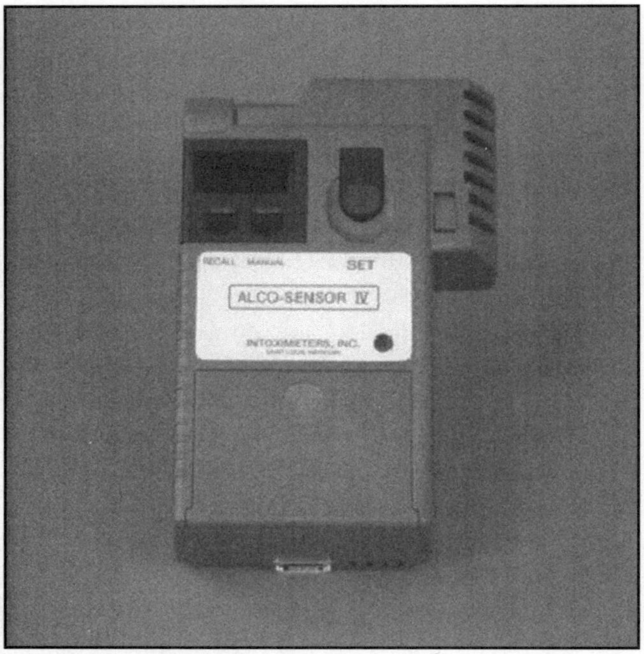

Figure 11.2 *Alco-Sensor IV*

The Intoxilyzer 300 can use a wet-bath simulator and a dry-gas tank for calibration purposes. There is no separate calibration port for introduction of the standard. It can be recalibrated in the field via the menu options on the machine and does not need to be sent back to the factory for recalibration.

Fuel cells have a limited life and will need to be replaced as their sensitivity is lost. Blowing tobacco smoke into the device will permanently damage the fuel cell.

The Intoximeter® Alco-Sensor IV®

The Alco-Sensor IV (see Figure 11.2) is the sensing unit portion of the Intoximeter RBT-IV (Roadside Breath Tester). Note that the RBT-IV was removed from the streets of Arizona in 1997 after a drawn out legal challenge over the accuracy of the device (although the device still remains listed as an "approved device" in Arizona).

The Alco-Sensor IV is DOT approved. It is $5\text{-}{}^{1}/_{2}$ inches tall by 3 inches wide and weighs just 11 ounces. The unit is powered by one heavy-duty 9-volt alkaline battery and has a test capacity of more than 300 tests per battery. It features a last-test recall function but may be equipped with a larger memory that is able to store more than 100 tests. The unit has a four-digit LED display and can be connected to a printer, whereas the Intoxilyzer 300 cannot. The unit is designed to operate at ambient temperatures between 32°F and 104°F. (There is a confirmed report from Arizona of a Tucson Police Department Motorcycle Officer who wanted to test a subject in the summertime, but his Alco-Sensor IV unit was too hot after being stored in his motorcycle's saddle-bag. He brought the unit into a grocery store and placed in the refrigerated food section long enough to cool it to within operating temperatures, then administered the test.)

Like the Intoxilyzer 300, the Alco-Sensor IV is a fuel-cell device as opposed to an infrared device. It uses two platinum electrodes that react chemically with alcohol, consuming the alcohol, and converting it to an electric signal that is then interpreted by software to be a particular breath alcohol concentration. All of the traditional breath testing errors applicable to infrared evidential machines apply, such as expired breath temperature, partition ratio, hematocrit levels and breathing patterns. The machine is claimed to be specific to alcohol, so it will not mistake other compounds, such as acetone, for alcohol. There is much dispute about specificity, however.

It will sample a specimen of breath automatically, but a manual sample can be taken by the operator in the event the operator believes that the subject is not blowing hard enough to trip the automatic sensor.

There is no radio-frequency interference detector or slope-detector.

For calibration purposes, the Alco-Sensor IV can use a wet-bath simulator and a dry-gas tank as well. There is no separate calibration port for introduction of the standard. The machine can be recalibrated in the field via the menu options on the machine and does not need to be sent back to the factory for recalibration.

Fuel cells have a limited life and will need to be replaced as their sensitivity is lost. Blowing tobacco smoke into the device will permanently damage the fuel cell.

The Intoximeter Alco-Sensor III

The Intoximeter Alco-Sensor III is a pocket-sized breath testing device, operated by a 9-volt alkaline battery, that is designed to read blood alcohol concentrations (see Figure 11.3). With normal usage, like its cousin the Alco-Sensor IV, it should provide thousands of tests before the sensor needs replacing. Supposedly, the Alco-Sensor IV will hold its calibration for months. The manual suggests having the device calibrated every 60 to 90 days by a qualified technician in order to maintain good working condition.

The Alco-Sensor III also comes with a 15-minute waiting period between contact with subject and administration of device to insure the elimination of any potential mouth alcohol which could contaminate any offered result.

The Alco-Sensor III is designed to operate at temperatures between 68°F and 98°F. Thus, as the rate of the electrochemical reaction is affected by temperature, temperature is an important factor for proper administration. The unit will operate at temperatures lower than 68°F / 20°C. The manual

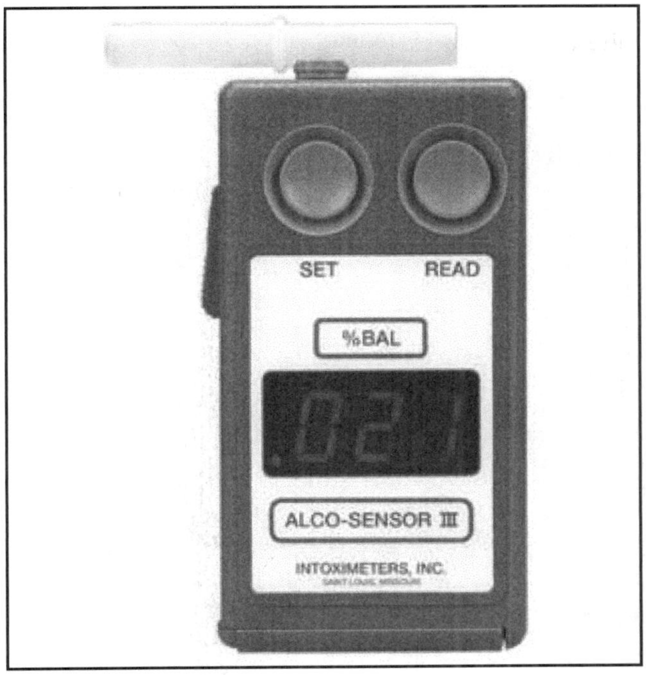

Figure 11.3 *Alco-Sensor III*

states that it will work as low as 0°C. However, the response is sluggish, with some sensitivity being sacrificed when the temperature is lower than 68°F / 20°C. The optimal temperature is between 68°F / 20°C and 98°F / 36°C.

Instrument temperature on the Alco-Sensor III can be checked by the liquid crystal thermometer built into the back panel of the device. It reads the temperature in centigrade degrees, and has a range of 20°C to 36°C. If no temperature figure is visible then the unit is either too hot or too cold. The manual suggests having the officer place the device in her "shirt pocket," which will cause the device to achieve appropriate operating temperature in a "short amount of time." Once the unit achieves appropriate operating temperature it will function properly in temperatures ranging from 0°C to 100°C, atmospheric pressure of 435 to 787 mm of mercury, and relative humidity of 0 to 100 percent.

The higher the operating temperature the more efficient the unit becomes. In theory, higher temperatures not only minimize condensation and assure rapid reading, but the unit also becomes reusable in a shorter period of time.

The manual suggests that with a "good deep lung breath sample" the Alco-Sensor III carries an accuracy rate, in comparison to a blood draw at the same time, of +/- 5 percent. However, the unit will lose sensitivity if more than five positive alcohol tests are run in an hour. The manual suggests avoiding mass testing of subjects of more than .10 BAC unless the unit is re-calibrated every five tests. Like the Intoxilyzer S-D2 and Alco-Sensor IV, the Alco-Sensor III is more specific to alcohol than infrared devices. Fuel

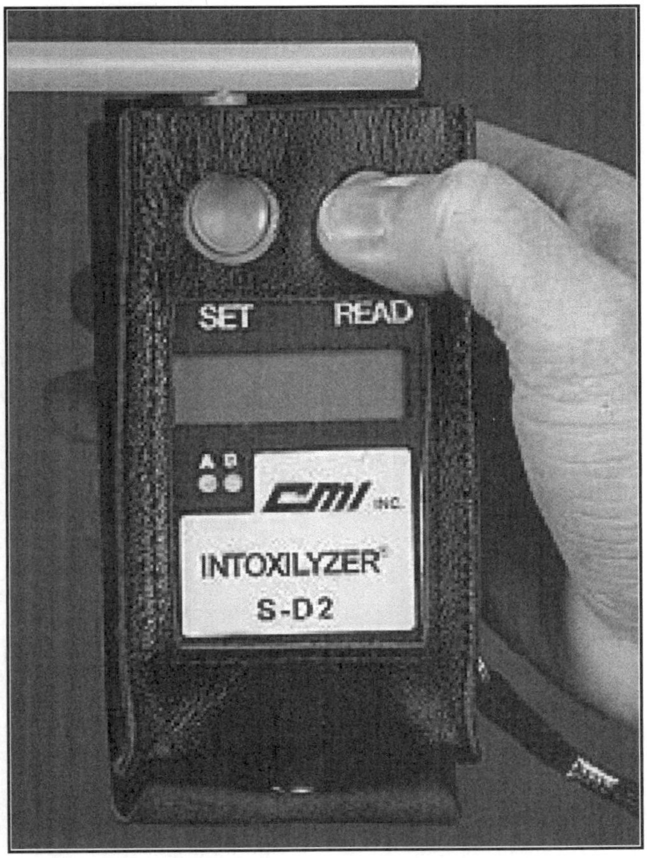

Figure 11.4 *Intoxilyzer S-D2*

cells for this device generally last 2 to 5 years. Like all fuel-cell-based devices, blowing tobacco smoke into it will permanently damage the fuel cell.

The Intoxilyzer S-D2

The Intoxilyzer S-D2, manufactured by CMI, Inc., is a small, handheld lightweight and portable device (see Figure 11.4). It weighs approximately 7.5 ounces, including pouch and battery, and is 2-$^{3}/_{4}$ inches wide by 1-$^{1}/_{2}$ inches thick by 5 inches tall. The Intoxilyzer S-D2 is powered by a 9-volt battery which should last for a minimum of 500 tests before needing to be replaced.

It has a three-digit illuminated liquid crystal display screen with a marketed +/- 5 percent accuracy rate when properly administered. The machine is designed to be used in temperature conditions between 32°F and 104°F.

The Intoxilyzer S-D2 is a fuel-cell device as opposed to an infrared device such as the CMI Intoxilyzer 5000 and 8000 models. A fuel cell device uses two platinum electrodes that react chemically with alcohol, consuming the alcohol and converting it to an electrical signal which is then interpreted by software to be a particular breath alcohol concentration. All of the traditional breath testing errors applicable to infrared evidential machines apply, such as expired breath temperature, partition ratio, hematocrit levels and breathing patterns. The machine, however, is more specific to alcohol than infrared devices which often mistake many different compounds, such as acetone, for alcohol.

There is no slope-detector for purposes of determining the presence of mouth alcohol. The machine's manual states that a 15-minute observation period must be maintained to ensure that there is no mouth alcohol affecting the result. Moreover, PBTs are generally only used as a screening device, so replicate testing is rarely performed with a PBT.

There is no radio-frequency interference detector with this device. The manual advises against use of this device in close proximity to radio transmitters while they are transmitting.

The device must be used carefully. Rapidly testing one subject after another could create false readings. At least two minutes must pass after a test of an alcohol-positive subject to allow the fuel cell to clear, otherwise the alcohol from the previous subject may have an additive effect to the next subject's reading. There is no ambient air check or air blank mode. Testing of a subject may be done sooner than two minutes after testing of an alcohol-free subject. The most commonly seen rapid-test problem occurs at parties where the police suspect underage drinking. The police may be hasty in their attempts to test all the underage subjects and not wait the proper amount of time between subjects. An alcohol-free subject may thus be deemed to have had alcohol because of the residual amount left in the machine and the lack of replicate testing and air blank safeguards.

The Intoxilyzer S-D2 will sample a specimen of breath automatically. It can use a dry gas standard or wet-bath simulator for calibration purposes. There is no separate calibration port for introduction of the standard. It can be recalibrated in the field via the menu options on the device. However, while the manual suggests the S-D2s will generally hold its calibration for months, it is recommended that to get good results the device must be calibrated every 60 to 90 days by a toxicologist or other qualified personnel.

Fuel cells have a limited life and will need to be replaced as their sensitivity is lost. Blowing tobacco smoke into the device will permanently damage the fuel cell.

The Alco-Sensor FST

The Alco-Sensor FST is the newest of the preliminary breath testing devices being used nationwide (see Figure 11.5). It is DOT-approved. It too is a handheld fuel-cell-based device and operates much like the SD-2 and Alco-Sensor III and IV models. The FST fuel cell is designed to respond only to alcohol in the human breath. It is operated by two AA batteries which are supposed to provide approximately 1,500 tests before needing replaced. The FST supposedly will not respond to hydrocarbons or acetone, which may be found in the breath of a diabetic, someone on a high-protein diet or someone who regularly exercises strenuously like a professional athlete or marathon runner. In fact, the manual boasts that the FST has no significant cross sensitivity to any substance that may be found in the human body after the mandatory minimum 15-minute waiting period is adhered from initial contact to administration. The fuel cell is supposed to last anywhere from 3 to 6 years before needing to be replaced. As with all other PBT devices, blowing tobacco smoke directly into the fuel cell will damage it. It is recommended that accuracy checks be performed on this device at least once a month. An external accuracy check and/or calibration, like other fuel-cell-based PBT devices, can be performed using a dry gas standard (approved by both NHTSA and Intoximeters) or a wet bath simulator with properly certified and maintained ethanol solutions. The wet bath simulator should also be approved for use by NHTSA and Intoximeters. In either case, the compressed gas tanks, simulators and simulator solutions are to be used and maintained only in accordance with quality assurance plans provided by the manufacturer.

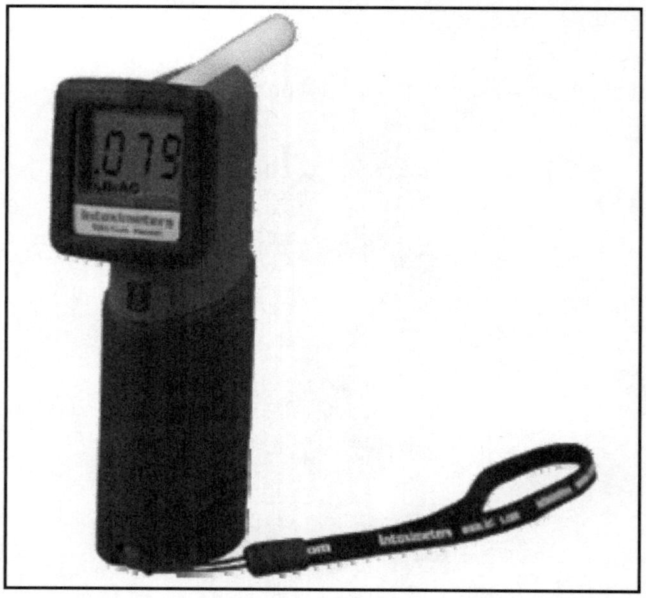

Figure 11.5 *Alco-Sensor FST*

The Alco-Sensor FST's casing is supposed to be designed to provide radio frequency interference (RFI) shielding from other electronics that are in operation in close proximity. The test will be voided and is to be restarted when RFI is detected by the device. When this occurs, the manual advises one to remove the mouthpiece, which turns the unit off, locate the source of the RFI, remove it and restart the test. Examples of commonly seen RFIs include officer walkie-talkies, cell phones and other radio-transmitting sources. The manufacturer claims that the Alco-Sensor FST also has a +/- 5 percent accuracy rate when compared to a known sample, even if working properly.

11.5 Henry's Law and the Blood-to-Breath Ratio

In 1803 a British chemist, William Henry, developed a principle concerning the actions of volatile substances when placed in water and brought into contact with air. This discovery is called Henry's Law and is stated as follows:

> Assume a closed system and constant temperature. After a period of time, some of the molecules of the liquid will have moved into the gaseous phase in the headspace above that liquid. The number of molecules that have passed into the gaseous phase will be directly proportional to the number of molecules remaining in the liquid.

Alcohol and many other substances are volatile substances, meaning that they have a tendency to rapidly change states (liquid to air, evaporation; or air to liquid, condensation), whether they are alone or in solution. If one places a volatile substance, such as alcohol, in solution with water in a sealed container, the air in the container above the liquid will become saturated with alcohol vapor. When the amount of alcohol evaporating into the air space above the solution equals the amount of alcohol condensing and returning to the water, equilibrium has been reached. At equilibrium, there is a fixed ratio between the alcohol in the water and the alcohol in the air above it. This ratio is dependent upon the temperature of the solution and atmospheric pressure within the container. If either the temperature or the pressure is changed, the ratio will change.

William Henry did not use alcohol in his experiments. However, later experimentation confirmed that water and blood solutions using alcohol do obey Henry's Law except when the alcohol concentration exceeds 20 percent (about 50 times lethal dosage) which far exceeds any concentrations found in humans.

Applying Henry's Law to the human body

Does the human body meet the requirements of Henry's Law? The answer is unclear. First, we must think of alcohol consumption as placing a volatile substance into a "container." There is water present with which the alcohol can come into solution. Although the body is only a "closed" container when the subject does not breathe in or out, conventional breath testing science ignores this fact. The body is, however, regulated at a fairly constant temperature (98.6°F or 37°C) and external atmospheric pressure does not change rapidly. Breathing, on the other hand, does change pressure within the body with normal inspiration and exhalation.

The human respiratory system quickly brings some gaseous and volatile substances contained in the blood into equilibrium with the alveolar air of the lungs. The air passages of the lung may be compared to an inverted tree. The windpipe or "trachea" is the trunk. From there, one large branch or "bronchus" goes into each lung. The branches further divide into smaller and smaller branches. These smaller branches or "bronchi" finally become microscopic tubes, each ending in a thin irregularly shaped sac. Each sac is composed of a number of smaller sacs called "alveolus." Each alveolus is approximately 0.1 millimeter in diameter; its wall is only two cells in thickness; and it is honeycombed with capillaries. A normal lung will contain about 750 million alveoli, creating a surface area of approximately 600 square feet. It is here, in the alveolar region, that the exchange of some gases occurs. Some scientists also believe that this is where alcohol exchange occurs. It is this belief, which has not been empirically proven, that provides the basis for the science of alcohol breath testing.

Each time we breathe, we take in oxygen. The oxygen is brought into the alveolar section of the lungs where it will pass from the alveolar sacs directly into the blood, thereby creating arterial or oxygenated blood. The arterial blood then travels throughout the body delivering oxygen to all body tissues. After the arterial blood delivers its supply of oxygen and other nutrients, it collects carbon dioxide and other waste products from the various bodily tissues. The blood carrying the carbon dioxide, now called "venous" or "deoxygenated blood," returns to the alveolar region; it passes the carbon dioxide into the alveolar sac before it receives new oxygen. When we exhale, the carbon dioxide which has been collected from body tissues will be passed out of the body. Alcohol in our system is thought to follow this same exit route. Conventional breath testing theory states that as blood which contains alcohol comes into contact with the alveolar region, the alcohol will pass from the blood into the alveolar sacs. This intimate contact between the alcohol-laden blood and the alveolar region supposedly satisfies the requirements for Henry's Law, not only with alcohol, but oxygen, carbon dioxide and many other volatiles. Current breath testing science relies on the ratio of alcohol between the air and the blood occurring in the alveolar region of the lungs.

The Development of the 2100:1 "Blood to Breath" Ratio

Dr. Rolla Harger first attempted to apply Henry's Law to analyze breath for alcohol concentration. In an effort to assist the law enforcement community in combating the intoxicated driver, Dr. Harger began experimenting with methods of quickly and accurately determining alcohol levels without the need for invasive testing or waiting for lengthy laboratory analysis.

Initial experiments were done by placing whole blood combined with known quantities of alcohol, into a rotating cylinder. By rotating the cylinder Dr. Harger believed he was able to simulate the gas exchange processes occurring in the lung system. Samples were drawn from the blood and the air until a constant ratio was established. Other types of blood and different concentrations of alcohol were used until Dr. Harger felt confident that the correct blood to breath ratio had been established. Dr. Harger then published his findings, and the science of breath analysis was born. It is critical to understand the exact basis of this "blood to breath" statement. Dr. Harger concluded that 2100 mL of alveolar air will contain the same weight of alcohol as does 1 mL of pulmonary blood.

This conclusion has prompted much debate in both science and law. Most of the legal debate, however, is based on a misunderstanding of the statement. In almost every court across the country this is referred to as the "blood to breath ratio." However this statement refers neither to breath in general, nor blood in general, but rather to alveolar air and pulmonary arterial blood.

Just as there are specific types of blood in the body—arterial, venous, capillary—and each have specific characteristics, there are different types of breath. It is thought that the type of breath where the alcohol is in greatest contact, and therefore the prime sample to collect for a breath analysis, is the alveolar air. However, collecting a pure sample of alveolar would cause the lungs to collapse. Obviously this type of sample capture cannot be conducted in a breath analysis. Breath analysis is mathematically based on the ratio involving the alcohol concentration in the blood and that of the alveolar air, but what is collected is actually deep lung air. A deep lung breath sample is the closest one can get to the actual sample mathematically required by breath analysis instrumentation. This type of breath is thought to be representative of the alcohol concentration ratio between the arterial blood and the alveolar air. The "blood to breath ratio" of 2100:1 is still generally accepted by police, prosecutors, crime lab personnel and some experts as the best ratio to date for the accurate analysis of breath in an effort to establish alcohol concentrations in the blood.

Is Alveolar Alcohol Exchange a Myth?

Does alcohol really exchange in the alveolar sacs of the lungs, or does it exchange elsewhere in the respiratory system? One of the premier respiratory physiologists in the world holds a different opinion than the originators of breath alcohol testing, and he has done much research and experimentation to prove his point.

Dr. Michael Hlastala has shaken the very foundations of the conventional evidential breath testing world. The result of his research is politically dangerous to the scientists who have founded and contribute to the conventional theories of evidential breath testing. Tens of millions of dollars have been spent on the application of the conventional theory of human respiratory physiology to modern breath testing. If the basic assumptions were to be proved wrong, breath testing devices would be useless unless modified to account for human respiratory physiology as it actually exists. Scientists who have staked their reputations on false assumptions would be unfairly vilified by the defense. Breath testing programs in every state would be thrown into utter chaos. In short, it is not in the best interests of the government to tell the truth to the citizens irrespective of what science dictates.

It is important to realize that the scientists who first proposed, and still support, the alveolar-air-ethanol-exchange model of the former paradigm are not doing so out of malice. They simply did not have the scientific tools available to them fifty years ago that scientists have today. Hardware in the form of infrared breath testing devices had not yet been invented. But, more importantly, computer software has allowed today's respiratory physiologists to go where scientists could never have imagined going fifty years ago. New studies have led to different conclusions about gas exchange within the lungs. Physiology has not changed, but our understanding of it has changed.

In a nutshell, Dr. Hlastala's work proves that although some gases, such as oxygen and carbon dioxide, exchange between the breath and the blood in the alveoli, other compounds such as ethanol, exchange much higher up in the airway. The location of exchange is directly related to the solubility of the substance. Substances such as sulfur hexafluoride and ethane have very low solubility, whereas oxygen, carbon dioxide and ether have intermediate levels of solubility. Acetone, ethyl alcohol and water have much higher solubility. Substances with higher solubility values exchange higher in the airway while those with lower solubility exchange lower in the airway—such as in the alveolar sacs.

Conventional evidential breath testing theory relies on an exchange of alcohol between blood and breath in the alveolar sacs of the lungs as seen in Figure 11.6. However, this paradigm is at its end. There are simply too many anomalies to the long-held (and never empirically proven) conventional theory for it to hold true.

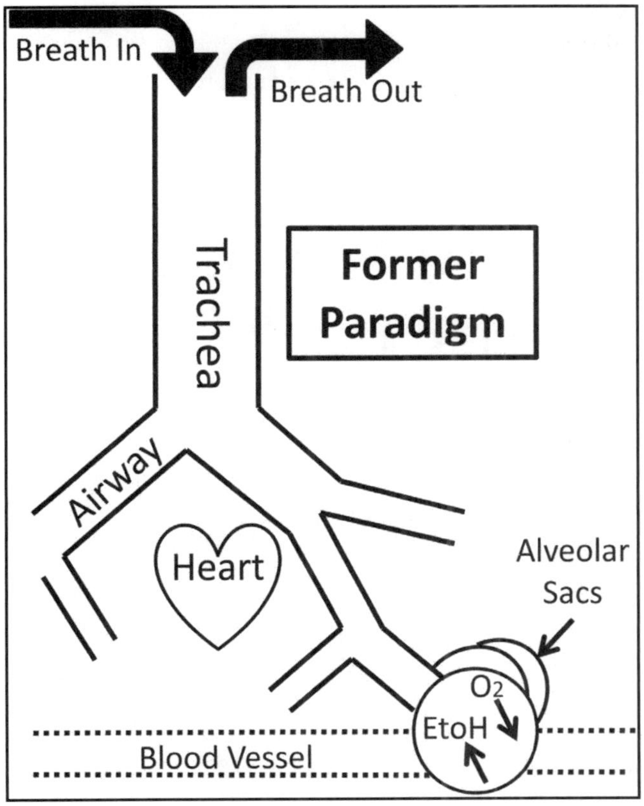

Figure 11.6 Former paradigm. Ethanol was thought to exchange in the alveolar sacs of the lungs.

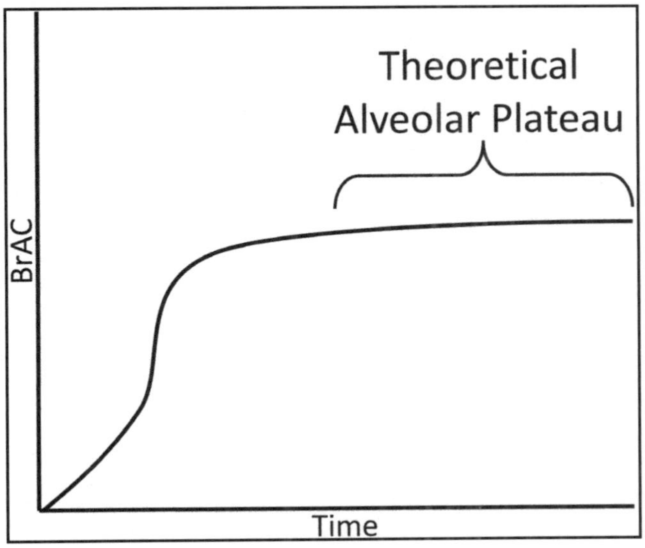

Figure 11.7 The alveolar pattern is an anomaly that cannot be explained by conventional breath testing theory.

For example, the conventional theory states that there is an "alveolar plateau" as seen in Figure 11.7. This supposed plateau is the point where enough air has been expelled from the subject's lungs such that the very end of the expiration contains mostly alveolar air. (It is impossible to get a sample

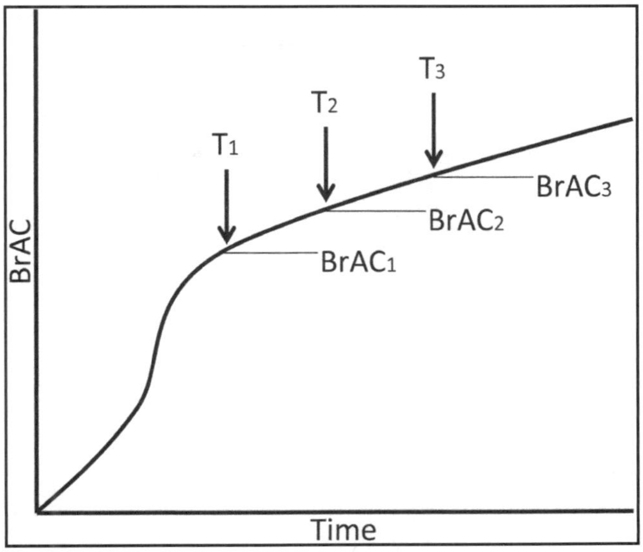

Figure 11.8 The longer the subject blows, the higher the reading goes.

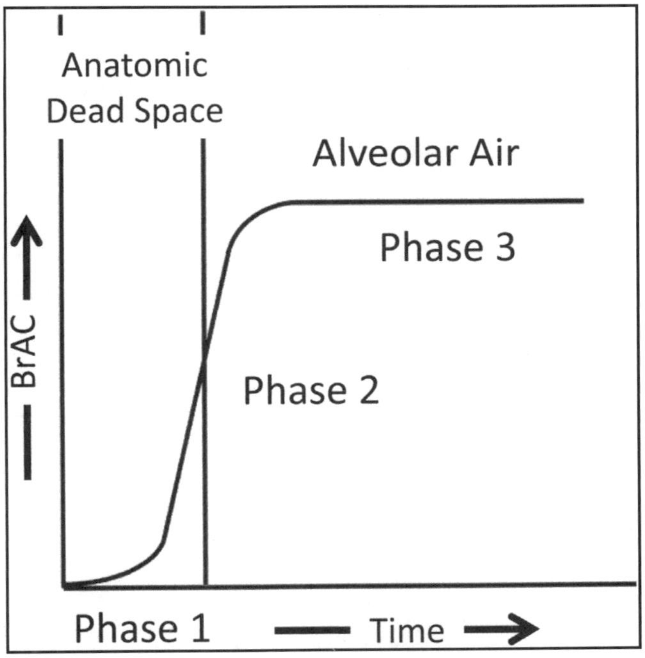

Figure 11.9 The "anatomic deadspace" is another anomaly not explained by conventional breath testing theory.

of pure alveolar air without collapsing the lungs and killing the subject—let's hope that the legislature never makes that type of testing a reality.) The conventional theory holds that when a breath sample is taken at any point during the alveolar plateau, the result will be the same as a sample taken at any other point during the alveolar plateau. Clearly, this is false. Anyone who has practiced in the DWI defense area knows that the longer the subject blows, the higher the result. There is no alveolar plateau (George et al., 1993; Ohlsson et al., 1990).

Dr. Hlastala's work has proven that there are significant differences when breath results are captured during the area which was previously thought to have been the alveolar plateau. In Figure 11.8, one can see significant differences between breath results at T1, T2 and T3. These differences should not exist if there is an alveolar plateau.

If conventional breath testing theory was correct, then there would be an "anatomic dead space" recorded for each subject test. In other words, there would be little or no alcohol at the beginning of the breath and it would rise only when alveolar air enters the mix as represented in Figure 11.9. Yet, we know that there is no anatomic dead space when a subject blows into a breath testing machine (George et al., 1993). This means that even after a deprivation period, there must still be some alcohol in the upper airways.

Moreover, if conventional breath test theory was correct, breathing patterns immediately before breath testing should have no effect on the reported result. Yet, breathing patterns immediately prior to a breath test can have a significant result as Dr. A. W. Jones discovered. Hyperventilation and hypoventilation will cause as much as a ±15 percent variation in a breath test result (Jones, 1990). The longer a person holds his breath, the higher the result. Short, rapid breaths tend to flush out the lungs and result in a lower reading. See Figure 11.10.

Dr. Hlastala's theory is graphically shown in Figure 11.11. The alcohol resides in the mucus lining of the trachea and other parts of the respiratory system. Alcohol is hydrophilic—that is, it can be found where there is water in the body. Mucus is mostly water, and alcohol, just like every other water-bearing substance in the body, will be in solution with it in higher concentrations than in other areas of the body such as bone and fat.

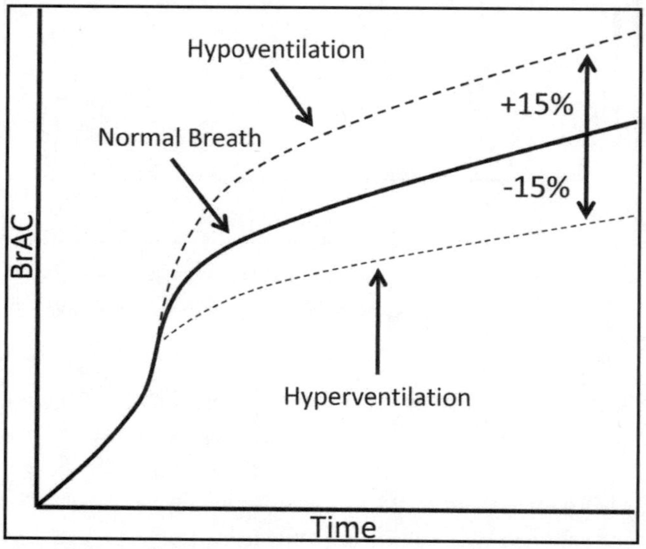

Figure 11.10 *If the conventional breath testing theory was correct, then breathing patterns would have no effect on the reported BrAC. Yet it can have up to a 15 percent effect in either direction.*

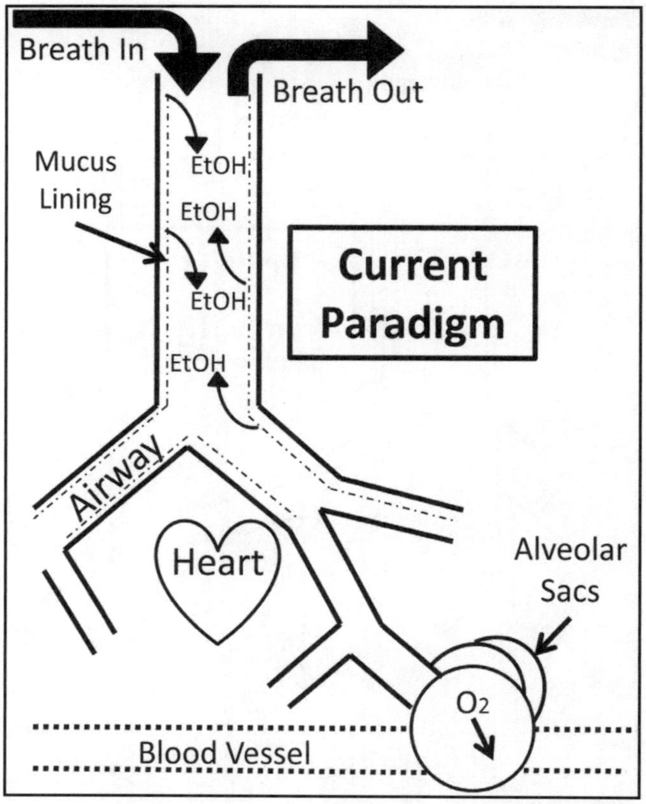

Figure 11.11 *Current paradigm. Ethanol exchanges in the upper airways of the lungs and trachea.*

When a subject breathes in and out, alcohol evaporates from the mucus lining and travels out of the mouth or nose with expiration. When the subject inhales, alcohol evaporates from one part of the mucus and is re-deposited into other parts of the mucus lining. This does not mean, however, that breath testing cannot be useful in an evidentiary sense. It simply means that it has to be performed differently.

Dr. Hlastala has advocated "re-breathing" as a means of more closely equilibrating the breath alcohol with the blood alcohol. When re-breathing, a subject inhales, then exhales into a device which captures the breath. The subject then "re-breathes" the air sample several times until the temperature and humidity of the sample is fairly constant. The "re-breathed" air sample is then analyzed through conventional means. It is ironic that Dr. Rolla Harger, widely credited with being the father of conventional breath testing theory, developed a method of re-breathing (see below) by having a subject breathe into a balloon a minimum of four times before the air was tested in order to assure that the sample was virtually the same composition as a purely alveolar sample. Harger's method, however, was limited because he did not control the temperature of the re-breathing bag. Condensation formed in the bag and ultimately lowered the reported breath alcohol result.

One of the government's arguments against using re-breathing as a part of breath testing is that it might be difficult to get an uncooperative subject to go through the steps necessary to re-breathe properly in order to provide a quality breath sample. Another argument is that the subject might be too intoxicated to re-breathe properly. Clearly these are valid arguments, but they provide no excuse for inaccurate breath test results. If the government cannot obtain valid, accurate and reliable results through current breath testing methods, perhaps the government should rethink the whole breath-testing proposition and gather evidence of intoxication by other means.

For conventional breath testing theory to be acceptable, there have to be explanations for the fact that there is no anatomic dead space, no alveolar plateau, that breath alcohol concentration depends upon exhaled volume, that the breath alcohol concentration depends upon pre-test breathing patterns and that re-breathing blood to breath values are lower than single-breath values.

The use of the "blood to breath" ratio in instrumentation

The first breath analysis instrument, known as the Drunkometer, was developed by Dr. Rolla Harger. The critical basis of the instrument was determining the exact amount of alveolar air contained in the sample since the instrument used "mixed expired" air which was composed of all the types of breath. The captured breath was bubbled into a reagent until the reagent had turned a specific color. The amount of breath it took to cause this reaction would vary depending on the alcohol concentration of the subject: the higher the alcohol concentration in the subject, the smaller the amount of captured sample it took to cause the reaction. The exact amount of alveolar breath then had to be determined. This was done by measuring the weight of carbon dioxide, which is found only in the alveolar air, captured by an ascarite tube, which had to be weighed before and after the test. Analysis also required applying mathematical formulas, assessing the exact amount of alveolar air, then correcting for the captured amount of alcohol. The instrument was later modified using a "re-breathing" technique whereby the individual would exhale into a "balloon," breathe the sample back in and then exhale again. By having the subject perform this technique a minimum of four times the sample that was then analyzed was believed to be virtually the same composition as alveolar air.

In 1954, Dr. Robert Borkenstein introduced the Breathalyzer. The Breathalyzer was designed to capture a specific amount of end-expired breath from the subject. Whereas the Drunkometer would use different amounts of breath, the Breathalyzer would capture only 52.5 cc of end-expired breath. The basis in this case was not the amount of breath used, but the amount of reagent destroyed based on a constant sample. The alcohol concentration would be proportional to the amount of reagent which reacted with the alcohol. To determine the amount of reagent destroyed in an ampoule, a "test" ampoule and a "standard" ampoule were used. The ampoules where placed in front of matched photocells and a movable light source was adjusted until the amount of light able to pass through the ampoules was equal. When the alcohol reacted in the test ampoule, a portion of the reagent was destroyed thereby altering the reagent's light absorption. The light source was readjusted until the amount of light passing through the ampoules was equal once again. The distance the light source had to move was directly proportional to the alcohol concentration.

In the 1960s investigations concerning the use of infrared light as a method of alcohol analysis were under way. A company called Omicron introduced the first infrared type of device. The basis of the infrared unit was to use an infrared light beam which when brought into contact with alcohol the alcohol molecule would absorb some of the infrared light energy. The blood to breath ratio is an integral part of the design of this type of instrument.

11.6 Evidential Breath Testing

Since 2009, when North Carolina discontinued use of the Intoxilyzer 5000, the Intoximeter EC/IR-II has been the approved breath test device throughout the state. Currently, the EC/IR-II is currently being used in only a handful of other states: Maryland, Wisconsin, Tennessee, Wyoming, West Virginia, Virginia and portions of California. (Indiana is currently in the process of implementing EC/IR-II use.) The EC/IR-II is believed to be the least expensive breath testing machine currently used in the United States.

The EC/IR-II is a DOT approved (desktop) device, encased in metal, that is approximately 7 inches in height, 17-3/4 inches wide, 18 inches deep and weighs about 22 lbs. It has a two line by twenty character fluorescent display screen that provides operator instructions and status information. See Figures 11.10-11.13.

It comes with a standard computer keyboard, a bar code scanner designed for reading and inputting coded driver's license and officer data, and an internal printer.

It has an internal clock and calendar which automatically updates the month, day, year and daylight savings time. It has a modem for communication purposes. The reinforced plastic breath tube is heated to prevent condensation from being introduced into the sample chamber.

The disposable mouthpiece fits in the end of the breath tube and its primary function is to prevent the subject from sucking air back from the instrument during testing (Figure 11.14).

11.7 Infrared Light Absorption

Both visible and IR light are wavelengths of what is known as the "electromagnetic spectrum." Humans and animals can see visible light. Other wavelengths of the electromagnetic spectrum are invisible to us, such as radio waves. The wavelengths in the spectrum vary in size from the height of skyscrapers to very short gamma rays, smaller than the nucleus of an atom.

Electromagnetic wavelengths are measured in terms of microns (one-millionth of a meter). The wavelength of the light that we see is from 0.4 microns (blue light) to 0.7 microns (red light).

The Electromagnetic Spectrum

Portion of the Spectrum	Wavelength in Microns
Radio Waves	Greater than 10^{+3}
Microwaves	25 to 10^{+3}
Far Infrared	15 to 50
Mid Infrared	2.5 to 15
Near Infrared	0.7 to 2.5
Visible Light	0.4 (blue) to 0.7 (red)
Ultraviolet	10^{-3} to 4×10^{-1}
X-rays	10^{-6} to 10^{-3}
Gamma Rays	Less than 10^{-6}

Organic molecules are made up of groups of atoms. IR light is absorbed by organic molecules, in this case ethanol, and converted into a type of energy called "molecular vibration." Certain groups of those atoms will absorb bands of IR light at or near predictable and characteristic wavelengths irrespective of the structure of the rest of the organic molecule. Alcohol is one of those molecules. Since alcohol molecules have characteristic wavelengths of absorption, breath testing devices are set to filter IR light at those particular wavelengths and measure it. Different devices use different filters (see Figure 11.12).

IR Breath Tester Wavelength Comparison

Intoxilyzer 5000 - - 3 Filters:

3.39 (acetone), 3.48 (EtOH), & 3.80 (reference) microns

Intoxilyzer 5000 - - 5 Filters:

3.40 (acetone), 3.47 (EtOH), 3.80 (reference) microns

3.36 (acetaldehyde), & 3.52 (toluene) microns

BAC DataMaster cdm - - 3 Filters:

3.37 (acetone), 3.44 (EtOH) microns & 3.50 (toluene)

Intoxilyzer 8000 - - 2 Filters:

3.4 (acetone) & 9.36 (EtOH) microns

Draeger Alcotest 7110 - - 1 Filter:

9.5 (EtOH) microns only—but also measures with a fuel cell

Figure 11.12

Notice that while both the three-filter and five-filter Intoxilyzer 5000 models absorb alcohol on a similar wavelength (3.48 and 3.47, respectively), the Intoxilyzer 8000 absorbs near the other end of the IR spectrum at 9.36 microns. The mid-infrared spectrum starts at only 2.5 microns and goes to 15 microns. This means that the Intoxilyzer 8000 measures absorption at a different part of the alcohol molecule than does either version of the Intoxilyzer 5000 or the BAC Datamaster cdm®.

The Intoxilyzer 5000 measures the C-H bonds (3.38 to 3.48 microns) of the methyl group and of the similar C-H bonds of the methylene group (3.43 to 3.51 microns), while the Intoxilyzer 8000 measures the C-O (7.93 to 10.00 microns) of the alcohol group. Below is a schematic representation of the molecular bonds within the ethanol molecule.

Structure of the EtOH Molecule

```
H = Hydrogen Atom      H   H
C = Carbon Atom         \ /
O = Oxygen Atom       H—C-C-O-H
                        / \
                       H   H
```

Chemical Subgroups of Atoms of the EtOH Molecule

```
                 Methylene Group CH2
     H               H
      \             /
     H—C           -C-            -O-H
      /             \             Hydroxy or
     H               H         Alcohol Group OH
Methyl Group CH3
```

11.8 Principles and Theory of Dry Gas Standards

The purpose of the dry gas standard is used to produce a sample gas of known ethanol concentration for use as a reference in a standard check on the EC/IR-II (see Figure 11.15). The purpose of this standard check, in theory and design, is to ensure and demonstrate that the instrument is working properly when conducting a breath test.

The dry gas standards are contained in a DOT-approved, pressurized, dry gas tank that is connected to the EC/IR-II through a single staged regulator. This tank contains a single-phased (gaseous), NIST-traceable, mixture of nitrogen and ethanol that is, by design, supposed to produce a .082% at sea level. During a standard performed by the machine, the regulator and internal components within the EC/IR-II is to automatically sample and analyze the reference standard.

The shelf life of a standard 105 liter tank is 24 months. Tanks are not to be transported on commercial airlines. Adjustments for barometric pressure, due to changes in weather or elevation, are necessary. Intoximeters claims that the machine automatically compensates for barometric variations. Use of the tank in a cold condition may ruin the standard resulting in a "standard file" error report.

Another consideration is to monitor the expiration date on the reference standard. Once the reference gas is loaded into the disposable tanks, the ethanol/nitrogen mixture is guaranteed stable for two years per the Intoximeter manual, with the expiration date labeled on each tank. Once the tank is approaching the date of expiration, two events will occur: an expiration warning 15 days prior to expiration and a tank expired indication on the date of expiration. The machine will then become disabled until a new tank is installed and the expiration date is reset within the machine. Be vigilant in your review of when the gas tank is set to expire, and how the police handle it when it occurs. The gas tank expiration date and the date entered into the database, may not match which presents fertile ground for attack.

11.9 Gas Tank Instrument Errors

The following are types of instrument errors that can occur with an EC/IR-II gas tank:

1. Standard Check Failed

The machine is out of calibration and needs to be calibrated.

The wrong target value was entered prior to accuracy check of machine. Officers are trained to check the "target value" on the ticket as compared to the result.

The machine may not have correctly compensated for barometric pressure.

2. Dry Gas Tank Empty

Gas tank is empty.

The flow from the regulator is not set properly and the instrument needs to be serviced.

The gas solenoid is not actuating properly and needs to be serviced.

3. Tank Is Expired

The gas tank has expired and needs to be replaced.

11.10 Principles of Fuel Cell Sensor

In its simplest form, the alcohol fuel cell consists of a porous, chemically inert disk coated on both sides with finely divided platinum (called platinum black). The porous disk is impregnated with an acidic electrolyte solution. Platinum wire electrical connections are applied to the platinum black surfaces. The entire assembly is mounted in a plastic case, which has a gas inlet that allows a fixed volume of breath to be introduced to the upper portion of the fuel cell.

In general terms, the reaction on the cell surface is simple: alcohol is converted to acetic acid. In the conversion process, two free electrons per molecule of alcohol are produced. The reaction takes place on the upper surface of the fuel cell. During the process, H^+ ions are freed and migrate to the lower surface of the cell where they combine with atmospheric oxygen to form water, consuming one electron per H^+ ion in the reaction. The process causes the upper surface of the disk to have an excess of electrons while the lower surface has a corresponding deficiency of electrons. When the two surfaces are connected electrically, a current flows through the external circuit to neutralize the charge. The current is called a "signal." The signal is electronically amplified and software interprets the amplified signal as a specific amount of alcohol consumed by the fuel cell. See Figure 11.1.

11.11 Principles of Infrared Cell

A basic principle of scientific analysis is that all organic molecules absorb infrared light. One can measure the infrared absorption of these molecules by directing infrared light through the sample, then measuring the amount of light hitting a detecting device. The amount of light that hits the detector is called a "signal." The signal is compared to the signal created when infrared light hits the detector without first passing through a breath sample. The difference between the signals is calculated and interpreted by software.

The software provides quantitative indications of the samples concentration, but not qualitative indications. The EC/IR-II is designed to process these signals to produce an output indicating the concentration of one or more of the constituents being analyzed (i.e., alcohol). Even in the gaseous state, these molecules exhibit absorption characteristics at specific wavelengths in the infrared spectrum.

In the EC/IR-II, the detector contains two channels—one for carbon dioxide and one for ethanol (alcohol)—that are selected by filtering the frequency of incident light reaching the detector. Thus, with no ethanol or carbon dioxide present, both develop approximately the same output voltage. When ethanol is introduced into the sample, the radiation reaching the ethanol detector is reduced, but the carbon dioxide channel is unchanged. Similarly, the presence of carbon dioxide reduces the signal output from the carbon dioxide detector.

The amount of signal decrease in either the carbon dioxide or ethanol channels is proportional to the concentration of the gas of interest according to "Lambert-Beer's law," which defines the exponential relationship between concentration and signal strength. See Figure 11.17.

11.12 General Operating Principles

The Intoximeter EC/IR-II employs two distinct analytical techniques to measure alcohol concentration: a fuel cell (i.e., an electrochemical sensor) and a miniaturized infrared absorption (IR) bench. The infrared (IR) sensor exhibits cross-sensitivity to several breath constituents (like acetone) and is a non-linear analytical device (difficult to calibrate), making it less attractive to use as the primary analytical system. The IR sensor supposedly makes continuous determinations of alcohol concentration, thus allowing the EC/IR-II to monitor a breath sample in near real time as it is delivered into the EC/IR-II. In theory, this is to help determine the correct moment at which to take a sample of the breath by the fuel cell for analysis and that the sample is not contaminated with mouth alcohol.

Intoximeters claims that the fuel cell sensor is specific alcohol and linear sensing, allowing for single-point calibration. This is supposed to ensure stable calibration across the full range of its sensing capabilities.

The breath sensing system in the EC/IR-II requires that sampling takes place at the end of an exhalation, if enough breath has been given to reach deep lung air. A thermistor monitors the flow rate of the breath through the instrument. The instrument will prompt the subject to keep blowing until it has reached the minimum volume of air (see Figure 11.18). After accumulating the minimum volume set by the software, the breath machine will initiate an automatic sample when a reduction in breath flow is sensed. This signifies the approaching end of exhalation. At the instant that the breath flow slows, the machine is designed to "take" a breath sample. The combined analytical techniques are used to quantify the amount of alcohol at the end of exhalation by the subject, once the infrared sensor has determined that a proper deep lung sample has been reached.

The manufacturer's goal was to use the two analytical systems to make accurate determinations of breath alcohol concentration as well as to ensure that the instrument takes a high-quality sample (see Figure 11.19). The sample is to be made up of alveolar breath, not a shallow breath sample or one tainted by alcohol from the upper respiratory tract of the subject. Note that if there is any reduction or cessation of breath flow rate by the subject, prior to the machine indicating it has received the minimum volume of breath sample needed for analysis, it will cause the machine to reset and request another breath sample. The subject is then required to provide another breath sample after the unit clears the delivered breath sample from the sample chamber.

PRACTICE TIP: Be sure to thoroughly inquire about your client's medical history. Someone who suffers from acid reflux disease and/or GERD could accidentally and unknowingly cause a significantly higher BAC reading on a breath machine due to the illness. Micro-belches, which may go undetected, are another way a false positive result can occur. Always inquire and thoroughly research as whether any of these potential defenses may be available to you.

11.13 Interferents

Since the fuel cell is unresponsive to some interferents that can be found on a subject's breath, like acetone or toluene, attention must be taken when low or zero readings occur on a client who was alleged to have been showing signs of impairment. The impairment could be due to diabetes, intoxicating inhalants such as paint thinner and the like, and/or the result of certain medications. One of these interferents, acetone, is produced in diabetics who have an extremely low blood sugar event. These individuals may become confused, disoriented and have poor balance along with some having spells of passing out. Yet, their BAC reading will be low or non-existent.

PRACTICE TIP: Whenever in doubt, seek the opinion of a qualified medical expert. You may have a client who suffers from medical illness or disease, or has a professional occupation which could provide false indicators of intoxication. Painters or tradesmen that work around paints or toxins that contain toluene can also unknowingly provide false positive breath samples.

11.14 The Operating Environment

Environments with heavy alcohol vapor, cigarette smoke, high levels of radio frequencies, or magnetic interference should be avoided. In addition, these machines are never to be placed in newly painted rooms. Further, the EC/IR-II is not designed for all-weather operation. The ideal environment for its proper use is indoors at room temperature. Prolonged exposure to these types of environmental factors may shorten the life of various components including the fuel cell. And just as with the PBT devices, any tobacco smoke introduced into the chamber will destroy the fuel cell.

11.15 North Carolina Operating Procedures

The North Carolina Department of Health and Human Services Forensic Tests For Alcohol BranchIntox EC/IR-II Manual lists the procedures for conducting a breath test. An operator begins a breath test by observing the accused for at least 15 minutes. The operator must ensure that the accused has not belched, burped, regurgitated, or placed anything in her mouth during this time. The operator then presses the enter key to start the machine and swipes his test operator's license like a credit card. The machine will then confirm whether the operator is licensed. The operator next swipes the accused's driver's license to input the accused's name, date of birth, and sex (this can also be entered manually), and then enters the appropriate jurisdiction and court.

After this information is received, the machine will conduct a diagnostic test. This test is internal and not visible. The manual does not describe what occurs during the Intox EC/IR-II's diagnostic test, but Department reports show that it records barometer readings.

If the diagnostic test shows proper operation, the machine will then "purge" itself. This means that it will open the test chamber to take a sample of air from the room—a "blank check." The operator must remove the mouthpiece while the machine does this. Then the machine will pump in a premeasured gas as a form of simulator. If the machine correctly recognizes the known value of this gas, the machine will do a second purge. This is to ensure that the simulator gas will not contaminate the accused's test.

At this point, the machine is ready for the accused to submit a breath sample. The operator puts a new mouthpiece on the breath tube, and instructs the accused to blow. The machine is looking for alveolar air, and this requires a sample of strong, steady breath. If there is any drop in pressure, the machine will do a quick purge/blank check sequence until it gets the steady breath needed. This can go on for three minutes.

Once the first sample is accepted by the machine, the operator takes off the mouthpiece and allows the machine to complete another purge. This can take up to two minutes. The operator again ensures that the accused has not burped or vomited, and again places the mouthpiece on the tube, and instructs the accused to blow a second time.

If the second sample is accepted, the operator removes the mouthpiece. The machine does a final purge and reports the lowest of the two breath results, truncated to the two digits past the decimal point (neither rounded up nor down). These two test results, filed with the Department and available to counsel, cannot be greater than .02 grams/210 liters apart from one another. If they are, the operator must take a third sample, using the same protocol as before. The lowest truncated result of the three readings will be the final reported test result.

11.16 Operator Instrument Messages

AMBIENT/RFI DETECTED—Radio Frequency Interference or High Ambient conditions detected in the purge cycle of the subject test and the subject test sequence is aborted. "Check Ambient Conditions, Ambient/RFI detected" is displayed on digital display. A certificate of analysis is printed. Identify and eliminate source, restart subject test.

DEFICIENT SAMPLE—Subject did not meet the minimum requirements for a proper breath sample. Subject did not provide a complete breath sample during the 3 minute "Please Blow" prompt. A certificate of analysis is printed and RETEST [Y/N]? is displayed on the instrument.

EXPIRED BADGE—Operator's license is expired. Check license, contact FTA.

INSTRUMENT DISABLED; CERTIFICATION REQUIRED—Contact FTA.

INTERFERENT DETECTED—A chemical other than ethanol was detected on the subject's breath; seek medical attention for the subject.

INVALID SAMPLE—Mouth alcohol detected while subject was providing a breath sample. If retesting the subject, an additional 15 minutes will be observed. A Certificate of Analysis with INVALID SAMPLE is printed and RETEST [Y/N]? is displayed on the instrument.

NO SAMPLE GIVEN—No pressure detected by the instrument during the 3 minute "Please Blow" prompt. Subject did not provide a sample. A Certificate of Analysis with NO SAMPLE GIVEN is printed and RETEST [Y/N]? is displayed on the instrument.

OPERATOR ABORT—Operator stopped subject test. If aborted after the diagnostics were complete, the instrument will not allow another test to be run on that subject for 15 minutes.

OUT OF TOLERANCE—Dry gas standard out of range (greater than ±5% of the target). Restart the subject test. After the second OUT OF TOLERANCE the instrument will disable itself and will contact FTA.

PRINTER OFFLINE—Printer attached to instrument is offline, check the printer.

PAPER OUT—Check printer to ensure it has Certificates loaded.

REMOTE ACCESS—DFS is in contact with the instrument.

RETEST [Y/N]?—This message is displayed for 25 minutes after the DEFICIENT SAMPLE, NO SAMPLE GIVEN, and INVALID SAMPLE instrument messages. If 'Y' is pressed, the instrument will go through diagnostics and prompt the subject to "Please Blow." If 'N' is pressed the instrument returns to Scroll Mode. After an INVALID SAMPLE message, an additional 15 minute observation period will be required for the subject. If neither 'Y' nor 'N' is chosen during the 25 minute prompt, the instrument automatically resets to Scroll Mode.

SAMPLE PARAMETERS NOT MET—There was no .02 agreement between the three breath samples provided by the subject. Restart the subject test.

SEQUENCE—Incorrect sequence during the subject test. Restart the subject test.

TEST RESULT OVER RANGE/SAMPLE RESULT OVER RANGE—Results exceed upper limit of the instrument (0.000-0.400 g/210L.) Seek medical attention for the subject.

PRACTICE TIP: Certain lung ailments, such as emphysema, can be the cause of an "insufficient sample" reading because the individual cannot provide the required volume of breath for the machine to respond. In these instances an officer might allege that your client "refused" the breath test, when in actuality she simply could not produce the required volume of air for breath sample analysis. Thus, it is imperative to know every aspect of your client's medical history.

11.17 Maintenance

The EC/IR-II must be placed on a hard surface (usually a desktop) in a location that is properly ventilated and at least 1 inch from a back wall so as not to interfere with the cooling fan of the breath chamber exit tube seen on the back in Figure 11.20. The machine is never to be covered by anything, such as a blanket or rug or dust cover. The machine must neither be exposed to extreme temperatures nor be placed in areas of extremely high or low humidity. The machine's operational temperature is to be between 50°F and 105°F. Placing the machine in close proximity to various radio frequency devices is not recommended either. A weekly test (F2 function key) with a breath sample is factory advised so as to help maintain requisite moisture in the fuel cell.

PRACTICE TIP: Consider filing a motion with the trial court for a view of the area in which the designated machine is located. You may find the placement of the machine to be in violation of the factory mandates. This of course provides areas of defense attack on the offered BAC sample and machine credibility, generally. Further, file a motion requesting when the last time an "F2 test" was conducted, as recommended in the factory manual for proper operation of the machine so as to help maintain moisture in the fuel cell. Again, this could well be fertile ground for a defense attack on the offered BAC sample and BAC result credibility.

11.18 Breath Testing: Methods of Attack

There are three areas of attack on any breath test presented by the prosecution. They are machine-based, operator-based, and subject-based.

Machine-based attacks

a. Intermittent problems

Intermittent problems include vibrations to the machine while it is working, inadequate or improper power supplies, bad chopper motors and fluctuating DVM. Some Intoxilyzers are used in the back of patrol cars or inside vans. In addition to the inherent vibration associated with a running engine, power supplies can fluctuate as well. Watch for calibration logs from these mobile machines. Often they are removed from the vehicle and tested inside a building with a stable power source.

b. Warranty

The breath testing device may not be warranted to test breath. Intoximeters does not warrant that any of its devices will test breath for alcohol accurately or reliably. The company simply warrants that the device is free from defects in material and workmanship for only 12 months from the invoice date. The warranty is available at Intoximeters' website. Introduce the warranty at trial with your expert witness, then leave it alone until closing argument when you can say to the jury—"And the manufacturer of this machine doesn't

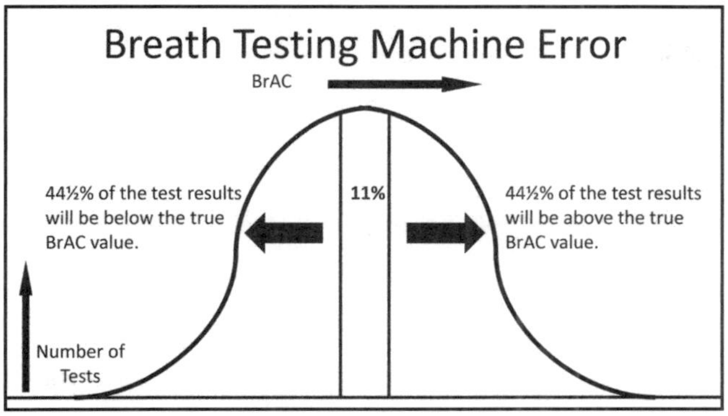

Figure 11.22 *At a 10 percent margin of error, if we run 1,000 tests using a simulator and plot them on a graph, 44.5 percent of the test results will be below the true BrAC value and 44.5 percent of the test results will be above the true BrAC value. But, it will only be "spot-on" accurate 11 percent of the time.*

even warrant that it will test breath accurately. Do you want to place your trust in that machine?"

c. Inherent margin of error

As stated, the purpose of the dry gas standard is to produce a sample gas of known ethanol concentration for use as a reference in a standard check on the EC/IR-II. The purpose of this standard check, in theory and design, is to ensure and demonstrate that the instrument is working properly when conducting a breath test. In accordance with the Bureau of Public Health, the reference standard check on dry gas is "accepted" if the reading on the EC/IR-II is 0.07 to 0.08. As such, always scrutinize these margins.

d. Stipulated accuracy/uncertainty range by manufacturer

North Carolina claims that their instruments will maintain a calibration of ±.005 at .100 g/210L from six months to more than one year. It is not clear what this means as that standard differs from state to state. For example, the Illinois EC/IR-II Manual states on page 3: "The Intox EC/IR-II is accurate to within ±.005 at .100 g/210L, or ±5%, whichever is greater." It seems that DFS is claiming that the uncertainty at .08 g/210L is ±.002, at .15 g/210L is ±.005 and at .25 is ±.006 g/210L. Obviously this differs from Illinois and it is also known that some of the basic assumptions of the machine are incorrect. It is doubtful that these claims would hold up when analyzed by an expert.

f. Radio Frequency Interference (RFI)

Probably the most overlooked and improperly used attack is RFI. RFI is an electromagnetic wave. We think of it most frequently as a police radio transmitting near a breath tester during the administration of a test. But that is not the most frequent source of RFI during a subject test. RFI is generated whenever and wherever an electric motor is running

g. Software and Source Code Issues

Software and source code issues have swept through some state courts as a challenge to the admissibility of breath test results, and the North Carolina Court of Appeals in State v. Marino 747 S.E.2d 633 (2013) rejected the defendant's argument that it violated the defendant's right to sixth amendment right to confrontation and ruled that it was not Brady material. The Court also said that the defendant had no right to pretrial discovery in a case appealed to Superior Court from District Court.

Source code is the human-readable version of software. Source code is the set of instructions for a particular device to operate; however, source code is unreadable by the computerized device because the device cannot read human language. The computerized device can only read and understand "machine language" which is also called "machine code," "firmware" or "software."

Source code is converted to software by another piece of software called a "compiler." Once converted, the software is burned onto a chip which is then installed in the target device—in this case, an Intoximeter® EC/IR-II. The chip from an EC/IR-II can easily be removed and the software contained in it can be stored onto a personal computer. The software can then be downloaded to a new chip in a commercially-available chip copier. If one were to obtain an EC/IR-II and make an exact replica of it, one could install the copied chip into the EC/IR-II copy and it should work exactly as the original. In fact, when one finds cheap foreign knock-offs of computerized goods, this is the typical way it is done. The blank chip itself is commercially available.

The source code for the EC/IR-II is not inside of the machine. Instead, the source code is kept by Intoximeters. There is no way to reverse-engineer the software to obtain the source code. When presented with requests for software, manufacturers almost uniformly complain that they cannot release the source code because it is a trade secret.

Assuming, arguendo, that the source code is a trade secret, however, this should not be a bar to disclosure in the right case. Federal law defines "fair use" of protected ideas under 17 U.S.C.A. §107. The statute states that use for purposes of "criticism" and "comment" are "not an infringement of copyright." The Code (17 U.S.C.A. §107) reads as follows:

> Notwithstanding the provisions of 106 and 106A, the fair use of copyrighted work, including such use by reproduction in copies or phonorecords or by any other means specified by that section, for purposes such as criticism, comment, news reporting, teaching (including multiple copies for classroom use), scholarship, or research, is not an infringement of copyright. In determining whether the use made of a work in any particular case is a fair use the factors to be considered shall include—
>
> (1) the purpose and character of the use, including whether such use is of a commercial nature or is for non-profit educational purposes;
> (2) the nature of the copyrighted work;
> (3) the amount and substantiality of the portion used in relation to the copyrighted work as a whole; and
> (4) the effect of the use upon the potential market for or value of the copyrighted work.

The use of allegedly confidential church documents by a plaintiff in a state tort action against a church was "fair use" and was not an infringement of copyright. The documents *were provided to expert witnesses in preparation of testimony* and were not used for any other purpose. *Religious Technology Center v. Wollershein,* 971 F.2d 364 (Cal. 1992).

In *Jartech, Inc. v. Clancy*, 666 F.2d 403, 213 U.S.P.Q. 1057, certiorari denied 103 S.Ct. 175, 459 U.S. 879, 74 L.Ed.2d 143, rehearing denied 103 S.Ct. 477, 459 U.S. 1059, 74 L.Ed.2d 1453, certiorari denied 103 S.Ct. 58, 459 U.S. 826, 74 L.Ed.2d 62, rehearing denied 103 S.Ct. 477, 459 U.S. 1058, 74 L.Ed.2d 624, certiorari denied 103 S.Ct. 59, 459 U.S. 826, 74 L.Ed.2d 62, the alleged copyright infringers made abbreviated copies of some films, not for subsequent use and enjoyment, but for evidence to be used in litigation. The use was held to be neither commercially exploitive of the copyright, nor commercially exploitive of the copyright holder's market.

Fair use even extends to disassembly of software and competition. In a reverse-engineering case, the federal courts have held that software can be "reverse engineered" under the Fair Use Doctrine. Take, for example, the case of *Sega Enterprises Ltd. v. Accolade, Inc.* C.A.9 (Cal.) 1992, 977 F.2d 1510, 24 U.S.P.Q.2d 1561, where the court found that the disassembly of computer object code of a copyrighted program was fair use of the copyrighted work, where disassembly was the only way to gain access to the ideas and functional elements embodied in the copyrighted program. Copying was performed for the purpose of competition in the marketplace for works of the same type. This case is very instructive, because if a copyrighted work can be disassembled for purposes of competition, then an uncopyrighted work can certainly be disclosed for purposes of the Sixth Amendment right to confrontation.

In *Atari Games Corp. v. Nintendo of North America Inc.*, C.A.Fed. (Cal.) 1992, 975 F.2d 832, 24 U.S.P.Q.2d 1015, rehearing denied, en banc suggestion declined, reverse engineering of the object code to discern unprotected ideas in the computer program for the purpose of understanding the ideas contained therein, was declared fair use.

The significant element of a trade secret is that it is *secret*. No hardware contained in the machine is a trade secret simply because of the fact that CMI has sold hundreds of Intoxilyzer 8000s to the State of Arizona and thousands nationwide. Most of their parts are from outside vendors and are patented, such as the light source and detectors. The operational and analytical principles are not only widely known, but are advertised by CMI. No data or software contained on the removable chip inside the machine is a trade secret because any purchaser can remove the chip and copy it without much difficulty.

Operator-based attacks

a. Inadequate deprivation period

Operators must ensure that the test subject has not ingested any alcoholic beverages or other fluids, vomited, eaten, smoked, or placed any foreign object in the mouth for at least 15 minutes immediately preceding the first sample. Anything less falls short of national standards where the operator must not only ensure that none of these things occur but must also watch the subject continuously for at least 15 minutes to ensure that the test subject has not burped. Technically (and in reality), police can place the subject in the back of a patrol car and know that the person has not put anything into his mouth because of being handcuffed behind the back; and that is good enough for government work—but is that good enough for a jury?

c. Breath holding

Operators are supposed to instruct subjects to take a deep breath and then immediately blow all of their breath into the machine. For officer safety, the police officers are instructed to hold the breath tube while the subject is blowing and not let the subject handle the breath hose. This is because the Intoximeter EC/IR-II can be used as a weapon by an uncooperative subject. Some subjects have been known to grab an Intoximeter EC/IR-II by the hose and swing it around, injuring the officer.

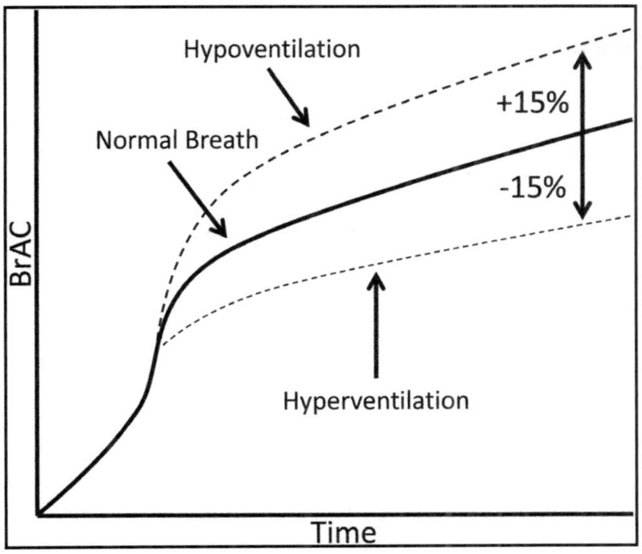

Figure 11.23

This instruction to the officer about holding the breath hose has led to both intentional and unintentional breath holding. An officer who wishes to make the breath test result higher may ask the subject to take a deep breath and then blow it into the machine as directed. The subject then takes a deep breath, but the officer does not immediately present the breath hose to the subject. Instead, the officer will hold onto the breath hose for a few moments while the subject is holding her breath. This can cause a heightened, inaccurate BAC reading than what is actually present.

Subject-based attacks

a. Breathing patterns

Hyperventilation and hypoventilation will cause as much as a ±15 percent variation in a breath test result (Jones, 1990). The longer a person holds her breath, the higher the result. Short, rapid breaths tend to flush out the lungs and result in a lower reading (see Figure 11.23).

This variance is most often seen when an operator has a subject hold her breath and then delays giving her the breath tube or when a subject is upset to the point of crying or nearly crying. People who are crying generally are not breathing in a normal pattern—which is required for accurate breath testing. The crying subject may take deep breaths and hold them or may also have short, shallow, rapid breathing. In any event, a crying subject is likely not breathing as expected for an evidential breath test.

b. Temperature

Temperature variations in the human body can change the amount of alcohol that is transferred from the blood to the breath. The amount of alcohol that passes from the blood into the breath is similar to that found in *Henry's Law of Partial Pressures*, which is the cornerstone of forensic breath testing.

Henry's Law—Assume a closed system and constant temperature. After a period of time, some of the molecules of the liquid will have moved into the gaseous phase in the headspace above that liquid. The number of molecules that have passed into the gaseous phase will be directly proportional to the number of molecules remaining in the liquid.

The concept is simple. The hotter a liquid, the more molecules of that liquid will pass into the gaseous phase. Take, for example, a small room with a very cold cup of black coffee sitting on a table in that room. It is likely that you would not smell the coffee unless you put your nose right at the lip of the cup. Take the same example, but substitute a steaming cup of coffee. Within minutes, the room would be filled with the coffee's aroma. This is because more molecules of the hot coffee passed into the gaseous phase and filled the room.

Every breath testing unit in the United States is programmed to expect a breath temperature of 34°C, but what they most often get is a breath temperature of 35°C. This is because breath testing machines were programmed based on a very small study of end-expired breath temperature. In 1950, Harger adopted a breath temperature of 34°C; however his study listed only six subjects. The range was 31°C to 35°C. In 1995, Schoknecht adopted a breath temperature that was a full degree centigrade higher than Harger's reported average temperature. Schoknecht adopted 35°C as the average human breath-temperature. The range was 33°C to 36.7°C. There were 700 subjects in that study.

Each degree centigrade of variance equates to 8.6 percent variance in the breath test result (see Fox and Hayward, 1989; Jones, 1990). Thus, someone with a .075 BAC will test at a .081 BAC if breath temperature is 35°C.

The IACT (International Association of Chemical Testers) Newsletter carried an article by Dr. Dale Carpenter and Dr. James A. Buttram (Carpenter and Buttram, 1998), which shows that while 34°C is the accepted breath temperature for breath testing, the human range starts at 31°C and rises to 35°C, with the average being 35°C. The argument is that if your client is the average human being, she is 1°C higher than what the machine is programmed to expect. Thus, the jury can give your client that extra 8.6 percent in addition to any other rises in temperature due to illness, infection or menstrual cycles.

c. Hematocrit

Hematocrit is a number expressing the size and number of red blood cells in proportion to rest of the blood. Hematocrit ratios vary in healthy human beings from 40.7 to 50 percent in men, and 36.1 to 44.3 percent in women. It can vary with altitude, illness, and state of hydration. The hematocrit level governs how much alcohol may be contained by the blood and, in turn, how much will pass into the breath. Normal hematocrit ratios will lead to a ±5 percent difference in a breath test result (Labianca, 1990; Payne et al., 1968; Smith, 1987).

d. Abnormal lung physiology

All breath testing machines are designed to test breath from average, healthy humans. When you have abnormal lung physiology, consult heavily with your expert witness before trial. Abnormal lung physiology could have three possible outcomes: raising the reported BAC, lowering the reported BAC or having no effect on the reported BAC. Sometimes you will know that your client has abnormal lung physiology, but you will not know what the result might be of that type of abnormal lung physiology—it might make the BAC higher or lower—but isn't that the essence of reasonable doubt?

e. Mouth alcohol

Mouth alcohol is residual alcohol that remains in the mouth after drinking or is introduced into the mouth via regurgitation. In either event, mouth alcohol can increase the result of a breath test result. The slope detector is a software program that looks at the slope of the graph of the ethanol in breath profile. If the slope does not fall within the parameters of the slope programmed into the device, the software is supposed to flag it as mouth alcohol, alert the operator and abort the test. The operator must conduct a new deprivation period before the next test. The three main parameters that must be followed to assure a valid test, free from the influence of mouth alcohol, are:

- A valid deprivation period.
- A working slope detector.
- Sample agreement within a scientifically accepted amount at sufficiently different times.

If any one of these three parameters is not met, scientific confidence in the validity of the results is lessened, and the test results may be inadmissible. The QAR should reflect a tested and working slope detector, and the breath test cards should reflect sample agreement of no more than .02 apart and consecutive tests within 5 to 10 minutes of each other.

Although a 15-minute deprivation period is required by Arizona law, 15 minutes may not be long enough. In a recent scientific study, "The Slope Detector Does Not Always Detect the Presence of Mouth Alcohol," *The Champion*, March, 2006, Dr. Michael P. Hlastala, Wayne J. E. Lamm, and James Nesci reported findings which showed that mouth alcohol can more than double the true breath test result in subjects who had consumed alcohol and go unnoticed by slope detectors in both the Intoxilyzer 5000 and the BAC Datamaster.

This confirms a long-held belief by many members of the DWI defense community—the manner of testing the slope detector by the state is inadequate. Normally, a technician has no alcohol in his system at the time of the quality assurance testing. The technician will swish an alcohol-containing liquid or spray Binaca® into his mouth, then blow into the machine to test the slope detector. Almost invariably, the slope does not fit the profile of a normal breath test slope, and the machine will flag it as mouth alcohol. However, the profile of the slope of an alcohol-free subject does not match the slope of a person who has a measurable BrAC *and* mouth alcohol. In fact, the breath profile of a person with a measurable BrAC and mouth alcohol will more likely fit the profile of a normal breath profile than will the alcohol-free subject with mouth alcohol. This will lead to false-positive readings for some individuals as seen in Figure 11.24. Breath test results that are contaminated with mouth-alcohol will always be higher than an uncontaminated sample.

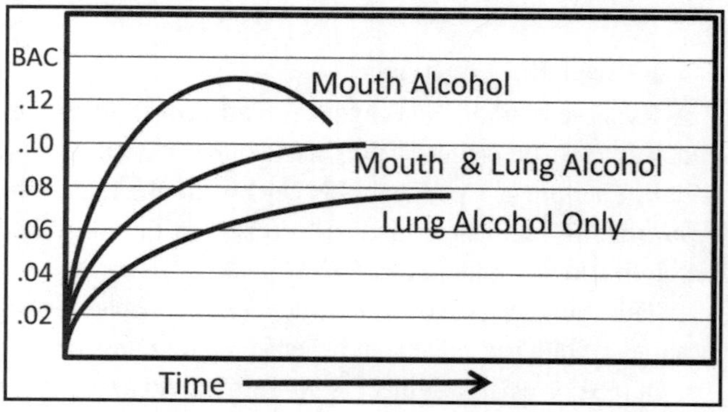

Figure 11.24

Dentures and Gastroesophogeal Reflux Disease (GERD) can contribute to mouth alcohol. The conclusion of the article was that a 15-minute deprivation period must be maintained with at least 15 minutes between replicate samples, agreeing by no more than .02.

f. Partition ratio

In courtrooms that still allow the truth to be told to juries, partition ratio can be a very powerful argument. All breath testing machines in the United States are set to a partition ratio of 2100:1. In other words, for every one part of alcohol in a subject's breath, the machine is programmed to assume that there is another 2,100 parts in the blood. Thus, the machines perform a mathematical calculation to convert a breath alcohol concentration to a blood alcohol concentration and display the results in grams of alcohol per 210 liters of blood. This would be fine if all human beings had a constant partition ratio of 2100:1. We do not. The normal, healthy human body varies from 900:1 to about 3400:1 (see Alobaidi et al., 1976; Mason, 1976; Yamamoto and Ueda, 1972).

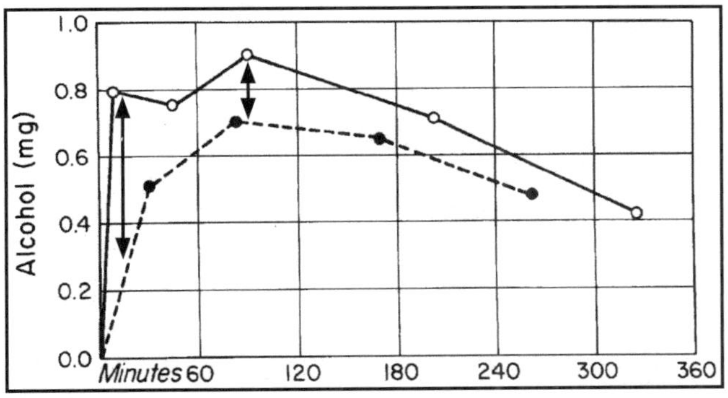

Figure 11.25 *Blood (dashed line, mg/cm³) and breath (solid line, mg/2l) alcohol concentrations after oral administration of alcohol to a subject. At about 15 minutes into absorption, the breath overestimates blood by almost four times. Even at about 90 minutes, the subject's breath is about a .090, while the subject's blood is significantly under the per se limit at about a .070 (Widmark, 1981).*

PRACTICE TIP: Conversion to different partition ratios is a simple mathematical formula. Take the breath test reading and divide it by 2,100 then multiply by the new partition ratio number that you have chosen. This will give the corrected breath test value.

Example

To convert a .100 BAC at 2100:1 to a new ratio of 1500:1 use the formula:

Step 1: (BAC Reading) ÷ 2100 = Y

Step 2:

Y × (New Partition Ratio Value) = Corrected Breath Test Value

Step 1: .100 BAC ÷ 2100 = 0.00004762

Step 2: 0.00004762 × 1500 = .071 BAC

Thus a .080 BAC at 1100:1 could be corrected to .042, and a .080 BAC at 2800:1 could be corrected to .107.

11.19 Calibration

Wet-bath simulators

Guth Laboratories makes simulators used all over the country. A simulator is used for calibration checks of the various breath testing machines and is supposed to simulate human breath.

The simulator consists of a glass jar about the size and shape of a typical peanut butter jar (see Figure 11.26). The jar is filled about two-thirds with a simulator solution which may be made by the lab or purchased through a commercial vendor. The jar is sealed, and the solution is heated and stirred by the apparatus screwed to the top of the jar. Temperature is monitored and automatically adjusted by the simulator.

At the top of the apparatus are two ports. One port is for the headspace vapor to be transferred to the breath testing machine and the other is for return of the vapor to the simulator. The simulator has no air pump—it relies on the breath testing machine's air pump to regulate flow of the headspace vapor.

The theory is that the simulator solution, when heated to 34°C, will release a vapor equivalent to 0.08%. This means that the simulator solution must be at a concentration higher than the headspace vapor. The mathematical formula used to determine the headspace concentration of an aqueous alcohol simulator solution at 34°C is:

$$\frac{\chi}{.121} \times .10 = \Omega$$

Where

χ = reported value from gas chromatograph of the liquid solution

Ω = headspace gas value at 34°C

Thus;

Value of the Alcohol Solution (χ)	Headspace Gas Value at 34°C (Ω)
.085	.070
.091	.075
.097	.080
.103	.085
.109	.090
.121	.100
.133	.110

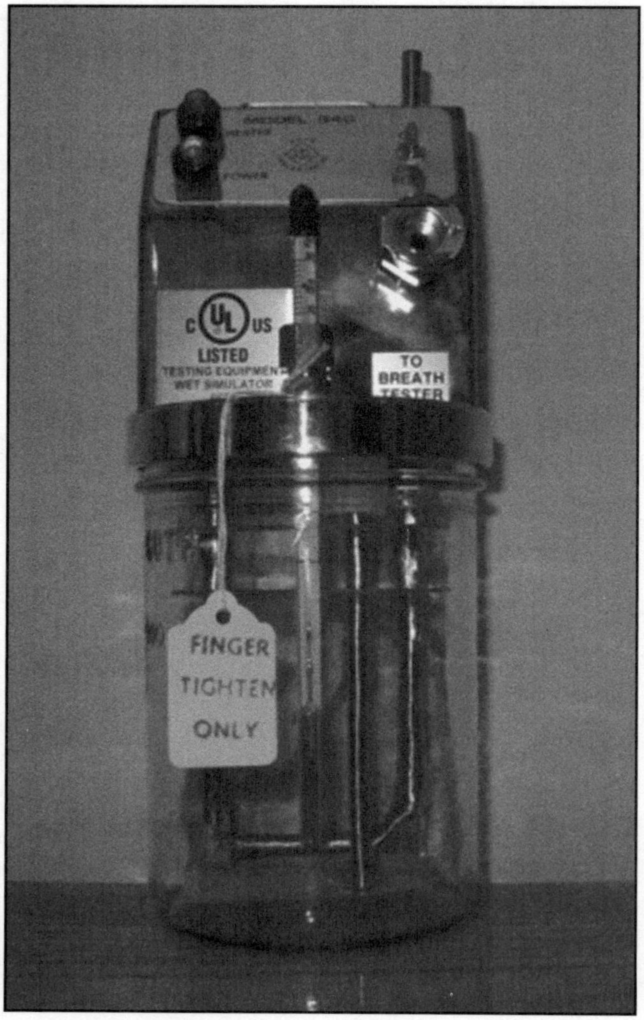

Figure 11.26 *Guth model 34C wet-bath simulator*

The value of the simulator solution is an important component of the overall discovery process in any breath test case. The lab must use a solution of known value in order to test the breath testing machine. The calibration logs rarely show anything other than a .080 or .10 solution as being used, but there are surprising variances from that number found when the simulator solution used is actually checked. This is most often a result of poor lab procedures when the solution is made in-house, rather than being purchased from a reputable supplier. Additionally, overuse of the solution can contribute to problems. The concentration of alcohol in the solution depletes with use and over time. Some agencies are simply too cheap to replace the solutions as necessary. Typically, the solution is checked by way of a headspace gas chromatograph, if it is checked at all. Sometimes the crime labs will simply rely on the claims of the manufacturer of the solution for accuracy.

In addition to possible problems with the solution, the simulator itself may be suspect. Guth makes simulators and guarantees them to be accurate when shipped, but if the crime lab ignores proper maintenance, care and use procedures, the simulator's accuracy will be compromised. Some improper maintenance procedures include replacing broken thermometers with lesser quality (and less accurate) thermometers, contamination of the simulator sample with cleaning agents such as acetone, toluene and other compounds, and heaters that go bad intermittently (some simulators have an alarm to alert the operator of an improper temperature—others require the operator to be vigilant). The bottom line is: no matter how high the quality of the simulator, it must be maintained and used properly to expect accurate and reproducible results.

Dry-gas standards

When a dry-gas standard is used to calibrate or check calibration of a device, an altitude correction must be made. This is not necessary for a wet-bath simulator because the wet-bath system will be adjusted to the barometric pressure due to the nature of the system itself. The dry-gas, however, comes from a sealed, pressurized tank and the concentration of alcohol contained in the inert gas (nitrogen) is dependent on pressure. The altitude correction chart below should be used to figure conversion rates. The math is quite simple.

If the dry-gas standard used has a value of .080 BAC at sea level but is being used at an altitude of 2,500 feet, the correction factor applied would be .907. In order to correct the value of the dry-gas standard to 2,500 feet, one would multiply the BAC at sea level by the altitude correction factor (.080 × .907 = .073 BAC). Thus, a dry-gas standard of .080 will read as a .073 at 2,500 feet.

Be aware that some instruments, such as the Intoxilyzer 5000EN and the Intoxilyzer 8000, have an automatic altitude compensation feature, so altitude correction is not necessary.

Altitude Correction Chart

Elevation from Sea Level	Correction Factor
0	1.000
500	.981
1000	.962
1500	.943
2000	.925
2500	.907
3000	.889
3500	.872
4000	.854

4500	.837
5000	.820
5500	.804
6000	.787
6500	.771
7000	.755
7500	.740
8000	.724

Source: CMI, Inc.

The dry-gas standard will usually be contained in a "SCOTTY® Tank" manufactured by Scott Specialty Gases. Scott dry-gas standards are traceable to N.I.S.T. which assures the high quality of its product. The tank will contain an expiration date, altitude correction chart and lot number. Typically, crime labs will use the SCOTTY 105 tank that holds 105 liters of gas at a pressure of about 1,000 psi. Unlike a wet-bath simulator, there is no specific temperature requirement for the dry-gas standard.

11.20 North Carolina Administrative Code on Breath Testing

10A NCAC 41B .0313 BREATH-TESTING INSTRUMENTS: REPORTING OF SEQUENTIAL TESTS

The Department approves breath-testing instruments listed on the National Highway Traffic Safety Administration, Conforming Products List of Evidential Breath Measurement Devices. Instruments are approved on the basis of results of evaluations by the Forensic Tests for Alcohol Branch. Evaluations are not limited in scope and may include any factors deemed appropriate to ensure the accuracy, reliability, stability, cost, and ease of operation and durability of the instrument being evaluated. History Note: Authority G.S. 20-16.5(j); 20-139.1(b); Eff. January 1, 1982; Amended Eff. May 1, 2007; April 1, 1993; September 1, 1990; March 1, 1989;

10A NCAC 41B .0322 INTOXIMETERS: MODEL INTOX EC/IR II

The operational procedures to be followed in using the Intoximeters, Model Intox EC/IR II are: (1) Insure instrument displays time and date; (2) Insure observation period requirements have been met; (3) Initiate breath test sequence; (4) Enter information as prompted; (5) Verify instrument accuracy; (6) When "PLEASE BLOW" appears, collect breath sample; (7) When "PLEASE BLOW" appears, collect breath sample; and (8) Print test record. If the alcohol concentrations differ by more than 0.02, a third or fourth breath sample shall be collected when "PLEASE BLOW" appears. Subsequent tests shall be administered as soon as feasible by repeating steps (1) through (8), as applicable. History Note: G.S. 20-139.1(b); Eff. November 1, 2007.December 1, 1987.

10A NCAC 41B .0323 PREVENTIVE MAINTENANCE: INTOXIMETERS: MODEL INTOX EC/IR II

The preventive maintenance procedures for the Intoximeters, Model Intox EC/IR II to be followed at least once every four months are: (1) Verify the ethanol gas canister displays pressure, or the alcoholic breath simulator thermometer shows 34 degrees, plus or minus .2 degree centigrade; (2) Verify instrument displays time and date; (3) Initiate breath test sequence; (4) Enter information as prompted; (5) Verify instrument accuracy; (6) When "PLEASE BLOW" appears, collect breath sample; (7) When "PLEASE BLOW" appears, collect breath sample; (8) Print test record; (9) Verify Diagnostic Program; and (10) Verify that the ethanol gas canister is being changed before expiration date, or the alcoholic breath simulator solution is being changed every four months or after 125 Alcoholic Breath Simulator tests, whichever occurs first. A signed original of the preventive maintenance record shall be kept on file for at least three years. History Note: G.S. 20-139.1(b2); Eff. November 1, 2007.

11.21 Blood Testing: From the Vein to the Lab

Health issues and allergies

A phlebotomist should always ask the subject about health issues regarding blood clotting, blood pressure and blood-borne diseases. The subject must also be asked about allergies, especially to latex, povidone iodine and shellfish (some people do not know that they are allergic to iodine, but shellfish contains a great deal of iodine, and if they are allergic to shellfish, they are likely allergic to iodine). A latex band is used as a tourniquet, hence the reason that the subject should be asked about latex allergies.

Proper site selection

In order to draw blood properly, a phlebotomist must first check for a suitable vein to puncture. Improper draw sites include the arm on the side of a mastectomy, scarred areas, arms with fistulas or vascular grafts, sites above an IV cannula, edematous areas and hematomas. The best sites for venipuncture are the superficial veins on the mid-to-upper arm including the median cubital vein found at the inside of the elbow. Also used is the cephalic vein, which can be found toward the top of the upper forearm and runs all the way up to the biceps. Another location is the basilic vein, found at the bottom side of the forearm near the median cubital vein. The back of the hand may also be used, but it may be especially painful. There are reports of police using the back of the hand as the first choice because it is easier for the officer to find a vein. There are also reports of officers using especially large-gauge needles because it allows a faster blood draw, despite the increased pain to the subject.

Once the vein is selected, the phlebotomist will wrap a latex band around the subject's arm. This causes the vein to bulge slightly because the heart can more easily pump blood through the arteries into the lower arm, but the latex band restricts blood flow back to the heart. Pressure builds in the vein and it expands, making it easier to find and puncture the vein to draw blood.

Subject positioning

Proper phlebotomy requires that the subject should be seated (or lying down) in a suitable chair that allows easy access to the arms. Care should be taken to ensure that if the subject passes out she will not fall to the ground. Contrast this scenario with the many reports of police drawing blood from subjects who are standing, unsupported, by the side of the roadway. The chair and surrounding area of the blood draw should be cleaned and disinfected with a suitable non-alcoholic anti-bacterial agent.

Proper officer and phlebotomist safety precautions need to be taken as well. The subject will be under arrest at this point and could be unpredictable, uncooperative and even violent. Sharp instruments will be used to complete a medical procedure. The potential for injury to officers, the phlebotomist and the subject exists which is clearly a reason that the subject should be taken to a hospital where a real, neutral phlebotomist can draw blood in an environment that is sanitary and safe for all parties.

The blood kit

The expiration date of the tubes should always be checked. The preservative and anti-coagulant do not lose potency after expiration, but the seal on the tube is not guaranteed. This means that room air could leak into the tube through a compromised seal, bringing with it Candida albicans or other contaminants. The antiseptic swab also has an expiration date crimped into the bottom edge of its foil wrapper. The tubes should be grey-topped, 10 mL tubes. BD Vacutainer® is a brand of vacuum tubes made by Becton, Dickinson and Company (BD) and is the most common type found in blood kits. BD, however, does not create the blood draw kit. Many kits are created by N.I.K., Public Safety, Inc., which is a division of Armor Holdings. Arizona also uses blood kits created by the Lynn Peavey Company and Tri-Tech (see Figures 11.27-11.29).

N.I.K., Lynn Peavey and Tri-Tech gather components from different manufacturers and assemble the kits. Some agencies actually gather their own components and assemble the kits themselves. One needs to be aware of the fact that some police agencies actually remove instructions supplied by the purveyor of the kit. Others simply do not include any instructions when assembling the kits. This prevents a defense attack when the officer or phlebotomist does not follow the instructions provided by the manufacturer.

Tri-Tech kits generally come with a Monoject® needle made by Tyco Healthcare Group in Mansfield, Massachusetts. N.I.K. and Lynn Peavey kits come with BD needles made by Becton Dickinson in Franklin Lakes, New Jersey. It is important to note that N.I.K. states in some of its kit literature that BD Vacutainer tubes should only be used with the other parts of the kit while Tri-Tech has no such requirements.

The grey top of the tube indicates a preservative and anti-coagulant has been added to the tube. Grey-top tubes are used in the medical world for glucose testing procedures and were not developed strictly for law enforcement purposes.

The preservative (or "antiglycolytic" agent) in a grey-top tube is sodium fluoride (chemical symbol: Na_2). The anticoagulant may be either EDTA (potassium edetate) or potassium oxalate. Note that tubes with sodium fluoride and EDTA have a white powder in the tube, while those with sodium fluoride and potassium oxalate generally have a slightly pinkish colored powder.

Other types of tubes are sometimes used when a forensic kit is unavailable. These must be scrutinized carefully for their chemical contents. As if the differing color tops were not confusing enough, the material used for the container makes a difference. Red-top glass tubes, for example, contain no chemicals. Red-top plastic tubes contain a clot-activator only.

Grey-top BD Vacutainer tubes come in three varieties with two different types of grey tops. They may contain sodium fluoride and potassium oxalate, or sodium fluoride and EDTA, or sodium fluoride alone. The latter of the three tubes is a serum tube and contains no anticoagulant. The grey tops, themselves, may be either a traditional stopper or a Hemogard® closure. Note that traditional stoppers are less expensive, and therefore more commonly seen.

The N.I.K. 4990 kit contains two 10 mL grey-top Vacutainers, each containing 20 mg of sodium fluoride and 10 mg of EDTA, while both the N.I.K. 4994 kit and the Lynn Peavey kit contain two 10 mL grey-top Vacutainers, each containing 100 mg of sodium fluoride and 20 mg of potassium oxalate. The N.I.K. 4994 kit and the Lynn Peavey kits were designed to meet the requirements of states mandating, by law, that sodium fluoride be at least 1% of the 10 mL blood sample. A lower-strength solution results in a lower price for the Vacutainers used in the kits. Whether it results in lower protections for the blood-draw subject is an issue to be argued to the jury.

Note in Figure 11.30 that the four tubes are different despite the fact that they are all 10 mL grey-top tubes used for law enforcement. From left to right we see a BD Vacutainer with EDTA and sodium fluoride designed to give a 1%-strength solution (N.I.K. 4990 and Lynn-Peavey). The second from the left is another BD Vacutainer with sodium fluoride and potassium oxalate, designed to create a 2%-strength solution (N.I.K. 4994 and Lynn-Peavey). Third from the left is a Monoject tube with sodium fluoride and potassium oxalate, designed to create a 1%-strength solution (various police-assembled kits). Lastly, on the far right is a Tri-Tech tube with sodium fluoride and potassium oxalate, designed to create a 2%-strength solution (Tri-Tech).

Site cleansing

The phlebotomist disinfects the draw site with povidone iodine unless the person is allergic to iodine. If so, then another non-alcoholic cleansing agent should be used. Wiping must be done in concentric circles moving outward from the intended puncture site, otherwise the bacteria is just being pushed around, not removed.

If the phlebotomist does not wipe the area properly, bacteria (Candida albicans) can be sucked into the Vacutainer. Candida is everywhere. It is a yeast. When yeast and sugars (as in blood) mix, there could be fermentation, creating ethyl alcohol. This is indistinguishable from the ethyl alcohol allegedly consumed. The blood tube, however, could be tested for presence of Candida.

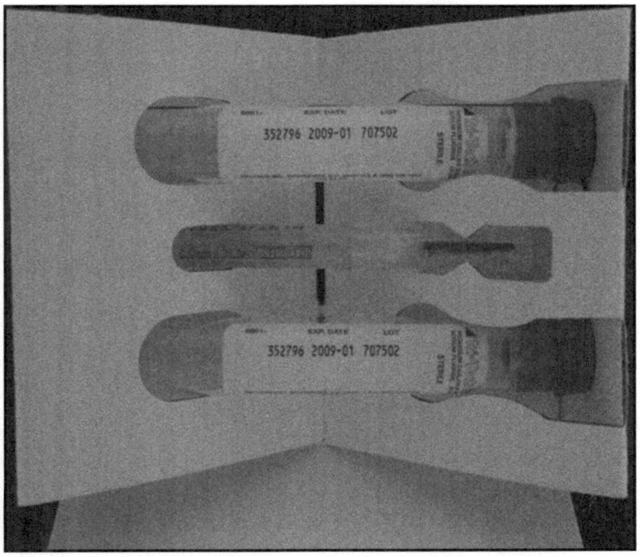

Figure 11.27 *Tri-Tech blood kit*

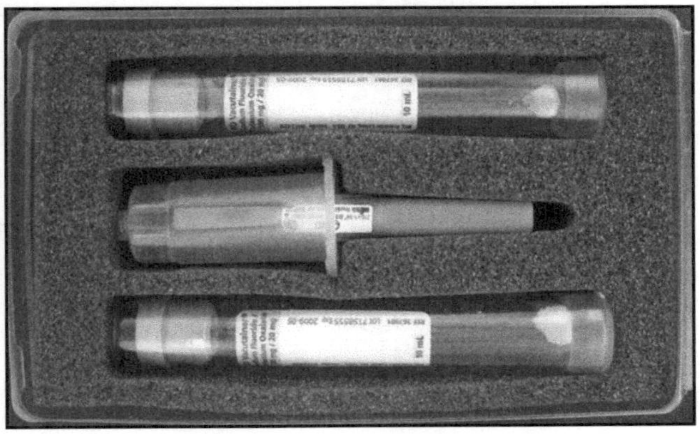

Figure 11.28 *Lynn-Peavey blood kit*

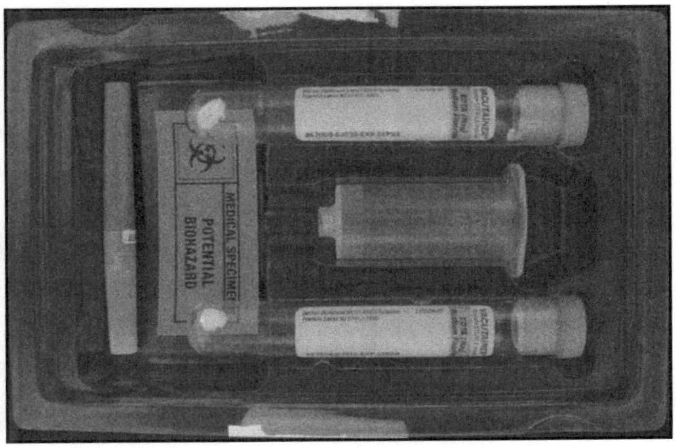

Figure 11.29 *NIK blood kit*

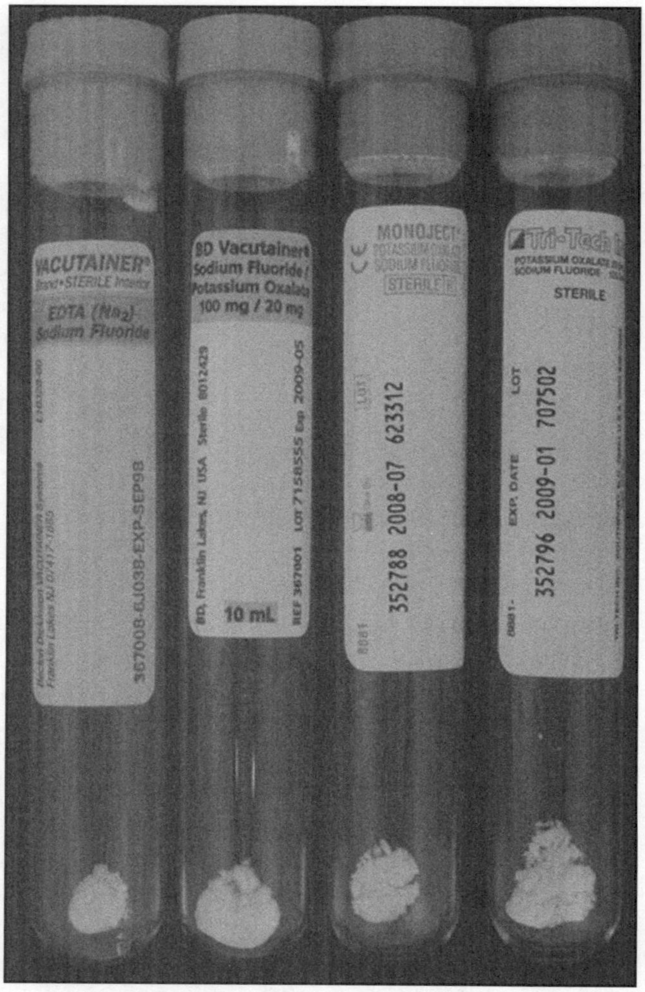

Figure 11.30 *(l – r) Two types of BD Vacutainer, Monoject blood tube, Tri-Tech blood tube.*

The blood draw

The phlebotomist will thread the safety needle supplied with the kit onto the hub until it is firmly seated. Note that a safety needle is double-ended (see Figure 11.31). One end punctures the vein while the other end punctures the stopper on the blood tube, breaking the seal. Note that the end of the needle which punctures the stopper has a retractable rubber sheath over it. As the needle penetrates the stopper, the rubber sheath is forced back, exposing the needle. The rubber sheath acts as a gasket, sealing against the stopper and allowing little outside air to enter the tube.

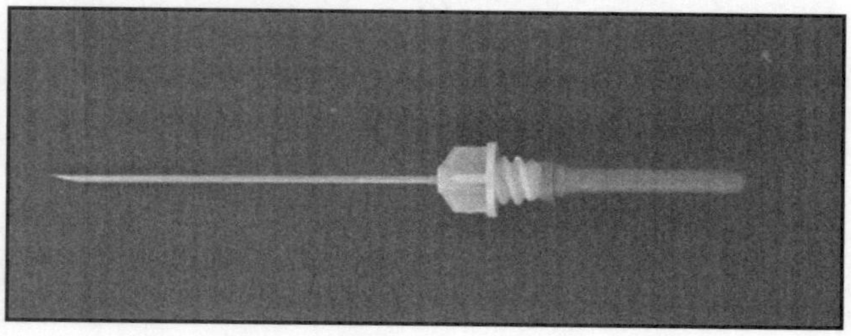

Figure 11.31 *Typical BD safety needle.*

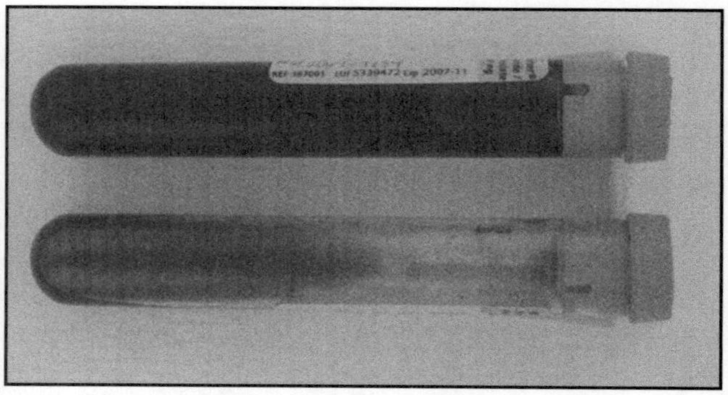

Figure 11.32 *Full and partially filled tubes*

The first tube is then placed into the hub, but not far enough to puncture the stopper on the tube. If the stopper is punctured before the needle pierces the vein, then the tube will fill with air and will not draw blood. The vein is then punctured, and the tube is pushed further into the hub, breaking the tube's seal and allowing blood to be sucked into the tube.

Although it is uncommon, a phlebotomist may improperly seat the tube inside the hub and on the needle. This could result in an incompletely punctured stopper which will not allow any blood to flow, or a partially punctured stopper which will allow a small amount to flow and draw in outside air. The needle may also be bent, causing further problems. Check the tubes to see if they have been filled to capacity. Sometimes a partially filled tube can be the result of a collapsed vein or some other issue. However, a partially filled tube can also be the result of an improper draw (see Figure 11.32).

The phlebotomist must also take care to insert the needle all the way into the vein, so as to prevent leakage of blood into the surrounding tissue, but not far enough to puncture both vein walls. The end of the needle is beveled for ease of insertion, but care must be taken to ensure that the bevel does not "seal" against the inner wall of the vein, causing obstructed blood flow.

The phlebotomist must keep the tube at a slight angle downward, so gravity will help prevent any backflow of the tube's contents into the subject's vein. This is a highly unlikely scenario because of blood pressure and vacuum, but backflow of chemicals from the tube into the subject could have disastrous results for the subject. The latex band should be removed as soon as blood begins to flow.

Once the first tube is filled, it should be removed and replaced with a second tube. When filled, the second tube should be removed from the hub and then the needle from the arm. The second tube can be contaminated when the phlebotomist withdraws the needle from the arm without withdrawing the second tube from the hub first. This will draw outside air, including Candida, into the second tube only. Some blood kit instruction sheets actually show the incorrect way to draw blood, causing contamination in this manner. Most phlebotomists and police do not distinguish first tube drawn from the second tube drawn.

Tube inversion

According to Becton Dickinson, the tubes are supposed to be gently inverted at least eight times immediately after the draw to mix the preservative and anti-coagulant. Note: Many blood kit instructions direct the phlebotomist not to shake the vials. This is for personal safety, as blood may splatter from vigorous shaking. Shaking may also affect the integrity of the blood sample if it causes hemolysis, which is the tearing and splitting of the red blood cells. Such damage can cause the blood testing process to be more akin to a plasma test which will cause a higher result.

The chemicals have to mix with the blood in a proper proportion; otherwise they do not work properly. Too much blood or too little chemical could cause the blood to ferment, and thus cause alcohol to form. Too little blood or too much chemical, and the chemicals could "salt out" the blood, causing a higher alcohol concentration under certain circumstances.

Chain of custody and proper handling of the specimens

The preservative is supposed to prevent *endogenous formation* of alcohol, but lesser-strength solutions available will slow, though not stop, endogenous alcohol formation. Studies show that a 2 percent solution will stop the growth of Candida albicans. Likewise, refrigeration only slows the decomposition; it does not stop it. After all, milk goes bad after a while even when refrigerated. Freezing will stop endogenous formation of alcohol, but blood tubes used for law enforcement blood kits are glass, and breakage becomes a problem. Generally, 4°C has been found to be a good compromise temperature for storage. Certainly, inquiries as to whether the blood remained in an unrefrigerated police car for some period of time should be made. In some jurisdictions it is not uncommon to mail the blood sample to a crime lab. *Chain of custody* is always worth investigating.

The blood storage facility at the crime lab should be investigated. Access and inventory control can be decisive, yet simple, issues in a blood test case.

Preparation of the sample for testing

At the crime lab, the blood is taken out of the refrigerator and allowed to come to room temperature. Usually the tube is placed in a rocker that gently rocks the contents back and forth, ensuring a good mix. What exactly was the room temperature? Generally, we do not know. Often, the analysts let the samples sit for a couple of hours to get to room temperature. They say that this cannot harm the mixture, but would you leave milk out for two hours? The second tube of blood should be repackaged and returned to the refrigerator in a timely manner. Due process issues may arise where the crime lab spoils the second sample.

Paperwork tracking the sample should be examined closely. Often, this will be reflected in the *analyst's bench notes*. Some labs assign a bar code label to each blood kit and each tube of blood is transferred. Tracking the blood from the tube to the actual computer-generated BAC printout is very important.

Once the tube is at room temperature, the top is removed by either cutting it off or pulling it out of the tube. Care should be taken either way as cutting requires the use of a sharp instrument and pulling could cause splatter. It should always be done under an exhaust hood, and adequate protective measures should be taken to avoid contact with the blood. Moreover, adequate ventilation in the lab and a proper hood design must ensure that airborne contaminants do not infiltrate the open sample.

Once the top is removed, the contents are poured into a container. A measured amount is removed from the container via a *pipette*. Ideally, the pipette should be electronic

Figure 11.33 *Autodilutor*

rather than manual to ensure greater accuracy and reliability. Maintenance and calibration records should be available for the pipette. Pipettes can be checked for accuracy by drawing a known amount of distilled water and depositing it onto a scale to check its weight.

The blood removed by the pipette is then transferred to a *headspace vial*. More sophisticated labs have pipettes that also draw a measured amount of *internal standard* and transfer the internal standard to the same headspace vial simultaneously with the blood. This is called an "auto-dilutor" and it will have a maintenance and calibration schedule as well. Figure 11.33. Two samples of blood should be prepared for testing, and the results should agree with each other to some adequate degree. Any somewhat competent lab should have no more than a 5 percent disagreement between samples.

The pipette must be rinsed clean between samples to avoid cross-contamination from previous blood samples. Only de-ionized water should be used to rinse the pipette because the flame ionization detector (FID) at the end of the process counts ions that hit it, counting them as alcohol. One would not want to introduce ions that could interfere with the result.

The headspace vials are often placed into an autosampler, which is an automated rack that will move each vial into place for sampling. The use of an autosampler allows the analyst to set the machine to run samples without the need to be present to inject each sample. The autosampler also heats and shakes the vials to ensure proper mixing of the components. Check the time at which your client's sample was injected. It might be well after working hours and leads to a good area of cross-examination. For example:

- You weren't at the crime lab at 2:02 A.M. when my client's blood was actually tested were you?
- You were home, asleep?
- If something went wrong with the process, would you expect the cleaning crew to take care of it?

11.22 Headspace Gas Chromatography

Chromatography is a separation science

Chromatography is a separation science. It relies on chemical or mechanical means of separating substances into more discrete units. Headspace gas chromatography is an indirect method of measuring the amount of a volatile substance contained in a liquid by measuring an equilibrated amount of the volatile substance in the headspace above the liquid.

Blood is prepared in a headspace vial by mixing it with a known amount of an internal standard (often a type of alcohol) as described above. The vial is crimp-sealed. The quality of the crimp at the top of the vial is important because it will be one factor that governs how much gas pressure builds up in the vial above the mixture.

The mixture is heated to a specific temperature in order to release the volatile compounds. The actual temperature is not as critical as the constancy of the temperature throughout the entire process. All vials must be heated to the same temperature. Colder temperatures result in longer times for the volatiles to move into the gaseous phase.

As the vial is heated, a gas rises above the mixture in the headspace vial like steam might rise above a pot of boiling water. The content of that gas is dependent upon *Henry's Law of Partial Pressures*. If the crimp is not perfect, it will change the pressure and the content of the gas. If the temperature varies, varying amounts of the volatiles will move into the gaseous phase as compared to other headspace vials.

Henry's Law—Assume a closed system and constant temperature. After a period of time, some of the molecules of the liquid will have moved into the gaseous phase in the headspace above the liquid. The number of molecules that have passed into the gaseous phase will be directly proportional to the number of molecules remaining in the liquid.

If we keep the temperature constant and the pressure constant, some of the alcohol molecules and the internal standard molecules will have passed from the liquid state into the headspace gaseous state. If we can measure the number of molecules in the headspace then we can, by conversion, quantify the amount of alcohol in the blood below it. Since the internal standard is mixed into the sample in a known amount and moves into the headspace at a known rate, the alcohol molecules are measured as a ratio in relation to the internal standard molecules released into the headspace.

Figure 11.34 *Hewlett-Packard GC Column*

Equilibration—Equilibration means that a constant proportion exists between the number of molecules in the gas above the liquid and the number of molecules in the liquid below, for any given volatile substance at a particular temperature and pressure. This does not mean, however, that there must be an equal amount of molecules in the gas and in the liquid.

If the temperature is not perfect, it will change the content of the gas. If the pressure is not constant, it will change the content of the gas.

In addition to the temperature and pressure, there is another factor that governs how much alcohol rises into the gas—that is called the *partition ratio*. Differing substances will have differing partition ratios, which are dependent upon many things, including the specific gravity of the substance.

Hematocrit, which is different but related to partition ratio, is also important. Hematocrit is a measure of the proportion of solid components to liquid components in the blood. Higher hematocrit means more solids. When pressurized, higher hematocrit levels push more hydrophilic molecules, such as alcohol, out of the liquid and into the gas. This can give a higher reported result if the internal standard passes into the gaseous phase at a slower rate than the alcohol.

The column

The column is a tube about as thin as a human hair and approximately 30 meters in length. It is heated in an oven inside the machine and is usually in a coil shape. The temperature in many headspace gas chromatographs used for blood testing is 60°C, but it may vary significantly and can be "ramped up" to bake-out impurities in the column between runs or as part of a maintenance procedure (see Figure 11.34).

An autosampler gently shakes and heats the headspace vials as it moves each one under a syringe. The syringe moves downward and punctures the crimped seal at the top of the headspace vial. It sucks a small amount of the headspace gas out and injects it into a transfer tube. Always check maintenance logs for syringe changes. Frequent changes may show problems with the process. Sometimes the syringes become bent because they miss the headspace vial. This is important if it happens during a blood run, and the run is continued without starting over. This means that the blood run was stopped and restarted without using new calibrators and controls.

At the same time that the headspace gas is being drawn out of the vial, an inert carrier gas (usually helium) is also introduced. The quality and content of the carrier gas should be documented as well as the intervals at which the filters for the carrier gas are inspected and changed. Ask for documentation regarding the purchase of the helium. Balloon grade helium is different from ultra-high purity scientific grade helium.

Separation of volatile substances, retention times and column maintenance

Both the carrier gas and the headspace sample move through the transfer tube and a Y-splitter. Half of the mixture flows through one column, while the other half flows through a second column. As the gases move through the column, the rate of flow of some molecules is slowed by chemical attraction to the column. Thus, separation is achieved over the course of several minutes. Each volatile compound has its own unique retention time. Retention times vary from column to column. Two columns from the same manufacturer, made to the same specifications will have different retention times for identical compounds.

It is important to realize that the column is designed to capture and slow molecules. In fact, the column has to be replaced every now and then because it gets packed with crud and blood from the samples. More often, however, the column needs to have its ends "clipped" with a file. Most problems with the column occur at either end and it can be remedied by removing the first or last inch of the column. This changes retention times. Columns are also routinely "baked out" to rid them of unwanted particulates. Baking out a column means that the temperature of the column is raised to a point much higher than that used for sampling purposes to incinerate particulate matter. Some GC programs also ramp up the temperature to a high level after each sample is run to bake out any particulates between samples. Column flow may also be reversed to dislodge particulates, much like the backwash function on a pool or spa.

Flame Ionization Detector

At the other end of the column from the injector is a Flame Ionization Detector (FID). The flame is powered by a mix of hydrogen gas and air supplied by the state. The purity of the gas mixture generally is not tested. Many labs create their own hydrogen supply with a hydrogen generator. The term *generator* is misleading as it does not actually create hydrogen, but separates it from other gaseous components.

The blood samples emerge (or *elute*) from the end of the column, striking the flame at a specific time. If we know how long it takes alcohol to move through the column and emerge at the end, we know that all substances that take the same amount of time are alcohol. The flame vaporizes every volatile substance in its path. The burnt and ionized particles

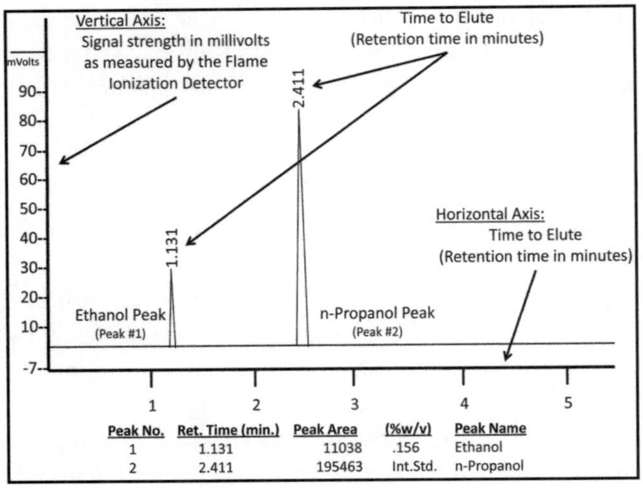

Figure 11.35 *Typical chromatogram explained.*

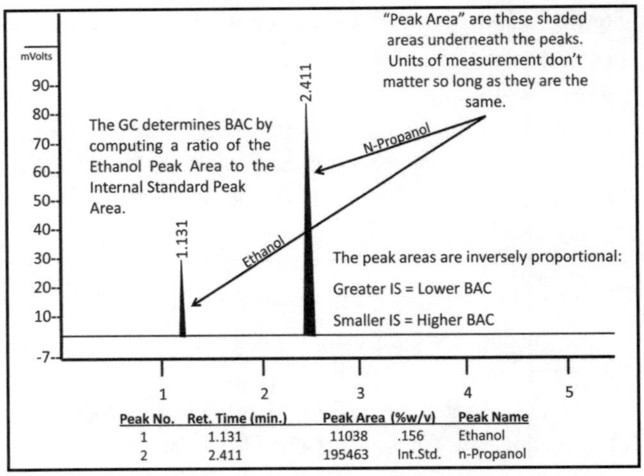

Figure 11.36 *How GC determines BAC.*

stick to an oppositely charged detector which counts them by measuring the electrical energy as each ion hits. The electrical signal strength is measured and reported in units called "millivolts."

The computer program calculates BAC

The GC then makes a mathematical calculation, and converts the electrical signal to a peak on a chromatogram (a computer-generated graph with peaks representing the electrical signal strength of volatile substances as they are ionized in the FID). There should be chromatograms for every sample introduced to the column. See Figure 11.35. Eventually, the blood alcohol report is generated and printed.

The mathematical calculation is unknown to the analyst because it is proprietary information that belongs to the manufacturer of the machine. The area underneath the peak represents the signal strength. One can calculate the peak area using geometry and algebra to check the result. One can also cut the peaks out with scissors and weigh them on a scale to calculate the results (assuming constant paper thickness, a very accurate scale, and extreme precision in cutting out the peaks from the graph). The amount of alcohol that is being detected is so small that it cannot be seen with the human eye.

The sizes of the peak areas are inversely proportional. In other words, if the ethanol peak area remains static, but the size of the internal standard peak area is increased, the ethanol peak area will "look smaller" to the computer program and it will report a lower BAC. If, however, the size of the ethanol peak area remains static and the size of the internal standard peak area is reduced (as when an analyst adds too little internal standard to the sample), the reported BAC will increase. See Figure 11.36.

Each time the GC is run, it must "learn" what differing levels of alcohol look like. Generally, four calibrators may be used to "teach" the machine to recognize, for example, 0.01, 0.10, 0.20 and 0.30 percent alcohol concentrations. Calibrators are used for this purpose and are commercially available or may be made in the lab. The important issue in calibration is to run the calibrators first in the run and then to run "verifiers" at the end of the run. The verifiers should, of course, be at the same levels as the calibrators (0.01, 0.10, 0.20 and 0.30 percent) but must come from a different source. If they do not come from a different source, and a calibrator is incorrect, the verifier will not catch the mistake. It will simply confirm the earlier mistake as being accurate.

The calibration run will generate a *calibration curve report* which is a graphical representation of the ratio of internal standard peak size versus alcohol peak size. All subject samples can, and should, be plotted on the calibration curve report to check for accuracy. The calibration curve report is a graphical representation of the calibrators. In Figure 11.37, all samples from .010 to .300 are linear, whereas samples above .300 are only assumed to be linear (and no one has any real interest in samples below .010, except in the very rare case).

To plot an individual subject's BAC on the calibration curve report, one must divide the ethanol peak area size by the internal standard peak area size. That number is then plotted on the vertical scale and a line is drawn horizontally to the point at which it intercepts the plotted curve. At the point of interception, the line is then dropped vertically to the horizontal scale. The point at which it intercepts the horizontal scale is the reported BAC.

Blanks must be run between samples at regular intervals to ensure no cross-contamination from one sample to the next. *Controls*, which are blood samples of a known value,

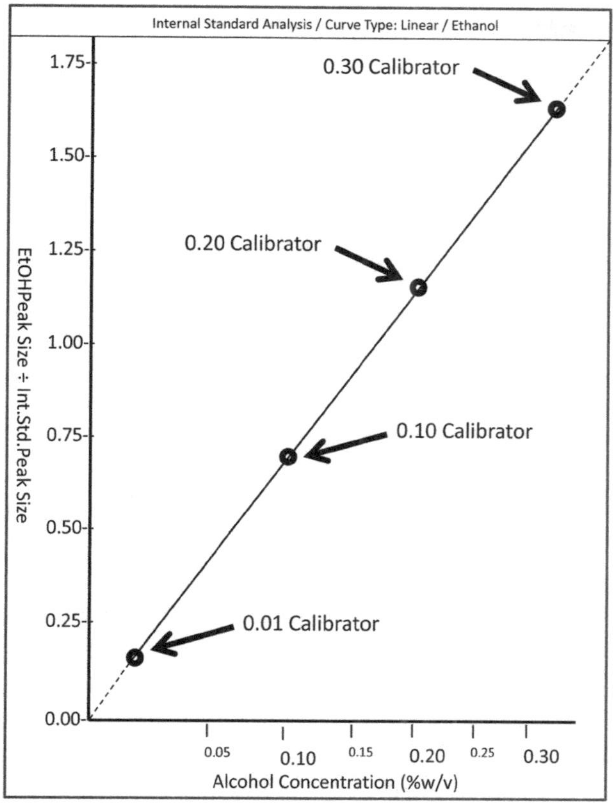

Figure 11.37 *Typical headspace gas chromatograph calibration curve report.*

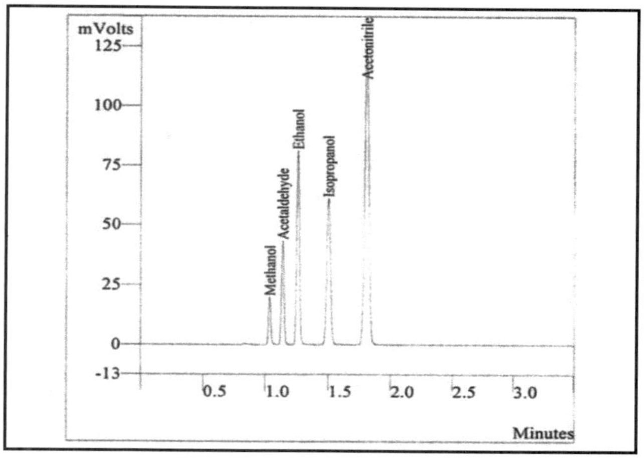

Figure 11.38 *Six compounds were analyzed. The GC could distinguish only five.*

should also be run at regular intervals with the blanks to ensure that the GC is operating accurately. Controls are commercially available or may be made in the lab. Either way, documentation should be available for each control batch.

A *mixed standard*, made up of several volatile compounds including ethanol, and internal standard must be run to ensure that the columns can separate different compounds.

Since chromatography is a separation science, if the GC cannot adequately distinguish between volatile compounds in blood, it is a useless tool for law enforcement. Figure 11.38 is an example where six compounds were analyzed, but the GC could distinguish only five. This column needs to be taken out of service and replaced. Watch out for explanations from the government that "It's OK. We know where the other volatile compound goes." That is a poor excuse for the obvious issue—the machine is broken.

Contamination: The Dirty Little Secret

Contamination is a real threat to the entire process and most crime lab personnel attempt to minimize its effect, both in the lab and in testimony. No lab is 100 percent contamination-free, despite the protestations of the criminalists who regularly testify in DWI cases.

Significant contamination issues are frequent in police crime labs and can come from unknown or known sources. Figure 11.39 is an example of significant contamination. The name of the contaminant and the source remain a mystery.

Not all contamination issues are mysterious, however. Some come from easily made mistakes and sloppy lab procedures. For example, toluene likely contaminated the sample in Figure 11.40 because an analyst switched caps on storage containers of ethanol and toluene. The next time ethanol was drawn from the container, it contained a significant amount of toluene which appeared in the actual calibration chromatogram in Figure 11.40.

Most disturbingly, however, is that the toluene also appeared at the same level in the .20 verification chromatogram at the end of the blood run. This means that the crime lab was using the exact same solution to calibrate the machine as was being used to verify the calibration of the machine. This is circular logic employed in its most dangerous form.

Co-elution of volatile compounds can cause a significantly increased BAC to be reported. As has been repeated over and over in this chapter, chromatography is a separation science. If the GC cannot separate compounds, it is worthless. And when compounds co-elute with ethanol, the innocent can go to prison. In this actual sample in Figure 11.41, ethanol co-eluted with acetone. Acetone was clearly present, but the GC reported its value as .000, whereas it reported a .320 BAC result. The subject of this test was tried and found Not Guilty, but a less-thorough attorney might not have asked for the chromatograms and would have missed this important issue.

Co-elution and the more common issue of poor baseline resolution do not always have to occur in a subject sample. The actual mixed standard chromatogram shows poor

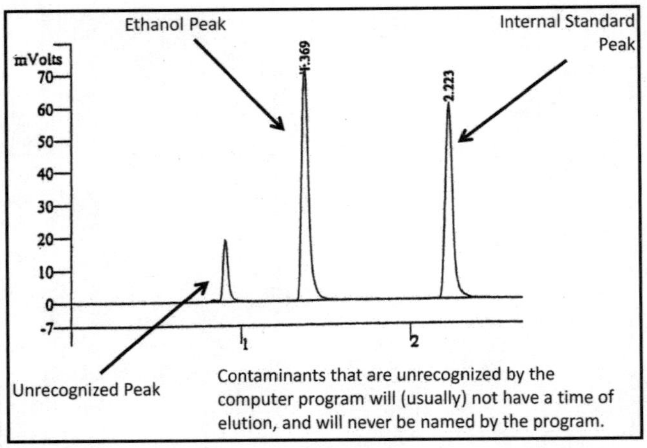

Figure 11.39 *Significant contamination.*

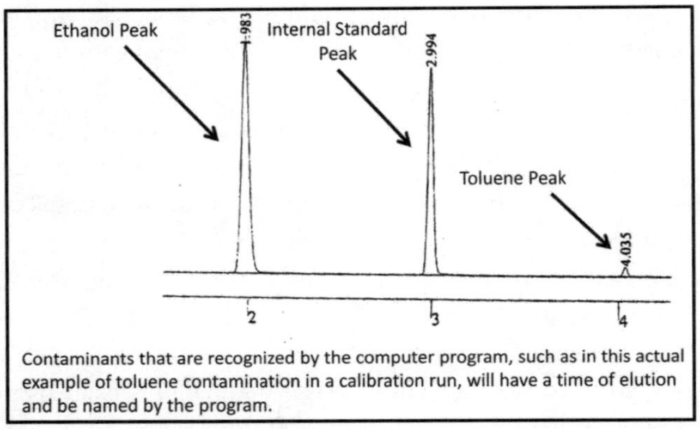

Figure 11.40 *Chromatogram example: contamination with toluene.*

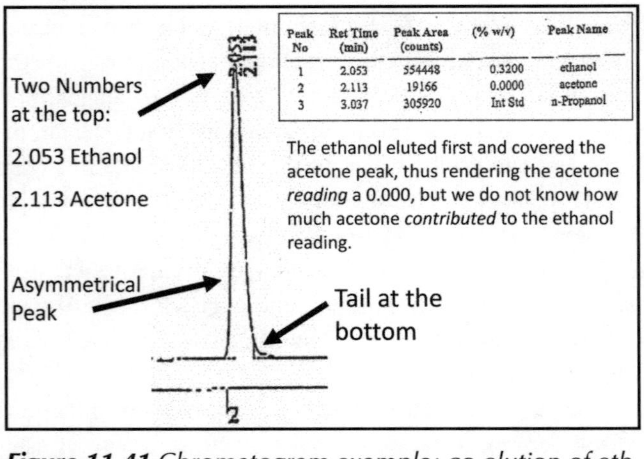

Figure 11.41 *Chromatogram example: co-elution of ethanol and acetone in a subject's blood sample.*

baseline resolution of ethanol and isopropanol. This column may have reached the end of its useful life and needs to be replaced. Watch out for explanations from the government that "this only happens on one column." That is a poor excuse for the obvious issue—the machine is broken.

An interruption of the gas flow can cause deleterious effects on a reported result. Most people don't even know what an interruption looks like, let alone how it occurs. An interruption can be caused by a physical blockage of the carrier gas line to the GC and it can also be caused by a leak in the gas line which allows gas pressure in the GC to drop. A leak is potentially more dangerous because the leak point can also suck in outside air and contaminate the sample. In either event, the entire GC run documentation should be saved for purpose of disclosure and maintenance. Then the blood should be rerun. As one can see in Figure 11.42, the evidence of interruption can appear as a very small detail on the chromatogram.

An odd situation is chronicled in Figure 11.43 where a volatile substance appears on one column, but not on the other column. The peak is too large to be any type of background noise or electronic interference. The program does not recognize the peak. Although it does not elute at the same time as any other compound such as ethanol on Column 2, it does not appear on Column 1. Since this compound actually exists, it must elute *somewhere* on the Column 1 chromatogram. It is possible for this compound to co-elute with another volatile substance on Column 1, or to remain trapped in the column until it is baked out.

Be aware that all chromatograms are susceptible to computerized manipulation. Figure 11.44 is an actual chromatogram showing manipulation. Fortunately, the analyst was exceedingly honest and documented the events that led to this in detail. She made proper disclosure of the issues and was forthright in her testimony. This underscores the extreme importance of integrity for all crime lab personnel. The national news is full of stories documenting how dishonest crime lab personnel have corrupted the system. It is unfortunate, but some crime lab personnel fall prey to the "us versus them" mentality and it affects the outcome of many cases.

"Peak shaving" is a common phenomenon which results from the CG's inability to properly integrate the peak size and shape into the software parameters. Remember that the area underneath the peak determines the amount of the measured substance. Since the area count is critical, the point at which the peak starts and ends, and where the baseline is drawn, is equally critical. The chromatograms may be manually or automatically manipulated to place an artificial start or end point and to draw a baseline. In the chromatogram in Figure 11.45,

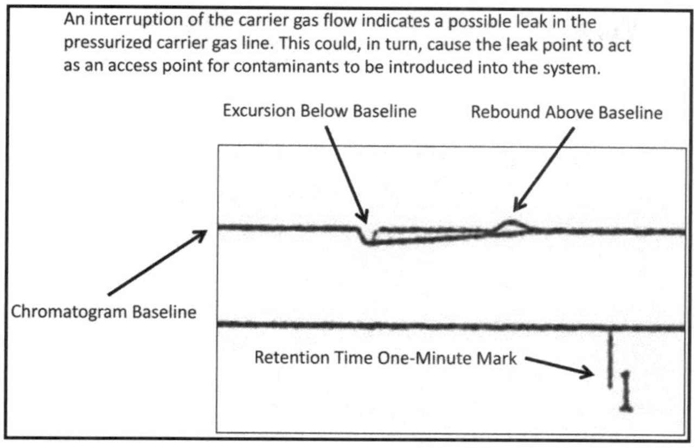

Figure 11.42 *Chromatogram example: interruption of carrier gas flow.*

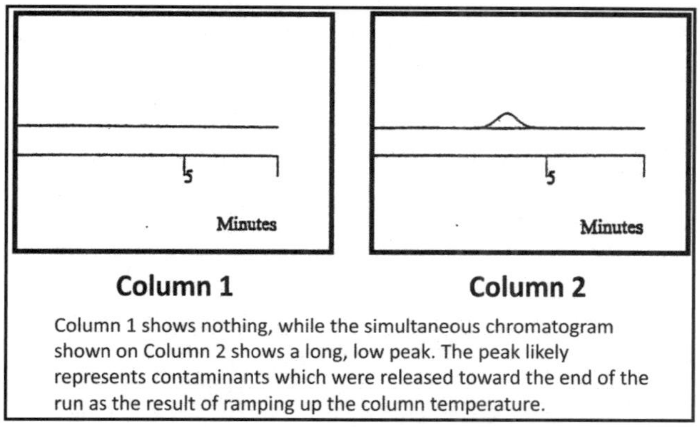

Figure 11.43 *Chromatogram example: late-eluting substance.*

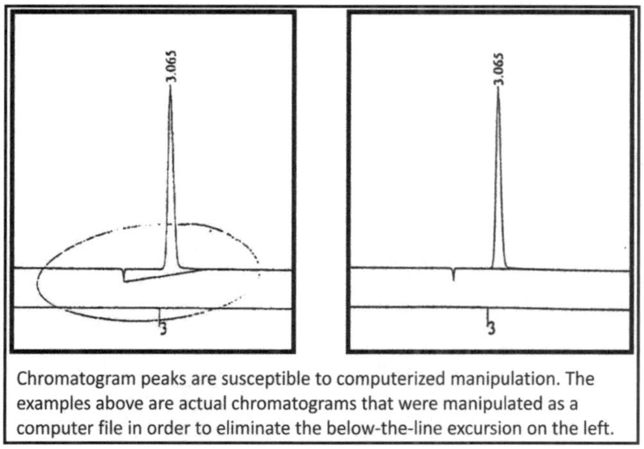

Figure 11.44 *Chromatogram example: Computer manipulation of chromatogram peaks.*

the peak is characterized by its asymmetry as well as the angled baseline which cuts off the lower portion of the peak. The area that is cut-out from the bottom edge of the peak is set by the "area-reject setting." In this particular case, the peak is the internal standard. Reducing the area count of the internal standard makes the ethanol peak appear larger in comparison, resulting in a higher reported alcohol concentration.

How can one tell if the peak has been manipulated to enhance the results? The analyst tries to avoid asymmetric peaks because they raise too many questions about the quality of the chromatography and the reported results. While some analysts try to avoid asymmetric peaks via strict adherence to proper scientific protocols, others simply manually manipulate the chromatography to hide the problems. Compare the chromatographs in Figure 11.46. The one on the left shows complete baseline resolution and good peak integration. The one on the right also shows complete baseline resolution and good peak integration. However, if one looks at the "tick marks" along the baseline, one can see the difference between good resolution and manipulation. The first tick mark signifies the beginning of the peak, which is where the software begins measuring area-count. The middle tick mark is where the peak reaches its highest point, and the final tick mark is where the software ends the area-count.

Notice that in the chromatogram on the left in Figure 11.46, the first tick mark is at the point where the baseline and the peak first intersect and the peak starts rising. The final tick mark is at the point where the baseline and the peak last intersect as the peak reaches the baseline again. In the chromatogram on the right in Figure 11.46, the first tick mark appears significantly prior to the intersection of the baseline and the start of the peak. The last tick mark ends significantly after the last point where the baseline and the peak intersect. This covers up any tailing, fronting, and asymmetry of the peak. Moreover, we do not know how much of the area was rejected from the area-count. The only way to discern the total effect is to view the actual data used to create the chromatogram and check the area-reject settings.

11.23 Breath, Blood, and Urine tests: Statutory Admissibility

§ 20-139.1. Procedures governing chemical analyses; admissibility; evidentiary provisions; controlled-drinking programs.

(a) Chemical Analysis Admissible. - In any implied-consent offense under G.S. 20-16.2, a person's alcohol concentration or the presence of any

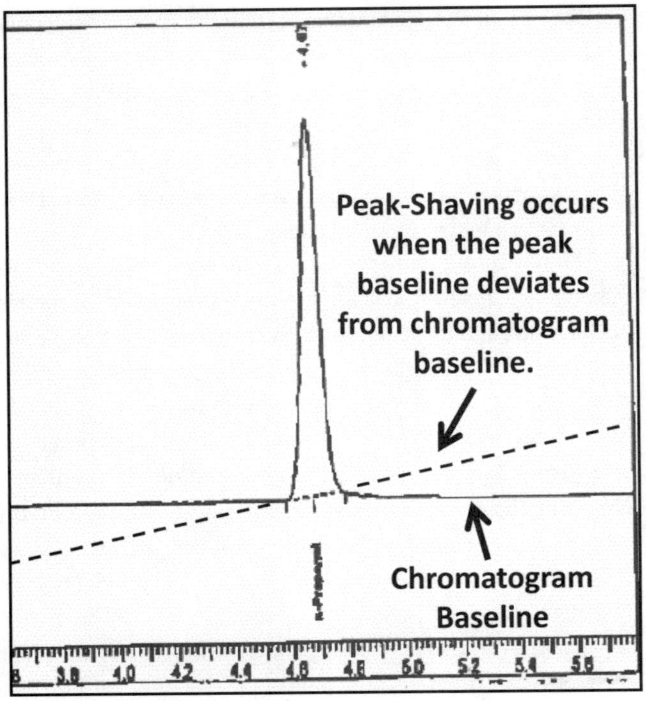

Figure 11.45 *Peak-shaving chromatogram.*

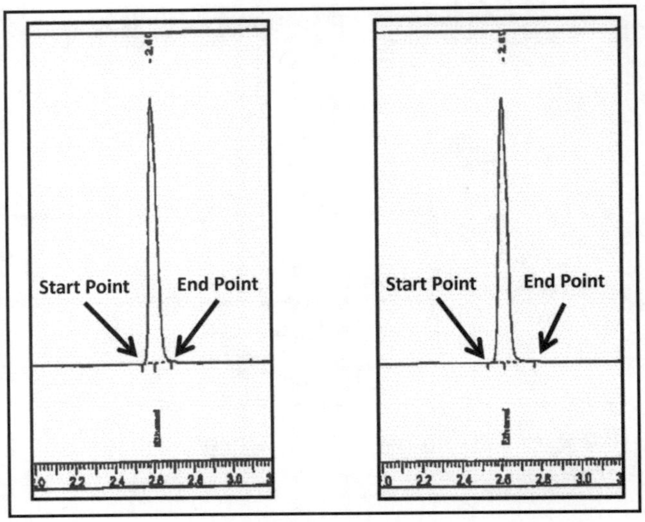

Figure 11.46 *Chromatograms by the same analyst, on the same column, five months apart.*

other impairing substance in the person's body as shown by a chemical analysis is admissible in evidence. This section does not limit the introduction of other competent evidence as to a person's alcohol concentration or results of other tests showing the presence of an impairing substance, including other chemical tests.

(b) Approval of Valid Test Methods; Licensing Chemical Analysts. - The results of a chemical analysis shall be deemed sufficient evidence to prove a person's alcohol concentration. A chemical analysis of the breath administered pursuant to the implied-consent law is admissible in any court or administrative hearing or proceeding if it meets both of the following requirements:

(1) It is performed in accordance with the rules of the Department of Health and Human Services.

(2) The person performing the analysis had, at the time of the analysis, a current permit issued by the Department of Health and Human Services authorizing the person to perform a test of the breath using the type of instrument employed.

For purposes of establishing compliance with subdivision (b)(1) of this section, the court or administrative agency shall take notice of the rules of the Department of Health and Human Services. For purposes of establishing compliance with subdivision (b)(2) of this section, the court or administrative agency shall take judicial notice of the list of permits issued to the person performing the analysis, the type of instrument on which the person is authorized to perform tests of the breath, and the date the permit was issued. The Department of Health and Human Services may ascertain the qualifications and competence of individuals to conduct particular chemical analyses and the methods for conducting chemical analyses. The Department may issue permits to conduct chemical analyses to individuals it finds qualified subject to periodic renewal, termination, and revocation of the permit in the Department's discretion.

(b1) When Officer May Perform Chemical Analysis. - Any person possessing a current permit authorizing the person to perform chemical analysis may perform a chemical analysis.

(b2) Breath Analysis Results Preventive Maintenance. - The Department of Health and Human Services shall perform preventive maintenance on breath-testing instruments used for chemical analysis. A court or administrative agency shall take judicial notice of the preventive maintenance records of the Department. Notwithstanding the provisions of subsection (b), the results of a chemical analysis of a person's breath performed in accordance with this section are not admissible in evidence if:

(1) The defendant objects to the introduction into evidence of the results of the chemical analysis of the defendant's breath; and

(2) The defendant demonstrates that, with respect to the instrument used to analyze the defendant's breath, preventive maintenance procedures required by the regulations of the Department of Health and Human Services had not been performed within the time limits prescribed by those regulations.

(b3) Sequential Breath Tests Required. - The methods governing the administration of chemical analyses of the breath shall require the testing of at least duplicate sequential breath samples. The results of the chemical analysis of all breath samples are admissible if the test results from any two consecutively collected breath samples do not differ from each other by an alcohol concentration greater than 0.02. Only the lower of the two test results of the consecutively administered tests can be used to prove a particular alcohol concentration. A person's refusal to give the sequential breath samples necessary to constitute a valid chemical analysis is a refusal under G.S. 20-16.2(c).

A person's refusal to give the second or subsequent breath sample shall make the result of the first breath sample, or the result of the sample providing the lowest alcohol concentration if more than one breath sample is provided, admissible in any judicial or administrative hearing for any relevant purpose, including the establishment that a person had a particular alcohol concentration for conviction of an offense involving impaired driving.

(b4) Repealed by Session Laws 2006-253, s. 16, effective December 1, 2006, and applicable to offenses committed on or after that date.

(b5) Subsequent Tests Allowed. - A person may be requested, pursuant to G.S. 20-16.2, to submit to a chemical analysis of the person's blood or other bodily fluid or substance in addition to or in lieu of a chemical analysis of the breath, in the discretion of a law enforcement officer; except that a person charged with a violation of G.S. 20-141.4 shall be requested to provide a blood sample in addition to or in lieu of a chemical analysis of the breath. However, if a breath sample shows an alcohol concentration of .08 or more, then requesting a blood sample shall be in the discretion of a law enforcement officer. If a subsequent chemical analysis is requested pursuant to this subsection, the person shall again be advised of the implied consent rights in accordance with G.S. 20-16.2(a). A person's willful refusal to submit to a chemical analysis of the blood or other bodily fluid or substance is a willful refusal under G.S. 20-16.2. If a person willfully refuses to provide a blood sample under this subsection, and the person is charged with a violation of G.S. 20-141.4, then a law enforcement officer with probable cause to believe that the offense involved impaired driving or was an alcohol-related offense made subject to the procedures of G.S. 20-16.2 shall seek a warrant to obtain a blood sample. The failure to obtain a blood sample pursuant to this subsection shall not be grounds for the dismissal of a charge and is not an appealable issue.

(b6) The Department of Health and Human Services shall post on a Web page a list of all persons who have a permit authorizing them to perform chemical analyses, the types of analyses that they can perform, the instruments that each person is authorized to operate, the effective dates of the permits, and the records of preventive maintenance. A court or administrative agency shall take judicial notice of whether, at the time of the chemical analysis, the chemical analyst possessed a permit authorizing the chemical analyst to perform the chemical analysis administered and whether preventive maintenance had been performed on the breath-testing instrument in accordance with the Department's rules.

(c) Blood and Urine for Chemical Analysis. - Notwithstanding any other provision of law, when a blood or urine test is specified as the type of chemical analysis by a law enforcement officer, a physician, registered nurse, emergency medical technician, or other qualified person shall withdraw the blood sample and obtain the urine sample, and no further authorization or approval is required. If the person withdrawing the blood or collecting the urine requests written confirmation of the law enforcement officer's request for the withdrawal of blood or collecting the urine, the officer shall furnish it before blood is withdrawn or urine collected. When blood is withdrawn or urine collected pursuant to a law enforcement officer's request, neither the person withdrawing the blood nor any hospital, laboratory, or other institution, person, firm, or corporation employing that person, or contracting for the service of withdrawing blood or collecting urine, may be held criminally or civilly liable by reason of withdrawing the blood or collecting the urine, except that there is no immunity from liability for negligent acts or omissions. A person requested to withdraw blood or collect urine pursuant to this subsection may refuse to do so only if it reasonably appears that the procedure cannot be performed without endangering the safety of the person collecting the sample or the safety of the person from whom the sample is being collected. If the officer requesting the blood or urine requests a written justification for the refusal, the medical provider who determined the sample could not be collected safely shall provide written justification at the time of the refusal.

(c1) Admissibility. - The results of a chemical analysis of blood or urine reported by the North Carolina State Crime Laboratory, the Charlotte, North Carolina, Police Department Laboratory, or any other laboratory approved for chemical analysis by the Department of Health and Human Services (DHHS), are admissible as evidence in all administrative hearings, and in any court, without further authentication and without the testimony of the analyst. For the purposes of this section, a "laboratory approved for chemical analysis" by the DHHS includes, but is not limited to, any hospital laboratory approved by DHHS pursuant to the program resulting from the federal Clinical Laboratory Improvement Amendments of 1988 (CLIA).

The results shall be certified by the person who performed the analysis. The provisions of this subsection may be utilized in any administrative hearing, but can only be utilized in cases tried in the district and superior court divisions, or in an adjudicatory hearing in juvenile court, if:

(1) The State notifies the defendant at least 15 business days before the proceeding at which the evidence would be used of its intention to introduce the report into evidence under this subsection and provides a copy of the report to the defendant, and

(2) The defendant fails to file a written objection with the court, with a copy to the State, at least five business days before the proceeding at which the report would be used that the defendant objects to the introduction of the report into evidence.

If the defendant's attorney of record, or the defendant if that person has no attorney, fails to file a written objection as provided in this subsection, then the report shall be admitted into evidence without the testimony of the analyst. Upon filing a timely objection, the admissibility of the report shall be determined and governed by the appropriate rules of evidence.

The report containing the results of any blood or urine test may be transmitted electronically or via facsimile. A copy of the affidavit sent electronically or via facsimile shall be admissible in any court or administrative hearing without further authentication. A copy of the report shall be sent to the charging officer, the clerk of superior court in the county in which the criminal charges are pending, the Division of Motor Vehicles, and the Department of Health and Human Services.

Nothing in this subsection precludes the right of any party to call any witness or to introduce any evidence supporting or contradicting the evidence contained in the report.

(c2) Repealed by Session Laws 2013-194, s. 1, effective June 26, 2013.

(c3) Procedure for Establishing Chain of Custody Without Calling Unnecessary Witnesses. -

(1) For the purpose of establishing the chain of physical custody or control of blood or urine tested or analyzed to determine whether it contains alcohol, a controlled substance or its metabolite, or any impairing substance, a statement signed by each successive person in the chain of custody that the person delivered it to the other person indicated on or about the date stated is prima facie evidence that the person had custody and made the delivery as stated, without the necessity of a personal appearance in court by the person signing the statement.

(2) The statement shall contain a sufficient description of the material or its container so as to distinguish it as the particular item in question and shall state that the material was delivered in essentially the same condition as received. The statement may be placed on the same document as the report provided for in subsection (c1) of this section.

(3) The provisions of this subsection may be utilized in any administrative hearing, but can only be utilized in cases tried in the district and superior court divisions, or in an adjudicatory hearing in juvenile court, if:

a. The State notifies the defendant at least 15 business days before the proceeding at which the statement would be used of its intention to introduce the statement into evidence under this subsection and provides a copy of the statement to the defendant, and

b. The defendant fails to file a written notification with the court, with a copy to the State, at least five business days before the proceeding at which the statement would be used that the defendant objects to the introduction of the statement into evidence.

If the defendant's attorney of record, or the defendant if that person has no attorney, fails to file a written objection as provided in this subsection, then the statement shall be admitted into evidence without the necessity of a personal appearance by the person signing the statement. Upon filing a timely objection, the admissibility of the report shall be determined and governed by the appropriate rules of evidence.

(4) Nothing in this subsection precludes the right of any party to call any witness or to introduce any evidence supporting or contradicting the evidence contained in the statement.

(c4) Repealed by Session Laws 2013-194, s. 1, effective June 26, 2013.

(c5) The testimony of an analyst regarding the results of a chemical analysis of blood or urine admissible pursuant to subsection (c1) of this section, and reported by that analyst, shall be permitted by remote testimony, as defined in G.S. 15A-1225.3, in all administrative hearings, and in any court, if all of the following occur:

(1) The State has provided a copy of the report to the attorney of record for the defendant, or to the defendant if that person has no attorney, as required by subsections (c1) and (c3) of this section.

(2) The State notifies the attorney of record for the defendant, or the defendant if that person has no attorney, at least 15 business days before the proceeding at which the evidence would be used of its intention to introduce the testimony regarding the chemical analysis into evidence using remote testimony.

(3) The defendant's attorney of record, or the defendant if that person has no attorney, fails to file a written objection with the court, with a copy to the State, at least five business days before the proceeding at which the testimony will be presented that the defendant objects to the introduction of the remote testimony.

If the defendant's attorney of record, or the defendant if that person has no attorney, fails to file a written objection as provided in this subsection, then the analyst shall be allowed to testify by remote testimony.

The method used for remote testimony authorized by this subsection shall allow the trier of fact and all parties to observe the demeanor of the analyst as the analyst testifies in a similar manner as if the analyst were testifying in the location where the hearing or trial is being conducted. The court shall ensure that the defendant's attorney, or the defendant if that person has no attorney, has a full and fair opportunity for examination and cross-examination of the analyst.

Nothing in this section shall preclude the right of any party to call any witness. Nothing in this subsection shall obligate the Administrative Office of the Courts or the State Crime Laboratory to incur expenses related to remote testimony absent an appropriation of funds for that purpose.

(d) Right to Additional Test. - Nothing in this section shall be construed to prohibit a person from obtaining or attempting to obtain an additional chemical analysis. If the person is not released from custody after the initial appearance, the agency having custody of the person shall make reasonable efforts in a timely manner to assist the person in obtaining access to a telephone to arrange for any additional test and allow access to the person in accordance with the agreed procedure in G.S. 20-38.5. The failure or inability of the person who submitted to a chemical analysis to obtain any additional test or to withdraw blood does not preclude the admission of evidence relating to the chemical analysis.

(d1) Right to Require Additional Tests. - If a person refuses to submit to any test or tests pursuant to this section, any law enforcement officer with probable cause may, without a court order, compel the person to provide blood or urine samples for analysis if the officer reasonably believes that the delay necessary to obtain a court order, under the circumstances, would result in the dissipation of the percentage of alcohol in the person's blood or urine.

(d2) Notwithstanding any other provision of law, when a blood or urine sample is requested under subsection (d1) of this section by a law enforcement officer, a physician, registered nurse, emergency medical technician, or other qualified person shall withdraw the blood and obtain the urine sample, and no further authorization or approval is required. If the person withdrawing the blood or collecting the urine requests written confirmation of the charging officer's request for the withdrawal of blood or obtaining urine, the officer shall furnish it before blood is withdrawn or urine obtained. A person requested to withdraw blood or collect urine pursuant to this subsection may refuse to do so only if it reasonably appears that the procedure cannot be performed without endangering the safety of the person collecting the sample or the safety of the person from whom the sample is being collected. If the officer requesting the blood or urine requests a written justification for the refusal, the medical provider who determined the sample could not be collected safely shall provide written justification at the time of the refusal.

(d3) When blood is withdrawn or urine collected pursuant to a law enforcement officer's request, neither the person withdrawing the blood nor any hospital, laboratory, or other institution, person, firm, or corporation employing that person, or contracting for the service of withdrawing blood, may be held criminally or civilly liable by reason of withdrawing that blood, except that there is no immunity from liability for negligent acts or omissions. The results of the analysis of blood or urine under this subsection shall be admissible if performed by the State Crime Laboratory or any other hospital or qualified laboratory.

(e) Recording Results of Chemical Analysis of Breath. - A person charged with an implied-consent offense who has not received, prior to a trial, a copy of the chemical analysis results the State intends to offer into evidence may request in writing a copy of the results. The failure to provide a copy prior to any trial shall be grounds for a continuance of the case but shall not be grounds to suppress the results of the chemical analysis or to dismiss the criminal charges.

(e1) Use of Chemical Analyst's Affidavit in District Court. - An affidavit by a chemical analyst sworn to and properly executed before an official authorized to administer oaths shall be admissible in evidence without further authentication and without the testimony of the analyst in any hearing or trial in the District Court Division of the General Court of Justice with respect to the following matters:

(1) The alcohol concentration or concentrations or the presence or absence of an impairing substance of a person given a chemical analysis and who is involved in the hearing or trial.

(2) The time of the collection of the blood, breath, or other bodily fluid or substance sample or samples for the chemical analysis.

(3) The type of chemical analysis administered and the procedures followed.

(4) The type and status of any permit issued by the Department of Health and Human Services that the analyst held on the date the analyst performed the chemical analysis in question.

(5) If the chemical analysis is performed on a breath-testing instrument for which regulations adopted pursuant to subsection (b) require preventive maintenance, the date the most recent preventive maintenance procedures were performed on the breath-testing instrument used, as shown on the maintenance records for that instrument.

The Department of Health and Human Services shall develop a form for use by chemical analysts in making this affidavit.

(e2) Except as governed by subsection (c1), (c2), or (c3) of this section, the State can only use the provisions of subsection (e1) of this section if:

(1) The State notifies the defendant at least 15 business days before the proceeding at which the affidavit would be used of its intention to introduce the affidavit into evidence under this subsection and provides a copy of the affidavit to the defendant, and

(2) The defendant fails to file a written notification with the court, with a copy to the State, at least five business days before the proceeding at which the affidavit would be used that the defendant objects to the introduction of the affidavit into evidence.

The failure to file a timely objection as provided in this subsection shall be deemed a waiver of the right to object to the admissibility of the affidavit.

Upon filing a timely objection, the admissibility of the report shall be determined and governed by the appropriate rules of evidence. The case shall be continued until the analyst can be present. The criminal case shall not be dismissed due to the failure of the analyst to appear, unless the analyst willfully fails to appear after being ordered to appear by the court. Nothing in subsection (e1) or subsection (e2) of this section precludes the right of any party to call any witness or to introduce any evidence supporting or contradicting the evidence contained in the affidavit.

(f) Evidence of Refusal Admissible. - If any person charged with an implied-consent offense refuses to submit to a chemical analysis or to perform field sobriety tests at the request of an officer, evidence of that refusal is admissible in any criminal, civil, or administrative action against the person.

(g) Controlled-Drinking Programs. - The Department of Health and Human Services may adopt rules concerning the ingestion of controlled amounts of alcohol by individuals submitting to chemical testing as a part of scientific, experimental, educational, or demonstration programs. These regulations shall prescribe procedures consistent with controlling federal law governing the acquisition, transportation, possession, storage, administration, and disposition of alcohol intended for use in the programs. Any person in charge of a controlled-drinking program who acquires alcohol under these regulations must keep records accounting for the disposition of all alcohol acquired, and the records must at all reasonable times be available for inspection upon the request of any federal, State, or local law-enforcement officer with jurisdiction over the laws relating to control of alcohol. A controlled-drinking program exclusively using lawfully purchased alcoholic beverages in places in which they may be lawfully possessed, however, need not comply with the record-keeping requirements of the regulations authorized by this subsection. All acts pursuant to the regulations reasonably done in furtherance of bona fide objectives of a controlled-drinking program authorized by the regulations are lawful notwithstanding the provisions of any other general or local statute, regulation, or ordinance controlling alcohol.

(h) Disposition of Blood Evidence. - Notwithstanding any other provision of law, any blood or urine sample subject to chemical analysis for the presence of alcohol, a controlled substance or its metabolite, or any impairing substance pursuant to this section may be destroyed by the analyzing agency 12 months after the case is filed or after the case is concluded in the trial court and not under appeal, whichever is later, without further notice to the parties. However, if a Motion to Preserve the evidence has been filed by either party, the evidence shall remain in the custody of the analyzing agency or the agency that collected the sample until dispositive order of a court of competent jurisdiction is entered.

11.24 Uncertainty of Measurement

The science of metrology tells us that the true value of any measurement cannot be known. Yet, we live in a world where we have to know the true values of many different measurements. When you go to the deli department of your local supermarket to buy a pound of roast beef, you don't seriously expect to get exactly one pound. You ask for a pound of roast beef, the deli worker tosses the roast beef onto a slicer, passes it back and forth a dozen or more times, then piles the slices onto an electronic scale. A sticker prints out from the scale that reads 1.05 pounds. You say "thank you" and go on with the rest of your shopping, but you did not get what you asked for—or did you?

Looking more closely at the factors that went into your roast beef purchase we find two major areas of uncertainty. The first area is human expectation/communication and the second area is the actual measurement.

The human expectation/communication component takes into account that you communicated very clearly that you wanted a pound of roast beef, but experience tells you that the deli worker will get as close to one pound as is reasonable. Will 0.05 pounds make any appreciable difference if you're going to make 4 roast beef sandwiches from that pound? No.

Will it make an appreciable difference in your budget? At $6.99 per pound, the difference would only be 35 cents. It's unlikely to make much of a difference in your budget, which is why the difference between what you ask for and what you get is no big deal.

Suppose, however, you are buying a pound of gold at $1,225 per ounce. The difference between 1.00 pounds and 1.05 pounds is $980. The difference between what you ask for and what you get may be a very big deal compared the roast beef example.

The human expectation/communication component depends on the consequences of the measurement. As the consequences resulting from the measurement become more serious, our expectations of accuracy become greater. For example, when someone's freedom hangs on the accuracy of a blood alcohol test result, most people expect a very accurate test. Some crime lab workers, however, subscribe to the "good enough for government work" philosophy.

The second area, actual measurement, has many different components. Every state has laws regarding weights and measures used for sale of goods. The deli counter's scale likely carries a state-issued sticker of calibration indicating that it has been checked and is operating within tolerances allowable by law. The scale that measures gold will also carry a sticker. Whether the deli scale and the gold scale have to be within the same tolerance is a matter of legislative discretion, but that doesn't change the fact that no matter what the tolerance allowable by law is, every measurement has a margin of uncertainty. That margin is due, in part, to the mechanical device used to make the measurement. Simply put, an inexpensive common bathroom scale that relies on springs may be less accurate that a very expensive balance-scale used in a hospital setting.

The unit of measurement employed makes a difference. A wooden yardstick may be graduated in quarter-inches, whereas a machinist's rule may be graduated in hundredths of an inch. Both are capable of accurate or inaccurate measurements, but the machinist's rule will make it far easier to discern a precise measurement. A digital scale which reads out to six decimal places will give a more precise measurement than one which reads out to just two decimal places.

The term "uncertainty of measurement" was previously known as the "margin of error." "Margin of error," however, is an unfortunate designation. Since all measurements, even very accurate ones, are subject to more precise methods, the term "error" is improper. Error implies that the measurement is incorrect. Uncertainty implies that the measurement is correct within a defined margin. One asks for a pound of roast beef and gets 1.05 pounds. That's not error, that's uncertainty in the measurement process. Calculating the value of each of the sources of uncertainty and adding them together to arrive at a set of parameters for the measurement is called an "uncertainty budget."

While the formulae that goes into calculating the uncertainty budget for blood alcohol content testing may be very complex, identifying the components which make up the uncertainty budget are less complex. A common way of defining the components is by using an Ishikawa diagram (sometimes called a "fishbone" diagram because of the resemblance to a fish skeleton).

The "backbone" of the Ishikawa diagram is the central point for which all sources of uncertainty are combined and lead to the ultimate "Uncertainty of Measurement" or "Uncertainty Budget." The individual sources of uncertainty are listed on the outlying bones and are categorized in a logical manner. It is important to realize that each category of uncertainty is made up of individual sources of uncertainty. Each individual source of uncertainty could have its own Ishikawa diagram. Moreover, each source of uncertainty within each category has an equation which calculates the magnitude of uncertainty. Each category has an equation which calculates the magnitude of combined sources of uncertainty for that category. Then, there is an equation which calculates the magnitude of the combined uncertainty of each category for the total "Uncertainty of Measurement" listed at the far right of the diagram.

Undertainty of Measurement Example: Arizona Department of Public Safety

Looking at the example in figure 11.47 we see that the sources of uncertainty fall into two categories: "reconciled" marked with a check and "not reconciled" marked with an asterisk. The reconciled sources of uncertainty have been removed from the budget. While a claim may be made that such factors are included elsewhere in the budget, the claim is not entirely credible. Let's look at the eight categories, individually.

Reproducibility

This category has the most included sources of uncertainty. The Master Budget includes certified reference materials from two manufacturers, Cerilliant and Cliniqa. They include five verifiers and one low aqueos control from Cerilliant, and three low whole-blood controls and two high-blood controls from Cliniqa. The problem, however, lies in the fact that the Cliniqa whole blood controls are not intended to be used in a forensic setting. In an August, 2013 email from Cliniqa responding to a DPS blood analyst at the Southern Regional Crime Lab, Cliniqa admits that their "Whole Blood Volatiles" (controls) have a 20% range established, but refuses to disclose their underlying uncertainty budget. Cliniqa states: "The justification for the establishment of the range is proprietary information." Cliniqa goes on to state: "Reason being the product is intended to be used in a clinical laboratory setting and is not technically supposed to be used in a forensic setting."

Additionally, the DPS Ishikawa Diagram does not tell us where the Cliniqa whole-blood controls figure into the budget. It could be figured under the Reproducibility category as "Historical QC Data" or under the Procedure category as "Bias-Systematic Error (CRM Uncertainty Bias)."

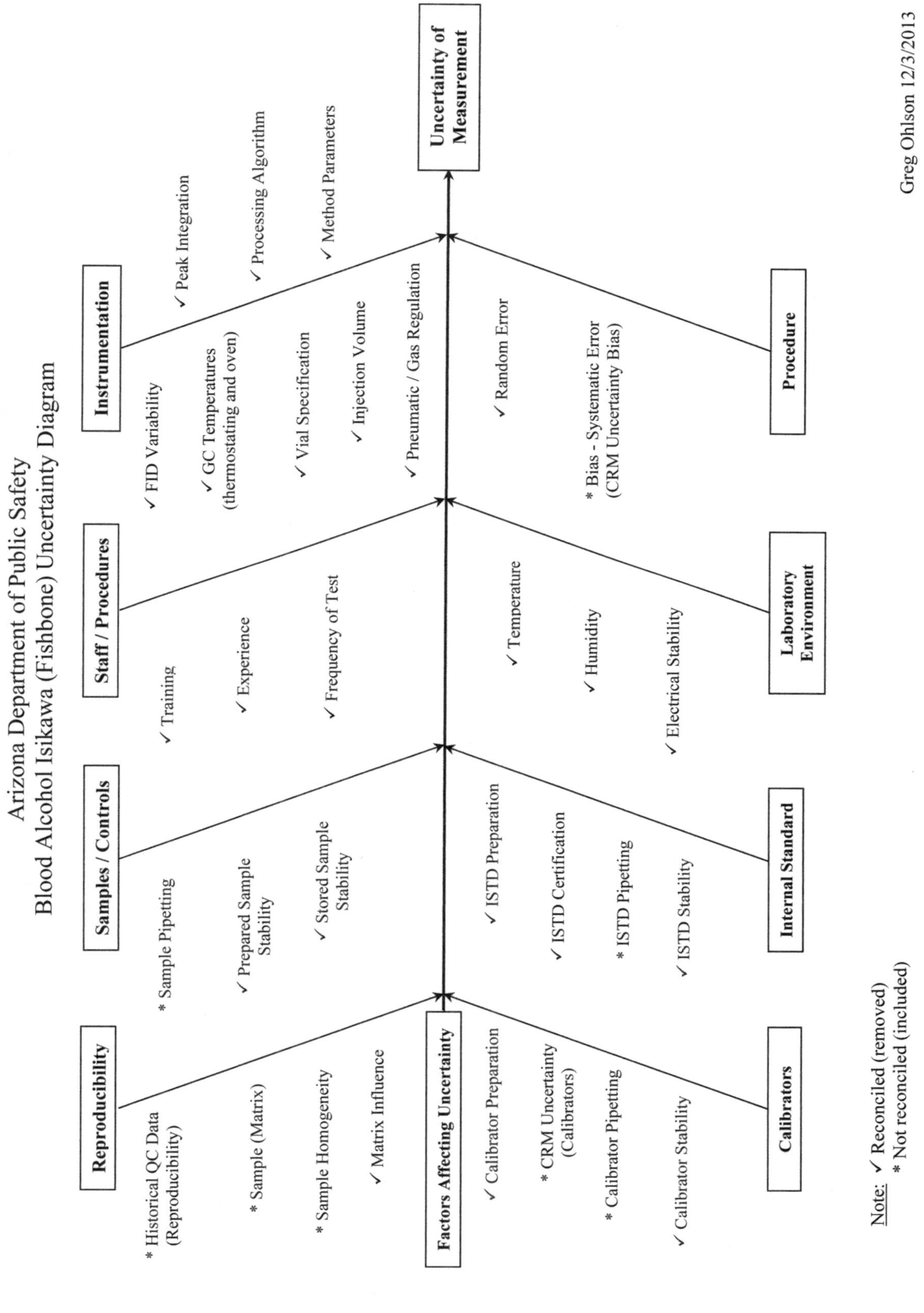

Figure 11.47 *Example: Isikawa [sic] (Fishbone) Uncertainty Diagram*

Samples/Controls

Sample Pipetting is included. In fact, Internal Standard Pipetting and Calibrator Pipetting are included under Internal Standard and Calibrator categories, respectively. This indicates that, overall, DPS considers pipetting to be the greatest source of uncertainty. Pipetting is an important laboratory technique and can easily be done incorrectly. Yet, training and experience are reconciled and not included. Did DPS include training and experience in the calculation for pipetting? To what degree were they included? We simply do not know. The Master Budget notes that pipettor MD96HB2387 used by the Southern Regional Crime Lab was recalibrated on November 6th, 2013 and the results were not used to establish the budget. This calls into question the entire budget if that pipettor was used to create blood alcohol test results. If the pipettor was recalibrated and used in the lab, but not considered in the data which contributed to the budget, what would the budget be if it had been included? An uncertainty budget cannot cherry-pick the best results and ignore poor results. It has to include all results to give an accurate representation of uncertainty.

Staff/Procedures

No uncertainty from this category is included (although it may be argued that a portion of it is included under Samples/Controls as "pipetting"). Removal of these sources of error would mean that whether it is an analyst's very first test, or an analyst with 25 years of experience, the source of uncertainty is not included. The master budget lists "Annual blood alcohol proficiency test results available for estimate of uncertainty evaluation" but fails to show how they were calculated into the budget.

Instrumentation

This manner in which the uncertainty of the instrumentation category is included is the most laughable of all calculations simply because it is not included. Each of the eight sources of uncertainty have been removed from the equation. Method Parameters is the software's control over the testing process. Method Parameters covers every aspect of the testing process. Without Method Parameters, there would be no test. Change the Method Parameters and you change the result.

Peak Integration can be either manual or automatic. Changing the peak integration will change the reported result.

FID Variability is the variability of the flame ionization detector. The FID must be replaced occasionally because it wears out. This source is ignored as well.

Calibrators

Even where the DPS included CRM (Certified Reference Material) Uncertainty for the calibrators, DPS still removed uncertainty related to the preparation and stability of the calibrator.

Internal Standard

Only pipetting has not been removed. Preparation, Certification and Stability each have their own sets of uncertainty, which remains unknown under this model.

Laboratory Environment

Nothing is included. While temperature and humidity may have negligible effects, electrical stability cannot be ignored.

Procedure

Either "Random Error" has been ignored, or it is included in the Reproducibility category as Historical QC (Quality Control) Data. Bias is also known as Systematic Error, which is not random error, but is introduced by an inaccuracy, as of observation or measurement, which is inherent in the system. Bias is may be very difficult to spot in a system because it should always result in an error in one direction, such as a scale that is not set to account for the tare weight. Moreover, the bias is from the Certified Reference Material with no differentiation from the CRM from the Calibrators category. Is it being counted twice? Is it different CRM? Is it a different measure of the uncertainty of the same CRM? We simply do not know.

When the entire Uncertainty Budget is reviewed, it becomes clear that it was poorly designed and seems almost haphazard in what has been included and excluded from the budget. Analysts will surely claim a very tight standard deviation from a true blood test result, but with little scientific and statistical evidence to back that claim. Strong, knowledgeable, and careful cross examination is the defense attorney's best strategy to expose the weaknesses in the uncertainty budget.

11.25 Blood Testing For Drugs

Overview

Blood is tested in a two-step process. The first step is a screening tool known as *Enzyme-Linked Immunosorbant Assay* (ELISA), and the second step is a confirmatory test known as *Liquid Chromatography Mass-Spectrometry* (LCMS).

Nothing is different in the manner in which the police collect blood samples in a DWI-drugs case as opposed to a DWI-alcohol case. What is irrelevant to the collection process, however, is the possibility of fermentation causing the neogenesis of cannabis or methamphetamine or any other drugs in the blood tube. That's not to say that the contents of the tubes could not be contaminated in some other manner, or that one drug could not be mistaken for another during the testing process, but blood collection and handling would never cause the formation of compounds of interest like cannabis in the blood tube.

As with any blood tube, the first area to check is chain-of-custody, and in some crime labs that is different from chain-of-custody in blood-alcohol cases. In a DWI-drugs analysis once the blood specimen is checked out of evidence control it may be opened by someone other than the LCMS analyst. This means that when the analyst arrives at her desk, she is working with a kit that has broken seals and is not in the same condition as when the officer submitted it into evidence. The criminalist who broke the seals is now a necessary witness in the chain of custody.

The analyst who opens the blood kit may not be the same analyst who performs the ELISA screening. Additionally, the analyst who performs the subsequent LCMS confirmation testing may not be the analyst who performed the ELISA screening. The series of analysts creates a problematic chain-of-custody issue for the prosecution. Chain-of-custody is usually unassailable when an officer seals a blood kit in the field and the analyst who performs the testing is the one who broke the original seal. As long as the original seal is intact, the prosecution can claim that there is no evidence of tampering and the sample is in substantially the same condition as it was when it was sealed. Obviously, environmental conditions and length of time in transit or storage may still be an issue.

When a second, or even third analyst receives the blood tube, the original seal will be broken and some of the sample will be missing. That is prima facie evidence of tampering. Once the defense establishes that the original seal was broken and that the sample is not in substantially the same condition as it was when the officer sealed it in the field, the people who broke the seal and handled the sample must appear and give testimony before the test result is admissible.

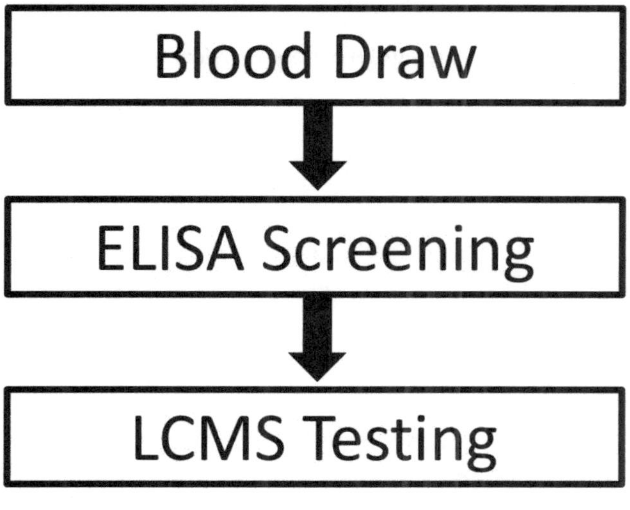

Figure 11.49 *The 3-Step Process*

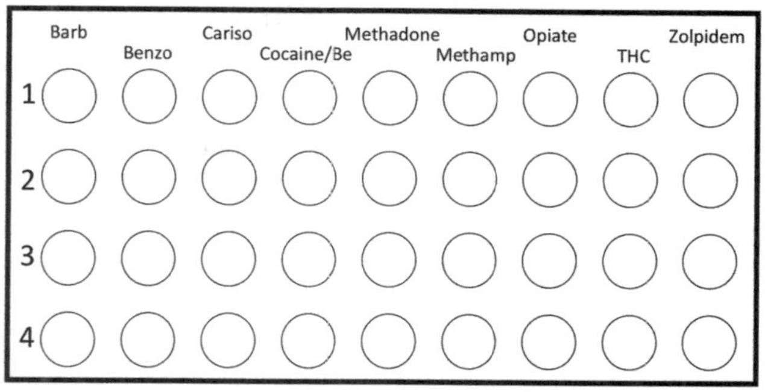

Figure 11.50 *ELISA Screening Plate. ELISA kits are commercially-available for different combinations of drug categories.*

The testing process is a three-step sequence (Figure 11.49).

A. ELISA—Enzyme-Linked Immunosorbant Assay

The first step in the actual analysis of the blood is called an "Enzyme-Linked Immunosorbant Assay" (ELISA). An "assay" is an analysis of a substance for identification, quality, or quantity of an unknown component. In the crime lab, they are assaying primarily for identification and secondarily for quantity.

An immunoassay is a "competitive binding" process commonly used in laboratories. Specific antigens with the same or similar chemical structure of the target compound compete to bind with specific binding sites on a particular antibody.

The ELISA analyst has a plate with "microwells" in rows across the plate (Figure 11.50). Microwells are simply small bowl-shaped containers molded into the plate. She pipettes a small amount of the blood sample into each of the microwells horizontally across the plate. Each horizontal row represents an individual subject's blood sample. Each well within the horizontal row represents one of the nine categories of drugs for which the crime lab has chosen to screen.

The ELISA analyst then pipettes one of the pre-determined antibodies (an enzyme-labeled drug) vertically down the plate.

The enzyme-labeled drug competes with possible drugs for antibody binding sites within a subject sample. The unbound material is then washed out of the microwells.

A chromogenic substrate is then added to the samples. The substrate develops color with the bound enzymes. The excess is washed away and a spectrophotometer is used to measure the color change to determine whether a drug category has been detected or not detected. This process is known as a "colorimetric assay."

Cross-reactivity can be a problem with ELISA. Despite the fact that the enzyme-labeled drugs are developed around a specific drug, other drugs or compounds with similar structures will also bind to the antibodies and produce a "detected" signal. This is why ELISA screening is only useful as a preliminary or presumptive tool. A second, confirmatory test must be done.

The ELISA specimen is just 0.1 mL of blood, serum or plasma. The enzyme-labeled drugs are purchased by the labs as "Immunalysis Reagent Kits" from a commercial vendor. There are specific kits for specific drug categories such as: Cocaine Metabolite, Methamphetamine, Opiates, Carisoprodol, Zolpidem, Cannabinoids, Benzodiazepines, Barbiturates, Methadone and others.

Calibrators are also purchased from a commercial vendor and are used to create high-calibrators, cutoff (low) calibrators and positive controls. Blanks are also created and used. At the end of the run, the high calibrators and positive controls should all be labeled as "detected" and the negative controls and blanks should be "not detected." But, what happens when it goes awry? Do they have to do it all over again? Not necessarily.

Data which does not meet all of the quality control criteria may be accepted at the discretion of the unit supervisor or designee. What this means in legal terms is that the unit supervisor can give all analysts the discretion to say "good enough for government work" when everything doesn't go according to plan.

While the ELISA screening is the preliminary step in the ultimate result, only a few areas are worth attacking by the defense. Realistically, ELISA is not needed by the crime lab for any purpose other than budgetary reasons. ELISA screening is not a scientific or legal prerequisite to LCMS testing. The crime lab could eliminate ELISA screening and simply test all blood samples by LCMS. They could also decide which categories of drugs to test for by LCMS by throwing darts at a dartboard labeled with the different categories of drugs. An attack on ELISA lies primarily in the chain of custody of the blood sample submitted to the crime lab. However, when a category of drugs is not detected, but is sent off for LCMS testing and results in a positive result, the conflict may provide an area of attack.

Below is an ELISA Preliminary Drug Screen result chart (Figure 11.51). It lists eight pieces of information for each of nine assays, and shows the presence of three drug categories. Note the Analyst's initials appear along with the date of analysis (Mar 19, 2013). There is also the Technical Reviewer's initials and stamp in the middle of the box, indicating review on the same date. The analyst also placed check-marks next to each category that was detected. The eight categories of information, from left-to-right, are explained below.

Assay

There are nine "Assay" categories which correspond to the nine wells across the ELISA plate. The names of the drug categories are programmed into the system, but are not necessarily limited to the specific drug named. For example, the assay category "THC" includes all forms of THC whether it is the active drug or the inactive metabolite. Likewise, "Methamp" includes all amphetamines, not just metham-

BLOOD EVO ELISA Preliminary Drug Screen

Assay	Result	Sample Abs.	Cutoff Level	Neg	Cutoff	High	High Level
Barb	ND	1.142	100 ng/mL	1.232	0.988	0.325	1000 ng/mL
Benzo	DETECTED	0.083	25 ng/mL	0.699	0.178	0.086	250 ng/mL
Cariso	DETECTED	0.085	100 ng/mL	1.358	0.607	0.225	1000 ng/mL
Cocaine/Be	ND	1.547	25 ng/mL	1.446	0.557	0.176	250 ng/mL
Methadone	ND	0.839	20 ng/mL	0.784	0.460	0.089	200 ng/mL
Methamp	ND	0.727	25 ng/mL	0.947	0.269	0.108	250 ng/mL
Opiate	DETECTED	0.919	5 ng/mL	2.204	1.130*	0.261	50 ng/mL
THC	ND	0.986	10 ng/mL	1.093	0.462	0.195	100 ng/mL
Zolpidem	ND	1.567	20 ng/mL	1.382	0.476	0.323	200 ng/mL

Tech Reviewed By MAR 19 2013

Analyst: 03/19/13 Print Date: 3/19/2013 DRE Opinion: □ CN □ CNS-D □ N.A. □ D.A. □ CNS-S □ INH □ HA

Batch ID#: 31913 Suspected Drugs: ____________

Figure 11.51 ELISA Preliminary Drug Screen result chart

phetamine. ELISA screenings are not uniform across all jurisdictions. The assay category is assembled based upon the drugs for which the crime lab has chosen. ELISA screening is not limited to forensic applications, either. It is used in many formats relating to healthcare and disease prevention applications.

Result

The result category for the ELISA Preliminary Drug Screen above indicates either "ND" which stands for "Not Detected," which appears in the Barbiturate, Cocaine, Methadone, Methamphetamine and Zolpidem categories, or "DETECTED," which appears in the Benzodiazepene, Carisoprodol and Opiate categories.

Samples with a result of detected are sent off for further confirmation and, at the analyst's discretion, those labeled not detected may also be sent off for further testing. If one is sent off for confirmation, yet has been labeled not detected the analyst's reasons should be scrutinized carefully for bias.

Sample Abs.

The category "Sample Abs." stands for "Sample Absorbance." This is a measure of light which was absorbed by the sample in that particular screen. The ELISA Screen is a colorimetric screening which is a type of spectroscopy where light is passed through the sample. A sample may absorb a little bit of the light, or a lot of the light, depending on the sample's properties. The absorbance of light is altered by the addition of the substrate by the analyst when the substrate binds to the drug. (A "substrate" is the substance upon which the enzyme acts).

In the assay example above, the Sample Absorbance level is inversely proportional to the amount of drug. In other words, more drug in the blood sample causes less absorbance of the light (i.e. more light makes it through the sample). Note that not all ELISA screening kits work on the principle of inverse proportionality.

The number stated in the Sample Absorbance category is a measure of the intensity of the color as light was passed through it. It does not correspond to traditional light measurements such as "lumens" but is a simple comparative reference used by the device. In the example, above, the Opiate category has a sample absorbance of 0.919.

Cutoff Level

Moving to the right, the Opiate category has a Cutoff Level of 5 ng/mL. The Cutoff Level is the amount of drug (reported as weight per volume) where the crime lab has chosen to say that the sample is "Detected" or "Not Detected." The term "Not Detected" does not mean that there is a complete absence of the drug. It simply means that the crime lab will not submit the sample for further confirmatory testing by Liquid Chromatography/Mass Spectrometry. Keep in mind that such decisions may be for scientific reasons, such as the limits of measurement may cause too many "Detected" samples to be sent on for confirmation which are actually negative. Confirmation testing costs more by adding more personnel, equipment and time to the equation.

Neg

The "Neg" category is a programmed sample-absorbance level which corresponds to a "negative" result (which may be different from a "Not Detected" result). In the Opiate category, above, the negative result is 2.204. If the sample absorbance result is 2.204 or higher, the result is considered to be "negative" or 0 ng/mL. However in this example, the result was 1.130, which is lower, and it was reported correctly as "DETECTED."

Cutoff

The "Cutoff" category is the sample-absorbance level that the crime lab has chosen to report a drug category as Detected or Not Detected (see "Cutoff Level" above). The Cutoff for the Opiate category is set at 1.130 which is equivalent to 5 ng/mL of the drug. If the sample absorbance result indicated something between Negative level of 2.204 and the cutoff level of 1.130, the reported result would be "DETECTED," but it should not be sent on for confirmation testing because it did not meet the sample-absorbance parameter of the cutoff level. In other words, the drug could actually be present, but because of the scientific levels of detection, it might be classified as background noise; or, it might not be economically feasible to run a confirmatory test on every detected opiate at that level; or, it might be a policy decision not to pursue prosecution of drivers at such low levels. It is likely a combination of these factors.

High

The "High" category is the upper sample-absorbance level chosen by the crime lab. It is dependent upon the ELISA kit purchased by the crime lab. Since the levels recorded by the ELISA screen are not typically admitted in court, it serves only to provide a linear calibration curve for the crime lab. In other words, the crime lab can plot a straight line from the Negative Level through the Cutoff Level to the High Level.

High Level

The "High Level" category is a programmed sample-absorbance level which corresponds to a specific weight per volume amount In the Opiate category, the high sample-absorbance result is 0.261. If the actual sample absorbance result was exactly 0.261, would be reported as "DETECTED" and, it would equal 50 ng/mL.

Referring again to the ELISA Preliminary Drug Screen illustration, we see that the category "Benzo" (benzodiazepine) has been detected. The reported sample-absorbance is 0.083. Remembering that the sample-absorbance is inversely proportional to the amount of drug, the 0.083 sample-absorbance result puts the amount of drug (weight-per-volume measurement) above the cutoff level of 0.178, and slightly below the High Level of 250 ng/mL (0.086 sample-absorbance).

B. Liquid Chromatography/Mass-Spectrometry

Overview

The forensic sciences are full of acronyms. One of the acronyms you will run into is GCFID, which refers to "Gas Chromatography with Flame Ionization Detection." GCFID is the most common method used for alcohol detection in blood. It is not used for drugs.

GCMS is Gas Chromatography with Mass-Spectrometry Detection which can be used for detection of certain drugs in blood or urine. Also used for detection of certain drugs in blood or urine is LCMS which is "Liquid Chromatography/Mass-Spectrometry." A more complex version is LCMSMS which is "Liquid Chromatography/Mass-Spectrometry/Mass-Spectrometry." A specific, and increasingly commonly-used type of LCMSMS is LC-QQQ-MS which is "Liquid Chromatography/Triple-Quadrupole/Mass-Spectrometry."

All forms of Chromatography which use Mass-Spectrometry are methods that both identify and quantify unknown substances. Unlike GCFID, both GCMS and LCMS use a different type of detector called a "mass spectrometer."

GCFID is used mainly for alcohol detection. The FID is sometimes known as a "dumb" detector because it cannot identify the volatile substance that it detects. For identification, the GCFID relies upon substances eluting at a known time. For example, if alcohol is known to elute at 1:00 minutes on Column A and at 2:00 minutes on Column B, then every substance which elutes at those times is presumed to be alcohol. This can only be determined by running many different known substances, several times, and recording the outcomes. If there is another compound that elutes at 1:00 minutes on Column A and at 2:00 minutes on Column B, the GCFID will mistake it for alcohol. As the compound elutes, it is burned or "ionized." The FID then quantifies the substance by recording the energy generated as the substance is burned.

The Mass-Spectrometer, on the other hand, is sometimes known as a "smart" detector. As the ion of interest (also known as a "resonant ion") elutes, it is fractured by one of many available methods into a known spectral pattern. Each ion has a specific pattern and, thus, identification is not governed by the time of elution, but by comparison to a spectral library. The spectral library is a series of patterns of shattered ions programmed into the database. The spectral patterns are compared by the computer and identification is made.

Definitions: An "ion" is an electrically-charged atom or groups of atoms. Typically, the number of electrons balances the number of protons in an atom making it electrically-neutral. An ion is created by the addition or loss of electrons. A "cation" has a positive charge and is created by the loss of electrons. An "anion" has a negative charge and is created by the addition of electrons. A "resonant ion" describes an ion with delocalized electrons that are contained within certain molecules.

The basic process is that a small portion of the prepared sample is injected through the sample inlet at high pressure into the mass spectrometer chamber. The mass spectrometer is housed inside of a vacuum which is created by a device called a "rough pump." The sample is struck by a high-energy ion beam which cleaves the molecular bonds of the sample. The ions created pass through a mass analyzer which sorts ions and further shatters the sample's molecules. The fragmented ions which make it to the end of the process enter an electron multiplier, causing an electron cascade, which goes to a detector for quantification. The signal from the detector is sent to an amplifier and finally to a computer which analyzes the result (Figure 11.52).

LC-QQQ-MS gets its name from the fact that it uses three quadrupoles, in sequence, to sort and identify ions of interest. A quadrupole, as the name suggests, is made up of four monopoles. A monopole is a rod, electrically neutral, but with oppositely charged ends. The strength and polarity of the monopoles is one factor that causes non-resonant ions to be sorted and filtered out of the ion stream (Figure 11.53).

LC-QQQ-MS uses three quadrupole arrays in sequence to shatter ions and filter the ion stream before it hits the detector. The first and third quadrupole arrays function as mass analyzers. The second quadrupole array is sometimes referred to as a "collision cell." All of the arrays are housed in a vacuum chamber (Figure 11.54).

The pressurized ion stream enters the first quadrupole array as it elutes from the column through a nebulizer called

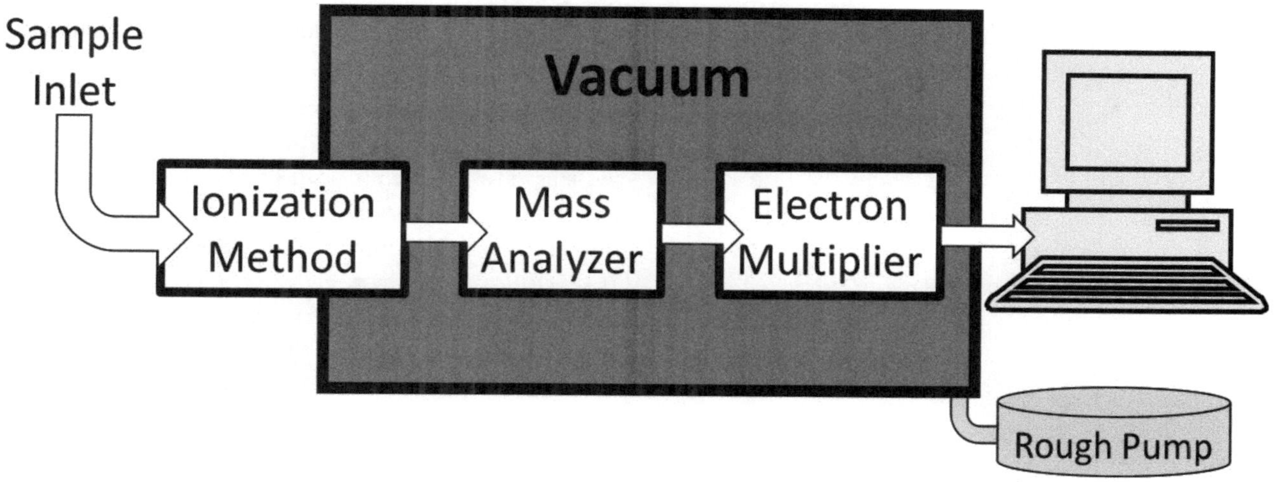

Figure 11.52

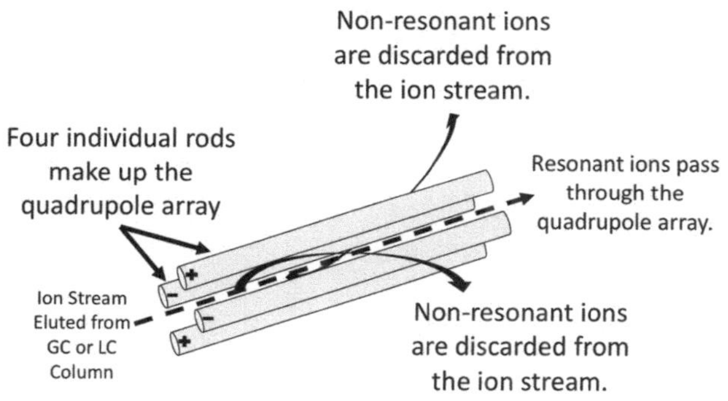

Figure 11.53 *Single-Quadrupole Mass-Filter Array. Non-resonant ions are not "ions of interest" and are filtered out. Resonant ions are "ions of interest" which identify the drug(s).*

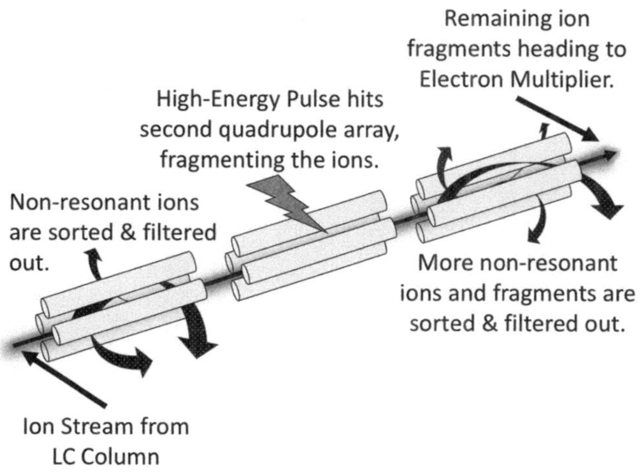

Figure 11.54 *Triple-Quadrupole Array*

an "inlet cone." Periodic maintenance should be done on the inlet cone to ensure that a full, fine spray is produced.

The first ionization process used is "EI" which stands for "Electron Ionization" and consists of a high-energy beam of ions which shatters the molecules in a predictable pattern as they exit the inlet cone (EI is sometimes referred to as a "hard" method of ionization). Another common method used in LCMS is "CI" which stands for "Chemical Ionization," although it is not commonly used in forensic labs when examining for drugs (CI is sometimes referred to as a "soft" method of ionization). The advantage to using EI over CI is that with EI, the spectral pattern that results from the shattering of the molecules can be compared to a spectral library for identification of the ions, irrespective of what type of device is used. CI, on the other hand, creates patterns that are generally dependent upon the device used and the manufacturer's specifications. ESI, or "Electrospray Ionization" is another ionization method and is used at atmospheric pressures and is not housed in a vacuum.

In LCMS the ions are separated, detected and measured according to their mass-to-charge ratios. The symbol for the mass-to-charge ratio is m/z where "m" is the mass and "z" is the charge. The term "Resolving Power" (abbreviation "res") designates the relative ability of a mass spectrometer to separate two masses.

The first quadrupole array electronically filters out non-resonant ions by superimposing a radio frequency (RF) across the constant DC current potentials between the four parallel rods. This leaves the resonant ion, also known as the "parent" ion in the stream. Non-resonant ions are discarded.

The ion stream is accelerated and enters the second quadrupole array. In the second array, the ion stream is

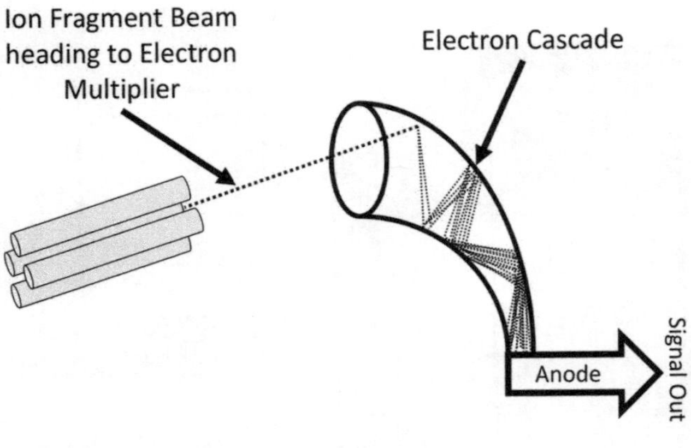

Figure 11.55 Electron Multiplier & Detector

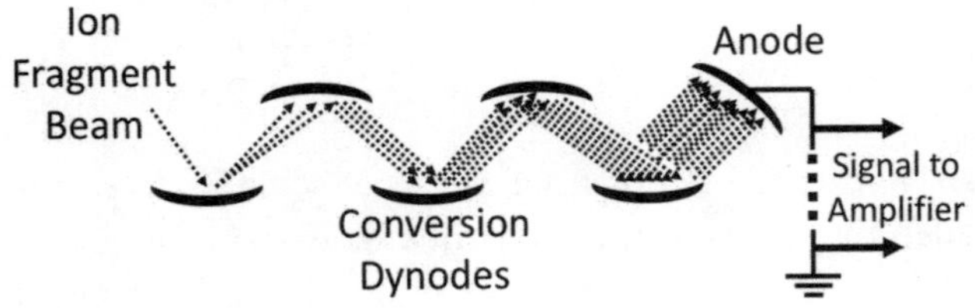

Figure 11.56 Electron Multiplier

bombarded with high kinetic energy electronic pulses in a nitrogen stream (helium and argon may also be used). This shatters, or "fragments," the resonant (parent) ions by breaking their molecular bonds. This is called "Collision-Induced Dissociation" (CID) or Collisionally-Activated Dissociation (CAD). The fragments continue on in the ion stream to the third quadrupole array. Non-resonant are discarded.

The ion stream is accelerated and enters the third quadrupole array. The third quadrupole array electronically filters out non-resonant ions much like the first quadrupole, leaving ion fragments. Non-resonant ions are discarded. The remaining fragments pass into a funnel-shaped device called an "Electron Multiplier."

Electron Multiplier/Detector

After the stream of ions has been filtered and shattered by the mass analyzer (triple quadrupoles), the surviving fragments enter an "Electron Multiplier" for the final phase of the detection and quantification process (Figure 11.55).

The stream of fragments is accelerated down a curved metal funnel-like structure which is highly charged with a few hundred, to over one thousand volts, depending on the system. The fragments strike the side of the structure known as a conversion dynode, which is made of a "secondary-emissive" material. This induces the emission of one or more electrons from the secondary-emissive material. The electrons ricochet across the funnel and strike another section, each releasing one or more electrons. They, in turn, ricochet back across the funnel releasing even more electrons. This multiplication of electrons creates a cascade effect as they work their way down the funnel.

At the small-end of the funnel is an anode, which collects the electrons and produces a signal proportional to the number of electrons that are collected (Figure 11.55). The signal is amplified, recorded, and printed as a quantity.

LCMS Chromatography

LCMS produces chromatograms which plots the abundances of the ions as a signal on a vertical axis and an "Acquisition Time" on the horizontal scale for a Total Ion Chromatogram (TIC). "TIC" is sometimes known as "Total Ion Current." The signal in LCMS is electron counts plotted against the "Acquisition Time." Acquisition Time is similar to the time

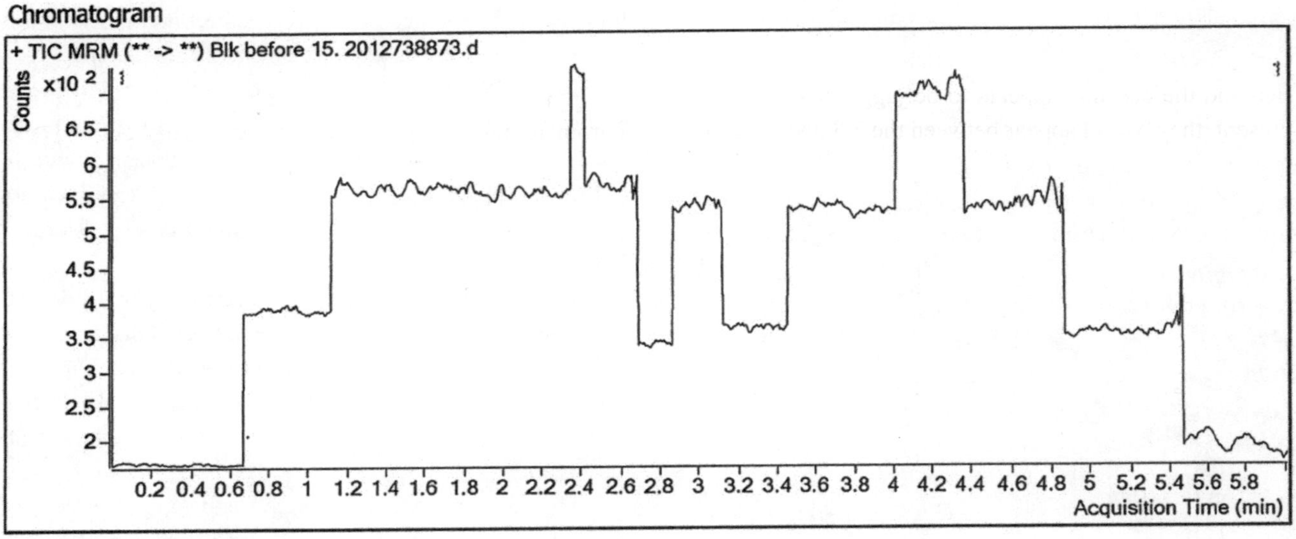

Figure 11.57 True-Blank Chromatogram—Opiates

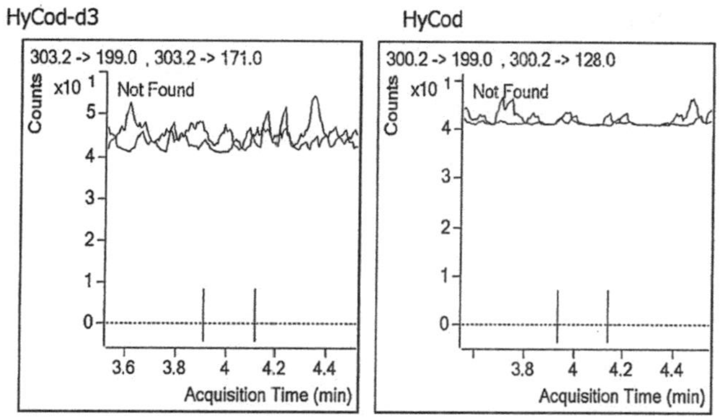

Figure 11.58 *True-blank chromatograms for Hydrocodone d3 (internal standard) and for Hydrocodone.*

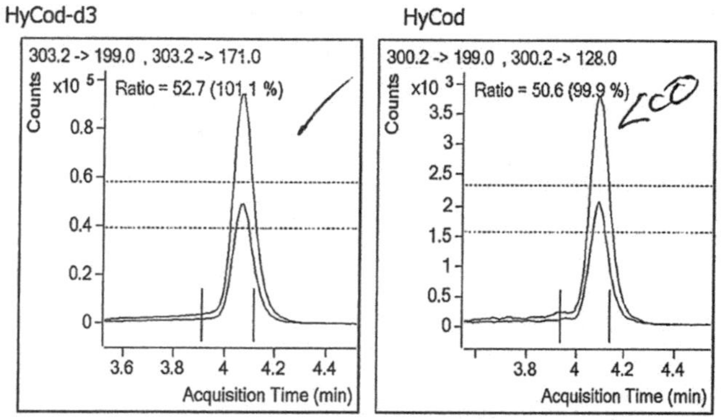

Figure 11.59 *Positive chromatograms for Hydrocodone d3 (internal standard) and Hydrocodone.*

of elution in GCFID testing. The chromatogram lists the term "+ TIC MRM" which stands for "Positive Total Ion Chromatogram, Multiple Reaction Monitoring." The chromatograms may look similar to the ones produced by GC-FID, used for alcohol detection.

MRM is accomplished by specifying the parent mass of the compound for MS/MS fragmentation and then specifically monitoring for a single fragment ion. The fragmentation results in a transition from the parent mass to the fragment mass known as a "transition" and can be written (parent mass -> fragment mass). For example 300.2 -> 199.

While positive LCMS chromatograms may look similar to GCFID, the LCMS blanks look much different than GCFID. The illustration, above, is a true-blank chromatogram for opiates prior to the opiate-detection chromatogram (Figure 11.57). It is referred to as a "true-blank" because it contains nothing—not even the internal standard.

Note that unlike a blank GCFID chromatogram for alcohol, this LCMS blank has what appear to be jagged and irregular peaks. In reality, the "peaks" are electronic "noise" from the instrument. Because the instrument is looking for such small amounts of opiates, the view is highly-magnified and the baseline appears to be jagged. If opiates were present, they would appear between the 3.8 and 4.2 minute-marks. Note the designation for TIC MRM in the upper left corner and the symbols (**->**) which indicates that it is monitoring transitions from parent ion to fragment ion (also known as a "daughter ion").

LCMS chromatograms also give a close-up view of the areas of interest. HyCod-d3 (Figure 11.58, left) is the internal standard used to measure for Hydrocodone, labeled "HyCod" on the chromatogram shown above (Figure 11.58, right). There are two lines present because it is tracking two different ions: ion 303.2 transitioning to 199.0, and; ion 303.2 transitioning to ion 171.0. If present, the internal standard (Hydrocodone-d3) would appear at the acquisition times bracketed by the vertical lines which appear at approximately 3.9 to 4.15 minutes. This is a "true-blank" as it has nothing in the sample—not even the internal standard.

The Hydrocodone chromatogram is blank as well. It tracks the ions of interest for Hydrocodone, which are: ion 300.2 transitioning to 199.0, and; 3002. Transitioning to 128.0. If present, the peak would appear at the acquisition times bracketed by the vertical lines which appear at approximately 3.9 to 4.15 minutes.

Looking more closely at the peak between 3.8 and 4.4, we see HyCod-d3, which is the internal standard used to quantify Hydrocodone (labeled "HyCod" on the chromatogram, Figure 11.59). Unlike the blank for this chromatogram, we clearly see the peaks for the internal standard and for the ion of interest, Hydrocodone, which was detected, but in an amount less than the lab's cutoff level (Figure 11.59, right). Note the analyst's handwritten checkmarks showing that he personally reviewed the results.

We can also see the two lines tracking both ions of interest: ion 303.2 transitioning to 199.0, and; ion 303.2 transitioning to ion 171.0.

Figure 11.60 is a chromatogram for showing presence of opiates and run after the blank. Note that unlike the blank chromatogram for opiates, this one has clearly-defined peaks which are smooth and not jagged. Hydrocodone appears as the sixth peak from the left, between 3.8 and 4.4 minutes.

HyMor-d3 (Figure 11.61, left) is the internal standard used to quantify Hydromorphone, which is labeled "HyMor" on the chromatogram shown, to the right of HyMor-d3. The internal standard appears in the chromatogram between the vertical lines, at approximately 1.5 to 1.7 minutes. Hydromorphone is "not found" (right) and the jagged peaks seen are merely noise.

When an ion of interest is detected, such as in the chromatogram for Carisoprodal (Figure 11.62), it contains one peak which is superimposed upon another peak.

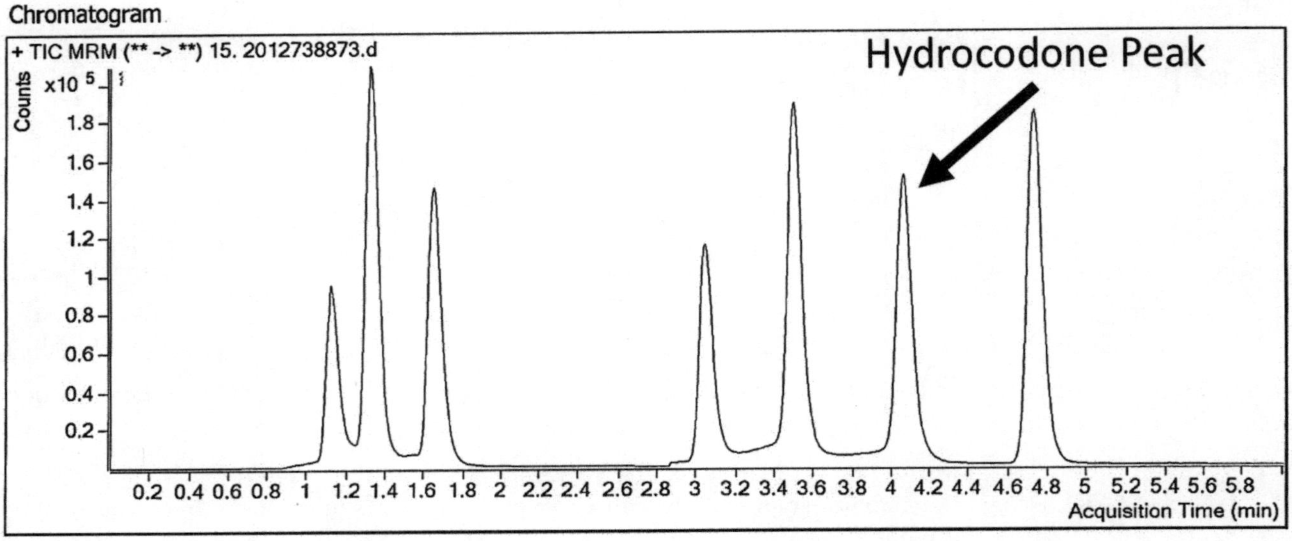

Figure 11.60 *Hydrocodone chromatogram*

Both peaks fall within the vertical acquisition time-lines which are programmed into the software as the expected acquisition time-range.

The peaks also fall within the horizontal dotted-lines programmed into the software for relative abundances of the ions of interest. The ions (261-transitioning-to-176, and 261-transitioning-to-55, must fall within a certain ratio of each other. In this case, the ratio is 65.4:1 which is 99.7% of the expected ratio for the ions. The reported ratio can also exceed the expected ratio.

On the next page is a true-blank chromatogram for Carisoprodal and Meprobamate (Figure 11.63). Compare it with the true-blank for opiates. It does not have the boxy characteristics of the opiate blank and, except for the spike at 4.8 minutes, it is relatively uniform in appearance.

The individual chromatograms, for Carisoprodal (Cari); Carisoprodal Internal Standard (Cari-d7); Meprobamate (Mepro), and; Meprobamate Internal Standard (Mepro-d7) confirm the fact that it is a true-blank (Figures 11.64 and 11.65).

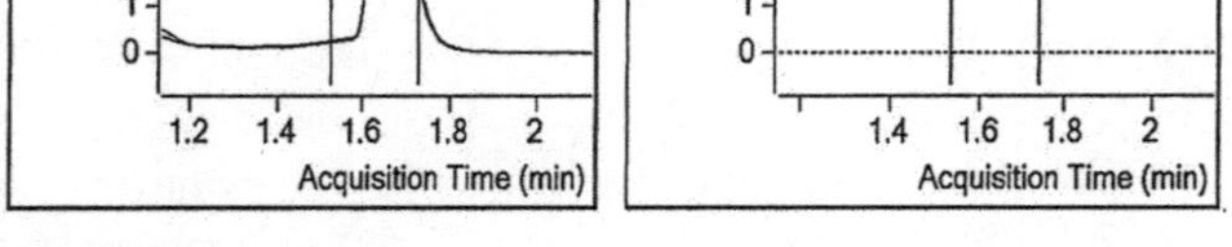

Figure 11.61 *Hydromorphone internal standard (positive) and Hydromorphone (negative) chromatogram*

Next page (Figure 11.66) is a chromatogram for Meprobamate (1.6 minutes) and Carisoprodal (3.4 minutes). Note the difference between the characteristics of this chromatogram compared to the jagged baseline of the blank.

The individual chromatograms (Figure 11.67) are for Carisoprodal (Cari); Carisoprodal Internal Standard (Cari-d7); Meprobamate (Mepro), and; Meprobamate Internal Standard (Mepro-d7). They show that each of the two drugs

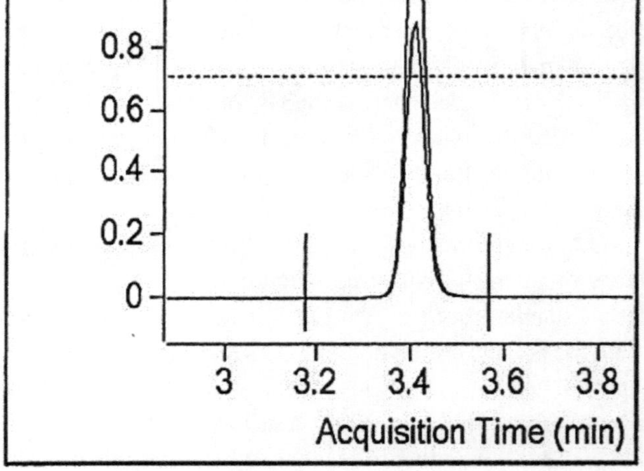

Figure 11.62 *Carisprodal*

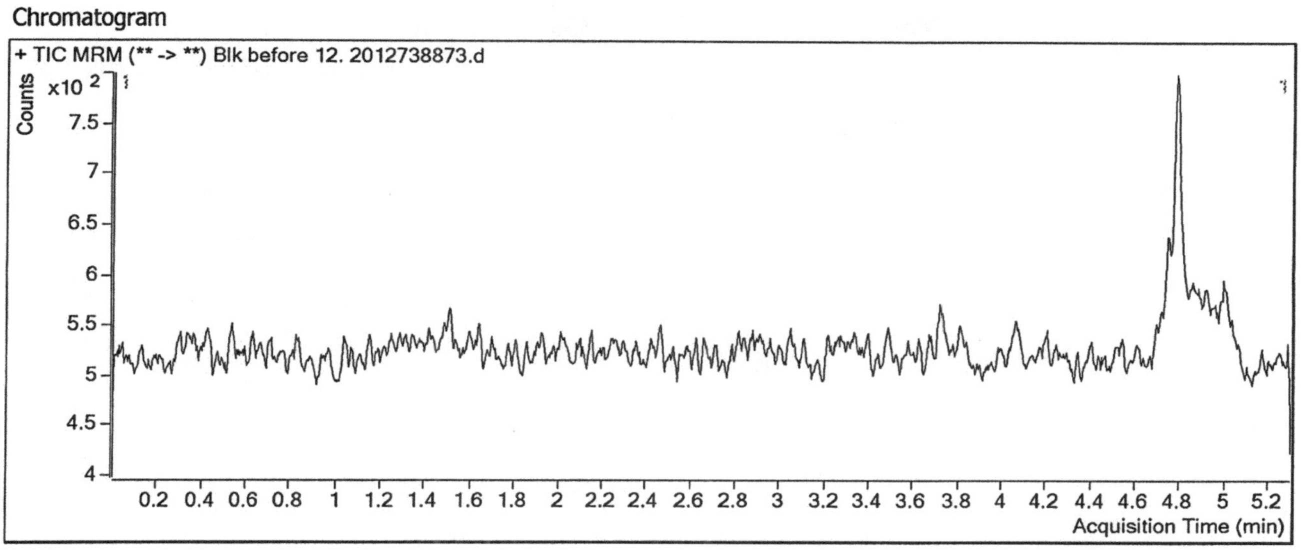

Figure 11.63 *Carisprodal and Meprobamate (blank)*

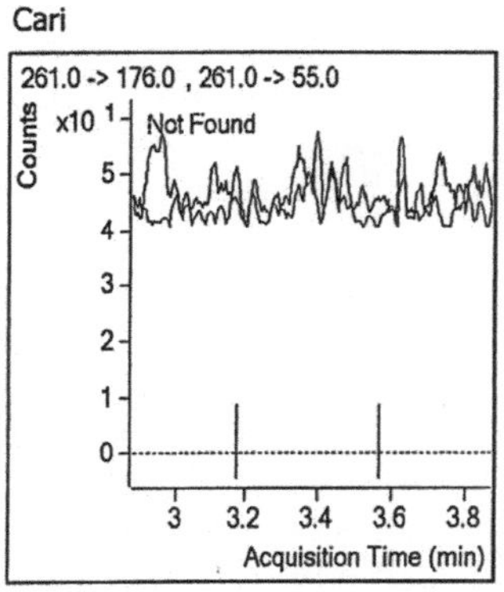

Figure 11.64 *Carisprodal (blank)*

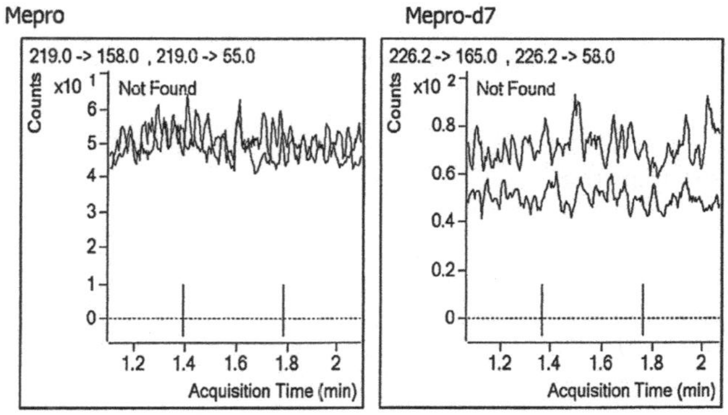

Figure 11.65 *Meprobamate (blank)*

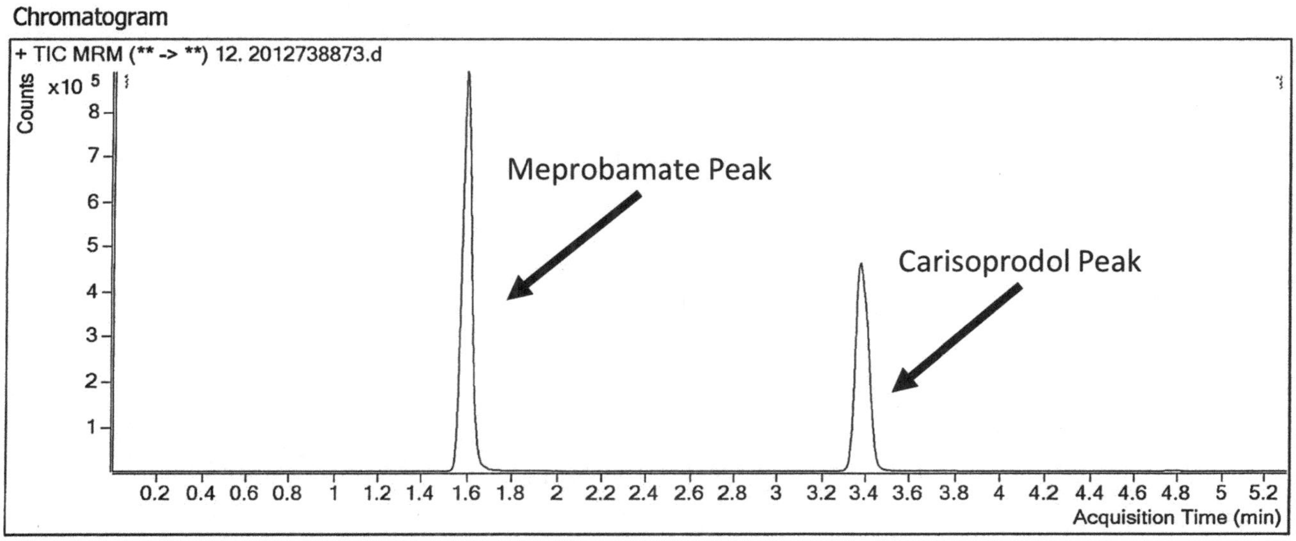

Figure 11.66 *Carisprodal and Meprobamate*

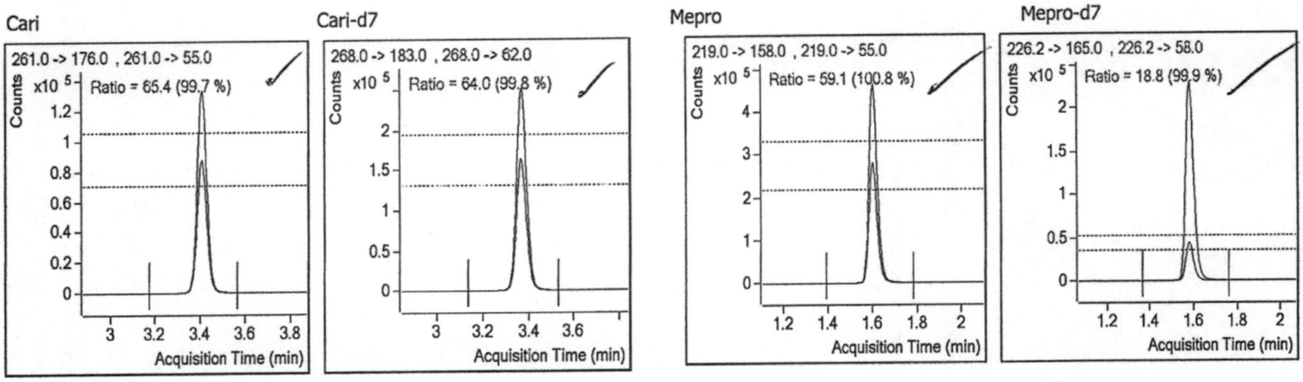

***Figure 11.67** Carisprodal and Meprobamate (positive)*

Compound	RT	ck	RT Range	Transition	Area	MI	Q1	g	lo	Q1 Range	ng/mL	
Cari	3.41		(3.21-3.55)	261.0 -> 176.0	401133		65.4			(52.5-78.7)	1937.52	+
Cari-d7	3.37		(3.17-3.51)	268.0 -> 183.0	778368		64.0			(51.3-77.0)		
Mepro	1.60		(1.52-1.68)	219.0 -> 158.0	1231199		59.1			(46.9-70.3)	9751.47	+
Mepro-d7	1.58		(1.49-1.65)	226.2 -> 165.0	614024		18.8			(15.0-22.5)		

***Figure 11.68** LC-QQQ-MS Printout*

were detected. None of the ratios was off by more than 0.8% of the expected range and all fell within the expected acquisition-time represented by the vertical lines.

The computer print-out which describes the Carispoprodal/Meprobamate chromatograms give a more-specific retention time, area counts, and a quantification measured in nanograms per milliliter (Figure 11.68). The program also reports these results as "positive" in accordance with the lab's protocols and the analyst circled the "+" signs as an indicator that he examined this report.

Compound	RT	ck	RT Range
Cari	3.41		(3.21-3.55)
Cari-d7	3.37		(3.17-3.51)
Mepro	1.60		(1.52-1.68)
Mepro-d7	1.58		(1.49-1.65)

***Figure 11.69** Compound and retention times*

The first three columns, from left to right, represent the drug's name, actual retention (or acquisition) time of the drug and the expected retention or acquisition time for each drug. (Figure 11.69.)

The "Transition" column names the ion-of-interest's mass spectral weights before it is shattered (261.0 for Carisoprodol) and after it is shattered (176.0). If the ion does not transition from 261.0 to 176.0, it is not identified as Carisoprodol. (Figure 11.70)

Likewise, the transition column identifies the Meprobamate ions-of-interest as transitioning from the mass spectral weight of 219.0 before it is shattered to 158.0 after it is shattered. The numbers in the smaller font, below the ions-of-interest are the ions for the internal standards for both drugs. The numbers in smaller font, below the ions of interest, are the internal standard ion transitions.

Transition
261.0 -> 176.0
268.0 -> 183.0
219.0 -> 158.0
226.2 -> 165.0

***Figure 11.70** Transition column*

The Area column is a measure of the peak area counts. Q1 is the ratio of the area counts and Q1 Range is the expected ratio range. Finally, ng/mL is the calculated quantification of the compound measured as weight-per-volume in units of nanograms per milliliter. (Figure 11.71)

Area	MI	Q1	g	lo	Q1 Range	ng/mL
401133		65.4			(52.5-78.7)	1937.52
778368		64.0			(51.3-77.0)	
1231199		59.1			(46.9-70.3)	9751.47
614024		18.8			(15.0-22.5)	

***Figure 11.71** Area counts, ratio, and quantification.*

11.26 Secondary Blood Testing

Independent test versus referee sample

The terms *independent test* and *referee sample* (or *second sample*) are two very different things. Although an independent sample is commonly blood, it does not necessarily have to be a blood sample (it could be breath). The key to an independent sample is that it is entirely separate from the police collection and testing procedures. In the case of blood, it requires a separate needle stick and collection tubes.

A referee sample, or second sample, is one of the two tubes of blood drawn by law enforcement. It does not have the added safeguards of an independent test because it relies upon the phlebotomist designated by the police, the integrity of the law enforcement blood kit and the handling of the tubes by law enforcement before it is picked up by the defendant's designee.

When picking up the second sample for defense testing, it is important that neither the defense attorney nor the defendant pick up the tube. The second sample should be retrieved by a third party designated by the defense. It should be delivered directly to the lab that will do the additional testing. Many messenger services provide this service at a reasonable fee. Private investigators may also perform this service. If the defense attorney picks up the sample, he becomes a witness regarding chain of custody. If the defendant picks it up, he also becomes a necessary witness for admissibility and leaves open the possibility of tampering.

References

Alobaidi, T. A. A., D. W. Hill and J. P. Payne. "Significance of Variations in Blood-Breath Partition Coefficient of Alcohol," *British Medical Journal*, December 18; 2(6050): 1479–1481. 1976.

Carpenter, Dale and James A. Buttram. "Breath Temperature: An Alabama Perspective," *International Association of Chemical Testers (IACT) Newsletter*. Volume 9, Number 2, July 1998.

Fox, Glyn R., and John S. Hayward. "Effect of Hyperthermia on Breath Alcohol Analysis." *Journal of Forensic Sciences.* Vol. 34 No. 4 July 1989, pp. 836-841.

George, S. C., A. L. Babb and M. P. Hlastala. "Dynamics of soluble gas exchange in the airways: III. Single exhalation breathing maneuver." *J.Appl.Physiol* 75:2439-2449, 1993.

Hlastala, M.P., W. J. E. Lamm and J. Nesci. *The Slope Detector Does Not Always Detect the Presence of Mouth Alcohol*, The Champion, 57-61 March, 2006.

Jones, A.W. "Physiological Aspects of Breath-Alcohol Measurement," *Alcohol, Drugs & Driving*, 6:1-25, 1990.

Labianca, D. "The Chemical Basis of the Breathalyzer," *J. Chemistry Education*, 76:261, 1990.

Mason, M.F. "Breath Alcohol Analysis: Uses, Methods and Some Forensic Problems," *J. Forensic Sci.* 21:9-41, 1976.

Ohlsson, J., D. D. Ralph, M. A. Mandelkorn, A. L. Babb and M. P. Hlastala. "Accurate Measurement of Blood Alcohol Concentration with Isothermal Rebreathing." *J.Stud.Alc.* 51:6-13, 1990).

Payne, J. P., D. W. Hill, and D. G. L. Wood. "Distribution of Ethanol between Plasma and Erythrocytes in Whole Blood," *Nature*, 217:963-964, 1968.

Smith, K., "Science, The Intoxilyzer and Breath Alcohol Testing," *The Champion*, May 1987 at 8.

Stuster, J. W., *The Detection of DWI Motorcyclists*, DOT HS 807 839, March 1993; Anacapa Sciences, Inc.

Stuster, J. and Burns, M.; *Validation of the Standardized Field Sobriety Test Battery at BACs Below .10 Percent*, August 1998, San Diego; ANACAPA Sciences, Inc.; Department of Transportation Number: DOT HS 808 839.

Tharp, V. et al., *Development & Field Test of Psychophysical Tests for DWI Arrests*, March, 1981; Southern California Research Institute; Department of Transportation Number DOT HS 805 864.

U.S. Department of Transportation, National Highway Traffic Safety Administration. Highway Safety Programs: *The Detection of DWI Motorists*, DOT HS 807 856, Revised; March, 2005.

U.S. Department of Transportation, National Highway Traffic Safety Administration. Highway Safety Programs: *The Visual Detection of DWI Motorists*, DOT HS 808 677.

Yamamoto, K. and M. Ueda. "Studies on Breath Alcohol Analysis for the Estimation of Blood Alcohol Levels," *J. Forensic Sci.* 1:207-224, 1972.

Chapter 12

Blood Alcohol Calculations for Attorneys

12.1 Blood Alcohol Calculations for Attorneys

Entire books have been devoted to blood alcohol calculations in humans. This chapter is not designed as a treatise on the disposition of alcohol in humans or as a reference for expert witnesses. Many formulae exist for the determination of BAC in humans. Most require conversion of Metric to English measurements. Some require the Body Mass Index (BMI) of the subject. All are complex.

This chapter is designed for attorneys who simply need to know how to calculate quickly the BAC numbers for use in court and in the office. The one-drink potential calculation is based on the Widmark formula. Metric units of measurement have been converted to English. Certain operations have been combined which necessitated moving variables from the numerator to the denominator position and vice versa.

12.2 Determining the One-Drink Potential

A *one-drink potential* is the maximum BAC that a person will reach after one drink. Every defense attorney needs to know how to estimate the one-drink potential for any client who walks in through the door. Fortunately, it is very simple. You will need only the following four pieces of information and a calculator:

1. Client's gender (for males use .13; females use .11 in the calculation)
2. Client's body weight in pounds
3. Type of drink (or alcohol content)
4. Size of drink in ounces

For example, the calculation for a 180 pound male who drank one 12-ounce, 4.16% alcohol beer (Bud Light) is as follows:

$$\frac{(12 \text{ oz. beer}) \times (.0416 \text{ alcohol content})}{(180 \text{ lbs}) \times (.13 \,♂)} = \frac{.499}{23.4} = 0.021 \text{ per drink}$$

The man has a one-drink potential of .021. In other words, .021 is the maximum BAC that he would reach after consuming one 12-ounce beer that is 4.16% alcohol.

If this man has four Bud Lights, the maximum his BAC could be would be .021 × 4 or .084. This does not account for elimination.

Men and women are different in so many ways, it is not surprising that they are also different in their one-drink potential. This is due to the fact that, on average, women have a higher body fat to water ratio than men. Although on average most women are shorter and lighter than most men, women tend to carry more fat in their breasts, buttocks and thighs than men. Clearly this may be reversed in some instances such as when we compare a very physically fit woman with an obese man, but the generalizations made here hold true enough for the attorney to estimate a BAC.

Take the same facts as above, but change the gender from male to female and we find a different one-drink potential:

$$\frac{(12 \text{ oz. beer}) \times (.0416 \text{ alcohol content})}{(180 \text{ lbs}) \times (.11 \,♀)} = \frac{.499}{19.8} = .025 \text{ per drink}$$

If this woman has four Bud Lights, the maximum her BAC could be would be .025 × 4 or .100. This, too, does not account for elimination.

The gender difference is embodied in Widmark's rho factor. Widmark's rho factor is a mathematical expression of the ratio of body fat to water in men and women. The rho factor has been moved from the numerator of Widmark's formula into the denominator of the formula above. For men, use .13 as the rho factor; for women, use .11 as the rho factor.

When figuring alcohol content for drinks that express alcohol content in terms of *proof*, simply divide the proof in half. Thus, 80-proof vodka has 40% alcohol. Sometimes proof is expressed as a small circle similar to a degree sign used for temperature. For example, "80 proof" can also be expressed as "80°".

Below is a quick reference chart for men and women from 100 to 240 pounds. It uses the formula above to calculate the one-drink potential BAC for a 12-ounce, 4% beer, or a 4-ounce, 12% glass of wine, or a 1-ounce shot of 96° distilled liquor. It does not account for elimination rates.

Weight (lbs)	Male	Female
100	.037/drink	.044/drink
110	.034/drink	.040/drink
120	.031/drink	.036/drink
130	.028/drink	.034/drink
140	.026/drink	.031/drink
150	.025/drink	.029/drink
160	.023/drink	.027/drink
170	.022/drink	.026/drink
180	.021/drink	.024/drink
190	.019/drink	.023/drink
200	.018/drink	.022/drink
210	.018/drink	.021/drink
220	.017/drink	.020/drink
230	.016/drink	.019/drink
240	.015/drink	.018/drink

12.3 Elimination and Retrograde Extrapolation

When DWI attorneys discuss elimination, we are mainly discussing the metabolization of the alcohol by the body, rather than the actual elimination of alcohol from the body.

A very small amount of alcohol leaves the body in an unchanged state (less than 6 percent). Most of the alcohol ingested is metabolized by enzymes in the *alcohol dehydrogenase pathway*. Alcohol dehydrogenase, aldehyde dehydrogenase, acetaldehyde and other enzymes play a part in the biological oxidation of alcohol and its metabolites. One can trace the path of alcohol elimination on a molecular level in great detail. Juries are bored by this, judges are confused by it and prosecutors do not know what to do with it on cross-examination.

What we need to know is that after alcohol has been consumed, it is eliminated at a relatively steady rate; rates of elimination have been recorded as low as .008 per hour and as high as about .035 per hour. Generally, alcoholics and binge drinkers with high BACs eliminate alcohol faster than inexperienced drinkers. The average rate used in court by many (but not all) forensic toxicologists is .010 to .017 per hour, depending on whom you talk to. It is not gender-dependent like one-drink potential calculations. Rather, it is dependent upon how "experienced" one's liver has become over time.

A man with a .100 BAC will be a .000 BAC in ten hours if the elimination rate is .010 per hour. Eliminating .010 per hour from his known BAC is called a *retrograde extrapolation* (sometimes known as *back extrapolation*). If the same man has an elimination rate of .015 per hour, he will be a .000 in less than seven hours. A retrograde extrapolation is nothing more than choosing an hourly elimination rate and subtracting that amount from the known BAC. The one caveat to a retrograde extrapolation is that the person must be in the elimination phase of alcohol consumption.

12.4 White's Retrograde Extrapolation

White's retrograde extrapolation calculates the number of drinks that need to be unabsorbed in the subject's stomach in order for the subject to be under the legal limit at the time of driving (this is also known as the *Rising BAC Defense* in many parts of the country).

In years past, before many state's legislatures eliminated the Affirmative Defense, White's retrograde extrapolation was the mainstay of the national DWI defense bar. Virtually the most important question for the attorney was to ask the client how many drinks were consumed in the hour before being stopped by the police. This is because those drinks could remain wholly or partially unabsorbed in the stomach at the time of driving, but could be partially or completely absorbed at the time of the chemical test. Alcohol sitting unabsorbed in the stomach (not in the blood) does not contribute to impairment any more than alcohol that remained in the bottle. A driver's BAC could have been substantially lower at the time of driving than at the time of the chemical test. The converse is also true where the driver is in the elimination phase at the time of driving. In fact, the driver might also be in the absorptive phase when stopped, reached a peak during the investigation, and be in the elimination phase at the time of the chemical test. Thus, the driver could be higher, lower, or have the same BAC at the time of the chemical test as he did at the time of driving. See Figure 12.1.

Now, the argument is virtually worthless where there is no Affirmative Defense because one has to start from the premise that the over-the-limit BAC was correct at the time of the chemical test but was under the limit at the time of

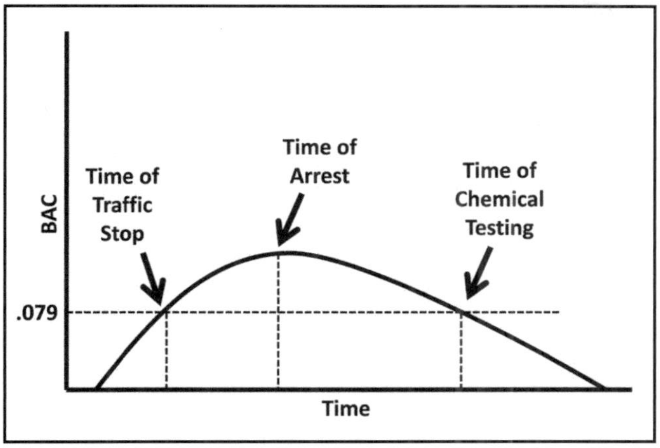

Figure 12.1 *This person would have a .079 at the time of the traffic stop because he was in the absorptive phase. The BAC rises to a point above the limit at the time of arrest, and back down to .079 at the time of the chemical test. A minimum of three measurements must be taken over time to determine which phase the subject is in.*

driving. If you concede the first premise and have no Affirmative Defense, you have lost the *per se* BAC charge.

White's retrograde extrapolation is still important in the scenario, for instance, where a defense rests not on the particular BAC within a specified period of time from driving, but on lack of impairment at the time of driving, such as in an accident case where impairment at the time of the accident is an issue.

Many people are charged with crimes involving injuries or worse along with a misdemeanor DWI. Sometimes one has to sacrifice losing the misdemeanor charge in order to have a chance of winning the more serious felony charges.

Take, for example, the scenario where your client is charged with two counts of assault after rear-ending a car with two passengers at a stoplight. The accident was at 2:15 A.M. The driver's BAC was measured just a half hour after the accident at 2:45 A.M., and it was .090. If he downed his last drink when the bar closed at 2:00 A.M., some of the alcohol could have remained unabsorbed in his stomach at the time of the accident, but fully absorbed at the time of the breath test.

If he is the 180 pound man from the one-drink potential example, the value of the 12-ounce beer could be subtracted from his reported BAC. Thus, we subtract .021 from .090, and the result is a .069. Because we do not know how fast he actually absorbed that 12-ounce beer into his bloodstream, he could have been anywhere from a .069 to the reported result of .090. Under these facts, you will never prove that your client was under the limit, but the prosecutor will never prove that he was over the limit either.

White's retrograde formula can be expressed as follows:

$$\frac{(\text{test result}) + \{[(\text{elapsed time*}) \times (\text{elimination rate } a)] - (.079)\}}{(\text{one-drink potential})}$$

$$= \text{\# of drinks unabsorbed in stomach}$$

* = Elapsed time from time of last drink to time of chemical test.
a = Choose the elimination rate within human limitations that suits your purpose.

$$\frac{(.090) + \{[(.75 \text{ hours})(.010/\text{hr})] - (.079)\}}{(.021)} = \frac{(.098) - (.079)}{(.021)} = \frac{.019}{.021}$$

$$= 0.88 \text{ drinks}$$

$$(0.88 \text{ drinks}) \times (12 \text{ oz. drink size}) = 10.6 \text{ oz.}$$

This means that if he had 0.88 drinks (or 10.6 ounces) unabsorbed in his stomach at the time of the accident, he was no higher than a .079.

For the most complete and thorough explanation of absorption, elimination, and retrograde extrapolations, refer to *Medicolegal Aspects of Alcohol, Fifth Edition*, edited by Dr. James C. Garriott and available from Lawyers & Judges Publishing Company.

12.5 Partition Ratio Conversions

The partition ratio is a way to account for the conversion of blood alcohol concentration to breath alcohol concentration. In simple terms, for every one part of alcohol on one's breath, there must be a proportional amount in that person's blood. If this were not true, breath testing would not work at all. The problem for the prosecution, however, is that the partition ratio varies from person to person, yet the breath testing machines all convert at 2100:1. Thus, if a subject's partition ratio is substantially higher than 2100:1, such as 2400:1, that person would benefit by a breath test because the result would be substantially lower than his true blood alcohol concentration. Conversely, a person with a 1700:1 ratio would find a breath test detrimental because a breath test would yield a result much higher than her true blood alcohol concentration.

Conversion to different partition ratios is a simple mathematical formula. Take the breath test reading and divide it by 2100 then multiply by the new partition ratio number that you have chosen. This will give the corrected breath test value.

Example:

To convert a .100 BAC at 2100:1 to a new ratio of 1500:1 use the formula:

Step 1: (BAC Reading) ÷ 2100 = Y

Step 2: Y × (New Partition Ratio Value) = Corrected Breath Test Value

Step 1: .100 BAC ÷ 2100 = 0.00004762

Step 2: 0.00004762 × 1500 = .071 BAC

Thus a .080 BAC at 1100:1 could be corrected to .042 and, a .080 BAC at 2800:1 could be corrected to .107

Mean Specific Gravity of whole blood is assumed to be 1.055.

Whole blood is assumed to be 80 percent w/w water.

Plasma is assumed to be 92 percent w/w water.

12.6 Unit Conversions

Conversions from among commonly used units of measurement are as follows:

mg/ 100 ml	g% w/v	mg/g	mmol/ L	mg/L	µg/L
50	0.05	0.47	10.8	0.24	240
100	0.10	0.94	21.7	0.48	480
150	0.15	1.41	32.3	0.72	720
200	0.20	1.88	43.2	0.96	960

g = grams
mg = milligrams
µg = micrograms
w/v = weight per volume
w/w = weight per weight
mmol = millimoles
ml = milliliters
L = liters

Chapter 13

Expert Witnesses

Synopsis

13.1 Overview

Expert Witnesses can be used for many different needs. The first thing that you should address is the cost of an expert witness with your client. The expert-cost discussion should take place at the initial interview and it is even wise to overstate the cost a little, just in case something arises during the investigation and trial preparation which would cause an increased cost. A good analogy is to tell your client not to buy the high-performance sports car and not be able to afford to put fuel in the tank.

Typically, we think of experts as forensic toxicologists; however, there are many other experts that may be useful in a DWI case, particularly if there is an accident or illness involved. In addition to a forensic toxicologist, you may consider using the following experts:

- Medical Doctor
- Ophthalmologist
- Registered Nurse
- Pharmacist
- Neuro-Pharmacologist
- Phlebotomist
- Chemist
- Paramedic
- Emergency Medical Technician
- Accident Reconstructionist
- Automotive Engineer
- Traffic Safety/Highway Engineer
- Retired Police Officer
- Dentist

The number and types of expert witnesses are as varied as the situations that you will encounter. While there are many types of experts to be used at trial, they can be broken down into two categories: "Our Experts" and "Their Experts." Good resources for experts are local universities as well as commercial expert witness lists. Carefully research an expert's history and education for both flaws and good points. A dishonest or overreaching expert does you more harm than good.

13.2 Pretrial Preparation

Your Expert Witness needs to know about all evidence that you expect will be admitted at trial. Police reports, calibration logs, blood testing documentation, even pretrial interview transcripts and evidentiary hearing transcripts are worth giving to your expert. Put these documents together in a detailed and easy-to-understand package for your expert's review. For pretrial hearings, it is wise to give your expert copies of the motions that are going to be argued along with a summary of your strategy.

Map out a guide for direct examination. If you are going to use a PowerPoint™ presentation with your expert witness, make sure that he approves of it and understands the slides in detail. Ask your expert what he expects the prosecutor or the judge to hit upon. You may have never before set foot in the courthouse that will handle your case, but your expert may have been there a dozen times before. Many prosecuting agencies have a "script" that they use for particularly well-known defense Expert Witnesses. Former prosecutors from that office may have left the office for private work and brought script copies with them. Ask for them. If that is not available, you can figure out what the script entails by getting a transcript of previous trials with the expert and a particular agency.

Do not give your Expert Witness evidence that has been suppressed. For example, imagine the scenario where your client is a seventy-two-year-old man in ill health. He has gout, arthritis and other problems. He was arrested for DWI, did Field Sobriety tests (poorly) and his blood test result was a 0.200. In a feat of sheer brilliance, you persuade the court to suppress the blood test results based on an illegal search and the per se charge is dismissed, but the DWI charge still remains.

Do not supply your Expert Witness with the suppressed blood test results and then ask him to make a determination as to the cause of the impairment in court! The expert will be bound to give you a truthful answer which will include the effects of the suppressed blood alcohol concentration. Clearly, you can (and should) ask the expert to base his opinion on the evidence as it appears in court, but a poorly-worded question can destroy the case in an instant.

There is nothing unethical, illegal, or underhanded about asking your expert to make a determination based on nothing but legally admissible evidence. In fact, that is exactly what the Expert Witness is supposed to do.

13.3 Direct Examination of the Defense Expert Witness

Juries can sometimes be "put off" by the use of a defense Expert Witness. They expect a prosecution witness, such as a blood analyst or a breath test technician to appear and testify about the chemical test or the maintenance of the machine because those witnesses are fact witnesses. That is, they had some physical role in the DWI investigation, whether it was receiving and analyzing the blood test and reporting the result or preparing the machine for use in the field.

Defense experts generally are not fact witnesses. They are brought in to do one of two things: They are there to dispute the prosecution's evidence, or they are there to interpret the prosecution's evidence in a different light. In either event, they are paid to be there and they are not fact witnesses. The only exception to this rule is where the defense expert witness retested a chemical sample or recreated some portion of the state's testing procedures.

Direct examination of the Defense Expert needs to start off gently, allowing the jury to get to know the expert before you get into the facts. Start off with basic biographical information; only then should you move into educational history and work history. Ask about committees he or she has served on, awards received, honors, articles published. Then move on to present employment before you get into the facts of the case. For example:

- Can you please introduce yourself to the jury?
- Where are you from (i.e. where do you work and live)?
- What do you do for a living?
- How long have you been a forensic toxicologist (doctor, criminalist, etc.)?
- What is your educational background that allows you to be a forensic toxicologist (doctor, criminalist, etc.)?
- What is your work history with regard to that?
- Do you belong to any professional organizations in your field?
- What positions have you held with those organizations?
- Do you have any awards or certifications?

Obviously, if your expert witness has no awards or special certifications, don't ask about any.

Strategy is of paramount importance when using your own expert. Your strategy will likely be that the state's evidence is worthless because of some flaw that invalidates it or that their evidence may be valid but misinterpreted. Do not confuse the two strategies.

The latter of the two strategies generally works best for many reasons. Sometimes it is difficult to chip away at the credibility of a blood test result when it is properly done. Sure, there are many things that can go wrong with it, but you don't have evidence to show that something actually did go wrong with it. This is where you must elicit the "I don't know" answer from your expert.

For example, in a blood test case where the analyst used a pipette to withdraw blood from a sample tube and we know that the analyst did not rinse the pipette between one subject's tube and the next. You can safely ask your expert if that *could* cause contamination of the next sample. The answer should be in the affirmative. Then you can ask your expert if it *did* cause contamination. The answer should be "I don't know." Next ask if there is any evidence that could *assure us* that there was no contamination. The answer will likely be negative. This is the essence of reasonable doubt and sets up your closing argument perfectly. Do not be afraid of telling the jury that you do not have to prove that your client was under the legal limit or unimpaired—it is the state that must prove she was over the limit or impaired. Since neither side can tell you that the lab procedures followed did not cause contamination, then they cannot assure you of an accurate result.

Always end your direct examination with the "payoff" question: "Based on all of the facts that were presented to you in court, is there a real possibility that Mr. Jones was not over the limit?" Or, "not impaired by alcohol." Or, whatever your particular issue happens to be. Do not put your own expert on the stand if you are not going to ask the payoff question. It is a waste of time and resources.

Prosecution attacks of the defense expert witness are going to come in some variant or combination of three forms:

- The defense expert is a "hired gun," who will say whatever he is paid to say.
- The defense expert is not qualified to render an opinion.
- The defense expert was not there.

Let's look at the counterpoint to these three arguments.

The "hired gun" argument is an attack on the credibility or the character of the witness. It generally has little substance (if it does have substance, maybe you should reconsider your choice of expert). It can be countered with work-history, education, and whether the expert has ever been retained by the prosecution. It is particularly helpful where an expert in a DWI case also works for civil litigants, doing both plaintiff and defense work. If you have a long-standing relationship with the expert, you may be able to ask if there were instances where the expert has advised against retaining him because he would not be able to say anything helpful for the defense.

The "not qualified" attack may be a legitimate attack on the credentials of the expert, rather than on the character of the expert. If it is a legitimate attack, that is the fault of the defense attorney for not retaining the proper expert, or by overreaching during direct examination. Your expert must fit the testimony and you must ensure that you hire the proper expert for the job. Moreover, you need to avoid asking questions that are legitimately outside of the expert's qualifications.

The "not there" argument is the one that you want the prosecution to have to make. When the prosecution makes this argument, you can counter by touting your expert's excellent character and qualifications that are beyond reproach. Don't be afraid to tell the jury what the job of an expert witness really is: It is to examine evidence as presented in court and to render an opinion about that evidence to help the jury make a decision. Don't be afraid to rehearse and use a simple line of questioning with your expert regarding this point. For example, most jurors have never heard of head-space gas chromatography with flame-ionization detection before being picked to hear a blood-test DWI case. It is unreasonable to expect them to make an intelligent decision without the proper information and opinions. You can ask your expert what the role of a defense expert is in a criminal trial. Your expert can answer that it is to examine, explain, and interpret evidence presented in court to help a jury reach a decision.

I use an expert witness in many of my DWI cases. The expert I used in the case below was Doug Scott. Mr. Scott is a retired police officer and former DRE. I have also used Mr. Scott in cases involving accident reconstruction and in speed measurement cases. Sometimes in the smaller counties, you may run into really poorly trained officers that don't want to admit their mistakes until they get backed into a corner. In these cases it's great to have an expert available to hold them to their training. The following exchange comes from a case I had a few years ago involving a speeding charge as the reason for the stop. I spent over sixteen hours preparing for this case by studying how the radar worked alongside my expert witness who guided me down the path. I also edited out the "ums" and "uhs" like my co-author Mr.Nesci. Here's my direct of my witness:

BY MR. SMITH:

Q. Good Afternoon, Mr. Scott. Could you state your full name for the record, please?

A. My full name is Julian Douglas Scott.

Q. Mr. Scott, what is your current occupation?

A. I'm a consultant, a certified substance abuse prevention consultant and a licensed private investigator.

Q. What is your educational background?

A. I have a bachelor's degree in political science with a concentration in criminal justice from NC State University, a post-grad certificate in administrative law enforcement management from NC State, a post-grad certificate in addiction gained from the University of Washington and I'm currently enrolled in the post-graduate study at the University of Florida in forensic drug chemistry.

Q. Mr. Scott, have you ever had any training or have you ever had any experience in law enforcement?

A. Yes, I have.

Q. What was that experience?

A. I was a sworn police officer with Fuquay-Varina Police Department from December 1981 through March of 1985 and then took a job with the Cary Police and as a patrol officer stayed there through June 2003 and then maintained my police certification as an auxiliary police officer through the Morrisville Police Department and also Capitol Special Police through 2010, summer of 2010.

Q. Can you tell me about some of the duties that you did and some of the assignments you had while employed with the Cary Police Department.

A. Yes. I was assigned with the Cary Police Department as a patrol officer initially and as a traffic safety officer. I was also select enforcement unit for the S.W.A.T. team, but it's really not relevant in this case. And then I was assigned as a Sergeant to develop a traffic safety program for the city. It was approximately 1990 and then so supervised that program that was funded through grants through the government safety program for about eight or nine years. Rose to the rank of lieutenant in that position, and then I was a watch shift commander, day shift watch shift commander and also commander of a drug unit for a short time.

Q. Now for the purposes of speed estimation, have you ever had any kind of training with the use of radar?

A. Yes, I have.

Q. Can you explain that?

A. My first training as a radar operator would have been about, it would seem I could approximate it around 1985. And I stayed certified as a radar operator with

Carolina, North Carolina Criminal Justice Education and Training Standards Commission through 2005, I believe, with the exception of about two years where I let my certification lapse due to my assignment as shift manager. I wasn't out running radar at that time. I received training on multiple devices including the Kustom Golden Eagle. I also attended VASCAR training with the highway patrol. I think that was in 2002, roughly. And I stayed certified as a speed measurement operator for about approximately four years.

Q. So you've heard the testimony of Officer Barbee regarding this incident with my client, Mr. Newman.

A. Yes, sir.

Q. I'm going to ask you some of the same questions that I asked him. You heard me mention a multi-path beam cancellation when I was speaking with him. I don't think he knew what that was. Can you describe for the Court what multi-path beam cancellation is?

A. A multi-path beam cancellation occurs when the radar for unknown reasons is unable to form a calculation and the screen just goes blank momentarily and you're unable to calculate the patrol speed or the target speed as a result until it resumes its functions.

Q. So what happens at that point? Do you have to begin a new tracking history?

A. Yes, sir. You have to start everything over.

Q. It's been your training that when you estimate the speed of moving vehicles you're supposed to have a technique or method. Is that correct?

A. That's correct. It's required and it's in the radar training that you have a method or technique to learn to estimate vehicles and then using that learned skill to estimate vehicles.

Q. What would be a common technique or method that an officer would use?

A. The radar training requires that you take your vehicle operated by someone, another police officer driving through measured distances that you know the exact distance and use a stop watch and complete time-distance formulas and learn what the relative motion of a vehicle at a given speed appears to be, say thirty five miles per hour. Then do that in practice with a vehicle running approximately forty five, fifty five and so on until you become very aware of what that relative motion appears to be and then do that as well in moving following another vehicle. And so, you use a police vehicle with someone driving that you can communicate with so you can verify what the speeds actually are. And then you begin to practice that until you become competent to do that.

Q. So you would agree with me that when you took this radar school you were required to estimate the speed of six vehicles in stationary radar, six vehicles moving opposite direction radar with a total variation of forty two miles per hour on twelve vehicles?

A. That's right. You can, and I did, have a leeway of three, average of three and a half miles per hour on the total average of the vehicles. But you can miss one vehicle by up to twelve miles per hour, plus or minus twelve miles per hour and still pass that portion of the daytime testing they do.

Q. Now you're familiar with the supplement of the radar operator training manual that lists all of the approved radar devices that are approved for the State of North Carolina to be used by police officers and speed measurement?

A. I'm familiar with it.

Q. And you heard officer Barbee talking about his setup and his prior procedures that are followed prior to use daily for his Kustom Directional Golden Eagle II moving stationary radar?

A. Yes, I heard.

Q. Did he omit anything in his testimony about setup?

A. He omitted, didn't tell what the numbers are in the light test segments, which is an insignificant detail, but most notably admitted that he did a setup for a moving opposite direction radar.

Q. And you also heard officer Barbee testify that the tuning fork test that they use to calibrate at the end of each stopping action?

A. Yes, I did.

Q. When you were a police officer when did you perform that accuracy test with the tuning fork?

A. The tuning fork test should be done at the beginning of the tour of duty and then immediately after each enforcement action and again at the end of each tour of duty. You do it immediately after each enforcement action so that if it didn't give you the correct numbers as far as plus or minus within one mile per hour with the tuning fork, you could know immediately not to issue any more citations, so that you now are out of work and having the citation you just issued dismissed because of some unreliability.

Q. So it would be a big deal if that never occurred?

A. It's absolutely mandatory. Yes, it's a big deal.

Q. You heard me ask officer Barbee about different types of things that may interfere with target speed, the actual target speed calculation by radar. One of those things was moving angular effect. Can you tell the Court what that is?

A. Sure. Moving angular effect is effect, well I guess I need to correct something. Officer Barbee testified that his speed was inputted from his speedometer in the Kustom Eagle II. That's incorrect. The radar determines the patrol speed and the target speed using the radar microwave energy. So, it's critical then that you don't have sources of interference like angular effect can cause an erroneous patrol speed to be calculated, and moving angular effect is in curves and hills. The beam of the radar can strike other objects on the side of the road, hill cuts, buildings, large signs, other vehicles, anything of that nature and can come back at an angle which can be a little lower in this case. No one would be concerned about, but lower than actual patrol speed which could then compute a higher than actual target speed.

Q. So you're basically saying that it could be wrong and it could be showing a speed that's not the actual speed of the patrol car, so now you've got a speed that's a lot higher than the target that you're actually trying to get.

A. That's correct.

Q. What about patrol speed shadowing? What is that and how can that cause an actual than higher target speed?

A. Patrol speed shadowing occurs when we have another vehicle larger in size and nearby in front which reflects microwave energy and the radar interprets or calculates the speed of that vehicle that reflected that.

Q. What about the double bounce effect? What is that?

A. Double bounce occurs when the microwave energy is transmitted through, police radar strikes another object, like a vehicle you may have passed going down the way. And if it's large and reflects enough microwave energy, has enough space to do that, goes back to the other vehicle then it comes back and of course is interpreted. If you're not listening, this is the purpose of the audio Doppler tone is to make sure that you are selecting the correct vehicle. You could be looking at another vehicle coming toward you, including an opposite direction radar for example and have that occurring and stop the vehicle that's approaching you thinking it's the one that's speeding when in fact it could be the vehicle behind you going in the opposite direction. So there's the point really about all this is it's critical that you listen and have an audio Doppler tone that is at a sufficient volume to hear above everything else in the vehicle so you can tell when it makes a subtle shift between vehicles, between objects, you know what it is that it's reflecting.

Q. That audio Doppler tracking feature is required, is that correct?

A. Yes, it's required. It's in one of those requirements in G.S. 8-50.2(b) I believe, is that you must follow the procedures of the North Carolina Criminal Justice Education and Training Standards Commission and that is one of the procedures.

Q. Now you heard Officer Barbee testify that he had a good tracking history. Would you agree with that statement?

A. I heard him say that.

Q. You've reviewed the video. Is that correct?

A. That's correct.

Q. And you've even made a chart about speed of the patrol vehicle versus the speed of my client's vehicle and all of that. Is that correct?

A. That's correct.

Q. And you've watched the different windows in the video showing the speed of the patrol vehicle and the speed of the target vehicle?

A. That's correct.

Q. Give me your expert opinion of what you saw in the video.

A. Okay. Well first there was no tracking history because there was no audio Doppler tone. You cannot have a tracking history without a audio Doppler tone sufficient volume to hear above everything else during all radar operations. If you can't hear the shift in microwave energy, you cannot tell what you're clocking. You can't tell if you are getting a moving angular effect. You can't tell if you've got a double bounce. You can't tell if you've got a vehicle coming, you know, beyond that vehicle. You have to listen to the audio Doppler tone. It is annoying. I've got a unit in the courtroom, and I can illustrate the sound so that it's clear that it would be heard and audible on that videotape if it had been present. It's an annoying sound to listen to for a full ten or twelve hour shift, but you've got to do it.

Q. Your Honor, could I have him demonstrate that tone for you?

THE COURT: Sure.

(Witness sets up Doppler unit)

THE WITNESS: Just for the purpose of hearing the tone, this would be a sixty five mile per hour tuning fork. And this is what you should hear while you're making your clock on your vehicle. And the higher the vehicle, that would be noticeable in a sharper, higher pitch than this. I think I can get this to come up now.

(Witness hits tuning fork and unit plays audio Doppler tone)

THE WITNESS: And of course, as the signal fades away, it becomes staticky. So, if you have a fluctuating signal that was mentioned earlier, you do not make the clock, because you've got selectivity issues. You've got signals for those issues. A lower speed vehicle, this is thirty five.

(Witness hits tuning fork two times)

(Witness hits tuning fork two more times and unit plays audio Doppler tone)

THE WITNESS: The lower tone is the lower speed. This is what sixty five sounds like.

(Witness hits tuning fork twice and unit plays audio Doppler tone twice)

Q. Mr. Scott, you didn't hear an audio Doppler tone in the video did you sir?

A. I did not hear an audio Doppler tone at any time in the video.

Q. Officer Barbee testified that he had a good tracking history and we also talked about tracking history using that type of moving same direction radar mode. Can you tell me what your knowledge form the training manual is as how long it would take to get a tracking history on a radar that's moving same direction?

A. Up to ten seconds. It would take six to ten seconds to do the target speed discrimination, vary your speeds, once you've gotten that good audio Doppler tone and had a steady tone and you were doing everything you're supposed to. So really it's close to ten seconds.

Q. Now from your recollection regarding the video that you saw from the stop, can you walk us through, I think you made a chart for purposes of explanation, can you walk us through the different things?

A. Sure, be happy to. The video has a box on the lower left corner that shows the target speed that is interfaced with the radar and the patrol speed. So, I used those speeds that were showing and stopped the camera. It's a little approximate, but I stopped it on each second and made a database of what the target speed was by second and then graphed that out on a graph just for illustrative purposes to show that there's a, it begins showing Officer Barbee driving approximately sixty one miles per hour in a fifty five mile per hour zone. And then about thirty seconds transpired, thirty one, and there's a vehicle coming towards the officer that he was clocking that vehicle and which would have had to have been opposite direction moving mode. And as soon as it went by, he picked up another speed. If it was Mr. Newman he would have had to change the mode to same direction moving at that point within a second and locked the speed with instantaneously. Then from that point, and at that point I guess it would be fair to say at about twenty six seconds or twenty seven seconds approximately, Officer Barbee up to seventy one miles per hour and accelerating and continued to accelerate. So that at the point that about three seconds later, four seconds later, they made that first lock. He was driving almost eighty one miles an hour and then continued to accelerate to ninety six miles per hour and in about twenty seconds. That would be what I would categorize as rapid acceleration. It's at that point that there appears to be a multi-path beam cancellation and there's no speed indicated in either box, target or patrol speed, on the radar interface on the video camera. It completely blanked out and it resumed in approximately a second later and one second from that also locked into a target speed instantaneously without any tracking history at all and then began. The officer drops speed to about eighty nine miles per hour and sped back up to about ninety eight and then dropped back off, just evened back to around eighty, eighty two, when he activated the blue lights and was still a fairly significant distance from the tractor trailer.

Q. In your expert opinion, would Officer Barbee been able to make of speed from that far away at night?

A. No, I took that and looked at Google. Earth and was able to see a left turn early in the video and approximated.

Q. Is this what you're referring to Mr. Scott?

A. Yes, this is the turn right here. Well no, this is where he stopped. The turn would be hard to see. It was up here (indicated). There's a left turn lane in this area of the picture. The stop was made on this exit ramp. And from that point using a speed of fifty five miles per hour for the truck and just make, it's an estimation, it appeared to me that there was about a three tenths of a mile difference between the two vehicles at that point and it appeared to be dark, unstreet lit, and I could not have estimated the speed of a vehicle at any time in this video because of the distance between the patrol car and the tractor trailer was too great to have any sort of reliable estimate of speed at that distance. That and had to be tied into the hilly, curvy nature of the road at some point. I don't know if I couldn't see the tractor trailer at some points in the video and the rapid acceleration of the vehicle, I think it would be impossible for anyone to accurately estimate the speed of a vehicle that's going much slower than they are while they're rapidly accelerating from a sixty to almost one hundred miles an hour, ninety six miles per hour, I think, in twenty four seconds.

Q. You were taught in radar school that you're not supposed to rapidly accelerate or decelerate, is that correct?

A. No, you should not rapidly accelerate or decelerate while making radar clocks.

Q. Why is that?

A. Because you can cause what's called batching and that's one of the things. The others you can't, you can confuse your closing speed for the speed of the vehicle you're trying to estimate. So you need to be close enough to make a reasonable estimate and essentially where you can see the vehicle. You can tell its relative motion between objects and have some sense of its speed. If you can't see objects it's passing, you can't develop a relative motion. You can't estimate the speed. You can't do, you can't corroborate your estimate without the audio Doppler tone. So there's a number of things wrong with this.

Q. Now, were you also taught that larger objects, like tractor trailer trucks and dump trucks, and things like that are harder to estimate than smaller objects?

A. Absolutely. They, it's part of the initial training. And they cost you because you may miss a vehicle and fail your test. It's not to try to estimate the speeds of large vehicles like school buses, dump trucks, tractor trailers or small vehicles like sports cars because the larger vehicles do appear to be going faster than they are and smaller vehicles often appear to be going slower than they are.

Q. Your Honor, I would just like for Mr. Scott to point out in the video where the multi-path beam cancellation comes into play if that's alright?

THE COURT: Yes, sir.

THE WITNESS: Do you want it to play?

MR. SMITH: Yes. Just where you can show me the windows and where the target speed and everything blanks out.

THE WITNESS: This is your target speed box and the patrol speed. I can't see that patrol vehicle. The tractor trailer is fairly in front. I think I missed it, your Honor. I think a lot of zero, zero. I'll try to back up. It's difficult to do it like this. It's quick. Right there. It's the register of zeros. Zero for the target, but ninety five miles for the officer's car. And then if you look in the lock box you'll see in about one or two seconds locked right there. So, he locked it in about one or two seconds.

Q. Is it your testimony, Mr. Scott, that from what you're seeing there that that's multi-beam cancellation? And as we discussed earlier, if a multi-beam cancellation event occurs, you're supposed to restart your tracking history?

A. Yes, and yes, that's correct. There wasn't a tracking history because there's no audio Doppler tone that you can hear.

Q. And once again, there was an instantaneous measurement made at that point?

A. Yes.

Q. That's when it locked back, as soon as it came back. I don't have any further questions right now for Mr. Scott.

13.4 Cross of the State's Expert Witness

The cross of the state's expert starts with the pretrial interview. Gather all documents related to the case, the expert's credentials, and past testimony, if it is available to you. Do a thorough interview. Do not be afraid to ask questions at the interview that may have bad answers—you want to know about them before you enter the courtroom.

To cross, or not to cross? That is the question. You may want to consider not cross-examining the state's witness. There are times when you will not dispute whether the breath tester was working properly. Your strategy might be that even where there were no problems with the machine, or the administration of the test, your client might not have been over the limit because of the inherent margins of error. If the state's witness simply testifies that the machine was properly calibrated and appears to have been properly used, leave it alone. Use your own expert to build upon that testimony. An important lesson for defense attorneys to learn is that we do not have to counter everything that the prosecution puts forth.

Unless there is something bad in the witness' educational or work history, stay away from it. There is one exception, however. That exception arises when your expert's credentials are far superior to that of the state's expert. You may be fortunate enough to have a medical doctor, a physics professor, or someone with advanced degrees and many years of work experience in the field. The state's expert will usually only have a bachelor's degree, and this will be his or her first job out of college. Compare the two backgrounds for the jury. Do not be condescending to the state's witness, simply point out the fact that your expert's credentials are far superior to the state's witness. Moreover, a subtle way to influence the jury is to refer to your expert's work history as "credentials" while referring to the state's witness' "work history." If your expert is a doctor, refer to her as "doctor." If the state's expert is a doctor, refer to him by name only—don't give him the added credibility of the title.

Like the prosecution attack of the defense expert, you can use three similar areas of attack for the government's expert as the prosecutor can use for your expert:

- The prosecution expert is a cop and will say whatever the prosecution wants him to say.
- The prosecution expert is not qualified to render an opinion.
- The prosecution expert was not there.

Let's look at how to effectively use them:

The prosecution expert is a cop. This is an attack on the credibility of the witness and it works best where the prosecution is overreaching. In a case where a crime lab technician is testifying, one of the best questions or areas of inquiry is to ask how many times the expert has come into court to say that the results obtained by the crime lab or that the breath test results were inaccurate. This tactic works especially well where a blood analyst has done thousands of blood tests. You can safely ask, "How many times have your results been incorrect?" If the answer is "never," the analyst loses credibility. Everyone makes mistakes. If the analyst says "a few times," or gives a number, then you have reasonable doubt. How many times has the expert testified that the accused was sober? How many times has the expert testified for the defense without a subpoena?

Be sure to ask the analyst if she has a badge, like the police, or special credentials that allow her access to secure spaces at the police station. You can ask if she conferred with the prosecutor or police in preparation for her testimony. Bias is inherent in the forensic science community.

"The prosecution expert is not qualified to render an opinion" is a valid argument in many more instances than are apparent to most attorneys. The fact that someone works in a crime lab does not mean that the person is qualified to render opinions on any aspect of forensic investigations. Generally, crime lab workers are not the best and brightest of their college classes. They're the people who could not get the high-paying jobs in private industry, but who have no criminal records. Many have little more than a bachelor's degree and some don't even have that much. College transcripts may be available to you and can provide a wealth of useful information. Would you want a D+ student analyzing your blood?

"The prosecution expert was not there" is the argument that you can make in addition to other arguments and to counter the argument that may be made by the prosecution about your expert. Clearly, this is ineffectual where the expert is an analyst who is testifying to the blood analysis and nothing more. It becomes effective where the analyst is asked to make assumptions about health, field sobriety testing, alcohol absorption, and elimination.

13.5 Direct Examination of the State's Expert as a Defense Witness

For one reason or another, you may find yourself using the state's Expert Witness as your own witness. Sometimes this occurs because your client has limited funds and cannot hire an expert. Other times, the court will be unreasonable and force a trial to take place when your expert is not available. Perhaps your Expert Witness will hurt you more than help you, so you would rather not call him or her.

Whatever the reason may be, there are inherent advantages and disadvantages to calling the state's expert as your own. My early career was virtually built on using the state's expert, and I became intimately familiar with the advantages and disadvantages. The advantages are that the state's expert is a police department employee. Thus anything he or she says that is favorable to your case can be magnified by the fact that it was said despite the inherent bias of the witness. Moreover, the jurors do not have to choose between "dueling" experts. Let's face it—most jurors are inherently biased toward the police and prosecutors. They want to believe them over some hired-gun defense expert.

The clear disadvantage is that the state's expert is a police department employee. Rarely will the state's expert volunteer information that will help your case. In fact, many of them will go out of their way to hurt your case. Using the state's expert is a dangerous tactic, but when done properly, the payoff is a "not guilty" verdict.

The following is an actual example of a direct examination of a state's Expert Witness in a breath testing case. The expert had been subpoenaed by the defense. It has been edited for non-fluencies such as "ums" and "uhs" and the names have been changed, but it remains true to the content of the cross-examination. Read along as it flows from inherent bias as a police department employee through the inherent margins of error in breath testing to the final conclusion.

BY MR. NESCI:

Q. Good afternoon.

Q. So you're a police department employee, am I correct?

A. City of Tucson employee assigned to the police department.

Q. And you have a, a City of Tucson payroll number, correct?

A. Yes.

Q. And you have a card that allows you to go into the police station, correct?

A. Yes, I do.

Q. Into the secure areas of the police station, am I correct?

A. Yes, that's correct.

Q. Where generally only other officers are allowed to go?

A. Officers and civilians who have clearance.

Q. All right. Can you tell the jury what it is you do at the crime lab?

A. Currently my title is Crime Laboratory Coordinator. I supervise two sections of the crime laboratory: chemical analysis section, which analyzes narcotics and dangerous drugs; and I supervise the toxicology section, which is responsible for maintaining breath testing instruments in the police department and testing blood samples for alcohol concentration.

Q. Now, physically yourself, you don't do the maintenance on the machines anymore, correct?

A. That is correct. Not on the instruments for breath testing. I do, however, continue to test blood samples for alcohol concentration.

Q. At some point in the past did you ever maintain the machines?

A. Yes. At some point in the past I have worked on almost every one of our instruments in the laboratory.

Q. What qualifications do you hold in order to do maintenance on the machines?

A. I have an Operator's Permit for the Intoxilyzer 5000, a Quality Assurance Specialist Permit, and an Instructor Approval, all given from the Department of Health Services. I also have performed maintenance and the required checks for the instruments when I was working as a quality assurance specialist.

Q. Have you ever worked on, or maintained, machine number 64-002659?

A. Yes, I have.

Q. Officer Smith says he's been using this particular machine since about 1987. Does that sound right to you?

A. It sounds right. Off and on he's had possession of that instrument.

Q. When you're doing a calibration check on one of these machines, can you describe for the jury how you do that calibration check?

A. Certainly. We take a simulator, which is a device designed to simulate alcoholic breath. It contains a solution of known alcohol concentration. The simulator heats that solution to 34 degrees Centigrade, which is approximately the temperature of exhaled human breath. The simulator device is attached to the Intoxilyzer through a side port. The quality assurance specialist places the instrument into the calibration mode by switching a switch on the Intoxilyzer to put it into that mode, and then simply follow the instructions on the instrument after you push the start test button. There's a checklist that's given to the QAS by the Arizona Department of Health Services to follow when performing this test. And if you follow the steps on the checklist, it has the instrument, with the attached simulator do a calibration check. That means it is checking to see if the instrument can accurately analyze that alcohol solution within a margin of error that's expected according to the Department of Health Services' rules.

Q. You said that you use a simulator and it accounts for, for a couple of different things, breath temperature being one of them and other things. But you don't just get some drunk guy in there and blow in the machine, right?

A. No. This is a device that is designed to simulate a breath sample of a known alcohol concentration. It's very difficult to do with an individual or a person to get them to a certain alcohol concentration and have them be a device to measure the accuracy of the instrument—much easier to use a device specifically for that purpose.

Q. Well, let's talk about the different things that are accounted for when you use a simulator as opposed to a human being. Would one of those things be the actual temperature of the vapor going into the machine?

A. Yes.

Q. What is that temperature supposed to be on a simulator?

A. The requirement is that it's 34 degrees Centigrade plus or minus .2 degrees Centigrade.

Q. Two-tenths of one degree?

A. Correct.

Q. What—if—say you're a quality assurance specialist, and you're going to do a test on the machine, call it a calibration check, and it's not within .2 degrees, can you do that check properly?

A. If your simulator fails to notify you that it's outside of the range, it's set to measure 34 degrees, plus or minus .2, and the simulators we use actually have an audible tone when the temperature exceeds that allowable range.

Q. If the simulator temperature higher—hotter—than it should be, will the breath alcohol result be higher?

A. Yes, due to the laws of physics that the hotter you heat a solution, the more alcohol will move from the liquid phase to the gas phase. So therefore, if it were hotter than 34 degrees, plus or minus .2, it would be a higher alcohol concentration.

Q. So if I were to walk into a room with a hot cup of coffee, I might smell it, but if I walk in the same room with a cold cup of coffee, I might not smell it, right? Same principle?

A. The same principle of once you heat a liquid and vaporize the components of that liquid, in our case it's alcohol, in your example it would be the aroma of coffee, then yes, that would be correct.

Q. How much does one degree Centigrade correlate to in a rise or fall of a resultant breath test?

A. For a human subject, there have been many measurements done and shows that for each degree in Centigrade change, you can expect a percentage change in the alcohol concentration measured on that subject, and I believe it's about 6 to 8 percent.

Q. And a normal healthy human being's core body temperature can vary through, throughout the day, am I correct?

A. Yes, it can.

Q. And it can vary as much as one degree, correct?

A. Well, it—the human body normal body temperature is 37 degrees, and, yes, it can vary.

Q. By about how much?

A. In Centigrade, probably about a degree at the most.

Q. Normal, healthy human being?

A. Yes.

Q. Not feverish or anything like that?

A. Correct.

Q. I understand that when you use the, the simulator, you're not actually blowing into the breath tube that Mr. Jones would blow into or any other subject, am I correct?

A. That is correct.

Q. The simulator vapor enters into a different port on the side, am I right?

A. Yes. It is attached to a side port specifically designed for calibration, or checking the calibration of the instrument.

Q. The breath tube that the subject would blow in is heated, am I correct?
A. Yes, it is.
Q. And it's heated for a reason, right?
A. Yes.
Q. To prevent condensation, correct?
A. Yes.
Q. You're assuming that there's no condensation as it goes in through the calibration port, am I correct?
A. Yes, that's correct.
Q. Can breathing patterns have an effect on the result?
A. The subject's breathing patterns can affect the subject test result.
Q. If we were to have a situation where the result was artificially low due to breathing patterns, about how much can that, can breathing patterns take off of somebody's breath test?
A. Well, again, we're looking at studies done on human subjects, and we see that the variability can range from about 15 percent to 20 percent depending on which way the subject is alternating their breathing pattern.
Q. Is that—which is that? Is it 15 percent low and 20 percent high or 20 percent low and 15 percent high? Do you know?
A. Yes. If you hold your breath, you can increase the alcohol concentration by up to 20 percent. And if you hyperventilate or breathe very quickly prior to the subject test, you can lower it by about 15 percent.
Q. Now, it doesn't have to be 20 percent. It could be less than that, am I right?
A. Oh, certainly. Up to 20 percent, but certainly any margin up to that amount.
Q. Somebody could only increase it 2 percent, correct?
A. Certainly, it's possible.
Q. Or lower it by 2 percent, right?
A. That's certainly possible.
Q. Now, that's breathing patterns, right?
A. Correct.
Q. There's something else I want to talk to you about, something called hematocrit. Are you familiar with what hematocrit is?
A. Yes, I am.
Q. Can you explain to the jury what hematocrit is?
A. It's a measure of the percent of red blood cells in a subject's blood sample.
Q. When somebody drinks alcohol, it eventually gets into the blood, am I correct?
A. Yes, it does.
Q. And when it's in the blood, alcohol is hydrophilic, is that correct term?
A. That would be a good term. That means that it goes to the water soluble tissues of the body.
Q. Does blood have a lot of water in it?
A. Yes, it does.
Q. What happens when we have a high hematocrit, as far as blood alcohol concentration?
A. With a higher hematocrit, you have more red blood cells circulating through the system, which means you have less water soluble portion of the blood, because the red blood cells actually don't allow very much or a very small amount of alcohol to penetrate into the cellular portion. So the alcohol concentration would be more concentrated the higher the blood, the cellular content or red blood cell content in the watery portion of the blood.
Q. And so if I have a low hematocrit, I might have a lower blood alcohol concentration after, after having consumed the same amount of alcohol if I have a higher hematocrit, I might have a higher, uh—boy, I didn't even say that right, huh?
A. There would—that theory is correct because depending on the number of blood cells you have, you could possibly change the way the alcohol is soluble into your bloodstream, and it's possible.
Q. And that could be, that could change the resulting breath alcohol concentration, am I correct?
A. Yes, it can.
Q. How much?
A. I believe the studies show that up to a 4 percent change due to hematocrit changes.
Q. High or low, right? Four percent high or low, either direction?
A. Yes, either direction is what I recall.
Q. All right. There is a, a error factor that's in all scientific instruments, am I correct?
A. Yes.
Q. Some instruments are way more accurate than other instruments depending on what they're being used for, right?
A. Yes.
Q. What is the allowable margin of error for the Intoxilyzer 5000 according to the Department of Health Services' regulations?
A. The regulations require the instrument to operate within plus or minus 10 percent accuracy or .01, whichever is the greater difference from a known solution of alcohol concentration.
Q. And this machine operates within those parameters, am I correct?
A. That's correct. And when it does not, it must be removed from service.
Q. Now, I have the calibration records here, which were introduced into evidence by the state. May I approach, Your Honor?
JUDGE. You may.
Q. If you'd like to look at them, I'd like to show you some specific stuff here and ask you about them. On one of these tests on December 4 the machine read .079 and .076, right?

A. Yes, that's correct.
Q. Certainly within the 10 percent?
A. Within .01 because at that level that is the greater difference from the known alcohol concentration level. In our case we're using a .08 solution, so the difference is .01.
Q. So this machine could read as much as a .090 or low as a .070 and it would not need to be taken out of service?
A. That's correct.
Q. And it read .075 and an .077 on November 6th?
A. Yes, that's correct.
Q. And here's one it read above the limit. It read .081 and .079 on October 9?
A. Yes, that's correct.
Q. And it read .079 and an .078 on September 10, correct?
A. Yes, that's correct.
Q. This is with the simulator, correct?
A. Yes, it is.
Q. This has—you have taken into account hematocrit, correct?
A. With a simulator it does not actually take into account hematocrit.
Q. It's not a factor?
A. That's correct.
Q. Certainly you take into account breathing patterns because the machine actually has a pump that sucks the air in from the simulator, am I correct?
A. Yes, that's correct.
Q. So we don't have to worry about hyper- or hypo-ventilating, correct?
A. That is correct.
Q. And it certainly takes into account the temperature because you can't do it if it's more than two-tenths of a degree outside of the temperature that it's supposed to be, right?
A. That's correct.
Q. So on a perfectly working Intoxilyzer with no problems whatsoever, these are tested in the lab, correct?
A. I'd have to check that.
Q. Sure.
A. That is true for two of the testing that was done in September and October. They were done in the laboratory at the Tucson Police Department. And the other two, November and December, were actually done at the DWI headquarters, which is located at the traffic substation.
Q. They were not done in the patrol car, am I correct?
A. That is correct.
Q. In this case we've had testimony his test was done with the machine that's in the back of the patrol car.
A. That's very likely. I don't know.
Q. When you do a test at either the DWI headquarters or in the lab, the machine gets plugged into a 110 volt outlet, correct?
A. Yes.
Q. It's not being run off of the car's engine with a voltage inverter or anything, right?
A. No, it's not.
Q. It's a clean environment to do, when you're doing the calibrations checks, correct?
A. Yes, our laboratory is clean, as well as the DWI headquarters.
Q. Certainly not like the back of a patrol car, right?
A. As far as cleanliness goes?
Q. Yeah.
A. Uh, I don't know—
Q. Right.
A. —that I could say.
Q. Lots of things happen in the back of a patrol car, right? I mean, you probably heard stories?
A. Well, these are designed only to have an Intoxilyzer and usually there are no individuals placed in the back.
Q. And you've accounted—for the calibration check you've accounted for breathing patterns, temperature, hematocrit's not a factor, and still this machine at one point read 7½ percent low, correct?
A. And you've calculated that?
Q. Yes.
A. I'm not going to repeat the math, but seeing that the lowest value is .075, I would probably agree.
Q. The breath temperature is independent of breathing patterns in many cases, am I correct?
A. The subject's breath temperature?
Q. Yeah.
A. Actually because of breathing patterns, you actually do cause a change to the exhaled breath temperature in, in some manner or a very slight change, but mainly it's due to the change at the air exchange in the lungs.
Q. And the breathing patterns and hematocrit are independent of each other, correct?
A. Yes.
Q. And the 10 percent error factor that's allowable by law and hematocrit are independent of each other, correct?
A. Yes, in this case.
Q. Yeah. All of these things could add up in one direction and make the breath test very, very high when it shouldn't be, correct?
A. That's certainly possible for the subject test, yes.
Q. Sure. All these things could add up and make it very, very low, am I correct?
A. That's certainly possible—for the subject test.
Q. For the subject test, yes. Now, you would agree with me that the odds of all of them adding up to make it

artificially high are very, very, it's almost astronomical, correct? Everything at their maximum, right?

A. If you multiplied the frequency possibility for each occurrence, then yeah, it's probably very, very high.

Q. And also same thing, very, very low. I mean, the, the odds of all these things canceling out to make the breath test artificially low as possible—the odds of that happening are astronomical, correct?

A. Not being able to put a number on it, I'd say it's high.

Q. Yeah, high. And statistically speaking, wouldn't it be also astronomical that they all exactly cancel each other out to make a breath test dead on accurate?

A. Certainly that's possible in the same way the others are possible.

Q. Statistically speaking, that has to be true?

A. Sure.

Q. When we're talking about somebody taking a breath test—actually let me, let me move onto something else, excuse me. When we're talking about somebody's blood alcohol concentration or breath alcohol concentration, is there a difference between blood or breath as far as possible alcohol concentration?

A. Well, you are measuring two different sources of alcohol, each one is measured in terms of the substance that's being measured. For instance, we're measuring breath in a specific measurement of weight per volume of breath and blood and weight per volume of blood.

Q. How does alcohol get from the blood into the breath?

A. It is exchanged at the alveolar sites of the lungs. You have the alcohol moving from the liquid of the blood to the vapor of the breath and being exhaled.

Q. There is in each human being some type of a conversion factor or a ratio from blood to breath, am I correct?

A. That is correct.

Q. If there isn't, breath testing doesn't work, am I right? I mean, if there's no conversion, it doesn't work?

A. It, it depends on how you would set it up.

Q. The Intoxilyzer 5000 is programmed at the factory with certain software?

A. Yes.

Q. And it's programmed to assume that for every 1 part of alcohol in one's breath, there's another 2100 parts in the person's blood, am I correct?

A. That is correct.

Q. Is everybody's blood to breath ratio 2100 to 1?

A. No.

Q. Is anybody's exactly 2100 to 1?

A. Not having measured everyone, I can't say for certain, but it's very likely that everyone is close to that value.

Q. And what is the reported range that, that you have heard and you, you believe?

A. I believe that the range is from about 1800 to 1 to about 2600 or 2700 to 1 has been the numbers I've most frequently seen.

Q. If you move to 1—I'm sorry, you said 2700 to 1?

A. 26 or 2700. I've seen both of those numbers.

Q. Which would you prefer to use for calculations here in front of the jury? Which would you feel comfortable using?

A. 2600.

Q. Say, for example, we have a person—oh, and by the way, we have two breath test numbers here. We have a .094, and we have a .102. The .094 came first. That was at 12:45. And the .102 was 12:51. Is there any significance to one being lower than the other as far as you can tell? In other words, what I'm asking is this: Is the person's blood alcohol content rising because we saw this or falling because we saw this or you can't tell?

A. With the—those two tests and the times which I didn't get exactly the times, but being very close in proximity to each other, I would say we could not predict a trend one way or the other based on those two tests.

Q. So you can tell us whether his, whether his blood alcohol content is rising or falling, correct?

Q. Which of those two breath test results would you like to go ahead and use for purposes of calculation in front of the jury?

A. I would choose the .094.

Q. Why would you choose the .094?

A. It's the lower of the two values. I would give the benefit of the two tests with the lower value to the subject.

Q. You work for the police department, right?

A. Yes.

Q. You're the person who chose the number here, .094 as, between the two for the calculations, right?

A. Yes.

Q. If you were to have an 1800 to 1 blood to breath ratio, how close to that .08 could he be? Go ahead, please tell us. What would—

A. I—

Q. If he had a .094 and the machine converted it 2100 to 1, what would his true blood alcohol content be if it was actually 1800 to 1?

A. I'm sorry. I thought you meant the accuracy requirements for that breath test.

Q. No.

A. .094 plus or minus .01. That's not the question you're asking.

Q. No, that's not the question. The question is he's a .094 and is tested by the Intox 5000, but he's really got an 1800 to 1 blood to breath ratio. That would put him at .081, am I correct or (inaudible).

A. Let me do the math, please.

Q. Sure.

PROSECUTOR. Your Honor, I'm going to object at this time. There's been no evidence presented about what the defendant's partition ratio is. And now the criminalist is making speculative calculations that she can make with any number.

JUDGE. Objection is overruled.

A. If we were to readjust to that value, to the 1800 to 1 partition ratio, then yes, it would be measured at .081.

Q. And if it was 2600 to 1, what could that .094 be?

A. .116.

Q. It's the amount of alcohol that reaches one's brain that affects impairment level, am I correct?

A. Yes, that is correct.

Q. So the amount of alcohol that's still in the bottle doesn't affect anything, right?

A. That's correct.

Q. The alcohol that's still in the stomach doesn't affect anything until it's absorbed, am I correct?

A. That is correct.

Q. So we got a .116 and a .081 as a possible true blood alcohol concentrations based on the .094 breath test, am I correct?

A. Well, these would be the measure of the breath if we had that partition ratio.

Q. Right.

A. Not a measurement of the blood.

Q. Sure. These numbers here are assuming that this .094 is dead on accurate?

A. It's only assuming the 2100 to 1 alcohol blood breath partition ratio and not taking into account any other factors.

Q. Right. So if we take this .094, and we were to go ahead and say add 8 percent because of breath temperature or core body temperature, 20 percent because of breathing patterns and 4 percent because of hematocrit, can you tell us what that number would be if you were to add those to it?

A. With all of those factors at the upper limits.

Q. Yes.

A. Of 8 percent for the change in body temperature, 20 percent for the breathing pattern, and 4 percent for the hematocrit difference?

Q. No. And—I'm sorry. Add in the 10 percent for the error factor as well on the machine. Forgot that one.

A. Well, I would use .01 since we're looking at a .094.

Q. Add that.

A. Sum—the sum total would say that the breath alcohol concentration would be .131.

Q. .131?

A. Correct.

Q. How low could it be taking into account these numbers?

A. .053.

Q. We're still talking breath here?

A. Correct. Because what we are measuring is the subject's breath with all of these variables associated with it.

Q. Now, if you have a .131—

A. Which I actually, uh, need to correct that.

Q. I'm sorry. Go ahead. Take your time.

A. Well, actually I'll leave that alone. I didn't use 15 percent on the low side. I actually used 20 percent as well.

Q. So it will be 5 percent higher than this?

A. Correct.

Q. So what would that be, .053 percent, about—

A. .058.

Q. .058.

A. About that.

Q. Close enough?

A. Yeah, close enough. .057.

Q. It was easier to convert the 3 to an 8, but I'll do it to a 7. .057 breath. We're still working in breath?

A. Correct.

Q. Now, if you were to actually have a .131 breath alcohol concentration, and the machine converted at 1800 to 1, what would, what would the conversion of the 1800 to 1 be for a .153?

A. .131?

Q. I'm sorry. .131. I apologize, .131.

A. .112.

Q. And if that .131 was done at 2600 to 1, what would it be?

A. .105.

Q. Now, with a .057, please do those two calculations at an 1800 to 1 and a 2600 to 1.

A. For the 1800 to 1.

Q. Uh-huh (affirmative).

A. You would be looking at a number measured at .067. For the 2600 to 1, you would be measuring at .046.

Q. So of all the calculations that we have done, it is possible for him to have a breath alcohol concentration under certain circumstances as high a .131?

A. Correct, with the cumulation of all of the changes to the high side.

Q. I'll put B-R-A-C, breath alcohol concentration as high a .131 and as low as a .057?

A. Correct.

Q. And based on the, on the breath tests, if we were talking about blood and blood to breath partition ratio, you could have a blood alcohol concentration as high as a .116?

A. Well, we're still measuring the breath alcohol concentration. We're just changing the ratio.

Q. Converting it to blood, to a possible blood alcohol concentration?
A. No, not at all. What we're doing is we're changing the way that the alcohol moves in the air passages of the lungs from the blood to the breath. We're still measuring breath alcohol concentration. We're just changing the ratio.
Q. But that's—
A. We're not measuring it as a blood alcohol concentration.
Q. But that's what the machine does. The machine says, okay, I've got a .094, and that's based on somebody having a 2100 to 1 blood to breath partition ratio?
A. Yes, that is correct.
Q. And the person, and that's, and that's based on something that's programmed into the machine?
A. Yes, that is correct.
Q. And if the person's blood to breath ratio is a 1800 to 1 and he blows an .094, that really could be as low as a .081?
A. That's correct.
Q. Breath alcohol concentration.
A. But we're still measuring the breath alcohol concentration.
Q. But here we've converted it to blood with the .131 and the .057?
A. All we've done is change the ratio that we, at which we're measuring the breath alcohol concentration.
Q. So how low could his blood—or how high could his blood alcohol concentration be based on his, based on the .094?
A. Based on the .094 with a different partition ratio, it could be measured as high as the .131 and the .057.
Q. And his blood alcohol concentration.
A. We're still measuring the breath alcohol concentration but converting it through a different measurement ratio to measure the breath.
Q. Can you convert it to blood?
A. I don't see any reason to because I can't measure it with a gas chromatograph. I'm not measuring it in terms of grams per 100 milliliters.
Q. I didn't ask you if you saw any reason to, I asked you could you?
A. I would be measuring it terms of grams per some volume of liters of breath. I would still be doing it that measurement. I would just change it from grams per 210 liters to grams per 260 liters or grams per 180 liters. I'd still be measuring a breath alcohol concentration.
Q. So there's no way to convert breath alcohol concentration to blood alcohol concentration?
A. I don't—I'm not inclined to do so because we're still measuring the person's breath alcohol.
Q. Oh, no, no. I'm not asking you whether you're inclined to do so. I'm asking you, can you convert one's breath alcohol concentration to a blood alcohol concentration?
A. I'm sure it's possible, but I believe that what we're doing here is not making that conversion. We're actually just changing the partition ratio of the subject.
Q. Can you—
A. And measuring the breath.
Q. Can you make that conversion? Do you know how?
A. Well, it's a ratio that you're going to use, but we would still be not measuring the same units for blood.
Q. Please, my question is: Can you, do you know how to convert a breath alcohol concentration to a blood alcohol concentration?
A. And measure—
Q. Do you know how? Yes or—
A. And measure it in terms of blood alcohol concentration, certainly I do. But we have to convert it through grams per 100 milliliters.
Q. Let's do it. Let's convert the .094 to a blood alcohol concentration.
A. And which ratio shall we use for—
Q. 1800 to 1.
A. This might take a few minutes, Your Honor.
JUDGE. Okay.
A. We could make sure that everyone understands that. I don't believe that it's a very simple calculation.
Q. I agree.
A. I don't think I'm going to be able to come up with an answer.
Q. No?
A. No.
Q. Now, you'd agree with me that the blood to breath partition ratio 2100 to 1 is—well, 2100 to 1 is an arbitrary number, am I correct?
A. Well, it was chosen based on scientific studies showing that subjects are at or near that value.
Q. You're familiar with the book Medical-Legal Aspects of Alcohol, correct?
A. Yes, I am.
Q. Edited by James C. Garriott?
A. Yes.
Q. Fourth Edition?
A. We actually have that edition in our laboratory.
Q. You folks use it at the laboratory, correct?
A. I've read through it, yes.
Q. You refer to it at times for certain things, correct?
A. Yes, I have.
Q. You find it to be reliable?
A. It has some glaring errors that I have found, but other than the errors in language, grammar and some numerical problems, for the most part it's correct.
Q. You understand who Dubowski is, am I correct?
A. Yes, I do.
Q. Can you tell the jury who Mr. Dubowski is?

A. Dr. Dubowski?
Q. Yes.
A. Yes. He was the, he's retired now, the head of the Oklahoma State Department of Health Services that was responsible for their blood and breath alcohol testing program. He's been a scientist who has published numerous publications on the subject of blood and breath alcohol testing since he's been working in the field, um, boy, since at least the 1950s, perhaps even earlier.
Q. You agree that his is a major figure in the breath testing and blood testing field?
A. Yes, at one time. He's retired now. I'm not sure what role he has maintained in his retired position.
Q. And do you believe that he is an authority on breath testing?
A. I believe that he's a very knowledgeable person about breath testing. I would refer to him for advice for many questions that I might have in the field, so I would say he is an authority.
Q. Would you agree with this quote: "In actual law enforcement practice when a breath sample is analyzed for alcohol, the quantity found cannot be used to calculate the simultaneously existing actual blood concentration without making assumptions, having uncertain validities in any given case because they have not been assessed"?
A. For each individual subject, yes, I would agree with that.
Q. Do you know what Mr. Smith's breath, or excuse me, core body temperature was on October 25th of 2003?
A. No, I do not.
Q. Do you know what his breathing patterns were like on October 25th of 2003?
A. No, I do not.
Q. Do you know what his hematocrit was on that day, October 25th, 2003?
A. No, I do not.
Q. Do you know what the particular error was on the particular test that he took in terms of that 10 percent error factor on October 25th?
A. I would give the margin of error for that test, plus or minus .01.
Q. So within that error factor?
A. Certainly.
Q. Do you know what his hematocrit was on October 25th of 2003?
A. I said I did not know that.
Q. Oh, I'm sorry. I went over that one twice. Do you know what his blood to breath partition ratio was on that day?
A. No, I do not.
Q. Based on all of the factors that we've talked about here, at the time he blew the .094, it is possible that his true breath alcohol concentration could be between, between .131 or .057, correct?
A. It's certainly possible, yes.
Q. And that's a real possibility, am I right?
A. Well, I think the astronomical odds for them all to be stacked one way or the other way, and that was what you said.
Q. Uh-huh (affirmative).
A. I think that they're high odds for them to be stacked either one way or the other way, but certainly possible it could be in that range.
Q. Still remains a real possibility that he was in that range?
A. Oh, yes, I believe so.
Q. Now, when we're talking about blood alcohol concentration or breath alcohol concentration, um, there's a manner in which you can calculate how many drinks it takes a person to get to a specific level, am I correct?
A. Yes.
Q. And the prosecutor and I will enter into a stipulation, because we didn't put it into evidence, with 175 pounds for Mr. Smith if that's acceptable to the court?
PROSECUTOR. That's fine Your Honor.
JUDGE. If you're going to stipulate to that then, that's a stipulated fact as far as the jury is concerned.
Q. Now, at 175 pounds—well, first off, let, let's just start with the basics. A really, really big guy and really, really little guy have the same amount of alcohol to drink, who's going to have the higher blood alcohol concentration?
A. The smaller the individual, the less area the alcohol has to disperse into, and so the person who's smaller will have a higher alcohol concentration, if they both drink the same amount and the same concentration.
Q. All right. Now, if we're talking about men and women, say we have 175 pound man and 175 pound woman and they both drink the exact same amount of alcohol over the same time period and everything, on average, who can have the higher blood alcohol concentration?
A. The woman's alcohol concentration will be higher than the man.
Q. And that is due to what?
A. That is due to the, again, the way the alcohol is distributed to the water tissues of the body. And women just naturally have more fat tissue than water soluble tissue. And therefore, they will have the higher concentration of alcohol. The alcohol only goes to the water soluble tissues, as we call it, hydrophilic.
Q. Now, what if we have a woman, 175 pound woman who's really athletic, not much fat, and we have a 175 pound man who's a couch potato, what's that going to, how's that going to make a difference?

A. You would actually have them be more equal in the alcohol concentration due to the way the alcohol would be distributed in their body.
Q. That's based on body fat to water ratio, am I correct?
A. Yes.
Q. Now, when we do this calculation, um, since we don't know what he was drinking or when he was drinking, we only have a number, a .094. How many drinks, and we'll define drinks, how many drinks or can you tell the jury how many drinks it would take that person to actually be a .094?
A. For a 175 pound male?
Q. Yes.
A. Standard drink?
Q. Yes.
A. Sure, I can do that.
Q. Tell the jury what a standard drink is first so we know.
A. Certainly. A standard drink is a regular 12-ounce beer, a glass of wine, which is usually 12 to 14 percent alcohol, and we usually have 4 to 6 ounces of wine in a glass, or a shot of distilled spirits. They're usually 80 proof, which means it's 40 percent alcohol. Each of those contains about one-half ounce of pure alcohol, some a little more, some a little less, but approximately one-half ounce.
Q. So if we're going to say a standard drink, we're talking about a 4 percent, 12-ounce beer, correct?
A. Yes, 4 to 4.8 percent.
Q. Or a, uh, 12 percent 4-ounce glass of wine?
A. Correct.
Q. Or a half shot?
A. One—
Q. Or a whole shot?
A. One shot.
Q. Whole shot of 80 proof? Or it would be 100 proof actually, correct?
A. Well—
Q. For the standard drink? One shot—
A. It's 1.25 ounces, usually in a shot. It's just slightly than an ounce. So 80 proof is about one-half ounce of alcohol.
Q. So those, those three drinks all have the same amount, the beer, the wine, and the shot that we're talking about?
A. Correct.
Q. Can you please tell us how you do that calculation?
A. I used the weight of 175 pounds. Since he's a male, I used a conversion factor that adjusts for various changes from pounds into grams.
Q. So—
A. And the ratio of body fat usually found in a man, but the number that I use is .13 when we combine all the variables that will be used in this calculation.
Q. So first, the first thing you're telling us is we have a 12-ounce beer times 4 percent or it could be a 1.25 times the, times the, uh—
A. Point—times 40 percent.
Q. Forty percent or, and 175 pounds times the Widmark RHO factor and the .13, correct?
A. Correct.
Q. What do you come up with?
A. I came up with using one-half ounce in the numerator .5 divided by the numbers on the denominator.
Q. Uh-huh (affirmative).
A. That it's equal to .022.
Q. Per drink?
A. Alcohol concentration per drink.
Q. So this man has one drink, he's a .022?
A. Correct. One standard drink, one-half of alcohol.
Q. Get me to the .094. How many drinks would he have to have absorbed in his system at the time?
A. I would simply divide .094 by .022. That's just over four drinks equivalent have accumulated in his system.
Q. Now, that's at the time of the test, right?
A. That is using the .094 test. I didn't catch the time. I didn't write it down. So I don't know.
Q. But the .094 was the time of the test?
A. Correct.
Q. Can the Intoxilyzer 5000 tell us how much alcohol was consumed over the evening?
A. No, it cannot. It's only measuring the accumulated amount of alcohol.
Q. Can it tell us the amount of alcohol at the time of driving?
A. Not unless the test was given at the time of driving.
Q. And without knowing the time of the last drink, you can't do a retrograde to the time of driving from the time of the test, am I correct?
A. Yes, that's correct.
MR. NESCI. I don't have any further questions.
JUDGE. All right. Counsel, approach.
[Bench conference]
JUDGE. (Juror question). If you know, is the blood to air or blood to breath conversion, conversion ratio normally distributed within the human population tested? If not, do you know the shape and the frequency of the distribution? If you know.
A. I do know. For the population statistics for blood to breath partition ratio show that the average is 2300 to 1. On average people are closer to that. If you do one standard deviation, you certainly cross over the 2100 to 1, and the outer ranges of 1800 and 2600 have a very small percentage of the population at those numbers. By and large, the average is close to 2300 to 1. And it's actually pretty normally distributed, but, uh, a very small distribution so that one standard deviation is very close to the average.

JUDGE. All right.
MR. NESCI. May I?
JUDGE. Yes, you may.
BY MR. NESCI:
Q. The only way to calculate somebody's blood to breath ratio is to actually draw blood and do a breath test simultaneously, right?
A. Actually several would be a better way to measure it, to do several tests and look at the average, and do them in ever close proximity in time so you don't have other factors influencing your measurement. But certainly that would be the most accurate way.
Q. When somebody's absorbing alcohol, the alcohol's going from the bloodstream, or excuse me, from the stomach into the bloodstream, it is true that a person's blood to breath ratio can change drastically, am I correct?
A. I'm sorry. Say that sentence again.
Q. When the person's in the absorptive phase of alcohol consumption, alcohol's going from the stomach into the blood, in other words, the blood alcohol concentration is rising, that person may have a different blood to breath ratio than when it's eliminating from the system, am I correct?
A. It may appear to be different but it's actually not, because you are still measuring the alcohol concentration at the lung exchange. What you see is the distribution of alcohol through the body during the absorption phase. You have a lag time that occurs. And therefore, when you're measuring someone in that phase, you may have the lag time due to absorption before it reaches the lungs and can be measured. It could be attributed to a different blood breath partition ratio, but I don't believe that that's correct. I believe it's more the difference in the way alcohol circulates during that time.
Q. You're—
A. It doesn't reach, reach equilibrium through all the tissues.
Q. Sure. There are cases where a breath alcohol concentration, when the person's in the absorptive phase, when the breath test can overestimate the person's true blood alcohol concentration, am I correct?
A. Yes, that is correct. In the absorption phase before the alcohol's been fully distributed.
Q. Sure. And sometimes if you've had food, it takes it longer to absorb, am I correct?
A. Correct.
Q. And so that active phase, alcohol, active absorptive phase can last for as much as two hours, am I correct?
A. The absorption phase can last for that long, but the huge variability is a short-term variability.
Q. There are some reported cases where a breath test can actually overestimate a person's true blood alcohol concentration by as much as 400 percent when the person's in the active absorptive phase, am I correct?
A. I've never read 400 percent. I have read up to 40 percent difference between blood and breath, differences when being measured simultaneously in the absorption phase.
Q. And when you're in the post absorptive phase, it can underestimate, am I correct?
A. That's correct. The studies do show that breath will underestimate a concurrent blood test by about 10 percent once you're fully absorbed. And knowing nothing but the time of the stop, being 12:10, the time of the breath test, the .094 anyway, being 12:45, just, uh, just 35 minutes later, without knowing when he stopped drinking, without knowing what his stomach contents were, you can't make any predictions about whether he's in the absorptive or post absorptive phase, am I correct?
A. I can only go with what the studies show for how long it takes to fully absorb alcohol, and without more information, I certainly couldn't even apply that.
Q. So we're just left with the possible ranges of, possible overestimation as much as 40 percent or underestimation, underestimation as much as how much?
A. If it, if they're in the post absorptive phase, about 10 percent.
Q. So if we were to apply that to the .094, .094 plus 40 percent and minus 40 percent, what do we get? Oh, I'm sorry. Minus 10 percent. I'm sorry. Is that right?
A. I actually—
Q. Has to be minus 40 percent and plus 10 percent. I did that backwards.
A. If we were to say that the breath is overestimating by 40 percent, then the alcohol concentration would be .05, .056. If we're saying that it's underestimating by 10 percent, then we're closer to .10, um, 4.
MR. NESCI. I don't have any further questions.

Chapter 14

DWI Jury Trial Warpack

14.1 Actual Physical Control (APC)

APC in North Carolina has been defined long ago by our statutes and Courts. Although the North Carolina General Statutes do not define "drives" or "operates" they do define "driver" as "the operator of a vehicle" N.C.G.S. §20-4.01 (7). An operator is "a person in actual physical control of a vehicle which is in motion or which has the engine running" N.C.G.S. §20-4.01(25).

In *State v. Fields*, the Court of Appeals found that Fields was in APC of the vehicle even though the defendant got "into the car behind the wheel and cranked the car up to turn the heat on because he was cold. Defendant further testified that he never put the car in gear and that the car never moved while he was behind the wheel" *State v. Fields,* 77 N.C. App. 404 (1985).

In *State v. Kelley*, an officer approached a car parked on the emergency strip of Interstate 40. "The engine was running and the car's flashers were on. On approaching the car, the officer observed defendant slumped over the steering wheel. *State v. Kelley* 65 N.C. App. 159 (1983). Once again the Court of Appeals found APC.

14.2 Aggravation

There is only one way to be charged with a felony DWI known as Habitual DWI in North Carolina. If your client has three convictions over the course of the last ten years and gets charged with DWI again during that same period. Other aggravating and grossly aggravating factors are also discussed in Chapter 3. In Superior Court, if your client appeals a DWI conviction, the State must give notice of any aggravating factors it plans to use pursuant to N.C.G.S. §20-179 at least ten days before trial.

Prior convictions

Even the most liberal jury in the world will convict when they hear that the defendant has two prior DWI convictions. In an effort to keep the jury unenlightened to the client's past, many defense attorneys attempt to stipulate to the prior offenses if it looks like the state will be able to prove them at trial. The legislature, however, understood that this would happen and made the prior convictions part of the elements of the offense. Thus, your client has two options: either stipulate to the past convictions (the jury does not get to hear about them this way) or not stipulate and have the prosecutor prove each of the past convictions in the State's case in chief. Obviously, it's best to stipulate in cases like this so the jury is unaware of the prior convictions.

14.3 Appellate Standard of Review

The most common standards of review in North Carolina are laid out below.

Abuse of discretion standard

"Abuse of discretion results where the court's ruling is manifestly unsupported by reason or is so arbitrary that it could not have been the result of a reasoned decision." *State v. Parker* 315 N.C. 249 (1985).

De novo standard

A motion to suppress is reviewed *de novo*. "This Court reviews the trial court's denial of a motion to dismiss *de novo*." *State v. Smith* 186 N.C. App. 57 (2007). Generally, this standard is also used when Constitutional rights are involved. Under this standard, the Court puts itself in the position of the lower court.

Plain error

Plain error is defined as an error so fundamental that without it, the jury would have reached a different result. *State v. Odom* 307 N.C. 655 (1983).

14.4 Arrest

Many times an arrest takes place long before the police utter the words "You're under arrest." But when does it take place? Generally, it is when a reasonable person would feel as if she is under arrest. Subjective intent of the officer, although relevant to credibility, is not relevant to the arrest decision if there is also objectively reasonable intent.

Display of official authority and the reasonable person standard

A display of official authority coupled with or without deprivation of movement is an arrest. It is the purpose of the display of authority that the court will consider in addition to whether a reasonable person would feel free to leave. In other words, detention for officer safety will be viewed differently than detention for purposes of extracting information from a subject. The court wrote: "we conclude that the officers mounted a show of authority when: (1) Officer Moore, who was armed and in uniform, initiated the encounter, telling the occupants of the truck that the area was known for drug crimes and prostitution; (2) Officer Moore called for backup assistance; (3) Officer Moore initially illuminated the truck with blue lights; (4) Officer Hedrick illuminated defendant's side of the truck with his take-down lights; (5) Officer Moore opened defendant's door, giving her no choice but to respond to him; and (6) Officer Moore instructed defendant to exit the truck and bring her purse. By the time defendant stepped out of the truck at Officer Moore's request, a reasonable person in defendant's place would have shared the officer's belief that she was not free to leave or otherwise terminate the encounter." *State v. Icard* 363 N.C. 303 (2009).

Freedom of movement restricted

Determining whether someone is seized for the purposes of the Fourth Amendment, our Court has based it on whether "in view of the circumstances surrounding the incident, a reasonable person would have believed that he was not free to leave." *State v. Gaines* 345 N.C. 647 (1997) *quoting United States v. Mendenhall* 446 U.S. 544 (1980).

Florida v. Bostick, 501 U.S. 429 (1991). A person is seized by the police and thus entitled to challenge the government's action under the Fourth Amendment when the officer, by means of physical force or show of authority terminates or restrains his freedom of movement.

Removal of suspect from field

Defense practitioners must also be on the lookout for situations in which DWI suspects are removed from the scene before field sobriety testing is complete. The removal from the scene can convert the investigation into an arrest before probable cause has been developed.

Parameters of arrest: federal case law

While an arrest definitely occurs with the use of physical restraint, an arrest certainly may occur without physical restraint by the police or even the magic words "You're under arrest" being uttered. The varied forms of arrest without physical restraint or an express statement are documented as follows:

United States v. Morrison, 546 F.2d 319, 320 (9th Cir. 1976). When a police officer commands a person to halt or stop, a seizure has occurred.

United States v. Palmer, 603 F.2d 1281 (8th Cir. 1979). Upon the police seeing a suspect walking down a residential street, but not committing any crime, the action of the officer waving his hand and calling the suspect over to the patrol car was deemed a seizure.

Johnson v. United States, 468 A.2d 1325 (D.C. App. 1983). A police officer ordering the driver of a car to "Halt. Come here. Police Officer." was classified as a seizure of the driver.

United States v. Davis, 94 F.3d 1456 (10th Cir. 1986). Escorting a suspect to a patrol car after ordering him to stop and take his hands out of his pockets was a seizure under the Fourth Amendment.

United States v. Wood, 981 F.2d 536 (D.C. Cir. 1992). Police who ordered a suspect to "Halt right there. Stop." had seized the person for Fourth Amendment purposes.

People v. Boodle, 46 N.Y. 2d 398, 391 N.E. 2d 1329 (1979). The order to "Keep your hands where I can see them" constituted a seizure.

Brown v. Texas, 443 U.S. 47 (1979). The act of officers asking a suspect for ID and an explanation for why he was in a public alleyway amounted to a seizure.

State v. Jones, 283 S.E. 2d 483, (1983). Ordering a suspect to step back from a car with his hands in plain view created a seizure under the Fourth Amendment.

United States v. Bowles, 625 F.2d 526 (5th Cir. 1980). Even where suspicious activity is seen, an illegal seizure may occur. A narcotics agent saw a suspect and another person engaged in what he believed to be suspicious activity in an airport. The agent's act of walking by the suspect, identifying himself as a narcotics agent by showing identification and asking him if he could talk for a moment constituted a seizure.

United States v. Turpin, 920 F.2d 1377 (8th Cir. 1990). A seizure occurred where a narcotics agent with a drug-sniffing dog at his side displayed his badge and requested that the suspect sit down.

United States v. Green, 783 F.2d 1364 (9th Cir. 1986). Police drew their weapons and ordered the suspects to place their hands on the car. Clearly, a seizure occurred.

Commonwealth v. Houle, 35 Mass. App. 474, 622 N.E. 2d 638 (1993). A seizure occurred where a uniformed officer asked a suspect if his name was "Bill," and upon seeing something in the suspect's mouth, the officer ordered that he spit it out.

A seizure that is justified under *Terry* standards can soon become an arrest requiring probable cause when the seizure is other than momentary. For instance, when the police order a suspect to halt and lie face down on the street, this conduct obviously amounts to an arrest and not a temporary detention. *United States v. Delgadill-Velasquez*, 856 F.2d 1292 (9th Cir. 1988).

United States v. Del Vizo, 918 F.2d 821 (9th Cir. 1990). A police officer stopped a vehicle, drew his weapon and ordered the occupants to get out and lie on the street and then handcuffed them. This amounted to an arrest.

The simple fact that the accused believes that he would be detained for a lengthy period of time without freedom to leave can be considered an arrest without actual force being used. See *Florida v. Royer* 460 U.S. 491, 103 S.Ct. 139, 75 L.Ed. 2d 229 (1983); *State of Arizona v. Winegar*, 147 U.S. 440, 711 P.2d 579 (1985).

Washington v. Lambert, 98 F.3d 1181 (9th Cir. 1996). It was deemed an arrest where police shined a search light into the suspect's car, handcuffed the occupants and placed them in the back of a patrol car for 5 to 25 minutes. An arrest occurred.

Subjective intent

The subjective intent of the arresting officer can provide "some evidence that the action taken was an arrest—but in and of itself it is not controlling." *State v. Logner* 148 N.C. App. 135 (2001) *quoting United States v. Perate* 719 F.2d

706 (4th Cir. 1983) *citing Taylor v. Arizona*, 471 F.2d 848 (9th Cir. 1972).

14.5 Authentication

DMV certified documents

Division of Motor Vehicles (DMV) records are allowed into evidence as long as they are certified by a DMV employee and if notice is required, by meeting that requirement under N.C.G.S. §20-48. The certification of the record is made possible by N.C.G.S. §8-35 and by N.C.G.S. §20-42 which allows for the certification of records. It's also interesting to look at N.C.G.S.§ 8-35.1.

§ 20-48. Giving of notice.

(a) Whenever the Division is authorized or required to give any notice under this Chapter or other law regulating the operation of vehicles, unless a different method of giving such notice is otherwise expressly prescribed, such notice shall be given either by personal delivery thereof to the person to be so notified or by deposit in the United States mail of such notice in an envelope with postage prepaid, addressed to such person at his address as shown by the records of the Division. The giving of notice by mail is complete upon the expiration of four days after such deposit of such notice. Proof of the giving of notice in either such manner may be made by a notation in the records of the Division that the notice was sent to a particular address and the purpose of the notice. A certified copy of the Division's records may be sent by the Police Information Network, facsimile, or other electronic means. A copy of the Division's records sent under the authority of this section is admissible as evidence in any court or administrative agency and is sufficient evidence to discharge the burden of the person presenting the record that notice was sent to the person named in the record, at the address indicated in the record, and for the purpose indicated in the record. There is no requirement that the actual notice or letter be produced.

(b) Notwithstanding any other provision of this Chapter at any time notice is now required by registered mail with return receipt requested, certified mail with return receipt requested may be used in lieu thereof and shall constitute valid notice to the same extent and degree as notice by registered mail with return receipt requested.

(c) The Commissioner shall appoint such agents of the Division as may be needed to serve revocation notices required by this Chapter. The fee for service of a notice shall be fifty dollars ($50.00).

§ 8-35. Authenticated copies of public records.

All copies of bonds, contracts, notes, mortgages, or other papers relating to or connected with any loan, account, settlement of any account or any part thereof, or other transaction, between the United States or any state thereof or any corporation all of whose stock is beneficially owned by the United States or any state thereof, either directly or indirectly, and any person, natural or artificial; or extracts therefrom when complete on any one subject, or copies from the books or papers on file, or records of any public office of the State or the United States or of any corporation all of whose stock is beneficially owned by the United States or by any state thereof, directly or indirectly, shall be received in evidence and entitled to full faith and credit in any of the courts of this State when certified to by the chief officer or agent in charge of such public office or of such office of such corporation, or by the secretary or an assistant secretary of such corporation, to be true copies, and authenticated under the seal of the office, department, or corporation concerned. Any such certificate shall be prima facie evidence of the genuineness of such certificate and seal, the truth of the statements made in such certificate, and the official character of the person by which it purports to have been executed.

§ 20-42. Authority to administer oaths and certify copies of records.

(a) Officers and employees of the Division designated by the Commissioner are, for the purpose of administering the motor vehicle laws, authorized to administer oaths and acknowledge signatures, and shall charge for the acknowledgment of signatures a fee according to the following schedule:

(1) One signature	$2.00
(2) Two signatures	3.00
(3) Three or more signatures	4.00

Funds received under the provisions of this subsection shall be used to defray a part of the costs of distribution of license plates, registration certificates and certificates of title issued by the Division.

(b) The Commissioner and officers of the Division designated by the Commissioner may prepare under the seal of the Division and deliver upon request a certified copy of any document of the Division for a fee. The fee for a document, other than an accident report under G.S. 20-166.1, is ten dollars ($10.00). The fee for an accident report is five dollars ($5.00). A certified copy shall be admissible in any proceeding in any court in like manner as the original thereof, without further certification. The certification fee does not apply to a document furnished for official use to a judicial official or to an official of the federal government, a state government, or a local government.

§ 8-35.1. Division of Motor Vehicles' record admissible as prima facie evidence of convictions of offenses involving impaired driving.

> Notwithstanding the provisions of G.S. 15A-924(d), a properly certified copy under G.S. 8-35 or G.S. 20-26(b) of the license records of a defendant kept by the Division of Motor Vehicles under G.S. 20-26(a) is admissible as prima facie evidence of any prior conviction of a defendant for an offense involving impaired driving as defined in G.S. 20-4.01(24a).

14.6 Blood Draws

Exigent circumstances

The United States Supreme Court in *Missouri v. McNeely* 133 S.Ct. 1552 (2013) basically answered the question to a degree in regard to blood draws in DWI cases without a warrant due to exigent circumstances. The question the Court answered was whether the natural dissipation of alcohol in the bloodstream establishes a per se exigency that suffices on its own to justify an exception to the warrant requirement of a no consent blood draw in a DWI case.

The Court found that it did not, saying "We hold that in drunk driving investigations, the natural dissipation of alcohol in the bloodstream does not constitute an exigency in every case sufficient to justify conducting a blood test without a warrant." 569 U.S.___ (2013).

Some in our State will still argue that *State v. Fletcher* 202 N.C. App. 107 (2010) is good law. I can see how this argument could be made seeing that there were other circumstances involved and not just the natural dissipation. However, I still believe that the *McNeely* case is the best argument.

Medical blood draws

It appears that as long as blood has been drawn in North Carolina it can be admitted. It doesn't matter if the blood was collected properly under N.C.G.S. §20-139.1 or not. As the State Supreme Court held in *State v. Drdak* 330 N.C. 587 (1992), the statute doesn't limit the inclusion of other tests.

14.7 Breath Testing

DHHS and certification

In *State v. Doggett* 41 N.C. App. 304 (1979), the Court of Appeals found that even though the officer may NOT have held a valid certificate from the Department of Human Resources (now the Department of Health and Human Services or DHHS) on the date of the offense stating that he was a qualified breathalyzer operator that this was not a problem. Since the officer's "testimony provides the basis for a reasonable inference that he possessed a valid permit at the time he administered the test. Nothing appears to the contrary; in fact, Richardson testified in detail about the simulator test he ran before testing the defendant, saying that when he got a reading he knew, "according to my training," that it was within the permissible limits." *State v. Doggett* 41 N.C. App. 304, 305-306 (1979).

The Court went on to say that this decision was made pursuant to *State v. Eubanks* 283 N.C. 556 (1973), which our State Supreme Court had ruled, holding that the testimony of the administering officer that he had attended the breathalyzer operator's school and received a certificate from the Board of Health found that testimony to be enough to establish the admissibility of the test results.

Partition ratio defense

The partition ratio is based on Henry's Law of Partial Pressures—a law of physics. The rule in North Carolina seems to be that when a DWI law conflicts with the laws of physics in such a way as to create a defense, the North Carolina Court system just doesn't let your expert testify: See *State v. Cothran* 120 N.C. App. 633 (1995), where the trial court did not let an expert witness testify to what the defendant's actual partition ratio was and the State Court of Appeals deemed that was fine.

The partition ratio is a way to account for the conversion of blood alcohol concentration to breath alcohol concentration. In simple terms, for every one part of alcohol on one's breath, there must be a proportional amount in that person's blood. If this were not true, breath testing would not work at all. The problem for the prosecution, however, is that the partition ratio varies from person to person, yet the breath testing machines all convert at 2100:1. Thus, if a subject's partition ratio is substantially higher than 2100:1, such as 2400:1, that person would benefit by a breath test because the result would be substantially lower than his true blood alcohol concentration. Conversely, a person with a 1700:1 ratio would find a breath test detrimental because a breath test would yield a result much higher than his true blood alcohol concentration.

Sample preservation

The Court of Appeals held that due process did not require state to provide DWI defendants with separate additional breath sample for independent testing so long as the testing device was properly maintained, two samples were taken, and the simulator test was ran. The Court went on to say in *State v. Tappe* 139 N.C. App. 33 (2000), that the "State's failure to take and preserve an additional breath sample or produce the control and test ampules for defendant's examination did not violate state and federal due process." The Court came to this understanding by relying on another Court of Appeals case *State v. Jones* 106 N.C. App. 214 (1992) which held that due process was not violated when a police officer disposed of control and test ampules used in performing the breathalyzer test in accord with standard procedures when the defendant did not challenge those procedures or present evidence to the contrary.

Units of measurement

"Blood alcohol concentration" is defined as grams of alcohol per 100 milliliters of blood, and "breath alcohol concentration" is defined as grams of alcohol per 210 liters of breath. Both are measured as weight per volume. If the state does not introduce the units (grams, milliliters or liters), the number produced is irrelevant. *City of Toledo v. Raider* 14 Ohio App.3d 198, 470 N.E.2d 418 14 O.B.R. 225 (1983), is directly on point, although it is not of precedential value in North Carolina. The case found that a necessary element for admission of a breath test result was testimony stating the units of weight per volume for the breath test result. Without such testimony the result is irrelevant and inadmissible. From the defense standpoint, one should not object to foundation for admission unless the defense feels that there is no real possibility that the state will be able to make the required foundational showing. The defense should, instead, allow the result to be admitted and then ask for a directed verdict based on a missing element of the charge. If the defense were to challenge foundation, is would be very simple for the prosecution to lay such foundation.

14.8 Burden of Proof

Prosecutor's burden

"When a prosecutor seeks to rely upon consent to justify the lawfulness of a search, he has the burden of proving that the consent was, in fact, freely and voluntarily given. This burden cannot be discharged by showing no more than acquiescence to a claim of lawful authority." *Bumper v. North Carolina*, 391 U.S. 543, 548-49, 88 S.Ct. 1788

14.9 Chain of Custody

Weight versus admissibility

State v. Campbell, 311 N.C. 386 (1984). "The trial court possesses and must exercise sound discretion in determining the standard of certainty that is required to show that an object offered is the same as the object involved in the incident and is in an unchanged condition. A detailed chain of custody need be established only when the evidence offered is not readily identifiable or is susceptible to alteration and there is reason to believe that it may have been altered. Further, any weak links in a chain of custody relate only to the weight to be given evidence and not to its admissibility." *Id.* at 389.

14.10 Circumstantial Evidence

The following cases are most often relevant to DWI cases where the alleged driver is found outside the vehicle.

Inference leading to verdict of guilty

"Circumstantial evidence may withstand a motion to dismiss and support a conviction even when the evidence does not rule out every hypothesis of innocence." *State v. Stone*, 323 N.C. 447, 452, 373 S.E.2d 430, 433 (1988). If the evidence presented is circumstantial, the court must consider whether a reasonable inference of defendant's guilt may be drawn from the circumstances. Once the court decides that a reasonable inference of defendant's guilt may be drawn from the circumstances, then " 'it is for the jury to decide whether the facts, taken singly or in combination, satisfy [it] beyond a reasonable doubt that the defendant is actually guilty.' " *State v. Thomas*, 296 N.C. 236, 244, 250 S.E.2d 204, 209 (1978) (alteration in original) (*quoting State v. Rowland*, 263 N.C. 353, 358, 139 S.E.2d 661, 665 (1965)).

Inference leading to acquittal

> "In the case before us, the evidence presented at trial satisfies the requirement that the defendant was under the influence of intoxicating liquor and that the accident occurred on a public highway. The State has been unsuccessful, however, in proving that the defendant drove or operated the vehicle. The only evidence presented by the State connecting the defendant with the automobile was the Public Safety Officer's testimony that he observed the defendant "halfway the front seat." This circumstantial evidence alone is insufficient to support a conclusion that the defendant was the driver. The State offered no evidence that the car had been operated recently or that it was in motion at the time the officer observed the defendant. See State v. Haddock. Nor did the State offer evidence that the motor was running with the defendant sitting under the steering wheel at the time the officer came upon the scene.."

State v. Ray 54 N.C. App. 473 (1981) 474,475

14.11 Closing Arguments—Ethical Considerations

The following two cases illustrate the same point: An attorney may not express ill will or animosity toward opposing counsel or engage in personality conflicts.

Abuse of opposing counsel

"It is well-established that a trial attorney may not make uncomplimentary comments about opposing counsel, and should 'refrain from abusive, vituperative, and opprobrious language, or from indulging in invectives.' " *State v. Sanderson*, 336N.C. 1, 10, 442 S.E.2d 33, 39 (1994) (quoting *State v. Miller*, 271 N.C. 646, 659, 157 S.E.2d 335, 346 (1967)).

Departure from the record

"[F]or an inappropriate prosecutorial comment to justify a new trial, it 'must **230 be sufficiently grave that it is prejudicial [error].' " *State v. Soyars*, 332 N.C. 47, 60, 418 S.E.2d 480, 487–88 (1992) (quoting *State v. Britt*, 291 N.C. 528, 537, 231 S.E.2d 644, 651 (1977) (alteration in original)). "In order to reach the level of 'prejudicial error' in this regard, it now is well established that the prosecutor's comments must have 'so infected the trial with unfairness as to make the resulting conviction a denial of due process.' " *State v. Green*, 336 N.C. 142, 186, 443 S.E.2d 14, 40 (quoting *Darden v. Wainwright*, 477 U.S. 168, 181, 106 S.Ct. 2464, 91 L.Ed.2d 144 (1986) (quoting *Donnelly v. DeChristoforo*, 416 U.S. 637, 94 S.Ct. 1868, 40 L.Ed.2d 431 (1974))), *cert. denied*, 513 U.S. 1046, 115 S.Ct. 642, 130 L.Ed.2d 547 (1994). However, this Court has held that when the trial court instructs the jury to disregard improper arguments and instructs counsel to confine his arguments to those matters contained in evidence, such an instruction renders the error caused by the improper arguments cured. See *State v. Sanders*, 303 N.C. 608, 618, 281 S.E.2d 7, 13, *cert. denied*, 454 U.S. 973, 102 S.Ct. 523, 70 L.Ed.2d 392 (1981).

State v. Peterson, 361 N.C. 587, 607, 652 S.E.2d 216, 229-30 (2007)

Misconduct as cause for reversal

Misconduct alone does not always cause reversal; however where the trial court finds that the outcome was affected by the misconduct and grants a new trial, the appellate court will customarily defer to the trial court's ruling.

Several rules have evolved with respect to alleged improper remarks by the prosecution. Argument of counsel must be left largely to the control and discretion of the presiding judge, and counsel must be allowed wide latitude in the argument of hotly contested cases. *State v. Seipel*, 252 N.C. 335, 113 S.E.2d 432 (1960); *State v. Barefoot*, 241 N.C. 650, 86 S.E.2d 424 (1955); *State v. Bowen*, 230 N.C. 710, 55 S.E.2d 466 (1949); *State v. Little*, 228 N.C. 417, 45 S.E.2d 542 (1947). Counsel may argue to the jury the facts in evidence and all reasonable inferences to be drawn therefrom, together with the relevant law, so as to **711 present his side of the case. *State v. Monk*, 286 N.C. 509, 212 S.E.2d 125 (1975); *State v. Noell*,284 N.C. 670, 202 S.E.2d 750 (1974). He may not, however, by argument, insinuating questions, or other means, place before the jury incompetent and prejudicial matters not legally admissible in evidence, and may not "travel outside of the record" or inject into his argument facts of his own knowledge or other facts not included in the evidence. *554 *State v. Phillips*,240 N.C. 516, 82 S.E.2d 762 (1954); *State v. Dockery*, 238 N.C. 222, 77 S.E.2d 664 (1953). It is the duty of the trial judge, upon objection, to censor remarks not warranted by the evidence or the law and, in cases of gross impropriety, the court may properly intervene, Ex meromotu. *State v. Britt*, 288 N.C. 699, 220 S.E.2d 283 (1975). On the other hand, when the prosecuting attorney does not go outside of the record and his characterizations of the defendant are supported by evidence, the defendant is not entitled to a new trial by reason of being characterized in uncomplimentary terms in the argument. *State v. Bowen*, supra.

State v. Brown, 39 N.C. App. 548, 553-54, 251 S.E.2d 706, 710-11 (1979)

Misstatement of the law

> At the conclusion of the arguments of counsel, the trial court gave proper instructions on the applicable law. We conclude that those instructions, in the context of this case, cured any prejudice to the defendant which may have resulted from the possible misstatements of law in the prosecutors' arguments to which the defendant has excepted.

State v. Anderson, 322 N.C. 22, 38, 366 S.E.2d 459, 469 (1988)

Timely objections

Whenever opposing counsel makes objectionable remarks (even during opening statements or closing arguments) counsel should object at the time that the remarks are made and ask for a remedy. Failure to do so may waive the objection. Some judges have specific courtroom rules about making objections during opening statements and closing arguments. If so, have those rules put in the record so that when an appeal is taken based on objectionable remarks, you can show the appellate court that you were prevented from making the objection in a timely manner or making a complete record for appeal.

Vouching is improper

Attorneys may not vouch for the credibility of their witnesses.

Our Supreme Court has recognized that while counsel may not personally vouch for the credibility of the State's witnesses or for his own credibility, counsel may give the jurors reasons why they should believe the State's evidence. *State v. Bunning*, 338 N.C. 483, 489, 450 S.E.2d 462, 464 (1994) (concluding **924 that a prosecutor's argument that a law enforcement officer would not risk his professional reputation merely to convict the defendant was proper); *587 *State v. Rogers*, 355 N.C. 420, 453, 562 S.E.2d 859, 880 (2002), *cert. denied*, 360 N.C. 294, 629 S.E.2d 283 (2006) (finding no impropriety in prosecutor's argument that the State's witness had no "axe to grind" or reason to lie).

State v. Jordan, 186 N.C. App. 576, 586-87, 651 S.E.2d 917, 923-24 (2007)

14.12 Collateral Estoppel in DWI Cases

Defendant Summers was charged with DWI and marked as a willful refusal. He appealed to the DMV and the revocation was upheld. He appealed to the Superior Court and was found NOT to have willfully refused. He was found guilty in his DWI trial in District Court and appealed *de novo* to Superior Court where he was found guilty again. He appealed to the Court of Appeals which granted him a new trial based on the fact that collateral estoppel barred the State from using his refusal in evidence since that matter had already been decided in Civil Superior Court by a Judge on appeal from the DMV. The State appealed and the Supreme Court agreed with the Court of Appeals saying:

In the case sub judice, all of the elements of collateral estoppel were satisfied: the interests of the State were represented in the civil appeal by the Attorney General, the district attorney is in privity with the Attorney General, and the issue in interest between the Attorney General in the civil action and the district attorney in the criminal action was material and relevant to the disposition of the civil action and was fully litigated. Therefore, we affirm the Court of Appeals' holding that the State was collaterally estopped from relitigating the issue of willful refusal when the prior court had determined as a matter of law that a refusal, in fact, did not exist. *Summers*, 132 N.C.App. at 645, 513 S.E.2d at 581. We also affirm the Court of Appeals' determination that the holding in this case is "limited to collaterally estopping the relitigation of issues in a criminal DWI case when those exact issues have been litigated in a civil license revocation hearing with the Attorney General representing DMV in superior court." *Id.*

State v. Summers, 351 N.C. 620, 626, 528 S.E.2d 17, 22 (2000)

14.13 Comment of Defendant's Silence

Plain error analysis

The *Moore* case found that although there was an improper question about the defendant's post-arrest silence, it did not prejudice the defendant. This case sits alone, based on the particular facts of the case. Usually, any comment by the prosecutor on the defendant's silence should cause a mistrial. Defense counsel should always bring a motion in limine to reinforce the issue and to bolster an argument for dismissal with prejudice based on prosecutorial misconduct should the prosecutor violate the motion *in limine*.

"In this case the admission of Officer Murphy's statements regarding defendant's post-*Miranda* exercise of his right to remain silent was not plain error. First, the prosecutor did not emphasize, capitalize on, or directly elicit Officer Murphy's prohibited responses. See *State v. Freeland*, 316 N.C. 13, 19–20, 340 S.E.2d 35, 38–39 (1986) (holding that the absence of an attempt by the prosecutor to directly elicit testimony or capitalize on the defendant's exercise of his Fifth Amendment rights weighed in favor of holding the error to be harmless). Officer Murphy's first statement regarding defendant's exercise of his rights was in response to the prosecutor's inquiry into whether *107 he arrested defendant after obtaining an arrest warrant from the magistrate. The prosecutor's question requested only a "yes" or "no" response. Officer Murphy's second statement came after an inquiry into whether he spoke to defendant or any party involved in the case after the arrest. While the wording of the question could be construed to be a reference to defendant's continued silence, the question appears likely to have been intended to establish the timeline of events and the extent of Officer Murphy's involvement in the case. In either event, the prosecutor did not emphasize or highlight defendant's exercise of his rights. Moreover, the prosecutor did not mention defendant's exercise of his rights **174 when he cross-examined defendant or in his closing argument. That the prosecutor did not emphasize, capitalize on, or directly elicit Officer Murphy's prohibited responses militates against a finding of plain error. See State v. Elmore, 337 N.C. 789, 792–93, 448 S.E.2d 501, 502–03 (1994) (holding error harmless beyond a reasonable doubt where a federal agent testified that the defendant said he wanted to consult with an attorney before talking about the matter; and noting that the violation, if any, was *de minimis*, that the statement was not solicited by the prosecutor, and that the prosecutor did not cross-examine the defendant about exercising his right to remain silent, nor did he refer to the statement in closing arguments); *State v. Alexander*, 337 N.C. 182, 196, 446 S.E.2d 83, 91 (1994) (holding no plain error where the prosecutor asked a State's witness, a police officer, if the defendant spoke or talked to him, and noting that the comments were "relatively benign" and that the prosecutor did not emphasize that the defendant did not speak with law enforcement after his arrest). Here, given the brief, passing nature of the evidence in the context of the entire trial, the evidence is not likely to have "tilted the scales?" in the jury's determination of defendant's guilt or innocence. See *State v. Black*, 308 N.C. 736, 741, 303 S.E.2d 804, 807 (1983)."

State v. Moore, 366 N.C. 100, 106-07, 726 S.E.2d 168, 173-74 (2012)

Yet, contrast the *Moore* case with the *Richardson* case: "As *Moore* establishes, however, our plain error analysis cannot end with an evaluation of the substantiality of the State's evidence. Instead, the Supreme Court's decision in *Moore* establishes that our plain error analysis must also focus on the nature, extent, and seriousness of the underlying error as well. Unlike the situation at issue in Moore, the prosecutor in this case did directly elicit, emphasize, and capitalize upon impermissible information in attacking Defendant's credibility. As a result, given that the relative credibility of the State's witnesses and those proffered by Defendant, including Defendant himself, was the critical issue before the jury at Defendant's trial; the fact that Defendant did elicit a significant amount of evidence, including his own denial of involvement in the assaults upon Mr. Kinard and Mr. Springs; the fact that the State did not elicit any evidence attacking Defendant's credibility (as compared to that of other witnesses) other than his post-arrest silence; and the fact that the prosecutor directly elicited and both emphasized and capitalized upon impermissible information concerning Defendant's decision to invoke his right to remain silent, we are unable, given the analytical framework set out in *Moore*, to reach any conclusion other than that the trial court's failure to preclude the challenged prosecutorial questions and comments rose to the level of plain error despite the fact that the State elicited substantial evidence, taken in isolation, of Defendant's guilt."

State v. Richardson, 741 S.E.2d 434, 446 (N.C. Ct. App. 2013)

The rule seems to be that while it is always improper to comment on the defendant's silence, in limited instances, and where no prejudice results, it will be harmless.

14.14 Confrontation

Personal appearance

Anyone who has tried a case knows that there is no substitute for face-to-face confrontation in court. However, the confrontation clause's face-to face requirement is not absolute. Mere convenience, however, is not a reason for telephonic testimony. The state must show some compelling reason for a violation of the face-to-face requirement.

Face-to-face, in-court testimony allows the fact finder to observe the demeanor, facial expressions and other body language of the witness. It helps to ensure that all statements are given under oath by the properly identified witness. In-court testimony ensures that the witness is not being coached or influenced during testimony and that the witness is not improperly referring to documents.

"We adopt the reasoning of *Jacobs* and *Topping* and hold that a defendant's confrontation rights are violated when telephonic testimony is admitted in a criminal trial and the State has not demonstrated a compelling reason or need for the telephonic testimony to substitute for in-person testimony." *United States v. Jacobs*, 97 F.3d 275 (8th Cir. 1996); *Topping v. People*, 793 P.2d 1168 (Colo. 1990).

Sixth Amendment concerns and limitations

"The right of confrontation confirms the common-law rule that, in criminal trials, the witnesses must be present and subject to cross-examination. *State v. Bumper*, 275 N.C. 670, 170 S.E.2d 457; *State v. Perry*, 210 N.C. 796, 188 S.E. 639; *State v. Hightower*, 187 N.C. 300, 121 S.E. 616; *State v. Thomas*, 64 N.C. 74. This same protection is granted by the Sixth Amendment to the United States Constitution and made applicable to the States by the Fourteenth Amendment. *State v. Moore*, 275 N.C. 198, 166 S.E.2d 652; *Pointer v. Texas*, 380 U.S. 400, 85 S.Ct. 1065, 13 L.Ed.2d 923. The right of confrontation is an absolute right rather than a privilege, and it must be afforded an accused not only in form but in substance. *State v. Bumper*, supra; *State v. Hightower*, supra; *State v. Hackney*, 240 N.C. 230, 81 S.E.2d 778."

State v. Watson, 281 N.C. 221, 230, 188 S.E.2d 289, 294 (1972)

Because the public records at issue were akin to business records, and were prepared and maintained regardless of their possible use in a criminal prosecution, the court concluded that they were not testimonial under *Crawford v. Washington*, 541 U.S. 36, 124 S.Ct. 1354, 158 L.Ed.2d 177 (2004).

Crawford v. Washington 541 U.S. 36, 124 S.Ct. 1354, 158 L.Ed.2d 177 (2004). Testimonial hearsay statements made for purposes of litigation are inadmissible if the witness who made the statement is not present for cross-examination.

Federal case law

Where the witness is a non-defendant, the trial court must consider not only the provisions of the Rules of Evidence but also the Sixth Amendment right of confrontation. The Sixth Amendment to the United States Constitution guarantees the right of a defendant "to be confronted with the witnesses against him." Such Sixth Amendment rights are secured for defendants in state as well as in federal criminal proceedings. *Pointer v. Texas*, 380 U.S. 400, 85 S.Ct. 1065, 13 L.Ed.2d 923 (1965).

Cross-examination is the principal means by which the credibility of a witness and the veracity of her testimony are tested. *Davis v. Alaska*, 415 U.S. 308, 316, 94 S.Ct. 1105, 1110, 39 L.Ed.2d 347, 353-54 (1974); *State v. Conroy*, 131 Ariz. 528, 642 P.2d 873 (Ariz.App. 1982).

The defendant has a right not only to cross-examination of a witness at trial, but to effective cross-examination of a witness at trial. *Davis v. Alaska*, 415 U.S. 308, 94 S.Ct. 1105, 39 L.Ed.2d 347 (1974).

Confrontation also includes as its "main and essential purpose" the ability to effectively cross-examine witnesses. *Delaware v. Van Arsdall*, 475 U.S. 673, 678, 106 S.Ct. 1431, 1435, 89 L.Ed.2d 674 (1986) (quoting *Davis*, 415 U.S. at 315, 94 S.Ct. at 1109).

Interest, bias, motive are fair game under cross-examination

Despite dicta, *State v. Stone*, 226 N.C. 97, 36 S.E.2d 704, *State v. Coleman*, 215 N.C. 716, 2 S.E.2d 865, and decision, *State v. Wray*, 217 N.C. 167, 7 S.E.2d 468, to that effect, evidence obtainable by cross-examination showing bias or interest of an opposing witness is not to be revealed in one case and concealed in another at the caprice or the discretion of the trial judge. Cross-examination of an opposing witness for the purpose of showing his bias or interest is a substantial legal right, which the trial judge can neither abrogate nor abridge to the prejudice of the cross-examining party. *State v. Roberson*, supra; *State v. Harston*, supra; *Common-wealth v. Taylor*, 319 Mass. 631, 67 N.E.2d 237; *Commonwealth v. Sansone*, 252 Mass. 71, 147 N.E. 574; *Commonwealth v. Russ*, 232 Mass. 58, 122 N.E. 176; *State v. Radon*, 45 Wyo. 383, 19 P.2d 177; 58 Am.Jur., Witnesses, s 715; 70 C.J., Witnesses, s 1165. A contrary rule would substitute the whim of the trial judge for the law of the land, which certainly contemplates that the causes of all men in like circumstances are to be determined by uniform laws, impartially administered.

State v. Hart, 239 N.C. 709, 711, 80 S.E.2d 901, 903 (1954)

14.15 Corpus

Independent evidence of driving must accompany a defendant's admission to driving because forced or coerced confessions at the hands of the police, mental illness, and other factors may play a significant role in an unreliable confession.

Evidence aliunde admissions by defendant which tends to establish the *corpus delicti* is as follows: (1) the fact that the overturned automobile was lying in the middle of the road and that a single person was seen leaving the automobile; (2) the fact that when defendant returned to the scene, he appeared to be impaired as a result of using alcohol; (3) the fact that defendant later blew 0.14 on a breathalyzer; and (4) the fact that the wreck was otherwise unexplained. This evidence is sufficient to corroborate defendant's admission that he drove the vehicle on a public highway or vehicular area after he had consumed alcohol and, when considered with his admissions, was sufficient to support a reasonable inference that at the time he was driving the motor vehicle he had consumed a sufficient amount of alcohol to raise his blood alcohol level to 0.10 or greater at a relevant time after driving.

State v. Trexler, 316 N.C. 528, 533, 342 S.E.2d 878, 881 (1986)

14.16 Court Rules

Traditionally, the decision to grant or deny a continuance rests within the discretion of the trial court. *Ungar v. Sarafite*, 376 U.S. 575, 589, 84 S.Ct. 841, 849, 11 L.Ed.2d 921, 931 (1964); *State v. Roper*, 328 N.C. 337, 348, 402 S.E.2d 600, 606, *cert. denied*, 502 U.S. 902, 112 S.Ct. 280, 116 L.Ed.2d 232 (1991). However, that discretion does not extend to the point of permitting the denial of a continuance that results in a violation of a defendant's right to due process. See *Roper*, 328 N.C. at 349, 402 S.E.2d at 606. This Court has long held that when a motion for a continuance is based on a constitutional right, the issue presented is an issue of law and the trial court's conclusions of law are fully reviewable on appeal. See *State v. McFadden*, 292 N.C. 609, 611, 234 S.E.2d 742, 744 (1977); *State v. Smathers*, 287 N.C. 226, 230, 214 S.E.2d 112, 114–15 (1975); *State v. Hackney*, 240 N.C. 230, 235, 81 S.E.2d 778, 781 (1954); *State v. Farrell*, 223 N.C. 321, 326, 26 S.E.2d 322, 325 (1943).

State v. Tunstall, 334 N.C. 320, 328, 432 S.E.2d 331, 336 (1993)

14.17 Credibility of Witnesses

Even though the subjective motives of a police officer are irrelevant to the issue of reasonable suspicion for a traffic stop, they are highly relevant to his or her credibility and the threshold question as to whether he or she actually saw a traffic violation or is lying about the event.

A legitimate purpose of cross-examination is impeachment of a witness's credibility, and any circumstance tending to show a defect in the witness's veracity is relevant for that purpose. 1 Stansbury, N.C. Evidence s 38 (Brandis rev. 1973).

State v. Harris, 49 N.C. App. 452, 453, 271 S.E.2d 579, 580 (1980)

14.18 Destruction of Evidence

State v. Williams, 362 N.C. 628 (2008) This case held that evidence destroyed by the State was favorable to the defendant, and that the Destruction of Evidence caused irreparable harm to the defendant meant a Due process violation for admitting that a material piece of evidence was no longer available.

State v. Dorman, 737 S.E.2d 452 (2013) If the evidence destroyed does not qualify as Brady material there must be bad faith on the part of state. Furthermore, bad faith alone is not enough to support a dismissal under N.C.G.S. §15A-954(a)(4), the Defendant must show irreparable prejudice to the preparation of his case to warrant a dismissal.

14.19 Discovery

No Discovery in District Court

We do decide that where a statute expressly restricts pretrial discovery, as does G.S. 15A-904(a), the trial court has no authority to order discovery. *State v. Hardy*, 293 N.C. 105, 125, 235 S.E.2d 828, 840 (1977)

§ 15A-904. Disclosure by the State - Certain information not subject to disclosure.

(a) The State is not required to disclose written materials drafted by the prosecuting attorney or the prosecuting attorney's legal staff for their own use at trial, including witness examinations, voir dire questions, opening statements, and closing arguments. Disclosure is also not required of legal research or of records, correspondence, reports, memoranda, or trial preparation interview notes prepared by the prosecuting attorney or by members of the prosecuting attorney's legal staff to the extent they contain the opinions, theories, strategies, or conclusions of the prosecuting attorney or the prosecuting attorney's legal staff.

(a1) The State is not required to disclose the identity of a confidential informant unless the disclosure is otherwise required by law.

(a2) The State is not required to provide any personal identifying information of a witness beyond that witness's name, address, date of birth, and published phone number, unless the court determines upon motion of the defendant that such additional information is necessary to accurately identify and locate the witness.

(a3) The State is not required to disclose the identity of any individual providing information about a crime or criminal conduct to a Crime Stoppers organization under promise or assurance of anonymity unless ordered by the court. For purposes of this Article, a Crime Stoppers organization or similarly named entity means a private, nonprofit North Carolina corporation governed by a civilian volunteer board of directors that is operated on a local or statewide level that (i) offers anonymity to persons providing information to the organization, (ii) accepts and expends donations for cash rewards to persons who report to the organization information about alleged criminal activity and that the organization forwards to the appropriate law enforcement agency, and (iii) is established as a cooperative alliance between the news media, the community, and law enforcement officials.

(a4) The State is not required to disclose the Victim Impact Statement or its contents unless otherwise required by law. For purposes of this Chapter, a Victim Impact Statement is a document submitted by the victim or the victim's family to the State pursuant to the Victims' Rights Amendment.

(b) Nothing in this section prohibits the State from making voluntary disclosures in the interest of justice nor prohibits a court from finding that the protections of this section have been waived.

(c) This section shall have no effect on the State's duty to comply with federal or State constitutional disclosure requirements.

As we have all heard from prosecutors all over the State "there's no discovery in District Court." This also rings true when your misdemeanor DWI client appeals to Superior Court *de novo*.Most jurisdictions that I've practiced in the State do offer open discovery in DWI cases, but some do not; you've been warned. If the case happens to start in Superior Court, like a habitual DWI, you do have a right to discovery. Just remember you also have to provide the State notice of any experts you intend to call and what the substance of the expert's testimony will be.

14.20 Motions to Dismiss/Motions for a Directed Verdict of Not Guilty

§ 15-173. Demurrer to the evidence.

When on the trial of any criminal action in the superior or district court, the State has introduced its evidence and rested its case, the defendant may move to dismiss the action, or for judgment as in case of nonsuit. If the motion is allowed, judgment shall be entered accordingly; and such judgment shall have the force and effect of a verdict of "not guilty" as to such defendant. If the motion is refused and the defendant does not choose to introduce evidence, the case shall be submitted to the jury as in other cases, and the defendant may on appeal urge as ground for reversal, the trial court's denial of his motion without the necessity of the defendant's having taken exception to such denial.

If the defendant introduces evidence, he thereby waives any motion for dismissal or judgment as in case of nonsuit which he may have made prior to the introduction of his evidence and cannot urge such prior motion as ground for appeal. The defendant, however, may make such motion at the conclusion of all the evidence in the case, irrespective of whether or not he made a motion for dismissal or judgment as in case of nonsuit theretofore. If the motion is allowed, or shall be sustained on appeal, it shall in all cases have the force and effect of a verdict of "not guilty." If the motion is refused, the defendant may on appeal, after the jury has rendered its verdict, urge as ground for reversal the trial court's denial of his motion made at the close of all the evidence without the necessity of the defendant's having taken exception to such denial.

§ 15A-1227. Motion for dismissal.

(a) A motion for dismissal for insufficiency of the evidence to sustain a conviction may be made at the following times:
   (1) Upon close of the State's evidence.
   (2) Upon close of all the evidence.
   (3) After return of a verdict of guilty and before entry of judgment.
   (4) After discharge of the jury without a verdict and before the end of the session.

(b) Failure to make the motion at the close of the State's evidence or after all the evidence is not a bar to making the motion at a later time as provided in subsection (a).

(c) The judge must rule on a motion to dismiss for insufficiency of the evidence before the trial may proceed.

(d) The sufficiency of all evidence introduced in a criminal case is reviewable on appeal without regard to whether a motion has been made during trial, as provided in G.S. 15A-1446(d)(5).

§ 15A-1414. Motion by defendant for appropriate relief made within 10 days after verdict.

(a) After the verdict but not more than 10 days after entry of judgment, the defendant by motion may seek appropriate relief for any error committed during or prior to the trial. (b) Unless included in G.S. 15A-1415, all errors, including but not limited to the following, must be asserted within 10 days after entry of judgment: (1) Any error of law, including the following: a. The court erroneously failed to dismiss the charge prior to trial pursuant to G.S.15A-954. b. The court's ruling was contrary to law with regard to motions made before or during the trial, or with regard to the admission or exclusion of evidence. c. The evidence, at the close of all the evidence, was insufficient to justify submission of the case to the jury, whether or not a motion so asserting was made before verdict. d. The court erroneously instructed the jury. (2) The verdict is contrary to the weight of the evidence. (3) For any other cause the defendant did not receive a fair and impartial trial. (4) The sentence imposed on the defendant is not supported by evidence introduced at the trial and sentencing hearing. This motion must be addressed to the sentencing judge. (c) The motion may be made and acted upon in the trial court whether or not notice of appeal has been given.

14.21 Double Jeopardy

Administrative hearings

> "Having examined N.C.G.S. § 20–16.5 in light of the two-part analysis established by Hudson, we reject defendant's argument that Hudson requires a conclusion that the driver's license revocation found in N.C.G.S. § 20–16.5 constitutes punishment for purposes of double jeopardy analysis under both the Double Jeopardy Clause of the United States Constitution and the Law of the Land Clause of the North Carolina Constitution. Because we conclude that N.C.G.S. § 20–16.5 is neither punitive in purpose nor effect, we need not reach *335 defendant's remaining assignments of error in which he argues that the limited driving privilege provided for in N.C.G.S. § 20–16.5(p) does not negate the punitive nature of the statute because N.C.G.S. § 20–16.5 violates the United States and North Carolina Constitutions."

State v. Evans, 145 N.C. App. 324, 334-35, 550 S.E.2d 853, 860 (2001)

14.22 DRE: Drug Recognition Evaluation Admissibility

People v. Quinn, 158 Misc.2d 1015 (1993) New York, 1993. The defense submitted the matter to a judge on stipulated facts rather than face a jury in order to challenge the DRE protocol on appeal. The case was reversed, however, because there was no waiver of a jury before submission on stipulated facts. Thus, the court did not consider the questions regarding the scientific reliability of a drug influence evaluation. Yet the court felt obliged to write: "However, we would note that in light of the overwhelming evidence of guilt, any error in admitting such testimony would clearly be harmless."

State v. Klawitter, 518 N.W.2d 577 (1994) Minnesota, 1994. Visual exam to determine nystagmus and convergence is scientific in nature but satisfies the Frye requirement. The remainder of the 12-Step DRE protocol is not scientifically new and, therefore, is not subject to Frye. The court specifically found that the 12-Step protocol is: "... essentially the same components that are used by police officers in evaluations for alcohol impairment or are routine examinations that can be competently performed by the police officer...."

One thing to keep in mind—the officer involved in this case was qualified to take medical vital signs and do an examination because he was a certified EMT.

The dissent is great. It finds that while the individual 12 steps are not new or novel, basing an opinion upon them is new and novel. The dissent reminds the rest of the court that the prosecution relies on the totality of the circumstances—not on 12 individual steps, isolated from each other.

U.S. v. Everett, 972 F.Supp. 1313 (1997) Nevada, 1997. DRE testimony is not scientific in nature, is based upon observations, training and experience and, therefore, is governed by Rule 702, not *Daubert*. The federal court wrote: "... the otherwise qualified DRE cannot testify as to scientific knowledge, but can testify as to 'specialized knowledge which will assist the trier of fact to understand the evidence.' "

Williams v. State, 710 So.2d 24 (1998) Florida, 1998. The court concluded that the 12-Step DRE protocol is not subject to *Frye* because tests are within the common experience and understanding of the average person and are not scientific within the meaning of *Frye*. The court wrote: "Contrary to the defendant's assertion, the DRE's opinion is not derived from the symptomatology matrix and does not constitute a medical diagnosis."

Horizontal Gaze Nystagmus (HGN), Vertical Gaze Nystagmus (VGN) and Lack of Convergence (LOC) are scientific within the meaning of Frye, but Frye does not apply because the tests are not new or novel. However, they do not immunize particular areas or principles based on longevity, but go on to say that longevity is helpful to exclude certain evidence from Frye analysis which would be wasteful of judicial resources. The court cites to the Minnesota case *Klawitter*.

State v. Baity, 140 Wash.2d 1, 991 P.2d 1151 (2000) Washington, 2000. DRE protocol meets *Frye*'s requirements, although many of the DRE steps are not scientific. HGN is scientific but is generally accepted and satisfies Frye requirements. With regard to DRE testimony, the court wrote: "This Court finds that the DRE can testify to the probabilities, based upon his or her observations and clinical findings, but cannot testify by way of scientific opinion, that the conclusion is an established fact by any reasonable scientific standard."

The court cautioned that its opinion is confined to situations where all 12 steps of the DRE protocol have been used.

State v. Sampson, 167 Or.App. 489, 6 P.3d 543 (2000) Oregon, 2000. DRE protocol and testimony are scientific evidence and admissible because they have achieved a significant degree of acceptance within the relevant scientific community to be sufficiently established. Scientific parts of the DRE include the following: BAC, VGN, LOC, vital signs, toxicological analysis. Other parts of the DRE are not scientific, yet admissible.

Evidence of the DRE examination is not more highly prejudicial than probative of any fact.

State v. Aman, 194 Or.App. 463, 95 P.3d 244 (2004) Oregon, 2004. Incomplete 12-Step DREs are not admissible as scientific evidence. In this case the urine sample was not taken because the defendant could not produce one. Reversed and remanded. Note that the state admitted that toxicology results do not directly relate to a suspect's impairment but furnish only circumstantial evidence to corroborate a DRE officer's opinion.

14.23 Due Process

See Pretrial Motions Chapter concerning the *Knoll* and *Ferguson* cases/motions

14.24 Evidence

Weight versus admissibility

"The admissibility of 404(b) evidence is subject to the weighing of probative value versus unfair prejudice mandated by Rule 403." *Thaggard*, 168 N.C.App. at 269, 608 S.E.2d at 779 (internal quotation marks omitted).

State v. Houseright, 220 N.C. App. 495, 498, 725 S.E.2d 445, 447 (2012)

Questions of credibility

A prosecutor's cross-examination of a defendant in which the defendant was forced to call a U.S. Marshall "a liar" was deemed prosecutorial misconduct because it called for the opinion on credibility of a witness. Note: The case was reversed on other grounds, so the court never reached the issue as to whether this was reversible error or not. *U.S. v. Sanchez*, 176 F.3d 1214 (9th Cir. 1999).

14.25 Expert Witnesses

Rule 702. Testimony by experts.

(a) If scientific, technical or other specialized knowledge will assist the trier of fact to understand the evidence or to determine a fact in issue, a witness qualified as an expert by knowledge, skill, experience, training, or education, may testify thereto in the form of an opinion, or otherwise, if all of the following apply:
  (1) The testimony is based upon sufficient facts or data.
  (2) The testimony is the product of reliable principles and methods.
  (3) The witness has applied the principles and methods reliably to the facts of the case.

(a1) A witness, qualified under subsection (a) of this section and with proper foundation, may give expert testimony solely on the issue of impairment and not on the issue of specific alcohol concentration level relating to the following:
  (1) The results of a Horizontal Gaze Nystagmus (HGN) Test when the test is administered by a person who has successfully completed training in HGN.
  (2) Whether a person was under the influence of one or more impairing substances, and the category of such impairing substance or substances. A witness who has received training and holds a current certification as a Drug Recognition Expert, issued by the State Department of Health and Human Services, shall be qualified to give the testimony under this subdivision.

(b) In a medical malpractice action as defined in G.S. 90-21.11, a person shall not give expert testimony on the appropriate standard of health care as defined in G.S. 90-21.12 unless the person is a licensed health care provider in this State or another state and meets the following criteria:

(1) If the party against whom or on whose behalf the testimony is offered is a specialist, the expert witness must:
  a. Specialize in the same specialty as the party against whom or on whose behalf the testimony is offered; or
  b. Specialize in a similar specialty which includes within its specialty the performance of the procedure that is the subject of the complaint and have prior experience treating similar patients.

(2) During the year immediately preceding the date of the occurrence that is the basis for the action, the expert witness must have devoted a majority of his or her professional time to either or both of the following:
  a. The active clinical practice of the same health profession in which the party against whom or on whose behalf the testimony is offered, and if that party is a specialist, the active clinical practice of the same specialty or a similar specialty which includes within its specialty the performance of the procedure that is the subject of the complaint and have prior experience treating similar patients; or
  b. The instruction of students in an accredited health professional school or accredited residency or clinical research program in the same health profession in which the party against whom or on whose behalf the testimony is offered, and if that party is a specialist, an accredited health professional school or accredited residency or clinical research program in the same specialty.

(c) Notwithstanding subsection (b) of this section, if the party against whom or on whose behalf the testimony is offered is a general practitioner, the expert witness, during the year immediately preceding the date of the occurrence that is the basis for the action, must have devoted a majority of his or her professional time to either or both of the following:
  (1) Active clinical practice as a general practitioner; or
  (2) Instruction of students in an accredited health professional school or accredited residency or clinical research program in the general practice of medicine.

(d) Notwithstanding subsection (b) of this section, a physician who qualifies as an expert under subsection (a) of this Rule and who by reason of active clinical practice or instruction of students has knowledge of the applicable standard of care for nurses, nurse practitioners, certified registered nurse anesthetists, certified registered nurse midwives, physician assistants, or other medical support staff may give expert testimony in a medical malpractice action with respect to the standard of care of which he is knowledgeable of nurses, nurse practitioners, certified registered nurse anesthetists, certified registered nurse midwives, physician assistants licensed under Chapter 90 of the General Statutes, or other medical support staff.

(e) Upon motion by either party, a resident judge of the superior court in the county or judicial district in which the action is pending may allow expert testimony on the appropriate standard of health care by a witness who does not meet the requirements of subsection (b) or (c) of this Rule, but who is otherwise qualified as an expert witness, upon a showing by the movant of extraordinary circumstances and a determination by the court that the motion should be allowed to serve the ends of justice.

(f) In an action alleging medical malpractice, an expert witness shall not testify on a contingency fee basis.

(g) This section does not limit the power of the trial court to disqualify an expert witness on grounds other than the qualifications set forth in this section.

(h) Notwithstanding subsection (b) of this section, in a medical malpractice action as defined in G.S. 90-21.11(2)b. against a hospital, or other health care or medical facility, a person shall not give expert testimony on the appropriate standard of care as to administrative or other nonclinical issues unless the person has substantial knowledge, by virtue of his or her training and experience, about the standard of care among hospitals, or health care or medical facilities, of the same type as the hospital, or health care or medical facility, whose actions or inactions are the subject of the testimony situated in the same or similar communities at the time of the alleged act giving rise to the cause of action.

(i) A witness qualified as an expert in accident reconstruction who has performed a reconstruction of a crash, or has reviewed the report of investigation, with proper foundation may give an opinion as to the speed of a vehicle even if the witness did not observe the vehicle moving.

14.26 Field Sobriety Test Admissibility

"Defendant argues that the trial court erred in allowing Deputy Goodwin to testify about the field sobriety tests when the State had failed to establish both that Deputy Goodwin was qualified to properly administer or interpret the field sobriety tests, and that the tests had been properly administered. However, we conclude that there was no error in admitting this evidence because it was relevant to Deputy Goodwin's lay testimony that defendant was impaired."

State v. Streckfuss, 171 N.C. App. 81, 88, 614 S.E.2d 323, 327 (2005)

14.27 Foundation

Admission of scientific evidence: the Daubert standard

North Carolina finally became a *Daubert* state in 2014. "It is the trial court's responsibility to determine "whether the expert is proposing to testify to (1) scientific knowledge" and whether that knowledge "(2) will assist the trier of fact to understand or determine a fact in issue." *Id.* at 592, 113 S.Ct. at 2796, 125 L.Ed.2d at 482. In deciding whether the proffered scientific theory or technique will assist the trier of fact, the trial court may consider, among other things, (1) "whether [a theory or technique] can be (and has been) tested," (2) "whether the theory or technique has been subjected to peer review and publication," (3) "the known or potential rate of error ... and the existence and maintenance of standards controlling the technique's operation," and (4) whether the theory or technique is generally accepted as reliable in the relevant scientific community. *Id.* at 593–94, 113 S.Ct. at 2797, 125 L.Ed.2d at 482–83. This inquiry is "a flexible one," *id.* at 594, 113 S.Ct. at 2797, 125 L.Ed.2d at 483–84, and remains reviewable under the abuse of discretion standard. *Gen. Elec. Co. v. Joiner*, 522 U.S. 136, 147, 118 S.Ct. 512, 519–20, 139 L.Ed.2d 508, 519 (1997).

State v. McGrady, 753 S.E.2d 361, 368 (N.C. Ct. App.) review allowed, 367 N.C. 505, 758 S.E.2d 864 (2014)

14.28 HGN

"Rule 702 of the North Carolina Rules of Evidence governs the testimony of expert witnesses; that rule states: "If scientific, technical or other specialized knowledge will assist the trier of fact to understand the evidence or to determine a fact in issue, a witness qualified as an expert by knowledge, skill, experience, training, or education, may testify thereto in the form of an opinion." N.C. Gen.Stat. § 8C-1, Rule 702(a) (2007). Per Rule 702(a1), an expert witness qualified under subsection (a) of this section and with proper foundation, may give expert testimony solely on the issue of impairment and not on the issue of specific alcohol concentration level relating to the following:

(1) The results of a Horizontal Gaze Nystagmus (HGN) Test when the test is administered by a person who has successfully completed training in HGN.

N.C. Gen.Stat. § 8C-1, Rule 702(a1) (2007).1

1 Before an expert witness may offer an opinion under Rule 702(a) of the North Carolina Rules of Evidence, the trial court must first make "a preliminary assessment of whether the reasoning or methodology underlying the testimony is sufficiently valid[.]" *State v. Goode*, 341 N.C. 513, 527, 461 S.E.2d 631, 639 (1995).

Before Officer Silsbee testified as to her administration of the HGN test, defense counsel subjected her to extensive voir dire regarding her training and her experience administrating the test. She also testified as to the accuracy rate of the test in assessing intoxication as measured by various studies.

2 Defendant's argument virtually ignores the above amendment to Rule 702(a1) specifying both the admissibility of HGN testimony and the admissibility of expert testimony on that test by "a person who has successfully completed training in HGN." We interpret this amendment to Rule 702(a1) as obviating the need for the State to prove that the HGN testing method is sufficiently reliable. Defendant would have us interpret this subsection to state that a person testifying as to the HGN test must be an expert on it, an interpretation which would make the subsection nothing more than an example of the requirements of subsection (a), which as mentioned above states that "a witness qualified as an expert by knowledge, skill, experience, training, or educa-

tion, may testify thereto in the form of an opinion." N.C. Gen.Stat. § 8C-1, Rule 702(a) (2007). Given that (1) Officer Silsbee was questioned at length as to her skill, experience, and training in administering the HGN test and (2) defendant's argument to this Court concentrates entirely on the method of proof rather than Officer Silsbee's qualifications, we find that the trial court did not err in admitting her testimony."

State v. Smart, 195 N.C. App. 752, 755-56, 674 S.E.2d 684, 686 (2009)

14.29 Impeachment

Prior inconsistent statements

"Under the hearsay rule, N.C.R. Evid. 801, an out-of-court statement is inadmissible if offered for the truth of the matter asserted. However, as the Court acknowledged in *Williams*, a witness may be impeached by confronting him with prior out-of-court statements inconsistent with his trial testimony. *Williams*, 322 N.C. at 455, 368 S.E.2d at 626. It is well established that "[p]rior statements of a witness which are inconsistent with his present testimony are not admissible as substantive evidence because of their hearsay nature. Even so, such prior inconsistent **203 statements are admissible for the purpose of impeachment." *State v. Mack*, 282 N.C. 334, 339–40, 193 S.E.2d 71, 75 (1972) (internal citations omitted)."

State v. Black, 223 N.C. App. 137, 150, 735 S.E.2d 195, 202-03 (2012)

14.30 Independent Test

Notice of right to independent test

Most other states follow the *Bunton* rule that we have re-embraced here. The majority rule is that when an accused is entitled to an independent test he must only be given reasonable opportunity to procure one. *Annotation, Drunk Driving: Motorist's Right to Private Sobriety Test*, 45 A.L.R. 4th 11 (1986). Most jurisdictions draw the line between police interference and police assistance, usually demanding no more than that the defendant be allowed a phone call. *Id.*

State v. Bumgarner, 97 N.C. App. 567, 573, 389 S.E.2d 425, 428 (1990)

Denial and Remedy of the right to an independent test

The burden of proving prejudice from a statutory violation is on defendant. N.C. Gen.Stat. § 15A–1443(a) (2001). "The defendant is not entitled to a new trial based on trial errors unless such errors were material and prejudicial." *State v. Alston*, 307 N.C. 321, 339, 298 S.E.2d 631, 644 (1983). Our standard of review is as follows:

> While charges pending against an accused may be dismissed for violations of his statutory rights, dismissal is a drastic remedy which should be granted sparingly. See *State v. Curmon*, 295 N.C. 453, 245 S.E.2d 503 (1978). Before a motion to dismiss should be granted, this court has held that it must appear that the statutory violation caused irreparable prejudice to the preparation *550 of defendant's case. *State v. Knoll*, 84 N.C.App. 228, 352 S.E.2d 463 (1987).

State v. Rasmussen, 158 N.C. App. 544, 549-50, 582 S.E.2d 44, 50 (2003)

14.31 Jurors and Jury Selection

Requirement of residency

§ 9-3. Qualifications of prospective jurors.

> All persons are qualified to serve as jurors and to be included on the master jury list who are citizens of the State and residents of the county, who have not served as jurors during the preceding two years or who have not served a full term of service as grand jurors during the preceding six years, who are 18 years of age or over, who are physically and mentally competent, who can understand the English language, who have not been convicted of a felony or pleaded guilty or *nolo contendere* to an indictment charging a felony (or if convicted of a felony or having pleaded guilty or *nolo contendere* to an indictment charging a felony have had their citizenship restored pursuant to law), and who have not been adjudged non compos mentis. Persons not qualified under this section are subject to challenge for cause. Also in the *Tirado* case, the Court speaks about the residency requirement. "The trial judge then asked if either the State or the defendants wished to be heard. When neither expressed any objection, the trial judge excused McMillan

from service because she was no longer a resident of Cumberland County. This record adequately establishes that the trial court properly executed its authority under N.C.G.S. § 15A-1211(b) to determine that prospective juror McMillan failed meet the statutory requirements to sit as a Cumberland County juror."

State v. Tirado, 358 N.C. 551, 574, 599 S.E.2d 515, 531 (2004)

Batson challenge

Batson v. Kentucky, 476 U.S. 79, 106 S.Ct. 1712, 90 L.Ed.2d 69 (1986) has two-fold protection. The first is that it affords the protection that a trial by jury is meant to secure—namely a trial by one's peers. It also protects, however, the rights of the citizenry to participate in the jury system as jurors.

A successful *Batson* challenge contains a prima facie case of discriminatory intent as demonstrated by a totality of the circumstances. Once the prima facie case is raised, the burden of production shifts to the opponent who must make an adequate race-neutral explanation. Although the burden of production shifts, the burden of persuasion never shifts from the party making the allegation of discrimination.

Challenge to the venire: racial composition

The Fourteenth and Sixth Amendments to the United States Constitution forbid a state's deliberate and systematic exclusion of an identifiable and distinct group from the jury lists because an accused is entitled to a jury drawn from a fair and representative cross section of the community. *Taylor v. Louisiana*, 419 U.S. 522, 95 S.Ct. 692, 42 L.Ed.2d 690 (1975); *Hernandez v. Texas*, 347 U.S. 475, 74 S.Ct. 667, 98 L.Ed. 866 (1954).

Mere observation that a particular group is underrepresented on a particular panel does not support a constitutional challenge. *U.S. v. Grose*, 525 F.2d 1115 (7th Cir. 1975), *cert. denied*, 424 U.S. 973, 96 S.Ct. 1477, 47 L.Ed.2d 743 (1976).

The use of voter registration lists as the sole source of the names of potential jurors is not constitutionally invalid, absent a showing of discrimination in the compiling of such voter registration lists. *United States v. James*, 453 F.2d 27 (9th Cir. 1971); *United States v. Parker*, 428 F.2d 488 (9th Cir. 1970), *cert. denied*, 400 U.S. 910, 91 S.Ct. 155, 27 L.Ed.2d 150.

14.32 Jury Deliberations

Hung jury

"Under certain circumstances language which informs the jurors that they may be kept for a specified period of time unless they reach a verdict may amount to coercion, tainting the verdict. *Pfeiffer v. State*, 35 Ariz. 321, 278 P. 63 (1929); *Canterbury v. Commonwealth*, 222 Ky. 510, 1 S.W.2d 976 (1928). It was said long ago in *Green v. Telfair*, 11 How.Pr. (N.Y.) 260 (1853), that "(a)n attempt to influence the jury, by referring to the time they are to be kept together, or the inconvenience to which they are to be subjected, in case they are so pertinacious as to adhere to their individual opinions, and thus continue to disagree, cannot be justified."

State v. Jones, 292 N.C. 513, 521-22, 234 S.E.2d 555, 559 (1977)

14.33 Jury Instructions

Direct vs. Circumstantial Evidence

"Finally, defendant contends the trial court erred in denying his special request for a jury instruction as to the effect of circumstantial evidence when no direct evidence is presented. The instruction requested by defendant should be given only when there is no direct evidence. If either the State or the defendant elicits direct evidence bearing on any issue for the jury's determination, then such an instruction is not appropriate."

State v. Bates, 309 N.C. 528, 537, 308 S.E.2d 258, 264 (1983)

Entitlement to instruction

"The trial court's jury instructions on possible theories of conviction must be supported by the evidence." *State v. Osborne*, 149 N.C.App. 235, 238, 562 S.E.2d 528, 531, *aff'd*, 356 N.C. 424, 571 S.E.2d 584 (2002).

Failure to instruct

While a specific intent is not an element of the offense of operating a motor vehicle on a public highway while one's license is suspended or revoked, the burden is on the State to prove that defendant had knowledge at the time charged that his operator's license was suspended or revoked; the State satisfies this burden when, nothing else appearing, it has offered evidence of compliance with the notice requirements of G.S. 20-48 because of the presumption that he received notice and had such knowledge. When there is some evidence to rebut this presumption, the issue of guilty knowledge is raised and must be determined by the jury under appropriate instruction from the trial court.

State v. Chester, 30 N.C. App. 224, 227, 226 S.E.2d 524, 526 (1976)

Refusal as evidence of guilt

Refusal to submit to a chemical test may be used as evidence of guilt. "An intoxilyzer test and field sobriety tests are not required to establish a defendant's faculties as being appreciably impaired under N.C. Gen.Stat. § 20-138.1. See, e.g., *State v. Rich*, 351 N.C. 386, 527 S.E.2d 299 (2000). Further, "it is a well-settled rule that a lay person may give his opinion as to whether a person is intoxicated so long as that opinion is based on the witness's personal observation." *Rich*, supra, 351 N.C. at 398, 527 S.E.2d at 306 (citing *State v. Lindley*, 286 N.C. 255, 258, 210 S.E.2d 207, 209 (1974)). An officer's opinion that a defendant is appreciably impaired is competent testimony and admissible evidence when it is based on the officer's personal observation of an odor of alcohol and of faulty driving or other evidence of impairment. *Rich*, supra; *Atkins v. Moye*, 277 N.C. 179, 176 S.E.2d 789 (1970); *State v. Hewitt*, 263 N.C. 759, 140 S.E.2d 241 (1965). The refusal to submit to an intoxilyzer test also is admissible as substantive evidence of guilt on a DWI charge. *State v. Pyatt*, 125 N.C.App. 147, 479 S.E.2d 218 (1997)."

State v. Gregory, 154 N.C. App. 718, 721, 572 S.E.2d 838, 840 (2002)

14.34 Jury Trial Right

DWI offense and other misdemeanors

The right to a jury trial *de novo* from an appeal of the District Court to the Superior Court has been found in our State Constitution as well as case law. "The offense here, of course, is a petty misdemeanor, but this court has held that the expression used in the Constitution, "with right of appeal," confers upon the defendant, when the appeal is taken, the right of trial by jury in the superior court, as will appear from these cases: *State v. Lytle*, 138 N. C. 738, 51 S. E. 66; *State v. Brittian*, 143 N. C. 668, 57 S. E. 352; *State v. Hyman*, 164 N. C. 411, 79 S. E. 284; *State v. Tate*, 169 N. C. 373, 85 S. E. 383; *State v. Pasley*, 180 N. C. 695, 104 S. E. 533. See, also, *State v.Rogers*, 162 N. C. 656, 78 S. E. 293, 46 L. R. A. (N. S.) 38, Ann. Cas. 1914A, 867.

Construing section 12 of article 1 with section 13, the court has held that, on these appeals from subordinate courts having jurisdiction of the subject-matter of the criminal action, a bill of indictment need not be sent in the court above against the defendant. When, however, a case reaches the superior court on appeal, it is heard de novo, as we have said, and, as a consequence, the right of a jury trial is secured thereby, according to the cases we have just cited."

State v. Pulliam, 184 N.C. 681, 114 S.E. 394, 395 (1922)

14.35 Motions

Untimely filed motions

Any motion can usually be made during the course of a trial; however, for implied consent offenses that are appealed to the Superior Court, you must file any suppression motion at least ten days before the trial. This is set out in the statute below. Pay close attention to subsection (d). Failure to do so can result in a dismissal.

§ 20-38.6. Motions and district court procedure.

(a) The defendant may move to suppress evidence or dismiss charges only prior to trial, except the defendant may move to dismiss the charges for insufficient evidence at the close of the State's evidence and at the close of all of the evidence without prior notice. If, during the course of the trial, the defendant discovers facts not previously known, a motion to suppress or dismiss may be made during the trial. (b) Upon a motion to suppress or dismiss the charges, other than at the close of the State's evidence or at the close of all the evidence, the State shall be granted reasonable time to procure witnesses or evidence and to conduct research required to defend against the motion. (c) The judge shall summarily grant the motion to suppress evidence if the State stipulates that the evidence sought to be suppressed will not be offered in evidence in any criminal action or proceeding against the defendant. (d) The judge may summarily deny the motion to suppress evidence if the defendant failed to make the motion pretrial when all material facts were known to the defendant. (e) If the motion is not determined summarily, the judge shall make the determination after a hearing and finding of facts. Testimony at the hearing shall be under oath. (f) The judge shall set forth in writing the findings of fact and conclusions of law and preliminarily indicate whether the motion should be granted or denied. If the judge preliminarily indicates the motion should be granted, the judge shall not enter a final judgment on the motion until after the State has appealed to superior court or has indicated it does not intend to appeal.

14.36 Miranda

Police must give Miranda warnings

Miranda v. Arizona, 384 U.S. 436, at 444, 86 S.Ct. 1602, at 1612, 16 L.Ed.2d 694 (1966) held that a person "deprived of his freedom in any significant way" could not be questioned unless he waived his rights after being advised of them. The simple rule is that if a person is not free to go, the police cannot begin interrogation unless first advising the suspect that he has the right to remain silent, to consult with counsel, to have counsel appointed if he cannot afford counsel and that anything said may be used against him in a court of law.

Routine background information not subject to Miranda

The routine gathering of background information of a defendant has generally been held not to constitute an interrogation. See also *State v. Garcia*, 233 Kan. 589, 664 P.2d 1343 (1983); *State v. Maximo*, 170 Ariz. 94, 821 P.2d 1379 (Ariz. App. 1991); *United States v. Crisco*, 725 F.2d 1228, 1232 (9th Cir.), cert. denied, 466 U.S. 977, 104 S.Ct. 2360, 80 L.Ed.2d 832 (1984)).

Juvenile Miranda Warnings

§ 7B-2101. Interrogation procedures.

(a) Any juvenile in custody must be advised prior to questioning:
   (1) That the juvenile has a right to remain silent;
   (2) That any statement the juvenile does make can be and may be used against the juvenile;
   (3) That the juvenile has a right to have a parent, guardian, or custodian present during questioning; and
   (4) That the juvenile has a right to consult with an attorney and that one will be appointed for the juvenile if the juvenile is not represented and wants representation.

(b) When the juvenile is less than 14 years of age, no in-custody admission or confession resulting from interrogation may be admitted into evidence unless the confession or admission was made in the presence of the juvenile's parent, guardian, custodian, or attorney. If an attorney is not present, the parent, guardian, or custodian as well as the juvenile must be advised of the juvenile's rights as set out in subsection (a) of this section; however, a parent, guardian, or custodian may not waive any right on behalf of the juvenile.

(c) If the juvenile indicates in any manner and at any stage of questioning pursuant to this section that the juvenile does not wish to be questioned further, the officer shall cease questioning.

(d) Before admitting into evidence any statement resulting from custodial interrogation, the court shall find that the juvenile knowingly, willingly, and understandingly waived the juvenile's rights.

Manner of informing suspect of Miranda Rights

Bell v. U.S., 382 F.2d 985 (9th Cir.1967) There is no requirement as to the precise manner in which the police communicate the required warnings to one suspected of crime. The requirement is that the police fully advise such a person of his rights. *See also U.S. v. Sledge*, 546 F.2d 1120, (4th Cir.1977) (holding that it is "not essential" that rights be given in oral rather than written form). In *Bell*, the Ninth Circuit rejected as "absurd" a claim that the police were obliged to advise a defendant of his *Miranda* rights orally rather than in writing. 382 F.2d at 987.

14.37 Necessity Defense

"Moreover, courts in other jurisdictions have specifically held that the defense of necessity is available in a DWI prosecution. *See, e.g., People v. Pena*, 149 Cal.App.3d Supp. 14, 22, 197 Cal.Rptr. 264, 269 (1983) (duress/necessity defense was available to a defendant charged with misdemeanor driving under the influence); *Stodghill v. State*, 881 So.2d 885, 889 (Miss.Ct.App.) ("[Defendant's] decision to drive after drinking may be excused as necessary."), *cert. denied*, 883 So.2d 1180 (2004); *State v. Shotton*, 142 Vt. 558, 562, 458 A.2d 1105, 1107 (1983) (in DWI prosecution, trial court erred in not instructing the jury on the defense of necessity). We likewise hold that the defense of necessity is available in a DWI prosecution."

State v. Hudgins, 167 N.C. App. 705, 710, 606 S.E.2d 443, 447 (2005)

14.38 DMV

Rules of Evidence Do Not Apply in DMV Hearings

After reviewing applicable statutes, we are not persuaded that the Rules of Evidence apply to these types of hearings. *See generally* N.C. Gen.Stat. § 8C–1, Rule 1101 (2011); N.C. Gen.Stat. § 20–16.2 (2011); N.C. Gen.Stat. § 150B–1(e)(8) (2011) (exempting the Department of Transportation from the contested case provisions of the Administrative Procedure Act); 19A N.C.A.C. 3A.0100 to 3J.0907 (2012) (outlining regulations concerning the DMV). N.C. Gen.Stat. § 16.2(d) only requires that the hearing officer subpoena witnesses or documents "that the hearing officer deems necessary." N.C. Gen.Stat. § 20–16.2(d) (2011). We hold the Rules of Evidence do not apply to DMV hearings held pursuant to § 20–16.2. Petitioner's argument is without merit.

Johnson v. Robertson, 742 S.E.2d 603, 606 (N.C. Ct. App. 2013)

14.39 Opinion Testimony

Witness May Not Testify About Legal Standard

Generally this type of testimony follows the North Carolina Rules of Evidence 701 through 704. A witness may not testify that a legal standard has or has not been met *State v. Daniels* 337 N.C. 243, 263 (1994).

The *Thibodeaux* Court determined that a witness may "testify as to whether the defendant had the capacity to understand certain words on the *Miranda* form, ...but he may not testify as to whether the defendant had the capacity to waive his rights." *State v. Thibodeaux* 341 N.C. 53 (1995).

14.40 Plea Agreements

The Alford plea

North Carolina v. Alford 400 US 25 (1970) allows your client to plead guilty without admitting guilt. It's still considered a guilty plea and your client is still treated and sentenced as if he or she were guilty. This type of plea just allows your client to say that while he or she did not do what the State claims, the client feels that a guilty verdict would ensue. This case actually comes from one of the main jurisdictions in which I practice.

14.41 Prior Convictions

Judicial Notice of Prior Convictions for Purposes of Habitual DWI

> "Defendant also contends that admission of State's Exhibit 6 during the State's case-in-chief violated N.C. Gen.Stat. § 15A-928(c)(1) (2003), as well as Rules 402 and 403 of our Rules of Evidence. We address defendant's argument because of the possibility of repetition on retrial.
>
> N.C. Gen.Stat. § 15A-928 (2003) governs the method of proof of previous convictions in superior court when the fact that the defendant has been previously convicted of an offense raises an offense of lower grade to one of higher grade and thereby becomes an element of the latter. It applies to prosecutions for habitual DWI, *State v. Scott*, 356 N.C. 591, 593, 573 S.E.2d 866, 867 (2002), and provides:
>
>> (c) After commencement of the trial and before the close of the State's case, the judge in the absence of the jury must arraign the defendant upon the special indictment or information, and must advise him that he may admit the previous conviction alleged, deny it, or remain silent. Depending upon the defendant's response, the trial of the case must then proceed as follows:
>>
>> (1) *If the defendant admits the previous conviction*, that element of the offense charged in the indictment or information is established, *no evidence in support thereof may be adduced by the State*, and the judge must submit the case to the jury without reference thereto and as if the fact of such previous conviction were not an element of the offense.
>
> N.C. Gen.Stat. § 15A-928 (emphasis added). "The purpose of this procedure is to afford the defendant an opportunity to admit the prior convictions which are an element of the offense and prevent the State from presenting evidence of these convictions before the jury." *State v. Burch*, 160 N.C.App. 394, 397, 585 S.E.2d 461, 463 (2003)

State v. Hudgins, 167 N.C. App. 705, 712, 606 S.E.2d 443, 448 (2005)

14.42 Probable Cause

Taylor v. Arizona, 471 F.2d 848 (9th Cir.1972), *cert. denied*, 409 U.S. 1130, 93 S.Ct. 948, 35 L.Ed.2d 262 (1973) (citing *United States v. Beck*, 598 F.2d 497 (9th Cir.1979)). Whether one is placed under arrest is a question of fact to be determined by the judge after a careful review of the facts. "The issue turns upon an evaluation of all the surrounding circumstances to determine whether a reasonable person, innocent of any crime, would reasonably believe that he was being arrested."

United States v. Beck, 598 F.2d 497 (9th Circuit 1979) "In determining whether an arrest has occurred, a significant consideration is the extent that freedom of movement is curtailed and the degree and manner of force used."

"The defendant was surrounded by police officers, deprived of her liberty of movement, and watched her companion be frisked. Defendant was then asked to accompany the officers across the street for further questioning. 'These circumstances surely amount to a show of official authority such that "a reasonable person would have believed he was not free to leave." ' "(quoting *Florida v. Royer*, 460 U.S. 491, 501, 103 S.Ct. 1319, 1326, 75 L.Ed.2d 229 (1983)).

The purpose of the detention requires scrutiny. Searches for the purpose of officer safety will generally be held constitutional, but searches for the purpose of evidence gathering will not. "Finally, we find that the illegal arrest had a 'quality of purposefulness' designed as an 'expedition for evidence' in the hope that defendant might confess." See *Dunaway v. New York*, 442 U.S. at 218, 99 S.Ct. at 2259 (1979)).

Another significant factor is the display of official authority such that "a reasonable person would believe that he is not free to leave." *Florida v. Royer*, 460 U.S. 491, 501, 103 S.Ct. 1319, 1326, 75 L.Ed.2d 229 (1983).

Remedy for Fourth Amendment violation

Evidence seized in violation of the Fourth Amendment should be suppressed under the "fruit of the poisonous tree" doctrine. *Wong Sun v. United States*, 371 U.S. 471, 83 S.Ct. 407, 9 L.Ed.2d 441 (1963).

14.43 Reasonable Suspicion

Not all traffic violations are cause for stop

"An investigatory stop of a motor vehicle constitutes a seizure under the Fourth Amendment. Because such stops are less intrusive than arrests, officers need not possess probable cause to justify them. Rather, they need only possess a reasonable suspicion that the driver has committed an offense. Under this standard, the officer must possess 'a particularized and objective basis for suspecting the particular person stopped of criminal activity.' When officers make traffic stops based on facts that neither constitute a violation of the law nor constitute reasonable grounds to suspect the driver has committed an offense, they run afoul of the Fourth Amendment requirement that they possess objectively reasonable grounds for the intrusion." (quoting *State v. Gonzales-Gutierrez*, 187 Ariz. 116, 118, 927 P.2d 776, 778 (1996) and *United States v. Cortez*, 449 U.S. 411, 417-18, 101 S.Ct. 690, 695, 66 L.Ed.2d 621, 629 (1996)).

The suspect's vehicle was observed to touch, not cross, the fog line and solid yellow painted line for approximately 10 seconds on two occasions—this was not a violation of the California statute which says that a car must be driven within the lane as nearly as practical and shall not change lanes without first being able to do so safely. The Fourth Amendment prohibition against unreasonable searches and seizures applies to investigatory traffic stops. To justify an investigative stop, the police must have reasonable suspicion that the suspect is involved in criminal activity. The cop's inferences that formed the basis for the stop must be grounded in objective facts and be capable of rational explanation; otherwise it is not reasonable suspicion. Defendants who were in the vehicle at the time of the stop had standing to challenge the stop, even though they had no possessory interest in the vehicle. *United States v. Colin*, 314 F.3d 439 (9th Cir. 2002).

A traffic stop is a seizure under the Fourth Amendment

Berkemer v. McCarty, 468 U.S. 420 (1984) There can be no question that the stopping of a vehicle and the detention of its occupants constitute a "seizure" under the meaning of the Fourth Amendment.

An investigatory stop of a vehicle is a seizure for Fourth Amendment purposes. *State v. Gonzales-Gutierrez*, 187 Ariz. 116, 118, 927 P.2d 776, 778 (1996). However, because investigatory stops are less intrusive than full-blown arrests, the officers do not need probable cause to justify them. *United States v. Brignoni-Ponce*, 442 US 873, 878, 881, 95 S.Ct. 2574, 2578, 2580, 45 L.Ed. 2d 607, 614, 616 (1975).

Police need only reasonable suspicion to believe that the driver has committed an offense in order to stop the driver. *Berkemer v. McCarty*, 468 US 420, 439, 104 S.Ct. 3138, 3149-50, 82 L.Ed. 2d 334 (1984);

When law enforcement officers make traffic stops based on facts other than a violation of the law or reasonable grounds to suspect that the driver has committed an offense, they are in violation of the Fourth Amendment requirement that they possess objectively reasonable grounds for the intrusion. *United States v. Mariscal*, 285 F.3d 1127, 1130-33 (9th Cir. 2002); *United States v. Lopez-Soto*, 205 F.3d 1101, 1105-1106 (9th Cir. 2000); *United States v. Lopez-Valdez*, 178 F.3d 282, 289 n. 6 (5th Cir. 1999); *United States v. Miller*, 146 F.3d 274, 279 (5th Cir. 1998).

Brendlin v. California, 551 U.S. 249, 127 S.Ct. 2400, 168 L.Ed. 2d 132 (2007). When police officers make a traffic stop, the passengers as well as the driver are seized for Fourth Amendment purposes. The passengers may challenge the stop's constitutionality.

Totality of the circumstances

By definition, reasonable suspicion is something short of probable cause. As the Supreme Court noted in *Illinois v. Wardlow*, 528 U.S. 119, 120 S.Ct. 673, 677, 145 L.Ed.2d 570 (2000), "[e]ven in Terry, the conduct justifying the stop was ambiguous and susceptible of an innocent explanation." One cannot isolate the individual factors and categorize each one as potentially innocent without looking at the whole picture. Instead, one must look at the totality of the circumstances to determine whether reasonable suspicion exists. See also *United States v. Cortez*, 449 U.S. 411, 101 S.Ct. 690 (1981).

Pretextual stops

Pretextual stops are valid, as long as the officer has reasonable suspicion. In other words, the subjective motives of the officer, unfortunately, do not matter. *Whren v. United States*, 517 U.S. 806, 813, 116 S.Ct. 1769, 1774, 135 L.Ed. 2d 89, 98 (1996);

Despite the fact that subjective motives are not relevant to the determination of reasonable suspicion, one can use the subjective motives of the officer to show that his credibility is lacking on the threshold question of whether he is lying about actually seeing a traffic violation.

Burden of proof and production

The State has the burden of showing the constitutionality of a search. *State v. Cooke*, 306 N.C. 132, 136, 291 S.E.2d 618, 620 (1982). Furthermore, the review of a search should be for constitutional errors, which the State has the burden of proving are "harmless **138 beyond a reasonable doubt." N.C. Gen.Stat. § 15A–1443(b) (2011).

State v. Schiro, 219 N.C. App. 105, 110, 723 S.E.2d 134, 137-38 (2012)

Remedy for Fourth Amendment violation

Evidence seized in violation of the Fourth Amendment should be suppressed under the "fruit of the poisonous tree" doctrine. *Wong Sun v. United States*, 371 U.S. 471, 83 S.Ct. 407, 9 L.Ed.2d 441 (1963).

Reasonable suspicion not required where there is no traffic stop

Officer Cloer approached defendant's vehicle and engaged in conversation with him, as the officer did in *Brooks*. He testified that he walked up to defendant's car on foot and asked to speak with him. During that conversation, Officer Cloer observed signs of intoxication (the odor of alcohol on defendant, an unopened can of beer, and slurred speech) leading him to investigate defendant further. Similar to *Isenhour*, Officer Cloer also did not use any "psychological barriers" while initiating contact with defendant. He testified that he did not activate his blue lights and there is no evidence that he removed his gun from his holster or used a threatening tone initiating contact with defendant. Thus, as found in *Brooks* and *Isenhour*, Officer Cloer engaged in a voluntary encounter with defendant.

State v. Veal, 760 S.E.2d 43, 47 (N.C. Ct. App.) appeal dismissed, 763 S.E.2d 392 (N.C. 2014)

14.44 Record Preservation for Appeal

This Court has repeatedly held that section 15A–1241 does not require recordation of "private bench conferences between trial judges and attorneys." *Cummings*, 332 N.C. at 497, 422 S.E.2d at 697; *accord Speller*, 345 N.C. at 605, 481 S.E.2d at 287. If, however, a party requests that the subject matter of a private bench conference be put on the record for appellate review, section 15A–1241(c) requires the trial judge to reconstruct the matter discussed as accurately as possible. See *Cummings*, 332 N.C. at 498, 422 S.E.2d at 698.

State v. Blakeney, 352 N.C. 287, 307, 531 S.E.2d 799, 814 (2000)

14.45 Refusal to Submit to Chemical Testing

Evidence of guilt and Right to Refuse

North Carolina allows a statutory right to refuse a breath test under N.C.G.S. §20-16.2; the consequences of the refusal however (the revocation of a driver's license for one year) are also set out in that same statute along with the fact that the refusal can be used as evidence at trial.

14.46 Relation Back

Relation back/retrograde calculations

Our Supreme Court has explained retrograde extrapolation as

> a mathematical analysis in which a known blood alcohol test result is used to determine what an individual's blood alcohol level would have been at a specified earlier time. The analysis determines the prior blood alcohol level on the bases of (1) the time elapsed between the occurrence of the specified earlier event (*e.g.*, a vehicle crash) and the known blood test, and (2) the rate of elimination of alcohol from the **512 subject's blood during the time between the event and the test.

State v. Cook, 362 N.C. 285, 288, 661 S.E.2d 874, 876 (2008). Our Courts have recognized retrograde extrapolation as a reliable method of proving BAC. *See State v. Davis*, 142 N.C.App. 81, 542 S.E.2d 236 (2001); *State v. Catoe*, 78 N.C.App. 167, 336 S.E.2d 691 (1985).

State v. Davis, 208 N.C. App. 26, 31, 702 S.E.2d 507, 511-12 (2010)

14.47 Replicate Testing

Schneckloth v. Bustamonte, 412 U.S. 218, 93 S.Ct. 2041, 36 L.Ed.2d 854 (1973); The state's duty to preserve evidence affects a defendant's fundamental right to a fair trial. Any waiver of that duty must be a voluntary and intentional relinquishment of a known right, otherwise it is void.

14.48 Restitution

A trial court's judgment ordering restitution "must be supported by evidence adduced at trial or at sentencing." *State v. Wilson*, 340 N.C. 720, 726, 459 S.E.2d 192, 196 (1995) (citations omitted). Issues at a sentencing hearing may be established by stipulation of counsel if that stipulation is " ' "definite and certain." ' " *State v. Alexander*, 359 N.C. 824, 828, 616 S.E.2d 914, 917 (2005) (quoting *State v. Powell*, 254 N.C. 231, 234, 118 S.E.2d 617, 619 (1961)) (citations omitted), *superseded by statute*, Safe Roads Act of 1983, ch. 435, sec. 29, 1983 N.C. Sess. Laws 332, 354–60 (codified as amended at N.C.G.S. § 20–179(a) (2003)) (as recognized in *State v. Denning*, 316 N.C. 523, 342 S.E.2d 855 (1986)).

9 Here we cannot agree with the State that defense counsel's statements quoted above amount to a definite and certain stipulation. There appeared to be some confusion over whether insurance payments had or had not been included in the restitution worksheets. We cannot be certain that defense counsel's statement was a stipulation *404 to the amount of the restitution or an affirmation that he was now clear on whether the insurance payments had been included on the worksheets. Moreover, we agree with defendant that the mere presentation of the worksheet by the prosecutor was not sufficient to support the award of restitution. *See, e.g., id.* at 827, 616 S.E.2d at 917 (stating that "a mere worksheet, standing alone, is insufficient to adequately establish a defendant's prior record level"). However, any error in the determination of restitution cannot be prejudicial to defendant because at the time the judgment is collected, defendant cannot be made to pay more than what is actually owed, that is, the amount actually due to the various entities that provided medical treatment to defendant's victims. Because defendant will pay the lesser of the actual amount owed or the amount ordered by the trial court, there is no prejudice to defendant. Accordingly, we reverse the decision of the Court of Appeals vacating the portion of the **918 trial court's judgment ordering payment of restitution.

State v. Mumford, 364 N.C. 394, 403-04, 699 S.E.2d 911, 917-18 (2010)

14.49 Right to Counsel

Remedy for violation of right to counsel

The proper remedy for violation of the right to counsel is dismissal of the DWI charges. In order to warrant dismissal of a charge under N.C.Gen.Stat. § 20-138.1(a)(2), a defendant must make a sufficient showing of a substantial statutory violation and of prejudice arising therefrom. *State v. Knoll*, 322 N.C. 535, 369 S.E.2d 558 (1988). *Knoll* involved three DWI cases (*State v. Knoll*, *State v. Warren*, and *State v. Hicks*) which had been consolidated for review. In *Knoll*, the magistrate set defendant's bond without inquiring into any of the conditions which affect the setting of a bond. Defendant had to wait in jail for an hour before he was allowed to call his father, and his father was told that he would not be allowed to post his bond for six hours. In *Warren*, the defendant was not informed of his right to communicate with counsel and friends. Two individuals attempted to post his bond but were told that defendant would have to remain in jail until 6:00 a.m. before he could be bailed out. In *Hicks*, the defendant was not informed of his right to communicate with counsel and friends. The magistrate set his bond without inquiring into any of the conditions affecting the setting of a bond, and refused to allow defendant to post his own bond despite the fact that he had the funds to do so. The Court held that each of the defendants had made a sufficient showing of a substantial statutory violation to warrant dismissal.

State v. Eliason, 100 N.C. App. 313, 315, 395 S.E.2d 702, 703 (1990)

14.50 Roadblocks (a.k.a. "DWI Checkpoints")

Note that the term "Roadblock" is used in this book rather than the police/prosecutor/court term "DWI Checkpoint." Early DWI cases used the term "roadblock" before it became politically unpopular for the courts to refer to them as such. Calling it a "checkpoint" serves to sanitize the unwarranted and unreasonable intrusion upon the liberty of ordinary, law-abiding citizens. How we as a society came to allow the police to stop our fellow citizens in absence of probable cause or reasonable suspicion simply to see if a crime has been committed is a complex issue. Misinformation and downright lies perpetrated upon the courts and the public by private lobby groups and the police played a large part in the formation of such laws which allow random stopping of motorists. Less than ten states have state constitutions which afford more protection to their citizens than the federal constitution.

Federal case law

United States v. Ortiz, 422 U.S. 891 (1975). The Supreme Court invalidated roadblocks designed to check for illegal immigrants because the roadblocks were too far removed from the borders, had unsubstantiated statistical effectiveness and left the officers with virtually unfettered discretion as to how to conduct the roadblocks.

United States v. Martinez-Fuerte, 428 U.S. 543 (1976). "The principal protection of Fourth Amendment rights at checkpoints lies in appropriate limitations on the scope of the stop."

Brown v. Texas, 443 U.S. 47 (1979) produced a three-part balancing test for roadblocks: "[T]he gravity of the public concerns served by the seizure, the degree to which the seizure advances the public interest, and the severity of the interference with individual liberty." Roadblock seizures are constitutional if they are "carried out pursuant to a plan embodying explicit, neutral limitations on the conduct of individual officers."

Michigan Department of State Police v. Sitz, 496 U.S. 444 (1990). DWI roadblocks were upheld based, in part, on the statistical data which showed that less than 2 percent of drivers passing through the roadblock were arrested for DWI. Specific rules must be followed to pass constitutional muster. Most importantly is that the police can have little, if any, individual discretion in deciding which cars to stop.

City of Indianapolis v. Edmond 531 U.S. 32 (2000). The Supreme Court invalidated a roadblock which was set up to discover evidence of "ordinary crimes." The roadblock was set up in an area declared by the police to be high in illegal drug sales. Cars were stopped and the occupants questioned in an effort to weed out the drug dealers and buyers. This was expressly not a DWI roadblock. "We decline to suspend the usual requirement of individualized suspicion where the police seek to employ a checkpoint primarily for the ordinary enterprise of investigating crimes. We cannot sanction stops justified only by the generalized and ever-present possibility that interrogation and inspection may reveal that any given motorist has committed some crime."

Illinois v. Lidster, 540 U.S. 419, 124 S.Ct. 885, 157 L.Ed. 2d 843 (2004). In *Lidster*, the police had set up a roadblock to question drivers and passengers about whether they had seen anything regarding a fatal hit-and-run accident. Mr. Lidster drove up to the roadblock and almost hit a police officer. Eventually, he was arrested for DWI and he had nothing to do with the hit-and-run accident that was being investigated.

The police stated that the objective was "to work out a fatal hit-and-run accident." In reality, *Lidster* only minimally differs from *Edmond* in that the police were not randomly seizing drivers as potential suspects for an unspecified crime as in *Edmond*, but were randomly stopping drivers to see if they knew anything about a specific crime. The government in *Lidster* claimed that they were not looking for the actual suspect at the roadblock, but were merely searching for witnesses. Unfortunately, the Supreme Court latched on to this obviously false claim by the government and used it to justify its ruling.

Moreover, the past line of roadblock cases always looked to whether there was a legitimate governmental interest in randomly seizing drivers in an effort to prevent future crimes by deterring DWI. In *Lidster*, the government was interested in solving a single alleged crime that had already occurred with a single victim. There were virtually no guidelines for this roadblock, yet it was held to be constitutional. "The relevant public concern was grave. Police were investigating a crime that had resulted in a human death. No one denies the police's need to obtain more information at that time. And the stop's objective was to help find the perpetrator of a specific and known crime, not of unknown crimes of a general sort."

Yet, there was no evidence that a crime was the cause of the death—it could have been a simple accident. The only crime was the driver leaving the scene which, under Illinois law, could be a misdemeanor.

Perhaps even more frightening is the Court's further justification: "Most importantly, the stops interfered only minimally with liberty of the sort the Fourth Amendment seeks to protect." So it seems that a small incursion into one's constitutionally protected rights will be tolerated, but where do we draw the line? In the opinion of the author of this book, *Lidster* was decided incorrectly.

Phantom Checkpoints

While it might be hard for some people to believe, it is true that the police lie to the public every now and then. Such is the case with "phantom checkpoints" set up by the police. A phantom checkpoint is a fiction created by the police wherein they set up DWI checkpoint signs with no roadblocks. Then the police wait to see who avoids the area. The police then follow the driver and either legitimately stop the driver, or sometimes make up a reason to stop the driver. There are no North Carolina cases that address phantom checkpoints, but at least one tenth circuit found them to be legal (United *States v. Flynn*, 309 F.3d 736 (10th Cir. 2002)).

14.52 Searches

Standing to challenge stop

The Fourth Amendment prohibition against unreasonable searches and seizures applies to clearly investigatory traffic stops. Defendants who were in the vehicle at the time of the stop had standing to challenge the stop, even though they had no possessory interest in the vehicle. Their consent to search the vehicle did not purge the taint of the illegal stop, thus their Fourth Amendment rights were violated. *United States v. Colin*, 314 F.3d 439 (9th Cir. 2002).

Terry stop

"For the search to come within the Terry stop and frisk exception, the trial court must have properly found that the officer reasonably feared for his safety or the safety of others. Under this exception, an officer may conduct a warrantless search if the circumstances are 'those in which a substantial risk of harm to the persons involved ... would arise if the police were to delay a search until a warrant could be obtained.' " *United States v. Robertson*, 606 F.2d 853, 859 (9th Cir.1979).

There are many types of warrantless searches permitted by law. One example would be search incident to arrest, another is where exigent circumstances exist. The police may do a *Terry* pat on a suspect when they reasonably believe that the suspect may have a weapon.

Exigent circumstances

Under the exigent circumstances exception to the Fourth Amendment, "... a warrantless entry can be made into a dwelling if the circumstances are 'those in which a substantial risk of harm to the persons involved or to the law enforcement process would arise if the police were to delay a search until a warrant could be obtained.' "(quoting *United States v. Robertson*, 606 F.2d 853, 859 (9th Cir.1979) (citations omitted).

The right to search, however, is dependent on "the reasonable cause the seizing officer has for belief that the contents of the automobile offend against the law." *Carroll v. United States*, 267 U.S. 132, 45 S.Ct. 280, 69 L.Ed. 543 (1925).

Chambers v. Maroney, 399 U.S. 42, 90 S.Ct. 1975, 26 L.Ed.2d 419 (1970); *Cardwell v. Lewis*, 417 U.S. 583, 94 S.Ct. 2464, 41 L.Ed.2d 325 (1974). The exception to the requirement of a search warrant is based on the fact that "[T]he circumstances that furnish probable cause to search a particular auto for particular articles are most often unforeseeable; moreover, the opportunity to search is fleeting since a car is readily movable."

The "automobile exception" provides that a search warrant is not necessary when probable cause exists to search a readily mobile vehicle that is stopped on the roadway or parked on a public street or in a parking lot. *California v. Carney*, 471 U.S. 386, 390, 105 S.Ct. 2066, 85 L.Ed.2d 406 (1985); *Cardwell v. Lewis*, 417 U.S. 583, 594, 94 S.Ct. 2464, 41 L.Ed.2d 325 (1974); *State v. Branham*, 191 Ariz. 94, 96, 952 P.2d 332, 334 (App.1997); *State v. Reyna*, 205 Ariz. 374, 71 P.3d 366 (Ariz.App. Div. 1 2003).

The Supreme Court created the automobile exception in *Carroll v. United States*, 267 U.S. 132, 153, 45 S.Ct. 280, 69 L.Ed. 543 (1925), in recognition of the impracticability of securing a warrant to search a vehicle that could be quickly moved from the jurisdiction.

California v. Carney, 471 U.S. 386, 390, 105 S.Ct. 2066, 85 L.Ed.2d 406 (1985). The Court eventually acknowledged that the automobile exception was also justified because the expectation of privacy with respect to one's automobile is significantly less than that relating to one's home or office.

In *Chimel v. California*, 395 U.S. 752, 89 S.Ct. 2034, 23 L.Ed.2d 685 (1969), the Supreme Court held that, when police make a lawful arrest, they may, without a warrant, search the person in custody as well as the "area from within which he might gain possession of a weapon or destructible evidence."

The U.S. Supreme Court later held that officers may search the entire passenger compartment of a vehicle, and all containers therein, as a "contemporaneous incident" of a lawful arrest. *New York v. Belton*, 453 U.S. 454, 101 S.Ct. 2860, 69 L.Ed.2d 768 (1981).

United States Constitution and North Carolina Constitution

The Fourth Amendment provides that "[t]he right of the people to be secure in their persons, houses, papers, and effects, against unreasonable searches and seizures, shall not be violated, and no Warrants shall issue, but upon probable cause, supported by Oath or affirmation, and particularly describing the place to be searched, and the persons or things seized." Its corollary in the North Carolina Constitution, Article 1, Section 20, states that "General warrants, whereby any officer or other person may be commanded to search suspected places without evidence of the act committed, or to seize any person or persons not named, whose offense is not particularly described and supported by evidence, are dangerous to liberty and shall not be granted."

Expectations of privacy

Cardwell v. Lewis, 417 U.S. 583, 94 S.Ct. 2464, 41 L.Ed.2d 325 (1974). The United States Supreme Court has never held that there is a reasonable expectation of privacy in the exterior of a vehicle. In fact, the opposite is true.

The fact that a person seeks to conceal evidence of a crime does not determine whether the person has an objectively legitimate expectation of privacy in the exterior appearance of his car. "The test of legitimacy is not whether the individual chooses to conceal assertedly 'private' activity," but instead "whether the government[al] intrusion infringes upon the personal and societal values protected by the Fourth Amendment." *Oliver v. United States*, 466 U.S. 170, 182-83, 104 S.Ct. 1735, 80 L.Ed.2d 214 (1984); *see also New York v. Class*, 475 U.S. 106, 114, 106 S.Ct. 960, 89 L.Ed.2d 81 (1986) ("We have recently emphasized that efforts to restrict access to an area do not generate a reasonable expectation of privacy where none would otherwise exist.").

United States v. Jacobsen, 466 U.S. 109, 104 S.Ct. 1652, 80 L.Ed.2d 85 (1984). A "search" under the Fourth Amendment occurs "when an expectation of privacy that society is prepared to consider reasonable is infringed."

Katz v. United States, 389 U.S. 347, 88 S.Ct. 507, 19 L.Ed.2d 576 (1967). The protection provided by the Fourth Amendment encompasses private information rather than formal definitions of property.

Smith v. Maryland, 442 U.S. 735, 99 S.Ct. 2577, 61 L.Ed.2d 220 (1979) (quoting *Katz*, 389 U.S. at 353, 88 S.Ct. 507). "To have a legitimate expectation of privacy protected by the Fourth Amendment, a person must show both an 'actual (subjective) expectation of privacy' and that the expectation is one that society is prepared to recognize as 'justifiable' under the circumstances." *See also California v. Greenwood*, 486 U.S. 35, 108 S.Ct. 1625, 100 L.Ed.2d 30 (1988) (holding Fourth Amendment protects only a "subjective expectation of privacy... that society accepts as objectively reasonable").

Inevitable discovery

Evidence obtained as a result of an unlawful search need not be suppressed when, in the normal course of police investigation and conduct, and absent the illicit conduct, the evidence would have been discovered inevitably or ultimately. *See also: Nix v. Williams*, 467 U.S. 431, 443-44, 447, 104 S.Ct. 2501, 2508-09, 2511, 81 L.Ed.2d 377 (1984);

Remedy for illegal search—the Exclusionary Rule

State v. McKinney 361 N.C. 53 (2006). The Fourth Amendment of the United States Constitution and Article 1, Section 20, of the North Carolina Constitution protect against unreasonable searches and seizures. When a violation of the Fourth Amendment or its state counterpart is determined to have occurred, the exclusionary rule generally requires the suppression at trial of any evidence directly or indirectly gained as a result of the violation.

14.53 Sentencing

Judicial notice of prior offense is acceptable

> In addition, however, defendant's counsel stipulated to the conviction at the probation hearing. The State asked the trial court to take judicial notice of defendant's DWI conviction "as satisfying the State's burden on that conviction." Defendant's counsel acknowledged that defendant had "[n]o objection to the judicial notice."
>
> Defendant acknowledges that his trial counsel's statement is arguably a stipulation, but contends that it is a stipulation to an issue of law and, therefore, not effective under *State v. Hanton*, 175 N.C.App. 250, 253, 623 S.E.2d 600, 603 (2006). *Hanton*, however, held that whether or not a defendant was convicted of a particular offense is a question of fact. *Id.* at 254, 623 S.E.2d at 604. *See also State v. Fair*, 205 N.C.App. 315, 318, 695 S.E.2d 514, 516 (2010) ("The existence of the conviction is an issue of fact."). As a result, defense counsel's statement that defendant did not object to the court's taking judicial notice of the conviction is sufficient evidence to support the trial court's finding that defendant committed a criminal offense in violation of his probation.

State v. Jacobs, 219 N.C. App. 648, 722 S.E.2d 798 (2012)

14.54 Subpoena

N.C.G.S. §15A-901 through 15A-910

N.C.Gen.Stat. § 15A–903(d) (1988) grants a defendant in a criminal case access as of right to documents and tangible objects that are "within the possession, custody or control of the State...." However, the reports and records at issue in this case were not within the prosecutor's possession, custody, or control; therefore, they were not subject to discovery as of right. *See State v. Newell*, 82 N.C.App. 707, 348 S.E.2d 158 (1986) (No common law right of discovery in criminal cases, therefore, criminal defendant's right of access to documents determined by statute). Another alternative for the production of documents not subject to the criminal discovery statute is the use of a subpoena *ducestecum*. The subpoena *ducestecum* is the process by which a court requires that particular documents or other items which are material to the inquiry be brought into court.

State v. Love, 100 N.C. App. 226, 229, 395 S.E.2d 429, 431 (1990)

14.55 Voir dire

The primary purpose of the voir dire of prospective jurors is to select an impartial jury. *State v. Lee*, 292 N.C. 617, 621, 234 S.E.2d 574, 577 (1977). Parties are allowed to question and strike potential jurors for cause. N.C. Gen. Stat. § 9-15(a). The trial court will determine whether the juror is fit or unfit and that decision is within the sound discretion of the trial court. *State v. Davis*, 349 N.C. 1, 16, 506 S.E.2d 455, 463 (1998). The decision will not be overturned on appeal without a showing of abuse of discretion. *Id.*

N.C. Gen. Stat. § 9-3 lists qualifications for prospective jurors. Any juror that does not qualify would be a proper challenge for cause. A challenge for cause would also be proper if a prospective juror states that he or she cannot follow the law as instructed by the judge. *State v. Cunningham*, 333 N.C. 744, 429 S.E.2d 718 (1993) (holding that it was an error to deny a challenge for cause when a juror was confused about, or refused to apply, presumption of evidence).

14.56 Voluntariness of Statements

Presumption of involuntariness

Statements made by a defendant are prima facie involuntary. *Jackson v. Denno*, 378 U.S. 368, 84 S.Ct. 1774, 12 L.Ed.2d 908 (1964).

Burden of proof

We next consider the effect of the first confession on the admissibility of the second confession. It is well settled in this jurisdiction that " 'where a confession has been obtained under circumstances rendering it involuntary, a presumption arises which imputes the same prior influence to any subsequent confession, and this presumption must be overcome before the subsequent confession can be received in evidence.' (Citation omitted.) The burden is upon the State to overcome this presumption by clear and convincing evidence. (Citations omitted.)"

State v. Siler, 292 N.C. 543, 551, 234 S.E.2d 733, 739 (1977)

Burden of Proof

Jackson v. Denno, 378 U.S. 368, 84 S.Ct. 1774, 12 L.Ed.2d 908 (1964). More than forty years ago the United States Supreme Court held that before a confession can be admitted into evidence, the trial judge must hold a hearing outside the presence of the jury and make a clear finding of voluntariness.

Schneckloth v. Bustamonte, 412 U.S. 218, 93 S.Ct. 2041, 36 L.Ed.2d 854, (1973). The voluntariness of a confession is assessed in light of "the totality of all the surrounding circumstances—both the characteristics of the accused and the details of the interrogation."

14.57 Warrants

No right to refuse a warrant

Although there seems to be no case law on point in North Carolina about forced blood draws, it is common for officers to compel the blood draw pursuant to N.C.G.S. §20-139.1 as a refusal under N.C.G.S. §20-16.2 and proceed after obtaining a search warrant. In fact the *McCrary* case even details restraints being used. The *McCrary* case, however, was a warrantless blood draw and is now on appeal to our State Supreme Court.

Deputy Fyle requested that hospital personnel assist him with obtaining defendant's blood sample. Deputy Fyle required the assistance of the other officers and used restraints to protect both the officers and hospital staff from defendant while his blood was drawn at 9:16 p.m., almost 3 hours after Lindsey's call. Deputy Fyle and defendant subsequently left the hospital at 9:29 p.m. and arrived at the magistrate's office for further processing at 9:43 p.m.

State v. McCrary, 764 S.E.2d 477, 479 (N.C. Ct. App. 2014) review allowed, writ allowed, 772 S.E.2d 718 (N.C. 2015) and cert. allowed, 772 S.E.2d 718 (N.C. 2015)

Appendix A

North Carolina Rules of Evidence

Chapter 8C. Evidence Code.

§ 8C-1. Rules of Evidence.

The North Carolina Rules of Evidence are as follows:

Article 1. General Provisions.

Rule 101. Scope.

These rules govern proceedings in the courts of this State to the extent and with the exceptions stated in Rule 1101. (1983, ch. 701, s. 1.)

Rule 102. Purpose and construction.

(a) In general. - These rules shall be construed to secure fairness in administration, elimination of unjustifiable expense and delay, and promotion of growth and development of the law of evidence to the end that the truth may be ascertained and proceedings justly determined.

(b) Subordinate divisions. - For the purpose of these rules only, the subordinate division of any rule which is labeled with a lower case letter shall be a subdivision. (1983, c. 701, s. 1.)

Rule 103. Rulings on evidence.

(a) Effect of erroneous ruling. - Error may not be predicated upon a ruling which admits or excludes evidence unless a substantial right of the party is affected, and

(1) Objection. - In case the ruling is one admitting evidence, a timely objection or motion to strike appears of record. No particular form is required in order to preserve the right to assert the alleged error upon appeal if the motion or objection clearly presented the alleged error to the trial court;

(2) Offer of proof. - In case the ruling is one excluding evidence, the substance of the evidence was made known to the court by offer or was apparent from the context within which questions were asked.

Once the court makes a definitive ruling on the record admitting or excluding evidence, either at or before trial, a party need not renew an objection or offer of proof to preserve a claim of error for appeal.

(b) Record of offer and ruling. - The court may add any other or further statement which shows the character of the evidence, the form in which it was offered, the objection made, and the ruling thereon. It may direct the making of an offer in question and answer form.

(c) Hearing of jury. - In jury cases, proceedings shall be conducted, to the extent practicable, so as to prevent inadmissible evidence from being suggested to the jury by any means, such as making statements or offers of proof or asking questions in the hearing of the jury.

(d) Review of errors where justice requires. - Notwithstanding the requirements of subdivision (a) of this rule, an appellate court may review errors affecting substantial rights if it determines, in the interest of justice, it is appropriate to do so. (1983, c. 701, s. 1; 2003-101, s. 1; 2006-264, s. 30.5.)

Rule 104. Preliminary questions.

(a) Questions of admissibility generally. - Preliminary questions concerning the qualification of a person to be a witness, the existence of a privilege, or the admissibility of evidence shall be determined by the court, subject to the provisions of subdivision (b). In making its determination it is not bound by the rules of evidence except those with respect to privileges.

(b) Relevancy conditioned on fact. - When the relevancy of evidence depends upon the fulfillment of a condition of fact, the court shall admit it upon, or subject to, the introduction of evidence sufficient to support a finding of the fulfillment of the condition.

(c) Hearing of jury. - Hearings on the admissibility of confessions or other motions to suppress evidence in criminal trials in Superior Court shall in all cases be conducted out of the hearing of the jury. Hearings on other preliminary matters shall be so conducted when the interests of justice require or, when an accused is a witness, if he so requests.

(d) Testimony by accused. - The accused does not, by testifying upon a preliminary matter, subject himself to cross-examination as to other issues in the case.

(e) Weight and credibility. - This rule does not limit the right of a party to introduce before the jury evidence relevant to weight or credibility. (1983, ch. 701, s. 1.)

Rule 105. Limited admissibility.
When evidence which is admissible as to one party or for one purpose but not admissible as to another party or for another purpose is admitted, the court, upon request, shall restrict the evidence to its proper scope and instruct the jury accordingly. (1983, c. 701, s. 1.)

Rule 106. Remainder of or related writings or recorded statements.
When a writing or recorded statement or part thereof is introduced by a party, an adverse party may require him at that time to introduce any other part or any other writing or recorded statement which ought in fairness to be considered contemporaneously with it. (1983, c. 701, s. 1.)

Article 2.
Judicial Notice.

Rule 201. Judicial notice of adjudicative facts.

(a) Scope of rule. - This rule governs only judicial notice of adjudicative facts.

(b) Kinds of facts. - A judicially noticed fact must be one not subject to reasonable dispute in that it is either (1) generally known within the territorial jurisdiction of the trial court or (2) capable of accurate and ready determination by resort to sources whose accuracy cannot reasonably be questioned.

(c) When discretionary. - A court may take judicial notice, whether requested or not.

(d) When mandatory. - A court shall take judicial notice if requested by a party and supplied with the necessary information.

(e) Opportunity to be heard. - In a trial court, a party is entitled upon timely request to an opportunity to be heard as to the propriety of taking judicial notice and the tenor of the matter noticed. In the absence of prior notification, the request may be made after judicial notice has been taken.

(f) Time of taking notice. - Judicial notice may be taken at any stage of the proceeding.

(g) Instructing jury. - In a civil action or proceeding, the court shall instruct the jury to accept as conclusive any fact judicially noticed. In a criminal case, the court shall instruct the jury that it may, but is not required to, accept as conclusive any fact judicially noticed. (1983, c. 701, s. 1.)

Article 3.
Presumptions in Civil Actions and Proceedings.

Rule 301. Presumptions in general in civil actions and proceedings.
In all civil actions and proceedings when not otherwise provided for by statute, by judicial decision, or by these rules, a presumption imposes on the party against whom it is directed the burden of going forward with evidence to rebut or meet the presumption, but does not shift to such party the burden of proof in the sense of the risk of nonpersuasion, which remains throughout the trial upon the party on whom it was originally cast. The burden of going forward is satisfied by the introduction of evidence sufficient to permit reasonable minds to conclude that the presumed fact does not exist. If the party against whom a presumption operates fails to meet the burden of producing evidence, the presumed fact shall be deemed proved, and the court shall instruct the jury accordingly. When the burden of producing evidence to meet a presumption is satisfied, the court must instruct the jury that it may, but is not required to, infer the existence of the presumed fact from the proved fact. (1983, c. 701, s. 1.)

Rule 302. Applicability of federal law in civil actions and proceedings.
In civil actions and proceedings, the effect of a presumption respecting a fact which is an element of a claim or defense as to which federal law supplies the rule of decision is determined in accordance with federal law. (1983, c. 701, s. 1.)

Article 4.
Relevancy and Its Limits.

Rule 401. Definition of "relevant evidence."
"Relevant evidence" means evidence having any tendency to make the existence of any fact that is of consequence to the determination of the action more probable or less probable than it would be without the evidence. (1983, c. 701, s. 1.)

Rule 402. Relevant evidence generally admissible; irrelevant evidence inadmissible.

All relevant evidence is admissible, except as otherwise provided by the Constitution of the United States, by the Constitution of North Carolina, by Act of Congress, by Act of the General Assembly or by these rules. Evidence which is not relevant is not admissible. (1983, c. 701, s. 1.)

Rule 403. Exclusion of relevant evidence on grounds of prejudice, confusion, or waste of time.

Although relevant, evidence may be excluded if its probative value is substantially outweighed by the danger of unfair prejudice, confusion of the issues, or misleading the jury, or by considerations of undue delay, waste of time, or needless presentation of cumulative evidence. (1983, c. 701, s. 1.)

Rule 404. Character evidence not admissible to prove conduct; exceptions; other crimes.

(a) Character evidence generally. - Evidence of a person's character or a trait of his character is not admissible for the purpose of proving that he acted in conformity therewith on a particular occasion, except:
   (1) Character of accused. - Evidence of a pertinent trait of his character offered by an accused, or by the prosecution to rebut the same;
   (2) Character of victim. - Evidence of a pertinent trait of character of the victim of the crime offered by an accused, or by the prosecution to rebut the same, or evidence of a character trait of peacefulness of the victim offered by the prosecution in a homicide case to rebut evidence that the victim was the first aggressor;
   (3) Character of witness. - Evidence of the character of a witness, as provided in Rules 607, 608, and 609.

(b) Other crimes, wrongs, or acts. - Evidence of other crimes, wrongs, or acts is not admissible to prove the character of a person in order to show that he acted in conformity therewith. It may, however, be admissible for other purposes, such as proof of motive, opportunity, intent, preparation, plan, knowledge, identity, or absence of mistake, entrapment or accident. Admissible evidence may include evidence of an offense committed by a juvenile if it would have been a Class A, B1, B2, C, D, or E felony if committed by an adult. (1983, c. 701, s. 1; 1994, Ex. Sess., c. 7, s. 3; 1995, c. 509, s. 7.)

Rule 405. Methods of proving character.

(a) Reputation or opinion. - In all cases in which evidence of character or a trait of character of a person is admissible, proof may be made by testimony as to reputation or by testimony in the form of an opinion. On cross-examination, inquiry is allowable into relevant specific instances of conduct. Expert testimony on character or a trait of character is not admissible as circumstantial evidence of behavior.

(b) Specific instances of conduct. - In cases in which character or a trait of character of a person is an essential element of a charge, claim, or defense, proof may also be made of specific instances of his conduct. (1983, c. 701, s. 1.)

Rule 406. Habit; routine practice.

Evidence of the habit of a person or of the routine practice of an organization, whether corroborated or not and regardless of the presence of eyewitnesses, is relevant to prove that the conduct of the person or organization on a particular occasion was in conformity with the habit or routine practice. (1983, c. 701, s. 1.)

Rule 407. Subsequent remedial measures.

When, after an event, measures are taken which, if taken previously, would have made the event less likely to occur, evidence of the subsequent measures is not admissible to prove negligence or culpable conduct in connection with the event. This rule does not require the exclusion of evidence of subsequent measures when offered for another purpose, such as proving ownership, control, or feasibility of precautionary measures, if those issues are controverted, or impeachment. (1983, c. 701, s. 1.)

Rule 408. Compromise and offers to compromise.

Evidence of (1) furnishing or offering or promising to furnish, or (2) accepting or offering or promising to accept, a valuable consideration in compromising or attempting to compromise a claim which was disputed as to either validity or amount, is not admissible to prove liability for or invalidity of the claim or its amount. Evidence of conduct or evidence of statements made in compromise negotiations is likewise not admissible. This rule does not require the exclusion of any evidence otherwise discoverable merely because it is presented in the course of compromise negotiations. This rule also does not require exclusion when the evidence is offered for another purpose, such as proving bias or prejudice of a witness, negativing a contention of undue delay, or proving an effort to obstruct a criminal investigation or prosecution. (1983, c. 701, s. 1.)

Rule 409. Payment of medical and other expenses.

Evidence of furnishing or offering or promising to pay medical, hospital, or other expenses occasioned by an injury is not admissible to prove liability for the injury. (1983, c. 701, s. 1.)

Rule 410. Inadmissibility of pleas, plea discussions, and related statements.

Except as otherwise provided in this rule, evidence of the following is not, in any civil or criminal proceeding, admissible for or against the defendant who made the plea or was a participant in the plea discussions:

(1) A plea of guilty which was later withdrawn;
(2) A plea of no contest;
(3) Any statement made in the course of any proceedings under Article 58 of Chapter 15A of the General Statutes or comparable procedure in district court, or proceedings under Rule 11 of the Federal Rules of Criminal Procedure or comparable procedure in another state, regarding a plea of guilty which was later withdrawn or a plea of no contest;
(4) Any statement made in the course of plea discussions with an attorney for the prosecuting authority which do not result in a plea of guilty or which result in a plea of guilty later withdrawn.

However, such a statement is admissible in any proceeding wherein another statement made in the course of the same plea or plea discussions has been introduced and the statement ought in fairness be considered contemporaneously with it. (1983, c. 701, s. 1.)

Rule 411. Liability insurance.

Evidence that a person was or was not insured against liability is not admissible upon the issue whether he acted negligently or otherwise wrongfully. This rule does not require the exclusion of evidence of insurance against liability when offered for another purpose, such as proof of agency, ownership, or control, or bias or prejudice of a witness. (1983, c. 701, s. 1.)

Rule 412. Rape or sex offense cases; relevance of victim's past behavior.

(a) As used in this rule, the term "sexual behavior" means sexual activity of the complainant other than the sexual act which is at issue in the indictment on trial.
(b) Notwithstanding any other provision of law, the sexual behavior of the complainant is irrelevant to any issue in the prosecution unless such behavior:
  (1) Was between the complainant and the defendant; or
  (2) Is evidence of specific instances of sexual behavior offered for the purpose of showing that the act or acts charged were not committed by the defendant; or
  (3) Is evidence of a pattern of sexual behavior so distinctive and so closely resembling the defendant's version of the alleged encounter with the complainant as to tend to prove that such complainant consented to the act or acts charged or behaved in such a manner as to lead the defendant reasonably to believe that the complainant consented; or
  (4) Is evidence of sexual behavior offered as the basis of expert psychological or psychiatric opinion that the complainant fantasized or invented the act or acts charged.
(c) Sexual behavior otherwise admissible under this rule may not be proved by reputation or opinion.
(d) Notwithstanding any other provision of law, unless and until the court determines that evidence of sexual behavior is relevant under subdivision (b), no reference to this behavior may be made in the presence of the jury and no evidence of this behavior may be introduced at any time during the trial of:
  (1) A charge of rape or a lesser included offense of rape;
  (2) A charge of a sex offense or a lesser included offense of a sex offense; or
  (3) An offense being tried jointly with a charge of rape or a sex offense, or with a lesser included offense of rape or a sex offense.

  Before any questions pertaining to such evidence are asked of any witness, the proponent of such evidence shall first apply to the court for a determination of the relevance of the sexual behavior to which it relates. The proponent of such evidence may make application either prior to trial pursuant to G.S. 15A-952, or during the trial at the time when the proponent desires to introduce such evidence. When application is made, the court shall conduct an in camera hearing, which shall be transcribed, to consider the proponent's offer of proof and the argument of counsel, including any counsel for the complainant, to determine the extent to which such behavior is relevant. In the hearing, the proponent of the evidence shall establish the basis of admissibility of such evidence. Notwithstanding subdivision (b) of Rule 104, if the relevancy of the evidence which the proponent seeks to offer in the trial depends upon the fulfillment of a condition of fact, the court, at the in camera hearing or at a subsequent in camera hearing scheduled for that purpose, shall accept evidence on the issue of whether that condition of fact is fulfilled and shall determine that issue. If the court finds that the evidence is relevant, it shall enter an order stating that the evidence may be admitted and the nature of the questions which will be permitted.
(e) The record of the in camera hearing and all evidence relating thereto shall be open to inspection only by the parties, the complainant, their attorneys and the court

and its agents, and shall be used only as necessary for appellate review. At any probable cause hearing, the judge shall take cognizance of the evidence, if admissible, at the end of the in camera hearing without the questions being repeated or the evidence being resubmitted in open court. (1983, c. 701, s. 1.)

Rule 413. Medical actions; statements to ameliorate or mitigate adverse outcome.

Statements by a health care provider apologizing for an adverse outcome in medical treatment, offers to undertake corrective or remedial treatment or actions, and gratuitous acts to assist affected persons shall not be admissible to prove negligence or culpable conduct by the health care provider in an action brought under Article 1B of Chapter 90 of the General Statutes. (2004-149, s. 3.1.)

Rule 414. Evidence of medical expenses.

Evidence offered to prove past medical expenses shall be limited to evidence of the amounts actually paid to satisfy the bills that have been satisfied, regardless of the source of payment, and evidence of the amounts actually necessary to satisfy the bills that have been incurred but not yet satisfied. This rule does not impose upon any party an affirmative duty to seek a reduction in billed charges to which the party is not contractually entitled. (2011-283, s. 1.1; 2011-317, s. 1.1.)

Article 5. Privileges.

Rule 501. General rule.

Except as otherwise required by the Constitution of the United States, the privileges of a witness, person, government, state, or political subdivision thereof shall be determined in accordance with the law of this State. (1983, c. 701, s. 1.)

Article 6. Witnesses.

Rule 601. General rule of competency; disqualification of witness.

(a) General rule. - Every person is competent to be a witness except as otherwise provided in these rules.

(b) Disqualification of witness in general. - A person is disqualified to testify as a witness when the court determines that the person is (1) incapable of expressing himself or herself concerning the matter as to be understood, either directly or through interpretation by one who can understand him or her, or (2) incapable of understanding the duty of a witness to tell the truth.

(c) Disqualification of interested persons. - Upon the trial of an action, or the hearing upon the merits of a special proceeding, a party or a person interested in the event, or a person from, through or under whom such a party or interested person derives his or her interest or title by assignment or otherwise, shall not be examined as a witness in his or her own behalf or interest, or in behalf of the party succeeding to his or her title or interest, against the executor, administrator or survivor of a deceased person, or the guardian of an incompetent person, or a person deriving his or her title or interest from, through or under a deceased or incompetent person by assignment or otherwise, concerning any oral communication between the witness and the deceased or incompetent person. However, this subdivision shall not apply when:

(1) The executor, administrator, survivor, guardian, or person so deriving title or interest is examined in his or her own behalf regarding the subject matter of the oral communication.

(2) The testimony of the deceased or incompetent person is given in evidence concerning the same transaction or communication.

(3) Evidence of the subject matter of the oral communication is offered by the executor, administrator, survivor, guardian or person so deriving title or interest.

Nothing in this subdivision shall preclude testimony as to the identity of the operator of a motor vehicle in any case. (1983, c. 701, s. 1; 2011-29, s. 2.)

Rule 602. Lack of personal knowledge.

A witness may not testify to a matter unless evidence is introduced sufficient to support a finding that he has personal knowledge of the matter. Evidence to prove personal knowledge may, but need not, consist of the testimony of the witness himself. This rule is subject to the provisions of Rule 703, relating to opinion testimony by expert witnesses. (1983, c. 701, s. 1.)

Rule 603. Oath or affirmation.

Before testifying, every witness shall be required to declare that he will testify truthfully, by oath or affirmation administered in a form calculated to awaken his conscience and impress his mind with his duty to do so. (1983, c. 701, s. 1.)

Rule 604. Interpreters.

An interpreter is subject to the provisions of these rules relating to qualification as an expert and the administration of an oath or affirmation that he will make a true translation. (1983, c. 701, s. 1.)

Rule 605. Competency of judge as witness.

The judge presiding at the trial may not testify in that trial as a witness. No objection need be made in order to preserve the point. (1983, c. 701, s. 1.)

Rule 606. Competency of juror as witness.

(a) At the trial. - A member of the jury may not testify as a witness before that jury in the trial of the case in which he is sitting as a juror. If he is called so to testify, the opposing party shall be afforded an opportunity to object out of the presence of the jury.

(b) Inquiry into validity of verdict or indictment. - Upon an inquiry into the validity of a verdict or indictment, a juror may not testify as to any matter or statement occurring during the course of the jury's deliberations or to the effect of anything upon his or any other juror's mind or emotions as influencing him to assent to or dissent from the verdict or indictment or concerning his mental processes in connection therewith, except that a juror may testify on the question whether extraneous prejudicial information was improperly brought to the jury's attention or whether any outside influence was improperly brought to bear upon any juror. Nor may his affidavit or evidence of any statement by him concerning a matter about which he would be precluded from testifying be received for these purposes. (1983, c. 701, s. 1.)

Rule 607. Who may impeach.

The credibility of a witness may be attacked by any party, including the party calling him. (1983, c. 701, s. 1.)

Rule 608. Evidence of character and conduct of witness.

(a) Opinion and reputation evidence of character. - The credibility of a witness may be attacked or supported by evidence in the form of reputation or opinion as provided in Rule 405(a), but subject to these limitations: (1) the evidence may refer only to character for truthfulness or untruthfulness, and (2) evidence of truthful character is admissible only after the character of the witness for truthfulness has been attacked by opinion or reputation evidence or otherwise.

(b) Specific instances of conduct. - Specific instances of the conduct of a witness, for the purpose of attacking or supporting his credibility, other than conviction of crime as provided in Rule 609, may not be proved by extrinsic evidence. They may, however, in the discretion of the court, if probative of truthfulness or untruthfulness, be inquired into on cross-examination of the witness (1) concerning his character for truthfulness or untruthfulness, or (2) concerning the character for truthfulness or untruthfulness of another witness as to which character the witness being cross-examined has testified.

The giving of testimony, whether by an accused or by any other witness, does not operate as a waiver of his privilege against self-incrimination when examined with respect to matters which relate only to credibility. (1983, c. 701, s. 1.)

Rule 609. Impeachment by evidence of conviction of crime.

(a) General rule. - For the purpose of attacking the credibility of a witness, evidence that the witness has been convicted of a felony, or of a Class A1, Class 1, or Class 2 misdemeanor, shall be admitted if elicited from the witness or established by public record during cross-examination or thereafter.

(b) Time limit. - Evidence of a conviction under this rule is not admissible if a period of more than 10 years has elapsed since the date of the conviction or of the release of the witness from the confinement imposed for that conviction, whichever is the later date, unless the court determines, in the interests of justice, that the probative value of the conviction supported by specific facts and circumstances substantially outweighs its prejudicial effect. However, evidence of a conviction more than 10 years old as calculated herein is not admissible unless the proponent gives to the adverse party sufficient advance written notice of intent to use such evidence to provide the adverse party with a fair opportunity to contest the use of such evidence.

(c) Effect of pardon. - Evidence of a conviction is not admissible under this rule if the conviction has been pardoned.

(d) Juvenile adjudications. - Evidence of juvenile adjudications is generally not admissible under this rule. The court may, however, in a criminal case allow evidence of a juvenile adjudication of a witness other than the accused if conviction of the offense would be admissible to attack the credibility of an adult and the court is satisfied that admission in evidence is necessary for a fair determination of the issue of guilt or innocence.

(e) Pendency of appeal. - The pendency of an appeal therefrom does not render evidence of a conviction inadmissible. Evidence of the pendency of an appeal is admissible. (1983, c. 701, s. 1; 1999-79, s. 1.)

Rule 610. Religious beliefs or opinions.

Evidence of the beliefs or opinions of a witness on matters of religion is not admissible for the purpose of showing that by reason of their nature his credibility is impaired or enhanced; provided, however, such evidence may be admitted for the purpose of showing interest or bias. (1983, c. 701, s. 1.)

Rule 611. Mode and order of interrogation and presentation.

(a) Control by court. - The court shall exercise reasonable control over the mode and order of interrogating witnesses and presenting evidence so as to (1) make the interrogation and presentation effective for the ascertainment of the truth, (2) avoid needless consumption of time, and (3) protect witnesses from harassment or undue embarrassment.

(b) Scope of cross-examination. - A witness may be cross-examined on any matter relevant to any issue in the case, including credibility.

(c) Leading questions. - Leading questions should not be used on the direct examination of a witness except as may be necessary to develop his testimony. Ordinarily leading questions should be permitted on cross-examination. When a party calls a hostile witness, an adverse party, or a witness identified with an adverse party, interrogation may be by leading questions. (1983, c. 701, s. 1.)

Rule 612. Writing or object used to refresh memory.

(a) While testifying. - If, while testifying, a witness uses a writing or object to refresh his memory, an adverse party is entitled to have the writing or object produced at the trial, hearing, or deposition in which the witness is testifying.

(b) Before testifying. - If, before testifying, a witness uses a writing or object to refresh his memory for the purpose of testifying and the court in its discretion determines that the interests of justice so require, an adverse party is entitled to have those portions of any writing or of the object which relate to the testimony produced, if practicable, at the trial, hearing, or deposition in which the witness is testifying.

(c) Terms and conditions of production and use. - A party entitled to have a writing or object produced under this rule is entitled to inspect it, to cross-examine the witness thereon, and to introduce in evidence those portions which relate to the testimony of the witness. If production of the writing or object at the trial, hearing, or deposition is impracticable, the court may order it made available for inspection. If it is claimed that the writing or object contains privileged information or information not directly related to the subject matter of the testimony, the court shall examine the writing or object in camera, excise any such portions, and order delivery of the remainder to the party entitled thereto. Any portion withheld over objections shall be preserved and made available to the appellate court in the event of an appeal. If a writing or object is not produced, made available for inspection, or delivered pursuant to order under this rule, the court shall make any order justice requires, but in criminal cases if the prosecution elects not to comply, the order shall be one striking the testimony or, if justice so requires, declaring a mistrial. (1983, c. 701, s. 1.)

Rule 613. Prior statements of witnesses.

In examining a witness concerning a prior statement made by him, whether written or not, the statement need not be shown nor its contents disclosed to him at that time, but on request the same shall be shown or disclosed to opposing counsel. (1983, c. 701, s. 1.)

Rule 614. Calling and interrogation of witnesses by court.

(a) Calling by court. - The court may, on its own motion or at the suggestion of a party, call witnesses, and all parties are entitled to cross-examine witnesses thus called.

(b) Interrogation by court. - The court may interrogate witnesses, whether called by itself or by a party.

(c) Objections. - No objections are necessary with respect to the calling of a witness by the court or to questions propounded to a witness by the court but it shall be deemed that proper objection has been made and overruled. (1983, c. 701, s. 1.)

Rule 615. Exclusion of witnesses.

At the request of a party the court may order witnesses excluded so that they cannot hear the testimony of other witnesses, and it may make the order of its own motion. This rule does not authorize exclusion of (1) a party who is a natural person, or (2) an officer or employee of a party that is not a natural person designated as its representative by its attorney, or (3) a person whose presence is shown by a party to be essential to the presentation of his cause, or (4) a person whose presence is determined by the court to be in the interest of justice. (1983, c. 701, s. 1.)

Rule 616. Alternative testimony of witnesses with developmental disabilities or mental retardation in civil cases and special proceedings.

(a) Definitions. - The following definitions apply to this section:
  (1) The definitions set out in G.S. 122C-3.
  (2) "Remote testimony" means a method by which a witness testifies outside of an open forum and outside of the physical presence of a party or parties.

(b) Remote Testimony Authorized. - A person with a developmental disability or a person with mental retardation who is competent to testify may testify by remote testimony in a civil proceeding or special proceeding if the court determines by clear and convincing evidence that the witness would suffer serious emotional distress from testifying in the presence of a named party or parties or from testifying in an open forum and that the ability of the witness to communicate with the trier of fact would be impaired by testifying in the presence of a named party or parties or from testifying in an open forum.

(c) Hearing Procedure. - Upon motion of a party or the court's own motion, and for good cause shown, the court shall hold an evidentiary hearing to determine whether to allow remote testimony. The hearing shall be recorded unless recordation is waived by all parties. The presence of the witness is not required at the hearing unless so ordered by the presiding judge.

(d) Order. - An order allowing or disallowing the use of remote testimony shall state the findings and conclusions of law that support the court's determination. An order allowing the use of remote testimony also shall do all of the following:
  (1) State the method by which the witness is to testify.
  (2) List any individual or category of individuals allowed to be in or required to be excluded from the presence of the witness during testimony.
  (3) State any special conditions necessary to facilitate the cross-examination of the witness.
  (4) State any condition or limitation upon the participation of individuals in the presence of the witness during the testimony.
  (5) State any other conditions necessary for taking or presenting testimony.

(e) Testimony. - The method of remote testimony shall allow the trier of fact and all parties to observe the demeanor of the witness as the witness testifies in a similar manner as if the witness were testifying in the open forum. Except as provided in this section, the court shall ensure that the counsel for all parties is physically present where the witness testifies and has a full and fair opportunity for examination and cross-examination of the witness. In a proceeding where a party is representing itself, the court may limit or deny the party from being physically present during testimony if the court finds that the witness would suffer serious emotional distress from testifying in the presence of the party. A party may waive the right to have counsel physically present where the witness testifies.

(f) Nonexclusive Procedure and Standard. - Nothing in this section shall prohibit the use or application of any other method or procedure authorized or required by law for the introduction into evidence of statements or testimony of a person with a developmental disability or a person with mental retardation. (2009-514, s. 1.)

Article 7.
Opinions and Expert Testimony.

Rule 701. Opinion testimony by lay witness.

If the witness is not testifying as an expert, his testimony in the form of opinions or inferences is limited to those opinions or inferences which are (a) rationally based on the perception of the witness and (b) helpful to a clear understanding of his testimony or the determination of a fact in issue. (1983, c. 701, s. 1.)

Rule 702. Testimony by experts.

(a) If scientific, technical or other specialized knowledge will assist the trier of fact to understand the evidence or to determine a fact in issue, a witness qualified as an expert by knowledge, skill, experience, training, or education, may testify thereto in the form of an opinion, or otherwise, if all of the following apply:
  (1) The testimony is based upon sufficient facts or data.
  (2) The testimony is the product of reliable principles and methods.
  (3) The witness has applied the principles and methods reliably to the facts of the case.

(a1) A witness, qualified under subsection (a) of this section and with proper foundation, may give expert testimony solely on the issue of impairment and not on the issue of specific alcohol concentration level relating to the following:

(1) The results of a Horizontal Gaze Nystagmus (HGN) Test when the test is administered by a person who has successfully completed training in HGN.

(2) Whether a person was under the influence of one or more impairing substances, and the category of such impairing substance or substances. A witness who has received training and holds a current certification as a Drug Recognition Expert, issued by the State Department of Health and Human Services, shall be qualified to give the testimony under this subdivision.

(b) In a medical malpractice action as defined in G.S. 90-21.11, a person shall not give expert testimony on the appropriate standard of health care as defined in G.S. 90-21.12 unless the person is a licensed health care provider in this State or another state and meets the following criteria:

(1) If the party against whom or on whose behalf the testimony is offered is a specialist, the expert witness must:

a. Specialize in the same specialty as the party against whom or on whose behalf the testimony is offered; or

b. Specialize in a similar specialty which includes within its specialty the performance of the procedure that is the subject of the complaint and have prior experience treating similar patients.

(2) During the year immediately preceding the date of the occurrence that is the basis for the action, the expert witness must have devoted a majority of his or her professional time to either or both of the following:

a. The active clinical practice of the same health profession in which the party against whom or on whose behalf the testimony is offered, and if that party is a specialist, the active clinical practice of the same specialty or a similar specialty which includes within its specialty the performance of the procedure that is the subject of the complaint and have prior experience treating similar patients; or

b. The instruction of students in an accredited health professional school or accredited residency or clinical research program in the same health profession in which the party against whom or on whose behalf the testimony is offered, and if that party is a specialist, an accredited health professional school or accredited residency or clinical research program in the same specialty.

(c) Notwithstanding subsection (b) of this section, if the party against whom or on whose behalf the testimony is offered is a general practitioner, the expert witness, during the year immediately preceding the date of the occurrence that is the basis for the action, must have devoted a majority of his or her professional time to either or both of the following:

(1) Active clinical practice as a general practitioner; or

(2) Instruction of students in an accredited health professional school or accredited residency or clinical research program in the general practice of medicine.

(d) Notwithstanding subsection (b) of this section, a physician who qualifies as an expert under subsection (a) of this Rule and who by reason of active clinical practice or instruction of students has knowledge of the applicable standard of care for nurses, nurse practitioners, certified registered nurse anesthetists, certified registered nurse midwives, physician assistants, or other medical support staff may give expert testimony in a medical malpractice action with respect to the standard of care of which he is knowledgeable of nurses, nurse practitioners, certified registered nurse anesthetists, certified registered nurse midwives, physician assistants licensed under Chapter 90 of the General Statutes, or other medical support staff.

(e) Upon motion by either party, a resident judge of the superior court in the county or judicial district in which the action is pending may allow expert testimony on the appropriate standard of health care by a witness who does not meet the requirements of subsection (b) or (c) of this Rule, but who is otherwise qualified as an expert witness, upon a showing by the movant of extraordinary circumstances and a determination by the court that the motion should be allowed to serve the ends of justice.

(f) In an action alleging medical malpractice, an expert witness shall not testify on a contingency fee basis.

(g) This section does not limit the power of the trial court to disqualify an expert witness on grounds other than the qualifications set forth in this section.

(h) Notwithstanding subsection (b) of this section, in a medical malpractice action as defined in G.S. 90-21.11(2)b. against a hospital, or other health care or medical facility, a person shall not give expert testimony on the appropriate standard of care as to administrative or other nonclinical issues unless the person has substantial knowledge, by virtue of his or her training and experience, about the standard of care among hospitals, or health care or medical facilities, of the same type as the hospital, or health care or medical facility, whose actions or inactions are the subject of the testimony situated in the same or similar communities at the time of the alleged act giving rise to the cause of action.

(i) A witness qualified as an expert in accident reconstruction who has performed a reconstruction of a crash, or has reviewed the report of investigation, with proper foundation may give an opinion as to the speed of a vehicle even if the witness did not observe the vehicle moving. (1983, c. 701, s. 1; 1995, c. 309, s. 1; 2006-253, s. 6; 2007-493, s. 5; 2011-283, s. 1.3; 2011-400, s. 4.)

Rule 703. Bases of opinion testimony by experts.

The facts or data in the particular case upon which an expert bases an opinion or inference may be those perceived by or made known to him at or before the hearing. If of a type reasonably relied upon by experts in the particular field in forming opinions or inferences upon the subject, the facts or data need not be admissible in evidence. (1983, c. 701, s. 1.)

Rule 704. Opinion on ultimate issue.

Testimony in the form of an opinion or inference is not objectionable because it embraces an ultimate issue to be decided by the trier of fact. (1983, c. 701, s. 1.)

Rule 705. Disclosure of facts or data underlying expert opinion.

The expert may testify in terms of opinion or inference and give his reasons therefor without prior disclosure of the underlying facts or data, unless an adverse party requests otherwise, in which event the expert will be required to disclose such underlying facts or data on direct examination or voir dire before stating the opinion. The expert may in any event be required to disclose the underlying facts or data on cross-examination. There shall be no requirement that expert testimony be in response to a hypothetical question. (1983, c. 701, s. 1.)

Rule 706. Court appointed experts.

(a) Appointment. - The court may on its own motion or on the motion of any party enter an order to show cause why expert witnesses should not be appointed, and may request the parties to submit nominations. The court may appoint any expert witnesses agreed upon by the parties, and may appoint witnesses of its own selection. An expert witness shall not be appointed by the court unless he consents to act. A witness so appointed shall be informed of his duties by the court in writing, a copy of which shall be filed with the clerk, or at a conference in which the parties shall have opportunity to participate. A witness so appointed shall advise the parties of his findings, if any; his deposition may be taken by any party; and he may be called to testify by the court or any party. He shall be subject to cross-examination by each party, including a party calling him as a witness.

(b) Compensation. - Expert witnesses so appointed are entitled to reasonable compensation in whatever sum the court may allow. The compensation thus fixed is payable from funds which may be provided by law in criminal cases and civil actions and proceedings involving just compensation for the taking of property. In other civil actions and proceedings the compensation shall be paid by the parties in such proportion and at such time as the court directs, and thereafter charged in like manner as other costs.

(c) Disclosure of appointment. - In the exercise of its discretion, the court may authorize disclosure to the jury of the fact that the court appointed the expert witness.

(d) Parties' experts of own selection. - Nothing in this rule limits the parties in calling expert witnesses of their own selection. (1983, c. 701, s. 1.)

Article 8.
Hearsay.

Rule 801. Definitions and exception for admissions of a party-opponent.

The following definitions apply under this Article:

(a) Statement. - A "statement" is (1) an oral or written assertion or (2) nonverbal conduct of a person, if it is intended by him as an assertion.

(b) Declarant. - A "declarant" is a person who makes a statement.

(c) Hearsay. - "Hearsay" is a statement, other than one made by the declarant while testifying at the trial or hearing, offered in evidence to prove the truth of the matter asserted.

(d) Exception for Admissions by a Party-Opponent. - A statement is admissible as an exception to the hearsay rule if it is offered against a party and it is (A) his own statement, in either his individual or a representative capacity, or (B) a statement of which he has manifested his adoption or belief in its truth, or (C) a statement by a person authorized by him to make a statement concerning the subject, or (D) a statement by his agent or servant concerning a matter within the scope of his agency or employment, made during the existence of the relationship or (E) a statement by a coconspirator of such party during the course and in furtherance of the conspiracy. (1983, c. 701, s. 1.)

Rule 802. Hearsay rule.

Hearsay is not admissible except as provided by statute or by these rules. (1983, c. 701, s. 1.)

Rule 803. Hearsay exceptions; availability of declarant immaterial.

The following are not excluded by the hearsay rule, even though the declarant is available as a witness:

(1) Present Sense Impression. - A statement describing or explaining an event or condition made while the declarant was perceiving the event or condition, or immediately thereafter.

(2) Excited Utterance. - A statement relating to a startling event or condition made while the declarant was under the stress of excitement caused by the event or condition.

(3) Then Existing Mental, Emotional, or Physical Condition. - A statement of the declarant's then existing state of mind, emotion, sensation, or physical condition (such as intent, plan, motive, design, mental feeling, pain, and bodily health), but not including a statement of memory or belief to prove the fact remembered or believed unless it relates to the execution, revocation, identification, or terms of declarant's will.

(4) Statements for Purposes of Medical Diagnosis or Treatment. - Statements made for purposes of medical diagnosis or treatment and describing medical history, or past or present symptoms, pain, or sensations, or the inception or general character of the cause or external source thereof insofar as reasonably pertinent to diagnosis or treatment.

(5) Recorded Recollection. - A memorandum or record concerning a matter about which a witness once had knowledge but now has insufficient recollection to enable him to testify fully and accurately, shown to have been made or adopted by the witness when the matter was fresh in his memory and to reflect that knowledge correctly. If admitted, the memorandum or record may be read into evidence but may not itself be received as an exhibit unless offered by an adverse party.

(6) Records of Regularly Conducted Activity. - A memorandum, report, record, or data compilation, in any form, of acts, events, conditions, opinions, or diagnoses, made at or near the time by, or from information transmitted by, a person with knowledge, if kept in the course of a regularly conducted business activity, and if it was the regular practice of that business activity to make the memorandum, report, record, or data compilation, all as shown by the testimony of the custodian or other qualified witness, unless the source of information or the method or circumstances of preparation indicate lack of trustworthiness. The term "business" as used in this paragraph includes business, institution, association, profession, occupation, and calling of every kind, whether or not conducted for profit.

(7) Absence of Entry in Records Kept in Accordance with the Provisions of Paragraph (6). - Evidence that a matter is not included in the memoranda, reports, records, or data compilations, in any form, kept in accordance with the provisions of paragraph (6), to prove the nonoccurrence or nonexistence of the matter, if the matter was of a kind of which a memorandum, report, record, or data compilation was regularly made and preserved, unless the sources of information or other circumstances indicate lack of trustworthiness.

(8) Public Records and Reports. - Records, reports, statements, or data compilations, in any form, of public offices or agencies, setting forth (A) the activities of the office or agency, or (B) matters observed pursuant to duty imposed by law as to which matters there was a duty to report, excluding, however, in criminal cases matters observed by police officers and other law-enforcement personnel, or (C) in civil actions and proceedings and against the State in criminal cases, factual findings resulting from an investigation made pursuant to authority granted by law, unless the sources of information or other circumstances indicate lack of trustworthiness.

(9) Records of Vital Statistics. - Records or data compilations, in any form, of births, fetal deaths, deaths, or marriages, if the report thereof was made to a public office pursuant to requirements of law.

(10) Absence of Public Record or Entry. - To prove the absence of a record, report, statement, or data compilation, in any form, or the nonoccurrence or nonexistence of a matter of which a record, report, statement, or data compilation, in any form, was regularly made and preserved by a public office or agency, evidence in the form of a certification in accordance with Rule 902, or testimony, that diligent search failed to disclose the record, report, statement, or data compilation, or entry.

(11) Records of Religious Organizations. - Statements of births, marriages, divorces, deaths, legitimacy, ancestry, relationship by blood or marriage, or other similar facts of personal or family history, contained in a regularly kept record of a religious organization.

(12) Marriage, Baptismal, and Similar Certificates. - Statements of fact contained in a certificate that the maker performed a marriage or other ceremony or administered a sacrament, made by a clergyman, public official,

or other person authorized by the rules or practices of a religious organization or by law to perform the act certified, and purporting to have been issued at the time of the act or within a reasonable time thereafter.

(13) Family Records. - Statements of fact concerning personal or family history contained in family Bibles, genealogies, charts, engravings on rings, inscriptions on family portraits, engravings on urns, crypts, or tombstones, or the like.

(14) Records of Documents Affecting an Interest in Property. - The record of a document purporting to establish or affect an interest in property, as proof of the content of the original recorded document and its execution and delivery by each person by whom it purports to have been executed, if the record is a record of a public office and an applicable statute authorizes the recording of documents of that kind in that office.

(15) Statements in Documents Affecting an Interest in Property. - A statement contained in a document purporting to establish or affect an interest in property if the matter stated was relevant to the purpose of the document, unless dealings with the property since the document was made have been inconsistent with the truth of the statement or the purport of the document.

(16) Statements in Ancient Documents. - Statements in a document in existence 20 years or more the authenticity of which is established.

(17) Market Reports, Commercial Publications. - Market quotations, tabulations, lists, directories, or other published compilations, generally used and relied upon by the public or by persons in particular occupations.

(18) Learned Treatises. - To the extent called to the attention of an expert witness upon cross-examination or relied upon by him in direct examination, statements contained in published treatises, periodicals, or pamphlets on a subject of history, medicine, or other science or art, established as a reliable authority by the testimony or admission of the witness or by other expert testimony or by judicial notice. If admitted, the statements may be read into evidence but may not be received as exhibits.

(19) Reputation Concerning Personal or Family History. - Reputation among members of his family by blood, adoption, or marriage, or among his associates, or in the community, concerning a person's birth, adoption, marriage, divorce, death, legitimacy, relationship by blood, adoption, or marriage, ancestry, or other similar fact of his personal or family history.

(20) Reputation Concerning Boundaries or General History. - Reputation in a community, arising before the controversy, as to boundaries of or customs affecting lands in the community, and reputation as to events of general history important to the community or state or nation in which located.

(21) Reputation as to Character. - Reputation of a person's character among his associates or in the community.

(22) (Reserved).

(23) Judgment as to Personal, Family or General History, or Boundaries. - Judgments as proof of matters of personal, family or general history, or boundaries, essential to the judgment, if the same would be provable by evidence of reputation.

(24) Other Exceptions. - A statement not specifically covered by any of the foregoing exceptions but having equivalent circumstantial guarantees of trustworthiness, if the court determines that (A) the statement is offered as evidence of a material fact; (B) the statement is more probative on the point for which it is offered than any other evidence which the proponent can procure through reasonable efforts; and (C) the general purposes of these rules and the interests of justice will best be served by admission of the statement into evidence. However, a statement may not be admitted under this exception unless the proponent of it gives written notice stating his intention to offer the statement and the particulars of it, including the name and address of the declarant, to the adverse party sufficiently in advance of offering the statement to provide the adverse party with a fair opportunity to prepare to meet the statement. (1983, c. 701, s. 1.)

Rule 804. Hearsay exceptions; declarant unavailable.

(a) Definition of unavailability. - "Unavailability as a witness" includes situations in which the declarant:

(1) Is exempted by ruling of the court on the ground of privilege from testifying concerning the subject matter of his statement; or

(2) Persists in refusing to testify concerning the subject matter of his statement despite an order of the court to do so; or

(3) Testifies to a lack of memory of the subject matter of his statement; or

(4) Is unable to be present or to testify at the hearing because of death or then existing physical or mental illness or infirmity; or

(5) Is absent from the hearing and the proponent of his statement has been unable to procure his attendance (or in the case of a hearsay exception under subdivision (b)(2), (3), or (4), his attendance or testimony) by process or other reasonable means.

A declarant is not unavailable as a witness if his exemption, refusal, claim of lack of memory, inability, or absence is due to the procurement or wrongdoing of the proponent of his statement for the purpose of preventing the witness from attending or testifying.

(b) Hearsay exceptions. - The following are not excluded by the hearsay rule if the declarant is unavailable as a witness:

(1) Former Testimony. - Testimony given as a witness at another hearing of the same or a different proceeding, or in a deposition taken in compliance with law in the course of the same or another proceeding, if the party against whom the testimony is now offered, or, in a civil action or proceeding, a predecessor in interest, had an opportunity and similar motive to develop the testimony by direct, cross, or redirect examination.

(2) Statement Under Belief of Impending Death. - A statement made by a declarant while believing that his death was imminent, concerning the cause or circumstances of what he believed to be his impending death.

(3) Statement Against Interest. - A statement which was at the time of its making so far contrary to the declarant's pecuniary or proprietary interest, or so far tended to subject him to civil or criminal liability, or to render invalid a claim by him against another, that a reasonable man in his position would not have made the statement unless he believed it to be true. A statement tending to expose the declarant to criminal liability is not admissible in a criminal case unless corroborating circumstances clearly indicate the trustworthiness of the statement.

(4) Statement of Personal or Family History. - (A) A statement concerning the declarant's own birth, adoption, marriage, divorce, legitimacy, relationship by blood, adoption, or marriage, ancestry, or other similar fact of personal or family history, even though declarant had no means of acquiring personal knowledge of the matter stated; or (B) a statement concerning the foregoing matters, and death also, of another person, if the declarant was related to the other by blood, adoption, or marriage or was so intimately associated with the other's family as to be likely to have accurate information concerning the matter declared.

(5) Other Exceptions. - A statement not specifically covered by any of the foregoing exceptions but having equivalent circumstantial guarantees of trustworthiness, if the court determines that (A) the statement is offered as evidence of a material fact; (B) the statement is more probative on the point for which it is offered than any other evidence which the proponent can procure through reasonable efforts; and (C) the general purposes of these rules and the interests of justice will best be served by admission of the statement into evidence. However, a statement may not be admitted under this exception unless the proponent of it gives written notice stating his intention to offer the statement and the particulars of it, including the name and address of the declarant, to the adverse party sufficiently in advance of offering the statement to provide the adverse party with a fair opportunity to prepare to meet the statement. (1983, c. 701, s. 1.)

Rule 805. Hearsay within hearsay.

Hearsay included within hearsay is not excluded under the hearsay rule if each part of the combined statements conforms with an exception to the hearsay rule provided in these rules. (1983, c. 701, s. 1.)

Rule 806. Attacking and supporting credibility of declarant.

When a hearsay statement has been admitted in evidence, the credibility of the declarant may be attacked, and if attacked may be supported, by any evidence which would be admissible for those purposes if declarant had testified as a witness. Evidence of a statement or conduct by the declarant at any time, inconsistent with his hearsay statement, is not subject to any requirement that he may have been afforded an opportunity to deny or explain. If the party against whom a hearsay statement has been admitted calls the declarant as a witness, the party is entitled to examine him on the statement as if under cross-examination. (1983, c. 701, s. 1.)

Article 9.
Authentication and Identification.

Rule 901. Requirement of authentication or identification.

(a) General provision. - The requirement of authentication or identification as a condition precedent to admissibility is satisfied by evidence sufficient to support a finding that the matter in question is what its proponent claims.

(b) Illustrations. - By way of illustration only, and not by way of limitation, the following are examples of authentication or identification conforming with the requirements of this rule:

(1) Testimony of Witness with Knowledge. - Testimony that a matter is what it is claimed to be.
(2) Nonexpert Opinion on Handwriting. - Nonexpert opinion as to the genuineness of handwriting, based upon familiarity not acquired for purposes of the litigation.
(3) Comparison by Trier or Expert Witness. - Comparison by the trier of fact or by expert witnesses with specimens which have been authenticated.
(4) Distinctive Characteristics and the Like. - Appearance, contents, substance, internal patterns, or other distinctive characteristics, taken in conjunction with circumstances.
(5) Voice Identification. - Identification of a voice, whether heard firsthand or through mechanical or electronic transmission or recording, by opinion based upon hearing the voice at any time under circumstances connecting it with the alleged speaker.
(6) Telephone Conversations. - Telephone conversations, by evidence that a call was made to the number assigned at the time by the telephone company to a particular person or business, if (A) in the case of a person, circumstances, including self-identification, show the person answering to be the one called, or (B) in the case of a business, the call was made to a place of business and the conversation related to business reasonably transacted over the telephone.
(7) Public Records or Reports. - Evidence that a writing authorized by law to be recorded or filed and in fact recorded or filed in a public office, or a purported public record, report, statement, or data compilation, in any form, is from the public office where items of this nature are kept.
(8) Ancient Documents or Data Compilations. - Evidence that a document or data compilation, in any form, (A) is in such condition as to create no suspicion concerning its authenticity, (B) was in a place where it, if authentic, would likely be, and (C) has been in existence 20 years or more at the time it is offered.
(9) Process or System. - Evidence describing a process or system used to produce a result and showing that the process or system produces an accurate result.
(10) Methods Provided by Statute. - Any method of authentication or identification provided by statute. (1983, c. 701, s. 1.)

Rule 902. Self-authentication.

Extrinsic evidence of authenticity as a condition precedent to admissibility is not required with respect to the following:

(1) Domestic Public Documents Under Seal. - A document bearing a seal purporting to be that of the United States, or of any state, district, commonwealth, territory or insular possession thereof, or the Trust Territory of the Pacific Islands, or of a political subdivision, department, officer, or agency thereof, and a signature purporting to be an attestation or execution.
(2) Domestic Public Documents Not Under Seal. - A document purporting to bear the signature in his official capacity of an officer or employee of any entity included in paragraph (1) hereof, having no seal, if a public officer having a seal and having official duties in the district or political subdivision of the officer or employee certifies under seal that the signer has the official capacity and that the signature is genuine.
(3) Foreign Public Documents. - A document purporting to be executed or attested in his official capacity by a person authorized by the laws of a foreign country to make the execution or attestation, and accompanied by a final certification as to the genuineness of the signature and official position (A) of the executing or attesting person, or (B) of any foreign official whose certificate of genuineness of signature and official position relates to the execution or attestation or is in a chain of certificates of genuineness of signature and official position relating to the execution or attestation. A final certification may be made by a secretary of embassy or legation, consul general, consul, vice consul, or consular agent of the United States, or a diplomatic or consular official of the foreign country assigned or accredited to the United States. If reasonable opportunity has been given to all parties to investigate the authenticity and accuracy of official documents, the court may, for good cause shown, order that they be treated as presumptively authentic without final certification or permit them to be evidenced by an attested summary with or without final certification.
(4) Certified Copies of Public Records. - A copy of an official record or report or entry therein, or of a document authorized by law to be recorded or filed and actually recorded or filed in a public office, including data compilations in any form, certified as correct by the custodian or other person authorized to make the certification, by certificate complying with paragraph (1), (2), or (3) or complying with any law of the United States or of this State.

(5) Official Publications. - Books, pamphlets, or other publications purporting to be issued by public authority.
(6) Newspapers and Periodicals. - Printed materials purporting to be newspapers or periodicals.
(7) Trade Inscriptions and the Like. - Inscriptions, signs, tags, or labels purporting to have been affixed in the course of business and indicating ownership, control, or origin.
(8) Acknowledged Documents. - Documents accompanied by a certificate of acknowledgment executed in the manner provided by law by a notary public or other officer authorized by law to take acknowledgments.
(9) Commercial Paper and Related Documents. - Commercial paper, signatures thereon, and documents relating thereto to the extent provided by general commercial law.
(10) Presumptions Created by Law. - Any signature, document, or other matter declared by any law of the United States or of this State to be presumptively or prima facie genuine or authentic. (1983, c. 701, s. 1.)

Rule 903. Subscribing witness' testimony unnecessary.

The testimony of a subscribing witness is not necessary to authenticate a writing unless required by the laws of the jurisdiction whose laws govern the validity of the writing. (1983, c. 701, s. 1.)

Article 10. Contents of Writings, Recordings and Photographs.

Rule 1001. Definitions.

For the purposes of this Article the following definitions are applicable:
(1) Writings and Recordings. - "Writings" and "recordings" consist of letters, words, sounds, or numbers, or their equivalent, set down by handwriting, typewriting, printing, photostating, photographing, magnetic impulse, mechanical or electronic recording, or other form of data compilation.
(2) Photographs. - "Photographs" include still photographs, x-ray films, video tapes, and motion pictures.
(3) Original. - An "original" of a writing or recording is the writing or recording itself or any counterpart intended to have the same effect by a person executing or issuing it. An "original" of a photograph includes the negative or any print therefrom. If data are stored in a computer or similar device, any printout or other output readable by sight, shown to reflect the data accurately, is an "original."
(4) Duplicate. - A "duplicate" is a counterpart produced by the same impression as the original, or from the same matrix, or by means of photography, including enlargements and miniatures, or by mechanical or electronic re-recording, or by chemical reproduction, or by other equivalent techniques which accurately reproduce the original. (1983, c. 701, s. 1.)

Rule 1002. Requirement of original.

To prove the content of a writing, recording, or photograph, the original writing, recording, or photograph is required, except as otherwise provided in these rules or by statute. (1983, c. 701, s. 1.)

Rule 1003. Admissibility of duplicates.

A duplicate is admissible to the same extent as an original unless (1) a genuine question is raised as to the authenticity of the original or (2) in the circumstances it would be unfair to admit the duplicate in lieu of the original. (1983, c. 701, s. 1.)

Rule 1004. Admissibility of other evidence of contents.

The original is not required, and other evidence of the contents of a writing, recording, or photograph is admissible if:
(1) Originals Lost or Destroyed. - All originals are lost or have been destroyed, unless the proponent lost or destroyed them in bad faith; or
(2) Original Not Obtainable. - No original can be obtained by any available judicial process or procedure; or
(3) Original in Possession of Opponent. - At a time when an original was under the control of a party against whom offered, he was put on notice, by the pleadings or otherwise, that the contents would be a subject of proof at the hearing, and he does not produce the original at the hearing; or
(4) Collateral Matters. - The writing, recording, or photograph is not closely related to a controlling issue. (1983, c. 701, s. 1.)

Rule 1005. Public records.

The contents of an official record, or of a document authorized to be recorded or filed and actually recorded or filed, including data compilations in any form, if otherwise admissible, may be proved by copy, certified as correct in accordance with Rule 902 or testified to be correct by a witness who has compared it with the original. If a copy which complies with the foregoing cannot be obtained by the exercise of reasonable diligence, then other evidence of the contents may be given. (1983, c. 701, s. 1.)

Rule 1006. Summaries.
The contents of voluminous writings, recordings, or photographs which cannot conveniently be examined in court may be presented in the form of a chart, summary, or calculation. The originals, or duplicates, shall be made available for examination or copying, or both, by other parties at a reasonable time and place. The court may order that they be produced in court. (1983, c. 701, s. 1.)

Rule 1007. Testimony or written admission of party.
Contents of writings, recordings, or photographs may be proved by the testimony or deposition of the party against whom offered or by his written admission, without accounting for the nonproduction of the original. (1983, c. 701, s. 1.)

Rule 1008. Functions of court and jury.
When the admissibility of other evidence of contents of writings, recordings, or photographs under these rules depends upon the fulfillment of a condition of fact, the question whether the condition has been fulfilled is ordinarily for the court to determine in accordance with the provisions of Rule 104. However, when an issue is raised (a) whether the asserted writing ever existed, or (b) whether another writing, recording, or photograph produced at the trial is the original, or (c) whether other evidence of contents correctly reflects the contents, the issue is for the trier of fact to determine as in the case of other issues of fact. (1983, c. 701, s. 1.)

Article 11.
Miscellaneous Rules.

Rule 1101. Applicability of rules.
(a) Proceedings generally. - Except as otherwise provided in subdivision (b) or by statute, these rules apply to all actions and proceedings in the courts of this State.
(b) Rules inapplicable. - The rules other than those with respect to privileges do not apply in the following situations:
    (1) Preliminary Questions of Fact. - The determination of questions of fact preliminary to admissibility of evidence when the issue is to be determined by the court under Rule 104(a).
    (2) Grand Jury. - Proceedings before grand juries.
    (3) Miscellaneous Proceedings. - Proceedings for extradition or rendition; first appearance before district court judge or probable cause hearing in criminal cases; sentencing, or granting or revoking probation; issuance of warrants for arrest, criminal summonses, and search warrants; proceedings with respect to release on bail or otherwise.
    (4) Contempt Proceedings. - Contempt proceedings in which the court is authorized by law to act summarily. (1983, c. 701, s. 1; 1983 (Reg. Sess., 1984), c. 1037, s. 14; 1985, c. 509, s. 2.)

Rule 1102. Short title.
These rules shall be known and may be cited as the "North Carolina Rules of Evidence." (1983, c. 701, s. 1.)

Appendix B

North Carolina Rules of Criminal Procedure

Chapter 15.
Criminal Procedure.

Article 1.
General Provisions.

§ 15-1. Statute of limitations for misdemeanors.
The crimes of deceit and malicious mischief, and the crime of petit larceny where the value of the property does not exceed five dollars ($5.00), and all misdemeanors except malicious misdemeanors, shall be presented or found by the grand jury within two years after the commission of the same, and not afterwards: Provided, that if any indictment found within that time shall be defective, so that no judgment can be given thereon, another prosecution may be instituted for the same offense, within one year after the first shall have been abandoned by the State. (1826, c. 11; R.C., c. 35, s. 8; Code, s. 1177; Rev., s. 3147; 1907, c. 408; C.S., s. 4512; 1943, c. 543.)

§§ 15-2 through 15-3. Repealed by Session Laws 1973, c. 1286, s. 26.

§ 15-4. Accused entitled to counsel.
Every person, accused of any crime whatsoever, shall be entitled to counsel in all matters which may be necessary for his defense. (1777, c. 115, s. 85, P.R.; R.C., c. 35, s. 13; Code, s. 1182; Rev., s. 3150; C.S., s. 4515.)

§§ 15-4.1 through 15-5.1. Repealed by Session Laws 1969, c. 1013, s. 12.

§ 15-5.2. Repealed by Session Laws 1969, c. 1013, s. 6.

§§ 15-5.3 through 15-5.4. Repealed by Session Laws 1969, c. 1013, s. 12.

§ 15-6. Imprisonment to be in county jail.
No person shall be imprisoned except in the common jail of the county, unless otherwise provided by law: Provided, that whenever the sheriff of any county shall be imprisoned, he may be imprisoned in the jail of any adjoining county. (1797, c. 474, s. 3, P.R.; R.C., c. 35, s. 6; 1879, c. 12; Code, s. 1174; Rev., s. 3151; C.S., s. 4517; 1973, c. 1141, s. 1.)

§ 15-6.1. Changing place of confinement of prisoner committing offense.
In all cases where a defendant has been convicted in a court inferior to the superior court and sentenced to a term in the county jail or to serve in some county institution other than under the supervision of the State Division of Adult Correction of the Department of Public Safety, and such defendant is subsequently brought before such court for an offense committed prior to the expiration of the term to be served in such county institution, upon conviction, plea of guilty or nolo contendere, the judge shall have the power and authority to change the place of confinement of the prisoner and commit such defendant to work under the supervision of the Division of Adult Correction of the Department of Public Safety. This provision shall apply whether or not the terms of the new sentence are to run concurrently with or consecutive to the remaining portion of the old sentence. (1953, c. 778; 1957, c. 65, s. 11; 1967, c. 996, s. 16; 2011-145, s. 19.1(h); 2012-83, s. 20.)

§ 15-6.2. Concurrent sentences for offenses of different grades or to be served in different places.
When by a judgment of a court or by operation of law a prison sentence runs concurrently with any other sentence a prisoner shall not be required to serve any additional time in prison solely because the concurrent sentences are for different grades of offenses or that it is required that they be

served in different places of confinement. (1955, c. 57.)

§ 15-6.3. Credit for service of sentence while in another jurisdiction.

When a person in actual confinement under sentence of another jurisdiction is brought for trial before a court of this State, the court may, upon sentencing, specifically impose a sentence to be concurrently served and direct that such person receive credit against the sentence imposed for all time subsequently served in the jurisdiction possessing physical custody of such person.(1971, c. 828.)

§ 15-7. Postmortem examinations directed.

In all cases of homicide, any officer prosecuting for the State may, at any time, direct a postmortem examination of the deceased to be made by one or more physicians to be summoned for the purpose; and the physicians shall be paid a reasonable compensation for such examination, the amount to be determined by the court and taxed in the costs, and if not collected out of the defendant the same shall be paid by the State. (R.C., c. 35, s. 49; Code, s. 1214; Rev., s. 3152; C.S., s. 4518; 1973, c. 1141, s. 2.)

§ 15-8. Stolen property returned to owner.

Upon the conviction of any person for robbing or stealing any money, goods, chattels, or other estate of any description whatever, the person from whom such goods, money, chattels or other estate were robbed or stolen shall be entitled to restitution thereof; and the court may award restitution of the articles so robbed or stolen, and make all such orders and issue such writs of restitution or otherwise as may be necessary for that purpose. (21 Hen. VIII, c. 11; R.C., c. 35, s. 34; Code, s. 1201; Rev., s. 3153; C.S., s. 4519; 1943, c. 543.)

§ 15-9. Repealed by Session Laws 1973, c. 1286, s. 26.

§ 15-10. Speedy trial or discharge on commitment for felony.

When any person who has been committed for treason or felony, plainly and specially expressed in the warrant of commitment, upon his prayer in open court to be brought to his trial, shall not be indicted some time in the next term of the superior or criminal court ensuing such commitment, the judge of the court, upon notice in open court on the last day of the term, shall set at liberty such prisoner upon bail, unless it appear upon oath that the witnesses for the State could not be produced at the same term; and if such prisoner, upon his prayer as aforesaid, shall not be indicted and tried at the second term of the court, he shall be discharged from his imprisonment: Provided, the judge presiding may, in his discretion, refuse to discharge such person if the time between the first and second terms of the court be less than four months. (1868-9, c. 116, s. 33; Code, s. 1658; Rev., s. 3155; 1913, c. 2; C.S., s. 4521.)

§ 15-10.1. Detainer; purpose; manner of use.

Any person confined in the State prison system of North Carolina, subject to the authority and control of the Division of Adult Correction of the Department of Public Safety, or any person confined in any other prison of North Carolina, may be held to account for any other charge pending against him only upon a written order from the clerk or judge of the court in which the charge originated upon a case regularly docketed, directing that such person be held to answer the charge pending in such court; and in no event shall the prison authorities hold any person to answer any charge upon a warrant or notice when the charge has not been regularly docketed in the court in which the warrant or charge has been issued: Provided, that this section shall not apply to any State agency exercising supervision over such person or prisoner by virtue of a judgment, order of court or statutory authority. (1949, c. 303; 1953, c. 603; 1957, c. 349, s. 10; 1967, c. 996, s. 13; 2011-145, s. 19.1(h); 2012-83, s. 21.)

§ 15-10.2. Mandatory disposition of detainers - request for final disposition of charges; continuance; information to be furnished prisoner.

(a) Any prisoner serving a sentence or sentences within the State prison system who, during his term of imprisonment, shall have lodged against him a detainer to answer to any criminal charge pending against him in any court within the State, shall be brought to trial within eight months after he shall have caused to be sent to the district attorney of the court in which said criminal charge is pending, by registered mail, written notice of his place of confinement and request for a final disposition of the criminal charge against him; said request shall be accompanied by a certificate from the Secretary of Public Safety stating the term of the sentence or sentences under which the prisoner is being held, the date he was received, and the time remaining to be served; provided that, for good cause shown in open court, the prisoner or his counsel being present, the court may grant any necessary and reasonable continuance.

(b) The Secretary of Public Safety shall, upon request by the prisoner, inform the prisoner in writing of the source and contents of any charge for which a detainer shall have been lodged against such prisoner as shown by said detainer, and furnished the prisoner with the certificate referred to in subsection (a). (1957, c. 1067, s. 1; 1967, c. 996, s. 15; 1973, c. 47, s. 2; c. 1262, s. 10; 2011-145, s. 19.1(i).)

§ 15-10.3. Mandatory disposition of detainers - procedure; return of prisoner after trial.

The district attorney, upon receipt of the written notice and request for a final disposition as hereinbefore specified, shall make application to the court in which said charge is pending for a writ of habeas corpus ad prosequendum and the court upon such application shall issue such writ to the Secretary of Public Safety requiring the prisoner to be delivered to said court to answer the pending charge and to stand trial on said charge within the time hereinbefore provided; upon completion of said trial, the prisoner shall be returned to the State prison system to complete service of the sentence or sentences under which he was held at the time said writ was issued. (1957, c. 1067, s. 2; 1967, c. 996, s. 15; 1973, c. 47, s. 2; c. 1262, s. 10; 2011-145, s. 19.1(i).)

§ 15-10.4. Mandatory disposition of detainers - exception as to prisoners who are mentally ill.

The provisions of G.S. 15-10.2 and 15-10.3 shall not apply to any prisoner who has been transferred and assigned for observation or treatment to any unit of the prison system which is maintained for those prisoners who are mentally ill or are suffering from mental disorders. (1957, c. 1067, s. 3.)

Article 2.
Record and Disposition of Seized, etc., Articles.

§ 15-11. Sheriffs and police departments to maintain register of personal property confiscated, seized or found.

Each sheriff and police department in this State is hereby required to keep and maintain a book or register, and it shall be the duty of each sheriff and police department to keep a record therein of all articles of personal property which may be seized or confiscated by him or it, or of which he or it may have become possessed in any way in the discharge of his duty. Said sheriffs and police departments shall cause to be kept in said registers a description of such property, the name of the person from whom it was seized, if such name be known, the date and place of its seizure, and, where the article was not taken from the person of a suspect or prisoner, a brief recital of the place and circumstances concerning the possession thereof by such sheriff and police department. Such sheriff and police department shall also keep in said register appropriate entries showing the manner, date, and to whom said articles are disposed of or delivered, and, if sold as hereinafter provided, a record showing the disposition of the proceeds arising from such sale. (1939, c. 195, s. 1; 1973, c. 1141, s. 3.)

§ 15-11.1. Seizure, custody and disposition of articles; exceptions.

(a) If a law-enforcement officer seizes property pursuant to lawful authority, he shall safely keep the property under the direction of the court or magistrate as long as necessary to assure that the property will be produced at and may be used as evidence in any trial. Upon application by the lawful owner or a person, firm or corporation entitled to possession or upon his own determination, the district attorney may release any property seized pursuant to his lawful authority if he determines that such property is no longer useful or necessary as evidence in a criminal trial and he is presented with satisfactory evidence of ownership. If the district attorney refuses to release such property, the lawful owner or a person, firm or corporation entitled to possession may make application to the court for return of the property. The court, after notice to all parties, including the defendant, and after hearing, may in its discretion order any or all of the property returned to the lawful owner or a person, firm or corporation entitled to possession. The court may enter such order as may be necessary to assure that the evidence will be available for use as evidence at the time of trial, and will otherwise protect the rights of all parties. Notwithstanding any other provision of law, photographs or other identification or analyses made of the property may be introduced at the time of the trial provided that the court determines that the introduction of such substitute evidence is not likely to substantially prejudice the rights of the defendant in the criminal trial.

(b) In the case of unknown or unapprehended defendants or of defendants willfully absent from the jurisdiction, the court shall determine whether an attorney should be appointed as guardian ad litem to represent and protect the interest of such unknown or absent defendants. Appointment shall be in accordance with rules adopted by the Office of Indigent Defense Services. The judicial findings concerning identification or value that are made at such hearing whereby property is returned to the lawful owner or a person, firm, or corporation entitled to possession, may be admissible into evidence at the trial. After final judgment all property lawfully seized by or otherwise coming into the possession of law-enforcement authorities shall be disposed of as the court or magistrate in its discretion orders, and may be forfeited and either sold or destroyed in accordance with due process of law.

(b1) Notwithstanding subsections (a) and (b) of this section or any other provision of law, if the property seized is a firearm and the district attorney determines the firearm is no longer necessary or useful as evidence in a criminal trial, the district attorney, after notice to all parties known or believed by the district attorney to have an ownership or a possessory interest in the firearm, including the defendant, shall apply to the court for an order of disposition of the firearm. The judge, after hearing, may order the disposition of the firearm in one of the following ways:

(1) By ordering the firearm returned to its rightful owner, when the rightful owner is someone other than the defendant and upon findings by the court (i) that the person, firm, or corporation determined by the court to be the rightful owner is entitled to possession of the firearm and (ii) that the person, firm, or corporation determined by the court to be the rightful owner of the firearm was unlawfully deprived of the same or had no knowledge or reasonable belief of the defendant's intention to use the firearm unlawfully.

(2) By ordering the firearm returned to the defendant, but only if the defendant is not convicted of any criminal offense in connection with the possession or use of the firearm, the defendant is the rightful owner of the firearm, and the defendant is not otherwise ineligible to possess such firearm.

(3) By ordering the firearm turned over to be destroyed by the sheriff of the county in which the firearm was seized or by his duly authorized agent if the firearm does not have a legible, unique identification number or is unsafe for use because of wear, damage, age, or modification. The sheriff shall maintain a record of the destruction of the firearm.

(4) By ordering the firearm turned over to a law enforcement agency in the county of trial for (i) the official use of the agency or (ii) sale, trade, or exchange by the agency to a federally licensed firearm dealer in accordance with all applicable State and federal firearm laws. The court may order a disposition of the firearm pursuant to this subdivision only if the firearm has a legible, unique identification number. If the law enforcement agency sells the firearm, then the proceeds of the sale shall be remitted to the appropriate county finance officer as provided by G.S. 115C-452 to be used to maintain free public schools. The receiving law enforcement agency shall maintain a record and inventory of all firearms received pursuant to this subdivision.

This subsection (b1) is not applicable to seizures pursuant to G.S. 113-137 of firearms used only in connection with a violation of Article 22 of Chapter 113 of the General Statutes or any local wildlife hunting ordinance.

(c) Any property, the forfeiture and disposition of which is specified in any general or special law, shall be disposed of in accordance therewith. (1977, c. 613; 1979, c. 593; 1994, Ex. Sess., c. 16, s. 1; 2000-144, s. 27; 2005-287, s. 1; 2013-158, s. 1; 2014-115, s. 24.5.)

§ 15-11.2. Disposition of unclaimed firearms not confiscated or seized as trial evidence.

(a) Definition. - For purposes of this section, the term "unclaimed firearm" means a firearm that is found or received by a law enforcement agency and that remains unclaimed by the person who may be entitled to it for a period of 30 days after the publication of the notice required by subsection (b) of this section. The term does not include a firearm that is seized and disposed of pursuant to G.S. 15-11.1 or a firearm that is confiscated and disposed of pursuant to G.S. 14-269.1.

(b) Published Notice of Unclaimed Firearm. - When a law enforcement agency finds or receives a firearm and the firearm remains unclaimed for a period of 180 days, the agency shall publish at least one notice in a newspaper published in the county in which the agency is located. The notice shall include all of the following:

(1) A statement that the firearm is unclaimed and is in the custody of the law enforcement agency.

(2) A statement that the firearm may be sold or otherwise disposed of unless the firearm is claimed within 30 days of the date of the publication of the notice.

(3) A brief description of the firearm and any other information that the chief or head of the law enforcement agency may consider necessary or advisable to reasonably inform the public about the firearm.

(c) Repealed by Session Laws 2013-158, s. 2, effective September 1, 2013, and applicable to any firearm found or received by a local law enforcement agency on or after that date and to any judicial order for the disposition of any firearm on or after that date.

(d) Disposition of Unclaimed Firearm. - If the firearm remains unclaimed for a period of 30 days after the publication of the notice, then the head or chief of the law enforcement agency shall order the disposition of the firearm in one of the following ways:

(1) By having the firearm destroyed if the firearm does not have a legible, unique identification number or is unsafe for use because of wear, damage, age, or modification and will not be disposed of pursuant to subdivision (3) of this subsection. The head or chief of the law enforcement agency shall maintain a record of the destruction of the firearm.

(2) By sale, trade, or exchange by the agency to a federally licensed firearm dealer in accordance with all applicable State and federal firearm laws or by sale of the firearm at a public auction to persons licensed as firearms collectors, dealers, importers, or manufacturers. The head or chief of the law enforcement agency shall dispose of the firearm pursuant to this subdivision only if the firearm has a legible, unique identification number.

(3) By maintaining the firearm for training or experimental purposes or transferring the firearm to a museum or historical society.

(e) Repealed by Session Laws 2013-158, s. 2, effective September 1, 2013, and applicable to any firearm found or received by a local law enforcement agency on or after that date and to any judicial order for the disposition of any firearm on or after that date.

(f) Disbursement of Proceeds of Sale. - If the law enforcement agency sells the firearm pursuant to subdivision (2) of subsection (d) of this section, then the proceeds of the sale shall be retained by the law enforcement agency and used for law enforcement purposes. The receiving law enforcement agency shall maintain a record and inventory of all firearms received pursuant to this section, as well as the disposition of the firearm, including any funds received from a sale of a firearm or any firearms or other property received in exchange or trade of a firearm. (2005-287, s. 2; 2013-158, s. 2; 2013-410, s. 17(a); 2014-115, s. 2.)

§ 15-12. Publication of notice of unclaimed property; advertisement and sale or donation of unclaimed bicycles.

(a) Unless otherwise provided herein, whenever such articles in the possession of any sheriff or police department have remained unclaimed by the person who may be entitled thereto for a period of 180 days after such seizure, confiscation, or receipt thereof in any other manner, by such sheriff or police department, the said sheriff or police department in whose possession said articles are may cause to be published one time in some newspaper published in said county a notice to the effect that such articles are in the custody of such officer or department, and requiring all persons who may have or claim any interest therein to make and establish such claim or interest not later than 30 days from the date of the publication of such notice or in default thereof, such articles will be sold and disposed of. Such notice shall contain a brief description of the said articles and such other information as the said officer or department may consider necessary or advisable to reasonably inform the public as to the kind and nature of the article about which the notice relates.

(b) Notwithstanding subsection (a) of this section or Article 12 of Chapter 160A of the General Statutes, when bicycles which are in the possession of any sheriff or police department, as provided for in this Article, have remained unclaimed by the person who may be entitled thereto for a period of 60 days after such seizure, confiscation or receipt thereof, the said sheriff or police department who has possession of any such bicycle may proceed to advertise and sell such bicycles as provided by this Article, or may donate such bicycles to a charitable organization exempt under section 501(c)(3) of the Internal Revenue Code. If the bicycles are to be donated, the notice shall state that as the intended disposition if they are not claimed. (1939, c. 195, s. 2; 1965, c. 807, s. 1; 1973, c. 1141, s. 4; 1997-180, s. 1.)

§ 15-13. Public sale 30 days after publication of notice.

If said articles shall remain unclaimed or satisfactory evidence of ownership thereof not be presented to the sheriff or police department, as the case may be, for a period of 30 days after the publication of the notice provided for in G.S. 15-12, then the said sheriff or police department in whose custody such articles may be is hereby authorized and empowered to sell the same at public auction for cash to the highest bidder, either at the courthouse door of the county, the county law enforcement headquarters if the sale is conducted by the sheriff, or at the police headquarters of the municipality in which the said articles of property are located, and at such sale to deliver the same to the purchaser or purchasers thereof. (1939, c. 195, s. 3; 1973, c. 1141, s. 5; 1991, c. 531, s. 2.)

§ 15-14. Notice of sale.

Before any sale of said property is made under the provisions of this Article, however, the said sheriff or police department making the same shall first advertise the sale by publishing a notice thereof in some newspaper published in the said county at least one time not less than 10 days prior to the date of sale, and by posting a notice of the sale at the courthouse door and at three other public places in the said county. Said notice shall specify the time and place of sale, and contain a sufficient description of the articles of property to be sold. It shall not be required that the sale lay open for increase bids or objections, but it may be deemed closed when the purchaser at the sale pays the amount of the accepted bid. (1939, c. 195, s. 4; 1973, c. 1141, s. 6.)

§ 15-14.1. Sale of property through electronic auction.

In addition to selling property as authorized in G.S. 15-13, a sheriff or police department may sell property in his or its possession through an electronic auction service. The sheriff or police department shall comply with the publication and notice requirements provided in G.S. 15-12 through G.S. 15-14 prior to any sale under this section. (2003-284, s. 18.6(c).)

§ 15-15. Disbursement of proceeds of sale.

From the proceeds realized from the sale of said property, the sheriff, police department or other officer making the same shall first pay the costs and expenses of the sale, and all other necessary expenses incident to a compliance with this Article, and any balance then remaining from the proceeds of said sale shall be paid within 30 days after the sale to the treasurer of the county board of education of the county in which such sale is made, for the benefit of the fund for maintaining the free public schools of such county. (1939, c. 195, s. 5; 1973, c. 1141, s. 7.)

§ 15-16. Nonliability of officers.

No sheriff, police department, or other officer shall be liable for any damages or claims on account of any such sale or disposition of such property, as provided in this Article. (1939, c. 195, s. 6; 1973, c. 1141, s. 8.)

§ 15-17. Construction of Article.

This Article shall not be construed to apply to the seizure and disposition of whiskey distilleries, game birds, and other property or articles which have been or may be seized, where the existing law now provides the method, manner, and extent of the disposition of such articles or of the proceeds derived from the sale thereof. (1939, c. 195, s. 7.)

Article 3.
Warrants.

§§ 15-18 through 15-24. Repealed by Session Laws 1973, c. 1286, s. 26.

§ 15-24.1. Amendment of warrant to show ownership of property.

Any criminal warrant may be amended in the superior court, before or during the trial, when there shall appear to be any variance between the allegations in the warrant and the evidence in setting forth the ownership of property if, in the opinion of the court, such amendment will not prejudice the defendant. This section shall be construed as enlarging and not limiting the conditions and situations under which a warrant may be amended. (1965, c. 285.)

Article 4.
Search Warrants.

§ 15-25. Repealed by Session Laws 1973, c. 1286, s. 26.

§§ 15-25.1 through 15-25.2. Repealed by Session Laws 1969, c. 869, s. 8.

§§ 15-26 through 15-27.1. Repealed by Session Laws 1973, c. 1286, s. 26.

Article 4A.
Administrative Search and Inspection Warrants.

§ 15-27.2. Warrants to conduct inspections authorized by law.

(a) Notwithstanding the provisions of Article 11 of Chapter 15A, any official or employee of the State or of a unit of county or local government of North Carolina may, under the conditions specified in this section, obtain a warrant authorizing him to conduct a search or inspection of property if such a search or inspection is one that is elsewhere authorized by law, either with or without the consent of the person whose privacy would be thereby invaded, and is one for which such a warrant is constitutionally required.

(b) The warrant may be issued by any magistrate of the general court of justice, judge, clerk, or assistant or deputy clerk of any court of record whose territorial jurisdiction encompasses the property to be inspected.

(c) The issuing officer shall issue the warrant when he is satisfied the following conditions are met:

(1) The one seeking the warrant must establish under

oath or affirmation that the property to be searched or inspected is to be searched or inspected as part of a legally authorized program of inspection which naturally includes that property, or that there is probable cause for believing that there is a condition, object, activity or circumstance which legally justifies such a search or inspection of that property;

(2) An affidavit indicating the basis for the establishment of one of the grounds described in (1) above must be signed under oath or affirmation by the affiant;

(3) The issuing official must examine the affiant under oath or affirmation to verify the accuracy of the matters indicated by the statement in the affidavit;

(d) The warrant shall be validly issued only if it meets the following requirements:

(1) Except as provided in subsection (e), it must be signed by the issuing official and must bear the date and hour of its issuance above his signature with a notation that the warrant is valid for only 24 hours following its issuance;

(2) It must describe, either directly or by reference to the affidavit, the property where the search or inspection is to occur and be accurate enough in description so that the executor of the warrant and the owner or the possessor of the property can reasonably determine from it what person or property the warrant authorizes an inspection of;

(3) It must indicate the conditions, objects, activities or circumstances which the inspection is intended to check or reveal;

(4) It must be attached to the affidavit required to be made in order to obtain the warrant.

(e) Any warrant issued under this section for a search or inspection shall be valid for only 24 hours after its issuance, must be personally served upon the owner or possessor of the property between the hours of 8:00 A.M. and 8:00 P.M. and must be returned within 48 hours. If the warrant, however, was procured pursuant to an investigation authorized by G.S. 58-79-1, the warrant may be executed at any hour, is valid for 48 hours after its issuance, and must be returned without unnecessary delay after its execution or after the expiration of the 48 hour period if it is not executed. If the owner or possessor of the property is not present on the property at the time of the search or inspection and reasonable efforts to locate the owner or possessor have been made and have failed, the warrant or a copy thereof may be affixed to the property and shall have the same effect as if served personally upon the owner or possessor.

(f) No facts discovered or evidence obtained in a search or inspection conducted under authority of a warrant issued under this section shall be competent as evidence in any civil, criminal or administrative action, nor considered in imposing any civil, criminal, or administrative sanction against any person, nor as a basis for further seeking to obtain any warrant, if the warrant is invalid or if what is discovered or obtained is not a condition, object, activity or circumstance which it was the legal purpose of the search or inspection to discover; but this shall not prevent any such facts or evidence to be so used when the warrant issued is not constitutionally required in those circumstances.

(g) The warrants authorized under this section shall not be regarded as search warrants for the purposes of application of Article 11 of Chapter 15A of the General Statutes of North Carolina. (1967, c. 1260; 1979, c. 729; 1983, c. 294, ss. 1, 2; c. 739, ss. 1, 2.)

Article 5.
Peace Warrants.

§§ 15-28 through 15-38. Repealed by Session Laws 1973, c. 1286, ss. 11, 26.

Article 6.
Arrest.

§§ 15-39 through 15-42. Repealed by Session Laws 1973, c. 1286, s. 26.

§ 15-43. House broken open to prevent felony.
All persons are authorized to break open and enter a house to prevent a felony about to be committed therein. (1868-9, c. 178, subch. 1, s. 4; Code, s. 1127; Rev., s. 3179; C.S., s. 4545.)

§§ 15-44 through 15-47. Repealed by Session Laws 1973, c. 1286, s. 26.

Article 7.
Fugitives from Justice.

§ 15-48. Repealed by Session Laws 1997-80, s. 10.

§ 15-49. Repealed by Session Laws 1975, c. 166, s. 26.

§§ 15-50 through 15-52. Repealed by Session Laws 1973, c. 1286, s. 26.

§ 15-53. Governor may employ agents, and offer rewards.
The Governor, on information made to the Governor of any person, whether the name of such person be known or unknown, having committed a felony or other infamous crime within the State, and of having fled out of the jurisdiction thereof, or who conceals himself or herself within the State to avoid arrest, or who, having been convicted, has escaped and cannot otherwise be apprehended, may either employ a special agent, with a sufficient escort, to pursue and apprehend such fugitive, or issue a proclamation, and therein offer a reward, not exceeding one hundred thousand dollars ($100,000), according to the nature of the case, as in the Governor's opinion may be sufficient for the purpose, to be paid to anyone who shall apprehend and deliver the fugitive to such person and at such place as in the proclamation shall be directed. (1800, c. 561, P.R.; R.C., c. 35, s. 4; 1866, c. 28; 1868-9, c. 52; 1870-1, c. 15; 1871-2, c. 29; Code, s. 1169; 1891, c. 421; Rev., s. 3188; C.S., s. 4554; 1925, c. 275, s. 6; 1967, c. 165, s. 1; 2013-276, s. 1.)

§ 15-53.1. Governor may offer rewards for information leading to arrest and conviction.
When it shall appear to the Governor, upon satisfactory information furnished to the Governor, that a felony or other infamous crime has been committed within the State, whether the name or names of the person or persons suspected of committing the said crime be known or unknown, the Governor may issue a proclamation and therein offer an award [reward] not exceeding one hundred thousand dollars ($100,000), according to the nature of the case as, in the Governor's opinion, may be sufficient for the purpose, to be paid to anyone who shall provide information leading to the arrest and conviction of such person or persons. The proclamation shall be upon such terms as the Governor may deem proper, but it shall identify the felony or felonies and the authority to whom the information is to be delivered and shall state such other terms as the Governor may require under which the reward is payable. (1967, c. 165, s. 2; 2013-276, s. 2.)

§ 15-54. Officer entitled to reward.
Any sheriff or other officer who shall make an arrest of any person charged with crime for whose apprehension a reward has been offered is entitled to such reward, and may sue for and recover the same in any court in this State having jurisdiction: Provided, that no reward shall be paid to any sheriff or other officer for any arrest made for a crime committed within the county of such sheriff or officer making such arrest. (1913, c. 132; 1917, c. 8; C.S., s. 4555.)

Article 8.
Extradition.

§§ 15-55 through 15-84. Transferred to G.S. 15A-721 to 15A-750 by Session Laws 1973, c. 1286, s. 16.

Article 9.
Preliminary Examination.

§§ 15-85 through 15-101. Repealed by Session Laws 1973, c. 1286, s. 26.

Article 10.
Bail.

§§ 15-102 through 15-103. Repealed by Session Laws 1973, c. 1286, s. 26.

§ 15-103.1. Repealed by Session Laws 1977, c. 711, s. 33.

§ 15-103.2. Repealed by Session Laws 1975, c. 166, s. 26.

§ 15-104. Repealed by Session Laws 1973, c. 1286, s. 26.

§ 15-104.1. Repealed by Session Laws 1975, c. 166, s. 26.

§§ 15-105 through 15-107. Repealed by Session Laws 1973, c. 1286, s. 26.

§ 15-107.1. Repealed by Session Laws 1975, c. 166, s. 26.

§§ 15-108 through 15-109. Repealed by Session Laws 1973, c. 1286, s. 26.

Article 11.
Forfeiture of Bail.

§§ 15-110 through 15-124. Repealed by Sessions

Laws 1977, c. 711, s. 33.

Article 12.
Commitment to Prison.

§ 15-125. Repealed by Session Laws 1973, c. 1286, s. 26.

§ 15-126. Commitment to county jail.

All persons committed to prison before conviction shall be committed to the jail of the county in which the examination is had, or to that of the county in which the offense is charged to have been committed: Provided, if the jails of these counties are unsafe, or injurious to the health of prisoners, the committing magistrate may commit to the jail of any other convenient county. And every sheriff or jailer to whose jail any person shall be committed by any court or magistrate of competent jurisdiction shall receive such prisoner and give a receipt for him, and be bound for his safekeeping as prescribed by law. (1868-9, c. 178, subch. 2, s. 33; Code, s. 1164; Rev., s. 3231; C.S., s. 4598; 1973, c. 1286, s. 26; 1975, c. 166, s. 25.)

§ 15-127. Repealed by Session Laws 1973, c. 1286, s. 26.

Article 13.
Venue.

§ 15-128. Repealed by Session Laws 1973, c. 1286, s. 26.

§ 15-129. In offenses on waters dividing counties.

When any offense is committed on any water, or watercourse whether at high or low water, which water or watercourse, or the sides or shores thereof, divides counties, such offense may be dealt with, inquired of, tried and determined, and punished at the discretion of the court, in either of the two counties which may be nearest to the place where the offense was committed. (R.C., c. 35, s. 24; Code, s. 1193; Rev., s. 3234; C.S., s. 4601; 1973, c. 1286, s. 26; 1975, c. 166, s. 25.)

§ 15-130. Assault in one county, death in another.

In all cases of felonious homicide when the assault has been made in one county within the State, and the person assaulted dies in any other county thereof, the offender shall be indicted and punished for the crime in the county wherein the assault was made. (1831, c. 22, s. 1; R.C., c. 35, s. 27; Code, s. 1196; Rev., s. 3235; C.S., s. 4602.)

§ 15-131. Assault in this State, death in another.

In all cases of felonious homicide, when the assault has been made within this State, and the person assaulted dies without the limits thereof, the offender shall be indicted and punished for the crime in the county where the assault was made, in the same manner, to all intents and purposes, as if the person assaulted had died within the limits of this State. (1831, c. 22, s. 2; R.C., c. 35, s. 28; Code, s. 1197; Rev., s. 3236; C.S., s. 4603.)

§ 15-132. Person in this State injuring one in another.

If any person, being in this State, unlawfully and willfully puts in motion a force from the effect of which any person is injured while in another state, the person so setting such force in motion shall be guilty of the same offense in this State as he would be if the effect had taken place within this State. (1895, c. 169; Rev., s. 3237; C.S., s. 4604.)

§ 15-133. In county where death occurs.

If a mortal wound is given or other violence or injury inflicted or poison is administered on the high seas or land, either within or without the limits of this State, by means whereof death ensues in any county thereof, the offense may be prosecuted and punished in the county where the death happens. (1891, c. 68; Rev., s. 3238; C.S., s. 4605.)

§§ 15-134 through 15-136. Repealed by Session Laws 1973, c. 1286, s. 26.

Article 14.
Presentment.

§§ 15-137 through 15-139. Repealed by Session Laws 1973, c. 1286, s. 26.

Article 15.
Indictment.

§§ 15-140 through 15-143. Repealed by Session Laws 1973, c. 1286, s. 26.

§ 15-144. Essentials of bill for homicide.

In indictments for murder and manslaughter, it is not necessary to allege matter not required to be proved on the trial; but in the body of the indictment, after naming the person accused, and the county of his residence, the date of the offense, the averment "with force and arms," and the county of the alleged commission of the offense, as is now usual, it is sufficient in describing murder to allege that the accused person feloniously, willfully, and of his malice aforethought, did kill and murder (naming the person killed), and concluding as is now required by law; and it is sufficient in describing manslaughter to allege that the accused feloniously and willfully did kill and slay (naming the person killed), and concluding as aforesaid; and any bill of indictment containing the averments and allegations herein named shall be good and sufficient in law as an indictment for murder or manslaughter, as the case may be. (1887, c. 58; Rev., s. 3245; C.S., s. 4614.)

§ 15-144.1. Essentials of bill for rape.

(a) In indictments for rape it is not necessary to allege every matter required to be proved on the trial; but in the body of the indictment, after naming the person accused, the date of the offense, the county in which the offense of rape was allegedly committed, and the averment "with force and arms," as is now usual, it is sufficient in describing rape to allege that the accused person unlawfully, willfully, and feloniously did ravish and carnally know the victim, naming her, by force and against her will and concluding as is now required by law. Any bill of indictment containing the averments and allegations herein named shall be good and sufficient in law as an indictment for rape in the first degree and will support a verdict of guilty of rape in the first degree, rape in the second degree, attempted rape or assault on a female.

(b) If the victim is a female child under the age of 13 years it is sufficient to allege that the accused unlawfully, willfully, and feloniously did carnally know and abuse a child under 13, naming her, and concluding as aforesaid. Any bill of indictment containing the averments and allegations herein named shall be good and sufficient in law as an indictment for the rape of a female child under the age of 13 years and all lesser included offenses.

(c) If the victim is a person who is mentally disabled, mentally incapacitated, or physically helpless it is sufficient to allege that the defendant unlawfully, willfully, and feloniously did carnally know and abuse a person who was mentally disabled, mentally incapacitated or physically helpless, naming such victim, and concluding as aforesaid. Any bill of indictment containing the averments and allegations herein named shall be good and sufficient in law for the rape of a mentally disabled, mentally incapacitated or physically helpless person and all lesser included offenses. (1977, c. 861, s. 1; 1979, c. 682, s. 10; 1983, c. 720, s. 1; 2002-159, s. 2(d).)

§ 15-144.2. Essentials of bill for sex offense.

(a) In indictments for sex offense it is not necessary to allege every matter required to be proved on the trial; but in the body of the indictment, after naming the person accused, the date of the offense, the county in which the sex offense was allegedly committed, and the averment "with force and arms," as is now usual, it is sufficient in describing a sex offense to allege that the accused person unlawfully, willfully, and feloniously did engage in a sex offense with the victim, naming the victim, by force and against the will of such victim and concluding as is now required by law. Any bill of indictment containing the averments and allegations herein named shall be good and sufficient in law as an indictment for a first degree sex offense and will support a verdict of guilty of a sex offense in the first degree, a sex offense in the second degree, an attempt to commit a sex offense or an assault.

(b) If the victim is a person under the age of 13 years, it is sufficient to allege that the defendant unlawfully, willfully, and feloniously did engage in a sex offense with a child under the age of 13 years, naming the child, and concluding as aforesaid. Any bill of indictment containing the averments and allegations herein named shall be good and sufficient in law as an indictment for a sex offense against a child under the age of 13 years and all lesser included offenses.

(c) If the victim is a person who is mentally disabled, mentally incapacitated, or physically helpless it is sufficient to allege that the defendant unlawfully, willfully, and feloniously did engage in a sex offense with a person who was mentally disabled, mentally incapacitated or physically helpless, naming such victim, and concluding as aforesaid. Any bill of indictment containing the averments and allegations herein named shall be good and sufficient in law for a sex offense against a mentally disabled, mentally incapacitated or physically helpless person and all lesser included offenses. (1979, c. 682, s. 11; 1983, c. 720, ss. 2, 3; 2002-159, s. 2(e).)

§ 15-145. Form of bill for perjury.

In every indictment for willful and corrupt perjury it is sufficient to set forth the substance of the offense charged upon the defendant, and by what court, or before whom, the oath was taken (averring such court or person to have competent authority to administer the same), together with the proper averments to falsify the matter wherein the perjury is assigned, without setting forth the bill, answer, information, indictment, declaration, or any part of any record or proceedings, either in law or equity, other than aforesaid, and without setting forth the commission or authority of the court or person before whom the perjury was committed. In indictments for perjury the following form shall be sufficient, to wit:

The jurors for the State, on their oath, present, that A.B., of______ County, did unlawfully commit perjury upon the trial of an action in ______ court, in ________ County, wherein ________ was plaintiff and ______ was defendant, by falsely asserting, on oath (or solemn affirmation) (here set out the statement or statements alleged to be false), knowing the said statement, or statements, to be false, or being ignorant whether or not said statement was true. (1842, c. 49, s. 1; R.C., c. 35, s. 16; Code, s. 1185; 1889, c. 83; Rev., ss. 3246, 3247; C.S., s. 4615.)

§ 15-146. Bill for subornation of perjury.

In every indictment for subornation of perjury, or for corrupt bargaining or contracting with others to commit willful and corrupt perjury, it is sufficient to set forth the substance of the offense charged upon the defendant, without setting forth the bill, answer, information, indictment, declaration or any part of any record or proceedings, and without setting forth the commission or authority of the court or person before whom the perjury was committed or was agreed or promised to be committed. (1842, c. 49, s. 2; R.C., c. 35, s. 17; Code, s. 1186; Rev., s. 3248; C.S., s. 4616.)

§ 15-147. Repealed by Session Laws 1973, c. 1286, s. 26.

§ 15-148. Manner of alleging joint ownership of property.

In any indictment wherein it is necessary to state the ownership of any property whatsoever, whether real or personal, which belongs to, or is in the possession of, more than one person, whether such persons be partners in trade, joint tenants or tenants in common, it is sufficient to name one of such persons, and to state such property to belong to the person so named, and another or others as the case may be; and whenever, in any such indictment, it is necessary to mention, for any purpose whatsoever, any partners, joint tenants or tenants in common, it is sufficient to describe them in the manner aforesaid; and this provision shall extend to all joint-stock companies and trustees. (R.C., c. 35, s. 19; Code, s. 1188; Rev., s. 3250; C.S., s. 4618.)

§ 15-149. Description in bill for larceny of money.

In every indictment in which it is necessary to make any averment as to the larceny of any money, or United States treasury note, or any note of any bank whatsoever, it is sufficient to describe such money, or treasury note, or bank note, simply as money, without specifying any particular coin, or treasury note, or bank note; and such allegation, so far as regards the description of the property, shall be sustained by proof of any amount of coin, or treasury note, or bank note, although the particular species of coin, of which such amount was composed, or the particular nature of the treasury note, or bank note, shall not be proven. (1876-7, c. 68; Code, s. 1190; Rev., s. 3251; C.S., s. 4619.)

§ 15-150. Description in bill for embezzlement.

In indictments for embezzlement, except when the offense relates to a chattel, it is sufficient to allege the embezzlement to be of money, without specifying any particular coin or valuable security; and such allegation, so far as regards the description of the property, shall be sustained if the offender shall be proved to have embezzled any amount, although the particular species of coin or valuable security of which such amount was composed shall not be proved. (1871-2, c. 145, s. 2; Code, s. 1020; Rev., s. 3252; C.S., s. 4620.)

§ 15-151. Intent to defraud; larceny and receiving.

In any case where an intent to defraud is required to constitute the offense of forgery, or any other offense whatever, it is sufficient to allege in the indictment an intent to defraud, without naming therein the particular person or body corporate intended to be defrauded; and on the trial of such indictment, it shall be sufficient, and shall not be deemed a variance, if there appear to be an intent to defraud the United States, or any state, county, city, town, or parish, or body corporate, or any public officer in his official capacity, or any copartnership or member thereof, or any particular person. The defendant may be charged in the same indictment in several counts with the separate offenses of receiving stolen goods, knowing them to be stolen, and larceny. (1852, c. 87, s. 2; R.C., c. 35, ss. 21, 23; 1874-5, c. 62; Code, s. 1191; Rev., s. 3253; C.S., s. 4621.)

§ 15-152. Repealed by Session Laws 1973, c. 1286, s. 26.

§ 15-153. Bill or warrant not quashed for informality.

Every criminal proceeding by warrant, indictment, information, or impeachment is sufficient in form for all intents and purposes if it express the charge against the defendant in a plain, intelligible, and explicit manner; and the same shall not be quashed, nor the judgment thereon stayed, by reason of any informality or refinement, if in the bill or proceeding, sufficient matter appears to enable the court to proceed to judgment. (37 Hen. VIII, c. 8; 1784, c. 210, s. 2, P.R.; 1811, c. 809, P.R.; R.C., c. 35, s. 14; Code, s. 1183; Rev., s. 3254; C.S., s. 4623.)

§ 15-154. Repealed by Session Laws 1973, c. 1286, s. 26.

§ 15-155. Defects which do not vitiate.

No judgment upon any indictment for felony or misdemeanor, whether after verdict, or by confession, or otherwise, shall be stayed or reversed for the want of the averment of any matter unnecessary to be proved, nor for omission of the words "as appears by the record," or of the words "with force and arms," nor for the insertion of the words "against the form of the statutes" instead of the words "against the form of the statute," or vice versa; nor for omission of the words "against the form of the statute" or "against the form of the statutes," nor for omitting to state the time at which the offense was committed in any case where time is not of the essence of the offense, nor for stating the time imperfectly, nor for stating the offense to have been committed on a day subsequent to the finding of the indictment, or on an impossible day, or on a day that never happened; nor for want of a proper and perfect venue, when the court shall appear by the indictment to have had jurisdiction of the offense. (7 Hen. VIII, c. 8; R.C., c. 35, s. 20; Code, s. 1189; Rev., s. 3255; C.S., s. 4625.)

Article 15A. Investigation of Offenses Involving Abandonment and Nonsupport of Children.

§ 15-155.1. Reports to district attorneys of Work First Family Assistance and out-of-wedlock births.

The Department of Health and Human Services by and through the Secretary of Health and Human Services shall promptly after June 19, 1959, make a report to each district attorney, setting out the names and addresses of all mothers who reside in his prosecutorial district as defined in G.S. 7A-60 and are recipients of assistance under the provisions of Part 2, Article 2, Chapter 108A of the General Statutes. Such report shall in some manner show the identity of the unwed mothers and shall set forth the number of children born to each said mother. Such a report shall also be made monthly thereafter setting out the names and addresses of all such mothers who reside in the district and who may have become recipients of assistance under the provisions of Part 2, Article 2, Chapter 108A of the General Statutes since the date of the last report. (1959, c. 1210, s. 1; 1973, c. 47, s. 2; c. 476, s. 138; 1987 (Reg. Sess., 1988), c. 1037, s. 50; 1997-443, ss. 11A.118(a), 12.23.)

§ 15-155.2. District attorney to take action on report of Work First Family Assistance and children born out of wedlock.

(a) Upon receipt of such reports as are provided for in G.S. 15-155.1, the district attorney of superior court may make an investigation to determine whether the mother of an out-of-wedlock child or who is a recipient of Work First Family Assistance, has abandoned, is willfully neglecting or is refusing to support and maintain the child within the meaning of G.S. 14-326 or 49-2 or is diverting any part of the funds received as Work First Family Assistance to any purpose other than for the support and maintenance of a child in violation of G.S. 108-76.1. In making this investigation the district attorney is authorized to call upon:
   (1) Any county board of social services or the Department of Health and Human Services for personal, clerical or investigative assistance and for access to any records kept by either such board and relating to the matter under investigation and such boards are hereby directed to assist in all investigations hereunder and to furnish all records relating thereto when so requested by the district attorney;
   (2) The board of county commissioners of any county within his district for legal or clerical assistance in making any investigation or investigations in such county and such boards are hereby authorized to furnish such assistance in their discretion; and
   (3) The district attorney of any inferior court in his district for personal assistance in making any investigation or investigations in the county in which the court is located and any district attorney so called upon is hereby authorized to furnish such assistance by and with the consent of the board of county commissioners of the county in which the court is located, which board shall provide and fix his compensation for assistance furnished.

(b) If following the investigation the district attorney has reasonable grounds to believe that a violation of G.S. 49-2, 14-326, 108-76.1 or any other criminal offense is being or has been committed, he shall send to the grand jury of the county in which he believes the offense is being or has been committed a bill of indictment charging the commission of the offense. Sole and exclusive jurisdiction of offenses discovered as a result of investigations under this section shall be vested in the superior court notwithstanding any other provisions of law, whether general, special or local. Provided nothing in this Article shall be construed to take from the inferior courts any authority or responsibility now vested in them by existing law or to compel the district attorney to again prosecute a crime that has been disposed of in the inferior courts.

(c) Repealed by Session Laws 1985, c. 589, s. 8. (1959, c. 1210, s. 1; 1969, c. 982; 1973, c. 47, s. 2; c. 476, s. 138; 1985, c. 589, s. 8; 1997-443, ss. 11A.118(a), 12.24; 2013-198, s. 4.)

§ 15-155.3. Disclosure of information by district attorney or agent.

No such district attorney, assistant district attorney, or any attorney-at-law especially appointed to assist the district attorney, or any agent or employee of the district attorney's office shall disclose any information, record, report, case history or any memorandum or document or any information contained therein, which may relate to or be connected with the mother or father of any child born out of wedlock, or any child born out of wedlock, unless in the opinion of the district attorney it is necessary or is required in the prosecution and performance of the district attorney's duties as set forth in the provisions of this Article. (1959, c. 1210, s. 4; 1973, c. 47, s. 2; 2013-198, s. 5.)

Article 15B.
Pretrial Examination of Witnesses and Exhibits of the State.

§§ 15-155.4 through 15-155.5. Repealed by Session Laws 1973, c. 1286, s. 26.

Article 16.
Trial before Justice.

§§ 15-156 through 15-158. Repealed by Session Laws 1973, c. 1286, s. 26.

§ 15-159. Repealed by Session Laws 1977, c. 711, s. 33.

§§ 15-160 through 15-161. Repealed by Session Laws 1973, c. 1286, s. 26.

Article 17.
Trial in Superior Court.

§ 15-162. Repealed by Session Laws 1973, c. 1286, s. 26.

§ 15-162.1. Repealed by Session Laws 1971, c. 1225.

§§ 15-163 through 15-165. Repealed by Session Laws 1967, c. 218, s. 4.

§ 15-166. Exclusion of bystanders in trial for rape and sex offenses.

In the trial of cases for rape or sex offense or attempt to commit rape or attempt to commit a sex offense, the trial judge may, during the taking of the testimony of the prosecutrix, exclude from the courtroom all persons except the officers of the court, the defendant and those engaged in the trial of the case. (1907, c. 21; C. S., s. 4636; 1973, c. 1141, s. 14; 1979, c. 682, s. 3; 1981, c. 682, s. 5.)

§ 15-167. Extension of session of court by trial judge.

Whenever a trial for a felony is in progress on the last Friday of any session of court and it appears to the trial judge that it is unlikely that such trial can be completed before 5:00 P.M. on such Friday, the trial judge may extend the session as long as in his opinion it shall be necessary for the purposes of the case, but he may recess court on Friday or Saturday of such week to such time on the succeeding Sunday or Monday as, in his discretion, he deems wise. The trial judge, in his discretion, may exercise the same power in the trial of any other cause under the same circumstances, except civil actions begun after Thursday of the last week. The length of time such court shall remain in session each day shall be in the discretion of the trial judge. Whenever a trial judge continues a session pursuant to this section, he shall cause an order to such effect to be entered in the minutes, which order may be entered at such time as the judge directs, either before or after he has extended the session. (1830, c. 22; R.C., c. 31, s. 16; C.C.P., s. 397; Code, s. 1229; 1893, c. 226; Rev., s. 3266; C.S., s. 4637; 1961, c. 181; 1973, c. 1141, s. 15.)

§ 15-168. Justification as defense to libel.

Every defendant who is charged by indictment with the publication of a libel may prove on the trial for the same the truth of the facts alleged in the indictment; and if it shall appear to the satisfaction of the jury that the facts are true, the defendant shall be acquitted of the charge. (R.C., c. 35, s. 26; Code, s. 1195; Rev., s. 3267; C.S., s. 4638.)

§ 15-169. Conviction of assault, when included in charge.
On the trial of any person for any felony whatsoever, when the crime charged includes an assault against the person, it is lawful for the jury to acquit of the felony and to find a verdict of guilty of assault against the person indicted, if the evidence warrants such finding; and when such verdict is found the court shall have power to imprison the person so found guilty of an assault, for any term now allowed by law in cases of conviction when the indictment was originally for the assault of a like character. (1885, c. 68; Rev., s. 3268; C.S., s. 4639; 1979, c. 682, s. 4.)

§ 15-170. Conviction for a less degree or an attempt.
Upon the trial of any indictment the prisoner may be convicted of the crime charged therein or of a less degree of the same crime, or of an attempt to commit the crime so charged, or of an attempt to commit a less degree of the same crime. (1891, c. 205, s. 2; Rev., s. 3269; C.S., s. 4640.)

§ 15-171. Repealed by Session Laws 1953, c. 100.

§ 15-172. Verdict for murder in first or second degree.
Nothing contained in the statute law dividing murder into degrees shall be construed to require any alteration or modification of the existing form of indictment for murder, but the jury before whom the offender is tried shall determine in their verdict whether the crime is murder in the first or second degree. (1893, c. 85, s. 3; Rev., s. 3271; C.S., s. 4642.)

§ 15-173. Demurrer to the evidence.
When on the trial of any criminal action in the superior or district court, the State has introduced its evidence and rested its case, the defendant may move to dismiss the action, or for judgment as in case of nonsuit. If the motion is allowed, judgment shall be entered accordingly; and such judgment shall have the force and effect of a verdict of "not guilty" as to such defendant. If the motion is refused and the defendant does not choose to introduce evidence, the case shall be submitted to the jury as in other cases, and the defendant may on appeal urge as ground for reversal, the trial court's denial of his motion without the necessity of the defendant's having taken exception to such denial.

If the defendant introduces evidence, he thereby waives any motion for dismissal or judgment as in case of nonsuit which he may have made prior to the introduction of his evidence and cannot urge such prior motion as ground for appeal. The defendant, however, may make such motion at the conclusion of all the evidence in the case, irrespective of whether or not he made a motion for dismissal or judgment as in case of nonsuit theretofore. If the motion is allowed, or shall be sustained on appeal, it shall in all cases have the force and effect of a verdict of "not guilty." If the motion is refused, the defendant may on appeal, after the jury has rendered its verdict, urge as ground for reversal the trial court's denial of his motion made at the close of all the evidence without the necessity of the defendant's having taken exception to such denial. (1913, c. 73; Ex. Sess. 1913, c. 32; C.S., s. 4643; 1951, c. 1086, s. 1; 1973, c. 1141, s. 16.)

§§ 15-173.1 through 15-174. Repealed by Session Laws 1977, c. 711, s. 33.

§ 15-175. Repealed by Session Laws 1973, c. 1286, s. 26.

§ 15-176. Prisoner not to be tried in prison uniform.
It shall be unlawful for any sheriff, jailer or other officer to require any person imprisoned in jail to appear in any court for trial dressed in the uniform or dress of a prisoner or convict, or in any uniform or apparel other than ordinary civilian's dress, or with shaven or clipped head. And no person charged with a criminal offense shall be tried in any court while dressed in the uniform or dress of a prisoner or convict, or in any uniform or apparel other than ordinary civilian's dress, or with head shaven or clipped by or under the direction and requirement of any sheriff, jailer or other officer, unless the head was shaven or clipped while such person was serving a term of imprisonment for the commission of a crime.

Any sheriff, jailer or other officer who violates the provisions of this section shall be guilty of a Class 1 misdemeanor. (1915, c. 124; C.S., s. 4646; 1993, c. 539, s. 296; 1994, Ex. Sess., c. 24, s. 14(c).)

§ 15-176.1. District attorney may argue for death penalty.
In the trial of capital cases, the district attorney or other counsel appearing for the State may argue to the jury that a sentence of death should be imposed and that the jury should not recommend life imprisonment. (1961, c. 890; 1973, c. 47, s. 2.)

§ 15-176.2. Repealed by Session Laws 1973, c. 44, s. 1.

Article 17A.

Informing Jury in Case Involving Death Penalty.

§ 15-176.3. Informing and questioning potential jurors on consequences of guilty verdict.
When a jury is being selected for a case in which the defendant is indicted for a crime for which the penalty is a sentence of death, the court, the defense, or the State may inform any person called to serve as a potential juror that the death penalty will be imposed upon the return of a verdict of guilty of that crime and may inquire of any person called to serve as a potential juror whether that person understands the consequences of a verdict of guilty of that crime. (1973, c. 1286, s. 12.)

§ 15-176.4. Instruction to jury on consequences of guilty verdict.
When a defendant is indicted for a crime for which the penalty is a sentence of death, the court, upon request by either party, shall instruct the jury that the death penalty will be imposed upon the return of a verdict of guilty of that crime. (1973, c. 1286, s. 12.)

§ 15-176.5. Argument to jury on consequences of guilty verdict.
When a case will be submitted to a jury on a charge for which the penalty is a sentence of death, either party in its argument to the jury may indicate the consequences of a verdict of guilty of that charge. (1973, c. 1286, s. 12.)

§§ 15-176.6 through 15-176.8. Reserved for future codification purposes.

Article 17B. Informing Jury of Possible Punishment upon Conviction.

§ 15-176.9. Loss of motor vehicle driver's license.
When a case will be submitted to a jury on a charge for which the penalty involves the possibility of the loss of a motor vehicle driver's license, either party in its argument to the jury may indicate the consequences of a verdict of guilty of that charge. (1973, c. 1286, s. 25.)

Article 18. Appeal.

§§ 15-177 through 15-178. Repealed by Session Laws 1973, c. 1141, s. 17.

§§ 15-179 through 15-186. Repealed by Session Laws 1977, c. 711, s. 33.

§ 15-186.1: Repealed by Session Laws 1973, c. 44, s. 1.

Article 19. Execution.

§ 15-187. Death by administration of lethal drugs.
Death by electrocution under sentence of law and death by the administration of lethal gas under sentence of law are abolished. Any person convicted of a criminal offense and sentenced to death shall be executed only by the administration of a lethal quantity of an ultrashort-acting barbiturate in combination with a chemical paralytic agent. The warden of Central Prison may obtain and employ the drugs necessary to carry out the provisions of this Article, regardless of contrary provisions in Chapter 90 of the General Statutes. (1909, ch. 443, s. 1; C.S., s. 4657; 1935, c. 294, s. 1; 1983, c. 678, ss. 1, 4; 1998-212, s. 17.22(a).)

§ 15-188. Manner and place of execution.
In accordance with G.S. 15-187, the mode of executing a death sentence must in every case be by administering to the convict or felon an intravenous injection of a substance or substances in a lethal quantity sufficient to cause death and until the person is dead, and that procedure shall be determined by the Secretary of the Department of Public Safety, who shall ensure compliance with the federal and State constitutions; and when any person, convict or felon shall be sentenced by any court of the State having competent jurisdiction to be so executed, the punishment shall only be inflicted within a permanent death chamber which the superintendent of the State penitentiary is hereby authorized and directed to provide within the walls of the North Carolina penitentiary at Raleigh, North Carolina. The superintendent of the State penitentiary shall also cause to be provided, in conformity with this Article, the necessary appliances for the infliction of the punishment of death and qualified personnel to set up and prepare the injection, administer the preinjections, insert the IV catheter, and to perform other tasks required for this procedure in accordance with the requirements of this Article. (1909, c. 443, s. 2; C.S., s. 4658; 1935, c. 294, s. 2; 1983, c. 678, s. 2; 1998-212, s. 17.22(b); 2012-136, s. 1; 2013-154, s. 3(a).)

§ 15-188.1. Health care professional assistance.
(a) Any assistance rendered with an execution under this

Article by any licensed health care professional, including, but not limited to, physicians, nurses, and pharmacists, shall not be cause for any disciplinary or corrective measures by any board, commission, or other authority created by the State or governed by State law which oversees or regulates the practice of health care professionals, including, but not limited to, the North Carolina Medical Board, the North Carolina Board of Nursing, and the North Carolina Board of Pharmacy.

(b) The infliction of the punishment of death by administration of the required lethal substances under this Article shall not be construed to be the practice of medicine. (2013-154, s. 1(a).)

§ 15-189. Sentence of death; prisoner taken to penitentiary.

Upon the sentence of death being pronounced against any person in the State of North Carolina convicted of a crime punishable by death, it shall be the duty of the judge pronouncing such death sentence to make the same in writing, which shall be filed in the papers in the case against such convicted person. The clerk of the superior court in which such death sentence is pronounced shall prepare a certified copy of said judgment or sentence of death, including therewith a copy of any notice or entries of appeal made in such case; if no entries or notice of appeal have been made or given in such case, a statement to the effect shall be included in the certificate of the clerk; it shall also be the duty of the district attorney, assistant district attorney, or attorney prosecuting in behalf of the State in the absence of the district attorney, to prepare and sign a certificate stating in substance that he prosecuted said case in behalf of the State and that notice or entries of appeal have or have not been made or given in said case, and further that he has examined a copy of said judgment or sentence of death certified by the clerk, including the copy of the notice or entries of appeal or statement to the effect that no appeal has been given, and to the best of his knowledge the same is correct; the certificate of said district attorney, or other prosecuting officer above named, shall be attached to the certified copy of said sentence of death, as prepared and certified by the clerk, and both certificates shall be transmitted by the clerk of the superior court in which said sentence of death is pronounced to the warden of the State penitentiary at Raleigh, North Carolina; at the same time and in the same manner, a duplicate original of said certificates shall be prepared by the clerk of the superior court and the district attorney, or other prosecuting officer above named, and the said duplicate original or said certificates shall be transmitted to the Attorney General of North Carolina. If notice of appeal is given or entries of appeal are made after the expiration of the term of superior court in which said sentence of death is pronounced, said certificates shall be prepared by the clerk of the superior court in which said sentence is pronounced and by the district attorney, or other prosecuting officer above named, prosecuting in behalf of the State, in the same manner and shall be transmitted as soon as possible to the warden of the State penitentiary at Raleigh, North Carolina, and to the Attorney General of North Carolina. The above certificates so prepared by the clerk of the superior court in which such sentence of death is pronounced and by the district attorney, or other prosecuting officer above named, shall be transmitted by the clerk of the superior court in which such sentence is pronounced to the warden of the State penitentiary at Raleigh, North Carolina, and to the Attorney General of North Carolina, not more than 20 or less than 10 days before the time fixed in the judgment of the court for the execution of the sentence; and in all cases where there is no appeal, said sentence of death shall not be carried out by the warden of the State penitentiary or by any of his deputies or agents until said certificates so prepared and transmitted by the clerk of the superior court in which said sentence of death is pronounced, and by the district attorney, or the prosecuting officer above named, have been received in the office of the warden of the State penitentiary at Raleigh, North Carolina. In all cases where there is no appeal from the sentence of death and in all cases where the sentence is pronounced against a prisoner convicted of the crime of rape it shall be the duty of the sheriff, together with at least one deputy, to convey to the penitentiary, at Raleigh, North Carolina, such condemned felon or convict forthwith upon the adjournment of the court in which the felon was tried, and deliver the convict or felon to the warden of the penitentiary. (1909, c. 443, s. 3; C.S., s. 4659; 1951, c. 899, s. 1; 1973, c. 47, s. 2.)

§ 15-190. Person or persons to be designated by warden to execute sentence; supervision of execution; who shall be present.

(a) Some guard or guards or other reliable person or persons to be named and designated by the warden from time to time shall cause the person, convict or felon against whom the death sentence has been so pronounced to be executed as provided by this Article and all amendments thereto. The execution shall be under the general supervision and control of the warden of the penitentiary, who shall from time to time, in writing, name and designate the guard or guards or other reliable person or persons who shall cause the person, convict or felon against whom the death sentence has been pronounced to be executed as provided by this

Article and all amendments thereto. At such execution there shall be present the warden or deputy warden or some person designated by the warden in the warden's place, and a licensed physician. Four respectable citizens, two members of the victim's family, the counsel and any relatives of such person, convict or felon and a minister or member of the clergy or religious leader of the person's choosing may be present if they so desire. The identities, including the names, residential addresses, residential telephone numbers, and social security numbers, of witnesses or persons designated to carry out the execution shall be confidential and exempted from Chapter 132 of the General Statutes and are not subject to discovery or introduction as evidence in any proceeding. The Senior Resident Superior Court Judge for Wake County may order disclosure of names made confidential by this section after making findings that support a conclusion that disclosure is necessary to a proper administration of justice.

(b) The warden shall report to the Joint Legislative Oversight Committee on Justice and Public Safety by April 1, 2014, and thereafter on October 1 of each year, on the status of the persons required by subsection (a) of this section to be named and designated by the warden to execute death sentences under this Article. The report shall confirm that the required persons are properly trained and ready to serve as an execution team. Alternatively, the Chairs of the Joint Legislative Oversight Committee on Justice and Public Safety may direct that the reports required under this subsection be made on other dates consistent with the Committee's schedule. (1909, c. 443, s. 4; C.S., s. 4660; 1925, c. 123; 1935, c. 294, s. 3; 1983, c. 678, s. 3; 1997-70, s. 1; 2004-124, s. 17.6A; 2004-199, s. 52; 2004-203, s. 22; 2013-154, s. 4.)

§ 15-191. Pending sentences unaffected.

Nothing in G.S. 15-187, 15-188, and 15-190 shall be construed to alter in any manner the execution of the sentence of death imposed on account of any crime or crimes committed before July 1, 1935. (1935, c. 294, s. 4.)

§ 15-192. Certificate filed with clerk.

The warden, together with the surgeon or physician of the penitentiary, shall certify the fact of the execution of the condemned person, convict or felon to the clerk of the superior court in which such sentence was pronounced, and the clerk shall file such certificate with the papers of the case and enter the same upon the records thereof. (1909, c. 443, s. 5; C.S., s. 4661.)

§ 15-193. Notice of reprieve or new trial.

Should the condemned person, convict or felon be granted a reprieve by the Governor or obtain a writ of error, or a new trial be granted by the Supreme Court of the State of North Carolina, or should the execution of the sentence be stayed by any competent judicial tribunal or proceeding, notice of such reprieve, new trial, appeal, writ of error or stay of execution shall be served upon the warden or deputy warden of the penitentiary by the sheriff of Wake County, in case such condemned person is confined in the penitentiary, or upon any sheriff having the custody of any such condemned person, also upon the condemned person himself. (1909, c. 443, s. 6; C.S., s. 4662.)

§ 15-194. Time for execution.

(a) In sentencing a capital defendant to a death sentence pursuant to G.S. 15A-2000(b), the sentencing judge need not specify the date and time the execution is to be carried out by the Division of Adult Correction of the Department of Public Safety. The Attorney General of North Carolina shall provide written notification to the Secretary of the Department of Public Safety of the occurrence of any of the following not more than 90 days from that occurrence:
   (1) The United States Supreme Court has filed an opinion upholding the sentence of death following completion of the initial State and federal postconviction proceedings, if any;
   (2) The mandate issued by the Supreme Court of North Carolina on direct appeal pursuant to N.C.R. App. P. 32(b) affirming the capital defendant's death sentence and the time for filing a petition for writ of certiorari to the United States Supreme Court has expired without a petition being filed;
   (3) The capital defendant, if indigent, failed to timely seek the appointment of counsel pursuant to G.S. 7A-451(c), or failed to file a timely motion for appropriate relief as required by G.S. 15A-1415(a);
   (4) The superior court denied the capital defendant's motion for appropriate relief, but the capital defendant failed to file a timely petition for writ of certiorari to the Supreme Court of North Carolina pursuant to N.C.R. App. P. 21(f);
   (5) The Supreme Court of North Carolina denied the capital defendant's petition for writ of certiorari pursuant to N.C.R. App. P. 21(f), or, if certiorari was granted, upheld the capital defendant's death sentence, but the capital defendant failed to file a timely petition for writ of certiorari to the United

States Supreme Court; or

(6) Following State postconviction proceedings, if any, the capital defendant failed to file a timely petition for writ of habeas corpus in the appropriate federal district court, or failed to timely appeal or petition an adverse habeas corpus decision to the United States Court of Appeals for the Fourth Circuit or the United States Supreme Court.

The Secretary of the Department of Public Safety shall immediately schedule a date for the execution of the original death sentence not less than 15 days or more than 120 days from the date of receiving written notification from the Attorney General under this section. The Secretary shall send a certified copy of the document fixing the date to the clerk of superior court of the county in which the case was tried or, if venue was changed, in which the defendant was indicted. The certified copy shall be recorded in the minutes of the court. The Secretary shall also send certified copies to the capital defendant, the capital defendant's attorney, the district attorney who prosecuted the case, and the Attorney General of North Carolina.

(b) The Attorney General shall submit a written report to the Joint Legislative Oversight Committee on Justice and Public Safety by April 1, 2014, and thereafter on October 1 of each year, on the status of all pending postconviction capital cases. Alternatively, the Chairs of the Joint Legislative Oversight Committee on Justice and Public Safety may direct that the reports required under this subsection be made on other dates consistent with the Committee's schedule. (1909, c. 443, s. 6; C.S., s. 4663; 1925, c. 55; 1951, c. 244, ss. 1, 2; 1973, c. 47, s. 2; 1981, c. 900; 1995 (Reg. Sess., 1996), c. 719, s. 5; 1997-289, s. 1; 1999-358, s. 2; 2011-145, s. 19.1(h), (i); 2013-154, s. 2.)

§ 15-195. Prisoner taken to place of trial when new trial granted.

Should a new trial be granted the condemned person, convict or felon against whom sentence of death has been pronounced, after he has been conveyed to the penitentiary, he shall be conveyed back to the place of trial by such guard or guards as the warden of the penitentiary shall direct, their expenses to be paid as is now provided by law for the conveyance of convicts to the penitentiary. (1909, c. 443, s. 7; C.S., s. 4664.)

§ 15-196: Repealed by Session Laws 1989, c. 353, s. 3.

Article 19A.
Credits against the Service of Sentences and for Attainment of Prison Privileges.

§ 15-196.1. Credits allowed.

The minimum and maximum term of a sentence shall be credited with and diminished by the total amount of time a defendant has spent, committed to or in confinement in any State or local correctional, mental or other institution as a result of the charge that culminated in the sentence. The credit provided shall be calculated from the date custody under the charge commenced and shall include credit for all time spent in custody pending trial, trial de novo, appeal, retrial, or pending parole, probation, or post-release supervision revocation hearing: Provided, however, the credit available herein shall not include any time that is credited on the term of a previously imposed sentence to which a defendant is subject. (1973, c. 44, s. 1; 1977, c. 711, s. 16A; 1977, 2nd Sess., c. 1147, s. 30; 1997-237, s. 3.)

§ 15-196.2. Allowance in cases of multiple sentences.

In the event time creditable under this section shall have been spent in custody as the result of more than one pending charge, resulting in imprisonment for more than one offense, credit shall be allowed as herein provided. Consecutive sentences shall be considered as one sentence for the purpose of providing credit, and the creditable time shall not be multiplied by the number of consecutive offenses for which a defendant is imprisoned. Each concurrent sentence shall be credited with so much of the time as was spent in custody due to the offense resulting in the sentence. When both concurrent and consecutive sentences are imposed, both of the above rules shall obtain to the applicable extent. (1973, c. 44, s. 1.)

§ 15-196.3. Effect of credit.

Time creditable under this section shall reduce the minimum and maximum term of a sentence; and, irrespective of sentence, shall reduce the time required to attain privileges made available to inmates in the custody of the Division of Adult Correction of the Department of Public Safety which are dependent, in whole or in part, upon the passage of a specific length of time in custody, including parole or post-release supervision consideration by the Post-Release Supervision and Parole Commission. However, nothing in this section shall be construed as requiring an automatic award of privileges by virtue of the passage of time. (1973, c. 44, s. 1; 1977, c. 711, s. 17; 1997-237, s. 4; 2011-145, s. 19.1(h); 2012-83, s. 22.)

§ 15-196.4. Procedures for judicial award.

Upon sentencing or activating a sentence, the judge presiding shall determine the credits to which the defendant is entitled and shall cause the clerk to transmit to the custodian of the defendant a statement of allowable credits. Upon committing a defendant upon the conclusion of an appeal, or a parole, probation, or post-release supervision revocation, the committing authority shall determine any credits allowable on account of these proceedings and shall cause to be transmitted, as in all other cases, a statement of the allowable credit to the custodian of the defendant. Upon reviewing a petition seeking credit not previously allowed, the court shall determine the credits due and forward an order setting forth the allowable credit to the custodian of the petitioner. (1973, c. 44, s. 1; 1997-237, s. 5.)

Article 20.
Suspension of Sentence and Probation.

§§ 15-197 through 15-200.1. Repealed by Session Laws 1977, c. 711, s. 33.

§ 15-200.2. Repealed by Session Laws 1975, c. 309, s. 2.

§§ 15-201 through 15-202. Repealed by Session Laws 1973, c. 1262, s. 10.

§ 15-203. Duties of the Secretary of Public Safety; appointment of probation officers; reports; requests for extradition.

The Secretary of Public Safety, or the Secretary's designee, shall direct the work of the probation officers appointed under this Article. Notwithstanding any other provision of law, the Secretary of Public Safety shall have sole discretion to establish the minimum experience requirements to receive an appointment as a probation officer. The Office of State Human Resources shall work with the Secretary to establish position classifications for probation officers based on the experience requirements established by the Secretary. The Secretary, or the Secretary's designee, shall consult and cooperate with the courts and institutions in the development of methods and procedure in the administration of probation, and shall arrange conferences of probation officers and judges. The Secretary shall make an annual written report with statistical and other information to the Governor. The Secretary is authorized to present to the Governor written applications for requisitions for the return of probationers who have broken the terms of their probation, and are believed to be in another state, and the Secretary shall follow the procedure outlined for requests for extradition as set forth in G.S. 15A-743. (1937, c. 132, s. 7; 1959, c. 127; 1963, c. 914, s. 2; 1973, c. 1262, s. 10; 2010-96, s. 2; 2011-145, s. 19.1(h), (i); 2012-83, s. 2; 2013-382, s. 9.1(c).)

§ 15-203.1. Repealed by Session Laws 1963, c. 914, s. 6.

§ 15-204. Assignment, compensation and oath of probation officers.

Probation officers appointed under this Article shall be assigned to serve in such courts or districts or otherwise as the Secretary of Public Safety may determine. They shall be paid annual salaries to be fixed by the Department of Public Safety, and shall also be paid traveling and other necessary expenses incurred in the performance of their official duties as probation officers when such expense accounts have been authorized and approved by the Secretary of Public Safety.

Each person appointed as a probation officer shall take an oath of office before the judge of the court or courts in which he is to serve, which oath shall be as follows:

"I, __________, do solemnly and sincerely swear that I will be faithful and bear true allegiance to the State of North Carolina, and to the constitutional powers and authorities which are or may be established for the government thereof; and that I will endeavor to support, maintain, and defend the Constitution of said State, not inconsistent with the Constitution of the United States, to the best of my knowledge and ability; so help me God,"

and shall be noted of record by the clerk of the court. (1937, c. 132, s. 8; 1973, c. 1262, s. 10; 2011-145, s. 19.1(h), (i); 2012-83, s. 23.)

§ 15-205. Duties and powers of the probation officers.

A probation officer shall investigate all cases referred to him for investigation by the judges of the courts or by the Secretary of Public Safety. Such officer shall keep informed concerning the conduct and condition of each person on probation under his supervision by visiting, requiring reports, and in other ways, and shall report thereon in writing as often as the court or the Secretary of Public Safety may require. Such officer shall use all practicable and suitable methods, not inconsistent with the conditions imposed by the court or the Secretary of Public Safety, to aid and encourage persons on probation to bring about improvement in their conduct and condition. Such officer shall keep detailed records of his work; shall make such reports in writing to the Secretary of Public Safety as he may require; and shall perform such other duties as the Secretary of Public Safety may require. A probation officer shall have, in the execution of his duties, the powers of arrest and, to the extent necessary for the performance of his duties, the same right to execute process as is now given, or that may hereafter be given by law, to the sheriffs of this State. (1937, c. 132, s. 9; 1973, c. 1262, s. 10; 1975, c. 229, s. 1; 1977, c. 711, s. 18; 2011-145, s. 19.1(h), (i); 2013-101, s. 3.)

§ 15-205.1. Repealed by Session Laws 1977, c. 711, s. 33.

§ 15-206. Cooperation with Division of Adult Correction of the Department of Public Safety and officials of local units.

It is hereby made the duty of every city, county, or State official or department to render all assistance and cooperation within the official's or the Department's fundamental power which may further the objects of this Article. The Division of Adult Correction of the Department of Public Safety, the Secretary of Public Safety, and the probation officers are authorized to seek the cooperation of such officials and departments, and especially of the county superintendents of social services and of the Department of Health and Human Services. (1937, c. 132, s. 10; 1961, c. 139, s. 2; 1969, c. 982; 1973, c. 476, s. 138; c. 1262, s. 10; 1997-443, s. 11A.118(a); 2011-145, ss. 19.1(h), (i); 2012-83, s. 24.)

§ 15-207. Records treated as privileged information.

All information and data obtained in the discharge of official duty by any probation officer shall be privileged information, shall not be receivable as evidence in any court, and shall not be disclosed directly or indirectly to any other than the judge or to others entitled under this Article to receive reports, unless and until otherwise ordered by a judge of the court or the Secretary of Public Safety. (1937, c. 132, s. 11; 1973, c. 1262, s. 10; 2011-145, s. 19.1(i).)

§ 15-208. Repealed by Session Laws 1975, c. 138.

§ 15-209. Accommodations for probation offices.

(a) The county commissioners in each county in which a probation office exists shall provide, in or near the courthouse, suitable office space for those probation officers assigned to the county who have probationary caseloads and their administrative support. This requirement does not include management staff of the Division of Adult Correction of the Department of Public Safety, nonprobation staff, or other Division of Adult Correction of the Department of Public Safety employees.

(b) If a county is unable to provide the space required under subsection (a) of this section for any reason, it may elect to request that the Division of Adult Correction of the Department of Public Safety lease space for the probation office and receive reimbursement from the county for the leased space. If a county fails to reimburse the Division for such leased space, the Secretary of Public Safety may request that the Administrative Office of the Courts transfer the unpaid amount to the Division from the county's court and jail facility fee remittances. (1937, c. 132, s. 13; 2009-451, s. 19.19; 2011-145, s. 19.1(h), (i).)

Article 21.
Segregation of Youthful Offenders.

§§ 15-210 through 15-216. Repealed by Session Laws 1967, c. 996, s. 17.

Article 22.
Review of Criminal Trials.

§ 15-217. Repealed by Session Laws 1977, c. 711, s. 33.

§ 15-217.1: Recodified as § 15A-1420(b1) by Session Laws 1995 (Regular Session, 1996), c. 719, s. 3.

§§ 15-218 through 15-222. Repealed by Session Laws 1977, c. 711, s. 33.

Article 23.
Expunction of Records.

§§ 15-223 through 15-224. Recodified as §§ 15A-145 and 15A-146 by Session Laws 1985, c. 636, s. 1, effective July 5, 1985.

Appendix C

North Carolina Department of Public Safety Alcohol Testing

SUBCHAPTER 41B – INJURY CONTROL

SECTION .0100 – GENERAL POLICIES

10A NCAC 41B .0101 DEFINITIONS

The definitions in G.S. 18B 101, G.S. 20 4.01, G.S. 130A 3 and the following shall apply throughout this Subchapter:

(1) "Alcoholic Breath Simulator" means a constant temperature water alcohol solution bath instrument devised for the purpose of providing a standard alcohol air mixture;

(2) "Breath testing Instrument" means an instrument for making a chemical analysis of breath and giving the resultant alcohol concentration in grams of alcohol per 210 liters of breath;

(3) "Controlled Drinking Program" means a bona fide scientific, experimental, educational, or demonstration program in which tests of a person's breath or blood are made for the purpose of determining his alcohol concentration when such person has consumed controlled amounts of alcohol;

(4) "Director" means the Director of the Division of Public Health of the Department;

(5) "Handling Alcoholic Beverages" means the acquisition, transportation, keeping in possession or custody, storage, administration, and disposition of alcoholic beverages done in connection with a controlled drinking program;

(6) "Observation Period" means a period during which a chemical analyst observes the person or persons to be tested to determine that the person or persons has not ingested alcohol or other fluids, regurgitated, vomited, eaten, or smoked in the 15 minutes immediately prior to the collection of a breath specimen. The chemical analyst may observe while conducting the operational procedures in using a breath testing instrument. Dental devices or oral jewelry need not be removed;

(7) "Permittee" means a chemical analyst possessing a valid permit from the Department to perform chemical analyses, of the type set forth within the permit;

(8) "Simulator Solution" means a water alcohol solution made by preparing a stock solution of distilled or American Society for Testing and Materials Type I water and 48.4 grams of alcohol per liter of solution. Each 10 ml. of this stock solution is further diluted to 500 ml. by adding distilled or American Society for Testing and Materials Type I water. The resulting simulator solution corresponds to the equivalent alcohol concentration of 0.08;

(9) "Verify Instrument Accuracy" means verification of instrumental accuracy of an approved breath testing instrument or approved alcohol screening test device by employment of a control sample from an alcoholic breath simulator using simulator solution and obtaining the expected result or 0.01 less than the expected result as specified in Item (8) of this Rule; or by employment of a control sample from an ethanol gas canister and obtaining the expected result or 0.01 less than the expected result as specified in Item (10) of this Rule. When the procedures set forth for approved breath testing instruments in Section .0300 of this Subchapter and for approved alcohol screening test devices in Section .0500 of this Subchapter are followed and the result specified herein is obtained, the instrument shall be deemed accurate;

(10) "Ethanol Gas Canister" means a dry gas calibrator producing an alcohol-in-inert gas sample at an accurately known concentration from a compressed gas cylinder. The resulting alcohol-in-inert gas sample corresponds to the equivalent concentration of 0.08.

History Note: *Authority G.S. 20 139.1(b); 20 139.1(g); Eff. February 1, 1976;*

Readopted Eff. December 5, 1977;
Amended Eff. November 1, 2007; April 1, 2001; January 1, 1995; January 4, 1994; October 1, 1990; September 1, 1990.

10A NCAC 41B .0102 CONSULTANT PANEL AND REVIEW BOARD FEES

History Note: *Authority G.S. 20-9; 143B-10;*
Eff. December 22, 1980;
Amended Eff. July 1, 2005; January 1, 1990; October 1, 1986;
Repealed Eff. November 1, 2005.

SECTION .0200 BLOOD ALCOHOL TEST REGULATIONS

10A NCAC 41B .0201 INITIAL PERMIT FOR BLOOD ANALYST

(a) Any person desiring an initial permit as a blood analyst shall make written application to the Director.

(b) In the application, the applicant shall set out his professional qualifications and experience and describe in detail the method intended to be used in performing chemical analyses of blood, the equipment and chemicals to be employed, the names and professional qualifications of any persons who will assist him in any of the incidental phases of the analyses to be made, and the location in and conditions under which the analyses shall be made. The Director shall prepare application forms to assist applicants in presenting the required information in an orderly fashion.

History Note: *Authority G.S. 20 139.1(b);*
Eff. February 1, 1976;
Readopted Eff. December 5, 1977.

10A NCAC 41B .0202 GRANTING PERMITS

(a) After receiving the application, the Director shall grant or deny permits to perform chemical analyses of the blood on the basis of his determination of the character and qualifications of the applicant and whether the method of chemical analysis proposed will be sufficiently reliable to meet generally accepted forensic standards.

(b) If from any application it appears that the chemical analysis of the blood will be done by persons under the supervision of the applicant, the Director shall require each person slated to perform chemical analyses of the blood to submit application. Where the Director is satisfied that the critical professional phases of the analysis will be performed by the applicant and that assistance from others will be incidental phases, he may grant the permit to the applicant.

(c) Permits granted under this Section shall be granted only to persons performing chemical analyses of blood for law enforcement officers under the provisions of G.S. 20 139.1. The Director may require such documentation or conduct such investigations as may be necessary to insure that applicants for initial or renewal permits meet this requirement before granting permits.

History Note: *Authority G.S. 20 139.1(b);*
Eff. February 1, 1976;
Readopted Eff. December 5, 1977;
Amended Eff. September 1, 1990; July 1, 1985; January 1, 1985.

10A NCAC 41B .0203 APPROVED PERMITS

(a) A blood analyst performing chemical analyses of blood in accordance with the description set out in the application for an initial, renewal, or modified permit shall be deemed to be performing such analyses in a manner approved by the Director.

(b) All initial, modified, and renewal permits shall be valid for a period of two years.

History Note: *Authority G.S. 20 139.1(b);*
Eff. February 1, 1976;
Readopted Eff. December 5, 1977;
Amended Eff. April 1, 1992; September 1, 1990; July 1, 1985.

10A NCAC 41B .0204 MODIFICATION OF PERMIT

Before making any material alteration in method or procedure for performing chemical analyses of blood, a blood analyst must be granted a modified permit from the Director. The provisions applicable for the granting of initial permits shall govern. When the blood analyst who holds a permit has assistants performing incidental phases of chemical analyses, replacement of these individuals with other assistants shall not be deemed a material alteration of procedure so long as any assistant has the same general qualifications and abilities as the person replaced.

History Note: *Authority G.S. 20 139.1(b);*
Eff. February 1, 1976;
Readopted Eff. December 5, 1977;
Amended Eff. September 1, 1990.

10A NCAC 41B .0205 RENEWAL OF PERMIT

(a) At least three months prior to the expiration of the permit, a blood analyst desiring to renew the permit must submit written application for renewal to the Director.
(b) The procedure applicable to the granting of initial applications shall govern the granting of renewal applications.

History Note: *Authority G.S. 20 139.1(b);*
Eff. February 1, 1976;
Readopted Eff. December 5, 1977;
Amended Eff. January 1, 1985.

10A NCAC 41B .0206 DETERMINATION OF RENEWAL OF PERMIT

(a) In determining whether to renew the permit of a blood analyst, the Director shall consider whether the method and procedure continues to meet the generally accepted forensic standards for chemical analyses of blood; he shall also take into account evidence available concerning the character and continuing ability of the blood analyst.
(b) If in acting upon an application for renewal of permit the Director returns the application for additional information, or requests a modification of method, so as to cause a delay in granting the renewal or modified permit, the Director at his discretion may grant the blood analyst a provisional permit under the conditions applicable to the expiring permit. A provisional permit shall be valid for the period stated in the permit, but shall not be issued for a period longer than three months. A provisional permit may be renewed once.

History Note: *Authority G.S. 20 139.1(b);*
Eff. February 1, 1976;
Readopted Eff. December 5, 1977;
Amended Eff. September 1, 1990; July 1, 1985.

10A NCAC 41B .0207 EVALUATION OF BLOOD ANALYSTS

The Director may institute a procedure for periodically testing the competence of blood analysts, which may include supervisory inspections of laboratories in which chemical analyses of blood are being performed.

History Note: *Authority G.S. 20 139.1(b);*
Eff. February 1, 1976;
Readopted Eff. December 5, 1977.

10A NCAC 41B .0208 REVOCATION OF PERMIT

(a) If the Director receives unfavorable information concerning the character or ability of any blood analyst, he shall direct an investigation to be made. If the Director becomes satisfied that the unfavorable information is accurate, and that the blood analyst would for this reason no longer be eligible to be granted an initial or renewal permit, he shall suspend or revoke the permit using the same procedures that are used for the suspension or revocation of permits in G.S. 130A 23.
(b) Appeals concerning the interpretation and enforcement of the rules in this Section shall be made in accordance with G.S. 150B.

History Note: *Authority G.S. 20 139.1(b);*
Eff. February 1, 1976;
Readopted Eff. December 5, 1977;
Amended Eff. September 1, 1990; December 1, 1987; April 1, 1987; January 1, 1982.

10A NCAC 41B .0209 REPORTING OF ALCOHOL CONCENTRATIONS BY BLOOD ANALYSTS

When performing chemical analyses of blood under the authority of G.S. 20 139.1 and the provisions of these rules, blood analysts shall report alcohol concentrations based on grams of alcohol per 100 milliliters of whole blood.

History Note: *Authority G.S. 20 139.1(b);*
Eff. October 1, 1986.

SECTION .0300 BREATH ALCOHOL TEST REGULATIONS

10A NCAC 41B .0301 APPLICATION FOR INITIAL PERMIT

(a) Application for an initial permit to perform chemical analysis of a person's breath to determine his alcohol concentration shall be made in writing to the Director. The applicant shall have the endorsement of his supervisor, or his supervisor's representative. The Director shall issue, deny, terminate, and revoke permits for individuals to perform chemical analyses.
(b) Permits shall be granted to individuals who:
    (1) demonstrate the ability to perform chemical analyses accurately and reliably;

(2) can explain the method of operation of the breath testing instrument for which he is applying for a permit to operate;
(3) provide a statement on the application from the applicant's supervisor attesting to the good character of the applicant; and
(4) are employed by a law enforcement agency, the Forensic Tests for Alcohol Branch or members of its instructional staff, or by some other federal, state, county or municipal agency with the responsibility of administering chemical analyses to drivers charged with implied consent offenses.

(c) Individuals successfully completing a minimum of 35 course hours conducted by the Forensic Tests for Alcohol Branch shall be deemed to have met the requirements of Subparagraphs (b)(1) and (2) of this Rule.

History Note: *Authority G.S. 20 139.1(b); Eff. January 1, 1982; Amended Eff. May 1, 2007; October 1, 1993; September 1, 1990; September 1, 1989; January 1, 1985.*

10A NCAC 41B .0302 LIMITATION OF PERMIT

(a) Permits shall be limited in scope to the methods or instruments for performing chemical analyses in which the individual applying for a permit has demonstrated competence. This limitation shall be upon the basis of the methods or instruments that received primary emphasis in the particular course of instruction attended by the applicant in the event that successful completion of the course is offered as proof of ability to perform chemical analyses. Initial and renewal permits shall state the date upon which they are to become effective and the date upon which they are to expire. The expiration date shall be no more than 24 months after the effective date.

(b) Permits granted under this Section, initial and renewals, shall be valid only during the period the permittee is employed by a law enforcement agency, the Forensic Tests for Alcohol Branch or a member of its instructional staff, or by some other federal, state, county or municipal agency with the responsibility of administering chemical analyses to drivers charged with implied consent offenses.

History Note: *Authority G.S. 20 139.1(b); Eff. January 1, 1982; Amended Eff. April 1, 2007; April 1, 1992; September 1, 1990; January 1, 1985; October 1, 1983.*

10A NCAC 41B .0303 RENEWAL OF PERMIT

The Director shall issue, deny, terminate, and revoke renewal permits for individuals to perform chemical analyses. Where there is a question on the need for a permit, the Director may require the individual to submit a written application for renewal. The applicant shall have the endorsement of his appropriate supervising law enforcement officer, or his designated representative, unless an exception is granted by the Director.

History Note: *Authority G.S. 20 139.1(b); Eff. January 1, 1982.*

10A NCAC 41B .0304 CONDITIONS FOR RENEWAL OF PERMIT

(a) Permits may be renewed at expiration, or at such time prior to expiration as is convenient for the Director, upon demonstration by the permittee of:
(1) continuing ability to perform accurate and reliable chemical analyses;
(2) ability to explain the method of operation of the breath testing instrument for which he is applying for a renewal permit to operate; and
(3) continued employment by a law enforcement agency, the Forensic Tests for Alcohol Branch or a member of its instructional staff, or by some other federal, state, county or municipal agency with the responsibility of administering chemical analyses to drivers charged with implied consent offenses.

(b) The permittee shall provide a statement on the application from the applicant's supervisor attesting to the good character of the applicant.

(c) Individuals successfully completing a forensic test for alcohol recertification course conducted by the Forensic Tests for Alcohol Branch prior to the expiration of their permits shall be deemed to have met the requirements of Subparagraphs (a)(1) and (2) of this Rule for the renewal of permits.

(d) In addition to meeting the requirements of Paragraph (a) of this Rule, individuals desiring renewal permits, after expiration of their permits, shall successfully complete the following Forensic Tests for Alcohol Branch course requirements prior to the granting of renewal permits:
(1) Forensic Tests for Alcohol Recertification Course if the permit has been expired less than six months;
(2) Forensic Tests for Alcohol Operators Course if the

permit has been expired six months or longer.

History Note: *Authority G.S. 20 139.1(b);*
Eff. January 1, 1982;
Amended Eff. May 1, 2007; October 1, 1993; April 1, 1992; September 1, 1990; September 1, 1989.

10A NCAC 41B .0305 RESERVED FOR FUTURE CODIFICATION

10A NCAC 41B .0306 TESTING OF EQUIPMENT

The Director or his representative shall have the authority to verify periodically the condition of all breath testing instruments used by permittees.

History Note: *Authority G.S. 20 139.1(b);*
Eff. January 1, 1982.

10A NCAC 41B .0307 EVALUATION OF PERMITTEES

The Director or his representative may at any time examine permittees to determine their continuing ability to perform accurate and reliable chemical analyses.

History Note: *Authority G.S. 20 139.1(b);*
Eff. January 1, 1982.

10A NCAC 41B .0308 REVOCATION OF PERMIT

(a) If the Director receives unfavorable information concerning the character or ability of any permittee, he shall direct an investigation to be made. If the Director determines, after investigation, that the permittee would no longer be eligible to be granted an initial or renewal permit, he shall suspend or revoke the permit using the same procedures that are used for suspension or revocation of permits in G.S. 130A 23.
(b) Appeals concerning the interpretation and enforcement of the Rules in this Section shall be made in accordance with G.S. 150B.

History Note: *Authority G.S. 20 139.1(b);*
Eff. January 1, 1982;
Amended Eff. September 1, 1990; December 1, 1987.

10A NCAC 41B .0309 QUALIFICATIONS OF MAINTENANCE PERSONNEL

History Note: *Authority; G.S. 20-139.1(b2);*
Eff. January 1, 1982;
Amended Eff. October 1, 1993; April 1, 1992; September 1, 1990; September 1, 1989;
Repealed Eff. May 1, 2007.

10A NCAC 41B .0310 RESERVED FOR FUTURE CODIFICATION

10A NCAC 41B .0311 LOG

History Note: *Authority G.S. 20 16.5(j); 20 139.1(b);*
Eff. January 1, 1982;
Amended Eff. April 1, 1992; October 1, 1990;
Repealed Eff. November 1, 2007.

10A NCAC 41B .0312 RESERVED FOR FUTURE CODIFICATION

10A NCAC 41B .0313 BREATH TESTING INSTRUMENTS: REPORTING OF SEQUENTIAL TESTS

The Department approves breath testing instruments listed on the National Highway Traffic Safety Administration, Conforming Products List of Evidential Breath Measurement Devices. Instruments are approved on the basis of results of evaluations by the Forensic Tests for Alcohol Branch. Evaluations are not limited in scope and may include any factors deemed appropriate to ensure the accuracy, reliability, stability, cost, and ease of operation and durability of the instrument being evaluated.

History Note: *Authority G.S. 20 16.5(j); 20 139.1(b);*
Eff. January 1, 1982;
Amended Eff. May 1, 2007; April 1, 1993; September 1, 1990; March 1, 1989; December 1, 1987.

10A NCAC 41B .0314 RESERVED FOR FUTURE CODIFICATION

10A NCAC 41B .0315 RESERVED FOR FUTURE CODIFICATION

10A NCAC 41B .0316 RESERVED FOR FUTURE CODIFICATION

10A NCAC 41B .0317 RESERVED FOR FUTURE CODIFICATION

10A NCAC 41B .0319 RESERVED FOR FUTURE CODIFICATION

10A NCAC 41B .0319 RESERVED FOR FUTURE CODIFICATION

10A NCAC 41B .0320 INTOXILYZER: MODEL 5000

The operational procedures to be followed in using the Intoxilyzer, Model 5000 are:

(1) Insure instrument displays time and date;
(2) Insure observation period requirements have been met;
(3) Press "START TEST"; when "INSERT CARD" appears, insert test record;
(4) Enter information as prompted;
(5) Verify instrument accuracy;
(6) When "PLEASE BLOW" appears, collect breath sample;
(7) When "PLEASE BLOW" appears, collect breath sample; and
(8) When test record ejects, remove.

If the alcohol concentrations differ by more than 0.02, a third breath sample shall be collected when "PLEASE BLOW" appears. Subsequent tests shall be administered as soon as feasible by repeating steps (1) through (8), as applicable.

History Note: Authority G.S. 20 139.1(b);
Eff. January 1, 1985;
Amended Eff. November 1, 2007; April 1, 2001; April 1, 1993; April 1, 1992; January 1, 1990; March 1, 1989.

10A NCAC 41B .0321 PREVENTIVE MAINTENANCE: INTOXILYZER: MODEL 5000

The preventive maintenance procedures for the Intoxilyzer Model 5000 to be followed at least once every four months are:

(1) Verify alcoholic breath simulator thermometer shows 34 degrees, plus or minus .2 degree centigrade;
(2) Verify instrument displays time and date;
(3) Press "START TEST"; when "INSERT CARD" appears, insert test record;
(4) Enter information as prompted;
(5) Verify instrument accuracy;
(6) When "PLEASE BLOW" appears, collect breath sample;
(7) When "PLEASE BLOW" appears, collect breath sample;
(8) When test record ejects, remove;
(9) Verify Diagnostic Program; and
(10) Verify alcoholic breath simulator solution is being changed every four months or after 125 Alcoholic Breath Simulator tests, whichever occurs first.

A signed original of the preventive maintenance record shall be kept on file for at least three years.

History Note: Authority G.S. 20 139.1(b)(b2);
Temporary Amendment Eff. September 1, 1989 for a period of 180 days to expire on February 28, 1990;
Eff. January 1, 1985;
Amended Eff November 1, 2007; April 1, 2001; April 1, 1993; April 1, 1992; January 1, 1990; March 1, 1989.

10A NCAC 41B .0322 INTOXIMETERS: MODEL INTOX EC/IR II

The operational procedures to be followed in using the Intoximeters, Model Intox EC/IR II are:

(1) Insure instrument displays time and date;
(2) Insure observation period requirements have been met;
(3) Initiate breath test sequence;
(4) Enter information as prompted;
(5) Verify instrument accuracy;
(6) When "PLEASE BLOW" appears, collect breath sample;
(7) When "PLEASE BLOW" appears, collect breath sample; and
(8) Print test record.

If the alcohol concentrations differ by more than 0.02, a third or fourth breath sample shall be collected when "PLEASE BLOW" appears. Subsequent tests shall be administered as soon as feasible by repeating steps (1) through (8), as applicable.

History Note: G.S. 20 139.1(b);
Eff. November 1, 2007.

10A NCAC 41B .0323 PREVENTIVE MAINTENANCE: INTOXIMETERS: MODEL INTOX EC/IR II

The preventive maintenance procedures for the Intoximeters, Model Intox EC/IR II to be followed at least once every four months are:

(1) Verify the ethanol gas canister displays pressure, or the alcoholic breath simulator thermometer shows 34 degrees, plus or minus .2 degree centigrade;

(2) Verify instrument displays time and date;
(3) Initiate breath test sequence;
(4) Enter information as prompted;
(5) Verify instrument accuracy;
(6) When "PLEASE BLOW" appears, collect breath sample;
(7) When "PLEASE BLOW" appears, collect breath sample;
(8) Print test record;
(9) Verify Diagnostic Program; and
(10) Verify that the ethanol gas canister is being changed before expiration date, or the alcoholic breath simulator solution is being changed every four months or after 125 Alcoholic Breath Simulator tests, whichever occurs first.

A signed original of the preventive maintenance record shall be kept on file for at least three years.

History Note: G.S. 20 139.1(b2);
Eff. November 1, 2007.

SECTION .0400 CONTROLLED DRINKING PROGRAMS

10A NCAC 41B .0401 APPLICATION OF REGULATIONS

(a) The regulations of this Section apply to the handling of alcoholic beverages in connection with one or a series of controlled drinking programs when any aspect of the handling would not be lawful except for the provisions of G.S. 20 139.1(g) and these regulations. If all aspects of the handling of alcoholic beverages in connection with one or a series of controlled drinking programs may be effected in accordance with North Carolina's laws and regulations of general application pertaining to the regulation of alcoholic beverages, compliance with these regulations is not necessary. In all events, governing provisions of federal law must be met in the handling of alcoholic beverages.
(b) Persons authorized to obtain and possess alcohol exempt from the taxes of the United States and of North Carolina may utilize such alcohol in controlled drinking programs to the extent authorized by law. Handling of such tax exempt alcohol shall not be governed by these regulations provided there is compliance with all the other applicable laws of the United States and of North Carolina.

History Note: Authority G.S. 20 139.1(g);
Eff. February 1, 1976;
Readopted Eff. December 5, 1977;
Amended Eff. January 1, 1982.

10A NCAC 41B .0402 AUTHORIZATION

(a) Any person may conduct a controlled drinking program without special authorization from the Director if such program is either under the supervision of a public agency or institution or presented with the participation of a public employee possessing a valid permit from the Director to perform chemical analyses of breath or blood and participation by the permittee has been authorized by his superiors.
(b) Any other person desiring to conduct a controlled drinking program under the authority of these regulations must apply for authorization from the Director. The Director may grant the authorization if it appears that the proposed controlled drinking program or series of programs will be conducted in a manner so as to minimize danger or annoyance to the public on the part of the drinking subjects and that the program or series of programs will in general further the bona fide objectives of the chemical testing programs within this state. Request for such authority shall be submitted so as to reach the Director at least 10 days prior to the proposed controlled drinking program or the initial program of a proposed series.

History Note: Authority G.S. 20 139.1(g);
Eff. February 1, 1976;
Readopted Eff. December 5, 1977;
Amended Eff. January 1, 1982.

10A NCAC 41B .0403 HANDLING ALCOHOLIC BEVERAGES

(a) Alcoholic beverage intended for use in a controlled drinking program authorized under these regulations shall be procured from alcoholic beverage control stores, from the North Carolina Alcoholic Beverage Control Commission, or from retail establishments duly licensed to sell wine or malt beverages. Each purchase shall be covered by a requisition, bill of sale, or other record evidence, showing the date, place of purchase, type of alcoholic beverage, and the quantity.
(b) An individual procuring alcoholic beverage for use in a controlled drinking program shall be of lawful age to buy alcoholic beverages.
(c) Alcoholic beverages required for use in a specific controlled drinking program shall be procured on the basis of estimated requirements and wherever feasible procured just prior to its use.

History Note: Authority G.S. 20 139.1(g);
Eff. February 1, 1976;
Readopted Eff. December 5, 1977;
Amended Eff. September 1, 1990; January 1, 1982.

10A NCAC 41B .0404 QUANTITY LIMITS

Any person handling alcoholic beverages in a manner consonant with the bona fide objectives of an authorized controlled drinking program may possess and transport such alcoholic beverage wherever necessary or desirable in furtherance of the objectives of the program within the quantity limits specified in this Rule. Any person handling alcohol beverages in conjunction with a controlled drinking program shall handle such beverages in accordance with G.S. 18B 303.

If the cap or seal on any container of alcoholic beverage has been opened or broken, such container may not be transported in the passenger area of a motor vehicle.

History Note: *Authority G.S. 20 139.1(g);*
Eff. February 1, 1976;
Readopted Eff. December 5, 1977;
Amended Eff. September 1, 1990; January 1, 1982.

10A NCAC 41B .0405 EXCESS OF QUANTITIES

(a) Any person responsible for the handling of alcoholic beverages in connection with an authorized controlled drinking program may procure, possess, and transport alcoholic beverages in excess of the quantities allowed by Rule .0404 of this Section provided the person or his employer holds a valid permit from the North Carolina Alcoholic Beverage Control Commission. Request for such a permit shall be forwarded to the Director, indicating the need for the permit, location of the testing program, the quantity and type alcoholic beverage to be procured and transported, and the name of the agency or individual to whom the permit should be issued.

(b) Where a series of controlled drinking programs are proposed, the request for the permit may generally state the nature, extent, and possible locations of such programs and the over all duration of the series. Permits shall not be valid for more than one year. The Director shall forward such requests to the North Carolina Alcoholic Beverage Control Commission with appropriate recommendations concerning the issuance of each permit.

History Note: *Authority G.S. 20 139.1(g);*
Eff. February 1, 1976;
Readopted Eff. December 5, 1977;
Amended Eff. September 1, 1990; January 1, 1982.

10A NCAC 41B .0406 RESTRICTED USE OF ALCOHOLIC BEVERAGES

(a) When not being used, all alcoholic beverages shall be stored in a safe place, if possible under lock and key.

(b) Alcoholic beverages procured for use in a controlled drinking program shall be used only for this purpose. Malt beverages, unfortified wine, fortified wine or spirituous liquor shall not be given or otherwise administered to anyone under 21 years of age.

(c) Any person, agency, or institution conducting a controlled drinking program is authorized to store such quantities of alcoholic beverages as may be required for the conduct of the program.

History Note: *Authority G.S. 20 139.1(g);*
Eff. February 1, 1976;
Readopted Eff. December 5, 1977;
Amended Eff. October 1, 1986; October 1, 1983; January 1, 1982.

10A NCAC 41B .0407 RECORDS

(a) Any person, agency, or institution acquiring alcoholic beverages for use in a controlled drinking program pursuant to these Rules shall keep records accounting for the disposition of all alcoholic beverages so acquired. Such records shall be made available for inspection upon the request of any federal or state law enforcement officer with jurisdiction over the laws relating to alcohol or alcoholic beverages.

(b) As a minimum, records on alcoholic beverages procured for use in controlled drinking programs will show the following:
   (1) the date, place, type, and quantity of alcoholic beverages procured;
   (2) the date and quantities of alcoholic beverages, by type, dispensed for controlled drinking purposes;
   (3) a running inventory, showing the quantity of each type alcoholic beverage on hand.

History Note: *Authority G.S. 20 139.1(g);*
Eff. February 1, 1976;
Readopted Eff. December 5, 1977;
Amended Eff. September 1, 1990; January 1, 1982.

SECTION .0500 ALCOHOL SCREENING TEST DEVICES

10A NCAC 41B .0501 SCREENING TESTS FOR ALCOHOL CONCENTRATION

(a) This Section governs the requirement of G.S. 20 16.3

that the Department examine devices suitable for use by law enforcement officers in making on the scene tests of drivers for alcohol concentration and that the Department approve these devices and their manner of use. In examining devices for making chemical analyses, the Department finds that at present only screening devices for testing the breath of drivers are suitable for on-the-scene use by law enforcement officers.

(b) This Section does not address or in any way restrict the use of screening tests for impairment other than those based on chemical analyses, including various psycho-physical tests for impairment.

History Note: *Authority G.S. 20 16.3; 20 16.3A;*
Eff. February 1, 1976;
Readopted Eff. December 5, 1977;
Amended Eff. April 1, 2007; October 1, 1993; October 1, 1983; January 1, 1982.

10A NCAC 41B .0502 APPROVAL: ALCOHOL SCREENING TEST DEVICES: USE

(a) Alcohol screening test devices that measure alcohol concentration through testing the breath of individuals are approved on the basis of results of evaluations by the Forensic Tests for Alcohol Branch. Devices shall meet the minimum requirements as set forth in the Department specifications for Alcohol Screening Test Devices. Evaluations are not limited in scope and may include any factors deemed appropriate to insure the accuracy, reliability, stability, cost, and ease of operation and durability of the device being evaluated. On the basis of evaluations to date, approved devices are listed in 10A NCAC 41B .0503 of this Section.

(b) When the validity of an alcohol screening test of the breath of a driver administered by a law enforcement officer depends upon approval by the Department of the test device and its manner of use, the test shall be administered as follows:

(1) The officer shall determine that the driver has removed all food, drink, tobacco products, chewing gum and other substances and objects from his mouth. Dental devices or oral jewelry need not be removed.

(2) Unless the driver volunteers the information that he has consumed an alcoholic beverage within the previous 15 minutes, the officer shall administer a screening test as soon as feasible. If a test made without observing a waiting period results in an alcohol concentration reading of 0.08 or more, the officer shall wait five minutes and administer an additional test. If the results of the additional test show an alcohol concentration reading more than 0.02 under the first reading, the officer shall disregard the first reading.

(3) The officer may request that the driver submit to one or more additional screening tests.

(4) In administering any screening test, the officer shall use an alcohol screening test device approved under 10A NCAC 41B .0503 of this Section in accordance with the operational instructions supplied by the Forensic Tests for Alcohol Branch and listed on the device.

History Note: *Authority G.S. 20 16.3;*
Eff. February 1, 1976;
Readopted Eff. December 5, 1977;
Amended Eff. April 1, 2007; April 1, 2001; September 1, 1990; January 1, 1990; October 1, 1983.

10A NCAC 41B .0503 APPROVED ALCOHOL SCREENING TEST DEVICES: CALIBRATION

(a) The following breath alcohol screening test devices are approved as to type and make:

(1) ALCO SENSOR (with two digit display), made by Intoximeters, Inc.

(2) ALCO SENSOR III (with three digit display), made by Intoximeters, Inc.

(3) ALCO SENSOR IV, manufactured by Intoximeters, Inc.

(4) ALCO-SENSOR FST, manufactured by Intoximeters, Inc.

(5) S-D2, manufactured by CMI, Inc.

(6) S-D5, manufactured by CMI, Inc.

(b) The agency or operator shall verify instrument calibration of each alcohol screening test device at least once during each 30 day period of use. The verification shall be performed by employment of an alcoholic breath simulator using simulator solution in accordance with the rules in this Section or an ethanol gas canister.

(c) Alcoholic breath simulators used exclusively to verify instrument calibration of alcohol screening test devices shall have the solution changed every 30 days or after 25 calibration tests, whichever occurs first.

(d) Ethanol gas canisters used exclusively to verify instrument calibration of alcohol screening test devices shall not be utilized beyond the expiration date on the canister.

(e) Requirements of Paragraphs (b), (c), and (d) of this Rule shall be recorded on an alcoholic breath simulator log or an ethanol gas canister log designed by the Forensic Tests for Alcohol Branch and maintained by the user agency.

History Note: *Authority G.S. 20 16.3;*
Eff. February 1, 1976;
Readopted Eff. December 5, 1977;
Amended Eff. July 1, 2007; November 1, 2005; April 1, 2001; January 1, 1995; January 4, 1994; April 1, 1993; January 4, 1993.

Appendix D

The Aging Process and Field Sobriety Tests

Mimi Coffey, Esq.

The Aging Process and Field Sobriety Tests

It is not surprising that every year 1.4 million Americans are diagnosed with cancer,[1] the second leading cause of death next to heart disease. It should be shocking that there are also approximately 1.4 million DWI/DUI arrests (1 of every 139 license drivers) in the country a year with 16,685 alcohol related fatalities in 2005.[2] "Alcohol related" fatalities defined as at least one driver or nonoccupant involved in the crash having a blood alcohol concentration of 0.01 grams per deciliter or higher. These figures include fatalities that were *NOT caused* by the presence of alcohol.[3] Boiled down, NHTSA has led a colossal campaign against DWI/DUI, arresting a disproportionate amount of people compared to the real threat of fatalities on the road (alcohol related fatalities representing 1 percent of the drivers being arrested). One does not need to be a mathematical genius to understand that this country has a problem, and it's not what MADD is concerned about.

The field sobriety tests are a mechanism to convict people not test whether or not they are sober. The standardized field sobriety tests are a witch-hunt cancer being perpetuated by law enforcement on our own people. Even a recent 2006 NHTSA publication admits, "Road tests have long been considered the gold standard for measuring driving ability. They have widely-recognized limitations."[4] One would not know this visiting the courtrooms across America. This paper addresses one of the most common sense problems contributing to false convictions, the condition and age of the subject.

Dr. Marcelline Burns, developer of the standardized field sobriety tests (SFSTs) has conceded that the tests were not designed to determine impairment of driving.[5] So what relevance do the SFST(s) have in determining whether or not a person is driving while intoxicated or driving while under the influence? Not much, particularly when you factor in their condition and age. It is well documented that the normal aging process is accompanied by deterioration in sensory functions and motor performance.[6] Sensory functions necessary in communication also show increased impairment with age.[7] Age-related slowing in cognitive and motor processes include longer reaction time and movement execution time. This is due to increased neural noise, which results in signals being less well detected in the central nervous system.[8] Before the SFSTs were developed, in the early decades of experimental psychology, it could already be shown that skill learning ability and motor performance accuracy deteriorate with increasing age.[9] The original SFST data seemed to take this in to account by setting 65 as the upper limit to SFST usefulness. Categorizing the effects of age chronologically as the SFST(s) do by stating a 65 year old age limit is both arbitrary and false. Aging actually results in increasing biologic diversity so that we become less alike as we age.[10] Biologic and chronologic ages are not the same, and body systems do not age at the same rate within an individual.[11] The bio-psychological state of a person is important, including most notably fitness and nutrition. It is empirically well supported that these factors improve attention and psychomotor performance across all age groups.[12] The National Highway Traffic and Safety Administration (NHTSA), much akin to their arbitrary cutoff, 65 years of age,[13] also references that an individual 50 lbs or more overweight may have difficulty with the one leg stand[14] test. Of relevance is the fact that 64.5 percent of Americans are overweight and 30.5 percent are obese.[15] Regarding physical fitness, the annual number of lives lost through physical inactivity is estimated at more than 250,000 per year.[16] With respect to the aging process there is a gradual decline in performance, as opposed to an abrupt drop off of cognitive and motor skills, as seen in the case of an acute stroke.[17] In short, a gradual decline in cognitive and motor processes results from chronological age, fitness, and nutrition in given individuals.

Changes within the brain are primarily responsible for a loss of motor skills. Poor performance on executive function tasks is associated with a smaller volume of prefrontal cortex mass and increased white matter hyperintensity burden.[18] Postmortem studies of individuals reveal age-related differences in brain structure including reduced brain weight and volume.[19] Sensory motor integration can be specifically linked to prefrontal activation of the brain, proving that the prefrontal cortex serves an executive function for motor skills. Age-related deterioration of the prefrontal cortex contributes to cognitive declines, which has significant consequences for motor behavior.[20] Simply put, the frontal lobes are more sensitive to the effects of and are directly related to motor functions.[21] Specifically, dopamine receptors within the brain are linked to locomotor functions and learning.[22] Dopamine neurons account for less than 1 percent of the total neuronal population of the brain but have a profound effect on motor function.[23] They act as chemical messengers similar to adrenaline connecting the brain processes that control movement.[24] Dopamine receptors are reduced up to 50 percent in the brains of aged humans.[25] Dopamine neurons in basal ganglia decline 5-10 percent per decade.[26] Parkinson's disease sufferers are a prime example of loss of control of motor activity in regards to dopamine neuron loss.[27] Early postmortem brain studies in the 1960s revealed significant loss of dopamine in Parkinson patients.[28] Treatments were developed with the aim of treating Parkinson's by addressing the prevention of dopamine[29] loss, or by stimulating the growth of dopamine receptors not natural in the human aging process.[30] Aging slows sensory processing, with 95 percent of the change attributable to aging of the central nervous system and only 5 percent attributable to slowing outside the brain.[31]

Declining hormone levels that occur naturally compound the effect of dopamine neuron loss. Several studies have shown that testosterone positively affects performance in certain cognitive domains such as memory and spatial ability.[32] In an academic study of men aged 48-80 it was shown that older men with less testosterone had lower levels of function in working memory, speed, and attention, as well as spatial relations. For men the use of synthetic hormones did not mediate the performance problem.[33] The same proving true for aged women in the administration of synthetic estrogen.[34] The average rate of decline of testosterone is about 3.2 ng/dL per year for men age 23-91,[35,36] and 11 ng/dL per year for men aged 61-87.

Memory of course becomes relevant under many scenarios of the DWI/DUI investigative process from short-term capacity that includes remembering instructions, to longer-term memory in cooperating with interrogations. The phenomenon of memory aging begins in the 20s among aging adults who report themselves in good health.[37] Aging memory affects us all, not just those with significant memory disorders such as Alzheimer's. In the periods of early and middle adulthood, the memory-aging phenomenon is associated with a shift of the entire distribution of memory. It is not simply attributable to a small percentage of individuals experiencing large memory loss due to pathology, with the remaining individuals maintaining the same level of performance.[38] With aging, there is a loss of neurons in the gray matter in the cerebellum and hippocampus, which seems to be involved in some aspects of memory function,[39] with less dramatic changes occurring in the deeper brain structures. In a study using a dual-task combination of walking and memorization it was revealed that older adults prioritized the sensorimotor brain function over the memory task to avoid a loss of balance, resulting in a performance decrease of the memory task.[40] This explains how the counting may suffer on various field sobriety tasks as the subject focuses more on the physical tasks of balance, regarding the walk and turn and one leg stand tests. There is a distinction in the memory regarding automated and effortful processing where the effects of aging increase the amount of effort required in the performance of new, unlearned or unnatural coordination patterns.[41] This explains why so many people perform a pivot on the walk and turn exercise versus taking a small series of steps. First, they do not comprehend the turn instructions well because of undue focus on the sensorimotor skills needed to maintain an unnatural and difficult positional stance. The turn itself is a new instruction on an unnatural turn pattern normally encountered in everyday settings. Older adults have much more difficulty with the performance of new tasks, albeit slight, due to the additional cognitive load that must be engaged for learning to occur.[42] Sensory memory lasts much less than a second and because of sensory changes that occur with aging this puts the aged at a disadvantage.[43] That explains why older people have much more difficulty in adjusting to the positional stance of the walk and turn, which requires a high level of sensorimotor control. Normally, this level of control is not required unless one is engaged in tightrope walking or gymnastics on the balance beam.

Clearly the SFST(s) are divided attention tests. It's known that the rate of shifting attention between different sources shows a clear-cut reduction with age.[44] A research project supported by a seed grant from the Center on Aging and Cognition demonstrated on a simple gripping test combined with recitation, that even after intense practice older adults needed more attentional resources than younger adults to perform a dual-task.[45] This proves that cognitive performance and force control are interconnected in older adults. In a dual-task bicycling and counting test where the subject had to bicycle in a certain direction and count the number of times an image appeared on a computer screen, it was found that performing the coordination patterns together with the attention task caused a decrease in phasing accuracy and stability in older versus younger people.[46] Driving is a divided attention task also but does not require the gravitational force control necessary in the one leg stand or memory number recitations to the degree called for in the walk and turn, one leg stand, or manual dexterity tests such as the finger count down. Older adults may experience temporary lapses of attention or executive control, which contributes to greater inconsistency of performance,[47] as seen in variations of the same field tests both at the roadside and in the station. Higher anxiety has also been associated with poorer divided attention performance in older but not younger adults.[48] Of course, basic psychomotor functions are required for a divided attention test, but basic too, is the premise that age-related changes in psychomotor functions will affect the performance scores.[49]

In a study involving 99 young people from ages 17 to 36, and 763 older people from ages 54-94 on a reaction time test, it was determined that variability between persons (diversity), variability within persons across tasks (dispersion) and variability within persons across time (inconsistency), were greater in older compared to younger adults even when group differences in speed were statistically controlled.[50] Studies contrasting younger and older adults have all found increased inconsistency in response time distributions with increasing age.[51]

It has been suggested that more studies need to be conducted in the field of experimental aging research to understand the effects of aging, anxiety and motor control.[52] An environmental stress study was conducted examining the performance of younger and older skilled miniature golf players during training and competition. Both younger and older adults showed a similar increase in heart rate and self reported anxiety, but whereas younger adults improved their performance during competitive play the older adults' deteriorated, demonstrating diminished capacity to cope with high arousal conditions due to age-related deficits in cognitive abilities.[53] This may be explained by the fact that aging is normally associated with neural degeneration in the hippocampus of the brain, which is critical for some forms of memory, and recent research suggests that anxiety and stress may have further detrimental effects on the hippocampus.[54]

Most DWIs/DUIs occur at night, also putting older people at a disadvantage. Across the adult lifespan there is a shift in the self-reported time of peak arousal or attention awareness. This shift reflects a tendency for the optimal time of day (TOD) to become earlier with advancing age.[55] Since the earliest days of experimental psychology it has been known that TOD can dramatically influence the efficiency of cognitive processing including short-term memory, sustained attention, inhibitory processing and semantic activation.[56] Age-related deficits of working memory are magnified at nonoptimal times of day.[57] It is undoubtedly obvious, that older subjects who have not been drinking at all will be disadvantaged compared to their younger counterparts. In an experiment regarding reaction time to a stop signal paradigm, there was a 20 percent difference in stopping efficiency between younger and older folks at nonoptimal times (11 percent difference at optimal times).[58]

Dizziness has been associated with stress. It is one of the most prominent symptoms of both panic attacks and hyperventilation.[59] As one grows older, however, the disturbances with balance are greater compared to younger people.[60] Of more notable concern is the fact that older people are less likely to view their dizzy condition as a self-perceived handicap.[61] People tend not to seek medical treatment for conditions associated with normal aging or ailments of which there are no known treatments. This is particularly true for dizziness. In a study of 100 consecutive outpatients in the United States with dizziness less than one-third received a diagnosis for which a treatment plan exists.[62] The symptomatic prevalence in the community for dizziness has been estimated at more than 20 percent, yet recorded annual consultation rates of less than 2 percent indicate this is a significant, silent, untreated problem.[63] The lifetime prevalence rate of dizziness of Americans resulting from outpatient self reports has been estimated at 25 percent.[64] What is alarming is the duration of dizzied impairment. In a London study of citizens aged 18 to 64, it was found that women were more likely to report dizziness than men; people under 36 were more likely to report nonhandicapping dizziness; and handicapping dizziness was significantly more common in individuals aged 36 to 64.[65] Of more concern is the duration of symptoms: 26 percent reported less than 6 months, 44 percent between 6 months and five years, and 30 percent more than five years.[66] More than half reported basic postural unsteadiness.[67] Dizziness is caused by both physical and psychological factors ranging from cardiovascular problems to anxiety.[68] Vertigo is episodic dizziness considered as an imbalance originating within the vestibular system.[69] It is interesting to note that several lines of research have suggested that dopamine has a protective role on cochlear[70] and vestibular function,[71] once again spotlighting dopamine's dramatic role of loss of executive motor control in the natural aging process.

Just to maintain a stance requires a greater portion of attentional resources in older compared to younger adults.[72] Postural stabilization has to do with the role of afferent/efferent signals related to eye movements.[73] Recent studies[74] have shown that postural sway during pursuit of a moving target or when looking straight ahead in the darkness is higher than when fixating on a stationary target or *nystagmus is suppressed.* In the latter two, extra-ocular signals are reduced,[75] resulting in less postural sway. Neck muscles are also involved in stabilizing the head during HGN; yet one's inability to keep one's head still is frequently used as a sign of intoxication or inability to follow directions. Horizontal gaze position is associated with head neck muscle activity. It is difficult to not move the head when focusing. In fixed head subjects there is a dynamic coupling of the neck splenius muscle, and horizontal eye position with the oculomotor brain command being distributed to both eye and neck muscles.[76] A moving platform experiment compared healthy young adults, older adults and older adults with a mild increase in fall risk. Participants were placed on a stationary platform under various conditions, and it was found that healthy older adults had considerable more difficulty maintaining balance both with and without the cognitive task of counting backwards.[77] Platform conditions varied with side-to-side and front to back movements simulating real-world conditions where one might be asked to perform the SFST(s) on inclined, or unleveled surfaces. It is preposterous that in the quest for more convictions, the recent NHTSA SFST manuals goes so far as to say, "Recent field validation studies have indicated that varying environmental conditions have not affected a suspect's ability to perform this test."[78] Motor control and postural control are inextricably linked.[79] If the surface area or testing conditions do not support basic postural control, performing a walk and turn or one leg stand test is inherently flawed. All motor tasks, unless performed while a subject is fully supported, require complex interactions of postural adjustments to maintain intersegmental coordination and equilibrium during the task.[80]

Although not a standardized test for DWI/DUI, in some jurisdictions the Romberg test is still administered. This is a medical test used to detect the presence of brain lesions, and is clearly inappropriate for forensic purposes. Police routinely use the test for sobriety testing purposes. The subject is asked to hold their head back, close their eyes and estimate the passage of 30 seconds. This test is skewed with or without alcohol or drugs because one's natural vestibular system sways to adjust for postural balance, becoming more pronounced with age. Head flexion or extension deteriorates postural stability as a result of vestibular input even where visual information is kept the same.[81]

The peripheral sensory functions of hearing and vision tend to show increased impairment with age, suffering remarkably after age 50.[82] Many visual changes accompany the aging process even in the absence of known visual pathology.[83] Among these changes that normal adults exhibit is a loss of contrast sensitivity,[84] shrinkage of the "useful field of view" (UFOV),[85] a decrease in central and peripheral acuity,[86] spatial vision,[87] and a weakening of the cognitive control of eye movements.[88] Translated to the real world practicality of HGN, older adults have difficulty converging their eyes to focus on a target at a close distance.[89] As far as lack of smooth pursuit, older adults are less able to smoothly pursue a moving stimulus.[90] Tracking an object shows clear-cut age deficits.[91] Following the stimulus in general is more difficult because reaction time in dealing with visuo-spatial tasks has been proven to slow for older adults.[92] Age differences in oculomotor control translate to saccadic movements (lack of smooth pursuit), which have greater latency and slower peak velocity.[93]

One might argue that the ultimate test in a DWI/DUI investigation is the actual operation of a motor vehicle with vehicle accidents reflecting intoxication. As there are obvious reasons for accidents outside of intoxication, it is important to note age-related concerns in automobile accidents. One age-related analysis of traffic accidents in Finland showed that attention fatigue is a drastic factor in traffic accidents.[94] Most DWI/DUIs are not occurring at optimal TOD for older people. One's useful field of view (UFOV), which diminishes with age, also turns out to be a good predictor of increased driving accidents.[95]

Age-related hearing loss (AHL) is the most common type of hearing impairment in humans.[96] 60 percent of people older than 70 years of age have hearing loss of at least 25 decibels[97] the prevalence of hearing loss among middle-aged people are not well known. In a comprehensive study of hearing loss in Beaver Dam, Wisconsin, of people aged 48-92, 46 percent had some form of hearing loss.[98] It was found that for every 5 years of age the risk of hearing loss increased by almost 90 percent with men being 4 times more likely to have hearing loss than women.[99] Education and income level were inversely associated; with people who had not completed high school being 2.42 times more likely to suffer hearing loss compared to those with a college education.[100] Those earning less than $30k a year were approximately twice as likely as those earning $60k a year to suffer hearing loss largely due to occupational exposure.[101] Hearing impairment increases with age. The most common hearing loss occurs at higher frequencies making speech especially difficult to understand against background noise,[102] like the roadside noise of a typical DWI/DUI setting. Temporal resolution is necessary to distinguish the background noise in everyday listening situations.[103] The precedence effect refers to the finding that short onset-to-onset stimulus delays and leading and lagging sounds will perceptually fuse into a single auditory image.[104] Even older people with normal hearing sensitivity perform more poorly than younger listeners on a precedence-effect task.[105] Both temporal resolution and the precedence effect deteriorate with age and hearing loss, with temporal resolution more closely associated with age than hearing loss.[106] We are all born with a set of sensory cells and at about age 18 we slowly start to lose them.[107] AHL is also known as presbycusis, or a decrease in hearing loss. Because presbycusis progresses slowly most people do not notice changes until well after age 50.[108] According to the National Institute on Deafness and other Communication Disorders (NIDCD), presbycusis usually affects both ears equally.[109] As people age, structures of the ear become less responsive to sound waves contributing to hearing loss.[110] More specifically, there is a progressive degeneration of the cochlea's sensory cells and spinal ganglion cells with the outer hair cells the most severely affected.[111] There are strong psychosocial concerns and consequences due to people not wanting to obtain hearing aids. One study, which addresses the stigma, estimated only 8 percent of an elderly population who could benefit from hearing devices requested one after an audiologic evaluation.[112] Considering the fact that the walk and turn test is not fully demonstrated to 9 steps, people who suffer temporal resolution even without hearing loss as well as those with hearing loss may miss the important instruction of taking only 9 as opposed to 10 steps making them appear intoxicated. A subject is not asked to repeat the instructions on the SFST(s) only that they are understood.

The walk and turn is a tightrope exercise requiring an unnatural coordination of muscles and balance. By the time one is aged 60, maximum muscular force is reduced by about 50 percent and the maximum movement speed up to 90 percent.[113] There are both automatic and effortful processes involved in movement control.[114] When it comes to walking, healthy older people select strategies that maximize stability when balance is perturbed.[115] For example, in a test where older people were asked to walk a figure 8, in order to maintain balance they shortened their steps.[116] Normal age-related decline in leg strength may be the primary limiting factor that prevents older people from walking at an equivalent speed to younger people.[117] Differences of walk are even more pronounced between older and younger people when walking on irregular surfaces.[118] Just general differences of gait between a younger officer and an older citizen on video reflect age-related declines in body systems, and yet are deceptively portrayed as signs of a slowed central nervous system due to alcohol or other depressants. In a walking coordination stability test comparing older and younger adults, it was proven that along with poorer visual acuity, contrast sensitivity, depth perception and vibration sense, older people also had less ankle dorsiflexion and quadriceps strength for walking.[119] We know that elderly people show a significant decrease in both cutaneous vibratory and joint sensations[120] essential for walking and limb coordination. The attentional cost associated with gait by means of dual-task paradigms have revealed that this common task requires a greater portion of attentional resources in older as compared to younger adults.[121] This reflects the essential fact that older brains need to recruit additional resources to manage executive functions of otherwise relatively simple tasks.[122]

Miscounting is often offered up as a sign of intoxication or the loss of the normal use of one's mental faculties. Although it is not a technical clue on the SFST guidelines, optional tests routinely used by officers such as the finger countdown or hand slap test, penalize a citizen for miscounting. In an exercise where the subject, while attempting to maintain balance on a moving platform, was asked to count backwards in threes starting from random numbers with no alcohol or drugs involved, out of 20 younger adults the average number of correct counting responses was 12.5 ± 2.9, and for 20 older adults it was 9.8 ± 2.6.[123] Recent brain imaging data has shown that during performance of repetitive finger or wrist movements, the aging brain must recruit additional sensorimotor regions.[124] In this way, age-related proprioceptive processing deficits compromise motor functions for which sensory information is of critical importance.[125]

Regarding the one leg stand, a study in two British towns administered the one leg stand to 70 participants upon leaving a bar or nightclub. The majority of those tested ranged in age from 18 to 36 (therefore not even inclusive of the older aged population) with only 23 deemed under the influence of alcohol or a drug, it was determined that the majority of people failed the one leg stand making it an unfit test to determine impairment.[126] In a massive research project conducted at the Center for Clinical and Lifestyle Research in late 1994 and 1995, involving tests on 349 men and women by Dr. James M. Rippe, M.D. the "Advil Fit over Forty" standards were developed. These standards have since been presented at a variety of national scientific and medical meetings including: The American College of Sports Medicine; The American Heart Association; and the Gerontological Society of America.[127] Interestingly enough, one of the tests in which a person can assess their health in terms of fitness and balance is the one leg stand test, in which a person merely lifts a leg (simpler than the SFST one leg stand test where one lifts and holds out their leg) for a timed 30 seconds. The following is based on a chart[128] that gauges one's level of fitness clearly indicating that the rigid grading criteria of the one leg stand is ludicrous. In the Fit Over Forty book by Dr. James M. Rippe, there is an enlightening chart on page 32 which includes among other things what would be considered average for holding one's leg back for middle aged people. Surprisingly enough woman in their 40s are considered average if they can hold their foot up in between 7.2-15.5 seconds. For corresponding males it is in between 4.1-14.7 seconds. This is a far cry from NHTSA's claim that a BAC can hold up their foot for 25 seconds but seldom 30.

In one analysis of the SFST(s) using data over a four-state area from 1986-1993, it was found that there was a significant trend toward decreased sensitivity with increasing driver age over 44 years,[129] sharply contrasting with NHTSA's 65 years of age. This study referenced some of the misclassification "to be a result of aging,"[130] and yet it is perilous and ignorant to associate aging by a mere chronological index. When evaluating the walk and turn and one leg stand tests overall, 50 percent of doctors in Strathclyde Scotland consulted in a law enforcement study expressed concerns that the tests were inappropriate for use in determining sobriety regardless of age.[131] The physicians with postgraduate qualifications were significantly more concerned about the tests than doctors without postgraduate qualifications.[132] The problem with the widespread promulgation of SFST(s) in the alcohol and drug arena by U.S. NHTSA-related psychologists, is the lack of true scientific reliability as opposed to purported self-serving statistics, which amount to "face validity." In a study analyzing a sample of 38 papers from 16 journals covering all the major drug types from 1972 to 1988 no papers were found to have documented true scientific reliability or validity.[133] Although Dr. Marcelline Burns has been widely quoted in her 1995 study, which claims "validation" for the SFST test battery, the validity of these tests has been questioned.[134] It is no different than the problem with the DRE validation: "It has to be acknowledged the author of the initial studies which tended to validate the DRE program, was intimately associated with the DRE protocol and involved in the L.A. test which 'touted' the DRE accuracy."[135] It has been published in the peer reviewed journal: the *Journal of Clinical Forensic Medicine*, that "No evidence has been presented that there is any correlation between a person's performance on any aspect of the battery of tests used in FIT (field impairment testing, SFST(s) in the United States) and that person's ability to drive. It is our belief that the use of these tests has led, and will continue to lead, to the arrest and conviction of motorists whose only crime is that they cannot 'pass' the FIT procedures."[136] The Association of Forensic Physicians has gone on record stating, "Field Impairment Testing (FIT) as currently performed in the UK has NOT been validated and there is increasing anecdotal evidence that errors of interpretation are being made which could lead to wrongful convictions."[137] Put simply, the problems with SFST(s) are that they only account for one variable: the person's performance at the time of testing, without accounting for any other variables. An experimental design systematically manipulates independent variables to discover their effects on dependent variables.[138] To attribute cause and effect correctly, all other variables must be controlled, usually by eliminating those that can't be eliminated, counterbalancing those that cannot, or measuring those that cannot be eliminated or counterbalanced.[139] The problem with the SFST(s) is that the variables such as age and pathology are not accounted for. Variables that are not accounted for can confound the results in the psychometrics of testing making it impossible to distinguish which variable has caused which effect.[140] The SFST(s) are an incorrect testing matrix by design. Any psychological test should be valid, reliable, and sensitive in that it should measure what it purports to measure, do so consistently, and be capable in basic design of detecting changes in what it measures.[141] Although these principles are commonly applied in areas of psychology such as personality, intelligence, and clinical occupational testing, they are rarely applied to performance assessment and hardly at all in the assessment of drugs on performance,[142] as can be seen with the SFST(s).

As we age, the rate of decline is intraindividual.[143] Individuals become less alike as a function of differences in change.[144] Age-related decreases in performance and increasing intraindividual variability in neurobiological mechanisms in the brain, drive increases in interindividual differences in performance.[145] Due to the fact that aging is a gradual process and most studies focus on the differences between the elderly and young populations, it is necessary to extrapolate across the ages that the physiologic decay of the body occurs over time. Middle-aged people largely reflect the biologic changes that produce chronic degeneration affecting the body systems. Hypertension (high blood pressure) is one of the most chronic conditions for men and women over the age of 40 with 1 out of every 3 Americans suffering this condition.[146] Blood pressure affects circulation within the brain, so vital to dopamine receptor health. High blood pressure has even been judicially recognized as a known cause for HGN.[147] In terms of circulation health, vital for good brain function, it is known that by the time a man is 50 years of age in the U.S., he has over a 30 percent chance of having coronary artery disease and by age 60, a 20 percent chance he has suffered a heart attack.[148] One of every four people over age 50 suffer from arthritis,[149] which of course has obvious implications on the walk and turn and one leg stand tests. Even one's ability to go to the bathroom (as sometimes commented on by police officers in DWI/DUI cases) is significantly affected by aging, as the kidney function of an average 70 year old is approximately 50 percent of an average 30 year old.[150]

In conclusion, age and the consumption of alcohol has its benefits. It has been widely recognized by the medical community that alcohol decreases the risk of heart disease by raising the level of healthy HDL cholesterol in one's blood.[151] Alcohol in the form of flavinoids, common in red wine, has also been proven to impede blood clots, which form in heart attacks.[152] It is pretty reasonable to assume that alcohol ingestion and driving are issues that shall continue to present themselves; the scientific and law community owe it to society to address the grave injustices currently employed in assessing whether or not one has operated a vehicle while intoxicated or impaired.

Endnotes

1. Denise Grady, *Cancer Patients, Lost in a Maze of Uneven Care*, New York Times, www.nytimes.com, (July 29, 2007).

2. NHTSA, DOT HS 810616, *Alcohol-Related Crashes and Fatalities*, Traffic Safety Facts, www.nhtsa.gov, (2005)

3. *See Id.*

4. NHTSA, DOT F 1700.7, *Identifying Strategies to Study Drug Usage and Driving Functioning Among Older Drivers*, Final Report of Polypharmacy and Older Drivers, www.nhtsa.gov, 1-89, (December 2006).

5. Lori Raye *Court Reporters, Examination under Oath of Marcelline Burns*, 1-62, (April 17 1998).

6. Sofie Heuninckx, Filiep Debaere, Nicole Wenderoth, Sabine Verschueren, and Stephan P. Swinnen, *Ipsilateral Coordination Deficits and Central Processing Requirements Associated With Coordination as a Function of Aging*, 59B J. of Gerontology 5, 225, (2004).

7. *See infra* note 9 at 465.

8. Deborah J. Serrien, Stephan P. Swinnen, and George E. Stelmach, *Age-Related Deterioration of Coordinated Interlimb Behavior,* 55B J. of Gerontology 5, 295, (2000).

9. Konrad Wolfgang Kallus, Jeroen A.J. Schmitt, and David Benton, *Attention, Psychomotor Functions and Age,* Eur J. Nur, 2005, 44, at 469.

    1. Source Cited: Thorndike EL, Bergman EO, Tilton J, and Woodyard E, *Adult Learning*, (1928), Oxford England.

10. Mark E. Williams M.D., *The American Geriatrics Society's Complete Guide to Aging and Health*, Harmony Books, NY, © by the Geriatrics Society, at 15, (1995)

11. *See Id.* at 14.

12. *See supra* note 9 at 482.

13. NHSTA, *DWI Detection and Standardized Field Sobriety Testing*, Participant Manual, (2004), re: WAT at VIII-11, re: OLS at VIII-14.

14. *See Id.* re: 50lbs, at VIII-14.

15. Dixie L Thompson, Jennifer Rakow, and Sara M. Perdue, *Relationship between Accumulated Walking and Body Composition in Middle-Aged Women*, Official J. of the American College of Sports Medicine, at 914, (Jan. 2004).

    1. Source Cited: Flegal K, M Carroll, C Ogden, and C Johnson, *Prevalence and trends in obesity among US adults*, 1999-2000, JAMA 288, 1723-27, (2002).

16. Ross C. Brownson PhD, Amy A Eyler PhD, Abby C. King PhD, David R. Brown PhD, Yuh-Ling Shyu MSW, and James F, Sallis PhD, *Patterns and Correlates of Physical Activity Among US Women 40 Years and Older*, 90 American Journal of Public Health 2, 264, (Feb. 2000).

    1. Source Cited: Powell KE, and Blair SN, *The public health burden of sedentary living habits: theoretical but realistic estimates*, *Med Sci Sports Exerc* 26, 851-56, (1994).

17. Joanna E. Condron BSc (Hons), and Keith D. Hill PhD Grad Dip Physio BappSc (Physio), *Reliability and Validity of Dual-Task Force Platform Assessment of Balance Performance: Effect of Age, Balance Impairment and Cognitive Task*, 50 J. of the American Geriatrics Society 1, 161.

18. Naftali Raz and Karen M. Rodrigue, *Differential aging of the brain: Patterns, cognitive correlates and modifiers*, Neuroscience and Biobehavioral Reviews, , 741, (2006).

19. *See Id.* at 731

20. *See supra* note 8 at 302.

21. Shannon Robertson, Joel Myerson, and Sandra Hale, *Are There Age Differences in Intraindividual Variability in Working Memory Performance?*, 61B J. of Gerontology 1, 18, (2006).

22. Charles A. Marsden, *Dopamine: the rewarding years*, British J. of Pharmacology, 140, (2006).

23. *See Id.* at 136.

24. *See supra* note 9 at 468

25. *See Id.* at 468.

    1. Source Cited: Rinne JO, Lonnberg P, and Marjamaki P, *Age-dependent decline in human brain dopamine D1 and D2 receptors*, 508 Brain Research 2, 349-52, (1990).

26. *See Id.* at 468.

    1. Source Cited: Naoi M, and Maruyama W, *Cell death of dopamine neurons in aging and Parkinson's disease*, Mech Aging 111 (2-3), 175-88, (1999).

27. Jackalina M. Van Kampen and Christopher B. Eckman, *Dopamine D3 Receptor Agonist Delivery to a Model of Parkinson's Disease Restores the Nigrostriatal Pathway and Improves Locomotor Behavior*, 26 Journal of Neuroscience 2, at 7272, (July 5, 2006).

28. *See supra* note 22 at 137.

29. *See supra* note 22.

30. *See supra* note 27 at 7273.

    1. "Interesting to note, rats injected with a form of methamphetamine showed restoration of dopaminergic nigrostriatal circuits." Baker SA, Baker KA, and Hagg T, *Dopaminergic* nigrostriatal projections regulate neural precursor cell proliferation in the adult *mouse subventricular zone, Eur J Neurosci* 20, 575-79, (2004).

31. *See supra* note 10 at 32.

32. Stephanie J. Fonda, Rosanna Bertrand, Amy O' Donnell, Christopher Longcope, and John B. McKinlay, *Age Hormones, and Cognitive Functioning Among Middle-Aged and Elderly Men: Cross-Sectional Evidence From Massachusetts Male Aging*, The Journal of Gerontology Series A: Biological Sciences and Medical Sciences 60, at 385, (2005).

33. *See Id.* at 388.

34. *See Id.* at 388.

    1. Source Cited: Janowsky JS, Oviatt SK, and Orwoll ES, Testosterone influences spatial cognition in older men 108, 325-32, (1994).

35. *See Id.* at 387.

    1. Source Cited: Harman SM, Metter JE, Tobin JD, Pearson J, and Blackman MR, *Longitudinal effects of aging on serum total and free testosterone levels in healthy men*, *J Clin Endocrinal Metab*, 86, 724-3, (2001).

36. *See Id.* at 387.

    1. Source Cited: Morley JE, Kaiser FE, and Perry HM 3rd, et al, *Longitudinal changes in testosterone, luteinizing hormone, and follicle-stimulating hormone in healthy older men*, *Metabolism* 46, 410-3, (1997).

37. Timothy A Salthouse PhD, *Memory Aging from 18 to 80*, 17 Alzheimer Disease Association Disorder 13, 166, (July-September 2003).

38. *See Id.* at 166.

39. *See supra* note 10 at 23.

40. *See supra* note 6 at 230.

    1. Study Cited: Li KZ, Lindenberger U, Freund AM, and Baltes PB, *Walking while memorizing: age-related differences in compensatory behavior*, *Psychological Science* 12, 230-37, (2001).

41. Laurie R. Wishart, Timothy D. Lee, Jason E. Murdoch, and Nicola J. Hodges, *Effects of Aging on Automatic and Effortful Process in Bimanual Coordination*, 55B J. of Gerontology 2, at 93, (2000).

42. *See Id.* at 93.

43. *See supra* note 10 at 35.

44. *See supra* note 9 at 468.

    1. Source Cited: Greenwood PM, and Parasutaman R, Scale of attentional focus in visual search, 61 Percept Psychophys 5, 837-59, (1999).

45. Claudia Voelcker-Rehage and Jay L. Alberts, *Effect of Motor Practice on Dual-Task Performance in Older Adults*, 62B Journal of Gerontology 3, at 147, (2007).

46. *See supra* note 6 at 230.

47. *See supra* note 16 at 112.

48. Michael J. Hogan, *Divided Attention in Older But Not Younger Adults Is Impaired by Anxiety*, Experimental Aging Research, at 111, (2003).

49. *See supra* note 9 at 463.

50. David F. Hultsch, Stuart W.S. MacDonald, and Roger A. Dixon, *Variability in Reaction Time Performance of Younger and Older Adults*, 57B J. of Gerontology 2, 101, (2002).

51. *See Id.* at 102.

52. *See supra* note 48 at 133.

53. *See Id.* at 113.

    1. Backman L, and Molander B, *On the generalizability of the age-related decline in coping with high-arousal conditions in a precision sport: replication and extension, Journal of Gerontology: Psychological Sciences* 46, 79-81, (1991).

54. *See Id.* at 133.

    1. Gurvits TG, Shenton MR, Hokama H, Ohta H, Lasko NB, Gilbertson MW, Orr SP, Kikinis R, Lasko FA, McCarley RW, and Pitman RK, *Magnetic resonance imaging study of hippocampal volume in chronic combat-related posttraumatic stress disorder*, *Biological Psychiatry* 40, 192-99, (1996).

55. Robert West, Kelly J. Murphy, Maria L. Armilio, Fergus I.M. Craik, and Donald T. Stuss, *Effects of Time on Age Differences in Working Memory*, 57B J. of Gerontology 1, at 3, (2002).

56. *See Id.* at 3.

57. *See Id.* at 4.

58. *See Id.* at 3.

    1. May CP, and Hasher L, *Synchrony effects in inhibitory control over thought and action*, *J. of Experimental Psychological Science* 24, 363-79, (1998).

59. Lucy Yardley, Natalie Owen, Irwin Nazareth, and Linda Luxon, *Prevalence and presentation of dizziness in a general practice community sample of working age people*, British J. of General Practice 48, at 1134, (1998).

60. Eva Ekvall Hånsson, Nils-Ove Månsson, and Anders Håkansson, *Balance performance and self-perceived handicap among dizzy patients in primary health care*, Scandinavian Journal of Primary Health care 23, at 215, (2005).

61. *See Id.* at 215.

62. *See supra* note 59 at 1134.

    1. Kroenke K, Lucas CA, and Rosenberg ML, *et al*, *Causes of persistent dizziness: a prospective study of 100 patients in ambulatory care*, *Ann Intern Med* 117, 898-904, (1992).

63. *See Id.* at 1134.

64. *See Id.* at 1131.

65. *See Id.* at 1133.

66. *See Id.* at 1133.

67. *See Id.* at 1133.

68. *See Id.* at 1131.

69. Kathleen C Horner PhD, Régis Guieu MD, Jacques Magnan MD, André Chays MD, and Yves Cazals PhD, *Prolactinoma in Some Ménière's Patients- Is Stress Involved?*, 26 Neuropychopharmacology 1, 135, (2002).

70. *See Id.* at 138.

    1. Study Cited: Eybalin M, *Neurotransmitters and neuromodulators of the mammalian cochlea*, Physiol Rev 73, 309-73, (1993).

71. *See Id.* at 138.

    1. Study Cited: Petrosini L, and Dell'Anna ME, *Vestibular Compensation is affected by treatment with dopamine active agents*, Arch Ital Biol 131, 159-71.

72. *See supra* note 6 at 225.

    1. Study Cited: Woollacott M, and Shumway-Cook A, *Attention and the control of posture and gait: A review of an emerging area of research*, *Gait and Posture*, 16, 1-14.

73. Zoï Kapoula, and Thanh-Thuan Lê, *Effects of distance and gaze position on postural stability in young and old subjects*, Exp Brain Res 173, 442, (2006).

74. *See Id.* at 442.

1. Study Cited: Brandt T, Paulus W, and Strube A, *Vision and Posture*, In: Bless W, Brandt T (eds) Disorders of posture, Elsewier, Amsterdam, 157-75.

2. Study Cited: Jahn K, Strupp M, Krafczyk S, Schuler O, Glasauer S, and Brandt T, Suppression of eye movement improves balance, Brain 125 (pt 9), 2005-2011, (2002).

3. Study Cited: Strupp M, Glasauer S, Jahn K, Schneider E, Krafczyk S, and Brandt T, *Eye movements and balance*, Ann NY Acad Sci 1004, 352-58, (2003).

4. Study Cited: Glasauer S, Schneider E, Jahn K, Strupp M, Brandy T, *How the eyes move the body* 65(8), 1291-93,(2005).

75. *See Id.* at 442.

76. *See Id.* at 442.

1. Study Cited: André-Deshays C, Berthoz A, and Revel M, *Eye-head coupling in humans*, I. Simultaneous recording of isolated motor units in dorsal neck muscles and horizontal eye movements, 69 Exp Brain Res 2, 399-406, (1998).

2. Study Cited: André-Deshays C, Revel M, and Berthoz A, *Eye-head coupling in humans*, II. Phasic components, 84 Exp Brain Res 2, 359-66, (1991).

77. *See supra* note 17 at 157.

78. *See supra* note 13 at VIII-11.

79. Nataliya Shkuratova BPht, Meg E Morris PhD, and Frances Huxham DipPT, *Effects of Age on Balance Control During Walking*, 85 Archives of Physical Medicine and Rehabilitation 4, 582, (April 2004).

80. *See Id.* at 582.

81. *See supra* note 73 at 443.

82. *See supra* note 9 at 465.

83. Charles T Scialfa, *Static and Dynamic Visual Sensitivity in Older Adults*, 30 Canadian Psychology/Psychologie Canadienne 4, at 703, (Oct 1989).

84. *See Id.* at 703.

85. *See supra* note 9 at 467.

86. Jochen Laubrock, Reinhold Kliegl, and Ralf Engbert, *SWIFT explorations of age differences in eye movements during reading*, Neuroscience and Biobehavioral Reviews 30, at 873, (2006).

87. *See supra* note 83 at 703.

88. *See supra* note 81 at 879.

89. *See supra* note 73 at 439.

90. *See supra* note 83 at 703.

91. *See supra* note 9 at 469.

92. K Dujardin, JL Bourriez, and JD Guieu, *Event-related desynchronization (ERD) patterns during memory processes: effects of aging and task difficulty*, Electroencephalography and clinical Neurophysiology 96, 181, (1995).

93. *See supra* note 86 at 874.

94. *See supra* note 9 at 466.

1. Source Cited: Summala H and MikkolaT, *Fatal accidents among car and truck drivers: effects of fatigue, age and alcohol consumption*, 36 Hum Factors 2, 315-26, (1994).

95. *See Id.* at 467.

1. Source Cited: Sekuler AB, Bennett PJ, and Mamelak M, *Effects of aging on the useful field of view*, 26 Exp Aging Res 2, 103-20, (1994).

96. Michael Anne Gratton and Ana Elena Vázquez, *Age-related hearing loss: current research*, Current Opinion Otolaryngology and Head and Neck Surgery 11, at 367, (2003).

97. *See Id.* at 367.

98. Karen J Cruickshanks, Terry L Wiley, Theodore S Tweed, Barbara EK Klein, Ronald Klein, Julie A Mares-Periman, and David M Nondahl, *Prevalence of Hearing Loss in Older Adults in Beaver Dam, Wisconsin*, 148 American Journal of Epidemiology 9, at 882.

99. *See Id.* at 881.

100. *See Id.* at 881.

101. *See Id.* at 881.

102. Margaret I Wallhagen PhD RN CS, William J Strawbridge PhD, Richard D Cohen MA, and George A Kaplan PhD, *An Increasing Prevalence of Hearing Impairment and Associated Risk Factors over Three Decades of the Alameda County Study*, 87 American J. of Public Health 3, at 440, (March 1997).

103. Richard A Roberts and Jennifer J Lister, *Effects of Age and Hearing Loss on Gap Detection and the Precedence Effect: Broadband Stimuli,* 47*J. of Speech, Language, and Hearing Research*, at 967(Oct 2004).

104. *See Id.* at 966.

105. *See Id.* at 966.

106. *See Id.* at 967.

107. Carol Rados, Sound *Advice About Age-Related Hearing Loss*, FDA Consumer Magazine, May-June 2005 issue, Pub No. FDA05-1340C.

   1. Source statement Cited: Statement by Dr. Hinrich Staecker, M.D., Ph.D, director of the Otology and Neurology Program at the University of Maryland Medical Center in Baltimore.

108. *See Id.*

109. *See Id.*

110. *See Id.*

111. *See supra* note 96 at 368.

112. Renato Peixoto Veras and Leila Couto Mattos, *Audiology and Aging: Literature review and current horizons*, 73 Rev Bras Otorrinolaringol 1, 126, (2007).

   1. Source Cited: Rosenhall ULF, et al, *The two faces of presbyacusis: hearing impairment and psychosocial consequences*, 41 Int J Audiol 2, 125-35, (2002).

113. *See supra* note 9 at 466.

114. *See supra* note 41 at 93.

115. *See supra* note 79 at 586.

116. *See Id.* at 586.

117. Hylton B Menz, Stephen R Lord, and Richard C Fitzpatrick, *Age-related differences in walking stability*, Age and Ageing, 32 British Geriatrics Society 2, at 141, (2003).

118. *See Id.* at 141.

119. *See Id.* at 139.

120. *See supra* note 6 at 231.

   1. Study Cited: Diener HC, Dichgans J, Gushlbauer B, and Mau H, *The significance of proprioception on postural stabilization as assessed by ischemia*, *Brain Research* 269, 103-109, (1984).

121. *See Id.* at 225.

   1. Study Cited: Woollacott M, and Shumway-Cook A, *Attention and the control of posture and gait: A review of and emerging area of research*, *Gait and Posture* 16, 1-14, (2002).

122. *See supra* note 50 at 112.

   1. Study Cited: Dixon RA, and Backman L, *Principles of compensation in cognitive neurorehabilitation*, In: DT Stuss, G Winocur, and IH Robertson (Eds), *Cognitive neurorehabilitation*, Cambridge England, Cambridge University Press, 59-72, (1999).

   2. Dixon RA, Hertzog C, Friesen IC, and Hultsch DF, *Assessment of intraindividual change in text recall of elderly adults*, In: HH Brownell, and Y Joanette (Eds), *Narrative discourse in neurologically impaired and normal aging adults*, San Diego CA: Singular, 77-101, (1993).

   3. Dixon RA, Hultsch DF, and Hertzog C, *A manual three-tired structurally equivalent texts for use in aging research* (CRGA Tech. Rep. No.2) Victoria, British Columbia, Canada: University of Victoria, Department of Psychology, (1989).

   4. Dixon RA, Wahlin A, Maitland SB, Hultsch DF, Hertzog L, and Backman L, (in Press), *Episodic memory change in late adulthood: Generalizability across samples and performance indices*, *Memory and Cognition*.

123. *See supra* note 32 at 159.

124. *See supra* note 6 at 231.

125. *See Id.* at 231.

126. Jackson PG, Turnbridge RJ, and Rohe DJ, *Drug recognition and field impairment testing: Evolution of trials*, In: Larrell Li, and Schlyter F (eds), Alcohol, drugs and traffic safety, Proceeding of the 15th International conference on alcohol, drugs and traffic safety, Stockholm, Sweden, (May 21-26 2000).

127. James M Rippe MD, *Fit Over Forty*, William Morah and Company Inc, New York, 17, (Copyright 1996).

128. *See Id.* at 32.

129. David C Grossman, Beth A Mueller, Tricia Kenaston, Philip Salzberg, William Cooper, and Gregory J Jurkovich, *The Validity of Police Assessment of Driver Intoxication in Motor Vehicle Crashes leading to Hospitalization*, 28 Accid. Anal. And Prev. 4, Elsevier Science Ltd., at 439, (1996).

130. See Id. at 441.

131. M O'Keefe, *Dugs driving-standardized field sobriety tests: a survey of police surgeons in Strathclyde*, 8 Journal of Clinical Forensic Medicine 2, 57, (June 2001).

132. See Id. at 60.

133. Anthony Wetherell, *Performance Tests*, 104 Environmental Health Perspectives 2, 252, (April 1996).

    1. Study Cited: Parrot AC, *Performance tests in psychopharmacology*, 2: Content Validity, Criterion Validity and Face Validity, Human Psychopharmacology, 6:91-98, (1991).

    2. Study Cited: Parrot AC, *Performance tests in psychopharmacology*, 3: Construct Validity and Test Interpretation, Human Psychopharmacology, , 6:197-207, (1991).

134. *17th Meeting of the International Council on Alcohol, Drugs, and Traffic Safety (TCADTS)*, held in Glassier, Scotland, United Kingdom, Aug. 8-13, 2004, and attended by some 400 delegates from around the world, at 5.

135. See Id. at 5.

    1. Study Cited: C.J. Trocino, "Drug Recognition Expert (DRE) Testimony Doesn't Pass Frye Test," *Williams v. Judicial Court Florida*, (1997).

136. See Id. at 5.

    1. Source Cited: Page, TE, *The Drug Recognition Expert Response, in the Effects of Drugs (other than alcohol) on Road Safety*, 1st Report of the Parliament of Victoria Road Safety Committee (May 1995).

137. See Id. at 5.

    1. Source Cited: AFP News, "AFP's View and Response: Field impairment Testing" 9, (December 2003).

138. See supra note 133 at 262.

139. See Id. at 262.

140. See Id. at 262.

141. See Id. at 252.

142. See Id. at 252.

143. See supra note 6 at 468.

144. See supra note 50 at 101.

145. See Id. at 112.

146. See supra note 127 at 280.

147. *Schultz v. State*, 664A. 2d60, 77 (Md. App. 1995).

148. See supra note 127 at 19.

149. See Id. at 277

150. See Id. at 265

151. See Id. at 217

152. See Id. at 217.

Appendix E

DWI—Modern Day Salem Witch Hunts

Mimi Coffey, Esq.

Modern Day Salem Witch Hunts

Judge Daryl Coffey of County Criminal Court number 8, in Tarrant County, Texas once remarked to me that all a prosecutor has to do to win a DWI case is just make sure that the three letters "DWI" are mentioned at least 15 times in a trial.[1] It is this type of environment that has allowed history to repeat itself. All we have to do is look back to the Salem Witch Hunt trials of 1692 where 19 convicted "witches" lost their lives on "specter" evidence.[2] Evidence in DWI trials has not come a long way from 1692 where claims of apparitions only visible to their victims were enough to get one hung. The greatest challenge to DWI practitioners these days and to those accused of DWI/DUI related crimes is that courtrooms have not kept pace with the science. Bad science is rubberstamped with approval by the majority of the judiciary as long as the government sponsors it.

Horizontal Gaze Nystagmus

The horizontal gaze nystagmus test, or HGN, is alleged to be 77 percent accurate (80 percent accurate with the W&T) in determining if a person is 0.10 BAC[3] or more.[4] The first problem with this test is the particularity. Police officers are not ophthalmologists trained in the detection of eye movements and or eye pathologies. There are forty-seven types of nystagmus in individuals, separate from Horizontal Nystagmus:

> (1) Acquired; (2) Anticipatory (induced); (3) Arthrokinetic (induced, somatosensory); (4) Associated (induced, Stransky's); (5) Audio kinetic (induced); (6) Bartel's (induced); (7) Brun's; (8) Centripetal; (9) Cervical (neck torsion, vestibular-basilar artery insufficiency); (10) Circular/Elliptic/Oblique (alternating windmill, circumduction, diagonal, elliptic, gyratory, oblique, radiary); (11) Congenital (fixation, hereditary); (12) Convergence; (13) Convergence-evoked; (14) Dissociated (disjunctive); (15) Downbeat; (16) Drug-induced (barbituate, bow tie, induced); (17) Epileptic (ictal); (18) Flash induced; (19) Gaze-evoked (deviational, gaze-paretic, neurasthenic, seducible, setting-in); (20) Horizontal; (21) Induced (provoked); (22) Intermittent Vertical; (23) Jerk; (24) Latent/Manifest Latent (monocular fixation, unimacular); (25) Lateral Medullary; (26) Lid; (27) Miner's (occupational); (28) Muscle-Paretic (myasthenic); (29) Optokinetic (induced, optomotor, panoramic, railway, sigma); (30) Optokinetic After-Induced (post-optokinetic, reverse post-optokinetic); (31) Pendular (talantropia); (32) Periodic/Aperiodic Alternating; (33) Physiologic (end-point, fatigue); (34) Pursuit After-induced; (35) Pursuit Defect; (36) Pseudo spontaneous; (37) Rebound; (38) Reflex (Baer's); (39) See-Saw; (40) Somatosensory; (41) Spontaneous; (42) Stepping Around; (43) Torsional; (44) Uniocular; (45) Upbeat; (46) Vertical; (47) Vestibular (ageotropic, geotropic, Bechterew's, caloric, compensatory, electrical/faradic/galvanic, labyrinthine, pneumatic/compression, positional/alcohol, pseudo caloric.[5]

It is unrealistic given this extensive laundry list—which includes medical conditions—that a police officer can make the important distinction that he is indeed observing horizontal gaze nystagmus. Even if he could, the next issue is causation. Officers jump to an incorrect premise that if they do isolate horizontal gaze nystagmus this must be indicative of ethanol intoxication. There are actually 38 different causes of horizontal gaze nystagmus unrelated to alcohol as judicially recognized in *Schultz v. State*:

> (1) problems with the inner ear labyrinth; (2) irrigating the ears with warm or cold water under peculiar weather conditions; (3) influenza; (4) streptococcus infection; (5) vertigo; (6) measles; (7) syphilis; (8) arteriosclerosis; (9) muscular dystrophy; (10) multiple sclerosis; (11) Korchaff's syndrome; (12) brain hemorrhage; (13) epilepsy; (14) hypertension; (15)

> motion sickness; (16) sunstroke; (17) eyestrain; (18) eye muscle fatigue; (19) glaucoma; (20) changes in atmospheric pressure; (21) consumption of excessive amounts of caffeine; (22) excessive exposure to nicotine; (23) aspirin; (24) circadian rhythms; (25) acute trauma to the head; (26) chronic trauma to the head; (27) some prescription drugs, tranquilizers, pain medications, anti-convulsants; (28) barbiturates; (29) disorders of the vestibular apparatus and brain stem; (30) cerebellum dysfunction; (31) heredity; (32) diet; (33) toxins; (34) exposure to solvents, PCBs, dry-cleaning fumes, carbon monoxide; (35) extreme chilling; (36) lesions; (37) continuous movement of the visual field past the eyes; and, (38) antihistamine use.[6]

Another real problem with the horizontal gaze nystagmus test is the timing of its presence and an actual alcohol concentration. The HGN, as administered by the National Highway Transportation Safety Administration's (NHTSA) protocol for the Standardized Field Sobriety Tests (SFST) has been cited as the only reliable index of blood alcohol when examined for its ability to distinguish BACs under and over 0.04 percent within the 0.00–0.08 percent range.[7] So it is a fallacy to use this test to determine that someone may be over 0.08 BAC. What is also alarming is the fact that nystagmus can remain for some time once the BAC has reached 0.000. In a dose/response study of 89 subjects,[8] 62 percent of the dosed subjects exhibited nystagmus in one or both eyes at BAC levels of 0.00 percent when tested immediately after all alcohol was cleared from their blood and 56 percent of those subjects still exhibited nystagmus one hour later.[9] In the same study, it was determined from 66 healthy, well-rested subjects[10] who did not consume any alcohol and completed 5.5 to 8.0 hours of sleep after being awake for 9 to 14.5 hours (average 11.2) that they had distinct nystagmus in one or both eyes.[11] Afterwards these same subjects were re-examined with an average awake time of 24.5 hours and distinct end position nystagmus was observed in one or both eyes in 55 percent of the group.[12] What is particularly troublesome is the stamp of imprimatur by the American Optometric Association[13] touted by prosecutors in laying the foundation for the test's admissibility.[14] It is important to distinguish that no such resolution of acceptance for the HGN exists by the American Academy of Ophthalmology. It is unsettling how eager the American Optometric Association has been to embrace the possibility of providing expert testimony as a puppet of the government without any legitimate scientific inquiry of their own. The seminal scientific research article on HGN states it best:

> In an article designed to inform optometrists how to provide expert testimony on the HGNT (HGN), the only evidence of a correlation between BAC and nystagmus given is a reference to the NHTSA's work. Specifically the article stated "through a series of studies, the National Highway Traffic and Safety Administration (NHTSA) has been able to establish a high correlation between alcohol concentrations in the body and performance on a series of field sobriety tests." It is interesting, and perhaps revealing, that no other evidence is referenced to support this correlation.[15]

One only needs to look at the criticism of NHTSA's foundational research[16]—which led to the development of the HGN test—to understand that this is yet another example of agenda government science which misses the mark. It is interesting to note that researchers have determined that percentages generally cited by the courts in support of HGN exist only in NHTSA publications.[17] Jurists and prosecutors in the United States have been quick to embrace the HGN test as hardcore science but this component has not been adopted by Great Britain.

Standardized Field Sobriety Tests

Outside of the HGN, DWI cases concentrate on psychomotor skills known as standardized field sobriety tests; but just how good are these tests? This requires some basic understanding of testing fundamentals. The first incorrect presumption with this framework is that these tests measure impairment related to driving. They do not.[18] The walk and turn and one leg stand are purported to have "face validity"[19]; that is, the tests relate to actual driving tasks. Face validity is the lowest form of validity a researcher can achieve and is generally not accepted by academia because "face validity rests on the investigator's subjective evaluation of the appropriateness of the instrument for measuring the concept rather than whether the instrument measures what the researcher wishes to measure."[20] For a test to be valid, there must be high reliability and validity both measured by a correlation coefficient ranging from 0 to 1.0 (highest end of the scale).[21] Reliability relates to the consistency of scores based on re-testing. Validity relates to the ability of a test to predict particular benchmarks. Intelligence tests such as the Wechsler Intelligence Test have a reliability of 0.90. According to the 1977 SCRI study which developed the three-part standardized field sobriety tests the validity correlation coefficient[22] was 0.48, the walk and turn was 0.55.[23] In layman's terms what this means is that using a one leg stand to predict a 0.10 BAC is only 25 percent better than chance.[24] The HGN interestingly enough had only a correlation coefficient of 0.67 equating to an approximate 33 percent better prediction than chance.[25] Use of the walk and turn is only 27-28 percent better than chance.[26] The overall error rate (wrong percentage of decisions to arrest) was 47 percent.[27] In 1981, laboratory field sobriety tests (this time just the HGN, walk and turn, and one leg stand) were researched again and the error rate was found to be 32 percent.[28] Validity correlation coefficients were not mentioned in this study. Reliability correlation coefficients were given for this study: HGN 0.66, walk and turn 0.72.[29] For a test to be reliable the coefficient must be 0.85 or higher.[30] When different officers performed the test on the same subject at the same BAC the coefficients dropped down to 0.59 for the HGN and 0.34 for the walk and turn, to whit a 66 percent error rate was indicated for the walk and turn and the one leg stand error rate equated to a 40 percent.[31] Dr. Burns herself indicated that the >77 and >81 error rates were unacceptable.[32] In response to a cross-examination question as to whether 32 percent was acceptable, she replied, "It is getting there."[33] This is the meat and potatoes of what still exists today.

Once one gets over the initial shock of how unacceptable these tests are according to government research, the next logical step is to look at the relevant scientific peer review community. Dr. Spurgeon Cole and Ronald Nowaczyk did just that in 1994 in a field sobriety study sponsored by Clemson University. According to this study, field sobriety tests which included the walk and turn and one leg stand test were compared to normal tasks such as reciting basic information and walking in normal manner for 21 sober individuals all with a BAC of 0.000. Forty-six percent of the officers determined the subjects intoxicated by SFST(s) with only fifteen percent of said subjects determined to be intoxicated by normal tests.[34] The promulgation of these tests, the HGN, walk and turn and one leg stand may be good enough for government work but are a far cry from reliable, scientific standards. Because of this, innocent people are being convicted every day on these premises, which are taken at face value and not questioned despite their invalidity. When most states lowered legal limits to 0.08, the government found itself in a quandary of which they still have not been able to solve; hence, the continuation of the misleading 1981 percentages of accuracy: HGN 77 percent, walk and turn 68 percent, one leg stand 65 percent.[35] The Colorado,[36] Florida[37] and San Diego[38] studies attempted to quantify accuracy at 0.08 but none proved worthy of the mission. Such roadblocks as documented by Steve Rubenzer, Ph.D, included but were not limited to the following critiques:

1. The field studies validated the arrest decisions of the officers in the studies, not the SFSTs.
2. The police officers and the degree of supervision in the field studies were not typical of typical DWI stops.
3. The studies were insufficiently documented for scientific papers as cited in *United States v. Horn*, 185 F. Supp.2d 530, 558 (D. Md. 2002).
4. The authors did not report the accuracy of arrest decisions for stops that were observed versus those that were not, or for SFSTs performed under adverse climate conditions versus those that were not.[39]

The new purported levels of accuracy in the recent validation studies regarding the same field tests at *lower* limits are proof of the tests' inherent low reliability correlation coefficient. How these statistically unreliable and invalid tests are somehow more purportedly valid at lower limits is yet proof positive how radical the DWI religion has become to lawmakers and jurists alike in blind disregard of the science.

Leading Jurisdictions

Despite ignorant, widespread acceptance of the validity of the HGN, walk and turn and one-leg stand tests, there are some jurisdictions which have started down a very unpopular but judiciously righteous path in respect of scientific principles and constitutional liberty. In *Homan v. State,* the court determined that in order for the results of a field sobriety test to serve as evidence of probable cause to arrest, the police must have administered the test in strict compliance with standardized testing procedures.[40] The court at least recognized that "testing" requires standardization and not haphazard administration if scoring criteria is to be used. What is key in this case is the court's threshold requirements merely address admissibility at the probable cause level. The mistake in *Homan* is to give the standardized tests any scientific evidentiary value at all. It, however, at least recognizes that adherence to protocol is necessary to admissibility as opposed to weight. In *United States v. Horn,* Judge Grimm wrote:

> There is no factual basis before me to support the NHTSA claims of accuracy for the WAT and OLS tests or to support the conclusions about the total number of standardized clues that should be looked for or that are missing a stated number means the subject failed the test. There is very little before me that suggests that the WAT and OLS tests are anything more than standardized procedures police officers use to enable them to observe a suspect's coordination, balance, concentration, speech, ability to follow instructions, mood and general physical condition—all of which are visual cues that

laypersons, using ordinary experience, associate with reaching opinions about whether someone has been drinking.[41]

Some of the more notable premises the *Horn* case stands for are that 1) The results of properly conducted tests may be considered for probable cause.[42] 2) The SFST(s) cannot be correlated with a specific BAC.[43] 3) The court where requested by counsel should take judicial notice of the fact that there are many causes of HGN outside of alcohol.[44] 4) Value added descriptive language regarding the SFST(s) such as "failed the test," "exhibited" a certain number of "standardized clues" or any other bolstering attempts by the officer is not allowed.[45] SFST(s) or any specialized information learned from law enforcement or traffic safety instruction should not be referred to as scientific, technical or specialized.[46] Judge Paul Grimm, much like Governor William Phipps of Salem, Massachusetts, who suspended the special court of Oyer and Terminer,[47] which based convictions on specious "specter" evidence, has through his opinion echoed some reason and common sense that is necessary in a court of law in the wake of mass hysteria over DWI prosecutions. Special recognition goes to courts responsible for cases like *State v. Doriguzzi*,[48] where HGN was ruled not admissible because the State had failed to show *Frye* acceptance and reliability and *Young v. City of Brookhaven*,[49] where the HGN test was ruled as a scientific test but not one generally accepted by the scientific community. These courts provide hope in proving that science is the voice of reason and we have a long way to go in spreading such reason to all parts of the country because science has no jurisdictional bounds.

Special thanks to:

- Dr. Ron Henson of Beron Consulting and Lab Works, Peoria, IL.
- Richard Essen of Essen, Essen, Susaneck, Canet, & Goodis P.A., Aventura FL 33180 (and paralegal Jason Hedges), Dr. Joe Citron, Atlanta, GA.
- Steve Oberman, Law Office of Steve Oberman, Knoxville, TN.

Endnotes

1. Unlike most jurists, Judge Coffey has a scientific background—a Bachelor of Science in Agriculture from Western Kentucky University.

2. *See* Rosemary Ellen Guiley, *The Encyclopedia of Witches and Witchcraft*, 234-299 (1989).

3. Indicating the chemical concentration of alcohol in the blood as being greater than 0.10 percent.

4. *See* V. Tharp, M. Burns, and H. Moskowitz, *Development and Field Test of Psychophysical Tests for DWI Arrest*, DOT-HS-805-864, U.S. Department of Transportation, NHTSA, Washington (1981).

5. Dr. L. F. Dell'Osso, *Nystagmus, Saccadic Intrusions/Oscillations and Oscillopsia*, 3 Current Neuro-Ophthalmology 147 (1989).

6. *Schultz v. State,* 664 A.2d 60, 77 (Md. App. 1995).

7. *See* A.J. McKnight et al., *Sobriety Tests for Low Blood Alcohol Concentrations*, Accid. Anal. Prev. 2002 May; 34(3): 305-11.

8. *See* J.L. Booker, *End-position nystagmus as an indicator of ethanol intoxication,* 41 Science and Justice 113, 115 (2001). (79 men and 10 women between the ages of 22 and 67 who were well rested and in good health, alcohol levels determined by blood and urine assays conducted by gas chromatography and breath concentrations determined by CMI Intoxilyzer 5000 instruments with wet-bath reference units operated at 34°C.)

9. *See Id.* at 115.

10. *See Id.* at 114-15. (The study consisted of 44 men and 22 women between the ages of 20 and 57 who denied use of alcohol or drugs within the preceding 24 hours.)

11. *See Id.* at 115.

12. *See Id.* at 115.

13. *See* Karl Citek, *HGN and the role of the Optometrist*, in Admissibility of Horizontal Gaze Nystagmus Evidence: Targeting Hardcore Impaired Drivers, 15 (Am. Prosecutors Research Inst. 2003). (The following resolution was adopted by the American Optometric Association House of Delegates, on June 1993:

Whereas drivers under the influence of alcohol pose a significant threat to the public health, safety, and welfare; and

Whereas optometric scientists and the National Highway and Traffic Safety Administration have shown the Horizontal Gaze Nystagmus (HGN) test to be a scientifically valid and reliable tool for trained police officers to use in field sobriety testing; now therefore be it

Resolved that the American Optometric Association acknowledges the scientific validity and reliability of the HGN test as a field sobriety test when administered by properly trained and certified police officers; and be it further

Resolved that the American Optometric Association urges doctors of optometry to become involved as professional consultants in the use of HGN field sobriety testing.)

14. *See Predicate Questions: Optometrist...Appendix K* (visited June 18, 2004) <http://nhtsa.com/people/injury/enforce/nystagmus/app_k.html>. (Direct Examination questions for the state's expert optometrist end with: 88. Are you familiar with the 1993 resolution "Horizontal Gaze Nystagmus as a Field Sobriety Test" passed by the House of Delegates of the American Optometric Association? 89. Is this a copy of the resolution? 90. Please read it to the court.)

15. Charles R. Honts, Susan L. Amato-Henderson, *Horizontal Gaze Nystagmus Test: The State of the Science in 1995*, 71 N.D. L.Rev. 671 at 6 (1995). (*citing* David V. Tiffany, *Optometric Expert Testimony: Foundation for the Horizontal Gaze Nystagmus Test*, 57 J. of Amer. Optometric Ass'n 705 (1986)).

16. *See Id.* at 15.

17. *See* Joseph R. Meaney, *Horizontal Gaze Nystagmus: A Closer Look,* 36 Jurimetrics J. 383, 385 (1996).

18. Jack Stuster and Marcelline Burns, *Validation of the Standardized Field Sobriety Test Battery at BACs Below 0.10 Percent*, DOT-HS-808-839 6, (1998).

19. *See Id*. at 27-28.

20. Chava Frankfort-Nachmias & David Nachmias, *Research Methods in the Social Sciences*, 150 (6th ed. Worth Pub. 2000).

21. *See* Trial Transcript at 14-16, later reported as *State v. Meador*, 674 So.2d 826 (Fla. Dist. Ct. App. 1996).

22. *See Id.* at 21, (The formula is actually the square root of 1.48.).

23. *See Id.* at 20.

24. *See Id.* at 21.

25. *See Id.* at 20, 22.

26. *See Id.* at 22.

27. *See Id.* at 29.

28. *See Id.* at 37.

29. *See Id.* at 42.

30. *See* R. Rosenthal and R.L. Rosnow, *Essentials of behavioral research: methods and data analysis* (2nd ed. McGraw-Hill 1991).

31. *See* Meador, *supra* note 21, at 31.

32. *See Id.* at 141.

33. *Id.* at 141.

34. *See* Spurgeon C. Cole and Ronald H. Nowaczyk, *Field Sobriety Tests: Are They Designed for Failure?,* Perceptual and Motor Skills, 79, 99-104, (1994).

35. *See* Tharp, *supra* note 4.

36. *See* Anderson, Ellen and Marcelline Burns, Ph.D., *A Colorado Validation Study of the Standardized Field Sobriety Test (SFST) Battery*, November 1995.

37. *See* Dioquino, Sgt. Teresa, et al., *A Florida Validation Study of the Standardized Field Sobriety (SFST) Battery*, (date of publication is unknown).

38. *See* Burns, *supra* note 18.

39. *See* Steven Rubenzer, *DWI- Part 1 The Psychometrics and Science of Standardized Field Sobriety Tests*, The Champion, May 2003, at 24-34.

40. *See Homan v. State,* 89 Ohio St.3d 421 (2000). Most unfortunately, and without any respect for scientific realities this case was later abrogated by legislation.

41. *United States v. Horn*, 185 F. Supp. 2d 530, 557 (D. Md. 2002).

42. *See Id.* at 532-33.

43. *See Id.* at 533.

44. *See Id.* at 533.

45. *See Id.* at 533.

46. *See Id.* at 533-34.

47. *See* Guiley, *supra* note 2 at 299.

48. 334 N.J. Super. 530 (App. Div. 2000)

49. 693 So.2d 1355 (Miss. 1997).

Appendix F

Fear and the DWI Field Sobriety Tests

Mimi Coffey, Esq.

The National Highway Traffic Safety Administration (NHTSA) developed the Standardized Field Sobriety Tests (SFSTs) in a vacuum. None of the original research simulated real life testing conditions; e.g., a person performing the standardized field sobriety tests with the fear of going to jail. This missing premise negates the validity of the tests as far as the "divided attention tests." The critical flaw of the SFSTs contributes to false convictions in the nationalized DWI testing protocol.

What is fear? Fear as a scientific term describes a behavioral, cognitive-emotional condition in which a set of biological adaptive responses activate in the presence of danger.[1] These physiological responses are hardwired to how our brain operates.[2] Fear is uncontrollably present in humans and animals when unpredictable, aversive events cause debilitating behavioral, cognitive and somatic effects.[3] Fear is controlled by ancient systems in the brain, primarily the amygdala, which acts relatively independent of later emerging higher cognitions.[4] Numerous studies have linked the amygdala with fear.[5] Much of fear's effects on the amygdala are subconscious with sensory information accessing the amygdala with minimal cortical processing.[6] It is important to note that fear is not related to intelligence or its effects negated by alcohol. Alcohol reduces *anxiety* but not fear.[7] Extreme experiments prove the symbiotic relationship of fear to the amygdala. In one, amygdala-lesioned rats approached a sedated cat, crawling over it and even nibbling on its ear.[8] In another, Rhesus monkeys had their amygdalae removed through a bilateral temporal lobectomy resulting in no innate fear of snakes, such as avoidance or freezing—a condition is known as 'psychic blindness'.[9] The function of fear is to motivate organisms to manage threats that jeopardize survival through the use of coping reactions clearly focused on escaping, attacking, and freezing.[10] Fear potentiated startle (FPS), a variant on freezing, is an instinctive response to a combination of light and noise stimuli.[11] A person's fear of police, at its basic element, is similar to that of rats to cats. In an experiment done by psychologists Blanchard and Blanchard, rats were exposed for 15 minutes to cats causing each to scatter into burrows and avoid open areas, in addition to curtailing non-defensive behaviors such as grooming, mounting, eating, and drinking, for the duration of the test.[12] The ability to focus one's attention while in fear requires first an understanding of the complex reactions occurring involuntarily in the body and beyond one's control.

Fear activates stress. Stress hormones will dramatically alter the turnover of several classes of neurotransmitters in the prefrontal cortex of the brain.[13] The prefrontal cortex has extensive projections from the limbic system, the mammalian part of the brain involved in emotion, which explains why strong emotions can adversely impact the quality of executive functions increasing the likelihood of imprudent or impulsive choices.[14] A study of threatening and neutral images established that the orbitofrontal cortex, as part of the fronto-parietal network has a key role in spatial attention; attention as well as emotion are two key components compromised in fear.[15] In particular, stress releases damaging hormones. Stress activates the hypothalamic-pituitary adrenal (HPA) axis which releases the glucocorticoids (cortisol) by the adrenal cortex and negatively interferes with brain structures central to memory.[16] Corticotrophin (CRH) released with physical and emotional stressors, causes increased blood glucose, heart rate and blood pressure, in addition to increased tolerance of pain and *changes in motor activity*.[17] Along with these physical reactions, an increase in glucocorticoid secretion is associated with immobilization or freezing.[18] Advances in the understanding of neuroendocrine and neurochemical behavioral responses have come a long way since 1911 when Walter Cannon confirmed the secretion of epinephrine after an emotional response with fight-or-flight.[19] Recently it was shown that norepinephrine and dopamine, also interactively involved in stress induced arousal, have effects on one's prefrontal cognition as well.[20] The problem with the body's natural reactions as a result of fear or stress is the deficits which result in the "loss of normal mental and physical faculties" judged for intoxication in a DWI. It is a recognized fact that when the basoleteral part of the amygdala is activated (such as in fear) and glucocorticoids are released, stress-induced retrieval deficits occur.[21] Retrieval deficits result in a negative effect on memory.[22] The compromised memory retrieval is due to the stress hormones and neurotransmitters switching the brain into a "memory consolidation" state allowing for strong recall of the event, thereby compromising memory retrieval during the event.[23] This makes sense as being able to recall and avoid threatening events is necessary for evolutionary survival, explaining why our brains' circuitry is programmed in this manner. Memory retrieval is critical in a DWI investigation for tasks such as NHTSA Phase II (e.g., alphabetic and numeric countdown) exercises. Such exercises are at times requested before exiting the vehicle so that the officer may test short-term memory recall prior to testing the subject's ability to memorize the instructions for the walk and turn and one leg stand tests. Participants in a study receiving cold pressor stress before memory retrieval recalled fewer words than the no stress control.[24] In another stress study done in 2009, a glucocorticoid (cortisol) administered to subjects impaired their memory during a weeklong word recall experiment.[25]

Memory is directly connected with the brain's processing of emotion and attention. Emotion and attention can interact either by emotion modulating attentional processing or attention influencing emotional processing.[26] In a DWI scenario, the emotion of fear precedes and interrupts task attention. Emotion functions importantly to help guide attention to emotionally valuable stimuli,[27] none of which is beneficial in a DWI investigation. Emotions result in abnormal excitation of the nervous network, which induces changes in heart rate and secretions or interrupts the normal relationship between the peripheral nervous system and the brain.[28] Simply put, emotions affect the central nervous system—the same system evaluated for 'normalcy' in a DWI. First, emotional information receives priority in neural processing.[29] Evidence suggests that once emotional stimuli are processed visual attention is often sustained.[30] One's inability to 'think straight' while mad or 'black out' in fear is due to emotional information receiving privileged access to attention and awareness.[31] To be 'paralyzed by fear' is due to emotions exerting their influence by modulating activity in regions involved in cognitive control.[32] Specifically, emotional signals modulate parietal and frontal brain regions involved in attention control.[33] This loss of attention control impedes the processing of task-relevant stimuli.[34] When the field sobriety tests were developed, the testing subjects had no emotional detractors to interfere with their ability to process the directions. One cannot perform the tests correctly without adhering to the proper instructions such as 'keep your arms by your side' or 'on the 9th step keep your lead foot planted and take a small series of steps'. Emotions are so powerful, evidence suggests, that outside of 'top down' mental processing, some automatic "preattentive" neural processing of emotional stimuli exists as well,[35] (Ohman proved this in a study that had snakes hidden in pictures).[36] Psychology literature reports several published studies that document the slowed brain processing when emotions are involved. One asked subjects to simply identify a target as a circle or square and found that when the shapes were preceded by emotional versus neutral images this slowed down the identification process.[37] Another proved that fear conditioned cues captured subjects' attention making it harder and slower to orient one's self to proper locations in a spatial attention/emotion study.[38] In another, participants found it more difficult to name colors of pictures or words when they had an emotional meaning attached to them, further proving the emotional hindrance is involuntary.[39]

Emotion potentiates the effect of attention.[40] Attention defined is the cognitive control involved in maintaining task rules in working memory, monitoring reward and error rates, filtering distracters, and suppressing prepotent and competitive responses.[41] Weak attentional control increases distractibility causing attentional lapses, impulsivity and attentional fatigue.[42] When a person loses the ability to orient attention towards relevant stimuli, sensory information can no longer be processed properly.[43] This processing occurs in the prefrontal cortex,[44] the same place shown to receive activation from threat-related signals.[45] The reason why one cannot focus attention during fear is because the amygdala activates the noradrenergic system projecting into and interfering with the locus coeruleus which modulates attention.[46] Without the effects of fear factored into the equation, DWI investigations attempt to prevent one from driving a vehicle when their central nervous system is impaired to the extent defined by the law for intoxication.[47] There are two central flaws to this end result. Dr. Marcelline Burns, developer of the SFSTs, has admitted that the tests were never designed to detect impairment and one's ability to safely operate a motor vehicle.[48] She attempts to bridge this fatal blow by advocating her second central flaw that the field tests are designed at judging one's ability to divide their attention.[49] Does driving a car involve the divided attention used as an objective in the field sobriety tests? Driving often consists of monitoring external stimuli for certain classes of events (pedestrians, looming cars, etc.) with the driving and thinking representing a case of 'simultaneous performance'.[50] There are specifically two neural conclusions about driving: (1) perceptual monitoring occurs at the same time as central processing and (2) central processing can be interrupted quickly on the basis of detections made while scanning and monitoring the environment.[51] Field sobriety tests under fear conditions do not fairly represent simultaneous perception monitoring and central processing. When it comes to divided attention tests many tasks interfere with each other quite drastically, although they are neither intellectually challenging nor physically incompatible.[52] One comprehensive analysis on the topic, published in the scholarly Psychological Bulletin referred to by specialists in the field of psychology, determined "the results show that people have surprisingly severe limitations on their ability to carry out simultaneously certain cognitive processes that seem fairly trivial from a computational standpoint".[53] Basic science counterbalances experiments with controls. If the control studies show unsuitability for divided attention without alcohol, much less negated by the presence of fear, it is time the National Highway Traffic Safety Administration be held accountable for substandard and ineffective protocol and testing measures.

Attention at its core is simply holding information in the working memory, necessitating a basic understanding of working memory as it relates to fear.[54] As mentioned above, memory retrieval processes are impaired with a high level of circulating glucocorticoids[55] which occurs in concert with changes in other neurotransmitter systems.[56] These neural systems extend from the frontal lobes into the primary cortices where attention and working memory show considerable overlap.[57] To paraphrase, in normal cognition, memory consolidation and retrieval processes occur simultaneously; thus, a single glucocorticoid rush can alter these reactions.[58] Specifically, stress levels of glucocorticoids influence the prefrontal cortex impairing short term memory retrieval.[59] In one study, rats experienced foot-shock exposure for thirty minutes, resulting in a temporary memory loss.[60] In a human study, subjects tested after glucocorticoid elevations showed the same impaired memory retention under various testing conditions,[61] including the recall of previously learned words.[62] The bottom line, emotionally distracting scenarios are associated with a decrease in dorsal lateral prefrontal cortex activity along with a concomitant drop in working memory performance.[63]

Although man is the most highly developed species, we are still animals largely controlled by instincts, one of the greatest of which is fear. The processing of fear-relevant stimuli was evolutionarily optimized for survival.[64] Our fear responses are innate, species-typical responses that are not learned or voluntary.[65] These responses kick into full gear when we see the flashing lights behind us, hear the sirens and are approached by men and women in uniform carrying guns. Known as tonic immobility, profound temporary motor inhibitions both physically and mentally occur when we perceive ourselves to be in these constraining and dangerous situations.[66] To disregard these natural reactions, particularly in the scenario of a DWI investigation where testing is conducted, is to ignore science which short-circuits truth, and justice. The social sciences have recognized that people who are depressed have attentional inflexibility which is linked to impairment in cognitive control mechanisms.[67] People with post traumatic stress disorder (PTSD) in the same light, fail to maintain and direct proper attention when faced with threatening information.[68] Modern science has recognized that with advances in brain research, we can pinpoint some of the mechanisms at work that cause a loss of normal mental and physical faculties in emotional states. Whereas doctors have cognitive goals for their patients in these emotional states, lawyers and judges must learn to differentiate such states to prevent false convictions, particularly in the area of intoxication related offenses. There are enormous intellectual differences between the worlds of science and law in the basic premises concerning causality and certainty.[69] It is time to close the gap.

Endnotes

1. J. J. Kim & K.M. Myers, *Fear: Psychological and Neural Aspects*, 8 International Encyclopedia of the Social & Behavioral Sciences 5428, 5428 (2001).

2. *See Id.* at 5430.

3. Ruben P. Alvarez et al., *Phasic and Sustained Fear in Humans Elicits Distinct Patterns of Brain Activity*, 55 NeuroImage 389, 389 (2011).

4. Arne Ohman, *The Role of the Amygdala in Human Fear: Automatic Detection of Threat*, 30 Psychoneuroendocrinology 953, 954 (2005).

5. *See generally* Steve R. Makkar et al., *Review: Behavioral and Neural Analysis of GABA in the Acquisition, Consolidation, Reconsolidation, and Extinction of Fear Memory*, 35 neuropsychopharmacology 1625, 1632 (2010); Joseph LeDoux, *The Emotional Brain, Fear, and the Amygdala*, 23 Cellular and Molecular Neurobiology 727, 727 (2003); Patrik Vuilleumier, *How Brains Beware: Neural Mechanisms of Emotional Attention*, 9 Trends in Cognitive Sciences 585, 588 (2005); Ralph Adolphs, *What Does the Amygdala Contribute to Social Cognition?*, 1191 The Annals of the New York Academy of Sciences 42, 42 (2010).

6. *See* Ohman, *Role, supra* note 4 at 954; Ralph Adolphs, *Fear, Faces, and the Human Amygdala*, 18 CURRENT OPINION IN NEUROBIOLOGY 166, 167 (2008).

7. *See* Christine A. Moberg & John J. Curtin, *Alcohol Selectively Reduces Anxiety but not Fear: Startle Response During Unpredictable vs. Predictable Threat*, 118 JOURNAL OF ABNORMAL PSYCHOLOGY 335, 345 (2009).

8. Rene Misslin, *The Defense System of Fear: Behavior and Neurocircuitry*, 33 NEUROPHYSIOLOGIE CLINIQUE 55, 61 (2003).

9. *Id.*

10. Arne Ohman et al., *On the Unconscious Subcortical Origin of Human Fear*, 92 PHYSIOLOGY & BEHAVIOR 180, 180 (2007) (freezing "is a behaviorally quiescent state that involves scanning of the environment to assess risks and opportunities").

11. *See* Amanda R. de Oliveira et al., *Conditioned Fear Response is Modulated by a Combined Action of the Hypothalamic-Pituitary-Adrenal Axis and Dopamine Activity in the Basolateral Amygdala*, EUROPEAN NEUROPSYCHOPHARMACOLOGY (forthcoming).

12. Misslin, *supra* note 8 at 58.

13. *See* Robert M. Sapolsky, *The Frontal Cortex and the Criminal Justice System*, 359 PHILOSOPHICAL TRANSACTIONS OF THE ROYAL SOCIETY B 1787, 1792 (2004).

14. *Id.*

15. *See* Jorge L. Armony & Raymond J. Dolan, *Modulation of Spatial Attention by Fear-Conditioned Stimuli: An Event-Related fMRI Study*, 40 NEUROPSYCHOLOGIA 817, 824 (2002).

16. Tom Smeets, *Acute Stress Impairs Memory Retrieval Independent of Time of Day*, 36 PSYCHONEUROENDOCTRINOLOGY 495, 495 (2011).

17. *See* T.M. O'Connor et al., *The Stress Response and the Hypothalamic-Pituitary-Adrenal Axis: From Molecule to Melancholia*, 93 QUARTERLY JOURNAL OF MEDICINE 323, 328 (2000).

18. Thierry Steimer, *The Biology of Fear-and Anxiety-Related Behaviors*, 4 DIALOGUES IN CLINICAL NEUROSCIENCE 231, 234 (2002).

19. *See* R. McCarty, *Fight-or-Flight Response*, in 2 ENCYCLOPEDIA OF STRESS 62, 62 (2d ed. 2007).

20. *See* Anreas Boehringer et al., *A Combination of High Stress-Induced Tense and Energetic Arousal Compensates for Imparing Effects of Stress on Memory Retrieval in Men*, 13 STRESS 444, 451 (2010).

21. *See* Smeets, *supra* note 16 at 500.

22. *See* Marie-France Marin et al., *Modulatory Effects of Stress on Reactivated Emotional Memories*, 35 PSYCHONEUROENDORINOLOGY 1388, 1388 (2010).

23. Benno Roozendaal, *Stress and Memory: Opposing Effects of Glucocorticoids on Memory Consolidation and Memory Retrieval*, 78 NEUROBIOLOGY OF LEARNING AND MEMORY 578, 590 (2002).

24. *See* Smeets, *supra* note 16 at 495.

25. *See* Marin, *supra* note 22 at 1389.

26. Armony & Dolan, *supra* note 15 at 817.

27. *See* N. Fragopanagos & J.G. Taylor, *Modelling the Interaction of Attention and Emotion*, 69 NEUROCOMPUTING 1977, 1982 (2006).

28. *See* Steimer, *supra* note 18 at 231.

29. *See* Marie T. Banich et al., *Cognitive Control Mechanisms, Emotion & Memory: A Neural Perspective with Implications for Psychopathology*, 33 NEUROSCIENCE & BIOBEHAVIORAL REVIEWS 613, 614 (2009).

30. *See* Greg Hajcak et al., The *Dynamic Allocation of Attention to Emotion: Simultaneous and Independent Evidence from the Late Positive Potential and Steady State Visual Evoked Potentials*, BIOLOGICAL PSYCHOLOGY (2011), *available at* http://www.sciencedirect.com/science/article/pii/S0301051111002973.

31. *See* Vuilleumier, *How Brains Beware*, *supra* note 5 at 586.

32. *See* Banich et al., *supra* note 29 at 620.

33. Vuilleumier, *How Brains Beware*, *supra* note 5 at 591.

34. *See* Hajcak et al., supra *note* 30.

35. Patrik Vuilleumier et al., *Effects of Attention and Emotion on Face Processing in the Human Brain: An Event-Related fMRI Study*, 30 NEURON 829, 829 (2001).

36. *See* Ohman et al., *Unconscious*, *supra* note 10 at 182.

37. *See* Hajcak et al., *supra* note 30.

38. *See* John G. Taylor & Nickolaos F. Fragopanagos, *The Interaction of Attention and Emotion*, 18 NEURAL NETWORKS 353, 358 (2005).

39. *See* Vuilleumier, *How Brains Beware*, *supra* note 5 at 585.

40. Ohman et al., *Unconscious*, *supra* note 10 at 183.

41. Martin Sarter & Giovanna Paolone, *Theoretical Review-Deficits in Attentional Control: Cholinergic Mechanisms and Circuitry-Based Treatment Approach*, 125 BEHAVIORAL NEUROSCIENCE 825, 825 (2011).

42. *Id.*

43. *See* Christina Lucas & Johan Lauwereyns, *Selective Working Memory Disables Inhibition of Visual Features*, 54 EXPERIMENTAL PSYCHOLOGY 256, 256 (2007).

44. See Taylor & Fragopanagos, *supra* note 38 at 353.

45. *See* Belinda J. Liddell et al., *A Direct Brainstem-Amygdala-Cortical 'Alarm' System for Subliminal Signals of Fear*, 24 NEUROIMAGE 235, 240 (2005).

46. Vuilleumier, *How Brains Beware*, *supra* note 5 at 592.

47. *See* TEX. PENAL CODE § 49.01 ("not having the normal use of mental or physical faculties by reason of the introduction of alcohol, a controlled substance, a drug, a combination of two or more of those substance, or any other substance into the body; or having an alcohol concentration of 0.08 or more.").

48. *See* Lori Raye Court Reporters, Examination under Oath of Marcelline Burns, 1, 39-40 (April 17, 1998).

49. *See* Jack Stuster & Marcelline Burns, *Validation of the Standardized Field Sobriety Test Battery at BACs Below 0.10 Percent*, (Contract No. DTNH22-95-C-05192) U.S Department of Transportation and National Highway Traffic Safety Administration, 1, 32 (August 1998).

50. *See* Harold Pashler, *Dual-Task Interference in Simple Tasks: Data and Theory*, 116 PSYCHOLOGICAL BULLETIN 220, 238 (1994).

51. *See Id.*

52. *See Id* at 220.

53. *Id* at 241.

54. *See* Lucas & Lauwereyns, *supra* note 43 at 262.

55. *See* Roozendaal, *supra* note 23 at 591.

56. *See Id* at 588.

57. *See* Lucas & Lauwereyns, *supra* note 43 at 256.

58. *See* Roozendaal, *supra* note 23 at 588.

59. *See Id* at 587.

60. *Id* at 585-86 (Rats in the study were trained in a water maze to find a platform located in a specific location. Immediately after exposure to foot-shock, the rats were unable to readily identify the location of the platform previously known to each rat tested. However, after a short time elapsed following the foot-shock, rats were able to easily find the platform location again.).

61. *See Id* at 585.

62. *See Id* at 587.

63. Banich et al., *supra* note 29 at 618.

64. *See* Taylor & Fragopanagos, *supra* note 38 at 356.

65. *See* LeDoux, *supra* note 5 at 728.

66. Misslin, *supra*, at 59.

67. *See* Banich et al., *supra* note 29 at 620.

68. *See Id.* at 624.

69. *See* Sapolsky, *supra* note 13 at 1789.

Appendix G

North Carolina Pattern Jury Instructions for Criminal Cases

North Carolina Pattern Jury Instructions for Criminal Cases, individual instructions listed below with date of most current instruction provided. Published the School of Government for the North Carolina Conference of Superior Court Judges: Committee on Pattern Jury Instructions.

- 202.20 Aiding and Abetting-Felony, Misdemeanor (June 2014)
- 206.55A Involuntary Manslaughter (Impaired Driving) (June 2014)
- 206.57A Felony Death By Vehicle (June 2014)
- 206.57B Aggravated Felony Death By Vehicle (June 2014)
- 206.57C Felony Serious Injury By Vehicle (June 2014)
- 206.57D Aggravated Felony Serious Injury By Vehicle (June 2014)
- 270.05A Punishment Levels for Impaired Driving (January 1999)
- 270.15 Aggravating Factors for Impaired Driving (June 2012)
- 270.20A Impaired Driving Misdemeanor (June 2014)
- 270.21A Impaired Driving In a Commercial Vehicle Misdemeanor (June 2014)
- 270.25A Habitual Impaired Driving-Including Chemical Test Felony (June 2015)
- 270.30 Driving by a Person Less Than 21 Years Old (While) (After) Consuming Alcohol or Drugs Misdemeanor (May 1999)
- 270A.25 Operating Vessel While Under the Influence of an Impairing Substance Misdemeanor (June 2008)

Credit Statement:

N.C.P.I.—CRIM 202.20
AIDING AND ABETTING—FELONY, MISDEMEANOR.
GENERAL CRIMINAL VOLUME
JUNE 2014
N.C. Gen. Stat. § 4-1; 14-5.2

202.20 AIDING AND ABETTING—FELONY, MISDEMEANOR.[1]

A person may be guilty of (*name crime*) although the defendant personally does not do any of the acts necessary to constitute that crime. A person who aids and abets another to commit a crime is guilty of that crime. You must clearly understand that if the defendant does aid and abet, the defendant is guilty of the crime, just as if the defendant had personally done all the acts necessary to constitute that crime.

For you to find the defendant guilty of (*name crime*) because of aiding and abetting, the State must prove three things beyond a reasonable doubt:

First, that the crime of (*name crime*) was committed by some other person(s).[2] (*Here give the elements of the crime as they relate to this case*).[3]

Second, that the defendant knowingly [advised] [instigated] [encouraged] [procured] [aided] the other person(s) to commit that crime.

(A person is not guilty of a crime merely because the defendant is present at the scene, even though the defendant may silently approve of the crime or secretly intend to assist in its commission. To be guilty the defendant must aid or actively encourage the person committing the crime, or in some way communicate to this person the defendant's intention to assist in its commission.)[4]

And Third, that the defendant's actions or statements caused or contributed to the commission of the crime by that other person.[5]

If you find from the evidence beyond a reasonable doubt that on or about the alleged date, some person(s) other than the defendant committed (name crime), that the defendant knowingly [advised] [instigated] [encouraged] [procured] [aided] the other person(s) to commit the crime, and that in so doing the defendant's actions or statements caused or contributed to the commission of the crime by the other person(s), it would be your duty to return a verdict of guilty of (name crime). If you do not so find or have a reasonable doubt as to one or more of these things, it would be your duty to return a verdict of not guilty.

Notes:

1. This charge may be given in connection with a charge on the principal crime where it is not clear whether defendant, if he committed the crime at all, actually committed the crime himself or did so as an aider and abettor. For special problems where the aider and abettor is tried alone, see *S. v. Jackson*, 270 N.C. 773 (1967).

2. *S. v. Bond*, 345 N.C. 1, 24 (1996), citing *S. v. Francis*, 341 N.C. 156 (1995).A showing of the defendant's presence, or lack thereof, is not required.

   Accessories before the fact who do not actually commit the crime and may not have been present can be convicted of the crime under a theory of aiding and abetting.

3. The parenthetical language should be given only if a mandate on the principal crime has not been given elsewhere.

4. This paragraph should be given only where there is support in the evidence for a finding that defendant was present at the scene of the crime. *S. v. Beach*, 283 N.C. 261, 267-268 (1973), states that there is an exception to the rule that mere presence does not make one an accessory:"'...when the bystander is a friend of the perpetrator, and knows that his presence will be regarded by the perpetrator as an encouragement and protection, presence alone may be regarded as an encouragement, and in contemplation of the law this was aiding and abetting.'" *See S. v. Walden*, 306 N.C. 466 (1982).

5. *See S. v. Davis*, 319 N.C. 620 (1987).

N.C.P.I.—CRIM 206.55A
INVOLUNTARY MANSLAUGHTER-(IMPAIRED DRIVING). FELONY.
GENERAL CRIMINAL VOLUME
JUNE 2014
N.C. Gen. Stat. § 20-141.4

206.55A INVOLUNTARY MANSLAUGHTER—(IMPAIRED DRIVING). FELONY.

NOTE WELL: This instruction is to be used for offenses occurring on or after December 1, 2006. For offenses occurring before December 1, 2006, use N.C.P.I. Crim. 206.56.

CAUTION: If the jury convicts the defendant of this involuntary manslaughter offense involving impaired driving[1] and driving while impaired, the court should arrest judgment on the driving while impaired offense.

The defendant has been charged with involuntary manslaughter.[2]

For you to find the defendant guilty of this offense, the State must prove four things beyond a reasonable doubt:

First, that the defendant was driving[3] a [vehicle][4] [commercial vehicle].

Second, that the defendant was driving that vehicle upon a [highway] [street] [public vehicular area] within the state.[5]

Third, that at the time the defendant was driving that [vehicle] [commercial vehicle] the defendant:

a) [was under the influence of an impairing substance.[6] ((*Name substance involved*) is an impairing substance.) The defendant is under the influence of an impairing substance when the defendant has taken (or consumed) a sufficient quantity of that impairing substance to cause the defendant to lose the normal control of the defendant's bodily or mental faculties, or both, to such an extent that there is an appreciable impairment of either or both of these faculties.[7]]
b) [had consumed sufficient alcohol that a chemical analysis[8] made at any relevant time after driving showed the defendant to have an alco-

hol concentration[9] of [0.08] [0.04][10] or more grams of alcohol [per 210 liters of breath] [per 100 milliliters of blood]. A relevant time is any time after driving in which the driver still has in the driver's body alcohol consumed before or during driving].[11]

c) [had any amount of [a Schedule I controlled substance] [metabolites of a Schedule I controlled substance] in the defendant's [blood] [urine] [breath]]. (*Name substance*) is a Schedule I controlled substance[12] or is a metabolite of a Schedule I controlled substance.].[13]

(If the evidence tends to show that [a chemical test known as a(n) [intoxilizer] [breathalyzer] [blood test] [urine test][14] was offered to the defendant by a law enforcement officer and that the defendant refused to take the test] [the defendant refused to perform a field sobriety test at the request of an officer], you may consider this evidence together with all other evidence in determining whether the defendant was under the influence of an impairing substance at the time the defendant (allegedly) drove a motor vehicle.)[15]

And Fourth, that the impaired driving by the defendant proximately caused the victim's death. Proximate cause is a real cause, a cause without which the victim's death would not have occurred, and one that a reasonably careful and prudent person could foresee would probably produce such [injury] [damage] or some similar injurious result. (The defendant's act(s) need not have been the last, or nearest cause. It is sufficient if [it] [they] concurred with some other cause acting at the same time which, in combination with, proximately caused the victim's death.)

If you find from the evidence beyond a reasonable doubt that on or about the alleged date the defendant drove a [vehicle] [commercial vehicle] on a [highway] [street] [public vehicular area] and that when the defendant did so the defendant [was under the influence of an impairing substance] [had consumed sufficient alcohol that a chemical analysis made at any relevant time after driving showed the defendant to have an alcohol concentration of [0.08] [0.04] or more grams of alcohol [per 210 liters of breath] [per 100 milliliters of blood]][had any amount of [a Schedule I controlled substance] [metabolites of a Schedule I controlled substance] in the defendant's blood or urine], and that defendant's impaired driving proximately caused the victim's death, it would be your duty to return a verdict of guilty. If you do not so find or have a reasonable doubt as to one or more of these things, it would be your duty to return a verdict of not guilty.[16]

Notes:

1. *See S v. Williams*, 90 N.C. App. 614, disc. *rev. den'd*, 323 N.C. 369 (1988), holding that felony death by vehicle is not a lesser included offense of involuntary manslaughter, but misdemeanor death by vehicle may be.

   See also State v. Mumford, 364 N.C. 394, 699 S.E.2d 911 (2010), holding that verdicts of guilty of the greater offense of felony serious injury by vehicle but not guilty on the lesser offense of driving while impaired were inconsistent but not mutually exclusive. N.C. Gen. Stat. § 20-141.1(a3), felony serious injury by vehicle, does not require a conviction of driving while impaired, but only a finding that defendant was engaged in the conduct described.

2. As a matter of law the violation of the driving while impaired statute, N.C. Gen. Stat. § 20-138.1 (1983), constitutes culpable negligence. *S. v. McGill*, 314 N.C. at 637 (1985).

3. N.C. Gen. Stat. § 20-4.01 defines the driver as the operator of a vehicle.

4. If there is any doubt, define "vehicle" under N.C. Gen. Stat. § 20-4.01(49), or "motor vehicle" under § 20-4.01(23).

5. If there is any doubt, define "highway" or "street" in accordance with N.C. Gen. Stat. § 20-4.01(13). "Public vehicular area" is defined in N.C. Gen. Stat. § 20-4.01(32).

6. An impairing substance includes alcohol, controlled substance under Chapter 90 of the General Statutes, or any other drug or psychoactive substance capable of impairing a person's physical or mental faculties, or any combination of these substances. N.C. Gen. Stat. § 20-4.01(14a).

7. N.C. Gen. Stat. § 20-4.01(48a).

8. N.C. Gen. Stat. § 20-4.01(3a) defines chemical analysis as "a chemical analysis of the breath or blood of a person to determine his alcohol concentration, performed in accordance with N.C. Gen. Stat. § 20-139.1. The term 'chemical analysis' includes duplicate or sequential analyses when necessary or desirable to insure the integrity of test results."

9. N.C. Gen. Stat. § 20-4.01(0.2) defines alcohol concentration as "the concentration of alcohol in a person, expressed either as (a) grams of alcohol per 100 milliliters of blood; or (b) grams of alcohol per 210 liters of breath.

10. Use 0.04 where a commercial vehicle is involved.

11. N.C. Gen. Stat. § 20-4.01(33a).

12. A metabolite is any substance produced or used during metabolism (digestion). In drug use, the term usually refers to the end product that remains after metabolism.

13. Driving with any Schedule I controlled substance, or its metabolites in one's blood or urine is a *per se* violation of impaired driving offense.

14. Note that if the offense occurred between December 1, 2006 and June 27, 2007, there was no statutory provision during this time that required the defendant to take a urine test.

16. N.C. Gen. Stat. § 20-139.1(f).

16. Note that Misdemeanor Death by Vehicle can be a lesser offense included within this offense. *See* note 1.

N.C.P.I.—CRIM 206.57A
FELONY DEATH BY VEHICLE. FELONY.
GENERAL CRIMINAL VOLUME
JUNE 2014
N.C. Gen. Stat. § 20-141.4(a1)

206.57A FELONY DEATH BY VEHICLE. FELONY. .

NOTE WELL: This instruction is to be used for offenses occurring on or after December 1, 2006. For offenses occurring before December 1, 2006, use N.C.P.I.–Crim. 206.57.

NOTE WELL: If a separate charge of driving while impaired is submitted, then the jury may only convict the defendant of this offense if it also convicts the defendant of driving while impaired. See State v. Mumford, 2010 No. COA09-300, N.C. App. LEXIS 35, (Jan. 5, 2010).

CAUTION: If the jury convicts the defendant of this offense and driving while impaired, the court should arrest judgment on the driving while impaired offense. If the jury finds the defendant not guilty of driving while impaired, the court must arrest judgment on this offense.

The defendant has been charged with felony death by vehicle.

For you to find the defendant guilty of this offense, the State must prove four things beyond a reasonable doubt:

First, that the defendant was driving[1] a [vehicle][2] [commercial vehicle].[3]

Second, that the defendant was driving that [vehicle] [commercial vehicle] upon a [highway] [street] [public vehicular area] within the state.[4]

Third, that at the time the defendant was driving that [vehicle] [commercial vehicle] the defendant:

NOTE WELL: If the evidence supports submission of the case under alternatives (A), (B) and (C), instructions on each alternative should be given.

(A) [was under the influence of an impairing substance. (*Name substance involved*) is an impairing substance.[5] The defendant is under the influence of an impairing substance when the defendant has taken (or consumed) a sufficient quantity of that impairing substance to cause the defendant to lose the normal control of the defendant's bodily or mental faculties, or both, to such an extent that there is an appreciable impairment of either or both of these faculties.[6]]

(B) [had consumed sufficient alcohol that at any relevant time after driving the defendant had an alcohol concentration[7] of [0.08[[0.04][8] or more grams of alcohol [per 210 liters of breath] [per 100 milliliters of blood]. A relevant time is any time after driving that the driver still has in the driver's body alcohol consumed before or during driving].[9] The results of a chemical analysis are deemed sufficient evidence to prove a person's alcohol concentration.[10]

(C) [had any amount of [a Schedule I controlled substance] [metabolites of a Schedule I controlled substance] in the defendant's blood or urine]. (*Name substance*) is a Schedule I controlled substance or is a metabolite[11] of Schedule I controlled substance.].[12]

(If the evidence tends to show that [a chemical test known as a(n) [intoxilizer] [breathalyzer] [blood test] [urine test][13] was offered to the defendant by a law enforcement officer and that the defendant refused to take the test] [the defendant refused to perform a field sobriety test at the request of an officer], you may consider this evidence together with all other evidence in determining whether the defendant was under the influence of an impairing substance at the time the defendant (allegedly) drove a motor vehicle.)[14]

And Fourth, that the impaired driving by the defendant proximately but unintentionally caused the victim's death. Proximate cause is a real cause, a cause without which the victim's death would not have occurred, and one that a reasonably careful and prudent person could foresee would probably produce such [injury] [damage] or some similar injurious result. (The defendant's act(s) need not have been the last, or nearest cause. It is sufficient if [it] [they] concurred with some other cause acting at the same time which, in combination with it, proximately caused the victim's death.)

If you find from the evidence beyond a reasonable doubt that on or about the alleged date, the defendant drove a [vehicle] [commercial vehicle] on a [highway] [street] (or) [public vehicular area] in this state and that when doing so the defendant [was under the influence of an impairing substance] [had consumed sufficient alcohol that at any relevant time after driving the defendant had an alcohol concentration of [0.08] [0.04] or more grams of alcohol [per 210 liters of breath] [per 100 milliliters of blood]] [had any amount of [a Schedule I controlled substance] [metabolites of a Schedule I controlled substance] in the defendant's blood or urine], and that defendant's impaired driving proximately but unintentionally caused the victim's death, it would be your duty to return a verdict of guilty. If you do not so find or have a reasonable doubt as to one or more of these things, it would be your duty to return a verdict of not guilty.[15]

Notes:

1. N.C. Gen. Stat. § 20-4.01 defines the driver as the operator of a vehicle.
2. If there is any doubt, define "vehicle" under N.C. Gen. Stat. § 20-4.01(49), or "motor vehicle" under § 20-4.01(23).
3. N.C. Gen. Stat. § 20-4.01(3d) a and b defines commercial vehicle. *See also State v. Jones* 140 N.C. App. 691, 538 S.E.2d 228 (2000).
4. If there is any doubt, define "highway" or "street" in accordance with N.C. Gen. Stat. § 20-4.01(13). "Public vehicular area" is defined in N.C. Gen. Stat. § 20-4.01(32).
5. An impairing substance includes alcohol, controlled substance under Chapter 90 of the General Statutes, or any other drug or psychoactive substance capable of impairing a person's physical or mental faculties, or any combination of these substances. N.C. Gen. Stat. § 20-4.01(14a).
6. N.C. Gen. Stat. § 20-4.01(48a).
7. N.C. Gen. Stat. § 20-4.01(1b) defines alcohol concentration as "the concentration of alcohol in a person, expressed either as (a) grams of alcohol per 100 milliliters of blood; or (b) grams of alcohol per 210 liters of breath."
8. Use 0.04 where a commercial vehicle is involved.
9. N.C. Gen. Stat. § 20-4.01 (33a).
10. The term "deemed sufficient" is not defined in N.C. Gen. Stat. § 20-141.4, other statutes or any appellate court decisions. Absent a specific definition, it can be presumed that the legislature intended the words to be given their ordinary meaning.
11. A metabolite is any substance produced or used during metabolism (digestion). In drug use, the term usually refers to the end product that remains after metabolism.
12. Driving with any Schedule I controlled substance, or its metabolites in one's blood or urine is a per se violation of impaired driving offense.
13. Note that if the offense occurred between December 1, 2006 and June 27, 2007, there was no statutory provision during this time that required the defendant to take a urine test.
14. N.C. Gen. Stat. § 20-139.1(f).
15. Note that Misdemeanor Death by Vehicle is not a lesser offense included within this offense. *See* N.C.P.I.–Crim. 206.58.

N.C.P.I.—CRIM 206.57B
AGGRAVATED FELONY DEATH BY VEHICLE. FELONY.
GENERAL CRIMINAL VOLUME
JUNE 2014
N.C. Gen. Stat. § 20-141.4(a5)

206.57B AGGRAVATED FELONY DEATH BY VEHICLE. FELONY.

NOTE WELL: This instruction applies to offenses occurring on or after December 1, 2006. See N.C. Gen. Stat. § 15A-928 for provisions regarding indictment, bifurcated trial, verdict, and judgment.

NOTE WELL: If a separate charge of driving while impaired is submitted, then the jury may only convict the defendant of this offense if it also convicts the defendant of driving while impaired. See State v. Mumford, 2010 No. COA09-300, N.C. App. LEXIS 35, (Jan. 5, 2010).

CAUTION: If the jury convicts the defendant of this offense and driving while impaired, the court should arrest judgment on the driving while impaired offense. If the jury finds the defendant not guilty of driving while impaired, the court must arrest judgment on this offense.

The defendant has been charged with aggravated felony death by vehicle.

For you to find the defendant guilty of this offense, the State must prove five things beyond a reasonable doubt:

First, that the defendant was driving[1] a [vehicle][2] [commercial vehicle].[3]

Second, that the defendant was driving that [vehicle] [commercial vehicle] upon a [highway] [street] [public vehicular area] within the state.[4]

Third, that at the time the defendant was driving that [vehicle] [commercial vehicle] the defendant:

NOTE WELL: If the evidence supports submission of the case under alternatives (A), (B) and (C), instructions on each alternative should be given.

(A) [was under the influence of an impairing substance. (*Name substance involved*) is an impairing substance.[5] The defendant is under the influence of an impairing substance when the defendant has taken (or consumed) a sufficient quantity of that impairing substance to cause the defendant to lose the normal control of the defendant's bodily or mental faculties, or both, to such an extent that there is an appreciable impairment of either or both of these faculties.[6]]

(B) [Had consumed sufficient alcohol that at any relevant time after driving the defendant had an alcohol concentration[7] of [0.08] [0.04][8] or more grams of alcohol [per 210 liters of breath] [per 100 milliliters of blood]. A relevant time is any time after driving that the driver still has in the driver's body alcohol consumed before or during driving].[9] The results of a chemical analysis are deemed sufficient evidence to prove a person's alcohol concentration.[10]

(C) [Had any amount of [a Schedule I controlled substance] [metabolites of a Schedule I controlled substance] in the defendant's [blood] [urine] [breath]]. (*Name substance*) is a Schedule I controlled substance or is a metabolite[11] of a Schedule I controlled substance.].[12]

(If the evidence tends to show that [a chemical test known as a(n) [intoxilizer] [breathalyzer] [blood test] [urine test][13] was offered to the defendant by a law enforcement officer and that the defendant refused to take the test] [the defendant refused to perform a field sobriety test at the request of an officer], you may consider this evidence together with all other evidence in determining whether the defendant was under the influence of an impairing substance at the time the defendant (allegedly) drove a motor vehicle.)[14]

Fourth, that the impaired driving by the defendant proximately but unintentionally caused the victim's death. Proximate cause is a real cause, a cause without which the victim's death would not have occurred, and one that a reasonably careful and prudent person could foresee would probably produce such [injury] [damage] or some similar injurious result. (The defendant's act(s) need not have been the last, or nearest cause. It is sufficient if [it] [they] concurred with some other cause acting at the same time which, in combination with [it] [them], proximately caused the victim's death.)

And Fifth, that on (*name date*) in (*name court*) defendant was convicted of driving while impaired and this conviction was within seven years of the defendant's driving.

If you find from the evidence beyond a reasonable doubt that on or about the alleged date, the defendant drove a [vehicle] [commercial vehicle] on a [highway] [street] (or) [public vehicular area] in this state and that when doing so the defendant [was under the influence of an impairing substance] [had consumed sufficient alcohol that at any relevant time after driving the defendant had an alcohol concentration of [0.08] [0.04] or more grams of alcohol [per 210 liters of breath] [per 100 milliliters of blood]] [had any amount of [a Schedule I controlled substance] [metabolites of a Schedule I controlled substance] in the defendant's blood or urine], that defendant's impaired driving proximately but unintentionally caused the victim's death, and that at the time the defendant was driving, the defendant had been convicted within the past seven years driving while impaired, it would be your duty to return a verdict of guilty. If you do not so find or have a reasonable doubt as to one or more of these things, you would not return a verdict of guilty of aggravated felony death by vehicle but would consider whether the defendant is guilty of felony death by vehicle. Felony death by vehicle differs from aggravated felony death by vehicle in that the State need not prove that the defendant had been convicted within the past seven years of an offense involving impaired driving.

If you find from the evidence beyond a reasonable doubt that on or about the alleged date, the defendant drove a [vehicle] [commercial vehicle] on a [highway] [street] [public vehicular area] in this state and that when doing so the defendant [was under the influence of an impairing substance] [had consumed sufficient alcohol that at any relevant time after driving the defendant had an alcohol concentration of [0.08] [0.04] or more] [had any amount of [a Schedule I controlled substance] [metabolites of a Schedule I controlled substance] in the defendant's [blood] [urine] [breath] and that defendant's impaired driving proximately but unintentionally caused the victim's death, it would be your duty to return a verdict of guilty. If you do not so find or have a reasonable doubt as to one or more of these things, it would be your duty to return a verdict of not guilty.[15]

Notes:

1. N.C. Gen. Stat. § 20-4.01 defines the driver as the operator of a vehicle.
2. If there is any doubt, define "vehicle" under N.C. Gen. Stat. § 20-4.01(49), or "motor vehicle" under § 20-4.01(23).
3. N.C. Gen. Stat. § 20-4.01(3d) a. and b. defines commercial vehicle. *See also State v. Jones* 140 N.C. App. 691, 538 S.E.2d 228 (2000).
4. If there is any doubt, define "highway" or "street" in accordance with N.C. Gen. Stat. § 20-4.01(13). "Public vehicular area" is defined in N.C. Gen. Stat. § 20-4.01(32).
5. An impairing substance includes alcohol, controlled substance under Chapter 90 of the General Statutes, or any other drug or psychoactive substance capable of impairing a person's physical or mental faculties, or any combination of these substances. N.C. Gen. Stat. § 20-4.01(14a).
6. N.C. Gen. Stat. § 20-4.01(48a).
7. N.C. Gen. Stat. § 20-4.01(1b) defines alcohol concentration as "the concentration of alcohol in a person, expressed either as (a) grams of alcohol per 100 milliliters of blood; or (b) grams of alcohol per 210 liters of breath."
8. Use 0.04 where a commercial vehicle is involved.
9. N.C. Gen. Stat. § 20-4.01 (33a).
10. The term "deemed sufficient" is not defined in N.C. Gen. Stat. § 20-141.4, other statutes or any appellate court decisions. Absent a specific definition, it can be presumed that the legislature intended the words to be given their ordinary meaning.
11. A metabolite is any substance produced or used during metabolism (digestion). In drug use, the term usually refers to the end product that remains after metabolism.
12. Driving with any Schedule I controlled substance, or its metabolites in one's blood or urine is a *per se* violation of impaired driving offense.
13. Note that if the offense occurred between December 1, 2006 and June 27, 2007, there was no statutory provision during this time that required the defendant to take a urine test.
14. N.C. Gen. Stat. § 20-139.1(f).
15. Note that Misdemeanor Death by Vehicle is not a lesser offense included within this offense. *See* N.C.P.I.–Crim. 206.58.

N.C.P.I.—CRIM 206.57C
FELONY SERIOUS INJURY BY VEHICLE. FELONY.
JUNE 2014
GENERAL CRIMINAL VOLUME
N.C. Gen. Stat. § 20-141.4(a3)

206.57C FELONY SERIOUS INJURY BY VEHICLE. FELONY.

NOTE WELL: This instruction applies to offenses occurring on or after December 1, 2006. See N.C. Gen. Stat. § 15A-928 for provisions regarding indictment, bifurcated trial, verdict, and judgment.

CAUTION: If the jury convicts the defendant of this offense and driving while impaired, the court should arrest judgment on the driving while impaired offense.[1]

The defendant has been charged with felony serious injury by vehicle.

For you to find the defendant guilty of this offense, the State must prove five things beyond a reasonable doubt:

First, that the defendant was driving[2] a [vehicle][3] [commercial vehicle].[4]

Second, that the defendant was driving that [vehicle] [commercial vehicle] upon a [highway] [street] [public vehicular area] within the state.[5]

Third, that at the time the defendant was driving that [vehicle] [commercial vehicle] the defendant:

NOTE WELL: If the evidence supports submission of the case under alternatives (A), (B) and (C), instructions on each alternative should be given.

(A) [was under the influence of an impairing substance. (*Name substance involved*) is an impairing substance.[6] The defendant is under the influence of an impairing substance when the defendant has taken (or consumed) a sufficient quantity of that impairing substance to cause the defendant to lose the normal control of the defendant's bodily or mental faculties, or both, to such an extent that there is an appreciable impairment of either or both of these faculties.[7]]

(B) [had consumed sufficient alcohol that at any relevant time after driving the defendant had an alcohol concentration[8] of [0.08] [0.04][9] or more grams of alcohol [per 210 liters of breath] [per 100 milliliters of blood]. A relevant time is any time after driving that the driver still has in the driver's body alcohol consumed before or during driving].[10] The results of a chemical analysis are deemed sufficient evidence to prove a person's alcohol concentration.[11]

(C) [had any amount of a [Schedule I controlled substance] [metabolites of a Schedule I controlled substance] in the defendant's [blood] [urine] [breath]]. (*Name substance*) is a Schedule I controlled substance or is a metabolite[12] of a Schedule I controlled substance.].[13]

(If the evidence tends to show that [a chemical test known as a(n) [intoxilizer] [breathalyzer] [blood test] [urine test][14] was offered to the defendant by a law enforcement officer and that the defendant refused to take the test] [the defendant refused to perform a field sobriety test at the request of an officer], you may consider this evidence together with all other evidence in determining whether the defendant was under the influence of an impairing substance at the time the defendant drove a motor vehicle.)[15]

Fourth, that the victim was seriously injured.[16]

And Fifth, that the impaired driving by the defendant proximately, but unintentionally, caused the victim's serious injury. Proximate cause is a real cause, a cause without which the victim's serious injury would not have occurred, and one that a reasonably careful and prudent person could foresee would probably produce such [injury] [damage] or some similar injurious result. (The defendant's act(s) need not have been the last, or nearest cause. It is sufficient if [it] [they] concurred with some other cause acting at the same time which, in combination with [it] [them], proximately caused the victim's serious injury.)

If you find from the evidence beyond a reasonable doubt that on or about the alleged date, the defendant drove a [vehicle] [commercial vehicle] on a [highway] [street] [public vehicular area] in this state and that when doing so the defendant [was under the influence of an impairing substance] [had consumed sufficient alcohol that at any relevant time after driving the defendant had an alcohol concentration of [0.08] [0.04] or more grams of alcohol [per 210 liters of breath] [per 100 milliliters of blood]] [had any amount of [a Schedule I controlled substance] [metabolites of a Schedule I controlled substance] in the defendant's [blood] [urine] [breath]] and that defendant's impaired driving proximately but unintentionally caused the victim's serious injury, then it would be your duty to return a verdict of guilty. If you do not so find or have a reasonable doubt as to one or more of these things, it would be your duty to return a verdict of not guilty.

Notes:

1. *See State v. Mumford*, 364 N.C. 394, 699 S.E.2d 911 (2010), holding that verdicts of guilty of the greater offense of felony serious injury by vehicle but not guilty on the lesser offense of driving while impaired were inconsistent but not mutually exclusive. N.C. Gen. Stat. § 20-141.1(a3), felony serious injury by vehicle, does not require a conviction of driving while impaired, but only a finding that defendant was engaged in the conduct described.

2. N.C. Gen. Stat. § 20-4.01 defines the driver as the operator of a vehicle.

3. If there is any doubt, define "vehicle" under N.C. Gen. Stat. § 20-4.01(49), or "motor vehicle" under § 20-4.01(23).

4. N.C. Gen. Stat. § 20-4.01(3d) a and b defines commercial vehicle. *See also State v. Jones*, 140 N.C. App. 691, 538 S.E.2d 228 (2000).

5. If there is any doubt, define "highway" or "street" in accordance with N.C. Gen. Stat. § 20-4.01(13). "Public vehicular area" is defined in N.C. Gen. Stat. § 20-4.01(32).

6. An impairing substance includes alcohol, controlled substance under Chapter 90 of the General Statutes, or any other drug or psychoactive substance capable of impairing a person's physical or mental faculties, or any combination of these substances. N.C. Gen. Stat. § 20-4.01(14a).

7. N.C. Gen. Stat. § 20-4.01(48a).

8. N.C. Gen. Stat. § 20-4.01(1b) defines alcohol concentration as "the concentration of alcohol in a person, expressed either as (a) grams of alcohol per 100 milliliters of blood; or (b) grams of alcohol per 210 liters of breath."

9. Use 0.04 where a commercial vehicle is involved.

10. N.C. Gen. Stat. § 20-4.01(33a).

11. The term "deemed sufficient" is not defined in N.C. Gen. Stat. § 20-141.4, other statutes or any appellate court decisions. Absent a specific definition, it can be presumed that the legislature intended the words to be given their ordinary meaning.

12. A metabolite is any substance produced or used during metabolism (digestion). In drug use, the term usually refers to the end product that remains after metabolism.

13. Driving with any Schedule I controlled substance, or its metabolites in one's blood or urine is a *per se* violation of impaired driving offense.

14. Note that if the offense occurred between December 1, 2006 and June 27, 2007, there was no statutory provision during this time that required the defendant to take a urine test.

15. N.C. Gen. Stat. § 20-139.1(f).

16. Serious injury may be defined as "such physical injury as causes great pain and suffering." *See S. v. Jones*, 258 N.C. 89 (1962), and S. v. Ferguson, 261 N.C. 558 (1964).

N.C.P.I.—CRIM 206.57D
AGGRAVATED FELONY SERIOUS INJURY BY VEHICLE. FELONY.
GENERAL CRIMINAL VOLUME
JUNE 2014
N.C. Gen. Stat. § 20-141.4(a4)

206.57D AGGRAVATED FELONY SERIOUS INJURY BY VEHICLE. FELONY.

NOTE WELL: This instruction applies to offenses occurring on or after December 1, 2006. See N.C. Gen. Stat. § 15A-928 for provisions regarding indictment, bifurcated trial, verdict, and judgment.

NOTE WELL: If a separate charge of driving while impaired is submitted, then the jury may only convict the defendant of this offense if it also convicts the defendant of driving while impaired. See State v. Mumford, *2010 No. COA09-300, N.C. App. LEXIS 35, (Jan. 5, 2010).*

CAUTION: If the jury convicts the defendant of this offense and driving while impaired, the court should arrest judgment on the driving while impaired offense. If the jury finds the defendant not guilty of driving while impaired, the court must arrest judgment on this offense.

The defendant has been charged with aggravated felony serious injury by vehicle.

For you to find the defendant guilty of this offense, the State must prove six things beyond a reasonable doubt:

First, that the defendant was driving[1] a [vehicle][2] [commercial vehicle].[3]

Second, that the defendant was driving that [vehicle] [commercial vehicle] upon a [highway] [street] [public vehicular area] within the state.[4]

Third, that at the time the defendant was driving that [vehicle] [commercial vehicle] the defendant:

NOTE WELL: If the evidence supports submission of the case under alternatives (A), (B) and (C), instructions on each alternative should be given.

(A) [was under the influence of an impairing substance. (*Name substance involved*) is an impairing substance.[5] The defendant is under the influence of an impairing substance when the defendant has taken (or consumed) a sufficient quantity of that impairing substance to cause the defendant to lose the normal control of the defendant's bodily or mental faculties, or both, to such an extent that there is an appreciable impairment of either or both of these faculties.[6]]

(B) [had consumed sufficient alcohol that at any relevant time after driving the defendant had an alcohol concentration[7] of [0.08]][0.04][8] or more grams of alcohol [per 210 liters of breath] [per 100 milliliters of blood]. A relevant time is any time after driving that the driver still has in the driver's body alcohol consumed before or during driving].[9] The results of a chemical analysis are deemed sufficient evidence to prove a person's alcohol concentration.[10]

(C) [Had any amount of a [Schedule I controlled substance] [metabolites of a Schedule I controlled substance] in the defendant's [blood] [urine] [breath]]. (*Name substance*) is a Schedule I controlled substance or is a metabolite[11] of a Schedule I controlled substance.].[12]

(If the evidence tends to show that [a chemical test known as a(n) [intoxilizer] [breathalyzer] [blood test] [urine test][13] was offered to the defendant by a law enforcement officer and that the defendant refused to take the test] [the defendant refused to perform a field sobriety test at the request of an officer], you may consider this evidence together with all other evidence in determining whether the defendant was under the influence of an impairing substance at the time *he* (allegedly) drove a motor vehicle.)[14]

Fourth, that the victim was seriously injured.[15]

Fifth, that defendant's driving proximately but unintentionally caused the victim's serious injury. Proximate cause is a real cause, a cause without which the victim's serious injury would not have occurred, and one that a reasonably careful and prudent person could foresee would probably produce such [injury] [damage] or some similar injurious result. (The defendant's act(s) need not have been the last, or nearest cause. It is sufficient if [it] [they] concurred with some other cause acting at the same time which, in combination with [it] [them], proximately caused the victim's serious injury.)

And Sixth, that on (*name date*) in (*name court*) defendant was convicted of (*name offense*) which involved impaired driving and this conviction was within seven years of the defendant's driving.

If you find from the evidence beyond a reasonable doubt that on or about the alleged date, the defendant drove a [vehicle] [commercial vehicle] on a [highway] [street] [public vehicular area] in this state and that when doing so the defendant [was under the influence of an impairing substance] [had consumed sufficient alcohol that at any relevant time after driving the defendant had an alcohol concentration of [0.08] [0.04] or more grams of alcohol [per 210 liters of breath] [per 100 milliliters of blood]] [had any amount of [a Schedule I controlled substance] [metabolites of a Schedule I controlled substance] in the defendant's [blood] [urine] [breath]], that defendant's driving proximately but unintentionally caused the victim's serious injury, and that defendant had been convicted within the past seven years of an offense involving impaired driving, then it would be your duty to return a verdict of guilty. If you do not so find or have a reasonable doubt as to one or more of these things, you would not return a verdict of guilty, but would consider whether the defendant is guilty of Felony Serious Injury by Vehicle. Felony Serious Injury by Vehicle differs from Aggravated Felony Serious Injury by Vehicle in that the State need not prove that at the time the defendant was driving while impaired, the defendant had been convicted within the past seven years of an offense involving impaired driving.

If you find from the evidence beyond a reasonable doubt that on or about the alleged date, the defendant drove a vehicle on a [highway] [street] [public vehicular area] in this state and that when doing so the defendant [was under the influence of an impairing substance] [had consumed sufficient alcohol that at any relevant time after driving the defendant had an alcohol concentration of [0.08] [0.04] or more grams of alcohol [per 210 liters of breath] [per 100 milliliters of blood]] [had any amount of [a Schedule I controlled substance] [metabolites a Schedule I controlled substance] in the defendant's [blood] [urine] [breath], and that defendant's impaired driving proximately but unintentionally caused the victim's serious injury, then it would be your duty to return a verdict of guilty of felony serious injury by vehicle. If you do not so find or have a reasonable doubt as to one or more of these things, it would be your duty to return a verdict of not guilty.

Notes:

1. N.C. Gen. Stat. § 20-4.01 defines the driver as the operator of a vehicle.

2. If there is any doubt, define "vehicle" under N.C. Gen. Stat. § 20-4.01(49), or "motor vehicle" under § 20-4.01(23).

3. If there is any doubt, define "highway" or "street" in accordance with N.C. Gen. Stat. § 20-4.01(13). "Public vehicular area" is defined in N.C. Gen. Stat. § 20-4.01(32).

4. An impairing substance includes alcohol, controlled substance under Chapter 90 of the General Statutes, or any other drug or psychoactive substance capable of impairing a person's physical or mental faculties, or any combination of these substances. N.C. Gen. Stat. § 20-4.01(14a).

5. N.C. Gen. Stat. § 20-4.01(48a).

6. N.C. Gen. Stat. § 20-4.01(3a) defines chemical analysis as "a chemical analysis of the breath or blood of a person to determine his alcohol concentration, performed in accordance with N.C. Gen. Stat. § 20-139.1. The term 'chemical analysis' includes duplicate or sequential analyses when necessary or desirable to insure the integrity of test results."

7. N.C. Gen. Stat. § 20-4.01(1b) defines alcohol concentration as "the concentration of alcohol in a person, expressed either as (a) grams of alcohol per 100 milliliters of blood; or (b) grams of alcohol per 210 liters of breath.

8. Use 0.04 where a commercial vehicle is involved.

9. N.C. Gen. Stat. § 20-4.01(33a).

10. The term "deemed sufficient" is not defined in N.C. Gen. Stat. § 20-141.4, other statutes or any appellate court decisions. Absent a specific definition, it can be presumed that the legislature intended the words to be given their ordinary meaning.

11. A metabolite is any substance produced or used during metabolism (digestion). In drug use, the term usually refers to the end product that remains after metabolism.

12. Driving with any Schedule I controlled substance or its metabolites in one's blood or urine is a *per se* violation of impaired driving offense.

13. Note that if the offense occurred between December 1, 2006 and June 27, 2007, there was no statutory provision during this time that required the defendant to take a urine test.

14. N.C. Gen. Stat. § 20-139.1(f).

15. Serious injury may be defined as "such physical injury as causes great pain and suffering." *See S. v. Jones*, 258 N.C. 89 (1962), and *S. v. Ferguson*, 261 N.C. 558 (1964).

16. *See* N.C. Gen. Stat. § 20-4.01(24a). If the prior conviction would not obviously involve impaired driving, *e.g.* death by vehicle, first or second degree murder, or involuntary manslaughter, then additional facts will have to be found by the jury and the elements of these offenses should be included in the instruction at this point.

N.C.P.I.—Crim. 270.05A, Page 1

(See Figure G.1, next page.)

NOTE WELL: Structured sentencing doe not apply. This applies for offenses occurring on or after December 1, 1997.

Level	One	Two	Three	Four	Five
AGGRAVATING / MITIGATING FACTORS	Two or more grossly aggravating factors	One grossly aggravating factor	Aggravating factors outweigh mitigating factors	No aggravating/mitigating factors or they counter-balance each other	Mitigating factors outweigh aggravating factors
FINEl'l	Up to $4,000	Up to $2,000	Up to $1,000	Up to $500	Up to $200
IMPRISONMENT : FULL MAXIMUM MAXIMUM UNDER SPLIT SENTENCE	2 years 6 months	I year 3 months	6 months (may suspend) I 1/2 months	120 days (may suspend) 48 hours	60 days (may suspend) 24 hours
MINIMUM REQUIRED SENTENCE	30 days in jail	7 days in jail	72 hours in jail or 72 hours community service or 90 days without driving or Combination of above	48 hours in jail or 48 hours community service or 60 days without driving or Combination of above	24 hours in jail or 24 hours community service or 30 days without driving or Combination of above
CONDITIONS OF PROBATION Probation note (2) is applicable to all five levels of punishment.	(I) required if probation imposed. The term of imprisonment may be suspended only if a condition of special probation is imposed to require the defendant to serve 30 days imprisonment.	(I) required if probation imposed. The term of imprisonment may be suspended only if a condition of special probation is imposed to require the defendant to serve 7 days imprisonment.	(I) required if probation imposed.	(I) required if probation imposed.	(I) required if probation imposed.
LENGTH OF DMV REVOCATION	No prior conviction involving impaired driving in past three years: I year revocation		One year	One year	One year
	One such conviction in past three years: four-year revocation, but may apply after two years if record good.		(If an indigent defendant's prior conviction was obtained without counsel, it may not be used to set the punishment level, but it would be counted by the DMV to impose more than a one-year revocation in factually appropriate cases.)		
	Two such prior convictions (latest one in past five years): permanent, but may apply after three years if record good.				
LIMITED DRIVING PRIVILEGE	No	No	Yes, after 6 months revocation, if no prior convictions for offense involving impaired driving within 7 years of date of new offense; provided other conditions are met. G.S. 20-16.2(el) (i.e., substance abuse assessment has been obtained and has completed recommended treatment or education).		

Figure G.1: *Punishment Levels for Impaired Driving*

N.C.P.I.—Crim. 270.05A, Page 2

PROBATION NOTES:

(1) If placed on probation, defendant must obtain a substance-abuse assessment and must either submit to treatment if the assessment shows it is needed or successfully complete an Alcohol and Drug Education Traffic School (see G.S. 20-17.6)
(2) The judge continues to have discretion to impose other appropriate conditions of probation.

SENTENCING NOTES:

I. Under G .S. 15A-1351(a), the imprisonment portion of a split sentence (special probation) may not exceed 6 months or one-fourth of the statutory maximum, whichever is less.
2. Pursuant to G.S. 15A-1351(a) the judge may order that a term of imprisonment imposed as a condition of probation under any level of punishment be served as an inpatient in a state facility for treatment of alcoholism or substance abuse. See also G.S. 20-179(k1).
3. Under G.S. 20-17.6 a person convicted of impaired driving, to be eligible for a driver's license after the period of revocation has run, must obtain a substance abuse assessment and complete either the education or treatment required . This requirement applies regardless of whether defendant is placed on probation.

NOTE WELL:

G .S. 20-138.5(b) HABITUAL IMPAIRED DRIVING states that for offenses occurring on or after December I, 1997 "a person convicted of violating this section shall be punished as a Class F felon and shall be sentenced to a minimum active term of not less than 12 months of imprisonment, which shall not be suspended ."

FOOTNOTES:

[1] For offenses occurring prior to December 1, 1998, the maximum fme a defendant may be subject to for a level one punishment is $2,000, for a level two punishment is $1,000, for a level three punishment is $500, for a level four punishment is $250, and for a level five punishment is $100. Effective December 1, 1998, the maximum fine a defendant may be subject to for a level one punishment is $4,000, for a level two punishment is $2,000, for a level three punishment is $1,000, for a level four punishment is $500, and for a level five punishment is $200.

N.C.P.I.—Criminal 270.15
AGGRAVATING FACTORS FOR IMPAIRED DRIVING.
GENERAL CRIMINAL VOLUME
REPLACEMENT JUNE 2012
G.S. 20-179

AGGRAVATING FACTORS FOR IMPAIRED DRIVING.

NOTE WELL: In a 2005 decision, the North Carolina Supreme Court concluded that any fact that increases the penalty for a crime beyond the prescribed presumptive range, other than the fact of a prior conviction, must be submitted to a jury and proved beyond a reasonable doubt. See State v. Speight, *359 N.C. 602 (1 July 2005), modifying and affirming, 602 S.E.2d 4 (N.C. Ct. App. 2004). In 2006, the General Assembly amended G.S. § 20-179 (Session Law 2006-253). This amendment made the statute largely conform to the* Speight *decision; however, there are some differences which are explained in Note Wells below.*

The court has several options on how to proceed, including adding the aggravating factor as an element of the offense, bifurcating the proceeding, or in the absence of the jury arraigning the defendant upon the special indictment or information and advising him that he may admit the aggravating factor alleged, deny it, or remain silent. For procedural guidance, see, e.g., G.S. § 15A-928. In the event the defendant admits the aggravating factor(s), a record of the plea should be made and preserved. See G.S. § 15A-1026.

In the event you find (have found) the defendant guilty of impaired driving, you must then consider and answer the following question:

Do you find from the evidence beyond a reasonable doubt the existence of the following aggravating factor(s)?

NOTE WELL: Submit to the jury the aggravating factors supported by the evidence. G.S. § 20-179(c). Some of these aggravating factors are self-explanatory and require no further definition. If a factor requires additional explanation, relevant pattern jury instructions, such as the capital sentencing instruction, may be consulted.

The factors listed in G.S. § 20-179(c)(1)(a) and (c)(1)(b) are not included below, because the statute specifically notes that "whether a prior conviction exists under subdivision (1) of the subsection shall be a matter to be determined by the judge, and not the jury." See also State v. Allen, *359 N.C. 425 (1 July 2005), modifying and affirming, 601 S.E.2d 299 (N.C. Ct. App. 2004);* Blakely v. Washington, *124 S. Ct. 2531 (2004).*

(01) At the time of the offense, the defendant's license was revoked because of impaired driving.[1 2]

(02) There was serious injury to another person caused by the defendant's impaired driving at the time of the offense.

(03) At the time of the offense, the defendant was driving while a [child under the age of eighteen years] [a person with the mental development of a child under the age of eighteen years] [a person with a physical disability preventing unaided exit from the vehicle] was in the vehicle.

<u>NOTE WELL:</u> The factors listed in (01) through (03) above are grossly aggravating factors. Pursuant to G.S. § 20-179(c), the court must impose the Level One punishment under G.S. § 20-179(g) if the jury determines that (3) above or two other grossly aggravating factors apply. The court must impose the Level Two punishment under G.S. § 20-179(h) if the jury does not find (3) above and determines that only one of the grossly aggravating factors applies. In imposing a Level One or Two punishment, the judge may consider the aggravating and mitigating factors in G.S. § 20-179(d), (e) in determining the appropriate sentence.

<u>NOTE WELL:</u> Below are listed additional aggravating factors. Submit to the jury the aggravating factors supported by the evidence. G.S. § 20-179(d). In contrast to G.S. 20-179(c)(1)(a) and (c)(1)(b), subsection (d) of the statute does not specifically provide that prior convictions should be determined by the judge. Accordingly, the factor listed in G.S. § 20-179(d)(5), dealing with prior convictions, is included as (09) below. While it is certainly acceptable to have the jury determine the factor, it would seem that a judge could also determine the existence of this factor, given the treatment of prior convictions in subsection (c) and recent case law. See State v. Allen, *359 N.C. 425 (1 July 2005), modifying and affirming, 601 S.E.2d 299 (N.C. Ct. App. 2004);* Blakely v. Washington, *124 S. Ct. 2531 (2004).* See also State v. Speight, *359 N.C. 602 (1 July 2005), modifying and affirming, 602 S.E.2d 4 (N.C. Ct. App. 2004).*

<u>NOTE WELL:</u> For aggravating factors (04), and (06) through (12) below, G.S. § 20-179 specifically provides that "the conduct constituting the aggravating factor shall occur during the same transaction or occurrence as the impaired driving offense." The instruction's reference to "at the time of the offense" should be suitable for most circumstances, but can be amended if necessary to fit the circumstances of a particular case.

(04) At the time of the offense, the defendant's faculties were grossly impaired while driving.

(05) The defendant had an alcohol concentration of .16 or more at the time of the offense or within a relevant time of the driving involved in this offense.

(06) At the time of the offense, the defendant was driving especially [recklessly] [dangerously].

(07) At the time of the offense, the defendant's negligent driving led to a reportable accident.[3]

(08) At the time of the offense, the defendant was driving while his driver's license was revoked.[4]

(09) The defendant has [two or more prior convictions of a motor vehicle offense not involving impaired driving for which at least three points are assigned under G.S. 20-16 or for which the convicted person's license is subject to revocation, if the convictions occurred within five years of the date of the offense for which the defendant is being sentenced] [one or more prior convictions of an offense involving impaired driving that occurred more than seven years before the date of the offense for which the defendant is being sentenced].

(10) The defendant was convicted under G.S. 20-141.5 for speeding while [fleeing] [attempting to elude apprehension] at the time of the offense.

(11) The defendant was convicted under G.S. 20-141 for speeding by at least 30 miles per hour over the legal limit at the time of the offense.

(12) At the time of the offense, the defendant was passing a stopped school bus in violation of G.S. § 20-217.

NOTE WELL: If alleged in the indictment and supported by the evidence G.S. § 20-179(d)(9) provides for the allegation of additional factors that aggravate the seriousness of the offense.

NOTE WELL: If the jury finds the existence of the aggravating factors listed in (04) through (12), the judge must consider whether any mitigating factors are present and, if so, then perform the weighing and balancing contemplated in G.S. § 20-179.

If you find from the evidence beyond a reasonable doubt that (insert aggravating factor(s) supported by the evidence), then you will write "yes" in the space after the(se) aggravating factor(s) on the verdict sheet. If you have found the existence of (one or more of) the aggravating factor(s) and have written "yes" in the space after the(se) aggravating factor(s), then you will also answer Issue One "yes" and write "yes" in the space after Issue One on the verdict sheet.

STATE OF NORTH CAROLINA
IN THE GENERAL COURT OF JUSTICE
COUNTY OF _____________
SUPERIOR COURT DIVISION

FILE NO. Verdict Sheet
STATE OF NORTH CAROLINA
vs.

____
Defendant

Issue One:
Do you find from the evidence beyond a reasonable doubt the existence of the following aggravating factor(s)?
Answer: ______________

Before you answer the question above, consider (each of) the following aggravating factor(s). If you find beyond a reasonable doubt that a (the) factor exists, you would write "yes" in the space after that factor. If you write "yes" in (one or more of) the following space(s), then you would write "yes" in the space after the question above.

NOTE WELL: Modify verdict sheet and submit to the jury only the aggravating factors supported by the evidence. G.S. § 20-179(c).

(01) At the time of the offense, the defendant's license was revoked because of impaired driving.
Answer: ______________

(02) There was serious injury to another person caused by the defendant's impaired driving at the time of the offense.
Answer: ______________

(03) At the time of the offense, the defendant was driving while a [child under the age of eighteen years] [a person with the mental development of a child under the age of eighteen years] [a person with a physical disability preventing unaided exit from the vehicle] was in the vehicle.
Answer: ______________

(04) At the time of the offense, the defendant's faculties were grossly impaired while driving.
Answer: ______________

(05) The defendant had an alcohol concentration of .16 or more at the time of the offense or within a relevant time of the driving involved in this offense.
Answer: ______________

(06) At the time of the offense, the defendant was driving especially [recklessly] [dangerously].
Answer: ______________

(07) At the time of the offense, the defendant's negligent driving led to a reportable accident.
Answer: ______________

(08) At the time of the offense, the defendant was driving while his driver's license was revoked.
Answer: ______________

(09) The defendant has [two or more prior convictions of a motor vehicle offense not involving impaired driving for which at least three points are assigned under G.S. 20-16 or for which the convicted person's license is subject to revocation, if the convictions occurred within five years of the date of the offense for which the defendant is being sentenced] [one or more prior convictions of an offense involving impaired driving that occurred more than seven years before the date of the offense for which the defendant is being sentenced].
Answer: ______________

(10) The defendant was convicted under G.S. 20-141.5 for speeding while [fleeing] [attempting to elude apprehension] at the time of the offense.
Answer: ______________

(11) The defendant was convicted under G.S. 20-141 for speeding by at least 30 miles per hour over the legal limit at the time of the offense.
Answer: ______________

(12) At the time of the offense, the defendant was passing a stopped school bus in violation of G.S. § 20-217.

Answer: ____________

(13) At the time of the offense, the defendant was (list any other factor alleged in the indictment and supported by the evidence that aggravates the seriousness of the offense).

Answer: ____________

This the ____ day of ____________, ________.

____

Foreperson

Notes:

1. For the requirements of proving revocation and knowledge see N.C.P.I. 271.10. See also G.S. § 20-28 and 20-28.2(a).

2. Because of the nature of the aggravating factor alleged, the proceeding may have to be bifurcated.

3. See G.S. § 20-4.01 for a definition of a reportable accident.

4. Because of the nature of the aggravating factor alleged, the proceeding may have to be bifurcated.

N.C.P.I.—CRIM 270.20A
IMPAIRED DRIVING. MISDEMEANOR. (OFFENSES OCCURING ON OR AFTER DECEMBER 1,2006.)
GENERAL CRIMINAL VOLUME
JUNE 2014
N.C. Gen. Stat. § 20-138.1

270.20A IMPAIRED DRIVING. MISDEMEANOR.

> *NOTE WELL: This instruction is to be used for offenses occurring on or after December 1, 2006. For offenses occurring before December 1, 2006, use N.C.P.I.—Crim. 270.20. This instruction is also to be used when the defendant is charged with habitual impaired driving and admits previous conviction(s) under N.C. Gen. Stat. § 20-138.1 (or an equivalent statute from another jurisdiction). See N.C. Gen. Stat. § 15A-928.*

The defendant has been charged with impaired driving.

For you to find the defendant guilty of this offense, the State must prove three things beyond a reasonable doubt:

First, that the defendant was driving[1] a vehicle.[2]

Second, that the defendant was driving that vehicle upon a [highway] [street] [public vehicular area] within the state.[3]

And Third, that at the time the defendant was driving that vehicle, the defendant:

> *NOTE WELL: If the evidence supports submission of the case under alternatives (A) (B) and (C), instructions on each alternatives should be given.*

a. [Was under the influence of an impairing substance. (*Name substance involved*) is an impairing substance.[4] The defendant is under the influence of an impairing substance when the defendant has taken (or consumed) a sufficient quantity of that impairing substance to cause the defendant to lose the normal control of the defendant's bodily or mental faculties, or both, to such an extent that there is an appreciable impairment of either or both of these faculties.[5]]
b. [Had consumed sufficient alcohol that at any relevant time after the driving the defendant had an alcohol concentration[6] of 0.08 or more grams of alcohol [per 210 liters of breath] [per 100 milliliters of blood]. A relevant time is any time after the driving that the driver still has in the body alcohol consumed before or during the driving].[7] The results of a chemical analysis are deemed sufficient evidence to prove a person's alcohol concentration.[8]
c. [Had any amount of [a Schedule I control substance] [metabolites of a Schedule I controlled substance] in the defendant's blood or urine]. (*Name substance*) is a Schedule I control substance or is a metabolite[9] of a Schedule I control substance.].[10]

(If the evidence tends to show that [a chemical test known as a(n) [intoxilizer] [breathalyzer] [blood test] [urine test][11] was offered to the defendant by a law enforcement officer and that the defendant refused to take the test] (or) [the defendant refused to perform a field sobriety test at the request of an officer], you may consider this evidence together with all other evidence in determining whether the defendant was under the influence of an impairing substance at the time the defendant (allegedly) drove a motor vehicle.)[12]

If you find from the evidence beyond a reasonable doubt that on or about the alleged date, the defendant drove a vehicle on a [highway] [street] (or) [public vehicular area] in this state and that when doing so the defendant [was under the influence of an impairing substance] [had consumed sufficient alcohol that at any relevant time after the driving the defendant had an alcohol concentration of 0.08 or more] [had any amount of [a Schedule I controlled substance] [metabolites of a Schedule I controlled substance] in the defendant's [blood] [urine] [breath], it would be your duty to return a verdict of guilty. If you do not so find or have a reasonable doubt as one or more of these things, it would be your duty to return a verdict of not guilty.

Notes:

1. N.C. Gen. Stat. § 20-4.01 defines the driver as the operator of a vehicle.

2. If there is any doubt, define "vehicle" under N.C. Gen. Stat. § 20-4.01(49), or "motor vehicle" under N.C. Gen. Stat. § 20-4.01(23). The Safe Roads Act of 1983 makes this offense applicable to drivers of vehicles owned or operated by the State or any political subdivision thereof while engaged in maintenance or construction work on the highways. N.C. Gen. Stat. § 20-168(b). Effective December 1, 2006, lawnmowers and bicycles are no longer exempt. Horses remain exempt.

3. If there is any doubt, define "highway" or "street" in accordance with N.C. Gen. Stat. § 20-4.01(13). "Public vehicular area" is defined in N.C. Gen. Stat. § 20-4.01(32).

4. An impairing substance includes alcohol, controlled substance under Chapter 90 of the General Statutes, or any other drug or psychoactive substance capable of impairing a person's physical or mental faculties, or any combination of these substances. N.C. Gen. Stat. § 20-4.01(14a).

5. N.C. Gen. Stat. § 20-4.01(48a).

6. N.C. Gen. Stat. § 20-4.01(0.2) defines alcohol concentration as "the concentration of alcohol in a person, expressed either as (a) grams of alcohol per 100 milliliters of blood; or (b) grams of alcohol per 210 liters of breath."

7. N.C. Gen. Stat. § 20-4.01(33a).

8. The term "deemed sufficient" is not defined in N.C. Gen. Stat. § 20.138.1 or N.C. Gen. Stat. § 20-141.4, other statutes or any appellate court decisions. Absent a specific definition, it can be presumed that the legislature intended the words to be given their ordinary meaning.

9. A metabolite is any substance produced or used during metabolism (digestion). In drug use, the term usually refers to the end product that remains after metabolism.

10. Driving with any Schedule I controlled substance, or its metabolites in one's [blood] [urine] [breath] is a *per se* violation of impaired driving offense.

11. Note that if the offense occurred between December 1, 2006 and June 27, 2007, there was no statutory provision during this time that required the defendant to take a urine test.

12. N.C. Gen. Stat. § 20-139.1(f).

N.C.P.I.—CRIM 270.21A
IMPAIRED DRIVING IN A COMMERCIAL VEHICLE. MISDEMEANOR.
GENERAL CRIMINAL VOLUME
JUNE 2014
N.C. Gen. Stat. § 20-138.2 & 20-138.2A

270.21A IMPAIRED DRIVING IN A COMMERCIAL VEHICLE. MISDEMEANOR.

NOTE WELL: This instruction applies to offenses committed on or after December 1, 2006. For offenses committed before that date, use N.C.P.I.-Crim. 270.21

NOTE WELL: This offense is not a lesser included offense of impaired driving under N.C. Gen. Stat. § 20-138.1, but if a person is convicted under this section and of an offense involving impaired driving under N.C. Gen. Stat. § 20-138.1 arising out of the same transaction, the aggregate punishment imposed by the Court may not exceed the maximum punishment applicable to the offense involving impaired driving under N.C. Gen. Stat. § 20-138.1.

The defendant has been charged with impaired driving of a commercial vehicle.

For you to find the defendant guilty of this offense, the State must prove three things beyond a reasonable doubt:

First, that the defendant was driving[1] a commercial motor vehicle.[2]

Second, that the defendant was driving that vehicle upon a [highway] [street] [public vehicular area] within the state.[3]

And Third, that at the time the defendant was driving that vehicle, the defendant:

NOTE WELL: If the evidence supports submission of the case under alternative (A), (B) and (C), instructions on each alternative should be given.

(A) [was under the influence of an impairing substance. (*Name substance involved*) is an impairing substance.[4] The defendant is under the influence of an impairing substance when the defendant has taken (or consumed) a sufficient quantity of that impairing substance to cause the defendant to lose the normal control of the defendant's bodily or mental faculties, or both, to such an extent that there is an appreciable impairment of either or both of these faculties.[5]]

(B) [had consumed sufficient alcohol that at any relevant time after driving the defendant had an alcohol concentration[6] of 0.04 or more grams of alcohol [per 210 liters of breath] [per 100 milliliters of blood]. A relevant time is any time after driving that the driver still has in the driver's body alcohol consumed before or during driving].[7] The results of a chemical analysis are deemed sufficient evidence to prove a person's alcohol concentration.[8]

(C) [had any amount of [a Schedule I controlled substance] [metabolites of a Schedule I controlled substance] in the defendant's [blood] [urine] [breath]]. (*Name substance*) is a Schedule I controlled substance or is a metabolite[9] of a Schedule I controlled substance.].[10]

(If the evidence tends to show that [a chemical test known as a(n) [intoxilizer] [breathalyzer] [blood test] [urine test][11] was offered to the defendant by a law enforcement officer and that the defendant refused to take the test] [the defendant refused to perform a field sobriety test at the request of an officer], you may consider this evidence together with all other evidence in determining whether the defendant was under the influence of an impairing substance at the time the defendant (allegedly) drove a motor vehicle.)[12]

If you find from the evidence beyond a reasonable doubt that on or about the alleged date, the defendant drove a commercial vehicle on a [highway] [street] [public vehicular area] in this state and that when doing so the defendant [was under the influence of an impairing substance] [had consumed sufficient alcohol that at any relevant time after driving the defendant had an alcohol concentration of 0.04 or more] [had any amount of [a Schedule I controlled substance] [metabolites of a Schedule I controlled substance] in the defendant's [blood] [urine] [breath]], it would be your duty to return a verdict of guilty. If you do not so find or if you have a reasonable doubt as one or more of these things, you would not find the defendant guilty of impaired driving of a commercial vehicle, you must determine whether the defendant is guilty of operating a commercial vehicle after consuming alcohol.[13] Operating a commercial vehicle after consuming alcohol differs from impaired driving of a commercial vehicle in that the State need prove only that the defendant had consumed sufficient alcohol that at any relevant time after driving the defendant had an alcohol concentration greater than 0.00 but less than 0.04.

If you find from the evidence beyond a reasonable doubt that on or about the alleged date the defendant drove a commercial vehicle on a [highway] [street] [public vehicular area] in this state and that when the defendant did so the defendant had consumed sufficient alcohol that at any relevant time after driving the defendant had a blood alcohol concentration of greater than 0.00 and less than 0.04, it would be your duty to return a verdict of guilty of operating a commercial vehicle after consuming alcohol. If you do not so find or have a reasonable doubt as to one or more of these things, it would be your duty to return a verdict of not guilty.

Notes:

1. N.C. Gen. Stat. § 20-4.01 defines the driver as the operator of a vehicle.
2. N.C. Gen. Stat. § 20-4.01(3d) a. and b. defines commercial vehicle. See also State v. Jones, 140 N.C. App. 691, 538 S.E. 2d 228 (2000).
3. If there is any doubt, define "highway" or "street" in accordance with N.C. Gen. Stat. § 20-4.01(13). "Public vehicular area" is defined in N.C. Gen. Stat. § 20-4.01(32).

4. An impairing substance includes alcohol, controlled substance under Chapter 90 of the General Statutes, or any other drug or psychoactive substance capable of impairing a person's physical or mental faculties, or any combination of these substances. N.C. Gen. Stat. § 20-4.01(14a).

5. N.C. Gen. Stat. § 20-4.01(48a).

6. N.C. Gen. Stat. § 20-4.01(0.2) defines alcohol concentration as "the concentration of alcohol in a person, expressed either as (a) grams of alcohol per 100 milliliters of blood; or (b) grams of alcohol per 210 liters of breath."

7. N.C. Gen. Stat. § 20-4.01(33a).

8. The term "deemed sufficient" is not defined in N.C. Gen. Stat. §§ 20-138.2 or 20-138.2A, N.C. Gen. Stat. § 20-141.4, other statutes or any appellate court decisions. Absent a specific definition, it can be presumed that the legislature intended the words to be given their ordinary meaning.

9. A metabolite is any substance produced or used during metabolism (digestion). In drug use, the term usually refers to the end product that remains after metabolism.

10. Driving with any Schedule I controlled substance, or its metabolites in one's [blood] [urine] [breath] is a *per se* violation of impaired driving offense.

11. Note that if the offense occurred between December 1, 2006 and June 27, 2007, there was no statutory provision during this time that required the defendant to take a urine test.

12. N.C. Gen. Stat. § 20-139.1(f).

13. N.C. Gen. Stat. § 20-138.2A became effective December 1, 1998.

N.C.P.I.—Crim 270.25A
HABITUAL IMPAIRED DRIVING—INCLUDING CHEMICAL TEST. FELONY
CRIMINAL VOLUME
REPLACEMENT JUNE 2015
N.C. Gen. Stat. § 20-138.2A

270.25A HABITUAL IMPAIRED DRIVING—INCLUDING CHEMICAL TEST. FELONY.

NOTE WELL: This instruction applies to offenses committed on or after December 1, 2006. For offenses committed before that date, use N.C.P.I.-Crim. 270.25.

The Court has several options on how to proceed, including adding the aggravating factor as an element of the offense, bifurcating the proceeding, or in the absence of the jury, arraigning the defendant upon the special indictment or information and advising the defendant that the defendant may admit the aggravating factor alleged, deny it, or remain silent. For procedural guidance, see, e.g. N.C. Gen. Stat. § 15A-928. In the event the defendant admits the aggravating factor(s), a record of the plea should be made and preserved. See N.C. Gen. Stat. § 15A-1026.

Use this instruction only if the defendant denies a previous conviction or remains silent. If the defendant admits the previous convictions, use N.C.P.I.-Crim. 270.20A. (And see N.C. Gen. Stat. § 15A-928).

If the defendant admits to having been convicted within the preceding ten years of three or more offenses involving impaired driving, that element of the offense is established and no evidence in support thereof may be adduced by the State. If the defendant denies having been convicted within the past ten years of three or more offenses involving impaired driving or remains silent, the State must prove the fourth element of the offense charged before the jury as part of its case. (See N.C. Gen. Stat. § 15A-928).

The defendant has been charged with (habitual)[1] impaired driving.

For you to find the defendant guilty of this offense, the State must prove four things beyond a reasonable doubt:

First, that the defendant was driving[2] a vehicle.[3]

Second, that the defendant was driving that vehicle upon a [highway] [street] (or) [public vehicular area] within the state.[4]

Third, that at the time the defendant was driving that vehicle, the defendant:

NOTE WELL: If the evidence supports submission of the case under alternatives (A) (B) and (C), instructions on each alternatives should be given.

a. [Was under the influence of an impairing substance. (*Name substance involved*) is an impairing substance.[5] The defendant is under the influence of an impairing substance when the defendant has taken (or consumed) a sufficient quantity of that impairing substance to cause the defendant to lose the normal control of the defendant's bodily or mental faculties, or both, to such an extent that there is an appreciable impairment of either or both of these faculties.[6]]
b. [Had consumed sufficient alcohol that at any relevant time after the driving the defendant had an alcohol concentration[7] of 0.08 or more grams of alcohol [per 210 liters of breath] [per 100 milliliters of blood]. A relevant time is any time after the driving that the driver still has in the driver's body alcohol consumed before or during driving].[8] The results of a chemical analysis are deemed sufficient evidence to prove a person's alcohol concentration.[9]
c. [Had any amount of a [Schedule I controlled substance] [metabolites of a Schedule I controlled substance] in his/her blood or urine]. (*Name substance*) is a Schedule I controlled substance or is a metabolite[10] of a Schedule I controlled substance.].[11]

(If the evidence tends to show that [a chemical test known as a(n) [intoxilizer] [breathalyzer] [blood test] [urine test][12] was offered to the defendant by a law enforcement officer and that the defendant refused to take the test] [the defendant refused to perform a field sobriety test at the request of an officer], you may consider this evidence together with all other evidence in determining whether the defendant was under the influence of an impairing substance at the time the defendant (allegedly) drove a motor vehicle.)[13]

<u>And Fourth,</u> that at the time the defendant was driving while impaired, the defendant had been convicted of the following three (or more) offenses, which all involve impaired driving, within the past ten years of the dates of this offense:

1. On (*name date*), the defendant in (**name court**) [was convicted of] [plead guilty to] the offense of (*name offense involving impaired driving*), that was committed on (*name date*); and
2. On (*name date*), the defendant in (*name court*) [was convicted of] [plead guilty to] the offense of (*name offense involving impaired driving*), that was committed on (*name date*); and
3. On (*name date*), the defendant in (*name court*) [was convicted of] [plead guilty to] the offense of (*name offense involving impaired driving*), that was committed on (*name date*).

If you find from the evidence beyond a reasonable doubt that on or about the alleged date, the defendant drove a vehicle on a [highway] [street] (or) [public vehicular area] in this state and that when doing so the defendant [was under the influence of an impairing substance] [had consumed sufficient alcohol that at any relevant time after driving the defendant had an alcohol concentration of 0.08 or more] [had any amount of a [Schedule I controlled substance] [metabolites of a Schedule I controlled substance] in the defendant's [blood] [urine] and that:

1. On (*name date*), the defendant in (*name court*) [was convicted of] [plead guilty to] the offense of (*name offense involving impaired driving*), that was committed on (*name date*); and
2. On (*name date*), the defendant in (*name court*) [was convicted of] [plead guilty to] the offense of (*name offense involving impaired driving*), that was committed on (*name date*); and
3. On (*name date*), the defendant in (*name court*) [was convicted of] [plead guilty to] the offense of (*name offense involving impaired driving*), that was committed on (*name date*), and that all of these convictions occurred within the past seven years of this offense for which the defendant is currently charged, it would be your duty to return a verdict of guilty. If you do not so find or have a reasonable doubt as to one or more of these things, you will not return a verdict of guilty of habitual impaired driving, but would consider whether the defendant is guilty of impaired driving which differs from habitual impaired driving in that the State need not prove that the defendant [was convicted of] (or) [plead guilty to] an offense involving impaired driving at least three times.

If you find from the evidence beyond a reasonable doubt that on or about the alleged date, the defendant drove a vehicle on a [highway] [street] (or) [public vehicular area] in this state and that when doing so the defendant [was under the influence of an impairing substance] [had consumed sufficient alcohol that at any relevant time after driving the defendant had an alcohol concentration of 0.08 or more] [had any amount of a [Schedule I controlled substance] [metabolites of a Schedule I controlled substance] in the defendant's [blood] [urine], it would be your duty to return a verdict of guilty. If you do not so find or have a reasonable doubt as one or more of these things, it would be your duty to return a verdict of not guilty.

Notes:

1. Only charge the defendant with a habitual impaired driving offense if the defendant did not admit to the prior convictions. In the absence of an inquiry by the trial court to establish a record of a guilty plea, a stipulation to a habitual felon status is not tantamount to a guilty plea. *State v. Gilmore*, 542 S.E.2d 694, 699 (N.C. Ct. App. 2001).

2. N.C. Gen. Stat. § 20-4.01 defines the driver as the operator of a vehicle.

3. If there is any doubt, define "vehicle" under N.C. Gen. Stat. § 20-4.01(49), or "motor vehicle" under N.C. Gen. Stat. § 20-4.01(23). The Safe Roads Act of 1983 makes this offense applicable to drivers of vehicles owned or operated by the State or any political subdivision thereof while engaged in maintenance or construction work on the highways. N.C. Gen. Stat. § 20-168(b). effective December 1, 2006, lawnmowers and bicycles are no longer exempt. Horses remain exempt.

4. If there is any doubt, define "highway" or "street" in accordance with N.C. Gen. Stat. § 20-4.01(13). "Public vehicular area" is defined in N.C. Gen. Stat. § 20-4.01(32).

5. An impairing substance includes alcohol, controlled substance under Chapter 90 of the General Statutes, or any other drug or psychoactive substance capable of impairing a person's physical or mental faculties, or any combination of these substances. N.C. Gen. Stat. § 20-4.01(14a).

6. N.C. Gen. Stat. § 20-4.01(48a).

7. N.C. Gen. Stat. § 20-4.01(0.2) defines alcohol concentration as "the concentration of alcohol in a person, expressed either as (a) grams of alcohol per 100 milliliters of blood; or (b) grams of alcohol per 210 liters of breath."

8. N.C. Gen. Stat. § 20-4.01(33a).

9. The term "deemed sufficient" is not defined in N.C. Gen. Stat. § 20-138.5 or N.C. Gen. Stat. § 20-141.4, other statutes or any appellate court decisions. Absent a specific definition, it can be presumed that the legislature intended the words to be given their ordinary meaning.

10. A metabolite is any substance produced or used during metabolism (digestion). In drug use, the term usually refers to the end product that remains after metabolism.

11. Driving with any Schedule I controlled substance, or its metabolites in one's blood or urine is a *per se* violation of impaired driving offense.

12. Note that for offenses occurring between December 1, 2006 and June 27, 2007, there was no statutory provision during this time that required the defendant to take a urine test.

13. N.C. Gen. Stat. § 20-139.1(f).

N.C.P.I.—Crim. 270.30
DRIVING BY A PERSON LESS THAN 21 YEARS OLD [WHILE] [AFTER) CONSUMING ALCOHOL OR DRUGS. MISDEMEANOR.
G.S. 20-138.3.

DRIVING BY A PERSON LESS THAN 21 YEARS OLD [WHILE] [AFTER) CONSUMING ALCOHOL OR DRUGS. MISDEMEANOR.

The defendant has been charged with driving by a person less than 21 years old [while] [after][1] consuming [alcohol] (and) [drugs].

For you to find the defendant guilty of this offense, the State must prove three things beyond a reasonable doubt:

First, that on (*name date*) the defendant was less than 21 years old.

Second, that at that time the defendant drove a motor vehicle[2] on a [highway][3] [public vehicular area][4] within this State.

And Third, that at the time the defendant was driving that vehicle, he [was consuming alcohol] (or) [had any alcohol remaining in his body][5] (or) [had remaining in his blood a previously consumed controlled substance. *(Name substance, e.g. marijuana is a controlled substance)*][6]

If you find from the evidence beyond a reasonable doubt that on (*name date*), the defendant was less than 21 years old, that he drove a motor vehicle on a [highway] [public vehicular area] in this State and that when he did so he [was consuming alcohol] [had alcohol remaining in his body] [had remaining in his blood a previously consumed controlled substance], it would be your duty to return a verdict of guilty. If you do not so find or have a reasonable doubt as to one or more of these things, it would be your duty to return a verdict of not guilty.

Notes:

1. Note that the statute punishes driving while or after consuming alcohol, or after consuming drugs. G.S. 20-138.3(a).
2. A "motor vehicle" is defined in G.S. 20-4.01(23).
3. "Highway" is defined in G.S. 20-4.01(13).
4. "Public vehicular area" is defined in G.S. 20-4.01(32).
5. G.S. 20-4.01(1a) defines alcohol.
6. A person is not in violation of the statute if he drives with a controlled substance in his body which was lawfully obtained and taken in therapeutically appropriate amounts. G.S. 20-138.3(a).

N.C.P.I.--Crim. 270A.25
OPERATING VESSEL WHILE UNDER THE INFLUENCE OF AN IMPAIRING SUBSTANCE. MISDEMEANOR.
GENERAL CRIMINAL VOLUME
N.C.G.S. 75A-10(b1).

270A.25 OPERATING VESSEL WHILE UNDER THE INFLUENCE OF AN IMPAIRING SUBSTANCE. Misdemeanor. N.C.G.S. 75A-10(b1).

The defendant has been charged with [operating a [motorboat] [vessel]] [manipulating [water skis] [a surfboard] [nonmotorized vessel] [similar device (*describe device*)]] while under the influence of an impairing substance.

For you to find the defendant guilty of this offense, the State must prove two things beyond a reasonable doubt:

First, that the defendant was [operating a [motorboat] [vessel]] [manipulating [water skis] [a surfboard] [nonmotorized vessel] [similar device (*describe device*)]] on the waters of this State.

And Second, that the defendant

(a) [was under the influence of an impairing substance.]
(b) [had consumed sufficient alcohol that the defendant had, at any relevant time after the boating, an alcohol concentration of 0.08 (or more).]

If you find from the evidence beyond a reasonable doubt that on or about the alleged date the defendant was [operating a [motorboat] [vessel]] [manipulating [water skis] [a surfboard] [similar device (describe device)] on the waters of this State and that the defendant

(a) [was under the influence of an impairing substance,]
(b) [had consumed sufficient alcohol that the defendant had, at any relevant time after the boating, an alcohol concentration of 0.08 (or more),]

it would be your duty to return a verdict of guilty. If you do not so find or have a reasonable doubt as to one or both of these things, it would be your duty to return a verdict of not guilty.

Notes:

1. *See* G.S. 75A-2(6). "Waters of this State" means any waters within the territorial limits of this State, and the marginal sea adjacent to this State and the high seas when navigated as a part of a journey or ride to or from the shore of this State, but does not include private ponds as defined in G.S. 113-129.

About the Author

J. Scott Smith received his undergraduate degree in English from Guilford College and then matriculated to Florida Coastal School of Law, where he received his Juris Doctor in 2005. Mr. Smith returned to North Carolina and opened LAWSMITH, The Law Offices of J. Scott Smith, PLLC in 2007. Mr. Smith is admitted to all North Carolina State Courts and to the Federal District Courts in the Western and Middle Districts. In January 2012, Mr. Smith was admitted to the United States Supreme Court.

In the criminal justice system, Mr. Smith handles traffic offenses, misdemeanors, and felonies. Most of his time, however, is devoted to defending those accused of Driving While Impaired in North Carolina. Mr. Smith is a member and recent Summer Session Graduate of the National College of DUI Defense, Inc. and constantly helps other lawyers throughout the State that defend those charged with DWI. Mr. Smith is also the State Ambassador for North Carolina and a founding member of the DUI Defense Lawyers Association. Mr. Smith has been named by the National Trial Lawyers as Top 100 in North Carolina since 2013. In 2015, the National Association of Distinguished Counsel named Mr. Smith as being in the top one percent. Mr. Smith travels the State and Country learning about defending impaired driving cases and has also successfully completed the National Highway Traffic Safety Administration (NHTSA) 24 hour Standardized Field Sobriety course as well as NHTSA's ARIDE (Advanced Roadside Impaired Driving Enforcement) class. Mr. Smith uses this knowledge to fight for his clients in the courtroom. He knows the value of an aggressive defense and has helped numerous clients fight their DWI charges in Winston-Salem, Greensboro, and throughout the State of North Carolina.

Memberships and Associations:
National College of DUI Defense, Inc.
National Association of Criminal Defense Lawyers
DUI Defense Lawyers Association, Founding Member
DUI Defense Lawyers Association, State Ambassador
American Association of Premier DUI Attorneys, Founding Member
Association of Plaintiff Interstate Trucking Lawyers of America
North Carolina State Bar
North Carolina Bar Association
North Carolina Advocates for Justice
American Bar Association
American Association for Justice
Forsyth County Bar Association
Forsyth County Criminal Defense Trial Lawyers Association
United States District Court, Middle and Western Districts
United States Supreme Court

James Nesci is a 1994 graduate of the University of Arizona College of Law and practiced on his own for ten years in Tucson, Arizona before becoming the managing partner of the firm; *Nesci, St. Louis & West, P.L.L.C.* in 2005. On January 1st, 2010, he and Joseph P. St. Louis created Tucson's premier law firm for DUI Defense: *Nesci & St. Louis, P.L.L.C.*.

Mr. Nesci often defends cases well into the .30 blood-alcohol range. He has caught more than one police officer lying during cross-examination and some police officers have even refused to grant pretrial interviews to him without a prosecutor or their own counsel present. He was one of the lead attorneys on the Intoximeters® RBT-IV breath-testing issue in Southern Arizona which resulted in the suppression of breath tests in over 7,000 cases and the removal of the RBT-IV from the streets of Arizona. He also spear-headed the effort to obtain the manufacturer's source code and software for the CMI Intoxilyzer 8000. Although the source code was never obtained, he almost single-handedly ground 90% of all DUI prosecutions within the City of Tucson to a halt for nearly three years and obtained breath test suppressions and dismissals in hundreds of DUI cases.

In addition to "traditional" DUI cases which involve alcohol, Mr. Nesci is a recognized expert on the defense of DUI/Drugs cases. Whether they be legal-over-the-counter-medications, prescription medications or illicit drugs, such DUI cases are far more complex and present cutting-edge issues for the courts.

Mr. Nesci is a team-player within the Southern Arizona DUI Defense Community. He is often involved in large-scale challenges to DUI investigative methods and chemical testing. His opinion is sought by DUI Attorneys across the nation on various issues. He is one of only a handful of attorneys in the country who has ever held a DOT-Compliant Permit to operate an Intoxilyzer® 8000. He owns both an Intoxilyzer® 5000 & 8000 which are used for in-court demonstrations and for research purposes. He is qualified to administer Standardized Field Sobriety Tests under National Highway Traffic Safety Administration & International Association of Chiefs of Police Guidelines.

In 2006, he was appointed Regent of the National College for DUI Defense, Inc. He was formerly the chair of the Curriculum Committee for the NCDD. Currently, he is the State Delegate Coordinator, a member of the Amicus Committee, Treasurer of the NCDD, Member of the Executive Committee and served as an oral argument judge for the Board Certification Committee.

Mr. Nesci is a co-author of DUI Defense books for Colorado, Florida, Iowa, New Hampshire, Oklahoma, Texas, Utah, Virginia, West Virginia and Wisconsin. He is a contributing author to the 5th and 6th Editions of the treatise: *Garriott's Medicolegal Aspects of Alcohol.* All of these books are published by Lawyers & Judges Publishing Company.

In addition to writing books on DUI Defense, Mr. Nesci works on large-scale challenges to DUI laws and investigatory techniques. He is AV-Preeminent-Rated® by Martindale-Hubbell, has been continuously named as one of The Best Lawyers in America® by Woodward/White since 2010, and also named as one Tucson's Top DUI Lawyers by Tucson Lifestyles Magazine.

In 1999 Mr. Nesci became a Sustaining Member of the National College for DUI Defense [www.NCDD.com]. In 2001, he was Board Certified by the National College for DUI Defense, Inc., which is recognized by the American Bar Association. He is one of only three Board Certified attorneys in the State of Arizona, and one of less than fifty Board Certified attorneys in the nation (as of January, 2015).

Mr. Nesci has lectured from coast-to-coast for such organizations as The University of Arizona James E. Rogers College of Law, Arizona State University College of Law Alumni Association, University of Mississippi CLE Department, South Texas College of Law CLE Department, Arkansas Association of Criminal Defense Lawyers, Arizona Attorneys for Criminal Justice, Arizona Public Defenders Association, California Attorneys for Criminal Justice, City of Phoenix Public Defender's Office, Colorado Criminal Defense Bar, Florida Association of Criminal Defense Lawyers, Indiana Public Defender's Council, Kansas Association of Criminal Defense Lawyers, Louisiana Association of Criminal Defense Lawyers, Maricopa County Bar Association, Maricopa County Public Defender's Office, Maryland Criminal Defense Attorneys Association, the Mexican-American Bar Association at Loyola, the National Association of Criminal Defense Lawyers, the National College for DUI Defense, the Nebraska Criminal Defense Attorney's Association, the Nevada State Bar Association, the New York State Bar Association, the Ohio Association of Criminal Defense Lawyers, the Pima County Bar Association, the Pima County Bar Association Young Lawyer's Division, the Texas Criminal Defense Lawyers Association, the Tucson City Public Defender's Office, the Tulare County (California) Public Defender's Association, the Utah Criminal Defense Lawyers Association, and the Washington Foundation for Criminal Justice.

He has taught seminars on the subjects of Ethics, 4th Amendment Law, Drug Recognition Evaluations (DUI-Drugs/DRE), Cross-Examination, Trial Tactics, Jury Selection, Field Sobriety Testing, Driving Behavior, Blood Alcohol Calculations, Opening & Closing Arguments, Source Code Litigation, Frye & Daubert Challenges, Intoxilyzer 8000 Operator's Course, Headspace Gas Chromatography, Blood and Breath Testing.

Mr. Nesci lives in Tucson with his wife and twin daughters. He is an honorably discharged veteran of the U.S. Navy where he spent much of his time working as an electrician in the Philadelphia Naval Shipyards. His interests are traveling, fine wines, vintage port and fast cars. He is an amateur race car driver, an accomplished mechanic, and a Corvette fanatic.

Admissions:

Supreme Court of the United States, 2010
United States Court of Appeals for the Ninth Circuit, 1995
United States District Court for the District of Arizona, 1994
State of Arizona, 1994

Index

P

S